examzone®

PASS THE 7™

A PLAIN ENGLISH EXPLANATION TO HELP YOU PASS THE SERIES 7 EXAM

ROBERT M. WALKER

PASS THE 7™ - A PLAIN ENGLISH EXPLANATION TO HELP YOU PASS THE SERIES 7 EXAM

By Robert M. Walker

Revised Edition – January, 2017 – 3rd Edition

NASAA Statements of Policy and Model Rules reprinted with permission.

FINRA rules and definitions from the FINRA manual reprinted with permission from FINRA; ©2017 Financial Industry Regulatory Authority (FINRA).

MSRB General Rules reprinted with permission from MSRB.

www.examzone.com

Pass the 7™, 2nd Edition ISBN-13 978-0-9831411-7-4

Library of Congress Control Number (LCCN) 2016900470

Publisher: Sure Fire Publications, LLC.® Chicago, IL (Acquired by Examzone, Inc. August 2016)

Printed in the U.S.A.

Table of Contents

How to Use This Book

We're happy you chose Examzone to help you pass the Series 7 exam. Our Pass the 7 Textbook is written in Plain English so you can learn concepts and assimilate the material quickly and easily. We hope you take advantage of our full **Series 7 Success Program™**, complete with test prep materials for each step of the learning process.

The Learning Components of the **Series 7 Success Program™** can be found at http://www.examzone.com/series7 and include:

- Pass the 7™ Textbook
- Pass the 7™ DVD Lesson Set
- Pass the 7™ Online Training Videos
- Pass the 7™ Online Test-Taking Strategies Videos
- Pass the 7™ Online Practice Question Bank
- Pass the 7™ Go/No Go Exams

Our research has shown that students who follow the entire **Series 7 Success Program™** have considerably higher pass rates than those who use only one or two of the Learning Components. Our Success Program integrates each of the Learning Components on a chapter-by-chapter basis. The sequence starts with each textbook chapter, followed by the requisite Practice Exams and finishes with the videos and DVDs for that chapter. You can see this sequence outlined on the next page in the Study Plan for the **Series 7 Success Program™**.

Additionally, our Pass the 7™ Go/No Go Exams are designed to test your readiness for the Series 7 exam. We recommend you take the Go/No Go at least two weeks prior to your scheduled test date. If you score an 80% or above, we think you're ready to take the Series 7 exam.

All of the Success Program materials mentioned above are available for purchase at http://www.examzone.com/series7. Email us at support@examzone.com or call us toll free at 1-855-EXAM-CARE – 1 (855) 392-6227 with any questions.

Thanks for studying with Examzone, and good luck!

Estimated Time Commitments:

- 6-8 weeks of study (60-80 hours)
- 3-5 days per week
- 2-4 hours per day

Weekly Study Plan:

WEEK 1 Goals:	<ul><li>Finish textbook through Chapter 1</li><li>Take Chapter 1 review exercise and quizzes in Online Practice Question Bank</li><li>Watch the DVD and/or Online Streaming Video Lessons 1 through 3</li><li>Video Lessons: 1, Economic Factors, 2, Business Information and Financial Reporting, 3, Investment Risk and Suitability</li></ul>
WEEK 2 & **WEEK 3** Goals:	<ul><li>Finish textbook through Chapter 2</li><li>Take Chapter 2 review exercise and quizzes in Online Practice Question Bank</li><li>Watch the DVD and/or Online Streaming Video Lessons 4 through 10B, 18</li><li>Video Lessons: 4, Equity Securities, 5, Debt Securities, 6, Investment Companies, 7, Annuities and Insurance, 8, DPPs, 9, Hedge Funds and Alternative Investments, 10/10A/10B, Options, 18, Primary Marketplace</li></ul>
WEEK 4 Goals:	<ul><li>Finish textbook through Chapter 3</li><li>Take Chapter 3 review exercise and quizzes in Online Practice Question Bank</li><li>Watch the DVD and/or Online Streaming Video Lessons 14, 15, 19</li><li>Video Lessons: 14, Taxation, 15, Tax-Advantaged Plans, 19, Secondary Marketplace</li></ul>
WEEK 5 Goals:	<ul><li>Finish textbook through Chapter 4</li><li>Take Chapter 4 review exercise and quizzes in Online Practice Question Bank</li><li>Watch the DVD and/or Online Streaming Video Lessons 11 – 13</li><li>Video Lessons: 11, Customer Accounts, 12, Margin Accounts, 13, Brokerage Office</li></ul>
WEEK 6 Goals:	<ul><li>Finish textbook through Chapter 5</li><li>Take Chapter 5 review exercise and quizzes in Online Practice Question Bank</li><li>Watch the DVD and/or Online Streaming Video Lessons 16, 17</li><li>Video Lessons: 16, Regulatory Requirements, 17, Professional Conduct and Ethical</li></ul>
WEEK 7 Goals:	<ul><li>Watch ALL – *Test-Taking Strategies* Online Videos</li><li>Take both Practice Exams (250 Questions) in Online Practice Question Bank</li><li>Take both GoNoGo exams and proceed accordingly.</li><li>Schedule tutoring if you need extra help@ **www.examzone.com/tutoring**</li></ul>

CHAPTER 1: Economic Factors & Business Information

Basic Economic Concepts

Are you saving and investing for retirement? If so, you know--as I do--that if we continue funding the accounts and investing wisely, we could reduce several years from our working lives. On the other hand, if we fail to make contributions, or if we invest those contributions unwisely, we could end up adding several years to our careers, whether we want to or not.

And, even if we prudently fund and invest the accounts, our financial futures are subject to inflation, interest rates, yield curves, credit spreads, currency valuations, the business cycle, economic indicators, fiscal policy, and monetary policy.

Let's start with inflation.

Inflation, Deflation

Some of my older relatives never trusted banks and, therefore, kept their cash in a coffee can. I never had the heart to explain that while their cash was sitting in the coffee can, prices overall were rising. Therefore, their money was losing **purchasing power** every year.

Even when we deposit money in an FDIC-insured bank, we usually find that the low rates of interest the bank pays do not keep pace with **inflation**. It might look as if we are earning more dollars, but because of inflation those dollars can't buy as much as they used to. We used to be able to afford a dozen eggs. Now because of inflation we can only afford ten and a half.

Inflation has to do with supply and demand. When the demand for goods and services exceeds their supply, prices system-wide begin to rise or inflate. Since many workers in the American economy have no ability to raise their own paychecks, inflation is a problem. At first, maybe consumers have more money for gasoline by cutting back on snack chips. Maybe they can pay the power bill if the whole family agrees to brown-bag their lunch. While it's nice to see American families pull together, the fact is we don't like to see the snack chip company or the local restaurants lose revenue, as those companies represent hundreds or thousands of working families, as well.

Sometimes economists worry about the opposite scenario, **deflation**. Deflation occurs when the supply of goods and services is greater than demand. While inflation can make things too expensive for consumers to buy, deflation can make things ever cheaper. With deflation at work profit margins at businesses will be squeezed, as the companies pay last month's prices for raw materials and then struggle to sell their finished goods at next month's cheaper prices.

That's assuming they can sell anything to anyone. Would you rush out to buy something today if you knew it would be cheaper tomorrow? Wouldn't we all be tempted to put off our purchases indefinitely, waiting for the prices of cell phones, clothing, and automobiles to drop in our favor? That would lead to lay-offs. And then those workers would have less money to spend and less confidence in their ability to buy on credit. About two-thirds of the American economy is driven by consumer spending, so if consumers aren't spending, that's a problem.

We'll look at the **Federal Reserve Board** and its **Federal Open Market Committee (FOMC)** in detail up ahead. For now, I will just point out that by moving their interest rate targets up or down, the Federal Reserve Board and its FOMC try to achieve maximum employment, stable prices and stable economic growth. The Fed raises interest rates to fight inflation. To stimulate a sagging economy, the Fed lowers interest rates.

Typically, inflation and economic expansion go hand-in-hand, as do deflation and economic stagnation. However, as we saw in the late 1970s, sometimes the overall economy suffers high inflation even as the economy shrinks and workers experience high unemployment rates. This rare situation is known as **stagflation**, a blend of the words "stagnation" and "inflation."

Inflation is measured by the **CPI**, or "**Consumer Price Index**." The CPI tracks the prices consumers are paying for the basic things consumers buy (groceries, movie tickets, milk, blue jeans, gasoline, etc.) and tracks the increases or decreases in those prices. Sometimes economists exclude certain items which are volatile--specifically food and energy--to track what's called **core inflation**. Why? A one-time weather event such as a hurricane could drastically disrupt production of food and oil, sending prices upward, but that one-time event would not necessarily indicate that prices are rising throughout all areas of the economy.

Investors adjust the returns on their investments by the CPI to calculate their **inflation-adjusted** or **real rate of return**. If an investor receives 4% interest on her bond when the CPI is 2%, her inflation-adjusted return is just 2%. Take the rate of return and then subtract out the CPI to calculate real or inflation-adjusted return. If an investor receives just 1% when the CPI is 2%, his return would be -1% in terms of inflation-adjusted return. He is, in other words, losing purchasing power.

Economists also monitor the **PPI**, or **Producer Price Index**. This is a family of indices showing the prices received by producers at various stages of the production cycle: commodity level, intermediate demand, and final demand. If the CPI and PPI are revealing inflation, the Fed's Federal Open Market Committee (FOMC) will raise interest rates to let some air out of the economy. If prices start to collapse we can end up with deflation, so "the Fed" will pump some air back into the economy by lowering interest rates.

Okay. So what are interest rates?

Interest Rates

If a business owner needs $50,000 to start a bakery, chances are she has to borrow the money. The $50,000 she borrows is the **principal** amount of the loan. The extra money she pays to borrow the principal over time is what we call **interest rates**. When there's a lot of money to be lent out, lenders drop their rates. When money is tight, however, lenders charge higher rates. One way corporations borrow money is by selling bonds to investors, who act as lenders. How much should the corporate borrower pay the buyers of the bonds?

How about zero? Zero percent financing sounds tempting to a borrower. Unfortunately, the buyers of debt securities demand compensation. They're the lenders of the money, and they demand the best interest rate they can receive in return for lending their capital. So, bond issuers pay investors only what they have to pay them. Interest rates, then, are the result of constant spoken and unspoken negotiations going on between providers of capital and those who would like to borrow it.

The exam may mention any of the following interest rates:

- **Discount rate:** the rate banks have to pay when borrowing from the Federal Reserve.
- **Fed funds rate:** the rate banks charge each other for overnight loans in excess of $1 million. Considered the most volatile rate, subject to daily change.
- **Broker call loan rate:** the rate broker-dealers pay when borrowing on behalf of their margin customers.
- **Prime rate:** the rate that the most creditworthy corporate customers pay when borrowing through unsecured loans.
- **LIBOR:** stands for London InterBank Offered Rate, a benchmark rate that many large international banks charge each other for short-term loans.

The **London Interbank Market** is where large international banks go to get short-term loans at the most competitive rates possible. The rate mentioned above, LIBOR, is fixed daily by the British Banker's Association and represents an average of the world's most creditworthy banks' interbank deposit rates for large loans with maturities between overnight and one year. LIBOR is the most frequently used benchmark for short-term interest rates. Creditworthy borrowers might be able to borrow at "LIBOR plus five basis points," while shaky borrowers would have to pay a much higher premium to LIBOR.

Let's briefly look at **swaps** that typically occur among banks and other financial institutions. A simple example of an interest rate swap would be an agreement over the next three years for Bank A to pay Bank B a fixed rate of interest on a sum, while Bank B will pay Bank A a floating rate of interest, e.g., LIBOR plus 1%. There is no principal exchanged between the parties, so the sum is known as the "notional value." Let's say the notional value is $10,000,000, and the fixed rate of interest is 5%. Over year one, Bank A would owe Bank B $500,000. If LIBOR was 4.5%, Bank B would owe Bank A $550,000, so Bank B would simply pay Bank A the $50,000. The following year, if LIBOR drops, Bank A might be the party sending payment to the other side.

Swaps are private arrangements between the two parties. That means they trade over-the-counter, as opposed to options and futures, which are standardized products that trade on regulated exchanges. We will look at options in detail in Chapter 2. While options and futures are traded with clearinghouses acting as a buffer between the two parties, swaps leave both parties with counterparty risk, which is the risk that the other side will default on the contract.

Yield Curves

The longer a bondholder's money is at risk, the more yield he demands. If your bond matures in 2028 while mine matures in 2020, isn't your money at risk for 8 more years? That's why your bond would be offered at a higher yield than mine. If I buy a bond yielding 3.65%, yours might be offered at 3.89%. The extra .24% is your reward for taking on extra risk.

In the world of fixed-income securities it is generally accepted that short-term = bonds with up to three-year maturities, intermediate-term = bonds with four to ten-year maturities, and long-term = bonds with maturities > 10 years.

A **yield curve** displays the yields offered by debt securities of similar credit quality across various terms to maturity. Typically, the longer the maturity on the bond, the higher the yield demanded by investors. This situation is known as a **normal yield curve**, where intermediate-term bonds yield more than short-term bonds, and then long-term bonds yield more than both short-term and intermediate-term bonds, as well.

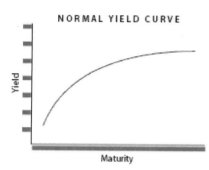

A normal yield curve implies that economic conditions are stable. For the majority of its history the yield curve for U.S. Treasuries has been in this state. Notice that though yields are higher, they also flatten out here rather than forming a steep slope. On the other hand, the test could mention a "steep yield curve" in which the curve buckles inward because the yields on longer maturities are so much higher than those on shorter maturities. This often happens before the economy goes into a rapid expansion.

As we'll see, the expansion phase of the business cycle often comes with higher interest rates and inflation, so fixed-income investors demand significantly higher yields on long-term bonds suddenly, causing a steep yield curve. We've seen that if the "Fed" sees inflation up ahead, they will raise interest rates. A steep yield curve suggests that this has already been factored into the bond market.

If we see the same yields among T-Bills, T-Notes, and T-Bonds, we are looking at a **flat yield curve**. The yield curve typically flattens when investor expectations for inflation are so low that they are not demanding higher yields to hold long-term debt securities. This typically occurs at the end of a Fed tightening cycle. At that point the Fed raises short-term interest rates until they are in line with intermediate- and long-term rates, and temporarily, with investors expecting no immediate threat from inflation, the yields are about the same across the board. A flat yield curve is thought to signal an economic slowdown.

So, when the economy expands, the Federal Reserve Board typically goes into a series of interest-rate tightening. Towards the end of this cycle, the yield curve can often flatten, which usually signals the party is over for the economy, at least for a while.

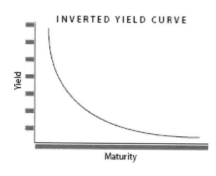

An **inverted yield curve** often follows a period of high interest rates. When bond investors feel that interest rates have peaked, they hurry to lock in the high interest rates for the longest period of time. In a rush of activity, they sell off their short-term bonds to buy long-term bonds at the best interest rate they're likely to see for a while. If the crowd is selling short-term bonds, the price drops [and the yield increases]. And if they're buying long-term bonds, the price increases [and the yield drops]. That causes the yield curve to invert, which is thought to be one of the surest signs that the economy is about to contract. The situation also signals lower inflation up ahead, possibly deflation.

Credit Spreads

A yield curve displays yields across different maturities. On the other hand, a yield or **credit spread** considers yields between different credit qualities. A credit spread shows the difference in yields between high-rated and low-rated bonds, or between Treasury and junk bonds. If investors demand a much greater yield on low-rated bonds than on high-rated bonds, that's a negative indicator for the economy. If investors don't demand a much higher yield on the low-rated bonds, that means they are confident about issuers' ability to repay, which is a positive indicator. So, when the yield spread narrows, that is good news, while, on the other hand, when the yield spread widens, there could be trouble up ahead.

If the 10-year U.S. Treasury Note currently yields 3%, while 10-year junk bonds yield 8%, the spread or "risk premium" is 5 percentage points. Investors are demanding a "risk premium" of 5 extra percentage points (500 basis points) of yield to buy the riskier bonds. If the T-Note is yielding 2% while high-yield bonds yield 5%, the credit spread has narrowed to just three percentage points, implying more confidence on the part of bond investors.

Global and Geopolitical Factors

As recently as the early 1970s the value of the U.S. dollar was tied to a specific weight of gold. I mean, if you really wanted to, you could require the federal government to give you a specific weight of gold for each dollar you presented to the Treasury Department. When a country ties its currency either to a commodity such as gold, or to another currency, they are using a **fixed exchange rate** system.

Like most world currencies, the U.S. Dollar's value is today determined by a free-market, supply-and-demand system known as a **floating-rate currency** system. How does a dollar compare to the yen, or the Euro in terms of its **exchange rate**? That is a question whose answer can change every day of the week, depending on many factors. Primarily, the exchange rate between the dollar and another currency is determined by the supply and demand for the currencies and the amounts held in foreign reserves. Is the U.S. suddenly the place to invest? If so, the value of the dollar will rise, and vice versa.

A while ago the Swiss central bank stopped using a fixed exchange rate system that kept the Swiss Franc from rising above 1.20 Euro. This sudden move from a fixed to a floating-rate system shocked currency and securities markets. Why?

Imports and exports are directly affected by the relative values of currencies. If the companies that export from Switzerland to other European nations face buyers whose currency is weak, they will not be able to sell to them. Similarly, the strength of the American dollar relative to foreign currencies affects our imports and exports. As our dollar strengthens, our exports become less attractive to consumers in other countries, whose weak currency can't buy our expensive goods.

When our dollar *weakens,* our exports become *more* attractive because suddenly their strong currencies can buy our relatively cheap products and services. Likewise, a strong dollar makes foreign travel less expensive for Americans, whereas a weak dollar makes foreign travel more expensive. It's just a way of asking how much of their stuff our dollar can buy.

The **balance of trade** number tracks money in and money out of the economy for imports and exports. If we export more to a country than we import from it, we have a balance of **trade surplus** with that nation. If we import more from a country than we export to it, we have a balance of **trade deficit** with that nation. The exam could refer to the difference between a country's exports and imports as their current account. Therefore, if a country imports more than it exports, it runs a current account deficit and a current account surplus when it exports more than it imports.

Also note that under "exports" and "imports" we include goods and services. So, whether the U.S. is manufacturing and exporting finished goods, we do export many services in terms of legal, accounting, investment banking, and professional consulting, etc. Know also that if the U.S. has a trade deficit with China, that means that China is holding a lot of our currency—that's how they pay for all those imports from us. We never want anyone to dump large quantities of our currency all at once and devalue it drastically in an act of retaliation or a sudden lack of confidence. That, of course, makes relations with China or other such trading partners tricky at times.

The strength of the dollar and trade deficits constantly work towards an equilibrium. If a weak dollar increases foreign demand for American-made goods, that increased demand for American-made goods will also increase the demand for dollars, making them stronger. And then it will be harder to export to foreign buyers. On the other hand, if a strong dollar hurts exports, the lack of foreign demand for American-made goods will also eventually drive down the value of the dollar, which should eventually increase the attractiveness of our exports again.

Interest rates also factor into the value of our currency. When interest rates in the United States are much higher than interest rates abroad, the demand for U.S. assets will increase the demand for the dollars needed to buy them (e.g., bank accounts, stocks, bonds, and real estate), and increase the value of the dollar compared to foreign currencies. On the other hand, if interest rates in the United States are lower than interest rates abroad, the demand for foreign assets will likely strengthen and the demand for U.S. assets will likely weaken. This will cause the demand for foreign currencies to strengthen, leading to a depreciation of the dollar compared to foreign currencies.

So, if we had a trade deficit with the European Union, would a strong dollar or a weak dollar help to bring us back to a surplus? Well, if we were already importing more from the EU than we were exporting, we would want to make our exports more attractive to the Europeans and our imports from the EU less attractive to Americans, which would happen as the dollar weakens. The dollar weakening is another way of saying the other currency is strengthening, remember.

The **balance of payments** statistic tracks all money coming in versus going out of the economy. So, it counts both imports vs. exports and also investments and other financial transactions. If more money is coming in than going out, we have a surplus. If more money is going out than coming in, we have a deficit. If a test question says that foreigners are paying off loans to American banks, this could lead to a balance of payments surplus for the U.S., for example. Or, the exam might want you to say, "a balance of payments deficit is financed by capital inflows from foreign investors."

The value of the dollar compared to another currency also comes into play when an investor buys an **ADR**. We look at ADRs in Chapter 2. For now, just know that American investors can buy shares of Toyota or Nissan, for example, as ADRs (**American Depository Receipts**), priced in American dollars. This way, we don't have to figure out how much we just paid for a stock priced at 176.453 yen. However, the relative value of the dollar to the yen comes into play, especially when it comes time to pay dividends. When the underlying stock pays the dividend in the foreign currency, the foreign currency received by the bank is converted to U.S. dollars. If the U.S. dollar is strong, the foreign currency purchases or converts to fewer U.S. dollars for the holder of the ADR. As a result, the dividend received by the holder of the ADR is lower. So, a *weak* dollar would be beneficial to the holder of an ADR, since the dividend paid would convert to *more* U.S. dollars.

Investing in an ADR involves currency exchange risk, but it also involves buying stock in a company. The success of the company's operations and financing affect the ADR investor, who often receives dividends from the issuer. On the other hand, some speculators trade the **foreign currencies** themselves. The foreign exchange market (abbreviated Forex) allows speculators to benefit from fluctuations between various currencies.

Trading currencies, however, is a high-risk strategy. As Fidelity's website explains, "Currency prices are highly volatile. Price movements for currencies are influenced by, among other things: changing supply-demand relationships; trade, fiscal, monetary, exchange control programs and policies of governments; United States and foreign political and economic events and policies; changes in national and international interest rates and inflation; currency devaluation; and sentiment of the marketplace. None of these factors can be controlled by you or any individual advisor and no assurance can be given that you will not incur losses from such events."

The site explains that there are 16 currencies that can be traded, with trades settling in any of these local currencies:

- Australian dollar (AUD)
- British pound (GBP)
- Canadian dollar (CAD)
- Danish krone (DKK)
- Euro (EUR)
- Hong Kong dollar (HKD)
- Japanese yen (JPY)
- Mexican peso (MXN)
- New Zealand dollar (NZD)
- Norwegian krone (NOK)
- Polish zloty (PLN)
- Singapore dollar (SGD)
- South African rand (ZAR)
- Swedish krona (SEK)
- Swiss franc (CHF)
- U.S. dollar (USD)

There may also be at least one ADR issued by companies in most of those nations above. If so, an American buying the ADR would *also* be exposed to currency fluctuations. But as the Swiss food giant Nestle explains, the currency fluctuation angle should not be overstated: The ADR share prices carry foreign currency risk depending on the movement of the US dollar against the Swiss franc. Most of the ADRs trade in line with the underlying security. The spread is in general small, reflecting the cost of foreign exchange conversion and other execution costs. If the currency of the underlying stock rises against the US dollar, the ADR price is expected to rise (and vice versa). That's from http://www.nestle.com/investors/faqs/adrs-faqs#exchange, btw, an excellent run-down on ADRs from a company that makes some really tasty products.

The standard of safety in the securities markets is provided by government debt issued by the United States Treasury in the form of T-Bills, T-Notes, and T-Bonds, etc. Not only do investors receive their interest from these debt securities, but also getting paid at maturity is never a concern. Another name for the debt of a national government is **sovereign debt.** Common abbreviations for such debt include U.S. Treasuries, U.K. Gilts, German Bunds, and French Oats.

Not all sovereign debt is stable. That's why investors must check credit ratings as they do when investing in corporate bonds. Sovereign debt is generally a riskier investment when it comes from a developing country, and a safer investment when it comes from a developed country. The stability of the government is a key factor in determining the credit risk. Nations with high rates of inflation or unpredictable currency exchange rates offer higher yields to investors and carry higher risk, as well.

When a nation or an entire region of the global economy suddenly has trouble servicing its sovereign debt, panic can hit the fixed-income, currency, and stock markets around the world. Lenders—the owners of the bonds—can't seize the assets of a government, so the only way out of the mess is for the government to secure financing and/or renegotiate the terms of the outstanding debt. For example, in the spring of 2010 several nations in the European Union (e.g., Greece, Turkey, and Portugal) suddenly appeared unable to meet their debt obligations. This, of course, sent the yields on their sovereign debt sky-high, as investors sold off the bonds in a panic. The European Union, along with the European Central Bank and the International Monetary Fund, had to intervene by offering a rescue package worth 750 billion euro to keep the economies of those nations afloat.

If an issuer of sovereign debt is experiencing strife of any kind, it may become less willing and able to meet its debt obligations. Sometimes issuing countries restructure their debt, which is usually bad news for bondholders. Restructured debt typically leaves bondholders with lower interest and principal payments. Sometimes maturity dates are extended, forcing investors to wait longer for their return of principal.

When a government has trouble meeting its debt obligations, it often devalues its currency. As we saw, a devalued currency can help increase a nation's exports; however, in these situations the currency's value tends to fall so far that citizens are unable to buy basic goods, and international confidence in the nation's economy tends to drop. Soon, stocks and bonds issued by companies in that nation falter on the secondary market, and international investors pull out of the nation or region entirely.

People often talk about the economy in terms of whether it is good or bad. But, how do we measure something as big and complex as the American economy? One way is by tracking **Gross Domestic Product (GDP)**. As the name implies, Gross Domestic Product measures the total output of a nation's economy. It's an estimate of the total value of all goods and services produced and purchased over a three-month period. If the GDP number comes in at 3%, that means the economy grew at an annual rate of 3% over the financial quarter. If GDP is −2%, the economy is shrinking at an annual rate of −2%. The GDP numbers that are factored for inflation are called "real GDP."

The Federal Reserve Board monitors many **economic indicators** to determine whether inflation is threatening the economy, or whether the Fed needs to provide stimulus to a sagging economy. The following **employment indicators** reveal how many people are working and how much compensation they're receiving. If people aren't working, that signals an economic slowdown, and the Fed might lend a hand by lowering interest rates to free up money in the economy. If too many people are working, that signals inflation, and the Fed might cool things down by raising interest rates.

- Average Weekly New Claims for Unemployment Insurance: if people are showing up for unemployment insurance at a higher rate, that's negative. If the number of new claims drops, that means economic activity is picking up—positive.
- Unemployment Rate (Non-farm Payroll): also called "payroll employment." Includes full-time and part-time workers, whether they're permanent or temporary employees. Tracks how many people are working in the private sector. Released monthly. Called "non-farm" because it doesn't measure seasonal agricultural jobs.
- Employment Cost Index (ECI): measures the growth of wages and benefits (compensation). Quarterly figure.

A **leading indicator** shows up before something happens and is used to predict. A **coincident indicator** tells us where we are right about now, and a **lagging indicator** gives us data about where we've just been, confirming a trend.

Leading (predict changes in the economy):

- the average weekly hours worked by manufacturing workers
- the average number of initial applications for unemployment insurance
- the amount of manufacturers' new orders for consumer goods and materials
- the speed of delivery of new merchandise to vendors from suppliers
- the amount of new orders for capital goods (equipment used to make products) unrelated to defense
- the amount of new building permits for residential buildings
- the S&P 500 stock index
- the inflation-adjusted monetary supply (M2)
- the spread between long and short interest rates
- consumer confidence
- bond yields

Coincident (current state of the economy):

- the number of employees on non-agricultural payrolls
- industrial production
- manufacturing and trade sales
- personal income levels

Lagging (confirm trends, do not predict):

- the value of outstanding commercial and industrial loans
- the change in the Consumer Price Index for services from the previous month
- the change in labor cost per unit of labor output
- inventories
- the ratio of consumer credit outstanding to personal income
- the average prime rate charged by banks
- length/duration of unemployment

The following table shows what the main indicators tend to reveal to an economist. For example, if the S&P 500 is up, that means the economy could be headed for an expansion, and when the S&P 500 is down, the economy could be headed for a contraction. The "Fed" typically intervenes to smooth out the otherwise rough patches in the economy, so if they see inflationary signals, they start tightening credit/raising interest rates. If they see deflationary signals, they provide economic stimulus by loosening credit/lowering interest rates.

INFLATIONARY/EXPANDING	DEFLATIONARY/CONTRACTING
S&P 500 Up	S&P 500 Down
Building Permits Up	Building Permits Down
# of Manufacturing Workers Up	# of Manufacturing Workers Down
Unemployment Claims Down	Unemployment Claims Up
Consumer Confidence Up	Consumer Confidence Down
Manufacturers' New Orders Up	Manufacturers' New Orders Down
Capital Goods Spending Up	Capital Goods Spending Down
Personal Income Up	Personal Income Down
Manufacturing & Trade Sales Up	Manufacturing & Trade Sales Down
Payroll Employment Up	Payroll Employment Down
Inventory Levels Down	Inventory Levels Up
Duration of Unemployment Down	Duration of Unemployment Up

Business Cycle

Gross Domestic Product (GDP) for the U.S. measures the value of goods and services produced and provided by workers stationed in the United States over a financial quarter. If GDP is increasing, the economy is growing. If GDP is declining, so is the economy.

The American economy is subject to the **business cycle** or the boom-and-bust cycle. The four phases of the business cycle are: **expansion, peak, contraction,** and **trough**. The period between the peak and the trough is called either a **recession** or a **depression**, depending on the severity. A depression is more prolonged and severe than the more frequently occurring recession. One definition of a recession is two consecutive quarters of inflation-adjusted GDP decline.

But, that is more likely a definition used by a journalist than an economist. As the former head of the San Francisco Federal Reserve Bank explains, "Economists use monthly business cycle peaks and troughs designated by the National Bureau of Economic Research (NBER) to define periods of expansion and contractions. The NBER website lists the peaks and troughs in economic activity starting with the December 1854 trough. The website also defines a recession as:

```
a significant decline in economic activity spread across the
economy, lasting more than a few months, normally visible in real
GDP, real income, employment, industrial production, and
wholesale-retail sales. A recession begins just after the economy
reaches a peak of activity and ends as the economy reaches its
trough. Between trough and peak, the economy is in an expansion.
Expansion is the normal state of the economy; most recessions are
brief and they have been rare in recent decades.
```

While there is no standard definition of a depression, economists generally consider a depression to be a more severe and prolonged version of a recession. For example, the Great Depression involved two severe economic downturns. The first lasted from August 1929 all the way through February 1933. After an expansion lasting 21 months, the economy went into a depression again, this time lasting from May 1937 all the way to June 1938.

Stocks of companies operating in certain industries are more dependent on this business cycle than others. These **cyclical** stocks tend to perform well during an expansion but poorly during a contraction. **Cyclical industries** involve expensive purchases and include: heavy equipment, steel, automobiles, durable goods such as refrigerators and dishwashers, travel, and aerospace. Large purchases are what consumers and businesses cut back on first when the economy hits a rough patch. During a robust economy, consumers begin purchasing new cars and refrigerators once again.

Other industries can survive a contraction more easily and are, therefore, called **defensive** or "non-cyclical." These industries include: food, clothing, pharmaceuticals, healthcare, alcohol and tobacco. Food is a defensive industry, but the test could say "restaurants."

That's not what we mean. We mean supermarkets and food supply companies. Restaurants get clobbered in a recession, as they are one of the first items consumers reduce or eliminate entirely from their budget. Similarly, clothing is a defensive industry, but we don't mean designer suits, which people cut back on in a recession. We mean the basics, like underwear, socks, gloves, and T-shirts.

If the industry space does better during a recession, it is considered **counter-cyclical.** Counter-cyclical stocks are negatively correlated to the business cycle. During a contraction, they thrive. During an expansion, they struggle. There are not many types of business models that improve when consumers have less money to spend, but during a period of high unemployment employment placement agencies typically see an increase in revenue. I remember in the summer of 1982 all factories at the local industrial park had signs taped to the front door--no applications accepted! Turned out the only way to find a job at any of the companies struggling to survive the recession was to go through such an employment agency. The factory that the agency eventually placed me with paid $6 and hour, and the agency took $2 from that, leaving me with $4 an hour before taxes. During normal economic times I am not likely to give up 1/3 of my paycheck, but when times are tight you do what you have to.

Similarly, education and training companies who prepare people for careers in automotive, electronics, or nursing, etc. are also countercyclical. When people lose a job, they tend to find other careers that they are willing to pay to enter.

While countercyclical stocks do well during a contraction, they also suffer during expansions. And expansions typically last longer. If unemployment is low, the two types of companies mentioned would see their revenue decrease.

Although we usually associate the term **interest-rate sensitive** with bonds and preferred stocks, there are also common stocks whose market prices tend to drop when interest rates rise. Companies who pay a generous and relatively fixed dividend tend to experience a drop in market value if interest rates rise. Also, companies who issue a lot of long-term bonds may see their stock price drop when interest rates rise. That's because their cost of borrowing will likely increase in the near future and hurt their profits. As we'll see, common stock is all about the expectation of future profits, so companies who do a lot of borrowing get hurt when interest rates increase.

On the other hand, some companies do better when interest rates rise. For example, banks, insurance companies, and certain broker-dealers often earn higher profits when interest rates increase, especially if the yield curve is steep. Broker-dealers make much of their profits by holding customer cash and earning interest on it until the customer buys stock or requests a withdrawal. The steeper the yield curve, the better the profits, as it is for banks and insurance companies.

So, the same economic climate produces winners and losers. During a recession, car makers and high-end retailers may suffer, but Wal-Mart and Priceline might report higher profits as Americans suddenly become cost-conscious. When interest rates rise, utility companies and heavy equipment makers might get hurt while, on the other hand, banks, insurers, payroll and certain broker-dealers might report better results.

If convinced a recession is coming an investor should purchase defensive stocks. People will, after all, keep buying razor blades, groceries, medicine, and liquor regardless of the current economic climate. If an expansion is expected, an investor should purchase cyclical stocks, like automobile and trucking or railroad companies.

How does the investor know when the recessions and recoveries are about to appear? He doesn't, but the stock market is always about speculation. As we'll see, some investors study overall economic trends to make investments along these lines; some investors buy stocks based only on the behavior of that stock in the marketplace; other investors refuse to pick investments but, rather, allocate percentages of their portfolio to this or that type of stock.

Also, we keep mentioning the more commonly used GDP, but the exam may ask about **GNP (Gross National Product),** too. Gross National Product for the U.S. counts the production of U.S. workers stationed here as well as working overseas for American companies. It does not count the production of, say, Japanese citizens working at a Toyota or Mitsubishi plant in Mississippi. Gross Domestic Product counts what is produced domestically, by both U.S. workers and foreigners working here in the United States. So, GNP tells us how much American workers are producing wherever they're stationed, while GDP tells us what is produced here in America, whoever is doing that work.

Monetary and Fiscal Policies

Economic policy makers use **monetary** and **fiscal policies** to influence the economy. Monetary policies are enacted by the Federal Reserve Board and its Federal Open Market Committee. Monetary policies involve setting targets for short-term interest rates to either fight inflation or stimulate a sagging economy.

The Federal Reserve Board (The Fed) requires that its member banks keep a certain percentage of their customer deposits in reserve. This is called the **reserve requirement**. If the Fed raises the reserve requirement, banks have less money to lend out to people trying to buy homes and start businesses. So if the economy is overheating, the Federal Reserve Board could raise the reserve requirement to cool things down, and if the economy is sluggish, they could lower the requirement to make more money available to fuel the economy.

However, of the three main tools of monetary policy changing the reserve requirement is the most drastic measure and, therefore, the tool used least often by the Federal Reserve. The exam could refer to a **multiplier effect** as the reason the tool is used less often than the others. In a nutshell that means that if banks can lend out maybe $10 for every $1 they have on reserve, when the Federal Reserve Board changes the amount required to be deposited in reserve by just a little bit, the effects are multiplied throughout the financial system. The multiplier effect is calculated by taking total bank deposits divided by the reserve requirement.

The Fed's Federal Open Market Committee (FOMC) can also use **open market operations** and either buy or sell U.S. Treasury securities on the secondary market. If they want to cool things down by raising interest rates, they sell Treasuries on the open market to depress their price and, thereby, increase their yield. If they want to fuel a sluggish economy by lowering interest rates, they buy Treasury securities, thereby driving up their price, which is the same thing as pushing down their yield. Yields and rates are the same thing, remember. It is the price of debt securities that moves in an inverse relationship to rates/yields. We will look at interest rates and bond prices in more detail up ahead.

When people say the FOMC is raising short-term interest rates by 25 basis points, they're talking about the **discount rate,** which is the rate the Federal Reserve Board charges banks that borrow directly from the FRB. If banks have to pay more to borrow, they will in turn charge their customers more to borrow from them. So, if the Fed wants to raise interest rates, they just raise the discount rate and let the banking system take it from there.

The Federal Reserve Board does not set tax policy—they enact monetary policy. And, typically, they only influence short-term interest rates, although if circumstances require it, they can also influence longer-term rates reflected by Treasury Notes and Treasury Bonds, discussed more in a later chapter.

As we'll also see later, the Securities Exchange Act of 1934 covers many aspects of the securities industry. This legislation gave the Federal Reserve Board the power to establish margin requirements under Regulation T and Regulation U. These regulations stipulate how much credit can be extended by broker-dealers and banks in connection with customer margin accounts. So, as with the other tools above, the Federal Reserve Board can make credit more available or less available through margin requirements, depending on the direction of their current monetary policy.

You can think of the Federal Reserve Board/FOMC as a sort of pit crew trying to perform tune-ups on an economy that never pulls over for a pit stop. If the economy starts going too fast, they let some air out of the tires by raising the reserve requirement, raising the discount rate, and selling Treasury securities. If the economy starts to slow down, they pump some air into the tires by lowering the reserve requirement, lowering the discount rate, and buying Treasuries.

Inflation is most likely to occur during the phase of the business cycle called the "peak," a time associated with the phrase "irrational exuberance," during which too many investors and entrepreneurs are convinced that things will keep improving forever. To fight inflation the Fed slows things down by raising interest rates. Deflation is found during the contraction. To fight deflation the Fed pumps air back into the economy by lowering interest rates.

There are many ways the exam can refer to the same thing here, too. If the Federal Reserve is fighting inflation, this could be referred to as "tight credit" or a "tight money policy." If the "Fed" is pumping inflation back into the economy, the exam could call this "loose credit" or a "loose money policy."

Fiscal policy is what the President and Congress do: tax and spend. **Keynesian** economists recommend that fiscal policy be used to increase aggregate (overall) demand for goods and services. To stimulate the economy, just cut taxes and increase government spending. Reduced taxes leave more money for Americans to spend and invest, fueling the economy. If the government is spending more on interstate highway construction, this means a lot more workers are going to be hired for construction crews. Or maybe the federal government orders military transport vehicles from a unit of GM. If so, GM will order a lot more parts from suppliers and hire more workers, who would make and spend more money to push the economy along.

On the other hand, if we need to cool things down, followers of Keynesian economics suggest that the federal government increase taxes and cut spending. Higher taxes leave less money for Americans to spend and invest, and decreased spending puts less government money into companies, who, in turn, spend less money on supplies, equipment, and salaries.

Financial Reporting

Accounting Fundamentals

Almost nothing moves the market price of a public company's stock more than the earnings announcements released four times a year in conjunction with their SEC and shareholder reports. Because investors rely on financial results so much these days, and because they receive the news and act upon it so quickly, the SEC is concerned that this information be accurate.

As the SEC explains on their website, "U.S. companies are required to present their financial statements according to a set of accounting standards, conventions and rules known as Generally Accepted Accounting Principles, or GAAP. An independent accountant audits the company's financial statements. For large companies, the independent accountant also reports on a company's internal controls over financial reporting. The auditor's report is a key part of the 10-K. Most audit reports express an 'unqualified opinion' that the financial statements fairly present the company's financial position in conformity with GAAP. If, however, an auditor expresses a 'qualified opinion' or a 'disclaimer of opinion,' investors should look carefully at what kept the auditor from expressing an unqualified opinion. Likewise, investors should carefully evaluate material weaknesses disclosed on internal controls over financial reporting."

Large public companies have internal controls over their financial reporting, but before a quarterly report is released it must be reviewed by their outside, independent auditor. And, before releasing the annual report the company must have the accounting firm audit the financial results and sign off on them. As we saw above, the issuer is hoping for an unqualified opinion from their independent auditor, since anything else is a red flag.

Issuers typically have an audit committee that oversees the financial reporting that is reviewed by the independent auditor, and the committee signs off on the financial statements released in required reports. The audit committee is, according to the Securities Exchange Act of 1934, "responsible for the appointment, compensation, and oversight of the work of any registered public accounting firm employed by that issuer (including resolution of disagreements between management and the auditor regarding financial reporting) for the purpose of preparing or issuing an audit report or related work, and each such registered public accounting firm shall report directly to the audit committee."

Auditing firms provide many other professional services to clients, and not so long ago it became common for a firm that was supposed to be auditing financial statements of a client to sell so many other lucrative services to that client that performing the rigorous type of audit the securities markets demand became awkward. The term "earnings management" became common, and it seemed that formerly trusted accounting firms were now asking their clients which earnings number they wanted to report before making the required adjustments to the financials. It must be fun for the CEO and CFO to watch their shares in the company rise with each announcement. However, when a public company finally has to come clean and announce it is re-stating all the financial statements it has released over the past several years, chaos typically follows.

Because the auditor needs to be objective and uncompromised, the Securities Exchange Act of 1934 prohibits a public accounting firm providing auditing services to a client from also performing any of the following services for that client:

- bookkeeping or other services related to the accounting records or financial statements of the audit client
- financial information systems design and implementation
- appraisal or valuation services, fairness opinions, or contribution-in-kind reports
- actuarial services
- internal audit outsourcing services

- management functions or human resources
- broker or dealer, investment adviser, or investment banking services
- legal services and expert services unrelated to the audit

At the annual meeting it is a routine matter for the shareholders to approve the board of directors' recommendation for the auditing firm. On the other hand, a sudden change of auditors can be a red flag. As the SEC explains, "The section of a 10K report called 'Changes in and Disagreements with Accountants on Accounting and Financial Disclosure' requires a company, if there has been a change in its accountants, to discuss any disagreements it had with those accountants. Many investors view this disclosure as a red flag."

The big idea here is that if you are an officer of the company, a member of the audit committee, or the independent auditor, you know that your signature on the financial statements released to the SEC and the securities markets is a big deal. Putting out bogus reports will not only get people in trouble with the SEC, but also shareholder lawsuits and even criminal actions may be taken against the offenders.

We mentioned that a public company's independent auditor reviews the financials presented in a quarterly report but goes so far as to audit the results presented in the annual report. In other words, the three 10Q reports filed each year are **unaudited**, while the annual 10K report is **audited**. Another name for an unaudited financial statement is "compiled." Compiled financial statements are not audited and no opinion as to the quality of the financial statements is given by the accounting firm. Statements and guarantees about the accuracy of the financial statements are much less than that given by certified/audited financial statements.

An accounting firm that compiles an issuer's financial statements is not required to verify the records. The firm also does not need to analyze the statements for accuracy. The accounting firm would have to notify management if they find erroneous, incomplete, or misleading information in the financial statements.

On the other hand, a certified financial statement has been audited and can be trusted the most by investors. The financial statements are reviewed carefully and audited by a certified public accountant. The CPA goes so far as to offer their opinion on the quality and accuracy of the issuer's financial statements and performs a careful analysis of the issuer and its financial reporting mechanisms.

Compiled (unaudited) financial statements are not as reliable as certified (audited) statements. The reason they are allowed is to provide the timely release of financial information that would be slowed down considerably if an audit were required. Investors typically find that a public company's audited financial statements are much more reliable than the unaudited statements, released more for their timeliness than their accuracy.

Cash vs. Accrual

The difference between **cash basis** and **accrual basis** accounting has to do with when sales and purchases are recorded on the income statement we will look at next. As its name implies, cash-based accounting records revenue only when payment is received and records expenses only when they are paid. Therefore, this system does not recognize accounts receivable or accounts payable. If a business sends out a $4,000 invoice in mid- December and receives payment 30 days later, that revenue would be recorded for January.

On the other hand, accrual-based accounting records revenue when it is earned and expenses when the invoices are received. That same business sending out a $4,000 invoice in mid-December would record the revenue for December using the accrual-based method, regardless of when payment is received. The accrual basis gives businesses a clearer picture of income and expenses over a period of time versus the cash basis. However, the accrual basis needs to be combined with a look at the statement of cash flow, because some businesses can appear to be profitable but have nearly empty bank accounts. Sending out invoices, in other words, is not always the same thing as getting paid, as many business owners have learned the hard way. Using the cash basis, the business would already see its cash position based on its bank account balance.

The cash basis is easier to maintain, and revenue is not taxed until it's received. Receivables and payables do not have to be tracked, and it is easy to see how much in cash resources are available to the business at any given time. The accrual basis is much more widely used. As mentioned, it provides a clearer picture of income and expenses over a period but also requires a careful look at the statement of cash flows, which are ignored under this method of accounting.

To illustrate the effects of the different accounting methods let's say a business presents an invoice for $10,000 to its biggest customer in December, receives a bill for $2,000 from a subcontractor, receives payment of $3,000 from a customer who was invoiced the previous month, and makes a payment of $250 on a bill received in late October. Using the cash basis of accounting, the net income (profit) for the month would be $3,000 - $250 or $2,750. Notice that neither the $10,000 invoice nor the $2,000 bill were factored into the income statement, as no cash was involved. On the other hand, using the accrual basis this same business would record a profit (net income) of $8,000 (the $10,000 invoice minus the $2,000 bill from the subcontractor). Notice that the money received and paid is not factored into the income statement using the accrual method, which is, again, why a look at the statement of cash flows is crucial.

These methods have an impact on taxes, as the accrual method would record the $10,000 invoice as revenue for December and, therefore, December's tax year. On the other hand, the business would record the revenue only when it is received by the customer if using the cash basis. The IRS allows many small businesses to use the cash method, but certain entities are required to use the accrual method. C-Corporations with annual gross receipts > $5 million, for example, are required to use the accrual method, as are partnerships that have a C-Corporation as a partner and receive > $5 million in annual gross receipts.

Many successful American businesses are privately owned. Five Guys Burgers & Fries and Toys 'R' Us, for example, are well-known companies, but we would have to estimate their revenue, expenses and profits since private companies don't report their financial results to the public. By comparison, if we want to know the revenue and net income after tax for Starbucks or Microsoft, we can go to the SEC's **EDGAR** site and pull up the company's most recent quarterly or annual reports.

It's not that Five Guys and Toys 'R' Us don't have income statements, balance sheets, and statements of cash flows. They don't publish their **financial statements**. Starbucks, Microsoft, and McDonald's, on the other hand, are reporting companies who must disclose all relevant information to the investing public, even to those who will never invest in their stock.

An issuer of securities can only pay the interest on their bonds if they have enough revenue to cover it. The preferred stockholders will only get paid if the profits are dependable, and the common stock will rise over the long term only if the profits at the company rise. The financial statements released by public companies disclose the company's revenue, expenses, and profits, as well as their financial condition and their cash flows. Each statement tells a different story about the same company.

Income Statement

The company's revenue and net income are disclosed on the **income statement**. We'll look at another financial statement called the **balance sheet** up ahead. For now let's point out the difference between the two statements, put out by the same company. The balance sheet is a snapshot of the company's financial strength right now, at some point in time. The income statement, on the other hand, shows the results of the company's operations over a period of time. So, if you want to see how solid a company's finances are, check the balance sheet. If you want to see how profitable a company's last fiscal year was, look at their income statement.

A public company had to register its securities offering with the SEC under the **Securities Act of 1933** when it went public. That same company is then a reporting company required to file quarterly and annual reports with the **SEC** under the **Securities Exchange Act of 1934,** as well as making these reports available to their shareholders. This allows the shareholders who invested in these public companies to see the financial condition (balance sheet) of their company and whether the sales and profits are increasing, decreasing, or flattening out (income statement). Because the issuer uploads the information to the SEC's EDGAR website, anyone with curiosity can see the details of the issuer's operations, not just current investors.

An income statement can also be referred to as a "statement of earnings" or "statement of operations," while the balance sheet is often referred to as the "statement of financial condition." Whatever we call it, although the reports are primarily for shareholders, this information is available to anyone who wants to see it.

That includes the company's competitors, which is another reason many companies stay private. For example, if Five Guys is in secret talks to acquire another fast food chain, they would rather keep that on the down-low as opposed to letting McDonald's see what they're thinking and maybe try to out-bid them. On the other hand, if McDonald's is planning to open a certain number of restaurants in

Africa next year, they would have to let the whole world know about it either on their next scheduled filing or by releasing an 8K.

If you go to your favorite financial website or search for a company's "10-K" or "annual shareholder report," you can see the financial statements for companies such as Microsoft, Oracle, and Starbucks. For now, though, let's start small. Let's say you're an 11-year-old kid again, and you have launched a lemonade stand for the summer. Each glass of lemonade sells for $1, and the dollars you pull in through your business this summer are called **sales** or **revenue**. Turns out you sell 10,000 glasses of lemonade, so your revenue is exactly $10,000 over the summer. Revenue is the top line of the income statement.

In some businesses there are returns, refunds, and discounts. Retailers, for example, often report their **net revenue** or **net operating revenue,** which is their revenue after all the returns, refunds, and discounts have been accounted for.

Your lemonade stand didn't do any discounting or experience any returns, so your revenue is what it is. However, $10,000 in revenue is not the same thing as $10,000 of profit. That lemonade you sold was produced by a combination of the following ingredients: purified water, fresh lemons, lemon juice, sugar, and ice. Those are the goods you bought to make the product you sold, which is why the money you spent on them is called the **cost of goods sold** or **cost of revenue.** You also have to serve your product in recyclable cups, which cost $1,000, on top of the $2,000 paid for the ingredients. So, now your $10,000 in revenue is down to $7,000 after subtracting the $3,000 for "cost of goods sold."

And, we're not done subtracting yet. Like all businesses, you have operating expenses to cover. Operating expenses are the expenses not directly associated with the production of the company's products: office rent, administrative salaries, office supplies, entertainment costs, travel costs, etc. You have a handful of operating expenses with your lemonade stand, as well. While you worked the stand yourself most of the time, you also hired your sister to come up with some marketing plans. Her $500 of compensation represents an operating expense to you. There are other operating expenses, including the advertising you do by putting up signs at both ends of the block and running a classified ad in the local paper. Your advertising expense was $500 over the summer.

Operating expenses are often referred to as "SG&A" for **"selling, general, and administrative"** expenses. At a manufacturing company, the labor of the workers on the production floor would generally be part of cost of goods sold, since that labor goes directly into the cost of the finished product. The compensation to the so-called "white-collar workers" out in the cozy offices is part of "selling, general, and administrative" expenses. If you hired baristas to serve up the lemonade, their labor is part of cost of goods sold (aka, cost of revenue), while the compensation for your sister's marketing work is an operating expense, not directly related to producing and serving your product.

Even though you're just an 11-year-old kid, you decided not to slap a piece of cardboard on a stick with the words "Cold Lemonade – $1." Instead, you got the boy next door to build you a stand for $200, and that is a different type of expense. See, you're going to be in business for the next five years, and you'll be using that stand each summer. So, you subtract 1/5 of that $200 on your income statement each year. Instead of subtracting $200 all at once, you only subtract $40 to "depreciate" this vital piece of equipment. Even though you spent the money all up front, next year you will also subtract $40 as a **depreciation** expense on your income statement. You will do that five times until you have depreciated the cost of the stand to zero.

To depreciate an asset means to spread its cost over its estimated useful life. A manufacturing company would not expense a $10 million piece of equipment out on the shop floor the way they would expense the paper and toner used up in the office. The latter are consumed and expensed all at once while the equipment is slowly subtracted/written down on the income statement to spread the cost over its estimated useful life.

Tangible assets are depreciated, while intangible assets are written down using **amortization.** If a company is manufacturing a drug under a patent with a limited life, they will amortize the patent over time, as they would depreciate a plastic injection molding machine over several years. In either case, an asset's cost is being spread over its estimated useful life by taking a series of charges on the income statement through these non-cash expenses called either depreciation or amortization.

There are other assets subject to depreciation at your lemonade stand. You had to buy several large thermoses, a couple of blenders, a little money drawer, a calculator, and a copy of QuickBooks™. These fixed assets all work out to $300, which you depreciate over three years, subtracting another $100 this year.

We have accounted for cost of goods sold, operating expenses, and depreciation. But there are **interest** payments and **taxes** to account for before arriving at the company's **net income** or **net loss** for the reporting period. Your mom had to spot you some credit to buy your first batch of ingredients and, unfortunately, she charges you interest on the loan. On the plus side, you get to deduct that interest before figuring your taxable income, just as homeowners deduct the interest paid on their mortgages. So, you subtract the $20 of interest, and your taxable income is $5,840. Your taxes work out to $40, and after paying those, you have a **net profit**, or **net income after tax**, of $5,800.

Let's review your lemonade stand's results of operations over the summer:

Sales/Revenue	$10,000
Cost of Goods Sold	− $3,000
Operating Expenses	− $1,000
Depreciation, Amortization	− $140
OPERATING INCOME	$5,860
Interest Expense	− $20
PRE-TAX INCOME	$5,840
Taxes	− $40

NET INCOME after tax	$5,800

Statement of Cash Flows

Some subtractions on the income statement do not involve an outlay of cash. Depreciation and amortization spread an asset's historical cost over an estimated useful life, but no cash is being spent when we record the expense on the income statement.

Therefore, since there's a difference between an accounting entry called "depreciation" and actual cash being spent, analysts ignore intangible expenses like that when focusing on **cash flow**, which is how much cash is being generated (or consumed) by a company. One way to estimate cash flow is to take the net income from the income statement and then add back two non-cash charges: depreciation and amortization. Your lemonade stand doesn't have a lot of depreciation and amortization going on, but companies that invest in expensive factories, warehouses, and equipment can show quite different figures for net income on the one hand and cash flow from operations on the other. When they add back the depreciation that reduced their net income, their cash flow is a much higher amount.

But, there's no need to estimate, since in the corporation's 10-K, we also find a separate **statement of cash flows** that shows how much cash has been provided or used by the business over the reporting period. You might think that is the same thing as the net income on the income statement (statement of earnings), but that's not the case. The accrual method of accounting is most widely used, and it involves the company booking revenue/sales before any cash has been exchanged. The statement of cash flows eliminates this sort of distortion, as well as intangible expenses like depreciation/amortization. A good fundamental analyst knows that some companies have been known to book "profits" when they're really not generating enough cash to stay afloat.

The statement of cash flows is separated into three distinct ways in which a company can generate (or exhaust) cash: cash flows from operating activities, cash flows from investing activities, and cash flows from financing activities. **Cash flows from operating activities** are what that phrase sounds like: the company provided or exhausted this much cash through their core operations. For example, Starbucks generates most of its cash by operating thousands of successful coffee shops, but it can also generate cash through investing activities and through financing activities. Most shareholders in SBUX would probably care most about the cash the company generates through its operations. I mean, they're not an investment company or a finance company, right? Cash flow from operations shows us the net income from the income statement, adds back depreciation/amortization, and then records the changes in working capital (from the balance sheet). After dealing with the change in the line items under current assets and current liabilities (working capital), the company can then calculate and report the net cash provided/used by operating activities.

Cash flow from investing activities indicates how much cash was used or generated, usually from investing in capital equipment, and to some extent buying and selling securities, e.g. U.S. Treasuries. Capital equipment ("capex") can be thought of as all the hard, tangible stuff that brick-and-mortar companies have to invest in to operate, stay afloat and maybe make a profit (buying a printing press, remodeling existing stores, building new stores, etc.). If a company is like MSFT or ORCL, they might go on a business buying binge, which is reflected in their cash used for acquisitions. Big increases in this number could indicate that the company is making strategic acquisitions of former competitors, or it could mean that they're generating too much of their returns by buying up smaller fish as opposed to operating successfully.

Cash flow from financing activities is the cash provided/used through basically any activity involving the shareholders (owners) or bondholders (creditors) of the company. If stock is issued, cash is generated, while if the company engages in share buyback programs, cash is used up. If a company issues bonds, cash is generated, while when it finally redeems or calls those bonds, cash is used up. Also, when the company pays dividends to shareholders, it's easy to see where that cash is ending up, right? Young, growing companies often issue stock to finance their operations. That may be fine, but new stock issues dilute the value of the existing shareholders' equity. More mature companies, with plenty of cash on hand, often buy back their shares to make each existing share more valuable. Either way, we could track these activities under this section of the statement of cash flows.

The terms "cash flows from investing activities" and "cash flows from financing activities" could be potentially confusing. Remember that if a company buys Government securities or shares of a public company on the open market, we'd see that under "cash flows from investing activities." And, if the company <u>invests</u> in a printing press, that's under cash flows from investing activities, too—no matter how much "sense" it might make to think of that as a "financing" activity. No, cash flow from financing activities includes the cash generated by issuing stocks or bonds and the cash flow exhausted buying back stock and/or retiring bonds. Would the test exploit this natural confusion? Anything's possible.

Balance Sheet

If you were applying for a loan, the lender would want to know two important things: how much money do you make, and what kind of collateral do you have? You could submit your statement of cash flow showing all your sources of income minus expenses. But the lender would also like to see what kind of **assets** you're holding minus your **liabilities.** Your lemonade stand might need to borrow money to expand someday. If so, the bank would want to see your balance sheet when you apply. The balance sheet reveals financial condition.

The basic formula for the balance sheet is expressed as:

$$\text{Assets} = \text{Liabilities} + \text{Stockholders' Equity}$$

or

$$\text{Assets} - \text{Liabilities} = \text{Stockholders' Equity}$$

Assets represent what a company owns. Liabilities represent what a company owes. You take what a company owns, subtract what it owes, and that's the **net worth** of the company. Another name for net worth is **stockholders' equity**, which implies that the stockholders are the owners of the company, so what we want to know is: what is that ownership worth?

Assets

Assets are divided into three types. The first type is **current assets**. Current assets represent cash and anything that could be converted to cash in the short-term: **cash & equivalents**, **accounts receivable**, and **inventory**. Cash is cash, and it's a good thing. "Equivalents" are money market instruments earning some interest, which is also a good thing. If they mature in the near term, commercial paper, bankers' acceptances, repurchase agreements, and T-Bills are considered "cash equivalents" here on the balance sheet.

From your profits at the lemonade stand, you wisely deposited $560 into a savings account at the end of the summer, as you know how important it is to have some cash on hand for expenses and investments into the business. File that under "cash." Accounts receivable is what customers owe the company. You were nice enough to sell lemonade on credit to two of your best friends over the summer, and they ran up a tab of $40 between them. You intend to be paid for those sales in the near-term, so you list that payment as an asset.

Inventory is the stuff the company makes and plans to sell just as soon as possible. When temperatures dropped suddenly and the cold rain started up in late August, you were left holding a rather large quantity of lemons, sugar, etc. You creatively made up as much lemonade as possible and turned it into popsicles. Next season, you intend to sell that inventory for $40, making the inventory a current asset.

The second type of assets, **fixed assets,** include office buildings, factories, equipment, furniture, etc. This is the stuff a company uses as opposed to putting directly into its finished products. Fixed assets could all be converted into cash, but this stuff was not purchased to be sold; it was purchased to generate revenue: printing presses, industrial control systems, fleet of delivery vans, etc. A large corporation would list the value of the real estate, as well as the value of the assembly line equipment, as well as the furniture and even the artwork hanging on the walls of the visitor lobby under fixed assets.

Then there are **intangible assets**. Intangible assets include patents, trademarks, and **goodwill**. When a company acquires another company, they usually pay more than just the value of the fixed assets. They're paying for the brand-identity, the customer base, etc. So, that excess paid above the hard, tangible value of assets you can touch and see is called "goodwill." Let's face it, your lemonade stand has no intangible assets at this point, but if you ever purchase the goodwill of a rival lemonade stand up the street, we would list that intangible asset here. Then, we would add all three types of assets and call the sum your **total assets**.

Liabilities

On the other side of the equation we find liabilities, which represent what a company owes. Anything that has to be paid out in the short term is a **current liability**. **Accounts payable**, **accrued wages**, and **accrued taxes** all represent bills the company has to pay currently, which is why they're called current liabilities. Your mom picked up a few batches of ingredients over the summer and put them on her credit card. Just as soon as she remembers doing so, you intend to pay her back the $60, listed under accounts payable. And, you owe your sister $100, which is listed under accrued wages.

The principal amount of a loan or a bond that has to be paid more than a year out is a **long-term liability**. You owe your mother $240 in principal, which is why it's listed under long-term liabilities. Add the current and the long-term liabilities together and you have **total liabilities** of $400.

Stockholders' Equity/Net Worth

Stockholders' Equity is sometimes called Shareholders' Equity or "net worth." Whatever we call it, remember that equity equals ownership, and the stockholders own a percentage of the company. What is that ownership worth at the time the balance sheet is printed? That's stockholders' equity. Companies place the total par value of their preferred stock under this heading. Common stock is assigned a par value of, say, $1, so if a company has 1,000,000 shares of common stock, they would list the par value as $1,000,000 and place it under stockholders' equity.

If investors bought the stock in the IPO at $11, that represents a surplus of $10 above the par value, so the company would list **paid-in surplus** of $10,000,000, as well. And then any earnings that have been retained are listed as **retained earnings**. Why did you only retain $600 this year? Because you're smart enough to know that a business that involves little capital equipment, little financing, and few recurring costs can afford to pay out big distributions to the owners. As the sole owner, you cut yourself a $5,200 dividend check on September 1st and smiled all the way to and from the bank.

Footnotes

In a company's quarterly and annual shareholder reports the financial statements are accompanied by **footnotes** that help clarify the numbers. For example, what does the company mean by "equivalents" in its "cash and equivalents" line item—debt securities with six months to maturity? Three months? When does a company recognize "revenue"? Is it when the company ships pies to a distributor, or only when someone has paid for the product? Also, unusual revenue events or charges need to be explained so that investors don't get the wrong idea about their long-term impact.

Whenever the numbers in a financial statement require further clarification, the footnotes section is used to provide it. A **10-K** or **annual shareholder report,** for example, presents the consolidated financial statements and then follows up with "notes to consolidated financial statements" that help clarify all the numbers presented from the balance sheet, income statement, and statement of cash flow.

Analytical Methods

This section explores many mathematical concepts and formulae. While both are important, the test is generally more concerned that you can recognize and work with a concept as opposed to leaning over your calculator and pushing buttons. Then again, there are calculations on the exam, which is why we write out the formulae and use them in our online practice questions.

 Just be prepared to deal with the information in this section from many different angles at the testing center. You might calculate a stock's price-to-earnings ratio. Or, you might choose which answer best describes the price-to-earnings ratio. Or, you might be asked which type of investor would care about the price-to-earnings ratio. Or, you might not see "price-to-earnings ratio" in your batch of questions at all.

So, there is really no reason to cover a white board or make a stack of flash cards with all the formulae we look at in this section and elsewhere in the book. Your time would be better spent reading the textbook and then doing the online exercises and practice questions.

Financial Ratios and Their Uses

Let's take a look at your lemonade stand's results in terms of various financial ratios pulled from your income statement and balance sheet. For a start-up lemonade stand $10,000 of revenue is impressive. But, your $10,000 of sales was immediately reduced by the $3,000 of cost of goods sold that went into producing the lemonade. The $7,000 that we are left with at this point represents your company's **gross profit.**

Gross Profit = Revenue – Cost of Goods Sold

To figure your **gross margin of profit,** or **gross margin,** we would divide that $7,000 by the $10,000 of revenue to arrive at a gross margin of 70%.

Gross Margin = Gross Profit / Revenue

If a company's cost of goods sold are too high, they have no hope of covering all the other expenses further down the income statement. A restaurant that sells a $5 hamburger with cost of goods sold of $4.50 will not survive, for example, yet if that same company could make a $5 hamburger for just $1.25, they might.

After cost of goods sold, we subtract the operating expenses and depreciation, and arrive at the **operating profit** or **operating earnings.** Some analysts call this line of the income statement **operating income** but whatever we call it, your lemonade stand had $5,860 at this point. If we divide that back into the revenue of $10,000, we see that your **operating margin** is 58.6%

Operating Margin = Operating Income / Revenue

As you're starting to see, this industry uses a lot of different terms for the same thing. Even though we used three names (operating earnings, operating income, and operating profit) so far, there is yet another name for "operating profit," called "**EBIT,**" or "earnings before interest and taxes." EBIT is a company's revenue minus all expenses other than interest and taxes. From the income statement, EBIT is the line we arrive at once we've taken revenue and subtracted cost of goods sold plus all operating expenses.

Companies that issue bonds must cover the interest payments, so bond analysts often compare the EBIT to the annual interest expense to arrive at the "**times interest earned.**" If a company has $3 million in "EBIT" and $1 million in interest payments to cover, their "times interest earned" is 3-to-1. In other words, the interest expense is earned three times over, which represents a cushion to the bondholders.

Similar calculations derived from the income statement include "EBT," which is "earnings before taxes," and EBITDA, which stands for "earnings before interest, taxes, depreciation, and amortization." EBITDA takes revenue and subtracts the cost of goods sold plus the basic operating expenses of running the business. It leaves off the fancier subtractions for interest, taxes, depreciation and amortization. Analysts often consider EBITDA for companies with a lot of fixed assets subject to depreciation. Such companies may show a net loss on their income statement due largely to depreciation and financing connected to those fixed assets, but when viewed through EBITDA may look more impressive.

For example, although a consulting firm might be able to show a profit the first year or two, a manufacturing company might have to invest so much in their property and equipment that profits are five years into the future. Looking at the company's EBITDA, however, analysts might see that the company is generating some rather impressive amounts of cash even while reporting a net loss on the income statement.

So, finally, we're at the bottom line. Net income, net income after tax, and net profit all mean the same thing. It is an amount of money, the $5,800 shown on the bottom line of your income statement. When we take that amount on the bottom line and compare it to the revenue on the top line, we arrive at the company's **net profit margin** or just **net margin**. If your lemonade stand shows net income of $5,800 on the bottom line, we divide that by the revenue on the top line of $10,000 to arrive at a 58% net margin.

Net Profit Margin = Net Income / Revenue

Lucky for you, your lemonade stand has no shareholders making claims on your profits of $5,800. To understand how it works at public companies, though, let's pretend you do have shareholders in your lemonade stand. You reported net income of $5,800. If you had raised your capital by issuing stock, you would have been issuing "shares," right?

Well, time to share. Who gets dividends first? Preferred stockholders. If you pay a preferred dividend of $800, that leaves exactly $5,000 of **earnings available to common**. If your company has $5,000 in earnings available to common with 1,000 shares of common stock outstanding, that represents $5 of **earnings per-share** (EPS). Each share of stock is attached to $5 of profit, in other words.

Earnings per-share = Earnings Available to Common / Shares Outstanding

We could apply a more stringent test that assumes all convertible securities (bonds, preferred stock, or warrants) are turned into common stock all at once. When these investors convert to common stock, your $5,000 in earnings would end up being divided among more shares. If your company ended up with 1,250 shares outstanding after conversion, your **diluted earnings per-share** would be only $4.

Now that we have our earnings per-share, we can also see how much gets paid out in dividends. Not surprisingly, we call this the **dividend payout ratio**. This takes the annual dividends paid and divides it by the earnings per-share (EPS). Your company has earnings-per-share (EPS) of $5. If you paid out $1 in common dividends, you paid out 20% of your earnings, which is called your "dividend payout ratio."

Dividend Payout = Annual Dividend / Earnings per-share

As we saw earlier, the income statement shows the sales, expenses, and profit or loss over a reporting period. The question, "Did we make our numbers this quarter?" would typically be answered with a quick look at the income statement over the financial quarter.

The balance sheet reveals the financial condition of the company, and there are many important ratios pulled from this statement. Bondholders are concerned about a company's **asset coverage** of the bonds and the safety of their promised income stream. We looked at the safety of income on the income statement. Now let's see how the balance sheet reveals the asset coverage of the bonds.

Current assets represent what a company owns. Current liabilities represent what a company owes. Hopefully, the company owns more than it owes. If not, it has a "burn rate" showing how quickly it could go bankrupt. Fundamental analysts take current assets and subtract current liabilities to measure **working capital** (sometimes called "net working capital"). This is a measure of how able a company is to finance current operations.

We're talking about short-term **liquidity** here. When a company's short-term liabilities exceed its current assets, that company is in great danger of getting behind in payments to suppliers and interest payments to creditors. On the other hand, if a company's current assets exceed its current liabilities, this company is in a strong position to fund current operations, just as your lemonade operation would be if you had $1,000 in total bills and $4,000 in the bank.

Working Capital = Current Assets – Current Liabilities

Your lemonade stand shows current assets of $640 and current liabilities of $160. Your working capital is, therefore, the difference of $480. Working capital is an amount of money. Analysts also express current assets and current liabilities as a ratio, known as the **current ratio**. Instead of subtracting $160 from $640, we would say that $640, divided by (over) $160, gives you a current ratio of 4 to 1. Basically, for every $1 of short-term debt, you have $4 of liquid assets to cover it. Not bad.

Current Ratio = Current Assets / Current Liabilities

Inventory is a current asset along with accounts receivable and cash & equivalents. But, inventory is not always a liquid asset. When we subtract inventory from current assets, we arrive at our **quick assets.** Quick assets include assets easily converted to cash: cash and marketable securities plus accounts receivable.

Looking at the quick assets of a company, analysts apply a more stringent test, known as the **quick ratio** or the **acid test**. The "i" in the words "quick" and "acid" reminds us that "inventory" is subtracted from current assets before we compare them to current liabilities. Why do that? Those frozen lemonade pops you made might go bad in storage, or might not strike your customers' fancy next summer. So, in case you didn't sell your inventory, what would your short-term financial condition look like then? We would deduct the $40 of inventory from your $640 of current assets first, and then compare that $600 to the $160 of current liabilities. At this point we would see a ratio of 3.75 to 1 for your quick ratio. For every $1 of short-term debt, you have $3.75 to cover it, even if the inventory completely spoils.

Quick Ratio = (Current Assets – Inventory) / Current Liabilities

Worth just $40, we can safely say that your lemonade stand has little inventory, but many manufacturing companies, car dealers, and supermarkets live and die by how effectively they manage their inventory. To measure this effectiveness analysts look at a company's **inventory turnover ratio**. This formula provides a link between the income statement and the balance sheet. To calculate it, we take the cost of goods sold from the income statement and divide that amount by the average inventory over the period. It is a ratio because it shows how many "times" inventory is turned over during the reporting period. If the turnover rate is too slow, that company is not deploying its capital effectively.

Current ratio, quick ratio, the acid test, and working capital measure short-term liquidity. A company's ability to meet current interest payments is reflected from a look at these concerns. The company's ability to repay the principal and avoid bankruptcy is reflected through a longer-term look at the balance sheet. For a picture of the company's long-term financial condition analysts calculate the **debt-to-equity ratio**. The debt-to-equity ratio shows us how leveraged the company is. It gives analysts an idea as to how much money was raised through borrowing/leverage compared to the money raised by selling ownership/equity stakes. The formula is:

Debt-to-Equity Ratio = Total Liabilities / Shareholders' Equity

The higher the ratio, the more leveraged the company is. Another formula that is frequently used for the same purpose is called the **debt ratio**, which compares the total debt of the company to its total assets. Again, the higher this number/ratio, the more leveraged the company is. The formula is:

Debt Ratio = Total Liabilities / Total Assets

another ratio that shows bondholders the risk of default is the **bond ratio**. This formula shows the percentage of the company's capitalization that comes from the issuance of bonds with maturities greater than one year. To calculate the bond ratio analysts take the value of the company's long-term debt and divide that by the long-term debt plus shareholder's equity. This shows what percentage the bonds make of the company's total capitalization. Except for utility companies, a bond ratio above 33% is generally considered a high amount of leverage.

We looked at "book value per-share" for common stock. Similarly, analysts often calculate an issuer's net asset value per bond to see how much in tangible assets is associated with each bond issued. To calculate this number, we take the net tangible assets of the company (not goodwill and other intangible assets) and divide that by the number of bonds issued by the company.

In a later chapter we'll see that ratings agencies including Moody's Investor Services and S&P use the concerns discussed above when assigning a credit rating to an issue of debt securities.

Bondholders are concerned about solvency and long-term liquidity. Shareholders are concerned about profitability, which is measured in many ways. Analysts call the hard, tangible asset value associated with a share of common stock the **book value per-share**. To calculate it, they take the stockholders' equity minus the preferred shares, divided by the shares outstanding. Value investors love to buy stocks trading at low multiples to book value. If they can buy the stock at or below book value, even better.

Book Value per-share = Stockholder's Equity / Shares Outstanding

To judge how effectively a company generates profits from its shareholders' investment into the company analysts calculate the company's **return on equity**. The return on equity (ROE) shows how much in profits each dollar of common stockholder's equity generates for the company. As with many measures of a company's financial health, this one combines a line from the income statement with a line from the balance sheet. The formula is:

Return on Equity = Net Income / Stockholders' Equity

Usually, "return on equity" relates only to common stock. Therefore, the preferred dividend is excluded from net income before comparing what's left to shareholder's equity. For more precision, some analysts use the term "return on common equity" to clarify that preferred stock is not being considered for this calculation.

Your lemonade stand has little inventory, but many manufacturing companies, car dealers, and supermarkets live and die by how effectively they manage their inventory. To measure this effectiveness analysts look at a company's **inventory turnover ratio**. This formula provides a link between the income statement and the balance sheet. To calculate it, we take the cost of goods sold from the income statement and divide that amount by the average inventory over the period. It is a ratio because it shows how many "times" inventory is turned over during the reporting period. If the turnover rate is too slow, that company is not deploying its capital effectively.

Valuation Ratios

Publicly traded stocks trade at various "multiples" such as the **price-to-earnings ratio**. The P/E ratio compares the market price of the stock to the earnings per-share. Growth stocks trade at high P/E ratios, while those trading at low P/E ratios are considered value stocks. The test could say that the P/E ratio shows the enthusiasm investors have for the company's profits, as reflected in the market price for their stock.

P/E = Market Price / Earnings per-share

Earnings are the bottom line of the income statement, which means they can be manipulated through creative accounting to some extent without necessarily being misleading. For this reason, many analysts prefer using **price-to-sales**. Sales/revenue is the first number reported on the income statement and is, therefore, probably the most reliable figure presented. Or, if the issuer is not yet profitable, there would be no earnings and, therefore, no "e" to compare to the "p." Price-to-sales compares the stock's market price to the revenue per-share.

Price-to-Sales = Market Price / Revenue per-share

If the issuer is not yet profitable, analysts typically focus on price-to-sales as well as **price-to-cash**. The price-to-cash ratio compares the stock's market price to the operating cash flow per-share.

Price-to-Cash = Market Price / Cash Flow per-share

If the issuer is not yet profitable, price-to-sales and price-to-cash are most instructive. For profitable companies, the price-to-earnings and **price-to-book** ratios are most instructive. As we saw, the book value is calculated from the issuer's balance sheet, sometimes considered a hypothetical liquidating value that indicates the tangible assets propping up a stock's value. A stock's price-to-book ratio is the market price compared to the book value per-share. If the ratio is high, we are looking at a growth stock. If the ratio is considered low, we are looking at a value stock.

$$\text{Price-to-Book} = \text{Market Price} / \text{Book Value per-share}$$

Time Value of Money

The **time value of money** means that a dollar can always earn some rate of interest in a savings account, CD, or T-Bill, so any amount of money is worth more the sooner it is received. We're about to look at **future value** and **present value**, where we will see that money earning 5% year after year grows magically into a large pile of cash due to "compounded returns" and the more frequently the principal compounds, the better. For now, let's just look at what happens in one year.

If you invest $100 today at 5% interest, you will have $105 in one year. We call that $105 the future value of the $100. It is calculated by multiplying $100 by 1.05. The number 1.05 represents that you will end up with 105% of what you started with—the $100 plus 5%. On the other hand, $100 received one year from now is worth only $95.24 today. Instead of multiplying $100 by 1.05 to calculate its future value, divide the $100 by 1.05 to find its present value. $100 divided by 1.05 = $95.24. In other words, if you invest $95.24 at 5% for one year, you'll end up with $100 at the end of the year. You can double-check that by taking $95.24 times 1.05 and getting back to $100. If the exam makes you calculate either future value or present value, I recommend double-checking your math.

Future Value

Of course, it's hard to get excited over the fact that $100 invested at 5% for one year takes the investment all the way up to $105. But, if you're patient and leave it in there a few years, it can grow quite nicely, even at just 5%. To see how large the investment would become, multiply $100 by 1.05, then multiply that by 1.05, and so on for every year you leave it in the account. These are **compound returns**, and through the magic of **compound interest** we see that $100 times 1.05 leaves us with $105 after year one. If we multiply that by 1.05, we have $110.25 after year two. Multiply that by 1.05, and we have $115.76 after year three, $121.55 after year four, and $127.62 after year five. So, the future value of $100 invested for five years at 5% compounded interest is $127.62. If that doesn't impress you, add zeros to your initial investment: $10,000 becomes $12,762 after five years, or $100,000 becomes $127,628 after five years, and so on.

The exam could say that a company's profits are $1 per-share—if they grow 7% per year for 5 years, what will the earnings per-share be at the end of the period? Just multiply the $1 by 1.07 five times in a row to get your answer. Or, the 25-cent dividend compounds at 6% for five years, and so on.

The formula for future value can be expressed a few different ways. One way is:

$$\text{FV} = \text{Principal} \times (1 + r)^t$$

Math is a language, and that is just the mathematical way to represent what we were doing by multiplying an investment by 1.05 for 5% or 1.10 for 10%, and so on. In this formula, "r" means "rate of return" and "t" means "time." Remember, our returns are compounded. So if you get 10% the first year, you'll have more money earning 10% the next year, and so on. Even if it's the same 10% rate of return, it's always 10% of a bigger number. So, if we expect to get 10% each year over a 5-year period, we would say that the FV (future value) of a dollar invested today will be $1 x (1.10)5. 1.10 is just the "1" plus 10%. The investment will multiply itself by 1.10 five times in a row. And remember that the "5" doesn't mean to multiply by 5. It means to multiply the 1.10 by itself five times. The exponent "5" means "to the fifth power."

So what we're doing in our example is multiplying our invested dollar by 1.10 five times in a row. The dollar would be worth $1.61 at the end of five years, and you can add as many zeroes as your client is willing to invest. $100,000 now would be worth $161,000 then (give or take). One million now equals about $1.61 million five years later.

Another way the formula can be written is:

$$Pn = P0 \ (1 + r)^n$$

"Pn" now stands for the future value of the investment. The little "n" is the number of years the portfolio will be compounding. P0 is the original investment or original amount. So, it's the same idea and formula expressed differently.

We just looked at a magical portfolio that compounds conveniently once per year, right on schedule. Well, if we had an investment that compounded more frequently—every six months, every quarter, or every month—that would be known as a "really good thing." The more frequently an investment compounds, the better that is for the investor.

When an investor buys a bond paying 5%, he receives 5% *simple* interest. That means the issuer pays 5% of the same $1,000 principal each year. If a corporate bond paid compound interest, it would work like our compounded returns above. In that case, a 5% bond would pay (but doesn't) $50 the first year, but then 5% of $1,050 the next year, and 5% of $1,102.50 the next, and so on. Which would be great, but the reality is that the issuer pays 5% <u>simple</u> interest on a bond. If you hold a bond for five years paying 5% simple interest, you get your $1,000 back plus total interest payments of $250.

So, compound interest pays interest on the principal plus the accumulated interest on that principal, while simple interest pays a rate applied only to the principal. Bank CDs pay compounded rates of interest. Unfortunately, the rates of interest are so low and the terms so short that one barely notices a difference between simple and compound interest on those safe-money products. So, where would an investor find a 5% compounded rate of return? There might not be any security guaranteeing that rate, but a diversified bond portfolio could easily return that much or more over the investor's holding period through reinvestments of interest payments.

Present Value

Future value answers this question: if I invest this much money and get this rate of return for this period of time, what will my money be worth in the future? **Present value** answers this question: if I need this much money in the future and can get this rate of return for this period, how much money do I have to put in now, in the present? Maybe you need a certain amount of money to put your child through college. Given a rate of return, how much do you need to invest today to get there? That's present value. I already sneaked it in when I said that $100 received in one year is worth only $95 today, since I could invest $95.24 right now at 5% and turn it into $100 in just one year.

The formula for Present Value is:

$$PV = FV / (1 + r)^t$$

So, for Future Value, we said that $100,000 invested today at 10% would be worth $161,000 in five years. What if your client said she needed exactly $190,000 in five years—how much must she invest at 10% to get there? Start with $190,000 and divide by 1.10 five times in a row. The investor needs to put in $117,975 in the present to end up with $190,000 at the end of her holding period. Not that we should tell her to expect 10% compounded returns for five years; just illustrating how these formulas work for the exam.

Internal Rate of Return and Net Present Value

Whenever a business is considering the opportunity to invest in a new call center, 3D printer, or other cash-generating asset, they first need to determine whether the investment will produce enough cash to not just cover the cost of borrowing the capital, but also to make a profit. In other words, they need to calculate the **Net Present Value (NPV)** of the expected cash flows for the project. To do this, they "discount" the cash flows by a required rate of return called the **internal rate of return**. Internal rate of return can be defined as "the discount rate that makes the net present value of the cash flows equal to zero." That sounds fancy, but it really just means that the investment will look attractive if it can generate any positive cash flow above our required rate of return.

Think of net present value (NPV) as the difference—positive or negative—between the present values of an investment's cash inflows and its cash outflows. If the net present value is negative, the project should be rejected as not financially feasible. A negative NPV means that it costs more to borrow the money than it's worth given the cash flows expected from the investment/project. If the net present value is positive, on the other hand, the investment may be attractive, since the cash inflows outweigh the outflows/costs associated with generating it.

Descriptive Statistics and Risk Measurements

Many people think of risk as the chance of losing money, but risk is generally defined in terms of the fluctuations of value an investment experiences. The words "unpredictable" and "risky" basically mean the same thing from this viewpoint. During the accumulation phase of our retirement savings plan, we can withstand some of these fluctuations. But, once we retire, if we are liquidating shares of mutual funds to meet living expenses, we can get hurt during bear markets for stocks or bonds. If one month the account is worth $300,000 and the next only $265,000, a retiree could burn through her investments quickly just by making scheduled sales and withdrawals.

I'm not saying that younger people should shrug off large fluctuations in value, either. I would think that at age 23 watching an investment drop by, say, $5,000 could also be alarming, considering how many hours most 23-year-olds have to work to make five grand. In a panic, such an investor might pull out of the securities markets entirely and never reach his retirement goal because he was talked into more volatility than he could handle on an emotional and psychological level.

Risk can be measured through descriptive statistics including both measures of central tendency such as the mean, median, and mode, and measures of variability or dispersion, such as standard deviation.

Measures of Central Tendency

Measures of central tendency provide a summary of a set of data and give investors an idea of what a typical return might be for a stock, bond, or mutual fund investment. The **mode** is the most common number in the set of data—maybe the portfolio returns 2% frequently, and that becomes the mode.

The **median** is the halfway point or "middle value," meaning that half the numbers are below this number, and half the numbers are above.

Then there is the **mean**, which is the average of the numbers. You may have read about the "average annual income" in your area and also the "median income." Those two numbers are not the same thing. The average annual income is figured by adding up everybody's income and dividing by that number of people. The median income tells us where the middle point of all the incomes is, where half are below and half above this number. If we want the average net worth of Bill Gates, Warren Buffet and a normal human being we might total up $80 billion for Bill Gates, plus $65 billion for Warren Buffet, plus $500,000 for the normal human being, divided by three. The average or mean financial net worth is $48.3 billion. On the other hand, the half-way point or median is the middle number, $65 billion.

Another name for "mean" is "arithmetic mean." This is not the same as the "geometric mean."

If we calculated an arithmetic mean, we would be figuring a simple average that could be misleading. For example, if an investor put $10,000 into a brokerage account and had the following returns, what would the account be worth at the end of the third year?

Year 1: −10%

Year 2: −20%

Year 3: +30%

If we take a simple "arithmetic mean" or average of −10, −20, and +30%, it might seem that the account should be back at $10,000. That is because the arithmetic mean does not account for the effects of compounded returns. For compounded returns each year's return is dependent on the one before it.

So, rather than trying to take the simple average of -10, -20 and 30, we can avoid misleading the investor by using a finance calculator to calculate the geometric mean. The geometric mean reveals that the account is worth only $9,360. When the value dropped 10%, the account value dropped to $9,000. When it lost 20%, it dropped to $7,200. If that account rises 30%, we're only back to $9,360.

To avoid misleading investors about their returns the geometric mean should always be used. The only time the arithmetic mean is accurate is when the account experiences no volatility, which is just about never in my experience.

Measures of central tendency indicate what typically happens. On the other hand, when we discuss **standard deviation**, we look at how much variability there is among an investment's returns. Through the perspective of standard deviation, an investment whose results are all over the road is risky, whether the surprises are on the plus or the minus side.

A piece of data that resides far from the central tendency of a set of numbers is called an outlier. If an investment has had an unusually high or low return in one year, that will skew the mean much more than it will the mode or median. In a set of results where there is an outlier, statisticians prefer to use the median over the other two m-words. When there are no outliers, the arithmetic mean is the best measure of central tendency.

Let's say the returns for a portfolio the past 9 years were: 5, 6, 5, 7, 6, 8, 9, 15, 5. The mode is the most common value of 5. The median is 6 because there are four values above and below that number. The mean is just the average of the nine numbers, 7.33%. And the returns are all positive because it's just an example.

Standard Deviation

Measures of central tendency give us an idea of what the typical returns have been for an investment, while a measure of dispersion tells us how far away from that average an investment's returns can be.

Standard deviation measures how much an investment deviates from its average return. Or, we could say that standard deviation measures the dispersion of a data set from its arithmetic mean. However we define it, standard deviation is understood in percentage terms, so a standard deviation of 5 means the investment typically deviates 5 percentage points above and below its average return. If the average return is 10% and the standard deviation is 5, the likely range of return outcomes is from 5% to 15%.

More accurately, that's what happens within "one standard deviation," which tells us what happens about 2/3 (68%) of the time. What happens about 95% of the time? Those returns lie within "two standard deviations." So, if the average return is 10 and the standard deviation is 5, two-thirds of the time the returns are within 5% and 15% (−5 and +5 from the mean); about 95% of the time the returns are within 0 and 20% (−10 and +10 from the mean). And, in virtually all cases (99.7% of the time), the returns in our data set will be within three standard deviations, which would put virtually all of our annual returns within −5% on the low end and 25% on the high end. What about that other .3%? What happens there? Well, those are the years that can really smart, which is why prudent investors don't trust their computer models too much.

As always, the exam can test a concept from many angles, so if you get a test question showing a table of numbers, understand that the set of numbers that hover more closely together is showing you a lower standard deviation. In other words, if the monthly returns for one stock were 3%, 5%, and 6%, that would represent a much lower standard deviation—less volatility—than a stock whose returns were −4%, 7%, and 17%. If a mutual fund gained 1% each month, its standard deviation would be zero, since every month it did the same thing—went up by 1%. Maybe you're wondering what the fund's standard deviation would be if it steadily lost 1% each month. Also zero. So, while it's nice to have a low standard deviation, this is not to be confused with making money.

The exam may ask you to identify which portfolio is the riskiest and/or has the highest standard deviation in a way that lets you eyeball your way to the answer. That's what we're hoping. Maybe it will say that one portfolio had a high return of 8% and a low of –10%, while another had a high of 4% and a low of –8%. Obviously, the second one has a lower standard deviation. It didn't go up as high or down as low. Similarly, an equity income mutual fund usually doesn't go up or down as much as a growth fund, so its standard deviation is lower, regardless of which fund has a higher total return. Another name for this simplified form of standard deviation is **range**.

Just in case the exam expects you to know the math behind standard deviation, here goes. If our portfolio had a high of 8% and a low of –10%, what was the average or the mean return? Just take – 10 plus 8 divided by two to get the average. The average or mean is –1%. If you're more of a visual person, imagine moving 9 spaces from either –10 or 8 on an imaginary number line—where do you end up?

Negative one percent. As we said, we now look at how far the returns were from that average. Positive 8% is 9 away from –1% and –10% is also 9 away from –1%. Since it's math, we now square both of those numbers. 9 squared = 81 and 9 squared = 81. We add those two 81s to get 162. Then, we divide 162 by (n–1) where "n" equals the number of values in our little data set. Since there are only two numbers, we divide 162 by (2–1), which is, of course, just 162. In case that wasn't enough steps, we now have to hit the little square root button on the calculator, and our answer is approximately 12.73. Yes standard deviation is also defined as "the square root of variance." So, 12.73 is the standard deviation of this portfolio. A portfolio with a standard deviation of, say, 9.2, then, is considered less risky.

Sharpe Ratio

The **Sharpe ratio** uses standard deviation to determine if an investor is getting enough return for the risk he's taking. The exam might say the Sharpe ratio measures the excess return per unit of risk. Mathematically, it is the actual return you get minus the "riskless rate of return," divided by the standard deviation.

Seriously. So, the Sharpe ratio measures **risk-adjusted returns**. And, the higher the number, the better. Also, the **riskless rate of return** we use as a comparison to what we're getting is the yield on 3-month T-Bills. So, if an investment gets a 10% return when the yield on 3-month T-Bills was 5%, we're down to 5% of excess return. If the standard deviation is 5, we would divide 5 by 5 for a Sharpe ratio of 1.

Notice how if the standard deviation had been 10, that Sharpe ratio would have been a lower number. Which is bad. The higher the Sharpe ratio, the better the investor is being compensated for the risk he's taking. That could be confusing—a high standard deviation is a red flag, but a high Sharpe ratio is a good thing.

Beta

If you click on the overview of a stock at your favorite financial website, chances are you'll see the **beta**, which is an investment's tendency to go up and down compared to the overall market. We use the S&P 500 as the measure of the overall market and then track how much the stock or portfolio moved compared to that index. So a beta of "1" means a security moves exactly in step with the overall market (S&P 500). A beta of more than 1 implies that the stock is more volatile than the overall market, while a beta of less than 1 implies that the stock is less volatile than the overall market.

A stock with a beta of more than 1 will out-perform the market when stock prices rise but under-perform the market when stock prices fall. Or, we could reverse that if the beta were less than 1, right? A stock with a low beta could be said to "under-perform a bull market and out-perform a bear market."

Alpha

If the expected return is 8%, but we only get a 6% return, we call that "negative alpha." The portfolio manager didn't do as well as expected. However, if the portfolio manager took a portfolio with an expected return of 8% and got a 10% return, that excess return could be referred to as "positive alpha." Portfolio managers who get excess returns or show positive alpha are said to be adding value with their money management skills. Those who consistently show "negative alpha" are eventually shown the door. I often see hedge funds described in terms of "alpha-driven" results, meaning that this portfolio's performance is almost entirely dependent on the skills of the portfolio manager, not on the movement of the overall market.

Like the Sharpe ratio, alpha measures performance on a risk-adjusted basis. Another way to define **alpha** is to say that it measures an investment's performance compared to a benchmark beyond what is predicted by beta.

The exam could have you figure alpha based on beta. For example, let's say an investment has a return of 8% and a beta of 1.5. The benchmark is the S&P 500, which was up 6% over the period. Because 8% is higher than 6%, this was a good investment, right? Well, a beta of 1.5 implies a volatility that is 50% greater than the benchmark. If the benchmark returned 6%, the beta of 1.5 implies that the returns should have been 9%. Because the return was only 8%, the alpha is -1, which means the investment was not good on a risk-adjusted basis.

R-Squared

R-squared is a statistical measurement that tries to explain how much of a portfolio's movement is explained by the movement in the benchmark index. For a fixed-income portfolio, T-Bills can serve as a benchmark. For stocks, the S&P 500 provides a useful benchmark. The values are from 0 to 100. If the R-squared value is 100, that means that 100% of the movement is explained by the movement of the benchmark index. A lower value (under 75, say) would indicate that the portfolio does not move in line with the index. Since index funds are so cheap to own, some investors don't like to pay for active portfolio management if the portfolio acts just like an index. So a lower R-squared value could be viewed as a sign that the portfolio manager is not just playing golf, mirroring an index, and charging unnecessary fees for active management.

Correlation

Alpha takes the volatility of an investment and compares its risk-adjusted performance to the benchmark that the investment most closely matches. Beta measures systematic risk, showing how much a security or portfolio moves compared to the overall market.

Correlation, on the other hand, shows how closely related—or unrelated—two investments are. The **correlation coefficient** between two investments ranges from 1 to -1. A positive correlation of 1 would indicate that two securities move in lock-step with each other. A negative correlation means that two securities move in opposite directions, with a coefficient of -1 meaning they move by the same amount but, again, in different directions. A correlation of zero means what it sounds like—there is zero correlation between two things. A correlation coefficient of .3 implies that two securities move in the same direction sharing a correlation of 30%. If one security rises 10%, the other rises 3%. A correlation coefficient of -.4 means that if one security rises 10%, the other one drops 4%.

The importance of correlation is that if a portfolio's securities are strongly and positively correlated, then when things go bad for one stock, they tend to go bad for the whole portfolio. If there is a slightly negative correlation among the securities in the portfolio, on the other hand, then when one part zigs, the other zags. Modern Portfolio Theory, with its efficient frontier approach, proposes that investors should seek portfolios with slightly negative correlations for this reason. The benefit of diversification is that investors can keep high expected return among assets that do not have a strong expected return correlation.

As with alpha and beta, there is no reason to assume that if two securities historically show a correlation of, say, .4 that they will continue to do so. Using statistical measures such as these merely provides a guide of likely outcomes.

Types of Risk

Saving money and investing money are not the same thing. In a savings account, the only risk is that your money will lose purchasing power. When you invest, on the other hand, you take the risk that you could lose your money. This is called **capital risk**. If you buy U.S. Treasury Bonds, you eliminate capital risk, but if you buy corporate bonds or common stock, you face the risk of losing some or all of your invested capital. Investing in common stock presents significantly more capital risk than investing in corporate bonds, which is why the potential reward is also higher on common stock.

I'm looking at the prospectus for a growth fund. It declares that its investment goal is "growth of capital," and then goes on to say that "dividend income, if any, will be incidental to this goal." In other words, the fund invests in growth stocks, but some companies expected to grow will also pay dividends, and this fund does not mind cashing their checks. It's just that the dividends have nothing to do with the fund's reasons for investing in the stock. It's the growth or capital appreciation they're after. The "principal strategy" is to focus on companies with $10 billion or more of market value using fundamental analysis to determine which companies show strength in terms of earnings, revenue, and profit margins.

Systematic Risk

The next section is called "important risks," such as:

```
Stock market risk, or the risk that the price of securities held
by the Fund will fall due to various conditions or circumstances
which may be unpredictable.
```

46

Market risk is a type of **systematic risk,** which means it affects securities across the board, as opposed to an **unsystematic risk,** which affects only particular stocks or bonds or industry sectors. Market risk is the risk that an investment will lose value due to an overall market decline. As the prospectus says, the circumstances may be unpredictable. For example, no one can predict the next war or credit crisis, but when events like that take place, they can have a devastating effect on the overall market.

Whether they panic because of war, weather, or whatever, the fact is when investors panic, stock prices plummet. We might think of stock market risk as the fact that even though the company might be doing well, the stock investment in that company could drop because the overall stock market panics.

Unfortunately, diversification does not help. If the overall market is going down, it doesn't matter how many different stocks we own; they're all going down. That's why we would have to bet against the overall market to protect against market risk. The S&P 500 index is generally used to represent the overall market; therefore, investors use options, futures, and Exchange-Traded Funds to bet that the overall market will drop. We will explore the investment vehicles used in this way in another section.

For now, just know that diversification does not protect against market or other systematic risks. Rather, an investor has to hedge by betting against the overall market with some part of his portfolio.

Beta is a risk measurement of how volatile an individual stock is compared to the overall market. If MSFT has a beta of .8, it goes up and down only 80% as much as the overall market as measured by the S&P 500. If the S&P 500 rises 10%, MSFT goes up only 8%, and when the S&P 500 drops 10%, MSFT drops only 8%. If SBUX has a beta of 1.3, it is 30% more volatile than the overall market—or 1.3 times as volatile, whichever clicks for you. If the S&P drops 4%, SBUX drops 5.2%, and so on.

A stock with a beta of 1 is in line with the overall market in terms of volatility. A stock with a beta of less than 1 is less volatile than the overall stock market. But, stocks in general are volatile, so that investment could scare off many investors.

Natural Event Risk

Natural event risk refers to the fact that a tsunami, earthquake, or hurricane could have a devastating effect on a country's economy, and possibly the economy of an entire area such as Europe or Southeast Asia. A recent annual report from Starbucks mentions a "global pandemic" as a major risk to the price of the stock, something I would not have thought of. In other words, if disease sweeps the globe or any part of it, public gathering places are going to be shut down, people will be too sick to pick coffee beans, and transportation routes may be closed to prevent the spread of illness. None of that would have anything to do with the taste of Starbucks coffee or the management skills of the company.

Unfortunately, natural event risk does not fit neatly in the systematic or unsystematic risk category. While a tsunami would have a negative impact on markets overall, there are many weather-related events that hit certain sectors or issuers only, making it an unsystematic risk. For example, food and energy producers are affected by weather events that might not impact other industries. A Florida frost impacts orange juice, unlike a tsunami, which impacts entire regions of the globe.

And, there are some industries that do better after natural disasters such as a flood or hurricane: mold remediation, construction, disaster recovery, etc.

Interest Rate Risk

Interest rate risk is the risk that rates will rise, pushing down the market prices of bonds. The longer the term on the bond, the more volatile its price, too. When rates go up, all bond prices fall, but the long-term bonds suffer the most. And, when rates go down, all bond prices rise, but the long-term bonds go up the most.

So, a 30-year government bond has no default risk, but carries more interest rate risk than a 10-year corporate bond. The reason we see short-term and intermediate-term bond funds is because many investors want to reduce interest rate risk. Maybe they have a shorter time horizon and will need this money in just a few years—they can't risk a big drop in market value due to a sudden rise in interest rates. They will probably sacrifice the higher yield offered by a long-term bond fund, but they will sleep better knowing that rising rates won't be as devastating to short-term bonds.

In a bond fund prospectus, we see that the important risks include:

```
Risk that the value of the securities the Fund holds will fall as
a result of changes in interest rates.
```

Interest rate risk. Rates up, price down—and it's more severe the longer the term to maturity.

Purchasing Power Risk

Purchasing power risk is sometimes called **inflation risk** and even constant dollar risk. If inflation erodes the purchasing power of money, an investor's fixed return can't buy what it used to. Fixed-income investments carry purchasing power or inflation risk, which is why investors often try to beat inflation by investing in common stock. The ride might be a wild one in the stock market, but the reward is that we should be able to grow faster than the rate of inflation, whereas a fixed-income payment is fixed. Retirees living solely on fixed incomes are more susceptible to inflation or purchasing power risk than people in the workforce, since salaries tend to rise with inflation. The longer the retiree has to live on a fixed income, the more susceptible she is to inflation risk.

Unfortunately, common stock is often too volatile for investors with shorter time horizons and high needs for liquidity. The solution is often to put the majority of a retiree's money into short-term bonds and money market instruments with a small percentage in large-cap stock, equity income, or growth & income funds. That way, the dependable income from the short-term debt securities will cover the living expenses, while the smaller piece devoted to conservative stock investments will likely provide some protection of purchasing power. Not to mention that blue chip stocks almost by definition pay dividends, and dividends tend to increase over time. So, putting a reasonable percentage of a retiree's money into blue chip stocks is not necessarily risky, as might have been thought in the past.

The bond fund prospectus on my desk also warns of **call risk**, or "the risk that a bond might be called during a period of declining interest rates." Most municipal and corporate bonds are **callable**, meaning that when interest rates drop, corporate and municipal bond issuers will borrow new money at today's lower rate and use it to pay off the current bondholders much sooner than they expected.

The problems for the current bondholders are that, first, the bond price stops rising in the secondary market once everyone knows the exact call price to be received. And, second, what do they do with the money they just received from the issuer? Reinvest it, right? And, where are interest rates now? Down—so they probably take the proceeds from a 9% bond and turn it into a 6% payment going forward. That means on a million dollars of principal they used to get $90,000 per year; now they can look forward to just $60,000 in interest income. Couldn't we protect ourselves by buying non-callable bonds? Sure, but they'll offer lower rates than what they pay on callable bonds. As they say, there is no free lunch.

Prepayment and Extension Risk

Prepayment risk is the form of call risk that comes with owning a mortgage-backed security. A homeowner with a mortgage will typically take advantage of a sudden drop in interest rates by refinancing. Therefore, if an investor holds **mortgage-backed securities** like those issued or guaranteed by GNMA, FNMA, or FHLMC (Ginnie, Fannie, Freddie), that investor will take a hit if interest rates drop suddenly and all the principal is returned sooner than expected. This is called **prepayment risk**.

When the investor receives the principal sooner than expected, she typically ends up reinvesting it into similar mortgage-backed securities and receiving a lower rate of interest going forward, while the homeowners in the pool of mortgages, on the other hand, are enjoying paying lower interest rates going forward.

On the other hand, if interest rates rise, homeowners will take longer than expected to pay off the mortgages. This scenario is called **extension risk**. Notice that most debt securities have stated maturities, while an investment in most mortgage-backed securities comes with an estimate only. Sort of like bonds without maturity dates.

Since GNMA (Ginnie Mae) securities are guaranteed by the U.S. Treasury, their main risk is prepayment—or extension—risk. An investment in FNMA or FHLMC securities have that plus credit/default risk.

Reinvestment Risk

Bonds paying regular interest force investors—if they don't just spend the money—to reinvest into new bonds every few months or so. What kind of yields will debt securities offer when they go to reinvest the coupon payments? Nobody knows, which is why it's a risk, called **reinvestment risk**. It's frustrating to take a 6% interest payment and reinvest it at 3%, but it does happen. To avoid reinvestment risk, some investors buy a debt security that pays nothing to reinvest along the way: zero coupons, i.e., Treasury STRIPS. A zero-coupon bond returns a higher principal amount to the investor rather than paying any regular interest over the term to maturity.

Even though bond investing is less risky than stock investing, notice how bondholders can get hurt many different ways. If it's a corporate bond—and plenty of municipal securities—they could end up with a default. Whether it's a corporate, municipal, or even a U.S. Treasury bond, when rates go up, the price of the bond drops. If rates go down, callable bonds are called, and the party's over, and with non-callable bonds they have to reinvest the interest checks every six months at a lower rate going forward. And, even if none of the above happens, inflation could inch its way up, making those

Political Risk

Political risk is part of the package with investments into **emerging markets**. An emerging market is a country or region where the financial markets are immature and unpredictable. They're not fully developed, a little awkward, a bit volatile, basically like teenagers—bright future, but some days you really aren't sure if they're going to make it. If you own stocks and bonds in companies operating and trading in undeveloped economies, what happens if the Chinese government gets tired of capitalism and seizes the companies whose shares you used to own? Total loss. Or maybe the transition from communism to "capitalism" doesn't go so well, and suddenly the whole country is shut down with riots in the streets and government tanks rolling in. When this type of thing happens, emerging market investments are affected, and not in a good way.

Investing in emerging markets is high-risk, but it also protects U.S. investors against a down year for the domestic stock market. Even if the S&P 500 drops, companies in Brazil or China may do well and take their related stock markets up with them.

Currency Exchange Risk

Since most countries use a different currency from the American dollar, **currency exchange risk** is also part of the package when investing in foreign markets, emerging or otherwise. The value of the American dollar relative to foreign currencies, then, is a risk to both international and emerging markets investors. So, even if it's a **developed market**, such as Japan, if we are investing internationally into Japanese stocks, the value of the yen versus the dollar presents foreign exchange or currency risk. If we are investing in China, we have that risk, plus the political risk of investing in companies operating in an immature capitalist system likely to suffer many setbacks before all the kinks are worked out.

Unsystematic Risk

While diversification does not reduce systematic risk, it does reduce the unsystematic risks we will look at next. Un-systematic risk relates to a particular issuer or industry space, as opposed to the overall market. The risk that regulators will increase regulations on the automobile industry is not system-wide, affecting only a few issuers and industries. Diversifying a portfolio reduces these more specific risks by spreading them out among stocks of different issuers operating in different industry sectors.

Or, a municipal bond investor might diversify her holdings geographically to avoid the risk that an area of the country could be hit by a weather event or an economic slump. Although municipal bond investors generally seek safety, they can also enhance their yield by purchasing some lower-rated municipal bonds with some percentage of the account assets. After all, even conservative bond funds frequently put 20% or so in so-called "junk" bonds issued by corporations or municipalities.

Municipal bonds come in many flavors, also, so investors might purchase bonds used for many different purposes—some general obligation and some revenue—to avoid being too dependent on just toll roads, for example, or airport revenues. While an individual bond investor could use a registered representative to put together a diversified portfolio, more likely the registered representative would find a mutual fund portfolio already designed to achieve what the investor is looking for.

Business Risk

Buying stock in any company presents **business risk**. Business risk includes the risk of competition, a labor strike, the release of inferior products, and the risk of **obsolescence**, which is the risk that a company's offerings suddenly become a thing of the past, or obsolete. Shareholders in companies producing telegraph equipment, typewriters, and 8-track players all felt the sting of obsolescence risk. Nowadays, investing in a bookstore chain carries more risk of obsolescence than investing in a company that manufactures underwear. The risk of poor management, of better competitors, or of products becoming obsolete are all part of business risk.

In other words, the stock we own is only as solid as the businesses who issued it. So, we also need to diversify the portfolio so that it's not all subject to the same type of business risk. Airlines, retailers, and financial services companies, for example, would face different business risks. And, this shows how inherently risky stock investing is. Investors can get hurt by the individual companies they invest in, as well as the fact that the stock market overall can drop in value, whether the individual companies do well or not.

Legislative or Regulatory Risk

Legislative or **regulatory risk** means that if industry regulations or the tax code changes, certain securities could be negatively affected. If the federal government announced that all car makers must get 35 mpg for their large SUVs and pickup trucks by the following year, this would probably depress the value of certain stocks and bonds issued by companies including Ford and GM. Or, what if an investor bought a portfolio of tax-exempt municipal bonds, and then Congress decided to eliminate the exemption for municipal bond interest? Most likely, investors would dump their municipal bonds, forcing the market prices down.

Different industries are subject to different regulatory risks, so diversification can protect the investor from legislative risk somewhat. For this reason mutual funds focusing on just one industry sector are riskier than the typical fund that is broadly diversified.

And, not all industries are harmed by increased regulations. For example, when legislation such as Dodd-Frank and the American Healthcare Affordability Act is passed, the need for consultants who can guide companies through the changes increases. When the tax code becomes more complex, CPAs and other tax-planning or tax-law professionals typically have more work to do, possibly at higher rates.

Credit/Default Risk

Credit risk is the risk that the issuer of a bond will be unable to pay interest or return principal to the bondholders. U.S. Treasury securities have little or no default risk, but some municipal securities and most corporate bonds carry default/credit risk to some degree. Even if the issuer never misses a payment, if S&P and Moody's downgrade their credit score, the market value of the bonds would also drop.

The terms credit risk and default risk are typically used interchangeably. I would prefer that the industry used credit risk to mean a downgrade of perceived creditworthiness and default risk to mean only an actual default, but the industry does not use terminology so rigidly. As we have seen, the industry prefers to use three or four names for the same thing whenever possible.

Liquidity Risk

Liquidity is the ability to quickly turn an investment into cash without having to sell at a loss. Government securities are more liquid than municipal securities, and listed stocks more liquid than those trading in the non-Nasdaq OTC market. So, thinly traded securities have **liquidity risk** compared to securities with more active secondary markets. Insurance companies invest their net premiums in liquid, investment-grade bonds because they often have to liquidate their portfolio to pay claims after, say, a hurricane or flood. If they had to find buyers for illiquid junk bonds or real estate holdings, they would likely end up selling at unfavorable prices.

Opportunity Cost

If we pass up an investment opportunity to make 5%, our **opportunity cost** is 5%, and we need to do better than 5% with the opportunity we choose instead. If we could have made 5% and end up making 7% with another investment, we made 2% better than your opportunity cost.

Finally, separating investment risks into two neat categories is an inexact science. While any resource worth its salt would call inflation a systematic risk and legislative risk unsystematic, it also appears that no two resources agree on where to put all of the risks we just discussed. I choose to put anything that is specific to an issuer or an industry group under the unsystematic heading and anything that would affect securities of many different issuers and across all industry groups as systematic.

INVESTMENT RISK	SIGNIFICANCE	NOTES	
Systematic	Affect the overall market	"Non-diversifiable"	Diversification won't help; investor must "hedge"
Un-systematic	Affect stocks only	Diversifiable	Buy many stocks in many industries
Market	Markets panic due to war, weather events, etc.	Measured by Beta	Hedge with options, futures, ETFs, etc.
Business	How strong is the issuer?	Competition, obsolescence	Diversify your holdings
Political	Emerging markets, e.g., China, Vietnam	Unstable political-economic systems	Don't confuse with "legislative risk"
Legislative/	Changes to	Tax code changes EPA	Could have negative effect

INVESTMENT RISK	SIGNIFICANCE	NOTES	
Regulatory	laws/regulations	requirements, OSHA mandates	on stock or bond price
Currency	Value of dollar	ADRs, international and global investing	Weak dollar makes ADR more valuable
Interest Rate	Rates up/Market price down	Long-term bonds most susceptible, measured by "duration"	Preferred stock is rate-sensitive, too
Credit, Default	Issuer could fail	Downgrade in credit rating lowers value of bond	Low bond values = high-yield
Purchasing Power	Inflation erodes buying power	Fixed-income presents purchasing power risk	Live and die by the CPI
Reinvestment Risk	Investing at varying rates of interest	If rates down, investor goes forward at lower rate	Zero-coupons avoid this risk
Liquidity Risk	Trying to sell when there are few or no buyers	Esoteric securities, partnerships, hedge fund investments are illiquid	Thinly traded stocks less liquid
Opportunity Cost	What you give up to invest elsewhere	If you give up a 5% T-Bond investment, 5% is your opportunity cost	Try to do better than 5%

Now What?

Reading a textbook takes time and effort. Unfortunately, it is only one important step in your learning process. The next important step is working with practice questions.

First up, we present simple questions designed to help you review and recall what you just read. When you work through these online review exercises, it is important that you do so with the textbook closed—no peeking!

The questions in the online review exercises generally have just two answer choices. They are designed to help you recall and review what you just read and move it into long-term memory. Please wait until you're completely done with the online review exercises before opening the textbook again.

After taking the online review exercises and skimming the textbook chapter, walk away from it for at least 20 minutes—sleeping on it is ideal. Either way, after this mandatory break, come back and take the chapter review quiz, again with the textbook closed. There is a "mastery score" for each quiz in our Pass the 7 Online Practice Question Bank, and it is usually higher than the passing score at the testing center. That's okay—you need to shoot for higher than a 72% in practice to get at least that score on your license exam.

The Series 7 requires you to know a lot of information and to be able to work with it from many angles. Students who report that they saw questions they'd never seen before on their Series 7 might as well report that the sky is blue and grass is generally green. FINRA pays testing companies big money to make sure that the questions you see on your test are not the same ones you've seen over and over again in practice.

That is why we have to help you both learn the information indicated on the exam outline and also improve your ability to take any question they throw at you on Exam Day, recognize what it's talking about, and quickly break it down in your favor. The trick there is to understand that the same concept can be presented in strikingly different ways.

For example, from the information in this textbook chapter you could see something like this:

The term "inflation" can also be thought of as which of the following?
A. Capital appreciation
B. An increase of purchasing power
C. An erosion of purchasing power
D. A demand for goods and services

EXPLANATION: the word "inflation" is logically linked to words such as "increase" or "appreciation." After all, if you inflate a football, doesn't it get bigger? Inflation is an overall increase in prices, but rising prices and decreasing purchasing power are the same thing. Now, look at the four answer choices. Capital appreciation means "growth," but this question isn't talking about the return on an investment—so we can eliminate Choice A. Inflation is not just demand but, rather, high demand relative to supply, so we can also eliminate Choice D, not because it's the opposite of what's true but because it doesn't work. Looking at the two choices left (B and C), we already decided that inflation is a loss of purchasing power, which allows us to eliminate Choice B. So, whether we were expecting to see the word "erosion" or not, the correct answer is the one that remains. . .

ANSWER: c

This shows why many exam candidates become frustrated at the testing center. They thought there were only one or two possible questions about inflation, because that's all they seemed to encounter over and over with their vendor's practice questions. They've never seen this question before and, therefore, refuse to even try to get the upper hand.

We can't approach the Series 7 that way. We have to know the information on a deeper level and be able to respond to various tactics the questions try to use against us. And, the question above is neither a difficult nor an easy Series 7 question. As usual, the answer choices try to take you in several directions and try to use the natural association between "inflate" and "getting bigger" against you. That is why you have to work through a test question as opposed to reading it and hoping you see the answer that just came to mind. The right answer is not necessarily what you want it to be. The right answer is the one you can't eliminate, as we just did by eliminating Answers A, B, and D.

Your license exam pulls questions surrounding a topic from large buckets of potential questions. If you liked the previous question, you might or might not like the following one, which could just as easily have shown up on your screen:

The Consumer Price Index (CPI) is used to:
A. Predict the direction of interest rates
B. Measure inflation and/or deflation
C. Determine short-term financing rates for Federal Reserve Banks
D. Establish intermediate-term rates on international business loans
EXPLANATION: notice that this question covers the same body of information, but in a different way. One of the biggest obstacles to success on the Series 7 is that test candidates merely skim their textbook, and then bang out the practice questions as if doing calisthenics. They quickly memorize a relatively small number of practice questions and then, thinking their test will look the same, they suffer a near meltdown at the testing center. Think about it—if any vendor knew exactly what your test questions looked like, why would they have competitors, and why would this vendor show you any more than the 250 questions they "know" will be on your exam? Just to make it look good for the regulators?
No. The only way to pass the test is to know the information from many angles so that whatever the question looks like, you can take it apart. The variation we just wrote is not difficult, but it went in a quite different direction. The ANSWER is B, by the way, as the other choices are trying to confuse someone over the difference between inflation and interest rates.

The same information might just as well show up like this:

Mary Ellen invested in a mutual fund, receiving a total return of 4% for the year. If the CPI was 2% over the year, which of the following is Mary Ellen's "real" rate of return?
A. 4%
B. 3%
C. 2%
D. 0%
EXPLANATION: again, on the surface, this looks like a completely different question. But, the question really just applies the concept of inflation in a different way—how it affects investors. To figure her real or inflation-adjusted return subtract the CPI from the return she got. 4% minus the 2% inflation rate leaves her with how much after inflation? 2%.
ANSWER: c

We have a lot of practice questions for you in our Pass the 7 Online Practice Question Bank. But, should you get through them all, we encourage you to write variations of our questions the way I just did above. Take a question on the income statement, for example, and make it more about the balance sheet or statement of cash flows. We'll worry about that later, since you already have a lot of homework to do. But recent educational research has shown that students who write their own questions learn more for the long-term than those using any other method of study. The same research also shows that students learn more from doing practice questions than they do from reading textbooks.

So, let's get you started on learning through practice questions. First, do the online review exercise for this chapter, closed-book. After at least a 20-minute break take the chapter review quiz online. If you have time to study, watch the related training video lessons, and then move onto the next chapter in the textbook.

CHAPTER 2: Investment Vehicle Characteristics

Securities investors do not avoid risk. Rather, they determine which risks they can take and substitute those for the ones they can't. If an investor avoids default risk by purchasing Treasury Bonds, he trades that risk for purchasing power, interest rate, and reinvestment risk. If he needs to protect against purchasing power risk by buying common stock, he trades that one for market risk, business risk, and legislative risk.

Investing in securities is like playing offense in football. Whether we run the ball by buying bonds or throw passes by purchasing common stock, we know that we will get hurt a few times before we finally reach the goal line.

Therefore, before playing offense with their money most investors first lay down some protection. Step one is usually to establish a rainy-day fund at the local bank. Step two is to talk to your insurance agent. To protect your family against a sudden loss of income your agent may discuss disability, long-term care, and life insurance products.

To protect against running out of income in retirement your agent may discuss annuities.

Insurance-Based Products

Annuities

An **annuity** is an investment sold by an insurance company that either promises a minimum rate of return to the investor or allows the investor to allocate payments to various funds that invest in the stock and bond markets. These products offer regular payments for the rest of the annuitant's life, but owners of annuities can instead take money out as lump sums or random withdrawals on the back end. Annuities are part of the retirement plans of many individuals, and they can either be part of the "safe-money" piece or can provide exposure to the stock and bond markets.

The three main types of annuities are fixed, indexed, and variable.

Fixed annuities

A **fixed annuity** promises a minimum rate of return to the investor in exchange for one big payment into the contract or several periodic **purchase payments**. The purchase payments are allocated to the insurance company's **general account,** so the rate of return is "guaranteed." But, that just means it's backed by the claims-paying ability of the insurance company's general account. So before turning over your money to an insurance company, expecting them to pay it back to you slowly, you might want to check their **AM Best** rating and their history of paying claims.

In a fixed annuity the insurance/annuity company bears all the investment risk. This product is suitable for someone who wants a "safe money" investment that is more dependable than anything in the stock or bond markets, something that promises to make dependable payments for the rest of his life, no matter how long he ends up living. The fixed annuity offers peace of mind if not a high rate of return.

Indexed Annuities

A special type of fixed annuity is the **equity-indexed annuity** or just **indexed annuity**. With this product the investor receives a guaranteed minimum rate of return when the stock market has a bad year. But, he/she receives a higher rate of return when an index—usually the S&P 500—has a good year. Do they receive the full upside, as if they owned an S&P 500 index fund? No, and that should be made clear by the sales representative. The contract is also not credited with the dividends associated with the S&P 500, and those dividends can easily be worth 2 or 3% of the index's total return for the year.

Equity indexed annuities have a **participation rate.** A participation rate of 70% means that the contract gets credited with 70% of the increase in the S&P 500. If the index goes up 10%, the contract makes 7% . . . unless that amount is higher than the annual **cap.**

Yes, these contracts also have a cap placed on the maximum increase for any year, regardless of what the stock market does. So with a participation rate of 70% and a cap of 6%, what happens if the S&P goes up 20%? Although 70% of that is 14%, if you're capped at 6%, then 6% is all the contract value will rise that year. As you can see, indexed annuities are really about the downside protection, which is why a securities license is not required to sell fixed annuities, equity-indexed or otherwise.

Variable Annuities

A **variable annuity** doesn't promise a rate of return, which is what they mean by a "variable" annuity—the return varies. Since investors are investing in accounts of their choosing, maybe they'll end up doing better than the modest rate that the fixed annuity guarantees. In a variable annuity the annuitant bears the investment risk rather than having the insurance company promise a certain rate of return. In exchange for bearing the risks we've looked at in the stock and bond markets, the variable annuitant gets the opportunity to do much better than he would have in a fixed annuity, protecting his purchasing power from the ravages of inflation.

Could he do worse? Sure, but if he wants a guarantee, he buys a fixed annuity where the insurance company guarantees a certain rate of return. Now he lives with purchasing power risk, because if the annuity promises 2%, that's not going to be sufficient with inflation rising at 4%. If he wants to protect his purchasing power by investing in the stock market, he buys a variable annuity, but now he takes on all the investment risks we've discussed.

Variable annuities use mutual fund-type accounts as their investment options, but we don't call variable annuities "mutual funds." We call the investment options **subaccounts.** Salespeople must go out of their way to avoid confusing customers into thinking an annuity *is* a mutual fund. It is not a mutual fund. Mutual funds aren't subject to early withdrawal penalties from the issuer or the IRS. Mutual funds don't offer a death benefit or add expenses to cover it. Also, mutual funds are not tax-deferred accounts. A mutual fund held in a taxable account will subject investors to taxation every year. The dividend and capital gains distributions are taxable, and if the investor redeems shares for a gain, that's also taxable for the year it occurs. This tax burden reduces the principal in the account each year, which is a major drag on long-term returns. A variable annuity, however, is really a retirement plan where we get to keep all the dividends and capital gains in the account, adding to our principal, and compounding our returns.

In a deferred annuity the annuitant defers taxation until he takes the money out, which is usually at retirement. The money grows much faster when it's not being taxed for 10, 20, maybe even 30 years, but every dance reaches the point where we have to pay the fiddler. It's been a fun dance, for sure, but the reality is that we will pay ordinary income tax rates on the earnings we have been shielding from the IRS all these years—if and when we decide to get our own hands on the money. Ordinary income rates, remember. If the individual is in the 35% marginal tax bracket, the gains coming out of the annuity are taxed at that rate.

Features of Annuities

An annuity comes with a **mortality guarantee**, which means that once it goes into the pay-out phase, the annuitant will receive monthly payments as long as he is alive (a mortal). Of course, the fixed annuity states what the check will be worth at a minimum, while the variable annuity—well, it varies, people. In the variable annuity, the annuitant will receive a check each month, but it could be mighty meager if the markets aren't doing well.

A fixed annuity is an insurance product providing peace of mind and tax deferral. A variable annuity functions like a mutual fund investment that grows tax-deferred and offers some peace of mind. But, whether it's fixed or variable, the insurance company offers a **death benefit** that promises to pay a beneficiary at least the amount of money invested by the annuitant during his life—period. In a regular old mutual fund investment, we could put in $80,000 and when we die the investment could be worth $30,000, which is all our heirs would inherit. In a variable annuity the death benefit would pay out the $80,000. And, if the value of your investment was more than the $80,000 cost basis, the heirs would receive the $90,000 or whatever the account was worth. Note that in the variable annuity, this death benefit is only in effect while the annuitant is deferring any payments from the contract. As we'll see, once we flip the switch to receive payments in a variable annuity, well, anything can happen.

Insurance companies sell peace of mind. Both the mortality guarantee and the death benefit help a lot of investors sleep better. Pretty tough to put a price tag on that. For maximum peace of mind, individuals should buy a fixed or indexed annuity. For some peace of mind and the chance to invest in the stock and bond markets, individuals should consider a variable annuity. A variable annuity offers the investment choices from a family of mutual funds (growth, value, high-yield bonds, etc.), the tax deferral from an IRA or 401(k) plan, plus a death benefit similar to a life insurance policy. A fixed annuity—or indexed annuity—offers the tax deferral, the death benefit, and a dependable stream of minimum payments, even if the annuitant lives to 100.

Interestingly, an annuity gives the insurance company a different kind of "mortality risk." In a life insurance policy, their risk is that someone will put in $10,000 and die the next year, forcing the company to pay out hundreds of thousands, maybe a million. In an annuity, their mortality risk is that the annuitant will end up living to 115. The insurance company makes a mortality guarantee, which promises to pay the annuitant each month for the rest of her life. But, they cover their risk with a fee, called a mortality risk fee.

An insurance company has the risk that their expenses will rise. They promise to keep expenses level, but they charge an expense risk fee to cover their risk. In fact, usually the two are combined and referred to as a "**mortality and expense risk fee**," or "M & E" for those in a hurry. Variable annuities use mutual fund–type accounts as investment vehicles, but they add charges in excess of what those mutual funds charge investors. The guarantees offered in the annuity contract can easily add an extra 1%-1.5% to annual expenses, which can really add up over 20 or 30 years.

A special feature is sometimes called a "rider," or a "bonus." Although these features can benefit the annuitant, they can also confuse him. For example, a deferred variable annuity can come with an "income guarantee," but that is all that is guaranteed. With this enhancement the insurance company guarantees an annual income stream that can be withdrawn starting a certain number of years into the future. This guaranteed income is not based on the investment performance of the subaccounts but, rather, on the claims-paying ability of the insurance company. Understand that even though the income stream does not depend on the account balance, the account balance can definitely drop due to poor investment performance.

So, is the investor guaranteed against a loss of principal? No. He's not even guaranteed a certain account balance. The investor is promised an income stream that can be withdrawn in a few years. The overview for a guaranteed deferred variable annuity that I'm looking at online includes this statement, "Guaranteed lifetime income that cannot be reduced due to market performance." The footnotes at the bottom of the page, however, point out that, "The contract value is subject to market fluctuations and investment risk so that, when withdrawn, it may be worth more or less than its original value."

And, how "guaranteed" is the income stream? As the footnotes also state, "Guarantees apply to certain insurance and annuity products and are subject to product terms, exclusions and limitations and the insurer's claims-paying ability and financial strength."

With a **bonus annuity** the annuity company may offer to enhance the buyer's premium by contributing an additional 1 to 5% of what he/she puts in. Of course, this comes with a price. First, there are fees attached and, second, the surrender period is longer. Third, if the investor surrenders the contract early, the bonus disappears. Remember that an investor is penalized by the annuity company with a "surrender charge" if they pull all their money out early. For bonus annuities that period where the investor could get penalized is longer.

Bonus annuities are not suitable for everyone. Variable annuities in general are not good for short-term investment goals, since the surrender charge is applied during the first 7 years or so. Should you switch a customer into a bonus annuity? Maybe. But, remember, even though the annuitant can avoid taxes through a 1035 exchange, when she exchanges the annuity, her surrender period starts all over again. And, yes, FINRA will bust you if it looks like you did the switch just to make a nice commission, forcing the investor to start the surrender period all over again. In general, investors should maximize their 401(k) and other retirement plans before considering annuities. Annuities are ideal for those who have maxed out those plans, since the annuity allows investors to contribute as much as they would like.

Variable annuities come with a **free-look period**, which is generally a minimum of 10 business days. If the consumer decides he or she doesn't want to keep the product, he or she can cancel without losing any premiums or surrender charges to the company. For fixed annuities, consumers have the same free look period their state requires of insurance policies.

Just like owners of mutual fund shares, owners of variable annuities get to vote their units on important decisions such as:

- Electing the Board of Managers
- Changing the Investment Objectives, Policies
- Ratifying the Independent Auditor/Accounting Firm

Purchasing Annuities

The categories of fixed, indexed, and variable annuities refer to the way payments are calculated on the way out. In terms of buying annuities the two major types are "immediate" and "deferred." These terms refer to how soon the contract holder wants to begin receiving payments—now, or later? These are retirement plans, remember, so you do need to be 59½ to avoid penalties. Therefore, some customers might want or need to wait 20 or 30 years before receiving payments. If so, they purchase a deferred annuity.

The tax deferral is nice, but if the individual is already, say, 68, she may want to retire now and start receiving payments immediately. As you can probably guess, we call that an immediate annuity. While there are immediate *variable* annuities, it is more common to buy the fixed *immediate* annuity. Why? The whole point of buying an immediate annuity is to know that—no matter what happens to social security and your 401(k) account—there is a solid insurance company contractually obligated to make a payment of at least X amount for as long as you live. An immediate *variable* annuity would work out well only if the investments did—while there is some minimal payment guaranteed, it is meager.

An immediate fixed annuity does not offer a high rate of return, but it does provide peace of mind to investors in retirement. Many financial planners would suggest that at least some of their customers' retirement money be in a fixed immediate annuity—maybe just enough to provide a monthly payment covering monthly expenses. Figuring withdrawal rates from retirement accounts is tricky, so having a payment of X amount from a solid insurance company could smooth out the bumps.

Customers can buy annuities either with one big payment or several smaller payments. The first method is called "single premium" or "single payment." The second method is called "periodic payment." If an investor has a large amount of money, she can put it in an annuity, where it can grow tax-deferred. If she's putting in a big single purchase payment, she can choose either to wait (defer) or to begin receiving annuity payments immediately. She has to be 59½ years old to annuitize, but if she's old enough, she can begin the pay-out phase immediately. That's called a **single-payment immediate annuity**. Maybe she's only 42, though, and wants to let the money grow another 20 years before taking it out. That's called a **single-payment deferred annuity** (SPDA).

Many investors put money into the annuity during the accumulation phase (pay-in) gradually, over time. That's called "periodic payment," and if they aren't done paying in yet, you can bet the insurance company isn't going to start paying out. So, if you're talking about a "periodic payment" plan, the only way to do it is through a **periodic *deferred* annuity**. There is no such thing as a "Periodic Immediate Annuity" since no insurance company I'm aware of would let me start sending in $100 a month while they go ahead and start sending me $110.

To review, then, there are three methods of purchasing annuities:

- Single-Payment Deferred Annuity
- Periodic-Payment Deferred Annuity
- Single-Payment Immediate Annuity

Again, understand that variable annuities use mutual funds (called subaccounts) as the investment vehicles in the plan. But, annuities add both features and extra expenses for the investor on top of all the investment-related expenses. Tax deferral is nice. So are the death benefit and the annuity payment that goes on as long as the individual lives. But, that stuff also adds maybe 1.0–1.5% per year in expenses to the investor. You can either slide that fact past your investor or fully disclose it. Depends on whether you want your name up on FINRA's website or not.

Receiving Payments (Settlement Options)

Some investors make periodic purchase payments into the contract while others make just one big purchase payment. Either way, when the individual gets ready to annuitize the contract, he tells the insurance company which payout option he's choosing. And, he is not able to change this decision—he makes the decision and that's that. Essentially, what's going on at this point in the contract is that the individual is about to make a bet with the insurance company as to how long he will end up living.

Seriously.

Same thing for a variable annuity, but it's probably not as surprising on the variable side. But, either way, if the individual throws the switch to receive payments and chooses **life only** or **straight life** he'll typically receive the largest monthly payout. Why? Because the insurance company sets those payments and the insurance company knows better than he does when he's going to die. Not the exact day or the exact method, of course, but they can estimate it with amazing precision. Since the insurance/annuity company only has to make payments for as long as he lives, the payments are typically the largest for a "life only" or "straight life" annuity settlement option. How does the individual win the "bet"? By living longer than the actuarial tables would predict. Not a bad motivation for exercising and eating right, huh? If this option seems too risky, the individual can choose a "unit refund life annuity." This way he is guaranteed a certain number of payments even if he does get hit by the proverbial bus. If he dies before receiving them, his beneficiary receives the balance of payments.

So, does the annuitant have family or a charity she wants to be sure receives the balance of her payments? If not, why not go with the life only/straight life option—tell the insurance company to pay her as much as possible for as long as she lives. If she dies—well, what does she care if State Farm or Northwestern Mutual comes out ahead? If she does have family, friends, or a charity that she'd like to name as a beneficiary, she can choose a **period certain** settlement option. In that case, the insurance company has to do what the name implies—make payments for a certain period of time. To either her or the named beneficiaries. For older investors, this option typically leads to a lower monthly payment, since the insurance company will now be on the hook for several years even if the annuitant conveniently expires early. If it's a 20-year period certain payout, the payments have to be made to the beneficiary for the rest of that period, even if the annuitant dies after the first month or two.

The annuitant could also choose **life with period certain**, and now we'd have a complicated either-or scenario with the insurance company. With this option the company will make payments for the greater of his life *or* a certain period of time, such as 20 years. If he dies after 2 years, the company makes payments to his beneficiary for the rest of the term. And if he lives longer than 20 years, they just keep on making payments until he finally expires. Please read that sentence again, because it seems that no one ever believes me when I say that if the annuitant chooses a 20-year life-with-period-certain settlement option and inconveniently lives 23 years, the insurance company makes payments for 23 years. When he dies, no more payments.

Finally, the **joint with last survivor** option would typically provide the smallest monthly check because the company is obligated to make payments as long as either the annuitant or the survivors are alive. The contract can be set up to pay the annuitant while he's alive and then pay the beneficiaries until the last beneficiary expires. Or, it can start paying the annuitant *and* the beneficiary until both have finally, you know. Covering two persons' mortality risks (the risk that they'll live an inconveniently long time) is an expensive proposition to the insurance company, so these monthly checks are typically smaller than either period certain or life-only settlement options.

Variable Annuities: Accumulation and Annuity Units

There are only two phases of an annuity—the **accumulation period** and the **annuity period**. An individual making periodic payments into the contract, or one who made one big purchase payment and is now just deferring the payout phase, is in the accumulation phase, holding **accumulation units**. When he throws the switch to start receiving payments, the insurance company will convert those accumulation units to **annuity units**.

In a fixed annuity, the annuitant knows the minimum monthly payment he can expect. A variable annuity, on the other hand, pays out the fluctuating value of those annuity units. And, although the value of annuity units fluctuates in a variable annuity during the payout phase, the *number* of those annuity units is fixed. To calculate the first payment for a variable annuity, the insurance company uses the following:

- Age of the annuitant
- Account value
- Gender
- Settlement option

Remember that health is not a factor—there are no medical exams required when determining the payout. This is also why an annuity cannot suddenly be turned into a life insurance policy, even though it can work in the other direction, as we'll discuss elsewhere.

As we said, once the number of annuity units has been determined, we say that the number of annuity units is fixed. So, for example, maybe every month he'll be paid the value of 100 annuity units.

Trouble is, he has no idea how big that monthly check is going to be, since nobody knows what 100 **annuity units** will be worth month-to-month, just like nobody knows what mutual fund shares will be worth month-to-month. So, how much is an annuity unit worth each month? All depends on the investment performance of the separate account compared to the expectations of its performance.

Seriously. If the separate account returns are better than the assumed rate, the units increase in value. If the account returns are exactly as expected, the unit value stays the same. And if the account returns are lower than expected, the unit value drops from the month before. It's all based on the **Assumed Interest Rate (AIR)** that the annuitant and annuity company agree to use.

If the **AIR** is 5%, that means the separate account investments are expected to grow each month at an annualized rate of 5%. If the account gets a 6% annualized rate of return one month, the individual's check gets bigger. If the account gets the anticipated 5% return next month, that's the same as AIR and the check will stay the same. And if the account gets only a 4% return the following month, the check will go down.

Don't let the exam trick you on this concept. If the AIR is 5%, here is how it could work:

Actual Return:	5%	7%	6%	5%	4%
Check:	$1,020	$1,035	$1,045	$1,045	$1,030

When the account gets a 7% return, the account gets much bigger. So when it gets only a 6% return the following month, that's 6% of a bigger account, and is 1% more than we expected to get. So, just compare the actual return with the AIR. If the actual return is bigger, so is the monthly check. If it's smaller, so is the monthly check. If the actual return is the same as the AIR, the check stays the same.

The Separate vs. General Account

An insurance company is one of the finest business models ever conceived. See, no one person can take the risk of dying at age 32 and leaving the family with an unpaid mortgage, a bunch of other bills, and a sudden loss of income, not to mention the maybe $15,000 it takes just for a funeral these days. But, an insurance company can take the risk that a certain number of individuals will die prematurely by insuring a large number of individuals and then using the precise laws of probability over large numbers that tell them how many individuals will die each year with only a small margin of error. Once they've taken the insurance premiums that individuals pay, they then invest what's left after covering expenses and invest it wisely in the real estate, fixed-income, and stock markets. They have just as much data on these markets, so they can use the laws of probability again to figure out that if they take this much risk here, they can count on earning this much return over here within only a small margin of error.

And, of course, most insurance companies not run by Warren Buffet are conservative investors. That's what allows them to crunch numbers and know with reasonable certainty they will never have to pay so many death benefits in one year that their investments are totally wiped out. This conservative investment account that guarantees the payout on whole life, term life, and fixed annuities is called the **general account**. In other words, the general account is for the insurance company's investments. Typically, it is comprised mostly of investment-grade corporate bonds.

Many insurance companies also create an account that is separate from the general account and, believe it or not, the industry calls it the **separate account**. It's really a mutual fund family that offers tax deferral, but we don't call it a mutual fund, even though it's also covered by and registered under the same Investment Company Act of 1940. The Investment Company Act of 1940 defines a separate account like so:

```
"Separate account" means an account established and maintained by
an insurance company pursuant to the laws of any State or
territory of the United States, or of Canada or any province
thereof, under which income, gains and losses, whether or not
realized, from assets allocated to such account, are, in
accordance with the applicable contract, credited to or charged
against such account without regard to other income, gains, or
losses of the insurance company.
```

When the **purchase payments** are invested in the general account, they are guaranteed a certain rate of return—whole life, fixed annuity. When the purchase payments are invested in the separate account, welcome to the stock and bond markets, where anything can happen.

From the perspective of the nice couple sitting across from a registered representative at the table, it all looks pretty much the same. He was talking about the Platinum Equity Income Fund a few minutes ago—now that he has switched to his variable annuity spiel, they're seeing the same Platinum Equity Income Fund.

It is the same fund, but if we buy it within a variable annuity contract, we call it a **subaccount**.

There are good reasons to avoid calling subaccounts "mutual funds." If the investor thinks he's in a "mutual fund," he might think he can take out his money whenever he wants. He also might not realize that he's paying an extra 1.0–1.5% a year to place the annuity wrapper around the "mutual fund" investments. So, be careful with the language out there, people.

Life Insurance

I've always felt it rude to die without insurance and leave family and friends footing the bill for my funeral. That's why I "rent" insurance coverage through something called **term life insurance**. It's cheap, but it's only good for a certain term—maybe it's a 5-, 10-, or 20-year term. The individual pays premiums in exchange for a guaranteed **death benefit** payable to a **beneficiary** if **the insured** dies during that period. If the insured does not die during that period, the policy expires. If the **policyholder** wants to renew, he can, but he's older now and more costly to insure. In other words, his premiums will go up, even though the death benefit will stay the same, because he's older and more likely to have some medical condition that raises his rates, too, or even that prevents him from being offered the insurance at all.

So, as with all products, there are pluses and minuses. Term insurance is cheap and offers nice protection, but it does not build any cash value and has to be renewed at higher and higher rates, just like renting an apartment.

Now would be a good time to note the language used in insurance:

- **Policyholder**: the owner of the policy, responsible for paying premiums
- **Insured**: the person whose life is insured by the policy, usually the policyholder
- **Beneficiary**: the party that receives the death benefit upon death of the insured
- **Death benefit**: the amount payable to the beneficiary upon death of the insured, minus any unpaid premiums or loan balances
- **Cash value**: a value in the policy account that can be partially withdrawn or borrowed against

So, let's say that Joe Smith buys an insurance policy with a $100,000 death benefit payable to his wife. He's the policyholder and the insured. If he dies, the death benefit of $100,000 is paid to the beneficiary, his wife. As we'll see, most insurance also builds up cash value, which can be withdrawn or borrowed while Joe is alive (note that term insurance does not build up this cash value, which is also why it's relatively cheap insurance).

Permanent vs. Temporary Insurance

As with housing, some people prefer to rent insurance for a term, and some prefer to buy it. Some feel that if you're going to be putting money aside, you might as well end up with something to show for it, so they purchase permanent insurance. The most common type of permanent insurance is called **whole life insurance**. The premiums are much higher than on the term insurance you sort of "rent," but insurance companies will guarantee a minimum **cash value**, and you can also pretty well plan for an even better cash value than that. This way it works to protect your beneficiaries if you die unexpectedly and also acts as a savings vehicle where the cash value grows tax-deferred. Maybe at age 55 you decide to borrow $50,000 of the cash value for whatever reason. Could come in really handy, yes?

So, term is cheap, but it builds no cash value. And, to keep it going, the policy owner usually has to pay more for the same benefit. Reminds me of how I spent five years paying "cheap" rent to a landlord. It was definitely lower than a mortgage payment would have been on a similar-sized house. But at the end of this 5-year term, I had turned over $40,000 to the landlord and was left with nothing but the opportunity to renew my lease at a higher rate. I covered myself with a roof for five years, and at the end of the five years I owned absolutely no part of that roof.

Whole life insurance is more like buying the house, which is exactly what I did after five years of renting. I had to come up with a down payment, and my monthly mortgage jumped by $200 above the monthly rent. The upside is that at the end of five years, I'll have some equity in the house that I can tap into for a loan maybe. Just like with a whole life policy, I'll be getting at least something back for all those payments I've made over the years. And the time will come when the full value is all paid up and mine.

So, whole life insurance involves premiums that are higher than those for term life insurance, but you end up with something even if you stop paying into the policy. There is a guaranteed cash value, whereas term leaves you with nothing. The death benefit is guaranteed, too, so whole life insurance is a popular product for people who want to protect their families and also use the policy as a savings vehicle, where all that increase in cash value grows tax-deferred.

If the exam asks which type of customer should purchase term insurance, look for a young, single parent, maybe, or someone who absolutely has to protect the kids from a sudden loss of income and wants to do it as cheaply as possible.

Since some customers crave flexibility, the industry bent over backwards to come up with a flexible form of permanent insurance called **universal life insurance**. Think "flexibility" when you see the words "universal life insurance." The death benefit and, therefore, the premiums can be adjusted by the customer. They can be increased to buy more coverage or decreased to back off on the coverage and save some money. If the cash value is sufficient, premiums can stop being paid by the customer and start being covered by the cash value. The cash value grows at a minimum, guaranteed rate, just like on traditional whole life polices, and if the general account does well, the cash value goes up from there. As mentioned, at some point the policyholder may decide to withdraw part of the cash value, or may usually borrow up to 90% of it.

Variable Policies

So, whether it's term, traditional whole life, or universal life insurance, we're talking strictly about insurance products. Death benefits and cash values are guaranteed by the insurance company, who invests the net premiums into their general account. Once they start attaching cash value and death benefits to the ups and downs of a separate account, however, they have created a new product that is both an insurance policy and a security. Opens a whole new market for the company, but it also means that those who sell them need both an insurance and a securities license.

Whole life and term life insurance policies tell customers exactly how much they will pay out upon death. So, in term and whole life policies, the investment risk is borne by the insurance company.

Well, with variable insurance products, the death benefit—as well as the cash value—fluctuates just like it does in a variable annuity. That's what they mean by "variable." It all varies, based on the investment performance of the separate account. The separate account, as we discussed under variable annuities, is made up of subaccounts. The investor chooses from these quasi-mutual funds that are trying to meet different investment objectives: growth, long-term bonds, short-term Treasuries, etc. He can even choose to invest some of the premiums into a fixed account, just to play it safe, and he can switch between the subaccounts as his investment needs change without a tax problem. This stuff all grows tax-deferred, remember.

The cash value is tied to account performance, period. So if the test question says that the separate account grew, it doesn't matter by how much. The cash value increases when the separate account increases. But death benefit is tied to actual performance versus AIR, just like an annuity unit in a variable annuity. So if the AIR is 6% and the account gets a 4% return, the cash value will increase due to the positive return, but the death benefit will decrease since the account returned less than AIR.

Variable Life Insurance (VLI) policies pay out the cash value/surrender value whenever the policyholder cashes in the policy. But, there's no way to know what the value might be at the time of surrender far into the future. If the subaccounts have performed well, the cash value might be better than expected. But if the market has been brutal, the cash value could go all the way to zero.

A minimum or fixed death benefit is guaranteed, however. Some refer to it as the "floor." No matter what the market does, the insurance company guarantees a minimum death benefit that could only be reduced or depleted by failure to pay premiums or taking out loans against the policy. Remember that any guaranteed payments are covered by the insurance company's general account. So, the minimum death benefit is guaranteed, and the policyholder also has the chance of enjoying an increased death benefit, depending on how well the subaccounts do. As we said, that's tied to AIR, so if the market is kind, the death benefit increases, but if the market is unkind, it could, theoretically, drag the death benefit all the way to the floor.

As with variable annuities, after the money's been allocated to the subaccounts of the separate account, the insurance company charges regular fees, just like they do in variable annuities:

- mortality risk fee
- expense risk fee (or "Mortality & Expense Risk Fee)
- investment management fees

The value of the subaccounts and, therefore, the cash value are calculated daily. The death benefit is calculated annually. If the separate account has several below-AIR months, it will take several above-AIR months after that before the customer's death benefit starts to increase.

Remember that flexibility we discussed that separates traditional whole life from universal life? Well, it probably isn't too surprising that someone eventually married that benefit to variable life to get **Variable Universal Life Insurance**. With VUL we have the death benefit and cash value tied to the separate account (variable), plus we have the flexible premium thing (universal) going on. Regular old variable life is called "scheduled premium." That means the insurance company puts your premium payments on a schedule, and you better stick to it. Variable Universal or Universal Variable Life policies are funded as "flexible premium." That means the customer may or may not have to send in a check. With a VUL policy, the customer has to maintain enough cash value and death benefit to keep the policy in force. If the separate account rocks, no money has to roll in from the customer. If the separate account rolls over and dies, look out. Since that's a little scary, some VULs come with minimum guaranteed death benefits.

The advantages of variable life over whole life insurance include the ability to invest some of the premiums into the stock market, which has historically enjoyed relatively high average returns and done well at beating inflation. A robust investment market can increase the cash value and death benefit, often faster than the rate of inflation. A traditional whole life policy, on the other hand, that promised to pay $50,000 when it was purchased in 1974 represented a lot of money then. But if it pays that $50,000 out in 2019, the $50,000 doesn't go far, due to inflation.

When selling variable insurance policies, the agent must remember that these are insurance policies first and foremost. He can discuss the benefits of investing in the subaccounts, but he can't present these insurance policies primarily as investment vehicles. Primarily, they're to be sold for the death benefit. They also offer the opportunity to invest in the subaccounts, but they're not to be pitched primarily as investment vehicles.

Four federal acts are involved with variable life insurance and variable annuities. The Securities Act of 1933 covers variable life insurance (and annuities). These products must be registered with the SEC and sold with a prospectus. Even though the company that issues these contracts is an insurance company, the subdivision that sells the securities products has to be a broker-dealer registered under the Securities Exchange Act of 1934. The separate account is defined as an investment company under the Investment Company Act of 1940 and is either registered as a UIT or an Open-End Fund as defined under that act. The "money manager" or "investment adviser" has to register under the Investment Advisers Act of 1940.

And, at the state level, both securities and insurance regulators are watching these products and those who sell them.

Policy Loans

Variable policies make 75% of the cash value available to the customer as a loan after three years. Guess what—they charge interest on that loan, just as they do on a whole life policy. If the loan is not repaid, that reduces both the cash value and the death benefit of the policy. And, if the customer takes out a big loan and then the separate account tanks, he'll have to put some money back in to bring the cash value back to a sufficient level, or risk having the policy lapse. Don't worry, though. Some people take out a loan with absolutely no intention of repaying it. They don't need as much death benefit at this point, so why not have some fun with the money right now?

Settlement Options for Insurance Policies

The policyholder can choose from many options concerning the method of payment to the beneficiary. These are called "settlement options." The "lump-sum" method is self-explanatory. "Fixed-period" means that the insurance company will invest the proceeds of the policy into an interest-bearing account and then make equal payments at regular intervals for a fixed period. The payments include principal and interest. How much are the payments? That depends on the size of the principal, the interest rate earned by the insurance company, and the length of time involved in this fixed period.

The "fixed-amount" settlement option has the insurance company invest the proceeds from the policy and pay the beneficiary a fixed amount of money at regular intervals until both the principal and interest are gone. The amount received is fixed, but the period over which the beneficiary receives payments varies.

So, for "fixed-period" versus "fixed-amount," the decision comes down to this: do you want to receive an uncertain amount of money for a fixed period, or do you want to receive a fixed amount of money for an uncertain period? Do you want to be paid something like $25,000 for exactly three years (fixed-period)? Or, would you prefer being paid exactly $25,000 for about three years (fixed-amount)?

In a "life-income" settlement option, the proceeds are annuitized. That means the insurance company provides the beneficiary with a guaranteed income for the rest of his/her life. Just like with annuities, the beneficiary's age expectancy is considered to determine the monthly payout, along with the size of the death benefit and the type of payout selected.

There is also an "interest-only" settlement option, whereby the insurance company keeps the proceeds from the policy and invests them, promising the beneficiary a guaranteed minimum rate of interest. The beneficiary might get more than the minimum, or not, and may receive the payments annually, semiannually, quarterly, or monthly. He/she also has the right to withdraw all the principal, or to change settlement options.

Types and Characteristics of Cash and Cash Equivalents

The first line of a corporation's balance sheet is "cash and equivalents," listed under current assets. Businesses can use cash and equivalents as a buffer against bad times or to make strategic acquisitions. When a business invests its excess cash in short-term interest-bearing securities, they are investing in **money market securities** as opposed to long-term bonds.

Debt securities maturing in greater than one year are sometimes called funded debt. Money market securities, on the other hand, are debt securities maturing in one year or less. They are considered safe, liquid investments that hold a steady value over the short-term. The exam may refer to money market securities as "cash equivalents" because, basically, they are just as good as cash. Better actually, because unlike cash hidden in a coffee can, money market instruments are earning interest. It's not necessarily a high rate of interest, but at least we are putting our cash to work and not risking it in the stock market, where anything can happen, or even the bond market, where interest rates could rise and knock down the value of our holdings.

The problem with investing too much money into cash equivalents is that we miss the big growth opportunities that arise when the stock or bond markets experience bull markets. That, as we have seen, is called opportunity cost. Also, these investments do not keep pace with inflation, leaving the investor with purchasing power risk.

T-Bills

The rate of return on a short-term U.S. Treasury Bill is considered the "riskless rate of return" for certain calculations we'll look at later. There is little time for interest rates or inflation to do any damage to a T-Bill. And, the issuer guarantees it against default.

That's right, the interest and principal are guaranteed, and the U.S. Treasury has never defaulted. So, if you don't need to withdraw a certain amount of money for several months or longer, you can buy the 3-month or 6-month T-Bill and usually earn higher yields than you'd earn in a savings account. There are no fees to buy T-Bills if you buy them directly through www.treasurydirect.gov.

Bank CDs usually yield about the same as T-Bills, but the bank's FDIC insurance stops at $250,000 per account. T-Bills, on the other hand, are guaranteed no matter how large the denomination. Any given Monday T-Bills are available by auction through the website mentioned above from as small as $100 par value to as large as $5 million. No matter how big the bill, it's guaranteed by the U.S. Treasury.

Bankers' Acceptances

A **bankers' acceptance** is a short-term credit investment created by a non-financial company and guaranteed by a bank as to payment. "BAs" are traded at discounts to face value in the secondary market. These instruments are commonly used in international transactions, and the exam might associate them with "importing and exporting." As with a T-Bill, bankers' acceptances are so short-term that it would make no sense to send interest checks to the buyer. Instead, these short-term debt securities are purchased at a discount from their face value. The difference between what we pay and what we receive is the interest income.

The "BA" or "bankers' acceptance" is backed both by a bank's full faith and credit and the goods being purchased by the importer. This is how the BA is created. First, a computer manufacturer in California imports computer parts from a Japanese company but is not ready to pay just yet. So, the California company issues a "time draft" to the Japanese company, which is really a post-dated check that is good on a future date and backed up by their bank's line of credit. The Japanese company can now sit on this time draft until the due date and receive the full amount. Or, they can cash it immediately at their bank at a slight discount. If they do the latter, the Japanese bank would then have a "bankers' acceptance" guaranteed by the American company's bank and the computer parts purchased by the American importer. The Japanese bank can either wait until the due date or sell it on the secondary market at a discount.

Commercial Paper

Commercial paper is typically used by companies as a source of working capital, receivables financing, and other short-term financing needs. To build major items such as an $800 million factory, a company generally issues long-term bonds (funded debt), and pays the lenders back slowly. But if Microsoft needs a mere $50 million for a few months, they would probably prefer to borrow it short-term at the lowest possible interest rate.

If so, they issue **commercial paper** with a $50 million face amount, selling it to a **money market mutual fund** for, say, $49.8 million. Again, the difference between the discounted price and the face amount *is* the interest earned by the investor. Commercial paper is generally issued only by corporations with high credit ratings from S&P, Moody's, or Fitch. Unfortunately, each of the three ratings agencies uses different nomenclature, so I have decided not to tell you about the P-1 down to P-3 ratings issued by Moody's, let alone the A1 down to A3 ratings issued by S&P or the F1 down to F3 ratings issued by Fitch. Do know that a rating below any of those "3's" is considered speculative commercial paper and would, therefore, not be found in the typical money market mutual fund portfolio.

Commercial paper could be described as an unsecured promissory note, as opposed to the repurchase agreements up ahead, which provide collateral to the lender. Some large corporations issue their commercial paper directly to investors, which may be mutual funds, pension funds, etc. The industry calls this "directly placed commercial paper." When corporations use commercial paper dealers to sell to the investor, the industry refers to this as "dealer-placed commercial paper."

Large financial institutions borrow money at low interest rates over the short term by taking money and paying whatever a savings account or CD currently offers. They then lend that money out to someone else long-term at a higher interest rate. If they're able to borrow at a lower rate than they lend it at to someone else, they're fine.

But this business model also puts them at risk in terms of fluctuating interest rates. Think of the flat and inverted yield curves we looked at, or even a positive yield curve with only a tiny difference between short-term and long-term interest rates. These interest rate environments are no good for bankers. If they suddenly have to pay high interest rates to borrow short-term while they're earning lower and lower rates when they lend the money out long-term, that's got to hurt.

To shield themselves from interest-rate risk over the short-term, large financial institutions engage in **repurchase agreements** and **reverse repurchase agreements**. Basically, one party buys a certain amount of the other party's fixed-income securities today and then sells them back at a set price in the near future. The difference between what the buyer pays at the start of the transaction and what they receive at the end of the agreement is their rate of return, expressed as a percentage per year. This rate is called the "repo rate." The repo rate is not set by any regulatory body but rather through negotiations between buyers and sellers in these arrangements.

Even though these agreements are structured as a purchase and a sale, they function more like a short-term loan. The buyer is really lending money short-term to the seller, and the loan is collateralized by the securities being purchased and held for, perhaps, 30 days. The risk is low, since even if the other party could not repurchase the securities, chances are the securities would be worth about what the buyer just paid for them. But that is not the same thing as a risk-free investment, so, no, repurchase agreements are not risk-free even though they are safe due to the collateral involved. Their main risk is **counterparty risk** because collateral is protection, not a 100% guarantee against loss.

So, a "repo" reduces the buyer's credit risk, and if the securities purchased are liquid, this also reduces their liquidity risk. Provided the assets are liquid, the buyer can either sell them or even refinance at any time during the life of a repo by selling or "repoing" the assets to a third party. If he got that fancy, the buyer would subsequently have to buy the same type of collateral back to return it to his counterparty at the end of the repo. This right of use on the collateral reduces the liquidity risk that the buyer takes by lending to the seller at the start of the transaction. And, because lending through a repurchase agreement exposes the buyer to lower credit and liquidity risk, repo rates are typically lower than unsecured money market rates—commercial paper, for example.

For the party of the transaction doing the selling to raise the cash, this is a repurchase agreement. To the party on the other side, who starts out as the buyer, the agreement is known as a reverse repurchase agreement. Although part of the money market, repurchase agreements (repos) are more of a private arrangement than a security that gets bought and sold. There is no active secondary market for these transactions. The interest rates are established through negotiations between the two parties to the transaction.

Most repurchase agreements have fixed terms. In the U.S., the majority are done on an overnight basis, with virtually all of them short-term. Then, there are repurchase agreements without fixed terms, called "open repos." With this on-demand agreement, the open repo can be terminated on any day in the future by either party, provided they give notice before an agreed daily deadline. Until an open repo is terminated, it automatically rolls over each day.

Tax-Exempt Municipal Notes

We'll look at municipal securities in a moment, but for now just know that cities, counties, and school districts, etc., can borrow money long-term by issuing bonds, and they can borrow short-term by issuing anticipation notes. For example, property taxes are collected twice a year. If the city wants some of that money now, they can issue a **tax anticipation note**, or TAN. If it's backed by revenues—from sewer and water services, for example—it's a **revenue anticipation note**, or RAN. If the note is backed by both taxes and revenues, they call it a **tax and revenue anticipation note**, or TRAN. Through a **bond anticipation note** or BAN the issuer borrows money now and backs it with part of the money they're going to borrow when they issue more bonds.

Seriously.

The interest paid on these municipal notes is lower than the nominal rates paid on a corporation's commercial paper, but that's okay—the interest paid is also tax-exempt at the federal level. So, if an investor or an institution is looking for safety, liquidity, and dependable, tax-exempt interest over the short-term, they purchase these anticipation notes directly or through a tax-exempt money market mutual fund.

Certificates of Deposit (CD)

To earn a higher interest rate than what their bank offers on savings or checking accounts, many bank customers put relatively large amounts of money into **certificates of deposit** or CDs. These are long-term deposits that pay higher rates of interest if the depositor agrees to leave the funds untouched during a certain time frame. CDs are typically offered in terms of three or six months, and as long as one, two, three or five years. Those are typical terms, but savers can find certificates of deposit with terms as short as seven days or as long as 10 years. Obviously, the bank would have to entice someone with a higher rate to get him to agree to leave a large deposit untouched for 10 years. And, a saver, on the other hand, could not expect a high rate of return when locking up funds for a mere seven days. Investors agree not to withdraw funds until the CD matures, which is why CDs usually offer higher yields than a regular savings account. As with any fixed-income investment, rates typically increase with the length of deposit terms.

Deposits in bank CDs are backed by the Federal Deposit Insurance Corporation for up to $250,000 per depositor and ownership category, per insured bank. Bank CDs are insured by the FDIC just like other bank deposits, so this is about as safe as "safe money" gets. As you might imagine, the yields on these government-insured deposits are also rather modest. Then again, for the liquid part of one's portfolio, bank CDs are often perfect.

The drawbacks include the fact that they are long-term deposits, not as liquid as a savings account or a money market mutual fund. If the individual wants her money out now to cover a roof replacement, she will be penalized and probably lose all or most of the interest she was going to make. Bank CDs are not bonds to be traded on the secondary market. CDs don't do much to protect purchasing power, either, but they are great at maintaining an investor's needs for liquidity and capital preservation. The rates offered on certificates of deposit can change every week.

A $250,000 investment is equally safe in a T-Bill or a bank CD. Above that amount, the T-Bill is safer. And, either way, T-Bills are securities that can be bought and sold any day the securities markets are open, while CDs, on the other hand, are commitments to keep money on deposit for a specified length of time.

Brokered CDS

As opposed to just walking into a local bank and accepting the yields they're currently offering on their certificates of deposit, investors who purchase brokered CDs open their portfolio up to yields offered by banks across the country. A brokered CD account would also provide liquidity for the investor since he could ask the broker/registered representative to sell the CD on the secondary market as opposed to taking an early withdrawal penalty from a bank. Assuming the CDs are all FDIC insured (up to $250,000), investors can put a substantial amount of money into brokered CD accounts and receive FDIC insurance on each individual certificate of deposit in the portfolio. All without opening accounts at dozens of different banks to avoid exceeding the $250,000 FDIC coverage. Of course, there are fees, and this works much like brokered mortgages—the interest rate you receive is less favorable after the broker takes his cut.

Although most CDs are short-term, there are also long-term certificates of deposit with maturities as long as 10 years. Although brokered CDs can be a great option for many investors, some investors have been shafted by brokers who put them into 10-year CDs which then led to large losses when the investors needed their cash. As one might imagine, these long-term CDs may have limited or even no liquidity and investors can lose money by selling these things on the secondary market. Also, the interest payments on long-term CDs are often complex and explained in fine print few investors understand. Broker-dealers and registered representatives selling these long-term CDs need to be sure that investors understand how these products differ from traditional bank CDs and must disclose all potential risks. Higher yields on the one hand, but the secondary market for the products might not be as liquid as one would hope. Suddenly, rather than sacrificing the interest on a bank CD, the individual could lose principal. I don't know about you, but "losing money" and "CDs" really don't go together in my mind. The regulators tend to have similar difficulty squaring the two notions.

Negotiable/Jumbo CDS

Some investors step outside the realm of FDIC insurance and purchase **jumbo** or **negotiable CDs**. The denominations here are often several millions of dollars. Therefore, jumbo CDs are usually not insured by the FDIC but are, rather, backed by the issuing bank. That makes their yields higher. Also, if you've ever pulled out of a bank CD early, you know how painful that can be. With a jumbo CD you have a negotiable security you can sell to someone else. That's what the word "negotiable" means—tradable. If you have one of those archaic things known as a "checkbook," you'll notice your checks are "non-negotiable." They're just bank drafts—not tradable or marketable instruments. Well, a "negotiable CD" is a tradable, marketable instrument as opposed to just a long-term deposit at a bank.

Banks typically lend out more money than they take in through deposits. In fact, it might be a ratio of $10 of lending for every $1 taken in from deposits. To keep the banks from going belly-up when the borrowers can't repay the loans, the Federal Reserve Board requires their member banks to maintain a minimum amount of their deposits in reserve. Like, in case someone wants her money this afternoon at the teller window in Conshohocken, Pennsylvania. If a bank in Conshohocken is a few million dollars short of meeting their reserve requirement, they might borrow excess funds from a bank in Pittsburgh or Poughkeepsie at the **fed funds rate**. The fed funds rate is the interest rate that banks charge other banks for overnight loans. The rate fluctuates daily and is considered an indicator of interest rate trends in general. For example, if the fed funds rate rises, it's likely that the prime rate that banks charge their most creditworthy corporate borrowers will also rise soon. As will rates charged on mortgages, car loans, and unsecured personal loans.

Types and Characteristics of Fixed-Income Securities

Insurance-based products provide financial protection. Investments in money market securities provide a rainy-day fund that earns interest and can be tapped in an emergency without having to sell at a loss. To earn higher rates of return investors purchase longer-term debt securities, provided they have a long enough time horizon. If the time horizon is 10 years, an investor would expect to receive a higher yield on a T-Note compared to purchasing and repurchasing T-bills over that period. After all, the yield curve is typically a normal or positive curve.

Businesses borrow money short-term by issuing money market securities. To borrow from investors over the long-term companies issue fixed-income securities that are usually called **bonds.** As we saw when looking at the balance sheet, businesses sell stock to some investors and bonds to others, forming their **capital structure**. Equity investors are owners; bond investors are loaners. Loaners are creditors who must be paid their interest and principal on time but don't get a vote in corporate management decisions. Owners don't have to be paid anything, but their potential reward is much bigger than those who buy the company's bonds.

For the issuing company there are advantages and disadvantages to both types of financing. Equity financing gives the business breathing room since there are no interest payments to meet. But, equity investors take a share of profits, have a voice in corporate matters, and never go away. Debt financing adds the burden of interest payments that could force the company into bankruptcy. However, if the company can meet the interest and principal payments, eventually the bondholders are paid off, never making a claim on the company's profits.

Corporate bonds are debt securities representing loans from investors to a corporation. Investors buy the bonds, and the corporation then pays them interest on the loan until the principal amount is returned with the last interest payment at the end of the term. The bonds are liquid, meaning that the lenders can sell the bonds to other investors if they need to convert to cash.

What separates them from, say, a money market mutual fund, then? Bond prices rise and fall based on many factors we discussed under investment risks. Even though a T-Bond is guaranteed against default, its market price could drop. If so, the investor would liquidate at a loss. The goal of a money market mutual fund is to maintain a stable share price of $1 so investors can liquidate without taking a loss.

Again, though, to earn a higher rate of return investors move into longer-term fixed-income securities.

A corporation issuing bonds is using **leverage**. A leveraged company has financed operations by issuing debt securities or taking out long-term bank loans. On the balance sheet, the par value of the bonds is listed under long-term liabilities. And, on the income statement the interest payments are recorded as an expense. Interest is, after all, the "I" in those EBIT, EBITDA, etc. abbreviations we looked at. So, an analyst assigning a bond rating spends much time with an issuer's financial statements to see if the issuer will have trouble making regular interest payments and returning the principal at maturity.

A bond has a specific value known as the **par value** or **principal** amount. Since it's printed on the face of the certificate, it is also called the **face amount** of the bond. Bonds usually have a par value of $1,000 and, occasionally, $5,000. This is the amount an investor will receive with the last interest payment from the issuer. Up to that point, the investor has only been receiving interest payments against the money he loaned to the corporation by purchasing their bond certificates.

The bond certificate has "$1,000" or whatever the par value is printed on the face, along with the interest rate the issuer will pay the investor e year. This interest rate could be referred to as the **coupon rate** or **nominal yield**. The interest rate a bondholder receives is a stated, known thing. That's a big difference from common stock, where investors own a piece of a company's profits and hope that company becomes more profitable all the time. On the other hand, if they buy a 5% bond, investors receive 5% of the par value ($1,000) every year, which is $50 per year per bond. In other words, if he owns $1,000,000 par value of a bond with a 5% nominal yield, the bondholder's interest income is $50,000 a year.

Form of Registration

A **bond certificate** is a paper or electronic document stating the details of the bond:

- issuer's name
- par value or face amount
- interest rate
- maturity date
- call date (if any)

There are four different forms that a bond can take in terms of the certificate itself. In the olden days, bonds were issued as **bearer bonds**, which meant that whoever had possession of the bond was assumed to be the owner. No owner name at all on the certificate. The bond certificate said "pay to the bearer," so whoever presented the bond at maturity received the principal. To receive the interest, investors holding bearer bonds used to clip coupons attached to the bond certificate every six months. There was no name on the interest coupon, either, so the IRS had no way of tracking the principal or the interest income. Bonds haven't been issued in bearer form since the early 1980s. That doesn't mean they don't exist. A few are out there in safe-deposit boxes surely.

Bonds also used to be **registered as to principal only**. That meant that we had a name on the bond certificate—the person who would receive the principal amount at maturity. But, again, we had the unnamed interest coupons. Therefore, only the principal was registered, thus the name "registered as to principal only."

In the early 1980s issuers started registering both pieces of the **debt service**. Ever since, the issuer has registered the name of the owner [principal] and automatically cuts a check every six months for the interest. We call these bonds fully registered, because both pieces of the debt service (interest, principal) are registered.

Book entry/journal entry bonds are also fully registered. It's just that it's done on computer, rather than on paper. The investor keeps the trade confirmation as proof of ownership, but the issuer's paying agent has an owner name on computer, and automatically pays interest checks to the registered owner. Book entry/journal entry is how virtually all securities are issued these days. But, since bonds often have 30-year maturities, there are investors out there with bond certificates in their possession.

Quotes

Bonds are quoted either in terms of their price, or their yield. Since the coupon rate or nominal yield doesn't change, if you give me the price, I can figure the yield. And, if you give me the yield, I can figure the price.

If we're talking about a bond's price, we're talking about bond points. A bond point is worth $10. So, if a bond is selling at "98," that means it's selling for 98 bond points. With each point worth $10, a bond selling for 98 bond points is trading for $980. A bond trading at 102 is selling for $1,020. Although fractions have been eliminated from stock and options pricing, they are alive in the world of bond pricing.

If a bond point is worth $10, how much is 1/2 a bond point worth? Five dollars. A quarter-point is worth $2.50. An eighth is $1.25. Therefore, if you see a bond priced at 102 3/8, how much does the bond cost in dollars and cents? The "102" puts the price at $1,020, and 3/8 of $10 is $3.75. So, a bond trading at 102 3/8 costs $1,023.75.

$$102 (\$1,020) + 3/8 (\$3.75) = \$1,023.75$$

Corporate and municipal bonds can be quoted in halves, quarters, and eighths. T-Notes and T-Bonds split the $10 into 32 parts, with each 32nd worth $.3125.

Not all bond prices are given in fractions these days, however. Often the price is a decimal indicating the percentage of par value one would pay to purchase the bond. For example, a bond that last traded at "97.65" traded for $976.50 per bond. Or, if a bond is trading at a price of $102.475, buyers pay $1,024.75 per bond, or 102.475% of the bond's face value. The exam could ask what the total cost is if the investor buys 10 bonds, or 100 bonds. For the bond trading at "97.65" 10 bonds would cost the investor $9,765 and 100 bonds would cost $97,650.

If we're talking about **basis points**, we're talking about a bond's yield. Yield to maturity, to be exact. If I say that a bond with an 8% coupon just traded on a 7.92 **basis**, I'm saying the price went up above par, pushing the yield to maturity down to 7.92%. In other words, the price pushed the yield to maturity to a certain percentage, or number of "basis points." A basis point is the smallest increment of change in a bond's yield. When the media talks about the Fed easing interest rates by fifty basis points, they're talking about 1/2 of 1 percent.

We would write 1% as .01, right? Well, basis points use a 4-digit display system, so .01 is written as:

$$.0\ 1\ 0\ 0$$

Then, we read that figure as "100 basis points." Two percent is 200 basis points. One-half of one percent is written as .0050 or "50 basis points." So, a bond trading at a 7.92 basis means that the YTM is 7.92% or 792 basis points.

An easy way to work with basis points is to remember that all the single-digit percentages are expressed in hundreds. 400 basis points means 4%. Anything less than 100 basis points is less than 1%. So, 30 basis points is only .3 of 1%.

When we look at mutual funds, we'll see that the fund's operating expenses are expressed as basis points so that the investment adviser's management fee could be .35% or 35 basis points per year of the fund's assets. The 12b-1 fees that agents earn on mutual fund sales are typically 25 basis points or .25% per year—also known as ¼ of 1%.

Notation

The exam might ask what the following means:

10M XYZ 8s debentures of '25, callable @103 in '18

Believe it or not, "10M" means $10,000 par value or 10 bonds. XYZ is the issuing corporation, and they pay "8s" or 8% in interest each year. The little "s" means you get the $80 in two semi-annual payments of $40 each. Remember that—a test question might ask how much the investor receives at maturity on this bond. The answer is $1,040. Remember that interest is always paid retroactively, meaning for the previous 6 months. So, when the bond matures, you get your final interest payment (for the previous 6 months) plus the principal/par value of $1,000. This investor owns 10 bonds, so she would receive $10,400 at maturity in 2025.

Assuming we make it that far. As we see above, if interest rates drop in 2018, the issuer can buy back the bonds for $1,030 each, end of story. That's what "callable at 103 in '18" means.

Accrued Interest

We have been discussing the annual interest paid to the owner of a bond. If we can express the interest per-year, we can also express what the interest per-day is, right? Bond interest is earned every day, so when a bond is traded, typically the buyer pays the seller for a certain number of days of interest earned since the last semiannual interest payment.

The tricky part is that different issuers use different days in their months and years. For a corporate or municipal issuer, we consider every month to have 30 days, and every year to have 360 days. Yes, even February has 30 days for corporate and municipal bonds. For U.S. Treasury securities actual calendar days are used:

Type	Settles	Months	Years
Corporate/Municipal bond	T + 3	30 days	360 days
Treasuries	T + 1	Actual	Actual

So, if a corporate bond pays $80 in annual interest, how much is that per day? Divide $80 by 360 days to get about 22.2 cents per day. That's what the owner of the bond earns in interest every day.

How often does the owner receive a check for her interest?

Twice a year, or semi-annually.

But, like most things in the securities industry, the payment months are abbreviated.

For a "J & J" bond, you'll have to think about which two "J" months would be six months apart.

January and July, right?

Here's how the chart works out for interest payment months:

J   J

F   A

M   S

A   O

M   N

J   D

Reading left to right, we pair January with July, February with August, March with September, April with October, May with November, and June with December. So if you buy an "A & O" bond, you'll receive your two interest checks on the first of April and the first of October. If it's the 8% bond we've been discussing, how much will you receive each time?

That's right, $40. $80 per year divided into two semi-annual payments.

If they don't add a number to the "A & O," that means the checks are received on the first of each month. If they add a "15" to the abbreviation, that means the checks are received on the 15th of each month, as in an "A & O 15" bond.

Now, the check might be received on the first day of April. That doesn't cover that day's interest, though. A bondholder earns interest every day she owns the bond, including weekends and holidays.

Doesn't matter when the check arrives. The check covers the previous six months' worth of interest, nothing more.

The concept behind accrued interest is that a bond is usually traded somewhere between the two interest payment dates. If the bond owner got her last interest check on the first of April, then sells the bond on July 16, what happens?

Well, who is going to receive the next interest check?

The buyer of the bond, who is about to become the new owner. Should we trust the buyer to deliver the seller's portion of that check when the buyer receives it?

Not a chance. So, the buyer is going to pay the seller her portion of the interest right up front. That's what the whole accrued interest concept comes down to. The buyer has to pay the seller the price of the bond, plus the interest that belongs to the seller, who hasn't gotten a check since the last payment date.

We can answer these questions step-by-step:

Dale Dawson sells Jim Jacobs an XYZ Corp. 8% A&O bond on Wednesday, June 19. How much in accrued interest must be paid, and who pays the interest?

I. Dale pays the interest.

II. Jim pays the interest.

III. Accrued interest is $18.44 per bond.

IV. Accrued interest is $1.84 per bond.

A. I, III

B. I, IV

C. II, III

D. II, IV

We know who pays the interest. Jim-the-buyer pays Dale-the-seller. How much does Jim pay Dale in accrued interest?

Step one, find the settlement date. Corporate and municipal bonds settle "T + 3," or three business days after the trade date. Weekends don't count as business days, so "T" is Wednesday. We count Thursday as one, Friday as two, and Monday as the third business day after the Trade date.

Monday will be June 24th.

Step two, count the days.

On the settlement date the buyer starts earning interest. So, the seller is entitled to every day up to—but not including—the settlement date. The settlement date's interest belongs to the buyer.

So, if the trade settles on the 24th of June, the seller is entitled to 23 days of interest.

This A&O bond last paid interest on the 1st of April. How many days in April is the seller entitled to?

Thirty. So, 30 days for April plus 30 days for May plus 23 days for June = 83 days of accrued interest.

Step three, find the interest-per-day that the bond pays. The bond pays $80 per year divided by 360 days, or 22.2 cents a day.

Step four, multiply the daily interest by the number of days that have accrued. Twenty-two cents a day times 83 days equals $18.44 per bond that Jim Jacobs must pay Dale Dawson, on top of the price of each bond.

The answer, then, is "C."

A question concerning U.S. Treasury securities might look like this:

A J & D 5% government bond trades on Wednesday, August 14th. How much accrued interest will the buyer pay the seller?

A. 13.7 cents

B. 28 cents

C. $1.65 per bond

D. $10.27 per bond

Step one—when does the trade settle? Thursday, August 15th. Treasuries settle on the next business day, T + 1.

Step two—count the days. This bond last made an interest payment on the first of June, so how many days have accrued?

June   30

July   31

Aug   14

Looks like 75 days total, right?

Step three—find the interest per day. $50 per year divided by 365 (actual) days = 13.7 cents per day.

Step four—multiply the days by the daily interest. 75 days times 13.7 cents = $10.27 per bond.

The answer is "D."

If an issuer issues bonds that all mature on the same date in the future, we call this a **term maturity**. On the other hand, if the bonds are issued all at once but then mature gradually over time, we call this a **serial maturity**. Municipal bonds are often issued as serial maturities. In this case, the municipality floats, say, a $50,000,000 issue in which a portion of the bonds will mature each year over, say, 20 years. The longer out the maturity, the higher the yield offered to those investors, and the lower the yield offered on the bonds coming due in just a year or two.

In a **balloon maturity,** some of the bonds issued come due in the near-term, while most of the principal is paid off all at once, usually at the final maturity date. The term "balloon maturity" only applies to bond issues not backed up with a sinking fund, which means such issues can put an issuer's cash flow under severe stress.

Special Types of Bonds

Zero Coupon, Step-Up Bonds

We saw that reinvestment risk is avoided by purchasing bonds that do not make regular interest payments to the investor. Such bonds are called **zero coupons**. Each year the investor's cost basis is accreted, but all interest income is delayed until the bond matures at a higher face amount than the investor paid. Because the value of the bond increases as opposed to the issuer paying interest, a zero coupon is also known as a **capital appreciation bond.**

Corporate and U.S. Government zero coupon bonds are taxable annually to the investor even though interest income is not received until maturity. Because there is no current cash flow, the market price of a zero coupon is more volatile than a bond with a similar term to maturity that pays interest.

A step-up bond makes higher interest payments in the future compared to the initial payment. Investors might receive a lower-than-current rate on the first payment, but in exchange for that, they might end up receiving higher payments going forward. Usually, the coupon rate resets annually, but after the call protection period has passed, the issuer also has the right to call the bonds. Some **step-up bonds** reset the coupon payment just once; most re-set it at regular intervals. If an investor is concerned that rates will rise in the future, a step-up bond may be suitable, as it would allow her to capture higher coupon payments should that happen.

Callable, Put-able, and Convertible

If a bond issue is **callable,** the issuer has the right to buy the bonds back for a stated price as of a certain date or on a series of dates. A bond might be callable starting in the year 2025 at 104, meaning that in the year 2025 the issuer can retire the debt by giving each bondholder $1,040 per bond plus any accrued interest. If the next call date is in 2027, maybe the issuer only has to pay 102 at that point, and so on. The terms of the call provisions are spelled out in the contract known as the bond **indenture.**

Why do issuers call bonds? When interest rates drop, bond issuers realize their current debt could be replaced with cheaper debt. If interest rates fall to 6%, they reason, let's issue new debt at 6% and use part of the proceeds to retire the debt we're currently paying 8% on. Maybe they have to pay a slight premium to par when retiring the bond early, but the issuer comes out ahead by refinancing a large amount of debt at a lower interest rate. The premium price of "104" or "102" just barely compensates the bondholders for having to give up their bonds early and go forward at a lower yield to their investment accounts.

Replacing one bond issue with another is called **refunding**. It tends to happen when interest rates fall. It allows the issuer to replace high-interest-rate debt with lower-interest-rate debt.

But, what can the bondholders do with the proceeds of the call? Reinvest them. At what rate? A lower rate. This is a form of reinvestment risk, but it could also be referred to as call risk. Whatever we call it, the fact is upon reinvestment, the bondholders will get a lower rate of return, since interest rates have now fallen.

And, what happens to bond prices as rates decline? They go up, only they stop going up the day the issuer announces that the bonds will be called, meaning the bondholder doesn't get the full appreciation in price he would have otherwise gotten.

So, since the bondholder takes on this call risk, callable bonds yield more than non-callable bonds. As always, if we want something good from the corporation, they take something away.

If a bond is callable, the issuer reserves the right to buy it back at a stated price as of a certain date or series of dates. On the other hand, if a bond is "put-able," this put feature gives the owner of the bond the right to sell the bond back to the issuer per the terms stated in the indenture. As with call dates, the indenture often spells out a series of dates on which the investor may sell the bonds. A "put-able" bond protects investors from interest rate risk. If interest rates rise, other investors will be holding bonds with depressed market prices while the owner of a put-able bond can sell his bond for the price stated in the indenture.

Both corporations and municipalities issue callable and put-able bonds. On the other hand, only corporations issue **convertible bonds**, as these bonds are convertible into shares of common stock. As with convertible preferred stock, the issuer offers some potential upside to fixed-income investors. What's the catch? The yield offered is lower.

For a convertible bond the investor applies the par value toward purchasing the company's stock at a pre-determined price. When a convertible bond is issued, it is given a conversion price. If the conversion price is $40, this means that the bond is convertible into common stock at $40. In other words, the investor can use the par value of her bond towards the purchase of the company's common stock at a set price of $40. If the par value is $1,000, she applies that $1,000 toward the purchase of stock at $40 per-share. When doing so, how many shares would she be able to buy?

25 shares. So, how much is this bond worth at any given moment? It's worth whatever 25 shares of the common stock are worth at that moment, give or take. Investors take the par value of the convertible bond and divide it by the conversion price to find out how many shares of common stock the bond could be converted into.

In this case, it's 25 shares, since $1,000 would go exactly that far when purchasing stock priced at $40 a share.

$$Par/Conversion\ price = \#\ common\ shares$$

$$1,000/40 = 25\ shares$$

As we will see with convertible preferred stock, another name for the 25:1 relationship here is conversion ratio.

Going forward then, how much is the bond worth? That depends—how much are 25 shares of the common stock currently worth? Since the bond could always be converted into 25 shares, it should be worth whatever 25 shares of the common stock are worth—give or take. When the bond trades for exactly what the 25 shares are worth, we call this relationship **parity**, which means "same" or "equal." Since one's price depends on the other, the two should have a price that is near "parity."

If the common stock started to trade above $40 in our example, the bond should trade for 25 times that amount. If the stock rises to $50, the convertible bond is worth $1,250 or more. If not, an investor would have an "arbitrage opportunity." That means he could buy the bonds for less than the underlying stock is worth. If the stock rose to $50, but for some reason, one could buy the bonds for just $1,200, this is an arbitrage opportunity where an alert trader could pay just $1,200 for $1,250 worth of stock.

What usually happens is the holder of a convertible bond experiences an increased market price if the underlying stock rises. The bondholder does not have to convert to profit. Rather, he can just sell his bond for a capital gain.

Unfortunately, most convertible bonds give the issuer the right to force investors to convert rather than wait for the stock price to rise even further. For that reason, most convertible bonds do not offer unlimited upside. Then again, these **hybrid securities** offer some downside protection to the investor holding a bond while also offering some upside to him by tying the value to the price of the common stock. The issuer benefits by issuing the bonds at a lower coupon rate than they would otherwise have to pay.

Common stockholders will see their equity diluted when convertible bonds are converted to shares of stock. That's why a company's EPS is often followed by its "diluted EPS" to factor in the earnings-per-share that would have been reported if all convertibles converted to the underlying common stock. While the interest payment to those bondholders would go away, unfortunately they would be getting a share of the net income of the company going forward. Looking at the most recent annual report for Starbucks, I noted yesterday that EPS was $1.84, while diluted EPS was just $1.82.

Risks

Let's do a quick review of the risks that bond investors face:

```
Credit/default risk: the risk that the issuer will miss interest
payments or be unable to return the principal to investors.
```

`Interest rate risk`: the risk that interest rates will rise, knocking bond market prices down. This is most severe on longer-term bonds.

`Purchasing power risk`: the risk that inflation will erode the value of the coupon/interest payment to the investor.

`Call risk`: the risk that when interest rates drop, issuers will buy back/redeem their bonds early. This forces bond investors to reinvest at lower rates going forward when they buy new bonds with the proceeds of the call. Not all bonds are callable, but those that are have this risk.

`Prepayment risk`: call risk for mortgage-backed securities.

`Reinvestment risk`: refers to the fact that e six months a fixed-income investor will reinvest interest payments into new bonds; when she does so, she will reinvest at lower rates if interest rates/yields have dropped compared to the stated interest rate on the existing bond in her portfolio.

`Market risk`: the risk that investors will panic and send bond prices downward.

Corporate Bonds

As the SEC explains in a notice to investors, "Companies use the proceeds from bond sales for a wide variety of purposes, including buying new equipment, investing in research and development, buying back their own stock, paying shareholder dividends, refinancing debt, and financing mergers and acquisitions."

As the SEC mentions, companies might even borrow money to buy back equity. A test question could ask about that in terms of how it would affect the issuer's balance sheet. If an issuer is trading debt for equity, they are using leverage, which is reflected in a higher debt-to-equity ratio. Whatever the earnings are going forward, by retiring equity the issuer could help boost the earnings per-share of the common stock, which is good news for the shareholders.

A default on a municipal bond is a rare thing, but many corporations end up unable to pay the interest on their bonds—or return the principal at maturity—and thereby go into default, which is always bad news for the bondholders. To protect bondholders from this, Congress passed the **Trust Indenture Act of 1939**. Under this act if a corporation wants to sell $5,000,000 or more worth of bonds that mature in longer than one year, they must do it under a contract or indenture with a trustee, who will enforce the terms of the indenture to the benefit of the bondholders. In other words, if the issuer defaults, the trustee can move to forcibly sell off the assets of the company so that bondholders can recover some of their money. The trustee is typically a large bank.

As we'll see, there are also federal bankruptcy laws that provide protections to both the issuers and investors of bonds.

A corporate bond pays a fixed rate of interest to the investor, and that bond interest must be paid, unlike a dividend on stock that is paid only if the board of directors declares it. We'll see that a bondholder doesn't suffer as much price volatility as a stock investor. But, unlike the owner of common stock, bondholders don't vote on corporate matters. The only time bondholders get to vote is if the corporation goes into bankruptcy. Creditors will be offered various scenarios by the corporation, and the bondholders will get to vote on these terms. In other words, the only time bondholders get to vote is when they wish they didn't have to.

Since bankruptcy is a concern, corporations often secure the bonds by pledging specific assets like airplanes, government securities, or real estate. These bonds secured by specific collateral are called **secured bonds.** The issuer of a secured bond pledges title of the assets to the trustee, who might end up selling them off if the issuer gets behind on its interest payments. Investors who buy bonds attached to specific collateral are secured creditors, the most likely creditors to get paid should the company become insolvent. If the collateral used is real estate, we call it a **mortgage bond**. If the collateral is securities, we call it a **collateral trust certificate**. And if the collateral is equipment, such as airplanes or railroad cars, we call it an **equipment trust certificate**. Since these bonds are usually the most secure bonds issued by the company, they offer the lowest coupon payment, too. Remember, if you take a small risk, you usually only get a small reward.

Most corporate bonds are backed by a promise known as the "full faith and credit" of the issuer. That's why we might want to see what S&P and Moody's say about an issuer's full faith and credit. If the credit is AAA, we won't be offered a large coupon payment. But if the issuer is rated right at the cut-off point of BBB (Baa for Moody's), then we demand a higher interest rate in exchange for buying bonds from an issuer just one notch above junk status. Regardless of the rating, if we buy a bond backed by the full faith and credit of an issuer, we are buying a **debenture**.

Debenture holders are general creditors with claims below those of the secured bondholders. In a bankruptcy, debenture holders must compete with all other unsecured creditors of the company, e.g., suppliers with unpaid invoices. Therefore, debentures pay a higher coupon than secured bonds, since they carry more risk.

Some bonds are **guaranteed bonds,** which means a party other than the issuer has promised to pay interest, principal, or both if the issuer of the bonds cannot. Often a parent company will guarantee the bonds issued by one of its smaller subsidiaries to improve the credit rating. A "guaranteed bond" does not imply the investor is guaranteed against loss. Outside of bank products backed by the FDIC, investors should never expect to be guaranteed against all investment risk. Being guaranteed against default is as good as it gets.

Subordinated debentures have a claim below debentures. Since these bonds are riskier, they pay a higher coupon than debentures.

Beneath all creditors, stockholders make their claims on the company's assets. Preferred stockholders get preference, and common stock is always last in line. Common stock represents the lowest claim on a company's assets, which is why it is called the most "junior" security issued by a company.

If a company becomes unable to pay its suppliers, employees, bondholders, etc., it files a petition for bankruptcy protection either under "Chapter 7" or "Chapter 11" of the federal bankruptcy laws. Under Chapter 11 the company could convince creditors to write off some of the debt or extend the terms of the debt they are currently unable to service. Or, in some cases the entity is completely re-organized under Chapter 11 and former creditors will typically become shareholders of the newly reorganized entity. The business entity often keeps functioning to the best of its abilities and is placed under a trusteeship as a company that is now a "debtor in possession." While the entity struggles along, the U.S. trustee oversees things, demanding that the debtor in possession file regular reports on the operations of the business. The U.S. trustee also appoints a creditors' committee whose role involves consulting with the debtor in possession on administration of the case, investigating the debtor's conduct and operation of the business, and participating in formulating a plan of reorganization. The creditors' committee ordinarily consists of unsecured creditors who hold the seven largest unsecured claims against the debtor.

Under Chapter 7 assets of the company are liquidated by a court-appointed trustee and paid out according to the priority of claims. A liquidation under Chapter 7 is done according to the "absolute priority rule." When the court-appointed trustee liquidates assets, the parties who are owed money would be paid according to the following order or priority:

1. Administrative expenses of the bankruptcy itself
2. Taxes, rents, wages, and benefits
3. Unsecured creditors, including suppliers and bondholders/lenders
4. Equity investors: preferred stock, common stock

As we saw, secured bondholders have a claim on specific assets, so they are outside the priority ordering. They can seize the assets or their value based on the indenture for their secured bonds. This is why a secured bondholder often gets paid, even when other creditors receive nothing. If secured creditors receive collateral that is insufficient to satisfy their claim, their excess claim becomes another claim by unsecured creditors.

Also, remember that an **income bond** only pays income if the company has income. It's usually issued by a company coming out of bankruptcy and usually offers a high coupon to compensate for the uncertainty of the interest payment. The idea here is that the re-organized company will get some breathing room from the creditors and maybe this breathing room will help it get its act together and start paying interest on its "income" or "adjustment" bonds." A potential trick question could try to confuse you into thinking that an "income investor" with a low risk tolerance should buy an "income bond."

No—only a bond investor with a high appetite for risk and little need for liquidity should do so.

Bonds pay interest-only until the end of the term. Since the issuing corporation must return the principal value of the bond at some point, they usually establish what's known as a **sinking fund**. If you held your interest-only mortgage 30 years, maybe your spouse would one day have to gently remind you, "Now, remember to add the $300,000 to this month's interest check, honey. Time to pay the principal back." Since that's how corporations pay back the principal, they set some money aside in escrow, which means they park it in safe, dependable U.S. Treasury securities. With this sinking fund established, the company would be able to return the principal or complete a "call." Having this money set aside can only help the rating by S&P and Moody's, too.

Some bonds—especially municipal bonds—are escrowed to maturity, which means the funds needed to retire that bond issue are already parked in a safe, interest-bearing account holding Treasury securities. Having the debt service covered by a verifiable escrow account tends to make such bond ratings AAA and easy to sell on the secondary market.

As we saw, a balloon maturity is a bond issue without a sinking fund and where most of the principal comes due at the end of the term.

U.S. Government Securities

The rate of default on high-yield corporate bonds has ranged in recent years from about 1% to 13%. On the other hand, the rate of default on U.S. Treasury securities has ranged from 0% to 0%, going all the way back to when Alexander Hamilton first issued them in the late 1700s. If you buy a bill, note, or bond issued by the United States Treasury, you eliminate default risk. You're going to get your interest and principal for sure. You just aren't going to get rich in the process. In fact, you usually need to be rich already to get excited about U.S. Government debt.

These fixed-income securities are for capital preservation. Working people need to save up for retirement through common stock or equity mutual funds. The less daring will save up by investing through corporate bonds or bond mutual funds. But if one already has millions of dollars, the goal might become preserving that capital as opposed to risking it trying to get bigger returns. If you sell your company for $10 million, for example, you might put $2 million into T-Bonds. If they yield 5%, that's $100,000 in interest income going forward, after all, with no risk to the principal.

U.S. Treasury securities are virtually free of default risk. They carry most of the other risks that corporate bondholders face, but default risk is eliminated. Therefore, if an investor compares the yield on, say, a 10-year Treasury Note to the yield on a 10-year corporate bond, the higher yield offered on the corporate bond indicates the market's perceived default risk. If the Treasury Note yields 3.0% while the 10-year corporate bond yields 4.5%, the **risk premium** demanded by investors is that difference of 1.5%. To take on default risk, investors require that much more yield.

As I write this, 1.5% happens to be exactly the risk premium investors are demanding to buy the lowest investment-grade rating (BBB/Baa). To buy the first level of junk a risk premium of 2.7% over U.S. Treasuries is currently required.

U.S. Government debt is safe and, therefore, low-yielding. T-Bills, T-Notes, T-Bonds, STRIPS, and TIPS are all securities that can be traded on the secondary market, what we call "negotiable" securities. I-Bonds, on the other hand, are not negotiable, meaning they can't be traded/sold to other investors.

T-Bills

T-Bills pay back the face amount, and investors try to buy them for the steepest discount possible on the front end. If the T-Bill pays out $1,000, investors would rather buy it for $950 than $965, right? In the first case, they earn $50 interest, in the second, only $35. That's why the BID looks higher than the ASK for T-Bills trading on the secondary market. The bid is the discount that buyers are trying to get; the asked price is the discount the sellers are willing to give up.

So, the quote might look like this:

BID	ASK
1.0%	.75%

In other words, the buyers want a 1% discount; the sellers are only willing to give up a .75% discount from the par value.

For a newly-issued T-Bill investors are able to purchase the security for less than the face amount they will receive in as little as 4 weeks or as long as 52 weeks. The U.S. Treasury operates a website that allows investors to purchase Treasury securities. The following explanation is from their website at www.treasurydirect.gov and reflects how low interest rates were at the time they published it:

For example, if a $1,000 26-week bill sells at auction for a 0.145% discount rate, the purchase price would be $999.27, a discount of $0.73.

In any case, T-Bills mature in one year or less (4 weeks, 13 weeks, 26 weeks, 52 weeks), so there are no coupon payments. Rather, the difference between the discounted purchase price and the face amount is the investor's interest on the short-term loan to the federal government. T-Bills are offered in minimum denominations of $100 and, like all Treasuries, T-Bills are issued in book entry/journal entry form. The maturities available change from time to time. Currently (as you can see at www.treasurydirect.gov) the available maturities are 4 weeks, 3 months, 6 months, 12 months, and the extremely short-term "cash management bills."

That website, by the way, offers an overview of bills, notes, bonds, etc. T-Bills are auctioned every Monday by the Federal Reserve Board. The big institutions put in "competitive tenders," trying to buy the bills for the lowest possible price. Small investors put in a "non-competitive" tender that will be filled. Institutions will probably get a better price on T-Bills today, but they also might not get their bid filled at all.

T-Notes, T-Bonds

T-Bills are ideal for the short-term, but investors may get tired of receiving low yields, and yields that tend to fluctuate each time they buy a new T-Bill. If the investor wants to receive interest payments for a few years and at a higher rate of interest, he will purchase T-Notes and T-Bonds instead. T-Notes are offered with 2- to 10-year maturities. T-Bonds mature in 30 years.

Both make semi-annual interest payments, and are both quoted in 32nds. A quote of 98.16 means $980 plus 16/32nds. A 32nd is worth thirty-one-and-a-quarter-pennies or $.3125. So, a T-Bond quoted at 98.16 is priced at $980 plus 16 times $.3125 ($5); a total of $985. A T-Bond quoted at 102.20 is trading for $1,020 plus 20 times $.3125 ($6.25); a total of $1,026.25.

The exam might ask you to calculate the **spread** on a quote for a T-Note or T-Bond. If a market maker says their bid is 98.16 while their offer is 98.20, the difference or "spread" between the prices is whatever 4 times $.3125 turns out to be on the calculator provided at the testing center. The spread in this example is $1.25 per bond or note. The question might then have you multiply that amount by the number of bonds or notes involved in the quote.

While corporate and municipal bonds are often callable just a few years after issue, 30-year T-Bonds are callable only in their last five years. The T-Bonds issued with super-high coupon rates back in 1983, for example, were not called until 2008.

STRIPS

The Treasury Department also takes T-Notes and T-Bonds and "strips" them into their various interest and principal components. Once they strip the securities into components, they sell interest-only or principal-only zero coupon bonds to investors. We call these STRIPS, an acronym that stands for the "separate trading of registered interest and principal of securities." If an investor needs to send kids to college, needs to have an exact amount of money available on a future date, and wants to avoid having to reinvest interest payments, put him into STRIPS. This way, he'll pay a known amount and receive a known amount on a future date, allowing him to lock into a yield long-term. He won't get rich, necessarily, but he won't lose the kids' college fund, either.

STRIPS present a peculiar tax problem called "phantom tax exposure." Even though interest income is not received until the STRIP matures, the investor pays tax on the amount of annual interest that has been added to the value of the security each year. A test question, might, therefore, point out that a STRIP or other taxable zero coupon forces investors to pay tax annually even though interest is received only at maturity.

Treasury Receipts

Broker-dealers sell zero coupons backed up by U.S. Treasury securities and call them **treasury receipts**. For both receipts and STRIPS, remember that they are purchased at a discount and mature at the face value. And remember that the STRIPS are guaranteed by Uncle Sam, while a Treasury Receipt is not.

TIPS

The Treasury Inflation-Protected Securities adjust for inflation, meaning that if inflation rises, investors receive more money, and when it falls, they receive less. Inflation is measured through the Consumer Price Index (CPI), which tracks the basic things that consumers buy.

If prices in general are rising (CPI is positive), the principal amount of the TIPS is adjusted upwards. That's a little surprising, since some readers would assume the principal amount/par value would stay the same, with the coupon rate adjusting. No. That would probably make too much sense to ever fly in Washington, DC. In any case, if the (fixed) coupon rate on the security is 3%, suddenly the investor could be receiving 3% of, say, $1030 to reflect inflation/rising consumer prices.

If the economy is experiencing falling prices (the CPI is negative), the principal amount of the TIPS could be lower than $1,000 when calculating the semi-annual interest payment. Even if the principal amount used to calculate an interest payment could be less than $1,000, the TIPS will pay out the $1,000 face amount at maturity, period. So, there is no default risk and no purchasing power/inflation risk on a TIPS. Basically, if you can find a safer security than a TIPS, please buy it.

Just don't expect to get much of a yield for your money.

An investor purchases an inflation-protected Treasury note (TIPS) with a coupon rate of 3%. Inflation in the first year is 4%. Therefore:
- A. The coupon payment becomes $31.20
- B. The principal becomes $1,030
- C. The coupon payment becomes $40
- D. The principal amount becomes $1,070

Answer: A. The rate of inflation is 4%, so the principal becomes 4% larger. Multiply the principal of $1,000 by 1.04 to get the new principal amount of $1,040. Then multiply that principal by 3%, and the new annual coupon rate is $31.20.

I-Bonds

Like all the other Government Securities above, TIPS are "negotiable securities," meaning you can sell them to other investors on the secondary market. I-bonds, on the other hand, are "non-negotiable," meaning there is no secondary market for them. An investor buys the I-bond from the U.S. Government and can only sell it by redeeming it to the U.S. Government for payment. In other words, they're not securities; they're merely "savings bonds." An I-bond is a savings bond issued by the U.S. Treasury, which means it's safe and also exempt from state and local income taxes.

An I-bond pays a guaranteed rate that is fixed but also pays more interest income when inflation rises. The semi-annual inflation rate announced in May is the change between the CPI (inflation) figures from the preceding September and March; the inflation rate announced in November is the change between the CPI figures from the preceding March and September. So, since they adjust the interest income to levels of inflation, there's no default risk and no real purchasing power risk, either. There are also tax advantages.

First, the interest isn't paid out; it's added to the value of the bond. You can, therefore, defer the taxes until you cash in the bond. And, if you use the proceeds for qualified education costs in the same calendar year that you redeem the bonds, the interest is tax-free. The investor does not even have to declare that the I-bonds will be used for educational purposes when she buys them. If she uses the proceeds in the same year she redeems the bonds—and meets the other requirements of the Education Savings Bond Program—the interest is tax-free.

Agency Bonds

Agency bonds or **agency issues** are debt securities issued by either Government Sponsored Enterprises (GSEs) or Federal Government agencies which may issue or guarantee these bonds. GSEs are usually federally-chartered but privately-owned corporations such as FNMA (Federal National Mortgage Association) and FHLMC (Federal Home Loan Mortgage Corporation). Government agencies include the Small Business Administration, GNMA (Government National Mortgage Association), and the FHA (Federal Housing Authority). A key difference here is that securities issued by GSEs are not direct obligations of the US Government, while those issued or guaranteed by GNMA (Ginnie Mae), the SBA, and the FHA are guaranteed against default just like T-Bills, T-Notes, and T-Bonds.

Agency securities tend to promote a public purpose. For example, FNMA and FHLMC purchase mortgages from lenders, which encourages lenders to make more loans and increase home ownership. Similarly, the Federal Farm Credit Banks provide assistance to the agricultural sector, while the Small Business Administration provides assistance to small businesses.

Fannie Mae (FNMA) and Freddie Mac (FHLMC) are public companies with common stock, unlike GNMA. While the US Government has provided financial assistance to these entities, it has not guaranteed their debt securities or preferred stock issues, let alone their common stock. So, while investing in Ginnie Mae involves no credit or default risk, this is not the case with Fannie and Freddie.

According to Ginnie Mae's website (www.ginniemae.gov), "At Ginnie Mae, we help make affordable housing a reality for millions of low- and moderate-income households across America by channeling global capital into the nation's housing markets. Specifically, the Ginnie Mae guaranty allows mortgage lenders to obtain a better price for their mortgage loans in the secondary mortgage market. The lenders can then use the proceeds to make new mortgage loans available. Ginnie Mae does not buy or sell loans or issue mortgage-backed securities (MBS). What Ginnie Mae does is guarantee investors the timely payment of principal and interest on mortgage-backed securities backed by federally insured or guaranteed loans — mainly loans insured by the Federal Housing Administration (FHA) or guaranteed by the Department of Veterans Affairs (VA). Ginnie Mae securities are the only MBS to carry the full faith and credit guaranty of the United States government, which means that even in difficult times, an investment in Ginnie Mae mortgage-backed securities is one of the safest an investor can make."

A minimum investment of $25,000 is required for GNMA mortgage-backed securities. Investors receive monthly interest and principal payments from a pool of mortgages. When will the mortgages in the pool be paid off? That is an uncertainty. If interest rates drop, the mortgages will be repaid sooner than expected, which we call prepayment risk. If interest rates go the other way, it will take longer than expected for the homeowners to pay off the mortgages, which we call extension risk. GNMA, FNMA, and FHLMC mortgage-backed securities all carry this risk, which we mentioned earlier.

GNMA is backed by the full faith and credit of the US Government. Still, the yields are typically higher than what one would receive on a Treasury security of a similar term due to prepayment and extension risk. Interest rates on mortgage securities from FNMA and FHLMC are also higher than on Treasury and higher than corporate bonds to reflect the compensation for the uncertainty of their maturity as well as their higher credit risk. While FNMA and FHLMC buy mortgages and issue mortgage-backed securities, GNMA adds her guaranty to mortgage-backed securities that have already been issued. FNMA and FHLMC do guarantee payment to investors, but, again, neither is the federal government, and both charge fees to provide the guarantee.

From an informative document put out by the Federal Reserve Bank of New York, I see that "The agencies use a variety of methods to distribute their securities including allocation to dealers, competitive dealer bidding, direct sales to investors, and sales to investors through dealers. A common distribution method for agency securities is to allocate them among members of a selling group or syndicate of dealers. The syndicate provides market and trading information to the issuing agency before and during the allocation, and may support secondary trading in the issue after allocation. In compensation for their services, the syndicate members retain a percentage of the proceeds from the sold securities."

Foreign Bonds

Some investors choose to purchase bonds issued outside the U.S., which typically offer higher yields. Does that imply that international investing is riskier? Absolutely. If the investor wants absolute safety, he sacrifices yield. If he wants high yield, he sacrifices safety. Investing in foreign bonds is risky, but there is a big difference between a developed market and an emerging market. In general, the following countries enjoy securities markets and economies that are considered developed: U.S., Canada, European Union countries, Australia, New Zealand, and Japan. Emerging markets would include everyone else, though South Korea and Singapore are much more advanced than China, India, and other "emerging" nations. If we purchase bonds issued and traded in emerging markets, we are investing in regions characterized by low per capita incomes, primitive securities markets, and/or economies that are not fully industrialized. In other words, there is a promising future, but it inconveniently hasn't shown up yet.

Whether the foreign market is considered developed or emerging, investors must deal with currency risk. If the bond pays interest and principal in yen or bot, the bondholder must convert that to U.S. dollars; if the dollar is strong, they receive fewer dollars. Luckily, not all foreign bonds pay interest and principal in foreign currencies. The exam might bring up the difference between "U.S. Pay Bonds" and "Foreign Pay Bonds." If a bond pays in U.S. dollars, currency risk is eliminated, but if it pays in another currency (foreign pay bond), then an American investor, obviously, does have currency exchange risk.

Types of "U.S. Pay Bonds" include "Eurodollar bonds," which are issued and traded outside the U.S. but are denominated in U.S. dollars. Another type is called the "Yankee bond," which allows foreign issuers to borrow money in the U.S. marketplace. Eurodollar bonds are not registered with the SEC and cannot be sold to U.S. investors until a certain number of days after being issued. Yankee bonds, on the other hand, are registered with the SEC.

The governments of emerging markets issue **Brady bonds**. Brady bonds are typically collateralized by U.S. Treasury securities, making these debt securities much safer than they seem on the surface.

CMOs

CMOs or **collateralized mortgage obligations** are inherently complex products. Generally, a financial institution takes either a pool of mortgages or a pool of mortgage-backed securities issued by GNMA, FNMA, or FHLMC and creates a CMO. The CMO offers various classes of bonds called **tranches**.

The tranches are bonds that offer different rates of interest, repayment schedules, and levels of priority for principal repayment. Investors can choose the yield, maturity structure, and risk level that best suits them. Let's look at a simple example of a "plain vanilla" CMO product. The investors in the CMO are divided up into three tranches: A, B, and C. Each tranche differs in the order that it receives principal payments, but it receives monthly interest payments until it is completely paid off. Class A investors are paid out the principal first with prepayments and repayments until they are paid off. Then class B investors are paid off, followed by class C investors. In a situation like this, class A investors bear most of the prepayment risk, while class C investors bear the least.

As with other mortgage-backed securities, investors never know if they'll get their money back sooner [rates fall] or later [rates rise]. The risk of receiving principal sooner than expected is called prepayment risk, which is associated with falling interest rates. The risk of receiving principal later than expected is called extension risk, and is associated with rising interest rates. As the SEC explains, "CMOs are often highly sensitive to changes in interest rates and any resulting change in the rate at which homeowners sell their properties, refinance, or otherwise pre-pay their loans. Investors in these securities may not only be subjected to this prepayment risk, but also exposed to significant market and liquidity risks."

Two specific types of CMOs are called **PACs** and **TACs**. A "PAC" is a **planned amortization class**, while a "TAC" is a **targeted amortization class**. Since there is a "plan" with the PAC, the exam might say that it protects the investor more against prepayment and extension risk. A TAC does offer some protection against prepayment risk but not extension risk. In either case, there is a "support class" created to protect against prepayments—if the principal is repaid more quickly than expected, it goes into a support class. For the PAC, if interest rates rise and principal is being repaid more slowly, money will be transferred from the support class to protect that PAC owner against extension risk. This would not happen for the owner of a TAC.

The exam might bring up the methods of estimating prepayment rates on CMOs. One method is called the "average life" method in which CMOs are compared to other types of fixed-income securities, with an average maturity calculated for each tranche. The "PSA model" estimates the speed of prepayments against a benchmark. If the "PSA" is 100, that means that prepayment rates will remain stable. If the PSA is greater than 100, prepayments are expected to speed up. If the PSA is less than 100, prepayments are expected to slow down.

Beyond the PAC and TAC, the exam might mention the Z-tranche, which is basically a zero-coupon bond inside the CMO that returns principal (and, therefore, accrued interest) only after all the other tranches have been paid off/retired. And, there are "principal only" and "interest only" securities which are pretty much what they sound like. The principal and the interest are separated so that principal-only investors are concerned with how quickly they receive the principal—the *faster* the better. Interest-only investors enjoy a higher yield when prepayments slow down and a lower yield when prepayments speed up. That is because interest payments are based on the remaining principal amount on the loans—as that principal declines, so does the amount of interest paid by homeowners and received by the interest-only investors in the CMO. The faster that principal declines, the lower the yield to the investor; the longer it takes homeowners to pay off the principal, the *higher* the yield to the investor.

CMOs are not extremely liquid and are often too complex to be suitable for many investors. Registered representatives should get the customer's signature on a suitability statement when selling these products. A term that is used interchangeably with CMO is **REMIC**, which stands for a Real Estate Mortgage Investment Conduit. As defined at www.investingbonds.com, both CMOs and REMICs "are multiclass securities which allow cash flows to be directed so that different classes of securities with different maturities and coupons can be created. They may be collateralized by raw mortgage loans as well as already-securitized pools of loans."

Asset-Backed Securities

Asset-backed securities (ABS), are bonds or notes backed by financial assets. Typically, these assets consist of receivables other than mortgage loans, such as credit card receivables, auto loans, manufactured-housing contracts, and home-equity loans. Asset-backed securities differ from most other bonds because their credit quality comes from sources other than the originator of the underlying assets. Financial institutions that originate loans turn them into marketable securities through a process known as securitization. These institutions sell pools of loans to a special-purpose vehicle (SPV), whose purpose is to buy the assets to securitize them. The SPV then sells them to a trust. The trust repackages the loans as interest-bearing securities and issues them. The securities, which are sold to investors by the investment banks that underwrite them, are "credit-enhanced" with one or more forms of extra protection—whether internal, external or both.

Most asset-backed securities are rated AAA/Aaa. Because they are secured by collateral and come with credit enhancements, investors can receive a safe investment that yields more than Treasury securities. In fact, the yields are more in line with corporate bonds and mortgage-backed securities with similar terms to maturity and credit quality.

The most interesting asset-backed securities that I know of were the "Bowie Bonds" sold by now-deceased glam rocker David Bowie. For an upfront payment, the bondholders received around 7% interest, backed by the royalties earned annually by the artist--around $1 million at the time of issuance. Interestingly, soon after issuance, the royalties dropped due to illegal downloading of music; however; the holders of the bonds received all their interest and their principal at maturity.

CDOs

Another product divided into tranches is the CDO or **Collateralized Debt Obligation.** A CDO is a structured asset-backed security paying cash flows to investors in a predetermined sequence, based on how much cash flow is collected from the package of assets owned. While a CMO focuses on mortgages, a CDO is a security that repackages individual fixed-income assets into a product that can be divided up and sold in pieces on the secondary market. The assets being packaged (mortgages, corporate bonds, corporate loans, automobile loans or credit card debt) serve as collateral for investors, thus the name "collateralized debt obligation."

The senior tranches in a CDO are safer than the junior tranches because they have first claim on the collateral in case of a default and because they have a higher claim on any interest payments. Therefore, the senior tranches receive higher credit ratings and pay lower yields to investors than the junior tranches. The most junior tranche is called the "equity tranche," which receives only residual cash flows after the more senior tranches have been paid by the prescribed formula.

Across the street from our office used to sit an old brick industrial building that was supposed to be turned into a major condominium and townhouse development back before the bottom fell out of the real estate market. Unfortunately, the developers borrowed $15 million but pre-sold only one condominium, sending the property into foreclosure.

So, the park district, whose land sits next to the foreclosed property, wanted to tear down the outdated structure for their operations. The park district needed $6 million to acquire and develop the property and, therefore, raised that amount by issuing **municipal bonds**. In a recent election, a majority of Forest Parkers voted to allow the park district to raise property taxes slightly to create the funds needed to pay off a $6 million bond issue to be used to better the community.

The bonds have already been issued, and the building has been torn down with part of the $6 million worth of **general obligation** bonds sold to finance the project. The bonds pay investors tax-exempt interest at the federal level. Illinois residents also escape state income tax on the bond interest.

For me, all it took to see the connection between this municipal securities section and the so-called "real world" was to walk 15 steps to the front window and see that the building pictured below has now been torn down and carted away brick-by-brick, all because a municipal taxing authority borrowed money by issuing bonds.

There are two main types of municipal bonds: **general obligation** and **revenue**. General obligation bonds are safer than revenue bonds because they are backed by the municipality's ability to collect and raise taxes from various sources. However, some states are considered safer issuers than others, and the same goes for counties, school districts, port authorities, etc. Revenue bonds are only as safe as the revenue source tied to the bonds.

To make the bonds more marketable and keep interest payments as low as possible, many municipal bonds come with a credit enhancement from an insurance company who insures against default. Remember that if interest rates rise, bond prices drop. That is not what is covered here. The insurance policies cover interest and principal payments, not market or interest rate risk. Examples of municipal bond insurance (or assurance) companies include AMBAC and MBIA.

Because some municipal bonds are insured and some are not, bond ratings agencies including Moody's and S&P typically indicate whether a rating is "pure" or "insured." A "pure" rating is based on the credit quality of the issuer only, while an "insured" rating implies the credit quality is based on the insurance policy backing the bonds against default.

The phrase **general obligation** means that the municipality is legally obligated to pay the debt service on the bonds issued. GOs are backed by the full faith and credit of the municipality. Where does a municipality get the money they'll need to pay off the bonds? If necessary, they'll dip into all the sources of general revenue available to a city or state or park district, like sales taxes, income taxes, parking fees, property taxes, fishing licenses, marriage licenses, whatever. And, if they have to, they'll even raise taxes to pay the debt service on a general obligation bond.

General obligation bonds are backed by the full taxing power of the issuer, and that's why GOs require **voter approval**. As I said, Forest Parkers first had to approve a $6 million bond issue before the park district could do the borrowing and back up the loan with their increased property taxes.

States get most of their revenue from sales and income taxes, while local governments rely on property taxes. Since local governments (cities, park districts, school districts) get much of their revenue from property taxes, a GO bond is associated with property taxes, called **ad valorem**. That phrase means that the property tax rises or falls "as to value" of the property.

A municipality might assess property at 50% of its market value. So, a home with a market value of $400,000 would have an **assessed value** of only half that, or $200,000. A homeowner takes the assessed value of his home and multiplies it by a rate known as the **millage rate** to find his tax bill. If the millage rate is "9 mills," that means we multiply the assessed value of $200,000 by .009 to get a tax bill of $1,800. That $1,800 goes to support many different overlapping municipalities, for example: water district, park district, school district, library & museum district, village government, and county government.

Some municipalities limit the number of mills that can be levied against property. If so, they might end up issuing **limited tax bonds**, which means there are limits on the taxes that can be used to pay the debt service. Maybe property tax rates can only go so high to pay the debt service on a GO, or maybe only certain taxes can be used but not others. School districts are often limited as to how high property taxes can go to support their bonds, while other governmental units have no such limits. So if you see limited tax bonds, associate the term with GOs.

Whenever the issuer's full faith and credit backs the bonds, we refer to the bonds as "general obligations." There is a peculiar type of municipal bond that is backed by that full faith and credit but also by the revenues generated at the facility being built with the bond proceeds. These bonds are called **double-barreled bonds**.

For example, a hospital is something all residents of a municipality benefit from, which is why the county or state might put its full faith and credit behind the bond issue. However, hospitals also generate revenues, which can be used to pay debt service. In this case, the issuer has two sources of revenue to pay debt service, which is why we call it a double-barreled bond. Anything backed by the issuer's full faith and credit as well as revenues is called a double-barreled bond. Since the full faith and credit of the issuer backs the issue, we consider this a GO.

Rather than putting the full faith and credit of the issuer behind it, a revenue bond identifies a specific source of revenue, and only that revenue can be used to pay the interest and principal on the bonds. Have you ever driven on a toll way or paid a toll to cross a bridge? What did you drop in the basket? A **user fee**. That money you put in the toll basket helped to pay the debt service on the revenue bond issued to build the toll way or toll bridge. If money problems arise, the issuer won't raise property taxes. They'll raise the user fees.

You don't like the higher tolls? Use the freeway. But, homeowners aren't affected one way or another since their property taxes cannot be used to pay off revenue bonds. Facilities that could generate enough revenue to pay off the bonds include airports, convention centers, golf courses, and sports stadiums. The Queens Ballpark or Citi Field, where the New York Mets play their home games, was built with the proceeds of a revenue bond. As I see from Bloomberg, "The Mets sold $613 million municipal bonds in 2006 backed by payments in lieu of property taxes, lease revenue and installment payments to finance the construction of Citi Field. The team also issued $82.3 million of insured debt in 2009, the year the 42,000-seat ballpark opened in Queens."

Unfortunately, the revenues a few years ago were significantly lower than what the consultants predicted. As you can imagine, that caused the bonds' rating to drop. At the time of this writing, however, with attendance up 20% last season, the revenues have improved just enough to boost the credit rating to one notch above junk. As you can see, revenue bonds are only as strong as the revenues being generated by the facility. When the revenues are tied to the success and popularity of a baseball team, it is not surprising that the credit rating could be upgraded and downgraded many times before maturity.

Since we don't have property tax on the table, the municipal government doesn't need any type of voter approval to issue a revenue bond. So we don't associate "voter approval" with a revenue bond. That belongs under the "GO" heading.

There are other ways that a municipality could identify specific sources of revenue for a bond issue. For example, if the residents of a county wanted their roads paved, the county could add a special tax on gasoline throughout the county and let motorists pay for the new roads each time they fill up their tanks. This **special tax** is used to pay the debt service on the revenue bonds, which are issued to raise the money required to pave the roads. That's an example of a **special tax bond**, a type of revenue bond. Any tax that is not a property or sales tax is considered a special tax, including special taxes on business licenses, excise taxes, and taxes on gasoline, tobacco, hotel/motel, bottled water, and alcohol. The exam might even refer to these as "sin taxes."

There are also **special assessment bonds**. Say that a wealthy subdivision in your community experiences problems with their sidewalks. The concrete is chipped, threatening the property values of the homes in the exclusive subdivision. The residents want the municipality to fix the sidewalks. The municipality says, okay, if you pay a special assessment on your property, since you're the only ones who'll benefit from this improvement. That special assessment will be the revenue used to pay the debt service on a special assessment bond, which is issued to raise the money to fix the sidewalks.

See how it works? They identify a future source of revenue, like tolls, ticket sales, or special taxes on gasoline. Then, since they need all that money right now, they issue debt securities against this new source of revenue they're creating. They take the proceeds from selling the debt securities and get the project built. Then those revenues they identified come in, and they use them to pay the interest and, eventually, the principal due to investors who bought the bonds.

Cities like Chicago and New York have public housing projects, which are under HUD, a unit of the federal government. Municipalities issue **PHA (Public Housing Authority)** or **NHA (New Housing Authority) bonds** to raise money for housing projects. The debt service is backed by the rental payments, which are in turn backed by contributions from Uncle Sam. PHAs and NHAs are considered the safest revenue bond because of this guaranteed contribution from the federal government. Sometimes they are referred to as "Section 8" bonds because something needs at least three names in this business. Note that they are not double-barreled bonds, because it's not the issuer's full faith and credit backing the things.

Industrial Development Revenue bonds are used to build or acquire facilities that a municipal government will then lease to a corporation. These **IDRs** carry the same credit rating as the corporation occupying the facility. The issuing municipality does not back the debt service in any way. Again, the debt service will be paid only from lease payments made by a corporation, so it's the corporation that backs the debt service. As you know, corporations have been known to go belly-up occasionally. If they're the ones backing up the debt service, you can imagine what happens when they themselves no longer have any assets behind them.

And if it happens, the issuer won't be there to bail out the bondholders. While revenue bonds are only serviced by specific sources of revenue, a **moral obligation bond** provides for the possibility of the issuer going to the legislature and convincing them to honor the "moral obligation" to pay off the debt service. This is a moral obligation, not a legal one, and it would take legislative action to get the money authorized.

Callable Bonds

A bond has a maturity date that represents the date when the issuer will pay the last interest check and the principal. At that point, it's all over—the debt has been paid in full, just like when you pay off your car, student loan, house, etc. This can be referred to as "maturity" or **redemption**. As we saw earlier, many bonds are repurchased by the issuer at a set price if interest rates drop. So, a bond might not make it to the maturity date because it might be called early. Either way, the debt would have been retired by the issuer.

Municipal bonds are frequently callable by the issuer. Refunding a current issue of bonds allows municipalities to finance their debt at lower rates going forward. Or, there could be a covenant in the bond indenture for the current issue that is burdensome, motivating the issuer to start over. An optional redemption gives the issuer the option to refinance/refund their debt as of a certain date at a stated price, or over a series of prices and associated call dates. Some bonds are issued with mandatory call provisions requiring the issuer to call a certain amount of the issue based on a schedule or on having enough money to do so in the sinking fund.

When issuers redeem callable bonds before the stated maturity date, they may call the entire issue or just part of it. For obvious reasons, the call provisions can, therefore, be referred to as in-whole redemptions or partial redemptions. The refunding is sometimes done through a direct exchange by bondholders of the existing bonds for the new issue. Usually, though, the issuer sells new bonds to pay off the existing issue.

When **refunding** an issue of bonds, issuers either perform a **current refunding** or an **advance refunding**. If the issuer uses the proceeds of the "refunding bonds" to promptly call (within 90 days) the "prior issue," we refer to this as a current refunding. On the other hand, when the issuer places some of the proceeds of the refunding issue in an escrow account to cover the debt service on the outstanding issue, we refer to this as an advance refunding. Because an escrow account is, literally, money in the bank, the prior issue whose debt service is now covered by the escrow deposit is not required to be included on the issuer's debt statement. Do we just take the issuer's word that the U.S. Treasury securities held in the escrow account are sufficient to cover the debt service on the prior issue?

No. Rather, an independent CPA issues a "verification report" verifying that the yield on the escrow deposit will be sufficient to pay off the outstanding or refunded issue of bonds. Because of the certainty surrounding a refunded issue of bonds, these bonds are typically rated AAA and are among the safest of all municipal bonds on the market. Because of their inherent safety, refunded bonds are also liquid.

The typical advance refunding is performed by placing proceeds from the sale of the refunding issue in an escrow account holding Treasury securities, with only the escrow account used to cover the debt service on the prior issue of bonds. In a "crossover refunding" the promised revenue stream backing the prior issue continues to be used to meet debt service until the bonds are called with proceeds from the escrow account.

Paying off a debt is sometimes referred to as a debt being "defeased." Therefore, the exam could refer to the refunding bonds as being issued to "defease" the prior issue of outstanding bonds.

Refunding bonds are not tax-exempt. Municipalities, in other words, can borrow money on the cheap for infrastructure, but if they could issue tax-exempt refunding issues, some governmental entities would do nothing but issue refunding bonds in a never-ending attempt to maximize their budgets.

United States Treasury bills, notes, bonds, etc., carry no default risk. On the other hand, while municipal bonds are generally safer than corporate bonds, municipal bonds do carry default risk. We don't expect state governments to fail, but some counties and certain projects built with revenue bond proceeds have been known to go belly-up.

How would an investor know a strong municipal securities issuer from a weak one? Same way he'd do it for a corporate bond—he would check the Moody's, S&P, and Fitch credit ratings. Perhaps you have seen recently that your county, city, or state has suffered a "credit downgrade" from Moody's, S&P, and/or Fitch. Maybe the issuer used to be a double-A borrower, but now has to pay the higher yields offered by single-A or triple-B borrowers. In other words it affects the borrower the same way a lower credit score would affect you when applying for a mortgage.

GO Analysis

A general obligation bond (GO) is backed by the full faith and credit of a municipality. Where does a municipality get the money needed to back up this sweeping promise to pay debt service? Mostly from taxpayers. So, how do these taxpayers generally feel about taxes and debt? A municipality whose voters typically approve bond issues will receive a higher rating than one populated by conservative voters who typically shoot down all bond referendums. Are residents moving in and bringing their tax dollars with them, or are they moving away and taking their tax dollars with them? Are jobs coming in or leaving the area? What's the economic health? High unemployment? Not good. Is the economic base diverse, or is it too dependent on just one industry or one or two big employers? Are the residents affluent? Let's hope so. What are the property values looking like? Trending upward? Excellent. Dropping? Not good. What is the issuer's **collection ratio**? The collection ratio is found by dividing the taxes collected by the taxes assessed, because no matter how many property tax bills get sent out, it only helps the issuer when people actually pay them. A high collection ratio is a positive sign to a GO bond analyst and vice versa.

The issuer has a **debt statement** that analysts review. On the debt statement we find the amount of general obligation debt that the issuer is fully responsible for and the debt it is partly responsible for. The **direct debt** is the GO debt that only the issuer is responsible for paying off. Sometimes a school district lies in more than one village. If so, the villages and the school district are **coterminous**. That means that when the analyst looks at the debt of the school district, they also factor in the debt of the village governments. This debt is called **overlapping** debt for obvious reasons. So the issuer's **net overall debt** is the total of GO bonds for which it is solely responsible and the total of overlapping debt for which it is partly responsible.

To protect residents from excessive taxes, municipalities typically impose a maximum on how much general obligation debt they can have outstanding at one time, so how close is the municipality to this **debt limit**? If it's already close to the limit, an analyst might not like to see another bond issue going out at this point, just as a mortgage lender is not going to be thrilled to see that you came up with your down payment by maxing out all your credit cards. What is the issuer's **debt per capita**, which is the debt divided by the population? If that's already a high number, this new GO issue is probably going to have a lower credit rating than the issuer would like.

What about the city's, county's or state's budget—are there any big **unfunded pension liabilities** that they are *also* legally obligated to pay? If an analyst is judging the issuer's ability to repay the bondholders and sees that the issuer has also promised to pay out about $2 billion more than they apparently have to teachers, police officers, or fire fighters, that fact is not going to help the credit rating.

In short, the issuer is the borrower. Do they have enough money from tax revenues versus their obligations to assure that bondholders will receive their interest and principal? If so, they get a high credit rating. If they're in over their heads like Illinois is currently, their bonds get a lower rating, which means they have to offer higher yields to investors, just as someone with a low credit score has to pay a higher rate on his mortgage.

Revenue Bond Analysis

Revenue bonds aren't backed by the issuer's taxing ability, so an analyst rating a revenue bond would not look at most of the things we just looked at for general obligation bonds. Revenue bond analysts need to know if the facility will be able to generate enough revenue to maintain operations and pay back the bondholders their interest and principal (debt service). A good place to start is the **feasibility study** that the issuer paid a consulting firm to put together. The feasibility study includes an **engineering report** that focuses on the design and construction of the facility. The feasibility study also predicts how many people will use the facility and how much they'll pay to use it, versus all the expenses and costs associated with the convention center, sports stadium, airport, etc.

The most important factor for assigning a credit rating to a revenue bond is the project's **debt service coverage ratio**. In the indenture, we see whether the project uses a **net revenue pledge** or a **gross revenue pledge**. The most common by far is the "net pledge," in which the issuer states that the first priority of payment will be operations and maintenance of the facility. After operations and maintenance are covered, then debt service is taken care of.

Under the rarer "gross pledge," the first priority is the debt service. Since most projects use a "net pledge," let's look at how the numbers might work out here. Let's say that a football stadium will pull in $20 million in revenue each year, with operations and maintenance at $10 million and debt service payments of $5 million. The first priority is operations and maintenance, so we take the $20 million of revenue and subtract the $10 million of operations and maintenance. The *net* revenue is now $10 million. That $10 million covers the $5 million of debt service at a 2:1 ratio.

A 2:1 debt service coverage ratio is considered adequate and would boost the revenue bond's credit rating as opposed to a lower coverage ratio. This might sound like rocket science at first, but that's only because the terminology is new. You, like the issuer of a revenue bond, like to borrow money at the lowest possible rate. Whoever issues your credit score looks at your income versus your expenses to calculate how likely you are to pay off your debts. You get your credit score from Experian, TransUnion, and Equifax. The revenue bond issuer would get their credit score from S&P, Moody's, and/or Fitch.

Revenue bonds are issued under what's known as an **indenture**. As we will see in later chapters, most corporate bonds have to be issued with an indenture, a contract in which the issuer makes promises to protect the bondholders, which are enforced by the trustee. Municipal bonds aren't covered by the

Trust Indenture Act of 1939, but since revenue bonds are only as solid as the revenue generated by the facility being built, usually revenue bonds are sold with an indenture in order to calm the lenders enough to buy the bonds. The indenture includes **protective covenants.** Some of the covenants include raising user fees to meet the debt service (**rate covenant**), keeping the facility properly maintained and insured (**maintenance covenant, insurance covenant**) and making sure the finances are subject to outside audit (**financial reports and audit covenant**). The **nondiscrimination covenant** is a promise that even local politicians and their girlfriends have to pay to park at the sports stadium or to drive through the toll booths along the turnpike. We would also see a **catastrophe call** described in the indenture, which means that if, for example, the convention center is destroyed by a hurricane, the entire bond issue will be called—assuming the place was properly insured, as the insurance covenant specified.

The **flow of funds** statement is also found in the bond indenture. Most revenue bonds use a series of funds/accounts that provide for the security of the bonds as funds generated by the facility are used to pay operations and maintenance expenses, debt service, and also a reserve fund for a rainy day. The flow of funds statement details the priority for allocating the revenues of the facility among the various accounts/funds. Basically, the revenues generated by the facility fill each account to a certain level and then flow to the next account. A fairly typical "flow of funds" would go in this order:

Revenue Fund: all receipts (gross revenue) are recorded and deposited here first

Operations and Maintenance Fund: a prescribed amount of gross revenue is deposited here to pay operations and maintenance expenses

Debt Service Fund: the required amount to meet interest on existing bonds and return principal on bonds that are about to mature

Debt Service Reserve Fund: extra money that might come in handy if revenues are a little light but bondholders expect to be paid anyway

Reserve Maintenance Fund: extra money to cover unexpected maintenance expenses

Replacement and Renewal Fund: extra money to cover new equipment and repairs to existing equipment, based on the engineering report

Sinking Fund: extra money that can be used to retire the bonds early through a refunding or advance refunding

Surplus Fund: extra money to be used in emergencies

A revenue bond indenture also includes the bond counsel's legal opinion and the maturity features of the bonds.

There's nothing worse than lending some corporation a few million dollars and then finding out they are not going to pay you back. This is known as a "default," and it's the worst thing that can happen to a bond investment.

How likely is it that a bond will go into default? It isn't going to happen on a United States Treasury security. It might happen on some municipal securities. But when you get into the category of corporate bonds, you see that it happens more than you'd like.

Luckily, Moody's, S&P, and Fitch all assign bond ratings designed to help investors gauge the likelihood of default. The highest quality issuers have AAA/Aaa (S&P/Moody's) ratings. The **investment grade** issues go from AAA/Aaa down to BBB/Baa. And below that, we're looking at high-yield or junk bonds.

Standard & Poor's (& Fitch)	Moody's
AAA	Aaa
AA	Aa
A	A
BBB	Baa
BELOW THIS IS JUNK, NON-INVESTMENT GRADE, HIGH-YIELD, SPECULATIVE	
BB	Ba
B	B
C	Caa

There is also a "D" rating indicating the bond is already in default. Only the savviest and most aggressive bond traders would likely trade a bond rated "D" or anything below "B" for that matter.

So, credit quality is the highest on the AAA/Aaa-rated bonds. As credit quality drops, you take on more default risk, so you expect to be compensated for the added risk through a higher yield. High yield and low quality go hand in hand, just as low yield and high quality do. How does a bond become "high yield" or "junk"? That means that a new issue of low-rated bonds would have to offer high coupon rates to get an investor interested in lending the money, and existing bonds would trade at lower and lower prices as people get more and more nervous about a possible default. As the price drops, the yield…increases.

It's not just interest rates that can push down a bond's market price. When S&P, Moody's, or Fitch downgrade an issuer's credit rating, the market price of those bonds will drop, increasing their yield.

How often do bonds default? To put it in perspective, here is the recent history of default rates on high-yield corporate bonds: the default rate in 2009 reached 13.7% before declining to 1.3% in 2010, as the economy began to recover, due in part to government initiatives and a general improvement in credit trends. Note this amount is significantly lower than the 16.4% default rate that occurred during the last financial downturn in 2002 (www.naic.org).

I noticed that the rate of default for investment-grade bonds was not even mentioned—it's that low. I also discovered that the main investment of insurance companies last year was corporate bonds. Insurance companies, in other words, can issue bonds to finance their operations, and they can also invest in bonds issued by other corporations. Investment-grade corporate bonds appear to be an ideal place for insurance companies to invest the net premiums paid on products like fixed annuities. According to the website cited above, 92% of those corporate bonds held by insurance companies are investment-grade. For good reason, insurance companies are not interested in stretching for every last bit of yield when they may be forced to sell their investments after a hurricane or other disaster strikes. Junk bonds are harder to sell in a hurry for a good price, so the higher the credit quality on the bond the higher its liquidity.

Methods Used to Determine the Value of Fixed-Income Securities

Investors purchase U.S. Treasury securities to eliminate credit risk. Unfortunately, because interest rates fluctuate, U.S. Treasury securities are just as exposed to interest rate and reinvestment risk as are corporate and municipal bonds.

Bonds are issued with a fixed interest rate. If the bond is an 8% bond, it will always be an 8% bond, and it will always pay 8% of the par value every year no matter who owns it at the time or how much she paid for it. For purposes of illustration, the par value is $1,000. 8% of $1,000 is $80 per year to the bondholder in interest income, split into two payments of $40 semiannually. With $1,000,000 in 8% bonds the investor would receive $80,000 a year in interest income.

Bonds are fixed-income securities. If it's a 5% bond, it pays $50 a year per $1,000 of par value. If it's a 13% bond, it pays $130 a year, which is an extremely high rate of interest.

So, if a bond pays a nominal yield of 8%, it will always pay 8% of par or $80 per $1,000 per year. Therefore, whenever interest rates change, they change the bond's market price—what it could sell for if the investor chose to sell it. When rates on new bonds go up, the existing bond's price drops. When rates go down, the existing bond's price rises.

Yields and Rates are the same thing. Bond Prices move in the other direction, which is called an **inverse relationship**, like this:

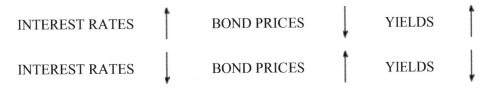

A test question could relate the Federal Reserve's actions to the bond market. For example, if the Fed is tightening credit, bond yields rise and bond market prices drop. If the Fed is stimulating the economy, yields drop and bond market prices rise. As with everything else in the economy, monetary policy creates winners and losers. People taking out mortgages win when the Fed pushes down interest rates, but fixed-income investors in retirement will have trouble making ends meet, for example.

Discount Bonds

Par value is what is returned to the bondholder at maturity and what the coupon rate is multiplied against. But, bonds are not bank deposits. Rather, they are securities that trade on a secondary market. Among other factors, a bond's market price fluctuates in response to changes in interest rates. If a bondholder has a bond that pays a nominal yield of 8%, what is the bond worth when interest rates in general climb to 10%? Not as much. If you had something that paid you 8%, when you knew you could be receiving more like 10%, how would you feel about the bond?

Not too good. But, when interest rates fall to 6%, suddenly that 8% bond looks good, right?

Current Yield

When we take a bond's market price into consideration, we're looking at **current yield**. Current yield (CY) takes the annual interest paid by the bond and divides it by what an investor would have to pay for the bond.

Current Yield = Annual Interest divided by Market Price

So, let's say that after an investor buys an 8% bond, interest rates rise, knocking down the market price to just $800. What is the current yield if that happens?

$80/$800 gives us a current yield of 10%.

Did the bond's market price just drop, or did its current yield rise? Those are two ways of saying the same thing. So, yes, it did.

"Yield" answers the question, "How much do I get every year compared to what I pay to get it?" So, if interest rates go up to 10%, suddenly this bond that pays only 8% isn't worth as much. The only motivation for buying this 8% bond is if an investor could get it at a **discount**. And, if she can get the $80 that the bond pays in annual interest for just $800, isn't she really getting 10% on her money? That's why we say her current yield is equal to 10%, higher than the nominal yield that never, ever changes.

Rates and yields up, price down. Rates are what new bonds pay. Yields are what existing bonds offer, after we factor in their market price.

A **discount bond** is a bond trading below par value. When you see a current yield higher than the coupon rate of the bond, you're looking at a discount bond. An 8% bond with a 10% current yield, for example, must be a discount bond. An 8% bond with a 6% current yield would *not* be a discount bond. As we'll see in a minute, it would, in fact, be a "premium bond."

Yield to Maturity

Yield to maturity (YTM) is the return an investor gets if she holds the bond all the way to maturity. It is sometimes called basis and represents the only yield that really matters to an investor. It factors in all the coupon payments and the difference between the market price paid for the bond and the par value received if the investor is holding at maturity. At maturity, an investor receives the par value, which is $1,000. If the investor puts down only $800 to buy the bond and receives $1,000 when the bond matures, doesn't she receive more at maturity than she paid?

She does, and that's why her yield to maturity is even higher than her current yield. She gets all the coupon payments, plus an extra $200 when the bond matures. If you see a yield-to-maturity that is higher than the coupon rate or the current yield, you're looking at a discount bond. For example, a 4% nominal yield trading at a 5.50 basis or yield to maturity is a discount bond.

Yield to Call

Like homeowners, sometimes issuers get tired of making interest payments that seem too high. That's why many bonds are issued as callable, meaning that after a certain period the issuer can buy the bonds back from investors at a stated price. A bond that matures in 10 or 20 years is often callable in just 5 years. If a bond is trading at a discount, rates have risen. Therefore, it is extremely unlikely that such a bond would be called. But, if it were called, the investor would make his gain faster than if he had to wait until maturity. That's why **yield to call** (YTC) is the highest of all for a discount bond.

Premium Bonds

So, that is what happens when interest rates rise. What happens when interest rates fall? Bond <u>prices</u> rise. If you owned this 8% bond and saw that interest rates had just fallen to 6%, how would you feel about your bond?

Pretty good. After all, it pays 2% more than new debt is paying. Do you want to sell it? Not really. But you might sell it if investors were willing to pay you a **premium**.

Current Yield

So, bond investors would have just pushed the price of the bond up as interest rates went down. Maybe your bond is worth $1,200 on the secondary market now. Dividing our $80 of annual interest by the $1,200 another investor would have to pay for the bond gives us a current yield of just 6.7%. That's lower than the coupon rate.

So, wait, did the price of this bond just rise, or did its current yield drop?

Yes, and yes.

When you see a coupon of 8% and current yield of 6.7% (or anything lower than that 8% printed on the bond), you're looking at a **premium bond**. A discount bond trades below the par value, while a premium bond trades above the par value.

The nominal yield of the bond doesn't change. Therefore, the only way to push a yield lower than the nominal yield stated on the bond is to have an investor pay more than par for the bond. Similarly, the only way to push the yield higher than the nominal yield stated on the bond is to have an investor pay less than par for the bond.

Yield to Maturity

If you sell your bond, you obviously don't care about the next investor's yield. But, when this investor's bond matures, how much does she get back from the issuer? Only $1,000. So, she put down

$1,200 and will only get back $1,000 at maturity. Her Yield to Maturity (YTM) goes down below both the nominal and current yields.

Yield to Call

Remember when we decided that a person who buys a bond at a discount wants the bond to return the principal amount sooner rather than later? Well, if you pay more than the par value for a bond, you're going to lose money when the bond returns your principal, no matter when that happens. So, if you're going to lose money, you want to lose it slowly to increase your yield. That's why a person who purchases a bond at a premium will have a lower yield to call than yield to maturity. He's going to lose money in either case, so he'd prefer to lose it over 10 or 20 years (maturity) rather than just 5 years (call).

So, yield to call is the lowest yield for a bond purchased at a premium. And, if there are successive call dates, the earliest call date will produce the worst or lowest yield to the investor.

Disclosing Yield on Customer Confirmations

When a customer purchases a bond, the broker-dealer sends her a **trade confirmation** no later than the settlement date. And, on this trade confirmation the firm must disclose either the YTM or the YTC. Should they disclose the best possible yield or the worst possible yield?

Always prepare the customer for the worst or most conservative yield, so there are no bad surprises, right? Okay, for a discount bond, which yield is lower, YTM or YTC? YTM. That's what the firm would disclose to a customer who purchases a bond at a discount.

For a premium bond, which yield is lower?

Yield to Call. So, that's what the firm would disclose to a customer who purchases a bond at a premium. The exam might call this calculation "yield to worst," by the way or even "YTW." The worst yield the investor can receive is the one based on the earliest call date.

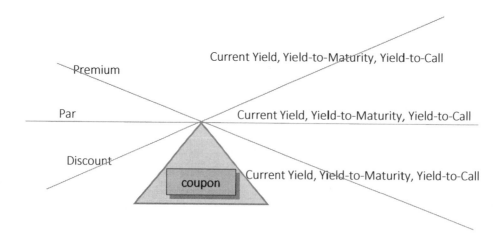

Duration

Duration measures the interest rate sensitivity of a bond, predicting how a small change in interest rates would affect the bond's market price. The longer/higher a bond's duration, the more sensitive it is to a change in interest rates. So, when interest rates go up, they push the prices of bonds with long/high durations down much more than those with lower durations.

Another way of talking about duration is to say that at some point all the coupon payments received by an investor will represent what the investor paid for the bond. If you pay par for a 30-year bond paying $40 a year, it would take you 25 years to receive $1,000 in the form of interest/coupon payments, right? So, the duration could be expressed as 25 years. A bond with a high duration is more susceptible to a rise in interest rates.

To express that mathematically, we could see how much the bond's price would decline if rates rose 1%. Just multiply the 20 (duration) by 1% to get an expected 20% decline in the bond's price should rates rise by just 1 point. That's volatile. If the bond paid a higher coupon, you'd get your original investment back sooner, knocking down the duration and making the bond's price less sensitive to interest rates.

Remember, the lower the coupon and the longer the maturity, the higher/greater the duration. And the greater the duration, the more susceptible the bond's price is to interest rate spikes.

For interest-paying bonds, the duration is always less than the years to maturity. But, for zero-coupon bonds, the duration *is* the maturity.

A common definition used for duration is "the weighted average of a bond's cash flows." As the formula shows, each cash flow is weighted by the amount of time the investor has to wait for the payment. For example, the first interest payment is multiplied by .5 and the next by 1.0 to represent that it takes ½ year to receive the first cash flow and one full year to receive the second. The principal payment is multiplied by the number of years it takes to receive it, and if it's a zero-coupon bond, all the cash flow is multiplied by the number of years to maturity.

Types and Characteristics of Equity Securities

Some investors seek income. They loan a corporation $100,000 and receive $4,000 a year in interest payments for 10 years. That 4% **yield** is nice, but at the end of the term, the investor will only receive $100,000, which will have lost purchasing power over 10 years due to inflation.

Other investors give up that steady income to reach for the risky and uncertain growth offered by the stock market. Rather than lending money to a corporation, these **equity** investors buy **common stock** in the company. This way, if the company becomes more valuable, so do the shares of common stock the investor holds.

Common Stock

While bondholders represent an expense on the income statement, common stock represents a claim on what is left after the company meets all their expenses. Common stock is all about the profits generated by the company. Unlike with bonds and preferred stock, common stock does not give the investor a stated rate of return. If shareholders receive 64 cents per-share of common stock as a dividend this year, they might or might not receive that much next year. In fact, the company might stop paying dividends if it hits a rough patch, and some companies—like Berkshire Hathaway—never pay dividends.

As a prospectus for a stock mutual fund would make clear, both the income produced by common stock and the market value of the stock itself are unpredictable. Therefore, common stock investors should only invest the money they could afford to lose.

Frank & Emma's Fruit Pies

To illustrate how common stock works let's consider the story of Frank & Emma's Fruit Pies. For fifty years this mom-and-pop baked goods maker in Maywood, Illinois made a modest profit on as much as $10 million in annual revenue. But, by the time the company hit that milestone Founder

Frank Kaminski and his wife Emma were in their 60s and getting tired of the daily grind. When some "private equity" investors from Chicago offered to buy them out, it did not take long for both to accept the deal.

Since then the private equity investors have installed their own business managers, who have helped to find new markets for the fruit pies while slashing costs. Now that sales are pushing $20 million annually, the private equity group is ready to do an initial public offering. To cash in on their investment, they will be offering through an underwriting syndicate up to 40% of the company for approximately $25 million. Frank & Emma's will use most of the proceeds to expand. The underwriters will keep 7% of the proceeds as their underwriting fee. And, investors buying the common stock will profit if the sales and earnings at Frank & Emma's Fruit Pies continue to rise. While investors could lose their money if the business fails, there is also no limit to what they could earn on their investment. Seventeen years ago I myself purchased shares of a little e-commerce company called Priceline for $21 a share. As I type this sentence, that stock now trades for just over $1,500 per-share.

Yeah, that's upside!

Rights and Privileges

Common stockholders are owners of the corporation and vote at all annual and special meetings. The owner of common stock has the right to vote for any major issue that could affect his status as a proportional owner of the corporation. Things like stock splits, board of director elections, and changes of business objectives all require shareholder approval.

Owners of common stock typically have the right to vote on:

- Members of the board of directors
- Proposals affecting material aspects of the business
- Ratifying the auditors
- Mergers & Acquisitions
- Stock Splits
- Liquidation of the company

One thing shareholders never vote on is whether a dividend is paid and, if so, how much. Letting shareholders propose and vote on dividends is like letting your kids propose and approve their own allowance. Like parents, the board of directors decides if a dividend is to be declared from profits and, if so, how much the payment per-share will be. Dividends benefit the shareholder now, while the profits that are reinvested back into the business should eventually help to increase the value of the stock, benefiting the shareholder in the long run.

At the annual meeting votes are cast per-share, not per-shareholder. Therefore, a mutual fund holding 45 million shares of Wells Fargo has a lot more votes than a retail investor holding 300 shares at the Wells Fargo annual meeting. In fact, the retail investor's vote is almost meaningless compared to what the mutual fund might decide to do with their 45 million votes. Either way, all shares get to be voted. The Board of Directors tells shareholders in the proxy statement how the Board recommends that shareholders vote, making it easy for a shareholder to just indicate that he wants to vote that way. Some shareholders might even go so far as to read the proposals and make up their own minds.

Either way, if a shareholder owns 100 shares of common stock, he has 100 votes to cast in corporate elections. Let's say there are three seats up for election on the Board of Directors. There are two ways that the votes could be cast. Under **statutory voting**, he can only cast the number of shares he owns for any one seat. So, he could cast up to 100 votes for any one seat, representing a total of 300 votes for three seats. Under statutory voting abstaining on any of the seats up for election provides no benefit to the shareholder.

Under cumulative voting, however, he could take those 300 votes and split them up any way he wanted among the three candidates. He could even abstain on the other seats up for election and then cast all 300 votes for one candidate. That's why **cumulative voting** gives a benefit to the small/minority shareholders. In other words, if we can get a candidate on the slate who will look out for us small shareholders, we can all cast all of our votes for her.

Beyond voting, common stockholders have the right to inspect the corporation's financials through quarterly (10-Q) and annual (10-K) reports. Public companies have to file these reports with the SEC, but even a shareholder in a private company has this same right. Shareholders may also see the list of stockholders and the minutes of shareholder meetings.

Common stockholders have a **pre-emptive right** to maintain their percentage of ownership. This means if Frank & Emma's wants to raise money in the future by selling more common stock, existing shareholders must get a chance to buy their percentage of the upcoming issue. If not, their ownership would be diluted. Investors buying the stock on the secondary market up to a certain date would also receive rights to buy more shares from the additional offering. Rights offerings avoid **dilution of equity** by giving owners a chance to maintain their percentage of ownership, if they choose to.

Should a corporation claim bankruptcy protection and have to be liquidated, common stockholders get in line for their piece of the proceeds. Unfortunately, they are last in line. They are behind all the creditors, including bondholders, and also behind preferred stockholders.

But, at least they are in line, and if there are any residuals left, they get to make their claim on those assets, known as a **residual claim** on assets or "residual rights." Common stock is the most "junior" security, since all other securities represent senior claims on the company's assets.

Shareholders have **limited liability**, which means they are shielded from the debts of the company and lawsuits filed against it. Unlike a sole proprietor whose business is going sour, shareholders of a corporation would not be sued by creditors.

Common stock owners have a claim on earnings and dividends. As owners, they have a share of the profits or net income that we looked at on the income statement. Some of the profits are reinvested into the business, which tends to make the share price rise. Some of the profits might be paid to shareholders as dividends.

Dividends

Not all shareholders are looking for dividends. An investment in Berkshire Hathaway today, for example, would be made without the issuer stating any plans to pay dividends, ever. The only type of investor interested in this stock, then, is a growth investor.

But, there are growth & income investors and also equity-income investors for whom dividends are important. Dividends are a share of profits paid out to shareholders if and when the Board of Directors for the corporation votes to declare them. The day that the Board declares the dividend is known as the **declaration date**. The board decides when they'll pay the dividend, too, and we call that the **payable date**. The board also sets the deadline for being an owner of stock if you want this dividend, and we call that the **record date** because an investor has to be the owner of record as of that date to receive the dividend.

Now, since an investor has to be the owner of record as of the record date to receive the dividend, there will come a day when it's too late for investors to buy the stock and also get the dividend.

Why? Because stock transactions don't "settle" until the third business day following the **trade date**, which means you might put in your purchase order to buy 1,000 shares of Frank & Emma's on a Monday, but you aren't the official owner until that transaction settles on Thursday. Your broker-dealer has to send payment to their clearing agency, and the seller has to deliver the 1,000 shares before the transaction has settled. This process takes three business days for common stock and is known as **regular way settlement**, or "T + 3," where the "T" stands for <u>T</u>rade Date. Assuming there are no holidays, a trade taking place on Monday settles on Thursday, while a trade on Tuesday settles on Friday.

So, if an investor has to be the owner of record on the record date, and it takes three business days for the buyer to become the new owner, wouldn't she have to buy the stock at least three business days prior to the record date? Yes.

On the other hand, if she buys it just two business days before the record date, her trade won't settle in time. We call that day the **ex-date** or **ex-dividend date**. Starting on that day investors who buy the stock will not receive the dividend. On the ex-date, it's too late. Why? Because the trades won't settle in time, and the purchasers won't be the owners of record with the transfer agent as of the record date. If the trade takes place on or after the ex-date, the seller is entitled to the dividend. If the trade takes place before the ex-date, the buyer is entitled to the dividend.

The regulators set the ex-date, as a function of "regular way" or "T + 3" settlement. The ex-date is two business days before the record date.

Investors don't qualify for the dividend starting with the ex-dividend date; therefore, the amount of the dividend is taken out of the stock price when trading opens on the ex-date. If the dividend to be paid is 70 cents, and the stock is set to open at $20, it would open at $19.30 on the ex-date.

Let's take a look at how the process looks from a press release:

```
Equity Office declares first quarter common dividend

Mar 16, 2005-- Equity Office Properties Trust (EOP), a publicly
held office building owner and manager, has announced that its
Board of Trustees has declared a first quarter cash dividend in
the amount of $.50 per common share. The dividend will be paid on
Friday 15 April 2005, to common shareholders of record at the
close of business on Thursday 31 March 2005.
```

March 16th is the Declaration Date. The Payable Date is April 15th. The Record Date is Thursday, March 31st. The article doesn't mention the Ex-Date (because that's established by the exchange regulators), but we can figure that it must be Tuesday, March 29th. If you bought the stock on Tuesday, your trade wouldn't settle until Friday, April 1st, which means the seller's name would be on the list of shareholders at the close of business on Thursday, March 31st.

A dividend can be paid in the following ways:

- Cash
- Stock
- Shares of a subsidiary
- Product

The Shares

A corporation files its articles of incorporation with the state where they are organized. These articles disclose the name and purpose of the business, its address, and how many shares of stock the corporation is authorized to issue, known as the **authorized** shares. If a public company is authorized to issue 1,000,000 shares of common stock, they will probably not sell all of them at once. When they first sell shares to the public during their IPO, the number they issue is known as **issued** shares. Let's say this corporation could issue 1 million, but they only issue 600,000 shares. If so, there would be 600,000 issued shares after the public offering. And, at that point, the **shares outstanding** would also be the 600,000 that were issued in the IPO.

For various reasons, the corporation might decide to buy back some of those shares that are out in the secondary market. These shares, which were issued but repurchased, are called **treasury stock**. Treasury stock has no voting rights and pays no dividends. The benefit to the shareholders who remain is that the value of their existing stock tends to rise when the company is reducing the number of shares on the secondary market. If this corporation had issued 600,000 shares and then purchased 200,000 for the treasury, they would have 400,000 shares outstanding.

600,000	Issued
-200,000	Treasury
400,000	Outstanding

When we look at a company's **earnings per-share,** or **EPS**, on the income statement, we only count the **outstanding shares**. That's why the company can boost its earnings per-share (EPS) by repurchasing their outstanding stock on the secondary market. Even if the company's total earnings stayed the same, the earnings per-share would rise if the company were reducing the number of outstanding shares. For example, if the company earned $1 million in net income, that is an earnings per-share of $1.67 when there were 600,000 shares outstanding. However, after the company buys back 200,000 shares for the treasury, that same $1 million profit would be $2.50 of earnings per-share. Right? Just like at a birthday party, with fewer guest showing up there is more cake for the rest of us.

Treasury stock doesn't vote, so the officers and directors of the company, who own large positions in the stock, end up with more influence during corporate elections after a large share buyback. Also note that the cash used buying back shares is reflected on the company's statement of cash flows under financing activities.

The articles of incorporation list the common stock as either having a minimal par value or having no par value at all. As we saw when examining the balance sheet, companies record the higher IPO price above par value as "paid-in surplus." While the specific par value of preferred stock and of bonds is important, the par value for common stock is not considered important to the investor.

Common stock is easy to transfer to another party. It can be sold, donated, gifted, or inherited. The issuer of the stock hires a financial institution to keep track of the transfers of ownership, and they're called the **transfer agent**. The transfer agent keeps the ownership records of the company's stock. They deal with issuing and validating stock and bond certificates, recording name changes when investors sell their certificates, and re-issuing lost, stolen, or destroyed certificates. If there's a problem with the ownership records of the security, contact the transfer agent. They can validate or re-issue certificates, for a fee, as the case may be.

The corporation hires another outside firm—typically a bank—and we refer to this bank as the **registrar**. The registrar audits/oversees the transfer agent, just to make sure there aren't more shares outstanding than the company is authorized to issue, and that all the ownership records are accurate.

With just one share of some stocks worth thousands—even hundreds of thousands—of dollars, I don't want the responsibility of protecting the certificates from damage or misplacement. I mean, I could get them re-issued by the  transfer agent if I lost them, but that's a pain in the neck, and there are fees involved. So, rather than having the securities in my account shipped to me, I could have the broker-dealer holding my account transfer the securities into my name and then hold them in the firm's vault (transfer and hold). The firm would likely charge a fee to do that. So, what I do is what most customers do these days. I have the broker-dealer hold the securities in street name. This means my broker-dealer is the named or "nominal owner" of the securities and I the customer am the "beneficial owner" of the securities.

As we're about to see, shareholders can now also use the direct registration method.

114

But, whatever the customer chooses, the fact is that most customers these days have never seen a stock or bond certificate because their broker-dealer holds them in street name and may have them on deposit at centralized "depositories" such as the **Depository Trust Company** (DTC). From there, the securities are transferred through electronic entries only, which explains why many registered representatives have also never seen a stock or bond certificate. From the Depository Trust Company's website at www.dtc.org we see how things currently work:

> With the implementation of direct registration, investors have three securities ownership options:
>
> *Physical Certificates*: Certificates are registered and issued in the investor's name. The investor will receive all mailings directly from the issuer or its transfer agent, including dividend or interest payments, annual reports, and proxies.
>
> *Street Name Registration*: Securities are registered in the street name of the investor's broker-dealer. While no physical certificate will be issued to the investor, the broker-dealer will issue, at least quarterly, account statements of the investor's holdings. The broker-dealer will pay dividends or interest to the investor, as well as provide the investor with mailing material from the issuer or transfer agent.
>
> *Direct Registration*: This option allows the investor to be registered directly on the books of the transfer agent without the need of a physical certificate to evidence the security ownership. While the investor will not receive a physical certificate, he or she will receive a statement of ownership and periodic (at least yearly) account statements. Dividend or interest payments, proxy materials, annual reports, etc., will be mailed from the issuer or its transfer agent.

If an investor holds paper stock certificates, he would have to sign them when selling or otherwise transferring them. He would sign the back of the certificate exactly as it is named on the front, and if the certificate is registered to two owners, both must sign the back. The process of signing a stock certificate to effect a transfer is called an endorsement. The owner of the certificate would also fill in his broker-dealer as the "attorney to transfer" so that only they can complete the transaction on his behalf.

Again, though, effecting these transfers is faster and easier for customers who use the street-name or direct registration method above, both of which would lead to electronic records as opposed to paper certificates.

Broker-dealers are not the only financial institutions holding securities and cash for investors. Banks also do this, especially for large institutional investors. We will explore options a bit later. For now, know that when an institutional investor has to prove ownership of a certain number of shares, the bank with custody of the account may issue what is known as an escrow receipt evidencing that a certain number of shares are in the bank's possession and control for the customer's account. A party who has sold call options, for example, must deliver the underlying shares if exercised. Therefore, the broker-dealer may require an escrow receipt (or escrow agreement), which is the document from the custodian bank showing that the shares are available for delivery if the account is assigned and forced to deliver the shares to the buyer of the call option.

We will look at calls and puts in some detail up ahead.

Stock Splits and Stock Dividends

Cash dividends are taxable because they involve a payment to the shareholder. Stock dividends, on the other hand, are not payments. Rather, investors end up with more shares in the company, with the shares worth less per-share. So, the big idea behind **stock splits** and **stock dividends** is that even when the investor ends up with more shares, the total value of his investment is unchanged. If he had 100 shares at $10 before, that was worth $1,000. No matter how many shares he has after the split or the stock dividend, the total value is $1,000. So, when a corporation does a 2:1 stock split, the investor would have twice as many shares. What would the price per-share be?

Half as much. The investor has $1,000 worth of stock both before and after the split. He used to have 100 shares worth $10 each. Now he has 200 shares worth $5 each. $1,000 worth, either way. The test might want you to work with an uneven split, like a 5:2 ratio. This is where the company gives investors five shares for every two that they own. So, let's say the question tells you the investor holds 100 shares of ABC, which she purchased for $50 each. What happens after a 5:2 stock split? All we have to do is multiply the number of shares by 5 and then divide that by 2. So, 100 times 5 equals 500, and 500 divided by 2 shows us the investor will have 250 shares after the split. Her cost basis is a total of $5,000 (100 shares @50), so take that $5,000 total and divide it by the new number of shares, which is 250. Her new cost basis is 250 ABC @20.

It's important to keep an investor's cost basis so that capital gains can be reported accurately in the future. But that is all that really happened in both examples—the investor's cost basis changes along with the lowered per-share price of the stock.

A stock dividend works the same way in terms of more shares/lower price. If an investor receives a 20% stock dividend, that's 20% more shares of stock, but the total value of the investment is the same. It's just divided among more shares. So an investor with 200 shares of XYZ common stock @40 would have $8,000 of XYZ stock. If XYZ declared a 20% stock dividend, she would then have 240 shares. Her $8,000 would then be divided among 240 shares, with a per-share price of $33.33. Companies in a growth phase are more likely to pay stock dividends than more established companies, who are more likely to pay cash dividends compared to small, growing companies.

Either way, nothing really changes for the investor after a stock dividend or a stock split. The investor has more shares at a lower price, which means her cost basis in the stock changes. 100 shares @50 might become 125 shares @40. Just keep track of your cost basis so that when you sell someday you can tell the IRS how much of a capital gain or loss you realized on the stock. But whether you have 100 shares @50 or 125 shares @40, you've paid $5,000 for a certain percentage of ownership. And, we'll deal with concerns such as "cost basis" and "capital gains" later in the book.

A forward stock split means investors end up with more shares. A 2:1, 3:2, or 5:4 split is a forward split that pushes the share price down.

Sometimes companies have the opposite problem. Their share price is so low that institutional investors won't touch it. These entities usually won't buy a stock trading below $5, so if our company's stock is trading for $1, we might need to increase that price. One way to do it is to perform a reverse stock split.

If JoAnne owns 100 shares of ABCD @$1, we might find ABCD doing a reverse split of 1:10. That means for every 10 shares she owns now, she'll end up with only one really big share. She'll have 10 shares when it's all over. If the shares were trading for $1 before the split and everybody now has shares that are 10 times bigger, the share price becomes $10 a share. JoAnne now owns 10 ABCD @$10.

Shareholders vote on stock splits, whether forward (5:4, 2:1, 3:2) or reverse (1:7, 1:10, etc.). Shareholders do not vote on dividends, whether cash or stock.

Sometimes a public company performs a type of "divestiture" known as a spin-off in which shareholders receive shares of a subsidiary or division of the company. For example, when Abbott Labs decided to make their business unit Hospira a separate company, they performed a spin-off in which ABT shareholders like me received a certain number of shares of HSP, which has since traded and operated as a completely separate company. If a company wants to exit a business line to concentrate on other areas, a spin-off may be completed. Usually, there are no tax consequences when the shareholders merely receive the shares of the spin-off. Rather, they have a cost basis, and are taxed on a capital gain if and when they sold the shares someday for a profit.

I have received shares of stock through spin-offs. Like many investors, I have also received shares of stock through mergers & acquisitions. If a larger company offers to give, for example, .75 shares of their stock for each share investors currently hold of the target company, shareholders will end up with a completely different holding. When they receive cash in an acquisition, shareholders record a capital gain or loss. But, if they're receiving shares of one company when turning in shares of their existing holding, investors record their cost basis in the shares for now. Someday, when they transfer those shares through a sale or gift, the tax consequences will be realized.

Interestingly, after holding those Hospira shares a few years common stockholders like me then voted to be acquired for cash by Pfizer. All in all, it turned out to be a decent investment, if I do say so myself.

ADRs

American Depositary Receipts (ADRs) are receipts issued to American investors against shares of foreign stock held on deposit by a U.S. bank outside the U.S. ADRs allow American investors to easily diversify their portfolio with foreign investments that trade, clear and settle in the U.S. financial system and U.S. currency while giving foreign companies easier access to U.S. capital markets. The ADR investor buys a negotiable certificate called an American Depositary Receipt that represents a certain number of American Depositary Shares of a foreign corporation's stock. The shares are held in a U.S. bank in the foreign country, which issues a receipt to the investor in

America. The custodian bank provides services including registration, compliance, dividend payments, communications, and recordkeeping. These fees are typically deducted from the gross dividends received by the ADR holders.

Or, if the issuer does not pay dividends, broker-dealers and banks cover the custody fees charged by depositary banks and then pass the charges on to their customers. ADRs file a registration statement called an F-6 which discloses information on the structure of the ADR including fees that may be charged to the ADR holders. Some ADRs grant voting rights to the investor; some do not.

If dividends are declared, they are declared in the foreign currency and then have to be converted into U.S. dollars. That is why ADR owners are subject to currency risk. Also, if the stock is worth a certain number of yen on the Japanese markets, that won't work out to as many U.S. dollars when our dollar is strong, although it would work out to more American dollars if our dollar is weak.

As the SEC explains in an investor bulletin, "Today, there are more than 2,000 ADRs available representing shares of companies located in more than 70 countries."

There are currently three levels of ADR trading, ranging from the more speculative issues trading over-the-counter to those, like Toyota, trading on the NYSE or NASDAQ. Level 1 ADRs trade over-the-counter. Level 2 ADRs trade on exchanges. Level 3 ADRs are part of a public offering that then trades on the NYSE or NASDAQ. In other words, some ADRs merely establish a trading presence in the U.S. while Level 3 ADRs also raise capital for the foreign issuer.

Subscription or Stock Rights

As we mentioned, one of the rights common stockholders enjoy is the right to maintain their proportionate ownership in the corporation. We call this a pre-emptive right because the existing shareholders get to say yes or no to their proportion of the new shares before the new shareholders get to buy them. Otherwise, if you owned 5% of the company, you'd end up owning less than 5% of it after they sold the new shares to everyone but you, called dilution of equity.

For each share owned, an investor receives what's known as a right. It works like a coupon, allowing the current shareholders to purchase the stock below the market price. If a stock is trading at $20, maybe the existing shareholders can take two rights plus $18 to buy a new share. Those rights act as coupons that give the current shareholders two dollars off the market price. So, the investors can use the rights, sell them, or let them expire.

Restricted Stock

The term **restricted stock** means the investor's ability to sell or transfer the stock is restricted because of a required holding period. Stock purchased in a private placement is restricted stock, restricted in terms of the investor's ability to sell it to another party. Officers and key employees may also receive restricted shares subject to a holding period as opposed to stock options that can be exercised right away. When purchasing restricted securities, investors typically receive a certificate with a legend stamped on it indicating that the securities may not be resold in the marketplace unless they are registered with the SEC or are exempt from the registration requirements.

The SEC does not want people acting like underwriters and funneling unregistered stock to the securities markets in a way that bypasses the Securities Act of 1933's concerns for full disclosure. **Rule 144** provides a safe harbor exemption for those who want to sell restricted stock without violating securities law. And, remember, though a registered representative will perhaps never own restricted stock, if he executes a sale for a customer who does, he could get in trouble if he doesn't know and follow the rules.

The first requirement for selling restricted stock is that the issuer must have been a reporting company under the Securities Exchange Act of 1934 for at least 90 days immediately before the sale. And, the issuer cannot have missed filing any of the 10Q or 10K reports they were required to file during the preceding 12 months. Without this requirement, worthless securities in companies no one knows anything about could be dumped onto the securities markets at great harm to investors.

So, first, the issuer must be someone about whom investors can receive material information. Even if the issuer is an insurance company or a company not subject to reporting (non-reporting company) under the Securities Exchange Act of 1934, the SEC requires that certain basic information on these issuers be available including information on the nature of its business, the identity of the officers and directors, and financial statements.

Otherwise, no sale.

Restricted stock is subject to a holding period. If the issuer is a reporting company subject to reporting requirements at least 90 days, purchasers must hold the securities a minimum of six months before reselling them. If the issuer is not a reporting company, the minimum holding period is one year.

Once the holding period is met a non-affiliate can sell his shares if he wants to. However, as the SEC explains, "Even if you have met the conditions of Rule 144, you can't sell your restricted securities to the public until you've gotten the legend removed from the certificate. Only a transfer agent can remove a restrictive legend. But the transfer agent won't remove the legend unless you've obtained the consent of the issuer—usually in the form of an opinion letter from the issuer's counsel—that the restrictive legend can be removed. Unless this happens, the transfer agent doesn't have the authority to remove the legend and permit execution of the trade in the marketplace. To begin the legend removal process, an investor should contact the company that issued the securities, or the transfer agent for the securities, to ask about the procedures for removing a legend. Removing the legend can be a complicated process requiring you to work with an attorney who specializes in securities law."

For **affiliates** of the company Rule 144 has further requirements, whether selling restricted or **control stock**. Restricted stock is unusual because of the way it was offered to investors. For control stock, on the other hand, it's the owner himself who triggers the requirements, not the securities. Control stock is held by people who can control the issuer or could harm the market price of the stock by dumping a large amount all at once. So, whether selling restricted or control stock, affiliates must file a **Form 144** with the SEC no later than at the time of the sale. The filing is good for 90 days. Also, if the transaction is not larger than 5,000 shares and $50,000, the sale can be made without filing a Form 144. Basically, a transaction that small does not make the regulators nervous, as it won't impact the price of the stock due to the low volume of shares traded.

Typically, affiliates sell large amounts of securities, but they must comply with the volume limits under Rule 144. For exchange-traded securities affiliates are allowed to sell the issuer's stock provided they sell no more than the greater of 1% of the outstanding shares or the average weekly trading volume over the four most recent weeks. If the company has 1 billion shares outstanding, the affiliate could sell whichever is greater over the next 90 days—10 million shares or the average weekly trading volume going back four weeks. For stocks that either don't trade or trade on the OTC Bulletin Board or Pink Quote, only the 1% figure is used.

That's the amount that can be sold. As for the method of sale the rule states, "If you are an affiliate, the sales must be handled in all respects as routine trading transactions, and brokers may not receive more than a normal commission. Neither the seller nor the broker can solicit orders to buy the securities."

Also, affiliates can never sell the company's stock short. And, although control stock is not subject to a holding period, an affiliate can't take a profit on their company's stock held less than 6 months. This is called a short-swing profit, which must be turned back over to the company with the gain being taxed by the IRS.

FINRA is concerned that agents and their firms sometimes help customers sell unregistered restricted securities, which violates federal securities law. In other words, if the customer does not conform to all the stipulations we just went over, but wants to just take his unregistered restricted shares and sell them, firms need to be sure they don't help him skirt securities law in this manner. FINRA alerts its member broker-dealers that some customers are companies trying to sell their shares illegally. If the customer deposits certificates representing a large block of thinly traded or low-priced securities, that's a red flag. If the share certificates refer to a company or customer name that has been changed or that does not match the name on the account, that's another red flag. If a customer with limited or no other assets under management at the firm receives an electronic transfer or journal transactions of large amounts of low-priced, unlisted securities, that's another red flag.

Broker-dealer firms need to do a reasonable inquiry to make sure that they are not helping people get around securities law. The SEC has said that "a dealer who offers to sell, or is asked to sell a substantial amount of securities must take whatever steps are necessary to be sure that this is a transaction not involving an issuer, person in a control relationship with an issuer, or an underwriter." For this purpose, it is not enough for him to accept "self-serving statements of his sellers and their counsel (attorneys) without reasonably exploring the possibility of contrary facts."

Rule 144's prohibitions on reselling restricted stock only apply to a sale to unsophisticated investors. **Rule 144a** allows the restricted securities that we just discussed to be re-sold to institutional investors including banks, insurance companies, broker-dealers, investment advisers, pension plans, and investment companies without meeting the usual registration requirements under the Securities Act of 1933. So, if an investor acquires restricted securities through a private placement, he/they can re-sell them to **qualified institutional buyers** such as those mentioned without destroying the exemption the issuer is claiming from the registration requirements. As usual, the regulators want to prevent the shares from being distributed in a general public offering without registration requirements being met. When the buyers are sophisticated institutions, the regulators can ease up.

120

This SEC rule also states that the seller needs to be reasonably certain that the buyers are qualified institutional buyers, which generally means that the institution invests on a discretionary basis at least $100 million, or is a registered broker-dealer, an investment company, a bank, or a federal covered investment adviser. To check that the buyers are qualified institutional buyers, the SEC says that the seller can rely on the buyer's most recent publicly available financial statements, or a certification from the CFO or other officer of the institution.

Preferred Stock

A common stock investor might receive dividends, but the dividend is not stated or promised going forward. In fact, the company may never pay a dividend on their common stock at all. Common stock investors are generally interested in growth or capital appreciation more than income. That means they want to buy the stock low and watch it increase in market price over time. On the other hand, income investors who want to buy stock would more likely buy **preferred stock** than common.

Preferred stock receives preferential treatment over common stock if the company has to be forcibly liquidated to pay creditors through a bankruptcy proceeding, and it always receives dividends before owners of common stock can be paid. Some investors refer to a preferred stock position in a private company as "first money out," because if there are distributions of profits, preferred stock gets theirs first.

And, unlike common stock, the preferred stock dividend is a stated percentage of par value. The par value for a preferred stock is assumed to be $100, though I think the test question would tell you what the par value is if it's required to answer the question. Whatever it is, the stated dividend is a percentage of the par value of the preferred stock. Six percent preferred stock would pay 6% of $100 per-share, or $6 per-share per year. Three percent preferred stock would pay a dividend of 3% of the par value each year.

We hope.

See, dividends have to be declared by the Board of Directors. Preferred stockholders aren't creditors. They're just proportional owners who like to receive dividends. If the board doesn't declare a dividend, do you know how much an owner of a 6% **straight preferred stock** would receive?

Nothing. However, if the investor owned **cumulative preferred stock**, the company would have to make up the missed dividend in future years before it could pay dividends to common stockholders. If the company missed the six dollars this year and wanted to pay a dividend to common shareholders next year, cumulative preferred stockholders would have to get their $12 first. Most preferred stock has this cumulative feature, and partial or skipped dividends are a rarity though always a possibility.

So far this 6% dividend works more like a maximum than a minimum. If an investor wants the chance to earn more than the stated 6%, he'd have to buy **participating preferred stock**, which would allow him to share in dividends above that rate, if the company has the money and decides to distribute it. Generally, if the issuer increases the dividend paid to common stockholders, they will also raise the dividend paid to participating preferred stockholders. A test question might say that participating preferred stock pays a dividend that is "fixed as to the minimum but not as to the maximum," while straight or cumulative preferred stock pays dividends that are "fixed both as to the minimum and the maximum."

Adjustable-rate preferred stock pays a rate of return that is tied to another rate, typically a U.S. Treasury security—T-Bill or T-Note, for example. If T-Bill rates rise, so does the rate paid on the adjustable-rate preferred stock, and vice versa. Because the rate adjusts, the price remains stable.

As with bonds, corporate issuers often get tired of paying preferred stockholders a high dividend rate when new investors would now accept a lower rate of interest. While most types of preferred stock go on for "perpetuity," **callable preferred stock** may be retired early at the issuer's discretion. If an investor had purchased 5.5% preferred stock a few years ago and then interest rates went down so that new investors would accept, say, 3%, the issuer would likely issue a new batch of 3% preferred stock to new investors and use some of the proceeds to retire the existing issue.

When investors bought the callable preferred stock, the call price and the first possible date were named. So, if rates go down at that point, the issuer might buy back the callable preferred stock, forcing shareholders to reinvest at lower rates. Because it can be retired early, callable preferred stock tends to pay the highest dividend rate of all types of preferred stock.

Preferred stock issued by a corporation does not derive its value from the market price of the common stock. Unlike preferred stock, common stock enjoys a share of the company's increased profits. Preferred stock, on the other hand, is just a fixed-income security constantly being re-compared to current interest rates. So, a 5% preferred stock—whether straight, cumulative, or callable—would not be expected to rise even if the market price of the issuer's common stock were to double or triple.

As always, there is an exception. But, there is only one type of preferred stock with a market price tied to the market price of the issuer's common stock. This type is known as **convertible preferred stock.** Unlike all other types of preferred stock, convertible preferred stock is not just a fixed-income security. This type lets an investor exchange one share of preferred stock for a certain number of the issuer's common shares. It works much like a warrant here, where the investor starts out on the fixed-income side, but also captures any upside on the common stock.

Say the convertible preferred stock is convertible into 10 shares of common stock. If so, the convertible preferred stock is usually worth whatever 10 shares of common stock are worth at a minimum. If the common stock rises, so does the convertible preferred stock it's tied to. If the common stock rises to $14, we would expect the convertible preferred stock to trade for at least $140. If it trades at exactly $140, it trades at **parity** to the common stock, the exam might say.

On another note, if a security has a fixed payment, the market compares that fixed payment to current interest rates. Current interest rates represent what investors could receive if they bought low-risk debt securities. If low-risk debt securities are paying 4%, and your preferred stock pays you a fixed 6%, how do you feel about your preferred stock? Pretty good, right, since it's paying a higher rate than current interest rates. If someone wanted to buy it, they'd have to pay a higher price. But, if interest rates shoot up to 10%, suddenly your 6% preferred stock doesn't look so great. In that case the market price would go down. Not the par value—par value is etched in stone. It's the market price that fluctuates.

Market prices adjust for interest rates: rates up/prices down, rates down/prices up. Well, as we mentioned, if the rate adjusts along with the T-Bill rate, the price doesn't need to move. But for other types of preferred stock, the price moves in the opposite direction of interest rates, just like bond prices. That's because the value is really determined by a comparison of the fixed rate of return to current interest rates.

But, if we add another variable, now the security's price isn't so sensitive to interest rates. Convertible preferred stock has a value tied to interest rates, like other preferred stock, but its value is also tied to the value of the common stock into which it can be exchanged or converted. If rates are up, preferred stock prices drop. But if you're holding a convertible preferred stock while the common stock is skyrocketing, the price of the preferred stock would skyrocket right along with it. Remember, it's worth a fixed number of common shares. If the value of the common stock goes up, so does the value of the convertible preferred stock it's tied to. So, convertible preferred stock is less sensitive to interest rates than other types of preferred stock.

For all other types of preferred stock the price has nothing to do with the price of the company's common stock, or even their increased profits. The exception there is convertible preferred stock, but all other types of preferred stock are fixed-income securities with market prices tied to credit quality and interest rates. Remember that unlike a bond, preferred stock generally does not have a **maturity date**, and unlike common stock, usually does not give the owner voting rights. Two specific cases where preferred stock *does* get to vote are: 1) the corporation defaults on the dividend payment a certain number of times and 2) the corporation wants to issue preferred stock of equal or senior status.

To review how common and preferred stock relate to each other, let's note the similarities and differences between the two.

SIMILARITIES	DIFFERENCES
dividends must be declared by the board of directors to be paid	preferred stock is a fixed-income security paying a stated rate of return
both are equity securities	preferred stock has a higher claim on dividends and on assets in a bankruptcy
	common stock has voting rights and pre-emptive rights

Yield vs. Total Return

There are only two ways to make money in equities. One, the stock price goes up, and, two, the stock pays a dividend. If I'm looking only for the share price to go up, I'm a "growth investor." If I'm solely interested in the dividends, I'm an "income investor." If I want both growth and income, guess what kind of investor I am?

Would you believe "growth and income"?

But, that's the only way to make money on stocks. You either sell the stock for more than you bought it someday, or the stock paid you dividends along the way. There is no third way to make money on common (or preferred) stock.

If you buy a stock at $10, and a year later it's worth $20, that's a capital appreciation of 100%. If a stock pays $2 in annual dividends and costs $200 on the open market, that's a yield of 1%. Yield shows how much an investor has to pay to receive how much in dividends.

Annual Dividend / Market Price = Dividend Yield

For **total return**, add the dividend received plus the capital growth/appreciation over the period. In other words, if you buy a stock for $10 and the market price rises to $12, you have $2 of capital appreciation. If the stock pays $1 in dividends, you're now "up $3" on a $10 investment.

That's a total return of "3 out of 10" or 30%. Or, sometimes the market price drops, dragging down total return. If an investor pays $10 for a stock and receives $1 in dividends, his total return is negative if the stock drops to $8, $7, or lower. If you invest $10, and the stock drops to $7, the $1 in dividends will improve that 30% drop to a negative 20% total return for the year.

Ouch. And that is not at all unusual for an investment in stocks or stock mutual funds.

Registered representatives must be careful when quoting yield or total return to investors. If a customer receives a 5% yield on a bond investment, a registered representative might want to talk only about that and ignore the fact that the market price is down, and the total return negative. The registered representative should give the customer the whole picture to avoid misleading her. Yield, remember, is always a positive number. Total return gives a more accurate picture of how the investment performed over the year.

Methods Used to Evaluate Equity Securities

Descriptive statistics and the related approaches we looked at search for patterns that can be exploited among securities and/or industry groups. That approach does not involve studying companies or following chart patterns, let alone performing detailed cash flow analysis on a securities issuer.

In this section we will look at traditional ways to value equity securities, all of which can be used to make a decision about a particular stock, as opposed to allocating a portfolio to 25% equities, 50% fixed-income, and 25% money market, for example, and then rebalancing along the way.

Fundamental Analysis

Fundamental analysis involves looking quantitatively at the financial statements we looked at as well as studying the company qualitatively in terms of its industry position, the skill of its management team, and the goodwill it has among customers and suppliers. The headlines about the company are important to fundamental analysts, as are the quarterly and year-end earnings figures. Fundamental analysts care about price-to-earnings and price-to-book ratios as well as revenue and net income.

In May 2009 I traveled to Omaha to listen to two successful fundamental analysts and investors named Warren Buffet and Charlie Munger. For over five hours the two men discussed the operations and performance of the companies they invest in while snacking on See's Candies and Dilly Bars. At one point Mr. Buffet said he had recently made a small investment in a company just by spending a half-hour studying their most recent 10K. Companies are often purchased or invested in based largely on the skill of the current owners and managers. Only fundamental analysts care about any of these things.

Top-down fundamental analysis starts by studying economic trends, and then considers which industry groups and then which issuers within those groups will be affected by the good or bad news up ahead. On the other hand, bottom-up fundamental analysis starts at the company level, what some refer to as the "granular level."

Technical Analysis

Either way, fundamental analysts look at the company who issued the common stock. **Technical analysis**, on the other hand, involves studying the behavior of the stock itself as it trades on the secondary market. Technical analysts don't want to hear about how a company's products have been selling or who the new CEO might be. They want to know how the shares of the company's stock have been trading in terms of market price and **volume** levels. Rather than studying companies, technical analysts study stock market data.

Charts and Patterns

Many people feel that in terms of stock prices, history tends to repeat itself. Therefore, many technical traders make decisions on whether to buy or sell by looking at charts of a stock's market price over a certain period of time. These days, **chartists** can review the price patterns over 200 days, 30 days, one day, five minutes, what have you. The idea is that by watching the chart pattern start to develop, the trader using charts can predict where the stock is headed next.

A popular type of chart is the candlestick chart. Each "candlestick" is a little vertical bar that indicates the opening price, the high price, the low price, and the closing price for the stock. At the left of the chart, we see what the "candle period" is, whether weekly, monthly, etc. Below the pricing information the chart also shows volume for the shares traded.

Reading the patterns that develop from such charts is part art and part science—just like fundamental analysis. The key is to find a **trendline**, defined as "local highs and local lows forming a straight line." In other words, a trendline allows us to step back from the trees to see the forest. Rather than obsessing over yesterday's high, low and close, a trendline shows us the bigger picture in terms of whether the price of the stock is generally moving upward, downward, or sideways. A basic premise of trendlines is that stock prices tend to bounce upward from a lower limit called **support** and also bounce downward off a higher limit called **resistance**, like this:

This means that whenever the stock goes up, it meets resistance, when all the sellers step in to depress the price, and whenever it falls, it finds support, where the buyers step in to bid the price back up again. A stock's arrival at the resistance threshold is often referred to as the market being **overbought**, and its fall to the support price is called an **oversold** market. A trader following charts might consistently try to buy close to support and sell as soon as it nears resistance. Or, maybe he waits until the stock breaks through resistance before buying it, reasoning that if it hits a **breakout** it will keep running up. Breakouts occurring on high volume—in either direction—are considered especially significant.

If the trendline's support and resistance lines run parallel, this pattern is referred to as a channel. If the parallel lines are going up, you're looking at a "channel up" pattern, and at a "channel down" pattern if the parallel lines are going down. If the lines are horizontal, the pattern is a "channel."

A trader using channel patterns tries to predict where the stock is about to go. If he sees a "channel up" pattern start to form, he's going to start buying the stock and probably ride it until he sees that things are about to turn around.

Parallel support and resistance lines form channel patterns. On the other hand, when the support and resistance lines start to converge, the pattern is called a wedge. A "rising wedge" pattern is considered a bearish signal. The rising wedge starts out wide at the bottom and then narrows as prices rise but the range gets smaller, with the lines squeezing together toward the top. A "falling wedge" pattern starts out wide at the top and then narrows as prices full with the range becoming smaller. A falling wedge is considered a bullish signal, a sign that the downtrend is about to turn the other way.

Insert graphics of channels and wedges.

Speaking of which, a **"head and shoulders"** price pattern on a chart also signals the reversal of a trend. A "head and shoulders" top pattern is characterized by a prior uptrend and then three distinct highs for the stock. A head and shoulders "top" indicates the bull trend is about to end, a **bearish** signal.

This is a head-and-shoulders top formation:

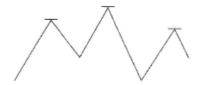

The stock makes a high represented as the left peak or "shoulder." It falls back and then really goes on a tear—the middle peak is called the "head." The stock then falls to the horizontal support line and makes one more big push. Unfortunately, the right shoulder is not as high as either the head or the left shoulder, which means the uptrend is about to end. So, when you see that right shoulder beginning to form, you're supposed to conclude that the stock price is headed for a big drop.

A head-and-shoulders top indicates the reversal of an uptrend and is a bearish indicator. A head-and-shoulders bottom or an **inverted head-and-shoulders** pattern, on the other hand, indicates the reversal of a downtrend and is a **bullish** indicator.

If a stock is trading in a narrow range between support and resistance, it is consolidating. A chart of a stock in **consolidation** appears to be moving sideways, like this:

The exam might talk about consolidation as the place where sophisticated investors (mutual funds, pension funds, etc.) are getting into or out of the stock. Since these institutional traders are presumed to be the experts, when we see them buying, it must mean the stock is going up, and when we see them selling, it must mean the stock is heading down. At this accumulation or distribution point, the price is, apparently, about to make a huge break on the up or down side. Consolidation and a "channel" pattern would be two ways of referring to the same phenomenon.

Other well-known chart patterns include the cup, the saucer, and the inverted saucer pattern. The cup pattern is a curved trendline. It usually starts to form just below resistance. The line curves downward as the closing prices drop, but then the line curves upward as prices rise. As the full curve is just about completed at the resistance line, many technical traders feel there is a high probability of a breakout. A cup pattern is formed over a few weeks. If the curve develops more slowly, chartists refer to the pattern as a "saucer" or a "rounding bottom." Either way, with a rounded bottom to its shape, this chart pattern indicates that the stock or index's level is about to rise. It is, in other words, a bullish indicator.

Well, as with the head-and-shoulders pattern, we could flip the saucer over and called it an "inverted saucer pattern." Here, with the curve flipped over, technical traders should conclude the stock's price is about to drop; the uptrend is about to end. Another name for this pattern is the "rounded top" pattern.

Whether it's an inverted or a regular-ole saucer pattern, the reason for the curve is a gradual shift from bearish-to-bullish or from bullish-to-bearish sentiment.

Advance-Decline Ratio

Technical analysts look to see how many stocks advance versus how many stocks decline. The name for this statistic is the **advance-decline ratio**. If advancers outnumber decliners by 2:1, that means that twice as many stocks finished up in market price as down that day. And if decliners outnumber advancers 2:1, that means that twice as many stocks went down that day as up. Maybe a technical analyst sees that advancers have outpaced decliners for several days and decides to go with the trend. Or, maybe he's a contrarian and figures that if advancers have been outpacing decliners consistently, that trend has to reverse itself soon because of other reasons. Again, notice how he's analyzing the overall movement of <u>stocks</u>, while the fundamental analyst focuses on the fundamentals of the <u>companies</u> underlying those stocks.

Volume

Volume is also of interest to the technical analyst. Volume indicates the total number of shares traded on, say, the NYSE, NASDAQ, or the regional exchanges in Chicago, Philadelphia, Boston, etc. Analysts expect stock prices to move on increasing volume. They would tend to place more significance on the fact that stock prices increased minutely on decreasing volume. Often, that situation is considered a reversal of a bullish trend, which is, of course, a bearish signal. It just means that the bull market is running out of steam—stock prices barely went up, and there was nowhere near as much trading going on.

Market momentum and sentiment

Market momentum is the ability of the market to sustain up or downswings in price. This concept combines both price changes and volume of trading. If a stock's price increases with large trading volumes, the momentum is much higher than if the share price rises on lower volume. The higher the momentum, the more likely the direction of the stock price will be sustained. Momentum is an "anticipatory indicator" used to predict price changes. Many technical analysts use stochastics to measure the momentum of stocks and stock indexes.

Market sentiment is a judgment of the mood or tone of a market. Markets are generally either bullish (going up) or bearish (going down). One way to gauge market sentiment is through the put/call ratio. We will look at puts and calls in depth in our chapter on Options. For now, understand that if an investor is worried about his stock dropping, he needs to "hedge" or protect his stock by buying puts. On the other hand, if he has bet against the market, he needs to hedge by purchasing calls. Therefore, technical analysts track the ratio of puts to calls and call this statistic the "put/call ratio" or "puts-to-calls." The ratio is > 1 if the volume of puts exceeds the volume for calls. When fewer puts are being traded than calls, the ratio is < 1. When the ratio is trading at relatively high levels, this is taken as an indication of bearish sentiment. Why? People must be worried about their stocks dropping, as evidenced by all the puts they've purchased to protect against that. When the ratio is trading at relatively low levels, this is taken as an indication of bullish sentiment.

Options are all about volatility. The more volatile/unpredictable a stock's price, the more one has to pay for options tied to that stock. Therefore, technical analysts are often interested in tracking option volatility. There are two types of volatility here—historical and implied. Historical volatility takes the daily price changes over a year for the underlying stock and finds the "standard deviation" showing if the stock is subject to wild price swings or, rather, trades more predictably. Implied volatility looks at the price of the options tied to a stock (or index of stocks) and determines what the market implies about the volatility of the stock up ahead.

Moving Average

A technical analyst looking at the put/call ratio would also factor in a **moving average** to make more sense of the information. A moving average replaces the oldest piece of data with the newest on a rolling basis. In baseball, if we say that someone is batting .286, that's over the whole season. A moving average would tell us how he's been hitting lately, and show graphically whether he's generally in a slump or on a hot streak. In other words, it would help us spot a trend. So, rather than focusing too hard on yesterday's or this week's closing price for a stock, we can use the moving average to see where the stock has been closing on average over the past so-many days.

The **200-day moving average** is probably the most commonly used. A technical analyst can track the 200-day moving average for a stock or for a index. He can also see what percentage of stocks have been closing above or below their 200-day moving average to get a feel for whether it's a bull or bear market. If a high percentage have been closing above their 200-day average, this is taken as a bullish indicator and vice versa for a low percentage.

Some technical traders assume that the movement of security index futures tied to the S&P 500, the Dow, etc., that happens before the market opens can predict the direction of the stock market. Therefore, if a customer has a large stock position to sell, he may be advised to wait until the market has opened and traded a while before placing a sell order, depending on the direction of the index futures. Most technical traders use the data on index futures to predict only the direction of the market in the short-term.

Theories

The technical analyst knows how smart he is. So much smarter than the small-time investor, in fact, that all he has to do is track what **odd-lot** investors are doing and bet the other way. If odd-lotters are buying, he sells. If odd-lotters are selling, he buys. Why? Because folks who can only afford an odd lot (<100 shares) of stock at a time always buy too high and sell too low. This is known as the **odd-lot theory**.

The **short interest theory** has to do with how many open short sales are out there. Now, as we'll see later, short sellers profit when a stock's price drops, but this theory also recognizes that short sellers eventually have to cover or buy back the shares that they borrowed to sell in the first place. So, if there are a lot of uncovered or "open" short positions out there, they might all suddenly be forced to buy the stock in a hurry. That would create buying pressure that could drive up the stock's price, which is why a large number of open short positions is a *bullish* indicator.

Discounted Cash Flow Analysis

We looked earlier at the net present value (NPV) of the anticipated cash flows from an investment in, say, a printing press or a new call center. This method is called **discounted cash flow analysis**. The basic question that this methodology tries to answer is, "how much cash can we generate from this investment adjusted for the time value of money?" Why adjust for the time value of money? Because, a company could always just park excess cash in a safe place and receive X amount on that cash; if they're going to, instead, aggressively invest that cash back into the business, they need to get a higher internal rate of return than what they could get parking the cash in T-Bills or bank CDs. If the company can't find any internal projects that provide a higher internal rate of return than what they can get in the securities markets, they might just invest their capital in the securities markets.

Of course, whether they're trying to calculate the cash flows generated by investing in, say, preferred stock of a public company or investing it internally into, say, a call center in Des Moines, Iowa, the company using discounted cash flow analysis always faces certain challenges:

- Small changes in inputs/assumptions can lead to large changes in results
- Estimating future cash flows is inherently imprecise

Dividend Discount

The **dividend discount model** is a way of valuing a common stock by using the dividends the investor predicts to receive in the future and then discounting them back to present value. If the value arrived at using this model is higher than the stock's current market price, the stock is thought to be undervalued and, therefore, a candidate for investment. The dividend discount model is considered the simplest method of valuing a common stock. The idea behind the model is that a common stock equals the present value of the expected dividends to be received. Of course, predicting dividends well into the future is no easy task, and if the company does not pay dividends, then this method can't be used.

FUNDAMENTAL ANALYSIS	TECHNICAL ANALYSIS
Financial Statements, e.g., balance sheet, income statement	Market Data
Revenue	Advance/Decline
Net Income	Moving Average
Profits, Profit Margins	Support/Resistance
Price-to-earnings, Price-to-book	52-week High/low
Working Capital	Price and Volume Levels
Qualitative judgments on the business	Market Sentiment, Momentum
Current Ratio, Quick Ratio	Short Interest
Debt-to-Equity or Debt Ratio	Charts, Patterns
Dividend Payout Ratio	Puts/Calls, Stochastics

Types and Characteristics of Pooled Investments

In the securities industry there are many ways to refer to the same thing. What some call a "pooled investment vehicle" others refer to as a "packaged product" or a "mutual fund." Whatever we call these investments, a **pooled investment** vehicle pools the capital of many investors together, with that capital then managed by a professional.

The best-known pooled investment vehicle is the mutual fund. While some investors buy shares of SBUX, many prefer to own shares of a mutual fund that devotes a percent of the portfolio to SBUX and other large-cap stocks. Similarly, rather than putting $100,000 into one issuer's bonds, many investors prefer the diversification and professional management offered by a bond fund.

Investment Companies

A mutual fund is an investment portfolio managed by an investment adviser. Investors buy shares of the portfolio. The adviser uses the money from investors to invest in stocks and bonds that the shareholders in the fund share ownership in, mutually. When an investor sends in money, the portfolio gets bigger, but it also gets cut into more slices to accommodate the investment into the fund. The only way for the slices to get bigger is for the portfolio to become more valuable. The portfolio value rises when securities in the fund increase in value and when they pay income to the portfolio.

That is the same way it happens in any securities account. When the market values of the securities in the account drop, the account value is down for the day unless income is received that outweighs the drop in price. For example, if an account was worth $100,000 when the markets opened and then just $98,817 when the markets closed, the investor is down for the day. . . unless he happened to receive dividends and interest of more than that drop in market value of $1,183.

Now, couldn't an investor bypass the mutual fund and just buy whatever securities he chooses? Sure, but most people refuse to change the oil in their car. Why would they suddenly become do-it-yourselfers with their retirement accounts? It takes work to decide which stocks or bonds to purchase.

Also, if an investor has $400 to invest, he can't take a meaningful position in any company's stock, and even if he tried, he would end up owning just one company's stock. Common stock can drop in a hurry, so we never put all our money in just one or two issues. Diversification protects against this unsystematic risk, and mutual funds own stocks and bonds from many different issuers, usually in different market sectors. Plus, the portfolio is run by professional investors called investment advisers.

Advantages of Mutual Funds
Advantages of investing through mutual funds vs. buying stocks and bonds directly include:

- Investment decisions made by a professional portfolio manager
- Ease of diversification
- Ability to liquidate a portion of the investment without losing diversification
- Simplified tax information
- Simplified record keeping
- Automatic reinvestments of capital gains and income distributions at **net asset value**
- Safekeeping of portfolio securities
- Ease of account inquiry

The first point is probably the main reason people buy mutual funds—they have no knowledge of stocks, bonds, taxation, etc., and they have even less interest in learning. Let a professional portfolio manager—often an entire team of portfolio managers—decide what to buy and when to buy or sell it. As we mentioned, it's tough to have your own diversified portfolio in individual stocks and bonds because a few hundred or thousand dollars will only buy a few shares of stock or a few bonds issued by just a few companies.

On the other hand, a mutual fund would usually hold stock in, say, 100 or more companies, and their bond portfolios are also diversified. Therefore, even with the smallest amount of money accepted by the fund, the investor is immediately diversified. This is called the "undivided interest concept," which means that $50 from a small investor owns a piece of all the securities in the portfolio, just as $1 million from a larger investor does.

Another bullet said, "Ability to liquidate a portion of the investment without losing diversification." That means if an investor owns 100 shares of IBM, MSFT, and GM, what is he going to do when he needs $5,000 to cover an emergency? If he sells a few shares of each, he'll pay three separate commissions. If he sells 100 shares of any one stock, his diversification is reduced. With a mutual fund, investors redeem a certain number of shares and remain just as diversified as they were before the sale. And, they can usually redeem shares without paying fees.

Mutual funds can diversify their holdings by:

- Industries
- Types of investment instruments
- Variety of securities issuers
- Geographic areas

If it's a stock fund, it is typically a growth fund, a value fund, an income fund, or some combination thereof. No matter what the objective, the fund usually buys stocks from issuers across many different industries. In a mutual fund prospectus there is typically a pie chart that shows what percentage of assets is devoted to an industry group. Maybe it's 3% in telecommunications, 10% retail, and 1.7% healthcare, etc. That way if it's a bad year for telecommunications or retail, the fund won't get hurt like a small investor who owns shares of only one telecom company and one retail company.

A bond fund can be diversified among investment interests. That means they buy debentures, secured bonds, convertible bonds, zero coupons, mortgage-backed securities, and even a few money market instruments to be on the safe side.

Even if the fund did not spread their investments across many different industries, they would purchase securities from a variety of issuers. If they like retail, they can buy stock in a variety of companies—Walmart, Target, Sears, Nordstrom, Home Depot, etc. And, since any geographic area could be hit by an economic slump, a tropical storm, or both, most funds spread their holdings among different geographic areas.

The Investment Company Act of 1940 defines a **diversified company** as:

> "Diversified company" means a management company which meets the following requirements: At least **75** per centum of the value of its total assets is represented by cash and cash items (including receivables), Government securities, securities of other investment companies, and other securities for the purposes of this calculation limited in respect of any one issuer to an amount not greater in value than **5** per centum of the value of the total assets of such management company and to not more than **10** per centum of the outstanding voting securities of such issuer.

So, how does the "Act of 1940" then define a **non-diversified company**?

> "Non-diversified company" means any management company other than a diversified company.

If the fund wants to promote itself as being diversified, it has to meet the definition above. For 75% of the fund's assets, no more than 5% of its assets are in any one company, and it doesn't own more than 10% of any company's outstanding shares.

If it doesn't want to abide by the definition, it must refer to itself as a "non-diversified fund." The term "management company" includes both open-end and closed-end funds. From there, each could be either diversified or non-diversified, leaving us with the following four types of management company:

- Diversified Open-End Fund
- Non-Diversified Open-End Fund
- Diversified Closed-End Fund
- Non-Diversified Closed-End Fund

Because closed-end funds use leverage, the most aggressive type above is the non-diversified closed-end fund. An example is found with the stock symbol KYN, of which I own a few shares.

I don't buy a lot of mutual funds, myself. That's because I like to own shares of companies of my own choosing and am willing to do a little homework. Unfortunately, I end up receiving proxy materials and annual reports from maybe 20 different companies, and keeping track of all the dividends I've received from the various sources is annoying. With a mutual fund, I'd get one **1099-DIV** showing all dividends and capital gains distributions, and I'd also get just one semi-annual report and one annual report from the fund.

Types of Funds

There are many types of open- and closed-end funds. Let's start with the most aggressive type, equity.

Equity

The primary focus of **equity funds** is to invest in common stock. Within equity funds, we find different objectives. **Growth funds** invest in companies likely to grow their profits faster than competitors and/or the overall stock market. These stocks usually trade at high p/e and price-to-book ratios.

Value funds, on the other hand, seek companies trading for less than the portfolio managers determine they're truly worth. These funds buy stock in established companies that are currently out of favor with investors. Since the share price is depressed, value stocks tend to have high dividend yields. Value funds are considered more conservative than growth funds.

What if he can't make up his mind between a growth fund and a value fund? There are funds that blend both styles of investing, and the industry calls these **blend funds**. In other words, no matter how creative the portfolio managers might get, they end up being either a growth fund, a value fund, or a blend of both styles.

If an investor's objective is to receive income from equities, an **equity income fund** may be suitable. These funds buy stocks that provide dependable dividend income. Receiving dividends tends to reduce the volatility of an investment, so equity income funds are lower risk than growth funds. They may also invest in debt securities to keep the yield consistent.

What if the investor can't decide between a mutual fund family's growth funds and its income funds? Chances are, he will choose their "growth and income fund." A growth and income fund buys stocks in companies expected to grow their profits and also in companies that pay dependable, respectable dividends. Since we've added the income component, growth and income funds have lower volatility than growth funds. Many allocate a percentage to fixed-income to assure a regular source of dividend distributions to the shareholders.

So, from highest to lowest volatility, we have growth, then growth & income, and then equity income funds. I have a catalog from a large mutual fund family that puts them in exactly that order, and even uses the color red for growth—as in, "Warning! This stuff can burn!" The bond funds and money market funds, on the other hand, use the colors blue and green.

Bond (Fixed-Income)

Stock is not for everyone. Even if an investor owns equity mutual funds, chances are he will put a percentage of his money into bond funds, as well. A rule-of-thumb is that whatever the investor's age, that's the percentage he should put into fixed-income. So, which type of fixed-income funds should the investor purchase? If the investor is not in a high tax bracket or is investing in an IRA, 401(k), etc., we'll recommend taxable bond funds—corporate and U.S. Government bonds.

The investor's time horizon determines if she should purchase short-term, intermediate-term, or long-term bond funds. Her risk tolerance determines if she needs the absolute safety of U.S. Treasury funds or is willing to reach for higher returns with high-yield funds. If the investor is in a taxable account and wants to earn interest exempt from federal income tax, her agent might put her into a tax-exempt bond fund, which purchases municipal bonds. If the investor is in a high-tax state such as Maryland, Virginia, or California, she might want the "Tax-Exempt Fund of Maryland," Virginia, or California. Now, the dividends she receives will generally be exempt from both federal and state income taxes.

Whichever tax-exempt fund she chooses, the next question is, "How much of a yield does she want, and how much risk can she withstand?" Her answers determine how long the average duration of the fund, and whether to focus on high-yield or investment-grade bond funds.

Money Market

An investor's need for liquidity determines how much to place in **money market mutual funds**. There are both taxable and tax-exempt money market mutual funds. The **tax-exempt money market funds** buy short-term obligations of states, counties, cities, school districts, etc. They pay low rates of interest, but since it's tax-free, investors in high marginal tax brackets come out ahead.

The benefit of the money market mutual fund is its **stable value**. The money investors put here can be turned right back into the same amount of money without worrying, unlike the money in a bond or stock fund. Investors earn low returns but can often write checks against these accounts, which are treated like a sale of so-many shares times $1 each.

Another use for these funds is as a vehicle in which to sweep a brokerage customer's cash after a deposit, dividend, interest payment, or sale occurs. Money market mutual funds are a holding place for cash that is not ready to be either invested long-term or spent by the customer.

As the SEC explains, "Money market funds pay dividends that reflect prevailing short-term interest rates, are redeemable on demand, and, unlike other investment companies, seek to maintain a stable NAV, typically $1.00. This combination of principal stability, liquidity and payment of short-term yields has made money market funds popular cash management vehicles for both retail and institutional investors."

Some of these funds keep at least 99.5% of their portfolio in Treasury securities and are called government money market funds. The funds that hold municipal securities are tax-exempt money market funds. Those holding corporate debt securities are known as prime money market funds. These three types can be for retail or institutional investors.

Because of the financial crisis of 2008 the SEC wants to prevent future runs on money market funds during extraordinary situations. The problem is that if funds artificially maintain an NAV of $1 when their portfolio may suddenly not be worth that amount, there is a first-mover advantage for investors to hurry up and pull out. To prevent this the SEC now requires institutional prime and tax-exempt money market mutual funds to value their NAV at the actual market value of the securities--called floating the NAV. This way, there is a natural disincentive to run for the exits and end up receiving only, say, 97 cents on the dollar.

Also, except for government money market funds, both retail and institutional prime and tax-exempt funds can now impose both liquidity fees of up to 2% to discourage redemptions and even a temporary halt to redemptions if the situation is dire. If the board of directors for the fund decides the redemption gate is in the best interest of the shareholders, they can impose it for up to 10 business days. No more than one 10-day gate or halt could be imposed, however, in any 90-day period.

As with all funds, investors agree to pay operating expenses in exchange for the benefits provided by the investment product. Money market funds do not charge sales charges, but typically impose a 12b-1 fee of .25% as well as management fees and transfer agent fees, etc.

So, while money market mutual funds are a safe and liquid investment, their liquidity is not as automatic and across the board as it once was, especially outside of government money market funds.

Specialty Funds

Specialty/specialized funds focus their approach to investing. Some funds specialize in an industry, some in geographic regions, some in writing covered calls, etc. Investors can buy the Latin America, the Europe, or the Pacific Rim fund. They would then hope that those regions don't go into a major economic slump or suffer a natural disaster. See, when the fund concentrates heavily in an industry or geographic region, it generally takes on more volatility.

Most equity funds hold stocks in many different industries. On the other hand, there are **sector funds** that do exactly as their name implies—focus on industry sectors. If we buy a "growth fund," so far we have no idea which industries the so-called "growth companies" compete in. On the other hand, if we buy the Communications Fund, the Financial Services Fund, or the Healthcare Fund, we know which industry space the companies operate in. Concentrating in just one sector is the definition of aggressive investing. Investment results are unpredictable year by year. So, make sure the investor has a long anticipated holding period and high risk tolerance before recommending sector funds in a test question.

There are **asset allocation** funds for conservative investors. Rather than maintaining one's own mix of, say, 20% large cap value, 20% small cap growth, 40% high-yield bond, and 20% short-term Treasuries and constantly having to rebalance, investors can invest in an asset allocation fund that matches their goals. A similar type of fund is called a **balanced fund**. Here, the portfolio is always balanced between stocks and bonds and generally diversified among various types of each. There is not a set percentage for us to know here. Rather, the fund's prospectus would explain the parameters established by the board of directors.

A popular way to invest these days is through **age-based portfolios** or **lifecycle funds**. These funds shift the allocation from mostly-equity to mostly-fixed-income gradually as the investor gets closer and closer to his goal of retirement. Another name for these investments is **target funds.** If she plans to retire in or around 2050, for example, the individual would invest in the Target 2050 fund offered by a mutual fund family. The investments would be diversified, and that mix would become more conservative as we get closer and closer to the year 2050.

529 Savings Plans typically offer an age-based portfolio that is much more aggressive for kids 1-6 years old than those who are now 18 and in need of the funds. For example, the allocation for the youngsters might be 90% equity/10% fixed-income, while those 18 years old would be in a portfolio closer to 70% fixed-income/20% money market/10% equity.

Both international and **global funds** appeal to investors who want to participate in markets not
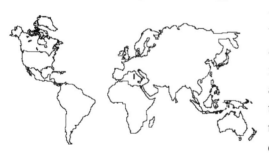
confined to the U.S. The difference between the two is that an **international fund** invests in companies located anywhere but the U.S., while a global fund would invest in companies located and doing business anywhere in the world, including the U.S. Remember that when investors move away from the U.S., they take on more political risk as well as currency exchange risk. For developed markets like Japan and Singapore, the political risk would be lower than in emerging markets such as Brazil and China. Both types of markets, however, would present currency exchange risk to U.S. investors.

Precious metals funds allow investors to speculate on the price of gold, silver, and copper, etc. by purchasing a portfolio usually of mining companies who extract these metals. Since a mine's costs are fixed, it only makes sense to open them for production when the price of what you're mining goes high enough to make it worth your while. Therefore, these funds typically hold stock in mining companies as opposed to holding precious metals themselves.

What if the investor does not believe that portfolio managers are likely to beat an index such as the S&P 500 with their active management over the long-term? He can buy an **index fund** that tracks an index as opposed to a fund trying to trade individual stocks. An index is an artificially grouped basket of stocks. Why are there 30 stocks in the Dow Jones Industrial Average, and why are the 30 stocks that are in there in there?

Because the company who put the index together says so. Same for the S&P 500. S&P decided that these 500 stocks make up an index, so there you have it. Investors buy index funds because there are no sales charges and low expenses. Since there's virtually no trading going on, the **management fees** should be—and typically are— low. So, for a no-brainer, low-cost option, investors can put their money into an index and expect to do about as well as that index.

Well-known indexes include the Dow Jones Industrial Average. The "Dow" is price-weighted, which means the stock price itself determines how much weighting the stock receives within the index. If a stock trades at $100, for example, its weighting is much higher than a stock trading at $11 per-share. The S&P 500, like most indexes, is market-cap-weighted. The share price of MSFT doesn't matter, but the fact that all of their outstanding shares are worth, say, $200 billion means MSFT could be weighted 20 times more heavily than other stocks within the index. Because the S&P 500 contains such a large percentage of the major stocks trading on the secondary market, its movement is considered to represent the movement of the overall stock market. We mentioned this when looking at beta, which measures how much one stock moves compared to the overall market, as measured by the S&P 500.

Note that neither the Dow nor the S&P 500 cares whether the stock trades on the NYSE or NASDAQ. It's the size of the company and the market cap that matter here. And, all 30 stocks within the Dow Jones Industrial Average would also be included with the 500 stocks in the S&P 500.

The most famous "Dow" is the **Dow Jones Industrial Average** (DJIA). But, there is also the Dow Jones Transportation Average and the Dow Jones Utility Average. Together, these three make up the Dow Composite, which provides what the publishers of the indices call a "blue-chip microcosm of the U.S. stock market."

As much as I hate to confuse you, the company that owns Standard & Poor's now owns the Dow Jones indices, too, so if you "google" it, you will find that the Dow Jones averages are now part of the "S&P Dow Jones Indices."

Another well-known market-cap-weighted index is the **NASDAQ 100.** This index represents the 100 largest non-financial company stocks, all trading on NASDAQ. Stocks such as Facebook, Google, Microsoft, and Amazon are found here.

A well-known small cap index is the **Russell 2,000.** There are also bond indices for bond investors who want to pay low management fees and engage in passive investing.

Open-end index funds are for long-term investors. If an investor wants to do as well as one of the indices above, this is where he goes. But, because it is an open-end fund, the shares must be redeemed, with everyone who redeems that day receiving the same NAV next calculated by the fund. In a few pages we'll see that Exchange-Traded Funds (ETFs) are another low-cost way to match the performance of a index, only these shares are traded throughout the day just as shares of MSFT or IBM are traded throughout the day. For a small investment of money, the open-end index funds are more cost-effective because the ETFs charge commissions. An investment of $100 into an ETF would be a bad move, even if the commission were just $9. That is like a self-imposed 9% front-end load!

But, for investments of several thousands of dollars, the ETF is at least as cost-effective as its open-end cousin.

The other night I helped a friend review the investments in her 401(k) plan, and I was able to quickly point out that her "35 and up" fund was a fund made up of several other funds, all from the same company, with the allocation based on her anticipated retirement date. Since this fund was comprised of other funds, your industry went ahead and named the product a **fund of funds**. Funds of funds are usually associated with higher fees as opposed to picking just one or two of the funds within the group.

Comparisons

Once we decide that the investor wants to invest in a growth fund or a value fund, how do we go about comparing one growth or value fund to another? The mutual fund prospectus is a good place to start. In this disclosure document we find the fund's investment objectives and style. Do they focus on companies valued at $5 billion and above? $1 billion and below? Do they use fundamental analysis, poring over income statements and balance sheets, possibly meeting with senior management of the companies whose stock they hold? Or, do they rely more on technical analysis—charts, patterns, trendlines, and volume, etc.? Is a company's dividend payout important when selecting investments for the portfolio, or is the fund only looking at the growth potential? Is this a small cap, mid-cap, or large cap fund, and how does the fund define "small, mid, and large cap"?

There are also investment policies disclosed in the prospectus. Maybe the fund discloses here that it may invest up to 10% of its assets in securities of issuers outside the United States and Canada and not included in the S&P 500. Or, that they allow themselves to invest 20% of their assets in lower-quality debt securities rated below BB/Ba by S&P and Moody's, or even in debt securities no one has rated. If that sounds too risky for the investor, well, that's why we're disclosing it here in the prospectus.

The prospectus provides information on the party managing the portfolio. We call that party the **investment adviser** or the portfolio manager. Often, it's a team approach, so we can see the names of the individual portfolio counselors and how much experience they have doing this sort of thing. The prospectus I am looking at now has a team of eight stock and bond pickers, and their experience in the industry ranges from 18 to 40 years.

One of the most misunderstood aspects of mutual fund investing has to do with the fees and expenses. You'll often hear people say, "No, I don't pay any expenses on my mutual funds—they're all no-load." As we'll see in more detail later, whether the fund is "no load" or not, all funds charge **operating expenses**. Investors might not get a bill for their share of the expenses, but the fund takes out enough money from the portfolio to cover their expenses, whether this happens to be a "no load" fund or one that charges either front- or back-end sales charges. Sales charges are one thing; expenses are another. Not all funds have sales charges, but all funds have expenses.

In the prospectus the investor can see how much of her check is going toward the sales charge, and how much of the dollars she then invests will be taken as ongoing operating expenses. If two growth funds have similar 10-year track records but one has expenses of 1.5% while the other charges just

.90%, this could certainly be the tiebreaker the investor is looking for. Expense ratios, in other words, are important factors when determining an investment into a mutual fund.

A mutual fund's **turnover ratio** tells us how actively the portfolio managers trade the portfolio securities. A turnover rate of 20 or 30% is considered a buy-and-hold strategy, while a turnover ratio greater than 100% indicates a fund that does a lot of buying and selling.

How well does the fund perform? The prospectus shows total return, usually as a bar chart and a table of numbers. Since I'm looking at a growth fund prospectus, the red bars are often long and pointing in both upward and downward directions. Over the past 10 years, the fund has gone up as high as 45% and down as much as 22% in any one year. As we said, investing in growth stocks requires a higher risk tolerance and a longer time horizon. There was a 3-year period here where the fund averaged returns of negative 9%.

That's why this would not be an account from which an investor should expect to make withdrawals. A growth fund is for an investor with a long time horizon, as these results make pretty clear. One could build up the account value over time in a growth fund but then shift some money out of that and into a money market mutual fund before taking withdrawals from the stable-value account.

What is total return? The point of buying a mutual fund share is that it might go up in value. The mutual fund will usually also pay out dividends from all those stocks and bonds they hold in the portfolio. And, at the end of the year if they took more profits than losses while trading their stocks and bonds, they distribute a capital gain to shareholders.

Total return takes all three of those things and compares it to where the fund started. If the fund started out with a "net asset value" or "NAV" of $10 and finished the year at $11 per-share, that's $1 of "capital appreciation." If the fund also paid a dividend of 50 cents per-share and a $1 capital gains distribution, we would add that $1.50 to the capital appreciation of $1 for a total of $2.50. Comparing that $2.50 to where we started—$10—gives us a total return of 25%.

How likely is it that a fund could have a total return of 25%? The prospectus I am looking at shows that the fund had positive total returns of 26%, 31%, and 45% during the first three years in the last 10-year period. So, naturally, it had a similar return the next three years, right? No, after that, it was anybody's guess: positive 7%, then negative 12%, followed by negative 22%. Which means the following year was probably even worse, right? No. The next year the fund had a total return of nearly 33% in a positive direction. Now we see why the prospectus says that "past results are not predictive of future results."

Most mutual funds are not short-term investments, especially not equity funds. Investors need a long time horizon, as the prospectus for this growth fund tells us on the first page. Nobody knows what will happen this year or next. We can show the returns over 1, 5, and 10 years and let investors be the judge. But no one can say which funds will go up this year, let alone which funds will go up the most.

Note that "total return" for a stock or bond is found the same way except that stocks and bonds lack that third component called a "capital gains distribution." For stocks and bonds, there is income (maybe), and then the security's market value either goes up or down. Those two amounts compared to the starting point equal the stock's or bond's total return.

The prospectus shows results after taxes have been figured in. Of course, this is a little tricky, as we see from the caveat in the prospectus on my desk:

```
Your actual after-tax returns depend on your individual tax
situation and likely will differ from the results shown below. In
addition, after-tax returns may not be relevant if you hold your
fund shares through a tax-deferred arrangement, such as a 401(k)
plan, IRA, or 529 Savings Plan.
```

Open-End Funds

Sales Charges vs. Expenses

Mutual funds are investment products, and it costs money to market these products to investors. To cover the costs of advertising and compensating sales people some open-end mutual funds charge **sales charges.** Unlike the ongoing operating expenses we'll look at, a sales charge is a one-time deduction taken out of an investor's investment into the fund.

Sales charges cover distribution expenses: printing and mailing sales literature, advertising the fund through magazines, radio, TV, and the internet, compensating sales people, etc.

If a mutual fund charges a maximum sales charge of 5.5%, that means that when the investor cuts her check, 5.5% of it goes to the distributor and the broker-dealer who sold her the fund. Only the other 94.5% goes into the mutual fund for investment purposes.

So, if the **net asset value (NAV)** is $9.45 but the **public offering price (POP)** is $10.00, the extra 55 cents is the sales charge. How big is that sales charge? It is exactly 5.5% of the investor's $10 check. The sales charge as a percentage equals:

(POP minus NAV) divided by the POP

If we plug our numbers into that formula, we see that $10 minus $9.45 is 55 cents. 55 cents divided by the POP of $10 equals 5.5%. Another way to refer to POP is the gross amount invested. NAV can also be referred to as the net amount invested, what is left after the front-end sales charge is deducted.

The fund is made up of perhaps 500 different stocks and bonds, all trading throughout the day. At the end of each day that the markets are open the fund recalculates the net asset value or NAV. Mutual funds use **forward pricing,** which means that when a customer puts in a purchase or redemption order at 10 AM, she won't know how many shares she'll buy or how many dollars she'll receive yet. Only when the NAV is next calculated are purchase and redemption orders processed.

If a mutual fund company were to allow certain large investors to see what the NAV is at about 4 p.m. Eastern and then receive the previous day's NAV, this is a violation known as late trading. As the SEC website explains, "Late trading refers to the practice of placing orders to buy or redeem mutual fund shares after the time as of which a mutual fund has calculated its net asset value (NAV), usually as of the close of trading at 4:00 p.m. Eastern Time, but receiving the price based on the prior NAV already determined as of that day. Late trading violates the federal securities laws concerning the price at which mutual fund shares must be bought or redeemed and defrauds innocent investors in those mutual funds by giving to the late trader an advantage not available to other investors. In , the late trader obtains an advantage – at the expense of the other shareholders of the mutual fund – when he learns of market moving information and is able to purchase or redeem mutual fund shares at prices set before the market moving information was released."

The NAV is the value of one share of the portfolio. The assets of the portfolio equal the value of the securities plus any cash they've generated, minus any liabilities. Where did the liabilities come from? The fund might borrow to handle redemptions because they don't always want to sell stocks and bonds to pay investors who are redeeming.

If the fund has $10,000,000 in assets and $550,000 in liabilities, the net assets of the fund are $9,450,000. If there are 1 million shares, the NAV per-share is $9.45. Investors will receive $9.45 per-share if they redeem their A-shares today, but they'll pay a POP higher than that if they're buying. Buyers of the B-shares will pay $9.45, but those redeeming/selling their shares will receive $9.45 per-share minus whatever percentage they leave behind to the contingent deferred sales charge.

A-, B- and C-shares

An open-end mutual fund that adds sales charges can take the sales charge from investors either when they buy or when they sell their shares of the fund. A-shares charge a **front-end load** when the investor acquires them. B-shares charge a **back-end load** when the investor sells them. For a B-share, the investor pays the NAV, but will leave a percentage behind when she sells. The percentage usually starts to decline in the second year, and after several years (6 to 8), the back-end load goes away completely. At that point, the B-shares are converted to A-shares.

B-shares are associated with **contingent deferred sales charges**. As the name implies, the sales charge is deferred until the investor sells, and the amount of the load is contingent upon when the investor sells. If the NAV is $10, the investor receives the $10, minus the percentage the fund keeps on the back end. So, if she sells 100 shares and there is a 2% back-end sales charge, she gets $1,000 minus $20, or $980 out the door.

Since the back-end or deferred sales charge eventually goes away, as long as the investor isn't going to sell her shares for, say, seven years, she should purchase B-shares, right?

Well, not exactly. While sales charges cover distribution costs, such costs are also covered by a **12b-1 fee**. Yes, a 12b-1 fee also covers distribution costs. You've heard of **no-load funds**, but you may not have gotten the whole story. A no-load fund can charge a 12b-1 fee, as long as it doesn't exceed .25% of the fund's assets. Every quarter, when they take money out to cover expenses, these no-load funds can also take an amount not to exceed 25 basis points—one-quarter of 1%.

But, while 12b-1 fees are associated with no-load funds, loaded funds also charge 12b-1 fees.

So, again, should the investor buy the A-share or the B-share? The choice has to do with the 12b-1 fee. The A-shares for the growth fund might charge a load as high as 5.5% on the front end, but the 12b-1 fee will often be .25%, while the B-shares will charge a 12b-1 fee of, say, 1.00%.

That complicates things. While the person who bought the B-shares is waiting for that contingent deferred sales charge schedule to hit zero, he's paying an extra .75% every year in expenses in this example. .75% times seven years is an extra 5.25%.

And, this 12b-1 fee is a percentage. As an investor's assets are growing over time, that .75% is also taking more money from him, even if it's a flat percentage.

As we'll soon see, 5.5% would probably be the maximum sales charge on the A-shares. If the investor puts in more money, she can reduce the sales charge to 3 or even 2%, which is why long-term investors with a large amount of money should almost always buy the A-shares. In fact, investors with $1 million or more will find that funds with sales charges waive those charges for investments of that size. Does that hurt the salesperson? No, the agent wants and earns most of the 12b-1 fee. The bigger the account value, the higher that fee.

Then, there are also **C-shares**, which usually don't charge an upfront load but do carry a 1% 12b-1 fee. The level 1% 12b-1 fee is the reason these are referred to as **"level load."** The level load shares are intended for shorter-term investments only.

So, which type of share should an investor buy? As a general guideline:

- Long-term investor with $50,000+ to invest – A-shares
- Long-term investor with small amount to invest – B-shares
- Short-term investor with up to $500,000 to invest – C-shares

The difference in expenses between A-shares on one hand and B- and C-shares on the other has to do with the 12b-1 fee. However, the 12b-1 fee is just one expense. The fund also charges a management fee to cover the cost of the investment adviser serving as portfolio manager. That fee is the same for all investors across the board and must be a separate line item. Management fees are not covered by any other charge. Rather, they must be clearly disclosed.

Other expenses cover transfer agent, custodial, legal and accounting services involved with running the fund. To see what the dollar amounts are investors can check the **statement of additional information or SAI**. For example, I just pulled up the SAI for the American Balanced Fund and saw that the investment adviser received $189 million managing the portfolio the previous year. The transfer agent, by comparison, received $74 million.

When we add the management fee, the 12b-1 fee, and the "other expenses" fee, we have the total operating expenses for the fund. Divide the total expenses by the assets of the fund, and we arrive at the fund's **expense ratio**. The expense ratio shows the administrative efficiency of the fund.

Both loaded and no-load open-end funds charge the following expenses, which are deducted from the fund's assets going forward:

- Management (investment advisory) fees
- Distribution fees
- Administrative service fees
- Transfer agent service fees

- Custodian fees
- Auditing and legal fees
- Shareholder reporting fees
- Registration statement and prospectus filing fees

Again, not all open-end funds have sales charges, but all open-end funds deduct operating expenses from portfolio income. Shareholders don't get a bill for the operating expenses, but whatever the fund takes out represents money that could have been paid to the shareholders in the form of dividends.

An open-end fund could be managed by an investment adviser, who then uses an outside distributor, transfer agent, etc. Management fees might be enough to interest the adviser to keep the fund open. At American Funds, on the other hand, the distributor, transfer agent, and investment adviser are all the same company. With over 50 different mutual funds all taking in fees from portfolio income it is not surprising that this company has grown since 1931 to be one of the biggest players in the industry.

Reducing the Sales Charge

Although A-shares charge a front-end load, investors can reduce that sales charge by employing various methods laid out in the prospectus.

Breakpoints

Breakpoints are quantity discounts. If the investor invests $1,000, he pays a higher sales charge than if he invests $100,000. For mutual funds, investors are rewarded with breakpoints. Let's say that the L & H Fund had the following sales charge schedule:

INVESTMENT	SALES CHARGE
<$50,000	5.5%
$50,000 – $99,999	5.0%
$100,000 – $149,999	4.0%
$150,000 – $199,999	3.0%

That means that an investor who buys $100,000 worth of the fund will pay a much lower sales charge than an investor who invests $20,000. In other words, less of her money will be deducted from her check when she invests. A breakpoint means that at this <u>point</u> the fund will give the shareholder this <u>break</u>. A lower sales charge means that an investor's money ends up buying more shares. For mutual funds, we don't pick the number of shares we want; we send in a certain amount of money and see how many shares our money buys us. With a lower sales charge, our money will buy us more shares. Keep in mind that fractional shares are common. For example, $1,000 would buy 12.5 shares if the POP were $80.

Breakpoints are available to individuals, husbands & wives, parents & minor child in a custodial account, corporations, partnerships, etc. So, if the mom puts in $30,000 and also puts in $20,000 for her minor child's UGMA account, that's a $50,000 investment in terms of achieving a breakpoint. The child cannot be an adult; he must be a minor. Corporations and other businesses qualify for breakpoints. About the only people who don't qualify for breakpoints are investment clubs.

Another important consideration for breakpoints is that a securities agent can never encourage an investor to invest a lower amount of money to keep him from obtaining a lower sales charge offered at the next breakpoint. That's called **breakpoint selling** and is a violation of FINRA rules. Likewise, if an agent fails to point out to an investor that a few more dollars invested would qualify for a breakpoint, that's just as bad as actively encouraging him to stay below the next breakpoint.

If a front-end-loaded fund has a breakpoint at $50,000, the registered representative should inform any investor who has even close to $50,000 to invest about that breakpoint. If the customer in the question has, say, $46,000, the agent must inform him about the breakpoint available for just $4,000 more.

Letter of Intent

What if the investor didn't have the $100,000 needed to qualify for that breakpoint? He could write a **letter of intent** explaining to the mutual fund his intention to invest $100,000 in the fund over the next 13 months. Now, as he sends in new money, say, $5,000 at a time, the fund applies the lower 4% sales charge, as if he'd already invested the full amount. The lower sales charge means he ends up buying more shares, right?

So, guess what the fund does? It holds those extra shares in a safe place, just in case he fails to invest that $100,000 he intended to. If he doesn't live up to his letter of intent, no big deal. He just doesn't get those extra shares. In other words, the higher sales charge applies to the money invested.

Also, that letter of intent could be backdated up to 90 calendar days to cover a previous purchase. If an investor bought $3,000 of the L & H fund on March 10, he might decide in early June that he should write a letter of intent to invest $50,000 over 13 months. He could backdate the letter to March 10 to include the previous investment and would then have 13 months from that date to invest the remaining $47,000.

If a test question says that one of your customers wants to invest today in a mutual fund with a front-end sales charge and is anticipating a large year-end bonus, make sure to inform the customer about the letter of intent (LOI) feature. That way he can approximate how much he'll be able to invest over the next 13 months and pay the lowest possible sales charge percentage.

Rights of Accumulation

If an investor's shares appreciate up to a breakpoint, the investor will receive a lower sales charge on additional purchases. In other words, when an investor is trying to reach a breakpoint, new money and account accumulation are counted the same way. So, if an investor's shares have appreciated to, say, $42,000 and the investor wanted to invest another $9,000, the entire purchase would qualify for the breakpoint that starts at $50,000. In other words, the $42,000 of value plus an additional $9,000 would take the investor past the $50,000 needed to qualify for the 5% sales charge.

This is known as **rights of accumulation**. Please note that this has nothing to do with a letter of intent. If you write a letter of intent to invest $100,000, you'll need to invest $100,000 of new dollars into the fund to get the breakpoint you're intending to get. Rights of accumulation means that you could save money on future purchases, based on the value of your account.

Combination Privilege

Most funds are part of a "family" of funds. Many of these fund families let investors combine a purchase in their Income Fund with, say, their Index or Growth Fund to figure a breakpoint. They call this a **combination privilege**. So, if the individual invests $20,000 in the Income Fund and $30,000 in the Growth Fund, that's considered a $50,000 investment in the family of funds, and that's the number they'd use to figure the breakpoint.

Conversion/Exchange Privilege

The fund might also offer a **conversion/exchange privilege**. This privilege allows investors to sell shares of, say, the L & H Growth Fund to buy shares of the L & H Income Fund at the NAV, rather than the higher POP. However, while buying the new shares on a net asset value basis is nice for the investor, the IRS considers the sale a taxable event. That means a capital gain or loss is realized on the date of the sale. An answer choice that mentions "deferring taxation until the new shares are sold," might sound logical but is also incorrect.

Structure and Operation

The following parties do not work for free. Who pays their expenses? The shareholders of the fund do, ultimately, as the following parties are paid through the deduction of operating expenses against the assets of the fund. The higher the expenses, the lower the dividend distributions to the shareholders of the fund, and vice versa.

Board of Directors

A mutual fund has a **board of directors** that oversees operations and policies of the fund or family of funds. The board's responsibilities include:

- establish investment policy
- select and oversee the investment adviser, transfer agent, custodian
- establish dividends and capital gains policy
- approve 12b-1 plans

As with a public company, the shareholders of the fund elect and re-elect the board members. Shareholders also vote their shares to approve the investment adviser's contract and 12b-1 fees. Independent board members have no other connection to the mutual fund sponsor or investment adviser, while the other board members either currently or recently had such a connection.

Investment Adviser

Each fund has an **investment adviser**, whose job is to manage the fund portfolio according to its stated objectives. For example, Capital Research and Management Company is the investment adviser for the American Funds. The board of directors sets the policies for investing, but it is Capital Research and Management making each purchase and sale for the portfolio.

Shareholders and the board vote to hire and retain investment advisers, who are paid a percentage of the fund's net assets. That's why they try so hard. The more valuable the fund, the more they get paid.

Their fee is typically the largest expense to a mutual fund. Investment advisers have to advise the fund (select the investments) in keeping with federal securities and tax law. They must also base their investment decisions on careful research of economic/financial trends. Since everything needs at least two names, the investment adviser is also called the "portfolio manager."

Custodian

The fund also keeps its securities and cash under the control of a **custodian**. Keeping track of all the dividends received from common and preferred stock held in the portfolio, interest payments from the bonds and money market instruments owned by the fund, purchases and sales, etc., is a big job, and the custodian performs it. The custodian is responsible for the payable/receivable functions involved when the portfolio buys and sells securities. That means they release the money and receive the securities purchased, and they accept the money and deliver the securities sold by the portfolio manager. When a security in the portfolio pays a dividend, the custodian receives it.

Transfer Agent

The **transfer agent** is the party that issues new shares to buyers and cancels shares that sellers redeem. Most of these shares are electronic files (book entry), but it takes a lot of work to issue and redeem them. While the custodian receives dividends and interest payments from the portfolio securities, it is the transfer agent that distributes income to the investors in the fund. The transfer agent acts as a customer service rep for the fund and often sends out those semi-annual and annual reports that investors have to receive. Investors can purchase and redeem shares directly with the transfer agent. The transfer agent also handles name changes when, for example, mutual fund shares are re-titled in the name of the estate for a now deceased investor.

Distributor

Funds are sponsored by broker-dealers acting as underwriters, who bear the costs of distributing the fund up front and are then compensated by the sales charge that they either earn themselves or split with the broker-dealers who make the sales. Underwriters (a.k.a. "wholesalers," "**distributors**," or "sponsors") also prepare sales literature for the fund, since they're the ones who will be selling the shares, either directly to the public or through a network of broker-dealers. If a fund acts as its own distributor, it usually covers the distribution costs through a 12b-1 fee, as we mentioned. The fund can call itself "no load" as long as the 12b-1 fee does not exceed .25% of net assets. To call itself "100% no-load" the fund could have neither a sales charge nor a 12b-1 fee.

These are the methods of distribution for mutual fund shares:

- Fund/to underwriter/to dealer/to investor
- Fund/to underwriter/to investor
- Fund/to investor (no-load funds)

Shareholder Voting

Mutual fund shareholders get to vote their shares in matters of major importance:

- Changes in investment policies and objectives
- Approval of investment adviser contract

- Approval of changes in fees
- Election of board members
- Ratification of independent auditors (PricewaterhouseCoopers, KPMG, etc.)

Closed-End Funds

The third type of investment company defined by the Investment Company Act of 1940 is the **management company**, under which we find both open-end funds and closed-end funds. So far, we've been talking mostly about the open-end funds. Let's say a few words on the closed-end variety at this point.

The main difference between the two is that open-end fund companies continually issue and redeem shares. When an agent finds an investor for an open-end fund, the fund issues new shares to the investor, which is why he had to sell them with a prospectus. Open-end funds don't do an IPO and then force shareholders to trade the fixed number of shares back and forth. Rather, they issue new shares every time someone wants to buy them, and they let the shareholders sell back the shares when they are ready to redeem them.

On the other hand, closed-end funds do an initial offering, at which point there is a fixed number of outstanding shares. What if a shareholder wants to sell his closed-end fund this afternoon? He trades it the same way he trades any other share of stock. How much will he receive? Whatever a buyer is willing to pay. These things usually trade at a discount to their NAV, or at a premium. It just depends on the supply and demand for the shares, and since this is such a small part of the secondary market, the pricing is less than efficient.

Therefore, if the test question says that the NAV is $9.45 with the POP at $9.00, something's up, right? Investors can't buy an open-end fund at a discount. As we saw, the cheapest they can buy them is at the NAV. B-shares are sold at the NAV and so are "no load" funds. But, no way can a public investor buy open-end shares at a discount. Only dealers, who are members of FINRA, get to do that. So, if the fund shares are selling below NAV, they have to be closed-end fund shares.

However, that doesn't mean that closed-end funds always trade at a discount. If people really want the shares, they might pay a premium. We're not saying that closed-end funds always trade at a discount to their NAV. We're saying that only the closed-end fund could do that. Really, it's because only the closed-end fund shares are traded between investors. The fund figures the NAV at the end of the day, but the shares trade back and forth all through the day, and not always in the most liquid or efficient market.

And, since closed-end shares trade the same way that GE or MSFT shares trade, investors can both purchase them on margin and sell them short. As we discuss elsewhere, "selling short" involves borrowing shares from a broker-dealer and selling them, with the obligation to buy them back and replace them later. If the price falls, you buy low after you already sold high. If the price rises, you're in trouble.

Another difference between open- and closed-end funds is that an investor would purchase, say, 100 shares of the closed-end fund and pay whatever that costs. For an open-end fund, he would cut a check for, say, $1,000, and see how many shares he ends up with next time they figure the NAV. In almost all cases, he will receive "full and fractional shares" with an open-end fund, which means that $100 would turn into 12.5 shares if the POP were $8.00. That little "point-5" of a share is the fractional share. For a closed-end fund, he would either buy 12 shares or 13 shares, not 12.5

Open-end funds only issue common stock to investors. Closed-end funds, on the other hand, issue preferred shares and use other forms of leverage, usually through bank borrowings or issuing auction rate preferred shares. These funds attempt to earn higher returns through such leverage, but the use of leverage also increases risks.

The investment objectives between an open-end and a closed-end fund could be exactly the same. There are closed-end corporate bond funds, tax-exempt bond funds, aggressive growth funds, etc. Nuveen Investments (www.nuveen.com) is the largest issuer of closed-end municipal bond funds. Why would an investor want those versus the open-end variety? Well, what happens to yield when the price of the bond drops—it goes up, right? So, if he can buy someone's closed-end bond fund at a discount, he just goosed his yield a little bit. What about when he wants to sell his shares someday? Nobody knows.

The expenses for closed-end funds include:

- Management fees
- Interest expense on borrowings
- Shareholder servicing
- Custodial fees
- Trustee fees
- Professional fees
- Shareholder reporting expenses
- Stock exchange listing fees
- Investor relations expenses

Open-end funds would not have stock exchange listing fees, as their shares do not trade among investors on the secondary market.

Although it's true that closed-end funds have a fixed number of shares, investors in the fund are able to reinvest their distributions into more shares. And, there are rights offerings for closed-end funds if the board of directors decides to do an additional offering of shares. The difference is that with open-end funds new investors can buy shares that are created on-the-fly by the open-end investment company.

Unit Investment Trusts (UITs)

Management companies are one type of registered investment company. **Unit Investment Trusts** are another. The Investment Company Act of 1940 defines a Unit Investment Trust (UIT) as:

```
an investment company which (A) is organized under a trust
indenture, contract of custodianship or agency, or similar
instrument, (B) does not have a board of directors, and (C) issues
only redeemable securities, each of which represents an undivided
```

```
interest in a unit of specified securities; but does not include a
voting trust.
```

The main differences between management companies and UITs include the fact that UITs do not trade their portfolio, do not therefore have an investment adviser, and do not have a board of directors. A UIT is a "supervised, unmanaged investment company," because while the portfolio is supervised by a trustee, the securities in it are not traded by an investment adviser the way most management companies would actively manage their assets. Running the trust does involve fees for bookkeeping, trustee fees, administrative fees, etc., but—again—no management fees are charged. When the shares are purchased an upfront sales charge is often added, or a deferred sales charge is imposed if and when the unit holder redeems.

Similar to a closed-end fund, a finite number of shares are offered to investors on the primary market. But, unlike, a closed-end fund, unit investment trust interests are redeemable as opposed to having to be traded at prices based on supply and demand. Also, unlike both open- and closed-end funds, unit investment trusts have a termination date, which means they have a limited duration. On the termination date, everything is liquidated, unit holders are paid out, and that's that.

Face-Amount Certificates

The Investment Company Act of 1940 defines a **face-amount certificate** company as:

```
an investment company which is engaged or proposes to engage in
the business of issuing face-amount certificates of the
installment type, or which has been engaged in such business and
has any such certificate outstanding
```

Think of a face-amount certificate as a debt security in which the certificate is purchased at a discount and redeemed at a future date for the higher face amount. Or, if presented early, the investor will receive the "surrendered value" at that point in time.

ETFs

As its name implies, an **ETF** or **exchange-traded fund** is a fund that trades on an exchange, as opposed to being redeemed or sold back to the issuer.

An ETF is typically an index fund, so if an investor wants to do as well as a particular index, she can track that index by purchasing an exchange-traded fund (ETF). To track the S&P 500, she can buy the "Spider," which is so named because it is an "SPDR" or "Standard & Poor's Depository Receipt." Of course, we already saw that she could do that with an S&P 500 open-end index fund. But, that is an open-end fund that has to be redeemed. No matter what time of day, if we put in a redemption order, we all receive the same NAV at the next calculated price. So, if the S&P 500 drops 80 points in the morning and rises 150 points by mid-afternoon, there is no way for us to buy low and then sell high. ETFs facilitate "intra-day trading," which means that you can buy and sell these things as many times as you want throughout the day.

Unlike the open-end versions, these ETFs can be bought on margin and can be sold short by investors who are "bearish" on the overall market or a particular index. If an investor is bearish on technology stocks overall, the answer might be for him to sell the QQQ short, as it represents the NASDAQ 100, the 100 hundred largest non-financial company stocks trading on NASDAQ. If he's right, he'll profit as those stocks drop in price. Or, an investor mostly in large cap stocks could hedge his risk by selling shares of the Dow ETF (Diamonds) short. This way if the index rises, his stocks make money, and if the index drops his short sale makes money.

So, are the ETFs cheaper than the open-end index fund versions?

Depends how you do it. For a small amount of money the open-end mutual fund is a great option. For larger amounts of money, though, the ETF is typically cheaper, as the flat commission paid becomes a smaller and smaller percentage of the amount invested. In other words, if the commission is $10 either way, a purchase of $300 is a bad idea, while a purchase of $30,000 would make that $10 insignificant.

As with the open-end index funds, ETFs offer diversification. For a rather small amount of money, an investor can own a little piece of, say, 500 different stocks with the SPDR, or 100 stocks with the QQQ. It is also easy to implement asset allocation strategies with ETFs. An investor can find ETFs that track all kinds of different indexes (small cap, value, growth, blue chip, long-term bonds, etc.). If an investor wanted to be 80% long-term bonds and 20% small-cap stock, that goal could be achieved with just two low-cost ETFs. This point is not necessarily a comparison to the open-end index funds, which would offer the same advantage. Rather, it is a comparison to purchasing individual bonds or small cap stocks. To spread the risk among many bonds and small cap stocks, an investor would have to spend large sums of money. With an ETF (as with the open-end index funds) diversification can be achieved immediately with a much smaller investment.

An ETF such as the SPDR (SPY) or Mid-Cap SPDR (MDY) is appropriate for most investors with a time horizon and risk tolerance suitable for stock (equity) investing in general.

FINRA Rule. Investment Company Securities

Mutual funds and variable annuities are both investment companies covered under the Investment Company Act of 1940. This rule tells member firms who act as underwriters/distributors of investment companies that they need to have a written sales agreement between themselves and other dealers spelling out all the terms of the business relationship. If the other dealer is not a FINRA member, they would have to pay the full public offering price, which would make it real tough for them to make a profit. Member firms must also transmit payment from customers to the mutual fund companies promptly.

Excessive Charges

This rule also tells member firms not to offer or sell shares of investment companies if the sales charges are excessive. What makes the sales charges excessive? 8.5% of the public offering price is the maximum sales charge. But, if the fund does not offer breakpoints and rights of accumulation that satisfy FINRA, the fund cannot charge 8.5%.

It would be a violation to describe a mutual fund as being "no load" or as having "no sales charge" if the investment company has a front-end (A shares) or deferred (B shares) sales charge, or whose 12b-1 fees exceed .25 of 1%.

Withhold Orders

This FINRA rule states that, "No member shall withhold placing customers' orders for any investment company security so as to profit himself as a result of such withholding." Another part of this rule says that member firms can only purchase investment company shares either for their own account or to fill existing customer orders—they can't just pick up a batch of shares and then see if anybody wants them, in other words.

Anti-Reciprocal Rule

Broker-dealers cannot decide to sell particular investment company shares based on how much trading business the investment company does or would consider doing through the firm. The old "pay to play" method is a big no-no, in other words. Be very broad in your understanding of this rule—if it looks at all as if a member firm is tying the promotion of particular funds to the amount of trading commissions they receive when the fund places trades through them, it's not passing the smell test. This would also apply to a member firm offering to compensate their branch managers and reps more for selling the shares of those investment companies who execute transactions through the firm, generating commissions.

So, I just told you that a broker-dealer (member firm) cannot sell mutual fund shares if the mutual fund trades through the broker-dealer, generating commissions for the member firm, right?

No. What I'm saying is that the firm can't tie the promotion/sale of the mutual fund to the level of trading the fund does or intends to do through the firm. Similarly, firms definitely compensate their branch managers and representatives for selling mutual fund shares; they simply can't compensate them more for selling the shares of the funds willing to "pay to play."

This all boils down to the fact that a broker-dealer should recommend a mutual fund because it's a suitable investment for a particular customer, not because the broker-dealer will make more money from the mutual fund when it executes its trades through the firm.

If a transaction involves the purchase of shares of an investment company that imposes a deferred sales charge when the investor redeems the shares someday, the written confirmation must also include the following legend: "On selling your shares, you may pay a sales charge. For the charge and other fees, see the prospectus." The legend must appear on the front of a confirmation and in, at least, 8-point type.

I am not making that up. 8-point type.

REITs

Investing in real estate has many advantages and disadvantages. The advantages are that property values often appreciate over time and that real estate provides diversification to a securities portfolio, since usually real estate and the stock market are not correlated. The disadvantages include the fact that real estate takes a lot of capital, and it isn't liquid. It often takes months or even years to get a property sold, or sold for a decent price, so the lack of liquidity keeps many investors from buying real estate, especially commercial real estate (shopping malls, skyscrapers, factories, etc.).

This is where publicly traded **REITs** come in. **A Real Estate Investment Trust** (REIT) is a company that owns a portfolio of properties and sells shares to investors. Investor can buy into REITs that own apartment buildings, office buildings, shopping centers, hotels, convention centers, self-storage units, timber—you name it. This way they can participate in real estate without having to be wealthy, and they can sell their shares as easily as selling shares of other publicly traded stock.

REITs are pooled investment vehicles that give the investor an ownership stake in a trust that owns real estate. They do not pass through losses (only real estate *partnerships* do that). REITS typically pay high dividend yields, but the dividend is taxed at ordinary income rates, not the kinder, gentler rate on qualified dividends that we will explore under Tax Considerations.

The type of REIT I just described is called an **Equity REIT**. A different type of REIT provides financing for real estate projects as opposed to just buying up and managing properties. These are called **Mortgage REITs,** and they provide financing as well as buy up mortgages and mortgage-backed securities. Some REITs do a little of both, and are called, fittingly, **Hybrid REITs.**

Private Funds

Investment company products are open to retail investors and can either be redeemed or traded whenever the markets are open. Publicly traded REITS are also open to retail investors, who do not have to sign net worth and risk acknowledgment statements the way they do for privately held REITS and the real estate limited partnerships we'll look at in a few pages. Private funds—including hedge funds, venture capital funds, and private equity funds—are also open only to sophisticated investors due to their risky investment strategies and relative lack of liquidity.

Hedge Funds

In general, **hedge funds** are only open to institutions and to individuals called **accredited investors.** An accredited investor has over $1 million in liquid net worth or makes > $200,000 per year. If it's a married couple, the assets held jointly count toward that $1 million figure, or the annual income needs to be > $300,000. The equity in the investor's primary residence is not counted toward the net worth minimum—we're talking about $1 million of net worth that could be invested.

Why does the investor need to meet net worth or income requirements? Because these hedge funds often use high-risk trading strategies including short selling, currency bets, and high levels of leverage, etc. If you're an average Joe and JoAnne, it wouldn't make sense to let you risk all of your investment capital on such high-risk investing. On the other hand, if you're a wealthy individual or an institution, chances are your hedge fund investment is just a percentage of the capital you invest. So, if you lose $1 million, chances are you have several more million where that came from.

A typical arrangement for a hedge fund is to have a limited number of investors form a private investment partnership. The fund typically charges 2% of assets as a management fee and extracts the first 20% of all capital gains. Then, they start thinking about their investors (we hope). Once you buy, there's a good chance you will not be able to sell your investment for at least one year. Rather than trying to beat an index such as the DJIA, hedge funds generally go for "absolute positive investment performance"—usually 8% or so—regardless of what the overall market is doing. In other words, hedge funds are designed to profit in *any* market environment, while index funds only work when the overall market—or the section of it represented by the index—is having a good year.

Now, although a **non-accredited purchaser** cannot invest directly in a hedge fund, there are mutual funds called **funds of hedge funds**, which she can invest in. As the name implies, these mutual funds would have investments in several different hedge funds. In most cases, the investor would not be able to redeem her investment, since hedge funds are illiquid (they don't trade among investors). Also, these investments would involve high expenses, since there would be the usual expenses of the mutual fund, on top of the high expenses of the hedge funds the mutual fund invests in.

The main testable points on hedge funds include:

- Designed to perform in any market environment
- Open to sophisticated, accredited investors with high net worth
- Illiquid—usually can't be sold for at least one year
- Employ riskier, more diverse strategies
- Charge high management fees and usually 20% of all gains
- Non-accredited purchasers can buy mutual funds that invest in hedge funds

Private Equity

Similar to a hedge fund, a **private equity fund** is structured as a limited partnership and is open only to sophisticated investors, as it is not liquid and generally takes on much greater risk than an open- or closed-end fund. As the name implies, private equity groups invest in securities that are not publicly traded. They often approach a company like Frank & Emma's Fruit Pies and cut a deal to buy all the common stock plus maybe a premium. After they appoint some better managers and board members, improve the profits at the acquired company, and get some good media buzz, maybe they then approach investment bankers to do an IPO so the owners can cash in as investors clamor for the stock. Private equity funds are typically set up for a period of time, maybe 10 years. After that, investors receive their money back from the general partner who set up the fund, plus—we hope—a profit.

The use of leverage is associated with private equity groups, whose acquisitions are often referred to as leveraged buyouts.

Venture Capital

Unlike private equity investors, **venture capital** firms typically focus on providing investments to early-stage companies, and rather than using leverage, VC firms typically use cash. Also, while private equity funds typically buy a company outright, venture capital funds typically make smaller investments in several companies in exchange for a minority stake.

 While private equity firms usually buy more mature companies, venture capitalists invest in much earlier-stage companies. Because most companies will fail, venture capital funds often invest smaller amounts in dozens of companies. The "VC" firms who invested early in companies such as Oracle, Microsoft, and Facebook realized mind boggling returns when those companies then offered shares to the public.

Uncovering the next grand-slam is the ultimate goal of a venture capitalist. Unfortunately, it's hard to see the future before it arrives.

Private equity investors buy a company that they expect to make more efficient and profitable, with—they hope—little risk of failure over the near-term. These investors plan to install new management and run the company for a while themselves. Venture capital investors, on the other hand, know that most of their investments will be losers; therefore, the returns are made on the handful of performers that survive and thrive. VC funds provide investment capital with a much more hands-off approach to running the companies in which they invest.

A private equity firm would purchase a company like the makers of Hostess snack cakes, fix it up, and then sell it. A venture capital firm would provide financing to an up-and-coming gluten-free snack cake maker who just did their first $1 million in revenue. And a hedge fund is more of a heavily traded portfolio of securities than a fund providing private investment capital to companies at various stages of their development.

Then again, the three terms (private equity, venture capital, and hedge funds) are subject to overlap. A hedge fund, for example, could end up buying a fast-food chain, although I would tend to think of that as "private equity." On the other hand, a private equity fund could provide capital to a less-mature enterprise, while a venture capital fund might occasionally purchase a young company outright.

Regardless, in all three cases the investors in the fund are taking on greater risk and are either institutions or accredited investors, with an investment adviser earning fees to manage the portfolio on their behalf.

Alternative Investments

Since mutual fund portfolios are open to retail investors, they can't focus on high-risk investment strategies. But, when the investors are all wealthy individuals and institutions, the regulators can relax a bit. Regulators, remember, provide necessary protection to investors, and sophisticated investors don't need so much protection to keep the playing field level. That's why such sophisticated investors can invest in the private funds we just looked at—private equity, venture capital, and hedge funds.

These investors can also invest in **direct participation programs**.

Limited Partnerships (DPPs)

A C-corporation is taxed as a business entity, with the owners then getting taxed on any dividend income that they distribute to themselves from the business's profits. C-corporations, in other words, lead to the double taxation of dividends for the owners.

On the other hand, in a direct participation program (DPP) the owners of the business take a share of the business entity's net income or net loss on their own personal income taxes. The partnership itself is not taxed. Rather, the partners are taxed on their share of the net income or net loss that flows through the business directly to them. Partnerships—like LLCs and S-corporations—are associated with **flow through** of net income/net loss to the owners.

There are partnerships organized to perform all kinds of business, from movie making to sports teams, from construction projects to law firms. Broker-dealers often raise capital for their investment banking customers looking to form natural resource or real estate ventures through DPP offerings.

Oil & gas programs could involve exploring for natural resources, developing proven reserves, or buying an income/production program. **Exploratory programs** for oil and gas are the riskiest programs with the highest return potential as well. The act of exploring for oil is sometimes called "wildcatting," which provides a hint of the risk/reward nature.

Exploration generates **intangible drilling costs** or **IDCs**. As opposed to capitalized costs sunk into the  oil rig and other equipment, intangible drilling costs are the costs/expenses that leave nothing to be recovered. IDCs include labor costs and the expense of the geological survey indicating there is—or should be—oil or natural gas down below. The IDCs in these programs are so high in the first few years that this type of program typically provides the most tax shelter to the investor, especially in the early years. Beyond IDCs, drilling programs take depreciation expenses on any equipment owned, which also may provide tax shelter to the LPs.

Sometimes DPPs drill for oil or gas in an area where these natural resources are already being extracted, with engineering studies confirming the existence of oil or natural gas below the ground. Such programs are called **developmental programs**. They're less risky than exploratory programs, but with a lower return potential. Some call these "step-out" programs, as if someone is starting at the existing well and stepping out so many paces before constructing another one. These programs also provide tax shelter through the intangible drilling costs we just looked at. And, there is depreciation on the expensive equipment if the partnership owns that equipment as opposed to leasing it.

The safest natural resources programs buy existing production and are called **income programs**. These investments provide immediate cash flow and are, therefore, the safest programs with the lowest potential reward. When I say they are "safe," I mean for a DPP. Even though income is expected, the prices of oil and natural gas are extremely volatile, making both the income and the investment's value difficult to estimate. And, as always, DPP investments are not liquid—there are no buyers standing ready should the investor wish to sell. The main tax advantage offered from these programs comes in the form of **depletion.** When oil or natural gas is sold, the partnership takes a charge/expense against their revenue, basically for depleting their assets. If the business entity owns the drilling equipment, depreciation may also provide tax shelter to the LPs.

In real estate, which is riskier, buying raw land or buying an apartment complex already filled with renters? **Raw land** is purely speculative and is, therefore, the riskiest type of real estate DPP. You buy parcels of land betting that an airport or industrial park will be built in the next few years. If you're right, the land appreciates in value. If not, it doesn't. And, you receive no income or tax benefits on raw land as you sit waiting for its value to go up. There is nothing to deplete, and land does not depreciate the way apartment buildings and oil rigs do.

New construction programs are aggressive programs, but once the projects are completed the townhouses or condominiums can be sold for capital gains. So they're safer than raw land and probably provide a lower reward potential. They also involve more costs, of course, as someone has to finance all that construction. For a construction program lasting several years, the LPs are likely to receive a share of net loss at the beginning, as the partnership sinks capital into building a townhouse community on the front end, hoping to sell enough units on the back end to turn a profit.

Existing properties DPPs are similar to income programs for oil. Here, the business is already up and running, with immediate cash flow. Investors can examine the financial statements and know what they're getting into, as opposed to an investment in raw land. Therefore, existing property DPPs offer lower risk and lower reward to investors. The tax shelter comes through depreciation of the buildings themselves as well as any maintenance equipment owned by the partnership.

Another common type of limited partnership is the **equipment leasing program.** These partnerships typically lease equipment that other companies do not want to own. For example, computers, transportation equipment, oil drilling and construction equipment, etc., might not be cost-effective for the users to own; therefore, it makes more sense to lease such equipment from an equipment leasing program. Tax benefits for equipment leasing would come largely through depreciation of the equipment.

Tax credits are the benefit for **government-assisted housing** programs. That means that if the partnership builds, acquires, or rehabs a government-assisted housing project, it will benefit from tax credits, and possibly from subsidy payments from the federal government. Or, a local government might provide tax credits to a partnership that does historic rehab or repurposing of former train stations or water pumping stations into shopping or restaurant districts, for example.

Either way, remember that a tax credit is always better than a tax deduction of an equal dollar amount. In fact, let's compare a $100,000 tax deduction to a $100,000 tax credit:

	$1,000,000	Income		$1,000,000	Income
-	$100,000	Deduction		x .30	30% tax rate
	$900,000	Net Income		$300,000	Tax
x .30		30% tax rate	-	$100,000	CREDIT
	$270,000	Tax		$200,000	Tax

Notice how a deduction is subtracted from the top line—revenue. For a credit, you figure the amount of tax you were going to have to pay, and then apply the credit dollar-for-dollar against that amount.

Surprisingly, there is no requirement that a "DPP" has to be formed as a limited partnership. Here is how FINRA defines the term "direct participation program":

> *...a program which provides for flow-through tax consequences regardless of the structure of the legal entity or vehicle for distribution including, but not limited to, oil and gas programs, real estate programs, agricultural programs, cattle programs, condominium securities, Subchapter S corporate offerings and all other programs of a similar nature, regardless of the industry represented by the program, or any combination thereof.*

GPs and LPs

The owners who provide most of the capital to the business are the **limited partners (LPs).** They are called "limited partners" because their liability is limited to their investment. If they invest $100,000, then $100,000 is all they can lose as passive investors in the partnership. Creditors can't come after the LPs for their personal assets if the business goes bankrupt. Lawsuits of all types could be filed against the partnership, but, again, the LPs would not have their personal assets at risk in such cases.

To maintain their limited liability status the limited partners need to stay out of day-to-day management of the business. Day-to-day management is left solely to the **general partner (GP).** As manager, the GP can also be compensated for these managerial efforts through a salary. While the LPs provide most of the capital, the GP (general partner) must have at least a 1% financial interest in the partnership as well. The GP is granted the authority to acquire and sell property on behalf of the business and sign any documents on behalf of the business required to carry out its management. The GP has to keep accurate books and records and must provide annual financial statements to the LPs. Typically, the GP can also admit new limited partners at his discretion.

Unlike an LP, the general partner has unlimited liability. That is why the GP is often a corporation, providing the individual controlling the business protection for his or her personal assets. The general partner is also a fiduciary to the limited partners. That means the GP has to maintain a duty of loyalty and good faith to the investors trusting him to manage the business using their invested capital.

The GP's fiduciary responsibility to the limited partners means he must put the interests of the partnership ahead of his own interests or the interests of other businesses in which he is involved. The GP can't compete with the partnership through some other business venture and, therefore, can't charge some bogus "no compete" payment—since they can't compete in the first place. When the GP sells a building, piece of equipment, or the business itself, he/they must refrain from receiving economic gain at the expense of the limited partners. As with an investment adviser, if there are any conflicts of interest involved, these must be fully disclosed to the LPs. Note that the LPs have no such duty to refrain from owning businesses that compete with the partnership.

The GP could provide a loan to the business, but as a fiduciary to the LPs, he would have to disclose any conflicts of interest he might have. For example, if he's lending money to the partnership through a savings & loan institution that he controls or owns shares in, this potential conflict of interest that could end up clouding his judgment must be disclosed. On the one hand, he wants to help the business. On the other hand, he likes to help his own lending institution. That is an example of a conflict of interest that an honest GP will consider and disclose to the LPs rather than waiting for them to sue for breach of fiduciary duty.

Limited partners stay out of day-to-day management decisions, but because of **partnership democracy** they do get to vote on major issues like suing the GP or dissolving the partnership. Why would they sue the GP? Maybe the oil & gas program turns out to be a scam in which the sponsor is using partners' money to fund other businesses or a high-rolling lifestyle. Viewers of *American Greed* know that stranger things have happened in the world of investments.

If the exam asks if LPs can make loans to the partnership, the answer is yes. In other words, some of the capital LPs provide to the partnership can be through debt securities paying a reasonable rate of interest. If you're in business for yourself, you may have fronted some cash to your business and then had the business pay you a rate of interest on the "promissory note." Same idea here. Some partnerships might have investors providing capital in exchange for debt securities that later to convert to equity in the business. There are many ways to structure the financing of a DPP.

Documents

The General Partner is responsible for filing the **certificate of limited partnership** with the state where the entity is organized. This is a public document that provides only the most basic information, including the name and address of the partnership, the name and addresses of all the general partners as well as the registered agent who would accept any "service of process" should a lawsuit arise against the business. The GP signs and files this document with the state where the business is organized.

The **partnership agreement** is signed by all partners and is the foundation for the partnership. In this agreement we would find the following information:

- business purpose of the partnership
- effective date and term of operation (if termination date or event is stated)
- required capital commitments now and in future for GP and LP
- name and address of GP
- principal place of business for the partnership
- powers and limitations of the GP's authority
- allocation of profits and losses
- distributions of cash
- transfer of interests
- withdrawal, removal of a partner

Corporations are presumed to go on for perpetuity. A partnership is also assumed to live on indefinitely unless the partnership agreement establishes a date or triggering event for dissolution of the entity. For example, a new construction program may dissolve when the last townhouse has been sold. Or, if the GP dies, the business may dissolve according to the stipulations in the agreement.

Suitability

While there are potential rewards to DPP investments, there are also plenty of risks. First, the business venture might strike out. Right across from our former offices in Forest Park, IL, we watched a large new construction program borrow $15 million and then go belly up when only one unit was sold. After spending untold sums sandblasting the original beams and posts, there must have been over 1,000 new windows installed in an old factory building, all of them eventually either broken by vandals, removed and sold for pennies-on-the-dollar, or smashed by the wrecking ball that eventually came. I'm thinking the partners in that program have made better investments.

Second, the IRS might determine that the partnership is an abusive tax shelter, set up to generate deductions through depreciation or depletion without ever intending to be economically viable. A DPP may be considered abusive if it's based on a false assumption or if the partnership overstated property values to take large depreciation deductions. If that happens, the IRS can suddenly disallow deductions that the partners previously claimed, causing investors to pay back taxes *plus* interest and penalties. If the IRS suspects the program was designed for tax losses without any intent to be run like a profitable business, they can go after everyone connected to the program with the full force of the IRS: audits, penalties, interest, seizure of assets, etc.

So, a registered representative must never recommend a DPP investment that has no chance of profitability based solely on the share of losses it will provide to the investor. When considering the economic viability of a direct participation program investment, a securities agent and his customer would consider:

- economic soundness of the program
- expertise of the general partner
- basic objectives of the program
- start-up costs

For example, if this is a real estate new construction program, has the General Partner already done a few successful programs like this, or is he doing his first big deal with the Limited Partners' money, therefore, at greater risk? If the price of oil and/or natural gas has plummeted, does it make sense to sink capital into start-up costs for an oil & gas exploration program?

Once economic viability of the business has been determined, the next consideration is tax benefits. If investors have **passive income**, they can use **passive losses** from DPPs to offset them for tax purposes. On the other hand, if they do not have passive income to offset, an agent may not recommend a program based on the tax shelter it provides, since they would not be able to benefit from that feature. And, some programs—including raw land—provide no tax benefits at all, regardless of the investor's tax situation.

The last thing a DPP investor should be in need of is liquidity because, basically, there isn't any. All investors must understand that a DPP investment is long-term and not liquid. A money market mutual fund investment is as liquid as one could find, while an investment in a DPP is on the other side of the liquidity spectrum. There are often estimates or target dates as to when LPs might be able to get some or all of their investment back, but these are only estimates.

Structured Products

As opposed to buying common stock or bonds issued by, say, GE, **structured products** are created and sold by financial intermediaries with terms that are mutually agreed upon by both parties.

We have looked at both bonds and ETFs in earlier sections. An **ETN (Exchange Traded Note)** has characteristics of both a bond and an ETF. An ETN is a type of unsecured debt security issued by a financial institution, e.g., Barclays Capital. This type of debt security differs from other types of bonds and notes because ETN returns are based upon the performance of an underlying benchmark minus fees. The benchmark could be a market index, a foreign currency, or commodities. No coupon payments are distributed during the investor's holding period and no principal protections exist. The issuer is borrowing the investor's money for a certain time frame, paying it all back (we hope) with interest at maturity, with the rate of interest dependent on the performance of the benchmark.

At maturity, the issuer pays the investor a sum of money based on the performance of the benchmark, investor fees, and the calculation explained in the prospectus for the ETN. During the holding period the value of the ETN fluctuates primarily based on two factors: the performance of the benchmark and the creditworthiness of the issuer. As with any bond, if the issuer's creditworthiness drops, so does the value of the security. ETNs can be traded on the secondary market, but, as with anything that can be traded on the secondary market, the price received could be less than what the investor paid. And, ETNs are generally not as liquid as stocks, bonds, and money market securities. The test might say that ETNs are subject to market risk, credit risk, and liquidity risk.

A big difference between ETNs and ETFs is that, while ETFs invest in securities that allow them to track the underlying benchmark, ETNs do not own what they are tracking.

OTC options are exotic options traded on the over-the-counter market, where participants can choose the characteristics of the options traded (offers flexibility).

HOLDRs are a financial product created by Merrill Lynch and traded daily on the American Stock Exchange that allows investors to buy and sell a basket of stocks in a sector, industry or other classification in a single transaction. The abbreviation stands for Holding Company Depository Receipt. There are currently 17 different HOLDRs currently trading on AMEX.

HOLDRs are often confused or lumped in with ETFs. As Think Advisor explains, "Essentially, a HOLDR is a static basket of stocks selected from a industry. As a result, HOLDRs do not track an underlying index like ETFs, and represent a rather narrow slice of an industry. Not only are HOLDRs completely unmanaged, their components almost never change. Furthermore, if a company is acquired and removed from a HOLDR, its stock is not replaced. This can result in even more concentration and added risk. In contrast, indexes that ETFs invest in can change and rebalance with some regularity, and generally contain more components. Such is the case with Barclay's 'iShares' and Vanguard's ETFs called 'VIPERs' (Vanguard Index Participation Equity Receipts), which collectively track Standard & Poor's and MSCI indexes." (http://www.thinkadvisor.com/2005/08/18/holdrs-vs-etfs-what-investors-should-know.

The term **leverage** sometimes refers to borrowed money but more generally refers to an investment promising higher returns on a percentage basis due to increased exposure to risk. For example, in a margin account the investor takes on the risk of borrowing money at a rate of interest, hoping to receive twice the returns he would have made on a percentage basis by being twice as exposed to the risks of the marketplace. With call options speculators can make much larger percentage gains than on the underlying stock and do so by putting down just a percentage of the stock's market price. On the other hand, options can lead to quick and painful losses when the speculator is on the wrong side of the market.

A **leveraged ETF** uses derivatives to increase the fund's exposure to the underlying index. Some funds are "2X," or exposed to the index in a way that will double the gains or losses. In other words, they are designed to go up or down 10% if the S&P 500 or other index goes up or down just 5%. Some funds are even "3X," designed to triple the exposure to the index and, therefore, triple the gains (or losses) to investors.

Leveraged funds are only for the short-term. In fact, the exposure is re-set each trading day and designed to capture the 2 or 3X returns for just that one day. The products are really designed for institutional and other sophisticated investors due to their complexity and amplified exposure to stock, bond, or commodities markets.

ETF shares can be sold short, as the shares trade throughout the day alongside shares of any public company you care to name. This allows investors to hedge their market risk by betting against the overall market with a percentage of their portfolio. If a trader thinks the S&P 500 will drop today, he can sell an ETF tracking the index short. If he's right, he'll make some money with that speculation, which will offset whatever he loses on his stock portfolio.

Inverse ETFs are designed to bet against an index, and most such funds do so at a 2 or 3X multiplier by using derivatives. This means that a leveraged inverse ETF is designed to move in the opposite direction of the index by a factor of 2 or 3. A 2X leveraged inverse fund is designed on a daily basis to, for example, rise 10% if the index drops 5%. Another name for a leveraged inverse fund is an "ultra-short fund." An example of a popular ultra-short fund is the *ProShares UltraShort S&P 500 ETF*, stock symbol SDS. As a helpful guide at the NASDAQ website explains, "Launched in July 2006, this fund seeks to deliver twice the inverse of the daily performance of the S&P 500 Index. With holdings of 500 securities, the fund has a certain tilt towards the technology sector with Apple Inc. (AAPL), Exxon Mobil (XOM) and General Electric (GE) as the top three firms. The product is largely concentrated in large cap firms with a 91% share, while the remainder goes to mid and small caps."

As tricky as an inverse and leveraged ETF might be, I would have to nominate the **viatical** or **life settlement** as the most alternative of all alternative investments. The investment vehicle is created when someone with a life insurance policy wants to receive most of the benefit right now while he's alive. If the policy has a $1 million death benefit, the viatical settlement would involve the buy-side purchasing the policy for more than its cash surrender value but at a discount to the $1 million death benefit. The third-party buyer then becomes the owner of the policy, paying any premiums due. Then, when the insured dies, the investor collects the full death benefit of $1 million.

But, wouldn't that imply that the sooner the insured dies the higher the investor's yield, and vice versa? Indeed. As I said—an extremely alternative approach to investing. A viatical settlement meets the definition of a security according to the state securities regulators. However, it is not liquid. If you purchase a viatical settlement, you may have to keep paying premiums, and you will only receive payment when the insured dies because there is no secondary market for these alternative investments. Unlike a bond investment, there is no annual return offered, and the actual return the investor receives is unpredictable since no one—except those relying on foul play—can accurately predict when someone is going to die.

The advantage is that this sort of investment would definitely provide diversification to the investor. And, since death benefits are not taxable, the gain made upon payout is tax-free.

Mortgages are pooled and sold to investors through Ginnie Mae and Fannie Mae securities. Life settlements are sometimes pooled into "death bonds." Here, investors buy shares of a diversified pool of life insurance policies. As with an individual life settlement, the investors will profit based on how long premiums must be paid on the policies versus how soon the death benefits in the pool are paid out to investors.

Other Assets

Shopping centers, office buildings, industrial centers, and apartments are all examples of real estate investment properties that take investors outside the world of securities. Historically, such investments have provided a hedge to a securities portfolio because the real estate market is not highly correlated with the stock and bond markets.

Real estate is not all upside, of course. It is often hard to sell an office building, or to sell it at an attractive price. In other words, it is illiquid. Also, rental property may require a management company or may require a major time commitment by the owner himself. And, unlike an investment in common stock, real estate investments often involve repairs, upgrades, insurance and many other expenses.

Bond investors face inflation risk. Therefore, some fixed-income investors hedge their risk by investing in gold, silver, and other **precious metals**. During inflationary periods or periods of financial uncertainty investors often bid up the price of such metals. Precious metals are used in coins, jewelry, and many varied industrial applications. The four main precious metals are gold, silver, platinum, and palladium.

There are several ways to invest in precious metals. Investors can buy bullion (bars of gold, silver, platinum, etc). Or, they can buy certain coins made of the four main precious metals. Some investors buy precious metals mutual funds that hold shares in mining companies. There are also ETFs that hold bullion in each of the four major precious metals. ETFs and mutual funds make it convenient to invest. Holding actual gold coins or bars of silver might be more fun. However, holding bullion or coins requires storage, security, and insurance.

Inflation makes it hard for consumers to keep up. It also means that commodity prices are high. Therefore, investors may add investments in cocoa, live cattle, or light, sweet crude oil to their portfolios to hedge their inflation or purchasing power risk.

To invest in **commodities** such as pork bellies, sugar, corn, and soybeans investors may open a commodity futures trading account or may purchase an Exchange Traded Note tied to the price of commodities. We will look at commodity futures contracts at the end of the next section.

When investors buy stocks and bonds on the primary market, they provide capital to an issuing corporation. If the company avoids default on the bonds, all the bondholders win at maturity. IPO investors who hold the stock long-term all win if the company continues to expand profits over their holding period.

This is not how it works with derivatives. With a derivative one side wins, the other loses. If a speculator buys options and wins $3,000, it is because the seller of the options lost $3,000. That's why they call derivatives a zero-sum game.

Derivative securities are contracts that derive their value from some other thing, known as the underlying instrument. Derivatives include warrants, options, futures, and forwards. The underlying instruments whose value drives the derivatives' value could be common stock or stock indexes, interest rates, or agricultural commodities such as corn and soy beans.

Warrants

A **warrant** gives the holder the right to buy the issuer's common stock for a set price regardless of how high the stock price rises on the secondary market. There are no dividends attached to a warrant. If an investor owns a warrant, all he owns is the opportunity to purchase a company's stock at a pre-determined price. If a warrant lets him buy XYZ for $30 per-share as of some future date, he will benefit if the stock price rises above $30 by that date.

When issued, the exercise price stated on the warrant is above the current market price of the stock. It usually takes a long time for a stock's price to go above the price stated on the warrant, assuming that ever happens at all. But, they're good for a long time, typically somewhere between two and ten years.

Warrants are often included in a bond offering. As we saw earlier, corporations pay interest to borrow money through bonds. If they include warrants, they can "sweeten the deal" and offer investors a lower interest payment. Why would one investor take 4% when his buddy gets 6% on his bond? Doesn't the buddy make $60 a year, while the other investor only makes $40 per $1,000? Yes. But if the company's common stock rises, the buddy will be making $60 a year, while the other investor could make a profit on the common stock.

Warrants are issued by the company itself. Equity options, on the other hand, are created by options exchanges and are based on the price of various public company stocks. So, MSFT might issue warrants to certain investors, but a MSFT call or put option is not issued by Microsoft. It is issued by the options exchanges, with Microsoft's permission but not their participation.

Options

A guy steps into a tavern. He sits down at the last open stool and slaps a stack of twenties on the bar, just loud enough to get the bartender's attention. The bartender looks up from the pitcher of pale ale she's pouring.

"Just a second," she says, afraid to take her eyes off the thick head of foam forming at the top.

"No hurry," the guy says, although it's clear he's not in the mood to wait.

163

Bartender finally comes up and takes his order. Bourbon and Pepsi. Not Coke—Coke's for losers. He wants *Pepsi* with his bourbon, okay?

The bartender shrugs and mutters something as she mixes his drink.

Three guys sitting to his right take the bait.

"You don't like Coke, huh, buddy?" says the dark-haired guy in the wrinkled white shirt.

"Nope," the guy says. "Don't like the drink, don't like the stock."

"What, you're a trader?" the blond guy with big shoulders says, wiping foam from his mustache.

"Just a guy who says Coke is headed where it belongs—in the toilet."

The three friends laugh and mutter among themselves for a while, not quite within earshot of the big guy badmouthing Coca-Cola.

"That's a bold statement," the dark-haired guy says. "My dad drove a route for Coke twenty years by the way."

"Good for him," the guy says. "Used to be a decent company—that's history, though. I say Coke is a dog, and I'll bet anybody at this bar it won't go above twenty-five bucks a share the rest of the year."

He says the last part loud enough to get everyone's attention. Even the jukebox seems to quiet down at this point.

"Oh yeah?" someone shouts from a corner booth. "I'll take that bet."

"Me, too!" someone yells from over by the pool tables.

Pretty soon the guy has over a dozen happy hour customers standing in line to bet that Coca-Cola common stock will, without a doubt, rise above $25 a share at some point between today (March 1) and the rest of the year.

The guy breaks out a stack of cocktail napkins and on each one he writes the following:

Anyone who thinks Coca-Cola common stock will rise above $25 a share has to pay $300. Guy ends up collecting $300 from 15 different customers, walking out with $4,500 in premiums.

What's his risk as he steps onto the rainy sidewalk outside?

Unlimited. See, no matter how high Coca-Cola common stock goes between today and the 3rd Friday of December, this guy would have to sell it to any holder of the cocktail napkin for $25 a share. Theoretically, his risk is unlimited, since there's no limit to how much he'd have to pay to get the stock.

What if the stock never makes it above $25 in the next 9 months? That's his best possible outcome. If it never makes it above $25, no one will ever call him to buy the stock for $25. In short, he'll walk away with the $4,500 in premiums, laughing at all the suckers at the bar who bet the wrong way.

What the guy sold at the bar was a Coca-Cola Dec 25 call @3. As the writer of that option, he granted any buyer willing to pay $300 the right to buy 100 shares of Coca-Cola common stock for $25 per-share anytime between today and the end of the contract. When would the person holding that option want to use or exercise it?

Only if Coca-Cola were worth more than $25 a share. In fact, since they each paid $3 a share for this right, Coca-Cola will have to rise above $28—their breakeven point—before it ever becomes worth the trouble of exercising the call. I mean, they *could* exercise it, but why bother?

Either way, the guy who wrote the calls gets the $4,500 in premiums. If Coke never makes it above $25, he'll never have to lift a finger. Just smile as the calls expire on the third Friday of December. We said derivatives are a zero-sum game. If an option expires, the seller realizes his maximum gain, while the buyer realizes his maximum loss. In this case, the buyers would lose a total of $4,500, and the seller would make/keep that amount.

Think of a call option as a bet between a buyer and a seller. The buyer says the price of something is going up. The seller disagrees. Rather than argue about it, they buy and sell call options.

The buyer pays the seller a **premium.** Because he pays some money, he gets the right to buy 100 shares of a particular stock for a particular price within a particular time frame. If the buyer has the right to buy the stock, the seller has the obligation to sell the stock to the buyer at the already agreed upon price, if the buyer chooses to exercise that right.

Buyers have rights. Sellers have obligations.

The buyer pays a premium, and he receives the right to buy the underlying stock at a stated price. That price is known as the **strike price** or **exercise price**.

Calls

A "MSFT Aug 70" **call** gives the call buyer the right to buy MSFT common stock for $70 at any time up to the **expiration date** in August. If the stock goes up to $90 before expiration, the owner of the call could buy the stock for $70. If MSFT went up to $190, the call owner could buy it at the strike price of $70. So you can probably see why call buyers make money when the underlying stock goes up in value.

Call buyers are betting that the stock's market price will go above the strike price. That's why they're called "bulls." Bull = up. If you hold an Aug 70 call, that means you're "bullish" on the stock and would like to see the underlying stock go above 70. How far above?

As far as possible. The higher it goes, the more valuable your call becomes. Wouldn't you love to buy a stock priced at $190 for only $70?

That's what call buyers are hoping to do.

So for a call, compare the strike price to the stock's market price. Whenever the underlying stock trades above the strike price of the call, the call is **in-the-money**. A MSFT Aug 70 call is in-the-money as soon as MSFT begins to trade above $70 a share. If MSFT were trading at $80 a share, the Aug 70 call is in-the-money by exactly $10.

Notice how we are not referring to a buyer or seller when we say a call is in-the-money. One problem with buying options is that you might end up paying, say, $5 a share and even though the call does go in-the-money by $3 a share, you lose that difference. We'll talk about buyers' gains and losses in a minute. For now understand that any time the market price is higher than the strike price, the call is in-the-money. Period.

The Premium

Option **premiums** represent the probability that a buyer could win. If the premium is cheap, it's a long shot. If the premium is expensive, things are probably already working in favor of the buyer with time left for things to get even better.

For example, if MSFT common stock now trades for $28 a share, the right to buy it next month for $40 is all but worthless, while the right to buy it for $30 has some chance of working out for the buyer and would, therefore, trade at a higher premium. The right to buy the stock for $30 through next month is also not worth as much as the right to buy it for $30 through the next three or four months, right? The premiums would show that this is exactly right. For call options, the premiums rise as the strike prices drop, and as time goes out.

If today were St. Patrick's Day, a MSFT Mar 20 call is worth more than a MSFT Mar 25 call, but a MSFT May 20 call is worth more than both. Why? The right to buy MSFT for $20 is worth more than the right to pay $25, and the right to do so for two extra months is worth even more.

Time and Intrinsic Value

There are only two types of value that an option can have: **intrinsic value** and **time value**. For calls, intrinsic value is another way of stating how much higher the stock price is compared to the strike price of the call. If the underlying stock is trading at $75, the MSFT Aug 70 call is how far in-the-money? Five dollars. The stock price is above the call's strike price by $5; therefore, the call has intrinsic value of five dollars. That means an investor could save $5 by owning that call and using it to buy the underlying stock.

But, if the stock is trading below the strike price, the option is out-of-the-money. With MSFT trading at $65, the Aug 70 call would have no intrinsic value. So, if there is a premium to be paid for this out-of-the-money call, it's only because there's plenty of time for things to improve. If the option doesn't expire for another three months, speculators might decide the stock could climb more than 5 points in that period. If so, the market will attach time value to the call. Time value means that the option could become more valuable given the amount of time left before expiration.

Whenever a call is at- or out-of-the-money, the premium represents time value only. Whenever a call is in-the-money, we can find the time value attached to it by subtracting intrinsic value from the premium. Let's say MSFT common stock is trading at $72, and the MSFT Aug 70 calls are selling for a premium of $3. That means the call is in-the-money by $2 ($72 market vs. 70 strike price), yet an investor has to pay a premium of $3. So, where is that extra dollar coming from?

Time value. If there is plenty of time on the option, speculators might gladly pay an extra dollar, even if the stock is only above the strike price by $2 at this point.

	PREMIUM	3
•	INTRINSIC VALUE	• 2
	TIME VALUE	1

For calls, intrinsic value is a way of stating how much higher the stock price is than the strike price. Time value equals whatever is left in the premium above that number.

What if MSFT were trading at $69 with the MSFT Aug 70 calls @3—how much time value would that represent?

	PREMIUM	3
•	INTRINSIC VALUE	• 0
	TIME VALUE	3

All time value. With the stock trading at only $69, the right to buy it at $70 has no intrinsic value. In fact, if the stock were trading right at the strike price of 70, there would be no intrinsic value to the MSFT Aug 70 call, right? If we want to buy a $70 stock for $70, do we need to buy an option?

No. We only buy the call because we want to end up buying the stock for less than it's currently trading, which will happen if the stock moves above the strike price.

So, if we pay $5 for a MSFT Aug 70 call with the stock trading at $70 (at-the-money) or below (out-of-the-money), we pay purely for the time value of the option.

Breakeven, Max Gain, Max Loss

So far we've been talking about the option itself. If we're looking at the investor, we have to remember that he won't begin to profit until the stock starts trading above the strike price by an amount greater than what he paid for the call. If an investor paid $5 for an Aug 70 call, he will only start making money when the stock goes above $75. So, he breaks even (BE) at $75 and begins to profit above $75.

$$\text{Strike Price} + \text{Premium} = \text{Breakeven}$$

$$70 \quad + \quad 5 \quad = \quad 75$$

What about the guy who sells the MSFT Aug 70 call @5. Where does that investor break even?

Same place: Strike price plus premium.

If the stock goes up to $75, the buyer's 70 call is worth $5 (intrinsic value). He could then sell it for exactly what he paid and be even. The seller, however, sold the option for $5 and could now (to avoid being exercised) buy it back for its intrinsic value of $5, leaving him even. In other words, the breakeven point is where the buyer and seller "tie." Nobody's made anything, but nobody's lost anything.

Breakeven, maximum gain, and maximum loss are all hypothetical situations. Sometimes we calculate what happened for an options investor. Sometimes we figure out what could happen. If the test is talking about breakeven, maximum gain, or maximum loss, it is asking us to look at what could happen. This is how it works for calls:

Buyers

The maximum loss is the premium they pay. Why? Because buyers can only lose whatever they pay for the option, end of story.

To find the breakeven point add the premium to the strike price. A MSFT Aug 70 call @5 would have a breakeven point of $75. Strike price of 70 + premium of 5 = 75.

There is no limit to the call buyer's maximum gain. How high can the price of the underlying stock go before expiration?

Nobody knows. That's why the buyer's maximum gain is unlimited. His purchase price is fixed as the "strike price." The sell price is unlimited; it's wherever the market takes the stock, with no limit on the upside.

Sellers

What's the most that the seller can win on this call option?

Sellers can only make the premium. Always. So, the seller's maximum gain is the premium.

The breakeven point is the same for buyers and sellers: strike price + premium.

The call seller's maximum loss is unlimited. His sale price is fixed at the strike price. His purchase price is wherever the market takes the stock, which could be as high as infinity. When the investor sells a call without first owning the stock, he is said to be establishing a **naked call** position. The maximum loss on a naked call is unlimited.

As we see, whatever the buyer can win, that's what the seller can lose. Whatever the buyer can lose, that's all the seller can win. Buyers and sellers break even at the same place. Again, zero-sum game.

CALL BUYER	CALL SELLER
Max Loss = Premium	Max Gain = Premium
Max Gain = Unlimited	Max Loss = Unlimited
Breakeven = Strike Price + Premium	Breakeven = Strike Price + Premium

Gains and Losses

Before we move forward, let's remember that options go in-the-money or out-of-the-money. People don't do that. People have gains and losses, based on how much they paid for an option versus how much they received for the option. So, terms such as time value, intrinsic value, in-the-money, out-of-the-money, and at-the-money refer only to options. Terms such as gains, losses, and breakeven refer to the options investor. Like this:

THE OPTION	THE INVESTOR
Time value	Gains
Intrinsic value	Losses
In-the-money, out-, at-the-money	Breakeven

The T-chart

When the exam wants you to tell it whether an investor ends up with a gain or a loss, and exactly how much he or she gained or lost, approach the problem step-by-step. These are essentially bookkeeping questions, where you track everything the investor paid and everything he/she received. This might seem complicated, but luckily you have a tool that can help called a "T-chart."

$ Out	$ In

The T-chart helps you track debits and credits. Whenever you buy or go long, you have a debit (Dr). Whenever you sell or go short, you have a credit (Cr). So debits are for the money going out of the account; credits are for money that comes into the account. If you end up with more money coming in than going out, you have a gain. If you end up with more money out than in, you have a loss. The rest involves running the numbers.

Here's a possible exam question:

An investor with no other positions buys an XYZ Jun 50 call @4 when the underlying instrument upon which the derivative is based is trading at 52. If the stock is trading at $52 at expiration and the investor closes his position for the intrinsic value, what is the investor's gain or loss?

    A. $1,000 loss

    B. $100 loss

    C. $200 gain

    D. $200 loss

First, draw a T-chart and use the labels you prefer: – and +, "$ out" and "$ in," "Dr" and "Cr," whatever works for you:

Okay. When the investor buys the call for $4, that's money out, so let's place "4" in the debit column.

The next part looks tricky but really isn't. The phrase "at expiration" means the last day of trading. At this point, all time value has evaporated. Since the option will soon expire, it is only worth the in-the-money amount. The intrinsic value. At expiration, an option either has intrinsic value, or it is worthless. So, what is the intrinsic value of the Jun 50 call when the stock is trading at $52? Two dollars. So, at expiration, the Jun 50 call is worth exactly $2. In this question the investor is closing his position for the intrinsic value. If he bought to open the contract, he sells it to close. When he sells the call for its intrinsic value of $2, this represents a credit, right? When you buy something, money comes out of your wallet. When you sell something, money comes into your wallet. Same for an options investor.

All right. So, if $4 went OUT of his account, and only $2 came back INTO his account, he ends up with a loss of how much? Two dollars. An option covers 100 shares, so multiply $2 by 100 to get a total loss of $200.

The answer to the question is "D," a $200 loss.

Notice how in the question the investor bought an option and sold it. That's called trading options, where we see terms such as "opening" and "closing." No stock is involved in that case. But, if the investor decides to exercise the option, now stock does change hands. Sometimes options are opened and closed; sometimes they are exercised; and sometimes they expire worthless. So, when figuring gains and losses for questions like the ones above, remember that only three things can happen once an option contract has been opened:

- Exercise
- Close Position
- Expire

If the call goes in-the-money, the investor could choose to exercise it. That means he buys stock at the strike price and sells it immediately at the current market price. If so, you'll be entering both the strike price (Debit) and the market price (Credit) into your T-chart. The investor could also close his position for the intrinsic value. To calculate intrinsic value, compare the higher market price to the strike price and place the difference in your T-chart. To close the position, remember that if he bought to open, he sells the option to close. If he sold to open, he buys the option back to close. And, finally, the option could expire worthless—put a zero in the T-chart to signify expiration.

The exam questions will give clues as to which of the three events has occurred. Just make sure you read the question carefully so you'll know what the exam expects.

In terms of expiration, know that ordinary options expire in 9 months or sooner. There are also long-term options called **LEAPS**, and these have much longer shelf lives—12 to 39 months. So, if you think it's hard to predict where common stock will close a week from next Friday, how about buying a LEAPS contract that allows you to predict where it will close 38 months from next Friday?

Because of the extra time on the contracts, LEAPS premiums are much higher than they are on similar ordinary options.

An American style option can be traded throughout each trading day and even exercised before the contract expires. That means that if you hold a MSFT May 30 call, you can exercise it in April, March, February, etc., if the common stock rises above $30 per-share. All equity options are American style. They can be exercised early if the buyer wants to do that.

Non-equity options, however, can be either American style or European style. A European style option can be traded throughout each trading day, but it can only be exercised at expiration.

The Terminology: Synonyms

It would be easier if we could just refer to the two parties in the options contract as the buyer and the seller. Unfortunately, we have other ways of referring to each. The exam might talk about the buyer of an option, or it might refer to him as being "long the option." Or, maybe he is referred to as the owner or the "holder" of the option.

It's all the same thing.

To sell an option is to write an option. If you sell an option, you are said to be "short" the option.

All means the same thing. Why would they use the word "hold" instead of "buy" or "own"? Think back to our guy in the tavern. When he sold the little cocktail napkins, the buyers were now holding the option in their hands. And, we call the seller the "writer," because, as you remember, our guy in the tavern literally wrote the terms of the contract on each cocktail napkin.

BUYER	SELLER
Long	Short
Holder	Writer
Owner	Grantor

So far, we've been talking about calls, which give investors the right to buy stock. Let's take a look at **puts** now, which give investors the right to sell stock at the strike price before expiration.

Puts

If we clipped the following coupon from the newspaper, what would it allow us to do?

That coupon represents an IXR Oct 40 put. As the holder/owner/buyer of this put we have the right to sell IXR stock for $40.

What if IXR is only worth $2?

Awesome! We get to sell the stock for $40 at any time before the end of trading on Friday, October 20, even if it's worth only two bucks on the open market. In fact, even if it's worth zero, we can sell it for the $40 strike price.

That's how a put works. A put buyer gets the right to sell IXR at the strike price before the contract expires. No matter how low IXR goes, the holder of an Oct 40 put has the right to sell 100 shares of IXR for $40 each before the end of trading on the third Friday of October.

Who buys puts? Investors who think a stock is about to drop in price. Bears. Bear = down. (Bulls point UP, like the horns on a Bull. Bears point DOWN, like the claws on a Bear, or just remember "bear down.")

Strange as it seems, as the stock price drops below the strike price, the value of the put goes up.

Think of it like this—if a stock is now at $20, wouldn't you like to sell it to someone for $40? If you were ready to exercise the put, you could buy the stock for $20, then immediately sell it to the put writer for $40. That would involve exercising the put. As we saw with calls, though, options investors don't always exercise their options, but, rather, close the positions for their intrinsic value. If they take in more than they spend, they end up with a profit. If they spend more than they take in, they don't.

For puts, intrinsic value is the amount of money that a put's strike price is above the market price, which is another way of saying that the market price has fallen below the strike price. An October 40 put has how much intrinsic value when the underlying stock trades at $20?

$20. Wouldn't you love to sell something worth only $20 for $40?

Talk about putting it to someone! The owner of a put profits when he can sell higher than the market price. He needs the stock price to go down, below the strike price. That's when he profits, when the stock is losing value.

Buying puts is a bearish strategy, as is selling stock short. Let's see what they have in common, and how they differ:

BUYING A PUT	SELLING STOCK SHORT
Bearish (profits when stock goes down)	Bearish (profits when stock goes down)
Limited loss (just the premium paid)	UN-limited loss
Less of a capital commitment	More capital, plus margin interest
Loses time value quickly	Stock can drop slowly, profitable

Time and Intrinsic Value

IXR Oct 40 put @5 with IXR trading at $38

	PREMIUM	5
•	INTRINSIC VALUE	• 2
	TIME VALUE	3

IXR Oct 40 put @5 with IXR trading at $40

Premium of $5 minus intrinsic value of $0 = time value of $5.

	PREMIUM	5
• INTRINSIC VALUE	•	0
TIME VALUE		5

So, in the first case, the put has $2 of intrinsic value, since it would allow the buyer to sell the stock for $2 more than it's worth. The premium is $5, so the additional $3 is time value. In the second case, the put has zero intrinsic value, since nobody needs the right to sell at $40 when the stock is at $40. So, the $5 premium is only time value.

Max Gain, Max Loss, Breakeven

When you buy an option, you're hoping to buy the stock low and sell it high, which you can do with either a call or a put. If you buy a call, you're picking your buy price—hopefully, the market price will go above that, so you can buy the stock low (strike price) and sell it high (market price). If you buy a put, you're picking your sell price—hopefully, the market price will go below that, so you can buy the stock low (market price) and sell it high (strike price).

Okay. So you can see why a bearish investor might buy puts.

Why would anyone sell them?

Back to our tavern. It's Monday after that third Friday in December, and our hero is back at the bar buying all the call buyers cheap beer just so they'll stick around long enough for him to rub it in.

Yes, unfortunately, for everyone but the seller/writer of the calls, Coca-Cola only made it to $22, and the calls all expired worthless. So, with the $4,500 in his pocket, the guy is in a pretty good mood. He's in such a good mood that he can't keep himself from not only trashing Coca-Cola but talking up his favored Pepsi. Pepsi is such an awesome stock, he swears, that it couldn't possibly fall below $70 a share in the next nine months. He's so confident his favorite stock won't fall below $70 that he'll take a bet with anyone who says the stock is a loser. You have to pay him three hundred dollars to make the bet, but it gives you the right to sell him 100 shares of Pepsi for $70, no matter how low it goes in the next nine months. Even if the stock drops to zero, you can put it to him and make him pay you $70 a share.

The 15 losers look at each other and decide the temptation is just too great. They imagine how much fun it will be to see the guy's face when they all make him give them $70 a share for a worthless stock. What if they're wrong? Then, just like before, they lose part or all of their premium. But that's all they can lose, too.

How much can our Pepsi-loving hero make? Same as before—just the premium. That's all the seller of an option can ever make. How much can he lose on this Pepsi put?

The good news for him as the writer of a put (as opposed to a call) is that his maximum loss is not unlimited. In fact, you won't see the word "unlimited" associated with puts. A stock can only go down to zero, which caps the maximum loss for the seller and the maximum gain for the buyer. If this guy collects $3 a share ($300 total) granting the right to sell him stock at $70 per-share, the worst that could happen is that he'd pay $70 for a stock worth zero and would have only collected $3 per-share. A maximum loss of $67 per-share, and it could only happen if PepsiCo, like, went out of business in the next nine months. Which could never happen, unless it did.

So, like before, the guy lines up the same 15 buyers and takes $300 from each one. He takes out a cocktail napkin for each buyer and writes:

So, after finishing his drink and buying the house another round, the guy walks out with $4,500 and

the obligation to buy Pepsi for $70 a share, no matter what it's worth at the time. Oh well. He's confident that the stock will remain at $70 or above. If so, those Pepsi puts will end up just as worthless as the Coke calls did.

So, the buyer and seller of a put have the following maximum gain, maximum loss, and breakeven:

BUYER	SELLER
Max Loss = Premium	Max Gain = Premium
BE = SP - Premium	BE = SP - Premium
Max Gain = BE down to zero	Max Loss = BE down to zero

So far we have only looked at single options positions. Now it's time to talk about establishing **multiple options** positions called straddles, spreads, and combinations. To establish a **straddle** an investor buys a call and a put with the same strike price (or sells a call and a put with the same strike price). To establish **spreads** investors buy *and* sell calls or puts with different strike prices, expiration months, or both. We will also see that if the multiple options position is neither a straddle nor a spread, we refer to it as a **combination.**

Straddles

Let's start with the straddle. If an investor feels that the quarterly earnings release for a company's stock—trading around $50 per share—could cause the price to shoot way up or way down, he would not be able to pick the direction of the stock. He would only be expecting volatility in this case.

If he wants to make a bet on volatility regardless of direction, he establishes a **long straddle,** buying a Jun 50 call <u>and</u> buying a Jun 50 put. In other words he is "straddling the market" at $50, with one foot on the call side, and one foot on the put side. As long as the stock advances in a big way, in either direction, he's happy. His risk is that the stock won't move. Remember that calls go in-the-money when the stock price goes above the strike price, and puts go in-the-money when the stock price goes below the strike price. One way or the other, this investor is convinced he'll make some money. One option will expire; the other one will go in-the-money.

Of course, he has to buy two options, which is why he has a total or combined premium. If he buys a Jun 50 call @3 and a Jun 50 put @2, he pays a total premium of $5. Like any other options buyer, if he starts with a debit (money out), he has to recover that amount just to break even. In other words, if the call goes in-the-money by $5, he breaks even; if the put goes in-the-money by $5, he breaks even there. In this case the breakeven points for the buyer are $45 and $55.

SP + Both Premiums and SP − Both Premiums

Now, what about the maximum gain and loss for the buyer of this straddle? The buyer can lose the total premium of five dollars per share. We've already established the two breakeven points—45 and 55. And, since the buyer holds a call, his maximum gain is unlimited.

The seller of a straddle is like all sellers—he's convinced the buyer is wrong. Maybe the stock will rise or fall, but not by as much as the two premiums he can collect. So, if the investor is convinced the underlying instrument will trade in a narrow range, he should be advised to sell a straddle.

A test question could look like this:

An investor sells a Jun 90 call @4 and a Jun 90 put @3.50. He closes both positions for their intrinsic value at expiration, when the underlying stock is trading at $111. What is the investor's gain or loss?
   A. $5 loss
   B. $13.50 loss

C. $13.50 gain

D. $1 loss on the put, breakeven on the call

Using a T-chart, we place the "4" and the "3.50" under the money-in or credit column, since he sold both options. That's the per-share amount—if you prefer using numbers like $400 and $350, that's fine, too. Just keep it all consistent. Okay. Now we have to find the intrinsic values because that's what he pays when he buys back both positions to close out the straddle. So, if the stock is at $111, what's the right to sell it at $90 worth at expiration?

Nothing. Place "0" under the money-out or debit column, then, since that's what he'd pay to buy back the put.

If the stock is at $111, what's the right to purchase it at $90 worth? $21 per share. That's a debit, because he'd have to buy back the call to close the position. Add it all up, and we see that $7.50 per share came in, with $21 going out. Looks like a loss of about $13.50 per share, doesn't it? The answer, then, is "B, $13.50 loss."

The maximum potential loss to the writer of a straddle is unlimited. Why? He's writing a naked call, and the stock could hypothetically go up forever. If the stock drops, the loss won't be as bad, but that, by definition, is not the maximum loss. The maximum loss is the worst-case scenario.

What's the best-case scenario for the writer of a straddle? As always, sellers can only make the premiums collected. So the investor in the practice question can make $750 per contract, since that's what he's collecting. And, I hope he's not expecting to make all that, since it could only happen if the stock ended up trading at exactly the strike price of $90. Any higher or lower, and he'll have to pay some money to close out either the call or the put. As long as he pays out less than $7.50 per share ($750 per contract) he wins.

His breakeven, as always, is the same as the buyer's. Strike price plus both premiums and strike price minus both premiums.

POSITION	EXAMPLE	STRATEGY	MAX GAIN	MAX LOSS	BREAKEVEN
LONG STRADDLE	Long ABC Oct 50 call Long ABC Oct 50 put	Expects volatility in either direction	Unlimited	total premiums	SP + and – total premiums
SHORT STRADDLE	Short ABC Dec 50 call Short ABC Dec 50 put	Expects stability	total premiums	unlimited	SP + and – total premiums

Spreads

A **spread** is another type of multiple options position. With a straddle, we saw that the investor bought two options or sold two options. The two options were different types. One was a call, the other a put.

177

For spreads, the **type** of option is the same. We're either talking about two calls for a **call spread**, or two puts for a **put spread**. To open a call spread, an investor buys a call and sells a call. To open a put spread, an investor buys a put and sells a put. Usually the expiration months are the same. For example, the investor buys a Jan 50 call and sells a Jan 55 call.

That would be a call spread. A debit call spread to be exact.

Debit Spread

Why is it a **debit spread**? Ask yourself which call is worth more, the Jan 50 or the Jan 55? In other words, would somebody rather buy a stock at $50 or at $55?

Fifty dollars. Calls with lower strike prices are always worth more money. So even before we attach premiums, do you suppose this investor has more money coming in or going out of his T-chart?

No matter where the underlying stock trades, the Jan 50 call is worth more—did he buy or sell it? He bought it. So he paid more for the Jan 50 call than he received for selling the Jan 55 call. We call this a **debit call spread** because the investor starts out with a debit. And, like any options investor who starts with a debit, the debit represents the investor's maximum loss.

Okay, let's say the investor bought the Jan 50 call @5 and sold the Jan 55 call @3. Go ahead and enter that in a T-chart. We place "5" in the debit column, since that's what he paid for the Jan 50 call. We place "3" in the credit column, since that's what he received for selling the Jan 55 call. He starts with a net debit of $2, so his maximum loss is $2.

What's his maximum gain? This part is easy. What's the difference between the two strike prices?

Jan 55 call

Jan 50 call

Five. Magically, in a spread, the maximum gain and maximum loss always add up to the difference between the two strike prices. Always. So just take five and subtract the maximum loss of two.

5 minus 2 = 3. So, his maximum gain is $3. Again, the max gain and max loss will always add up to the difference between the two strike prices.

Max gain + Max loss = Strike price difference

So, if the max loss is 2, the max gain is 3 when the difference between strike prices is 5. You'll never see the word "unlimited" associated with spreads, because the max gain and max loss are always going to be known numbers that add up to the difference between the two strike prices.

Breakevens for spreads are even easier. For call spreads, just add the net premium of $2 to the lower strike price. The lower strike price is $50 in our example. Add 2 to get $52. That's where the investor would break even.

So, how does the investor who establishes a debit call spread make money? When both options go in-the-money, becoming much more valuable.

If the stock goes up to $70 a share, how much is the right to buy it at $55 worth?

$15.

Long Jun 50 call

Short Jun 55 call @3 (now worth) $15

What's the right to buy it at $50 worth?

$20.

Long Jun 50 call @5 (now worth) $20

Short Jun 55 call @3 (now worth) $15

So the option he bought for $5 he could sell back for $20. And the option he sold for $3, he could buy back for $15. If he did that, he'd have a total of $20 per share going out of his T-chart and $23 coming in. That would represent his maximum gain of $3 per share. Both options went in-the-money, meaning they were "exercisable." That's what the investor behind a debit spread always wants—for both options to become more valuable. When we started, the difference between the two premiums was $2. When the options went in-the-money, the difference widened to $5. For a **debit spread**, the investor wants the difference in premiums to WIDEN and/or wants both options to be EXERCISED.

Debit = widen and exercise.

It might help to remember that "d-e-b-i-t" has five letters, as does the word "w-i-d-e-n."

Also, if you look at the investor's position, you can see why he'd love to see both options exercised:

Long Jun 50 call

Short Jun 55 call

Looking at the position, we see that he's obligated to sell stock at $55, but if so, that means he has the right to buy it for $50. Buy for $50, sell for $55. Not a bad thing. So, he can make a maximum of that $5 difference, minus his initial debit.

To establish a put spread an investor buys a put and sells a put. If he spends more than he takes in, he has a debit put spread. For example, if you purchase a June 50 put and sell a June 45 put, you are paying more than you're taking in—debit spread. Right? The contract granting someone the right to sell stock for $50 is always worth more than the one granting the right to sell stock for just $45. So, you would establish a debit put spread in this case. If you paid $6 for the Jun 50 put and received $3 selling the Jun 45 put, you start with a net debit of $3. Your maximum loss is, therefore, that $3 per share, and your maximum gain is $5 – $3, or $2 per share.

Credit Spread

To make the debit spread a **credit spread** all we'd have to do is switch the words "buy" and "sell" so that our investor sells the Jan 50 call @5 and buys the Jan 55 call @3. If he did that, he'd start out with a net credit of $2. As always, if the investor starts with a credit, that credit represents his maximum gain. So, his maximum gain is 2. The difference in strike prices is still 5, right? 5 – 2 = 3.

So the investor's maximum loss is $3.

Now, if the underlying stock were at $40 at expiration, how would the investor fare? If the stock is trading at $40, what's the right to buy it at $50 worth?

Zero. What's the right to buy it at $55 worth? Zero. A premium of zero means the options have expired worthless, and the difference between nothing and nothing is nothing. When we started, the premiums were $3 and $5, exactly two dollars apart. Now how far apart are they?

Not at all. Their difference has narrowed, and they have expired. Credit spread investors want the difference between premiums to narrow and for the options to expire worthless. Narrow and expire. Might help to remember that "n-a-r-r-o-w" and "e-x-p-i-r-e" have six letters, just like the word "c-r-e-d-i-t."

And, if you look at his position, you see that he is obligated to sell at $50 and has the right to buy at $55. Buying at $55 to sell at $50 is the worst that can happen, which is why he can lose that $5 difference, minus his initial credit.

No Premiums Provided

The exam might ask you to identify whether the investor has established a debit spread or a credit spread without providing the premiums. For example, try to name the following four spreads as either "debit spread" or "credit spread"…

Buy 1 ABC Apr 55 call

Sell 1 ABC Apr 50 call

Buy 1 ABC Apr 55 put

Sell 1 ABC Apr 50 put

Buy 1 XYZ Jun 50 call

Sell 1 XYZ Jun 55 call

Buy 1 XYZ Jun 50 put

Sell 1 XYZ Jun 55 put

Step 1) determine which of the two options is worth more. In all four spreads, which option is worth more? In order, it's the Apr 50 call, the Apr 55 put, the Jun 50 call, and the Jun 55 put. Why? The right to buy low, and the right to sell high are more valuable. Right? In the first spread, the right to buy ABC for $50 is worth more than the right to buy it for $55. In the second spread, the right to sell ABC for $55 is worth more than the right to sell it for just $50. And so on.

Now, Step 2) if he bought that more valuable option, it's a debit spread; if he sold it, it's a credit spread.

Let's apply that to the four spreads above. In the first one, the investor SELLS the more valuable option (credit spread). In the second one, he BUYS the more valuable put (debit spread). In the third, he BUYS the more valuable call (debit spread), and in the fourth he SELLS the more valuable put (credit spread).

Bull and Bear Spreads

What if the exam asked you to identify the two spreads as either "Bull" or "Bear?"

Use the following memory jogger:

B

U

L

L

S

Which stands for "Because U are Long the Lower Strike." If you are long the lower strike, then you are a bull. If not, you're a bear.

So, the following spreads are all BULL spreads, because "u" are long the lower strike:

Long MSFT Oct 50 call @4

Short MSFT Oct 60 call @1

Long IBM Mar 45 put @4

Short IBM Mar 50 put @7

Notice this "BULL" thing works for both call and put spreads. If you're long the lower strike price number (50 vs. 60, 45 vs. 50), you're a BULL. Which is why the following would be BEAR spreads:

Short MSFT Oct 50 call @4

Long MSFT Oct 60 call @1

Short IBM Mar 45 put @4

Long IBM Mar 50 put @7

More Terms

There are still other ways to refer to spreads. Rather than explain them in detail, I'm going to opt for the handy-dandy table format:

EXAMPLE	DESCRIPTION	NAME(S)
Long Jun 50 call Short Jun 60 call	Same expiration, different strike PRICE	Price spread, vertical spread
Long Jun 50 call Short Aug 50 call	Same strike price, different expiration	Time spread, calendar spread, horizontal spread
Long Jun 50 call Short Aug 40 call	Different strike price, different expiration	Diagonal spread

If the exam really wanted to make you sweat, it could use several different terms at once. For example, the following position can be referred to as a bear call spread, a credit call spread, a price spread, and/or a vertical spread:

> Long XYZ Jun 50 call
>
> Short XYZ Jun 40 call

Combinations

This is a straddle:

> Long 1 XYZ Jun 50 call
>
> Long 1 XYZ Jun 50 put

Notice how everything is the same except for the "type" of option. One is a call, the other a put. The same is true of a short straddle:

> Short 1 XYZ Jun 50 call
>
> Short 1 XYZ Jun 50 put

The investor buys a call and a put with the same strike price and expiration, or he sells a call and a put with the same strike price and expiration.

This, on the other hand, is a s-p-r-e-a-d:

> Long 1 XYZ Jun 50 call
>
> Short 1 XYZ Jun 40 call

Now, the only thing that is the same is the type—they both have to be calls, or they both have to be puts. The investor always buys one option and sells the other. Something is always different about the two calls, or the two puts—different strike price, different expiration month, or both.

A spread could also look like this:

> Long 1 XYZ Jun 50 call

Short 1 XYZ Aug 50 call

That's a horizontal/time/calendar spread in which the Aug 50 call is worth more than the June 50 call.

So, what if the test gives you a position that is not quite a straddle, and not quite a spread? Identify it as a **combination**. For example, take a look at the following and tell me whether it's a straddle or a spread:

Short 1 XYZ Jun 50 call

Short 1 XYZ Jun 45 put

It can't be a straddle, because the strike prices are not the same. It can't be a spread, because they're not both calls or puts. Remember, they call them call spreads and put spreads for a reason. So, this position is neither a straddle nor a spread. Instead, we call it a "combination." Since he sold both positions, it could be called a "short combination."

Chances are, you will only have to identify the position as a combination. If you have to calculate a gain or loss, use the T-chart and figure out the intrinsic value of the two options based on the stock price. For example, in the position above, what happens if XYZ trades for $52 at expiration? The Jun 50 call would be worth $2, while the Jun 45 put would expire worthless. Or, if XYZ trades for $42, the Jun 50 call expires worthless, and the Jun 45 put is worth $3.

Another example of a combination would look like this:

Long 1 XYZ Jun 50 call

Long 1 XYZ Jun 45 put

The position can't be a spread because he's buying two options, and they're not the same type.

If the test says that the Jun 50 call trades @3 and the Jun 45 put @1, you could figure the breakeven by adding the total premium ($4) to 50 and subtracting the total premium from 45. The two breakeven points, then, would be $54 and $41.

Hedging (Risk Modification Techniques)

If you buy stock, you're betting that it's going up. If it doesn't go up, or—worse—if it goes down, you lose. If you sell a stock short, you're betting that it's going down. If it goes up, you lose. Maybe the problem with both strategies, then, is that the investor is betting all one way. What he could do, instead, is hedge his bet.

To **hedge** a stock position means to "bet the other way, too." The term "hedge" is based on the way people grow hedges to establish the boundaries around their property. In this case, the property is stock—with a hedge, the owner can establish the boundaries in terms of what he's willing to lose.

Let's say one of your favorite stocks looks like it's about to drop. What should you do? Sell the stock? Yes, but that is a drastic measure, especially when it's also possible that the stock will rally, and you'd sure hate to miss out if it did. If you've ever taken a 50% profit on a stock, only to watch it go up 300% from there, you know exactly what I'm talking about.

So, instead of taking a drastic measure, maybe you could buy an option that names a selling price for your stock. Let's see, which option gives an investor the right to sell stock at a particular price?

A put. So, if you thought one of your stocks might drop sharply, you could buy a put, giving you the right to sell your stock at the put's strike price, regardless of how low it goes.

It's like a homeowner's insurance policy. If you own a home, you buy insurance against fire. Doesn't mean you're hoping your house burns down, but, if it does, aren't you glad you paid your premium? Buying puts against stock you own is a form of insurance. Insuring your downside, you might say.

A question might look like this:

Jimmy Joe purchases 100 shares of QSTX for $50 a share. Mr. Joe is bullish on QSTX for the long-term but is nervous about a possible downturn. To hedge his risk and get the best protection, which of the following strategies would you recommend?
A. sell a call
B. buy a call
C. sell a put
D. buy a put

If an investor buys stock, he is bullish, or betting the price will go up. To hedge, he'd have to take a bearish position, betting that the stock might go down. There are two "bearish" positions he can take to bet the other way or "hedge." He could sell a call, but if the test wanted you to recommend that strategy, the question would have said something about "increasing income" or "increasing yield."

And this one doesn't. This one gives you the key phrase:

"...and get the best protection..."

Whenever you see the word "protection," remember that the investor has to BUY an option. If an investor is long stock, he would buy a put for protection.

So, Mr. Jimmy Joe paid for protection in the question. If he has a put, he has the right to sell his stock for a minimum price rather than seeing how far the price drops on the secondary market. On the other hand, the question might have looked like this:

Barbara Bean purchases 100 shares of QSTX for $50 a share. Barbara is bullish on QSTX for the long-term but is afraid it may trade sideways in the short-term. To hedge her risk and increase income, which of the following strategies would you recommend?
A. sell a call
B. buy a call
C. sell a put
D. buy a put

As we saw, you don't increase your income by buying a put. When you buy something, money comes out of your wallet. In this case, Barbara Bean has to sell an option. What's the only bearish option she could sell?

A call. Call sellers are bearish. Or, bearish-neutral. If the stock goes "sideways," the call will expire in Barbara's favor. Since Barbara already owns the stock, this would be a **covered call**. Let's say she bought the stock at $50, then writes a Sep 60 call at $3. If the stock shoots up to the moon, what would happen? This investor would be forced to honor her obligation to sell the stock at the strike price of $60. Well, she only paid $50 for the stock, so she just made ten bucks there. And, she took in $3 for writing the call. So, she made $13, which represents her maximum gain.

Her maximum loss is much larger than the investor who bought the put in the preceding question. In this case the investor has not purchased a sale price for her stock. All she did was take in a premium of $3. That is the extent of her downside insurance. She paid $50 for the stock and took in $3 for the call. So, when the stock falls to $47 she has "broken even."

After that what's to prevent her from losing everything from that point down to zero? Nothing at all. So $47-per-share is her maximum loss. This illustrates why buying puts is for protection of a long position, while selling covered calls is just a way to generate premiums if the investor feels the stock is likely to trade in a narrow range for the duration of the call options.

Since they sell something they'll eventually have to buy back, short sellers are hoping the stock's price goes down. Short sellers have heard all about "buy low–sell high." They just prefer to do it the other way around: Sell high; buy back low. So if an investor sells a stock short for $50, he hopes it will drop to maybe $1 or $2 a share. If the stock goes up instead, what's his risk?

That the stock could go above $50—forever. Unlimited loss potential. Remember, he still has to buy this stock back, and he definitely doesn't want to buy it back for more than he first sold it for. Which option gives an investor the right to buy stock at the strike price?

Calls. So, if this investor wants protection, he'll have to buy a call.

A test question could look like this:

An investor sells short 100 shares of ABC at $50. In order to protect against an increase in price, which of the following strategies would you recommend?
   A. buy a put
   B. sell a put
   C. sell a call
   D. buy a call

The answer is "D," buy a call. Again the word "protection" means the investor has to buy an option. If he is concerned about his purchase price, he buys a call, which gives him the right to purchase stock at a strike price. Maybe he's willing to risk having to repurchase the stock at $55 but not a penny higher. Therefore, he buys a Sep 55 call for $2. Using our T-chart, where would we plug in the numbers? If he sells the stock at $50, that's a credit to his account, so let's place $50 in the credit column. He paid $2 for the call, so that's "2" in the debit column.

Okay, where does this investor break even, then? $48. 50 in the credit column, 2 in the debit column, so 48 would make things even.

And if you prefer to analyze the position, start with step one—look at the stock position. He shorted the stock at $50, which means he wants it to go down. If he paid $2 for the option, doesn't the stock have to work his way by exactly $2 before he breaks even?

It does. So when the stock goes down to $48, this investor breaks even. Is there anything to prevent him from making everything from that point down to zero? No. So $48 is his maximum gain, too. Breakeven down to zero.

What about his maximum loss? Well, let's say disaster strikes. The stock skyrockets to $120 a share. Does he have to buy it back at that price in order to "cover his short"? No. At what price could he buy back the stock?

The strike price of $55. That was the protection he bought. And, if he exercised his call, his T-chart would show that $50 came in when he sold short, while $57 came out (when he bought the stock at $55 after buying the call at $2). That's a loss, but it's only a loss of $7, which isn't too bad considering how risky it is to sell a security short.

So if a short seller needs protection, he buys a call. It's the same thing as long stock–long a put, only upside down.

Now, let's look at the mirror image of the covered call. Say this same short seller wanted to hedge his bet while also increasing income. If he starts out bearish, he hedges with a bullish position. To increase income, he'll have to sell a position. Only bullish position he can sell is a put. So, he ends up short the stock and also short a put. In other words, he sells the stock short and also sells a put on that underlying stock. If the stock gets put to him, presumably he'll use those shares to cover his short stock position.

If he shorts the stock at $50 and sells a Jun 40 put @ 3, where would he break even? Well, short sellers want to see the stock go down. However, since he took in $3, he can let his stock position work against him by $3. This investor breaks even at $53.

Right? That's what selling an option does for a hedger; it offsets the potential loss by the amount of premium collected. And, your T-chart tells you that $50 came in when he sold the stock short, plus $3 that came in for selling the put. So 53 is the breakeven point.

What's the most he can lose? Well, how high could the stock jump? Unlimited. Does he have the right to buy the stock back at a particular price? No. So, his maximum loss is unlimited.

Like the covered call writer, he has also capped his "upside" or his maximum gain. His upside is down, remember. When the stock goes down to zero, does he get to buy it back at zero?

Not after writing that put option. The investor who bought the Jun 40 put is going to make him buy the stock for $40. Now the investor realizes his maximum gain. Sold the stock at $50, bought it back at $40. That's a gain of $10. He also took in $3 for writing the put. So, his maximum gain is $13. Stock price vs. Strike price + Premium.

CBOE VIX

Perhaps you have heard of the "investor fear gauge" or "volatility index" known as the VIX. The proper name for this index is the **Chicago Board Options Exchange Market Volatility Index.** As the CBOE website explains: The CBOE Volatility Index® (VIX®) is a key measure of market expectations of near-term volatility conveyed by S&P 500 stock index option prices. Since its introduction in 1993, VIX has been considered by many to be the world's premier barometer of investor sentiment and market volatility. Several investors expressed interest in trading instruments related to the market's expectation of future volatility, and so VIX futures were introduced in 2004, and VIX options were introduced in 2006." On another section of the website, we see that, "The New VIX uses options on the S&P 500 Index, which is the primary U.S. stock market benchmark. The original VIX was based on S&P 100 Index (OEX) option prices."

As the website goes on to explain, the S&P 500 and the VIX move opposite of each other, though not at a perfect 1-to-1 relationship. Rather, about 80% of the time one closes up when the other drops and vice versa. Although it is sometimes called the "fear index" or "fear gauge," a high value for the VIX is not necessarily bearish for the stock market. This is because expected market volatility over the next 30 days could be pointed in either a bullish or bearish direction. The highest VIX readings occur when investors overall anticipate large price moves in either direction. A low VIX value would imply that investors expect little movement in the overall stock market.

Non-Equity Options

The options we have covered are called **equity options** because the underlying instrument is an equity security, common stock. The options we'll cover now are not based on common stock. That's why they're called **non-equity options.**

Equity options are **American style options,** which means they can be exercised before the expiration date if the holder so chooses. Some of the non-equity options we are about to examine are **European style.** A European style option can be traded throughout each trading day, but it can only be exercised at expiration.

Index Options

The first type of non-equity option, the **index option,** derives its value from various stock indexes. We talked about index funds and ETF based on the S&P 500 index. Some traders also buy puts and calls on the value of that index. Here's how it works. The S&P 500 index is a big basket of stocks hand-picked by the experts at Standard & Poor's. These 500 stocks represent the most important in the overall market. By tracking these 500 stocks, we can track the overall movement of the market. When investors buy or write calls on the SPX (symbol for the S&P 500 index), they're betting on the point value of the S&P 500, which gets figured every trading day.

The buyer of an SPX call says the point value of the S&P 500 is going up in the short-term, while the writer says the point value of the index is not. Exercise involves the delivery of cash rather than stock.

That's right, when the buyer exercises the call, the seller pays the buyer cash. How much cash? The intrinsic value or "in-the-money" amount.

Let's say the call has a strike price of 500. If the holder exercises the call when the index is at 520, the call would be in-the-money 20 points, so the seller would have to send the buyer 20 points' worth of cash. How much is a point worth?

$100. Twenty points times $100 each equals a total of $2,000 that the seller would deliver to the buyer. And he would deliver it by the next business day. No need for a T + 3 settlement, since no stock is changing hands, only money.

The premium is also multiplied by $100.

Here's an example:

Long 1 SPX Jun 500 call @ 8

In this case, the investor has a strike price of 500 (or 50,000), for which he pays 8 X $100, or $800. In order to break even, the SPX option would have to go in-the-money by 8 points. That would be 508.

Let's look at a practice question:

An investor buys 1 SPX Mar 600 call when the index is @590 for a premium of 9. What is the investor's gain or loss if he exercises the option when the SPX closes at 612?
  A. $100 loss
  B. $300 loss
  C. $300 gain
  D. $100 gain

As always, let's get serious and break out the T-chart.

The investor buys the call for $9, so let's place "9" in the debit column. How much money comes in upon exercise? How much is the call in-the-money? It's in the money by 12 points, so let's place "12" in the credit column. That's what the writer would pay the buyer upon exercise. Total it up, and we see that $9 went out, while $12 came in, for a net gain of $3. Multiply $3 by 100 to get our answer, which is "C, $300 gain."

Remember that the index is valued as of the end of the trading day, so it would be dangerous to exercise your index option in the morning. If your call went deep in-the-money at 11 o'clock in the morning, you would still need to wait and see where the index closes. The S&P and other indexes often go up for part of the day before finishing in negative territory. The OCC Disclosure Document indicates that if you exercise an option before the index has been officially totaled up for the day, and that option ends up going *out-of-the-money*, you would have to pay the *seller* the amount that your option is out-of-the-money.

Key points on index options:

- exercise involves delivery of cash, not stock
- index is valued at the end of the trading day
- multiplier is $100

The S&P 500 and the Dow Jones Industrial Average are **broad-based indexes**. That means they don't focus on a particular industry. Even if the Dow is only 30 stocks, the companies are so diverse as to include Microsoft, Home Depot, Johnson & Johnson, Walmart, American Express, and Disney. Then again, these stocks are all issued by large companies with a large number of shares outstanding—the way those shares trade is pretty close to what the whole market is doing that day.

A **narrow-based index** is pretty easy to spot, since it names the industry it focuses on. A "transportation index" would be narrow based, as would a "utilities index." So, even though the Dow Jones Industrial Average is broad-based, there are also the Dow Jones Utilities Index and the Dow Jones Transportation Index, both of which are obviously following just one sector at a time and are, therefore, narrow-based indexes.

So, if an investor is heavily weighted in a particular industry sector, he needs to hedge his risk with the associated narrow-based index options. If the investor is over-weighted in pharmaceutical stocks, he needs to find a pharmaceutical index that mirrors his own portfolio—the broad-based indexes won't help him. On the other hand, an investor exposed to the broad market would hedge with broad-based index options such as the S&P 500 and the DJIA. Index options are frequently used to hedge stock portfolios. They can also be used to speculate that the market, or a market sector, is about to go up, down, or stay the same.

Capped Index Options

Hypothetically, there is no limit to how high an index can rise, and that's what makes selling calls on an index so risky. Therefore, **capped index options** may be available. If we set the cap interval at 30 points, as soon as the buyer's option goes up that high, it's automatically exercised. That way the seller knows what his maximum loss is and, therefore, the buyer knows his maximum gain. If it's an SPX Aug 400 call, it would be automatically exercised as soon as the S&P 500 hit 430 or higher, assuming the cap interval is 30. If it's an OEX (S&P 100) Aug 400 put, it would be automatically exercised if the S&P 100 hit 370 or lower.

Very similar to the way commodities will stop trading once they "hit the limit" for the day. To prevent the price of cocoa or corn from spiraling out of control, once the price moves a certain amount, the contract stops trading. The movement is "capped."

Interest Rate Options

Price-based Options

Remember the "bond see-saw" diagram from Debt Securities? It might have seemed a bit overwhelming, but all it does is provide a model of what happens when interest rates go up or down. Remember that on a bond the borrower/issuer prints a stated interest rate. Since that rate is fixed, whenever prevailing interest rates change, they change in relation to that fixed rate on the bond. So, the price or value of the bond changes accordingly, as does its yield.

If interest rates go up, bond prices go down. If interest rates go down, bond prices go up.

And yields move with interest rates.

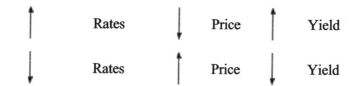

The OCC's *The Characteristics and Risks of Standardized Options* explains that while price-based options have been approved for trading and have traded in the past, currently there are no priced-based options being issued by the OCC and traded on the options exchanges. So, one would not expect the Series 7 to ask a lot of questions on the topic. In fact, the topic is not specifically listed on their exam outline, which is why we are not going to drill down in detail. Rather, since the outline definitely mentions the next type of option (yield-based), we will just discuss the basic concepts.

A priced-based option could be used to speculate on the direction of interest rates. Or, it could be used to hedge an investor's risk that interest rates will move the wrong way. With options, there are always two ways to hedge. If you want protection, you buy an option. If you want to increase income, you sell an option.

Therefore, since the portfolio manager of a bond mutual fund is bullish on bond prices, she'd have to take an appropriate bearish position to hedge. Bears buy puts and sell calls; therefore, the portfolio manager could hedge against rising interest rates by selling calls to increase income or buying puts for protection.

Yield-Based Options

Let's say that a test question brings up a mutual fund portfolio manager concerned that interest rates might go up and push down the price of her bonds. Now, if interest rates go up, what else goes up?

Yields. Yields go the same way interest rates go.

It's price that moves the other way. So, the portfolio's enemy is higher yields. If she can't beat them, why not join them? That's the concept behind hedging. If the other side is about to win, you bet on the other side a while. You profit from a temporary situation that otherwise would have left you with a loss.

So if the portfolio manager is bearish on prices, she's bullish on yields. Therefore, if she wants protection, she can either buy a price-based put, or buy a yield-based call. Right? If bond prices are going down, bond yields are going up. To increase income, she could sell price-based calls, or sell yield-based puts. Both options would work for her if she's right about interest rates rising.

Remember, it's all based on simple math. You just have to break things down and organize them properly. Never forget the premise:

If rates are up, prices are down, and yields are up.

If rates are down, prices are up, and yields are down.

Let's say our portfolio manager wanted protection. Her hedge is a bearish position on bond prices, which is the same thing as a bullish position on bond yields. So, she might protect against a drop in price by betting on the corresponding increase in yields. Maybe she goes long the following position:

Long 1 Mar 75 call @1

That "75" is notation for a yield of "7.5%." In basis points, it would be expressed as 750 basis points. The premium of $1 needs to be multiplied by $100, which is what the investor would pay to buy this yield-based call. Remember, no Treasury securities are delivered upon exercise—just cash.

So if she pays $100 for the call, she has to make $100 to break even. She needs to make 10 basis points. Each basis point is worth $10, so she needs to make ten of them to break even. That would happen if yields go to 7.6%, or 760 basis points. Upon exercise, she would receive 10 basis points times $10 each, or $100, and break even because 760 basis points is 10 points above her strike price of 750 basis points.

Simple, right?

Finally, yield-based options are "European style," meaning they can be traded at any time but only exercised on the expiration date.

Foreign Currency Options

When you're talking about currency exchange rates, this is what it all comes down to:

If one currency goes up, the other goes down.

That's what you have to remember about foreign currencies. If the U.S. dollar's value goes up, the other currency you're measuring it against goes down, and vice versa. The easy way to attack these questions is to remember the following mnemonic:

E

P

I

C

American Exporters buy Puts. American Importers buy Calls. And, of course they sell the opposite positions.

Let's say we make computers in Keokuk, Iowa. We import hard-drives from a company in Canada that insists on being paid in Canadian dollars within 60 days of issuing the purchase order. Okay, so we have to pay a certain number of Canadian dollars for those hard-drives 60 days from now. What's our risk? That the value of the Canadian dollar could skyrocket, forcing us to use more of our American dollars to buy enough Canadian dollars to satisfy the contract terms. Let's say the contract price is $1 million Canadian. How much is that in U.S. dollars?

Depends on the exchange rate, which is why importers and exporters constantly have to hedge their foreign currency risks with **foreign currency options**. If the exchange rate between the U.S. dollar and

the Canadian dollar is one of ours for one of theirs, then we will be paying $1 million American for those hard drives. That's because we'll take one of our dollars and turn it into one of their C$, one million times.

But if the exchange rate should tip, and suddenly their C$ has shot up in value against our weak

dollar, it's going to take more of our dollars to buy their C$. If our dollar weakens against a strengthened Canadian dollar, it might take three of our dollars to convert to just one C$. We have to pay 1 million C$, regardless of the exchange rate. If it takes three of ours to get one of theirs, how much are we really going to pay for those hard drives? Three million dollars. A call gives us the right to buy C$ at a strike price, even if the underlying C$ goes up in value.

That's why American "Importers buy Calls."

Now, let's say that we're going to export our assembled personal computers to a retailer in Japan, who is going to pay us in yen in 60 days. We agree that they'll pay us 100 million yen for a certain number of our computers. What's that amount going to be worth to us in 60 days? That's our risk, right?

If the exchange rate right now is 100 yen = 1 U.S. dollar, then we actually receive U.S. $1,000,000, when we take their 100 million yen and divide them into 1 million piles of a hundred. Not too bad. But what if our dollar strengthens against their suddenly weakened yen? Suddenly, their currency is so weak that it takes not 100, but 1 million of theirs to equal one of ours? Yikes! Sixty days later they send us that box of 100 million yen, and we put 1 million yen in each pile, ending up with 100 piles, each one worth exactly a dollar.

In other words, we get $100 when we were expecting $1,000,000!

Oops. Hope somebody bought a put on the yen. Or at least sold a call to offset the major loss we just took on the exchange rate. You can now answer some of the exam questions, just by understanding the risks, and remembering that American Exporters buy Puts, American Importers buy Calls.

E

P

I

C

What if the test question is talking about a *foreign* company? Think through the story problem. If the Japanese country is going to receive American dollars in 90 days, they worry that its value could drop. Since there are no puts on the U.S. dollar, they simply buy calls on the yen. Remember, if one currency is dropping, by definition, the other one is rising.

The size of each foreign currency option varies by currency, so the exam should give you the amount in the question, like this:

Canadian dollar (50,000) Oct 75 call at .60,

The "50,000" refers to the number of Canadian dollars covered by this one contract. The "75" is the strike price. Remember that these options are quoted in terms of American cents. So, the "75" means that each Canadian dollar can be purchased at the strike price of 75 American cents, regardless of how high the Canadian dollar goes relative to the American dollar. The ".60" means "six-tenths of one penny," so it just has to be multiplied by the penny (.01) to get .006. This contract covers 50,000 Canadian dollars, so multiply that by .006 to get $300.

$300 is what an investor would pay for this call.

If this investor were concerned that the Canadian dollar might skyrocket, chances are he's an importer who has to pay for a product in Canadian dollars. This call would tell him the maximum cost of the contract, and could also be used to profit, should his risk materialize.

Japanese yen are actually quoted in hundredths of American cents. So, if you're given a premium of ".52," you'll have to put two zeroes in front of it (.0052) before multiplying by the penny (.01).

Physically settled foreign currency options are no longer traded—instead retail investors settle all foreign currency options in U.S. dollars. This eliminates the risks associated with physical delivery of currency (which has to be stored, could be lost or destroyed). The exam might expect you to know that "New World Currency Option" contracts (WCOs) have been created to better fit the needs of retail investors by making the contracts smaller and having them settled in U.S. dollars.

Options Accounts

The OCC Disclosure Brochure is called "Characteristics and Risks of Standardized Options," and it's the prospectus used by the OCC (which *issues* the options) to comply with the Securities Act of 1933. When a customer opens an options account, he/she must receive this disclosure brochure, which explains how options work and discloses all the many risks involved. At what point must the customer receive this document? No later than when the account is approved for trading by the registered options principal.

Opening the Account

Here are the steps for opening an options account:

1. Registered rep discusses suitability issues with the customer: net worth, experience with options, types of options trades anticipated.
2. Registered rep sends OCC Disclosure Brochure either now or at the time the Options Principal approves the account. Registered rep also indicates when the OCC **Disclosure Brochure** called "Characteristics and Risks of Standardized Options" was sent/delivered to customer.

3. As soon as the Options Principal approves account, first options trade may occur.

4. Customer has 15 days to return a signed options agreement. If not, only closing transactions would be allowed—no new positions.

Position Limits

The customer's signature on the options agreement means that he/she understands the risks associated with options but chooses to trade anyway, and that he/she will abide by the rules of the options exchange. For example, they won't take the electronic quotes they get and re-sell them on a website. They won't write calls and then flee the country whenever they go deep in-the-money. And, they'll abide by any position limits that may be in place.

A **position limit** means that a customer, or a group of customers "acting in concert," will not try to corner the market, so to speak. If a standardized option has a position limit of 25,000, that means that an investor can have no more than 25,000 bull or bear positions in that option. If he buys 20,000 calls, there are 5,000 bull positions left. He could, therefore, buy 20,000 calls and write 5,000 puts. I'm talking about "per class" here, meaning all MSFT calls or puts, not all MSFT Oct 30 calls, which would be a series. He could also establish 25,000 bear positions (buy puts, sell calls) on a particular underlying security.

The same numbers used for position limits are used for exercise limits. That means if the option is subject to a limit of 25,000, 25,000 represents the maximum number of open bull or bear positions a trader can have at one time on a class of options and also the maximum number of contracts he can exercise over five consecutive business days. The CBOE regularly publishes a list of position limits associated with various options.

Regulatory Issues

As CBOE Rule 9.2 declares:

> No member organization shall be approved to transact options business with the public until those persons associated with it who are designated as Options Principals have been approved by and registered with the Exchange. Persons engaged in the management of the member organization's business pertaining to option contracts shall be designated as Options Principals.

Adjusting Contracts

If you own a MSFT Oct 50 call, you own the right to buy 100 shares of MSFT for $50, meaning you get to buy $5,000 of Microsoft common stock if you want to between now and late October. Well, what if you had attended the annual meeting in Redmond, Washington, last year after a few shots of Jack Daniel's and started giving Steve Ballmer a hard time, calling him an "incompetent, bald-headed bureaucrat" and calling the board of directors a "den of do-nothing dunces." They might then find out you're holding calls on the stock and decide to make them go suddenly out-of-the-money. They get wind that you own 100 Oct 50 calls that have just gone in-the-money. So, they effect a 2:1 stock split. Suddenly, the stock drops from $52 a share to $26 a share, sending your calls from in-the-money to worthless.

Well, they could try that, except it wouldn't work. If they do a 2:1 stock split, each MSFT Oct 50 call you own would become 2 MSFT Oct 25 calls. Remember, with each contract you have the right to buy $5,000 worth of MSFT stock, no matter how they decide to slice $5,000 worth of stock.

If it's a 5:4 or 3:2 split, just treat the test question like a question on 100 shares of stock. If you have 100 shares of stock @50, it becomes 125 shares of stock @40 after a 5:4 split. Actually, it becomes the same thing after a 25% stock dividend, too. Either way, an Oct 50 call would become an Oct (125 shares) 40 call. So, rather than me creating some handy-dandy table, just know the concept. If it's a 2:1 split, you get twice as many contracts at half the strike price. If it's an uneven split or a stock dividend, just treat the question as if it were asking what happens when somebody is long 100 shares at that particular strike price.

Position	Event	Becomes
Jul 50 call	2:1 split	2 Jul 25 calls
Jul 50 call	5:4 split, 25% stock dividend	Jul (125 shares) 40 call
Jul 50 call	3:2 split	Jul (150 shares) 33.33 call

1. A MSFT Jun 50 call is in-the-money when MSFT trades at which of the following prices?

   A. $49.00

   B. $50.00

   C. $51.00

   D. $49.05

2. How far is a MSFT Jan 90 call in-the-money with MSFT trading at $85?

   A. $5

   B. $90

   C. $87.50

   D. None of the above

3. How far are the IBM Aug 70 calls in-the-money if IBM trades at $77?

   A. $77

   B. $7

   C. $0

   D. None of the above

4. Joe Schmoe is long an XYZ Dec 50 call @2.50. On the third Friday of December, XYZ is trading @56 and Joe closes the contract for its intrinsic value. What is the result?

   A. gain of $250

   B. loss of $250

   C. gain of $350

   D. loss of $350

5. Joe Schmoe buys an ABC Apr 85 call @3.25. With ABC trading @89.50, Joe exercises the call and immediately sells the stock for a

   A. loss of $125

   B. gain of $125

   C. loss of $50

   D. gain of $450

6. Joe Schmoe sells an XYZ Jun 50 call @3.75. With XYZ @51, Joe closes the contract for its intrinsic value, realizing a

    A. loss of $375

    B. gain of $3752

    C. gain of $275

    D. loss of $1,000

7. A MSFT Jun 65 put @3 has how much intrinsic value with MSFT @65?

    A. $3

    B. $2

    C. $65

    D. 0

8. An IBM Mar 75 put @3 has how much time value with IBM @74?

    A. $1

    B. $3

    C. $2

    D. None of the above

9. If today is mid-July and IBM is trading at $93, which of the following options would command the highest premium?

    A. IBM Aug 90 call

    B. IBM Oct 90 call

    C. IBM Aug 95 put

    D. IBM Nov 100 put

10. Which position exposes the investor to the greatest risk?

    A. Long XYZ Mar 80 call @3

    B. Long XYZ Mar 85 put @4

    C. Short XYZ Mar 80 put @2

    D. Short XYZ Mar 20 put @2

11. Paula purchases a put for $300. Three hundred dollars represents

    A. The price per share

    B. Paula's maximum gain

    C. Paula's maximum loss

    D. Paul's breakeven

12. An investor buys an ABC Apr 45 put @2.50. With ABC trading @41, he exercises his put for a

    A. loss of $250

    B. gain of $250

    C. gain of $150

    D. loss of $4,500

13. An investor writes an ABC Apr 45 put @2.50. Which of the following stock prices would prove the most profitable?

    A. $44

    B. $43

    C. $42

    D. $45

14. If an investor expects the price of a stock to remain unchanged over the next three months, which of the following would be most suitable?

    A. long straddle

    B. short call

    C. short put

    D. short straddle

15. What are the breakeven points for the following position?

Long XYZ Oct 50 call @1.50

Long XYZ Oct 50 put @1.50

I. $53.00

II. $51.50

III.$47.00

IV. $48.50

A. I, IV

B. I, III

C. II, III

D. II, IV

16. An investor is long 1 Oct 40 call and short 1 Oct 35 put. This position is best described as

A. a long straddle

B. a debit spread

C. a combination

D. an iron butterfly

17. An investor buys an ABC Apr 45 call @1 and sells an ABC Apr 45 put @2. At expiration, ABC trades at $46. Therefore the investor realizes a

A. loss of $300

B. gain of $300

C. gain of $200

D. loss of $500

18. If an investor anticipates volatility but does not have an opinion on market direction, he would most likely

A. sell a straddle

B. buy a call

C. buy a straddle

D. buy a put

19. All of the following positions represent spreads EXCEPT:

    A. Long 10 XYZ Oct 50 calls, short 10 XYZ Oct 60 calls

    B. Long XYZ Oct 50 call, short XYZ Oct 40 put

    C. Long XYZ Nov 30 call, short XYZ Nov 40 call

    D. Long XYZ Nov 70 put, short XYZ Nov 60 put

20. Which of the following positions is BULLish?

    A. Short XYZ Dec 20 put, long XYZ Dec 30 put

    B. Short XYZ Jan 40 call, long XYZ Jan 30 call

    C. Buy DFZ Sep 90 put, write DFZ Sep 80 put

    D. Hold XYZ Oct 30 call, write XYZ Oct 20 call

21. What does an investor with the following position need in order to profit?
Long XYZ Oct 40 call

    Short XYZ Oct 50 call

    I. difference in strike prices narrows

    II. difference in premiums widens

    III. both options expire

    IV. both options are exercised

A. I, III

B. I, IV

C. II, III

D. II, IV

22. What does an investor with the following position need in order to profit?

    Long XYZ Oct 40 put

    Short XYZ Oct 50 put

    I. difference in premiums narrows

    II. difference in premiums widens

    III. both options expire

IV. both options go in-the-money

A. I, III

B. I, IV

C. II, III

D. II, IV

23. An investor with a long stock position would receive the best protection if she

    A. bought calls

    B. sold puts

    C. sold calls

    D. bought puts

24. An investor with an established long stock position wants to hedge and increase income.

    What should he do?

    A. buy puts

    B. sell puts

    C. sell calls

    D. buy calls

25. An investor with a short stock position would best protect the position by

    A. buying puts

    B. selling calls

    C. selling puts

    D. buying calls

26. An investor with a short stock position wants to hedge and increase yield. She should

    A. buy calls

    B. buy puts

    C. sell puts

    D. sell calls

27. What is the maximum loss for the following position?

Long 100 shares XYZ @60

Long 1 XYZ Apr 60 put at 3.35

Answer: _____

28. What is the maximum loss for the following position?

Long 100 shares XYZ @60

Short 1 XYZ Apr 75 call at 3.85

Answer: _____

29. What is the maximum loss for the following position?

Short 100 shares XYZ @60

Long 1 XYZ Apr 60 call at 3.75

Answer: _____

30. What is the maximum loss for the following position?

Short 100 shares XYZ @60

Short 1 XYZ Apr 40 put at 3.20

Answer: _____

Answers

1. C, only one price is above $50.

2. D, no one would pay $90 for an $85 stock.

3. B, take the market price minus the strike price.

4. C, he pays the premium of $250, so put that in the debit column. When he closes the contract, he sells it, so he takes in the intrinsic value of $6 per share or $600 total. $250 out - $600 in. That's a gain of $350.

5. B, step one, he pays $3.25, so place that in the debit column. When he exercises the call he has the "right to buy stock at the Strike Price," so place the strike price in the buy/debit column, too. Now we have $3.25 per share and $85 per share in the debit column. He sells the stock for $89.50, so place that in the credit column. With $88.25 in the debit column and $89.50 in the credit column, he gains the difference of $1.25 or $125 total.

6. C, anything "short" goes in the credit column, so place $3.75 per share in the credit column. He buys it back to close, and it's worth exactly $1 per share when he does. He makes the difference between $3.75 and $1 per share, or $275 total.

7. D, the right to sell a $65 stock at $65 has no intrinsic value. The premium represents pure speculation or "time value."

8. C, there is $1 of intrinsic value, since the $74 stock can be sold for $75. The rest of the premium ($2) equals its "time value."

9. D, the option with the most intrinsic value ($7) AND the most time would have to be the most expensive.

10. C, the most risk is always on the short side of the contract. Which put has a bigger maximum loss? The first one has a max loss of $78, which is much more than the max loss of $18 in choice D.

11. C, Paula, like any buyer, can only lose what she pays.

12. C, he pays $2.50 per share for the put and pays $41 for the stock. $43.50 in the debit column. He has the "right to sell stock at Strike Price," so put the $45 in the credit column. The difference of $1.50 per share or $150 total is his gain.

13. D, when you sell an option, you want it to expire worthless. Only the price of $45 would cause the option to expire worthless. The other three prices would leave intrinsic value on the contract, which the seller never wants to see at expiration. If you sell something, you want to walk away and never pay another dime. That happens if the thing expires at-the-money or out-of-the money. At which point it's worthless.

14. D, never buy an option if you think the market will remain unchanged. If you buy an option, you need the market to change in a hurry. Otherwise, the time value comes off your option and you sell it for less than you paid, if it doesn't expire on you. If you think the market will be flat, sell an option. Why sell just one, though, when you can sell both a call and a put with the same strike price? Short straddle.

15. B, for a straddle, enter the premiums in the T-chart. Add and subtract their total from the strike price. $50 plus $3 and $50 minus $3. It's really nothing new from single calls and single puts. Just that we're doing both at the same time.

16. C, if it's not quite a straddle and not quite a spread, we call it a combination.

17. C, he breaks even on the call, and the put expires, letting him pocket the premium.

18. C, volatility assumed, direction unknown. Buy/long a straddle.

19. B, a spread is two calls or two puts. One is long, the other short.

20. B, go to the lower strike price. If they're long, they're a bull. If not, they're a bear.

21. D, it's a debit spread, since he bought the more valuable call.

22. A, it's a credit spread, since she sold the more valuable put.

23. D, to "protect," we buy an option. If we already own stock, we hedge by betting the other way—buy a put.

24. C, to increase income/yield we have to sell an option. Its "arrow" has to be pointed the other way. Long stock—sell a call.

25. D, to "protect," we buy an option. If we are short stock, we hedge by betting the other way—buy a call.

26. C, to increase income/yield we have to sell an option. Its "arrow" has to be pointed the other way. Short stock—short a put.

27. $335, if we buy at 60 and can sell at 60, we can't lose on the stock. We can only lose the premium in this case. It's like a "zero deductible" insurance policy.

28. $5,615, if that stock goes to zero, the only thing working in the investor's favor is the premium. If we lose $6,000 on a stock but take in $385, we lose our maximum of $5,615.

29. $375, if we sell and buy stock at the same price, we lose zero. We can only lose the premium in this case.

30. Unlimited. The investor is short stock. If it goes up, he has no "right to buy." He would only be forced to buy if the stock went his way—down. If it goes up, it just keeps going up.

Futures

The buyer of an options contract has the right to do something. On the other hand, a **futures contract** is a binding agreement between two parties that obligates the two sides to buy and sell something for a set price, with delivery occurring at a specified future date. In the world of commodities including corn, orange juice, and crude oil there is today's cash price—known as the spot price. And then, there is the futures price specifying what the commodity can be bought or sold for as of some future delivery date. Will the price of corn, orange juice or crude oil rise above or fall below that futures price by next December? That is why they open the markets for trading every day.

A grain farmer typically does not wait to harvest 1,000 acres of corn and soybeans in the fall and then see how much the cash or spot price might be at that point. With futures contracts the farmer can sell some corn and soybean futures to buyers who want to lock in a purchase price now for delivery, say, next November. The farmer, this way, can lock in a minimum price he'll receive for some of his corn and beans in case crop prices drop by the time he harvests them. And the buyers who need his corn and beans can lock in a maximum purchase price on what they need to buy in the near future.

Those who use futures to lock in purchase or sale prices related to their businesses are called hedgers. Those who use futures to bet on the near-term price movement of a commodity are called speculators. Common commodities traded include, corn, soybeans, crude oil, live cattle, sugar, and cocoa, to name just a few.

If a farmer is producing corn, and a cereal maker needs to buy corn, the farmer can sell some of his crop even before it's harvested, while the cereal maker can lock in a maximum price for corn set for delivery as of a certain month. In this case, the farmer producing the commodity is short, while the cereal producer is long in the futures contract.

Long positions profit when the price of the commodity rises, while short positions profit when the price of the commodity drops, just as they do with options and common stock. What the two sides are doing, then, is identifying their risk and betting that way. The cereal producer is hurt if the price of the commodities they need rises. Therefore, they bet that way and profit if their risk materializes. The farmer can't take the chance that all of his grain will be sold at depressed prices in the future; therefore, he sells some contracts now representing what could end up being the highest price for delivery the market sees for years. In other words, he'll be glad he sold the corn at $12 a bushel back then if it ends up being worth only $3.50 on the spot market by the time it's harvested.

Futures contracts are standardized by the exchange where they trade. That means that the quantity, the quality, and the delivery are all standard terms so that the prices of the commodities traded mean exactly the same thing to everyone in the market. For example, the quality specifications of each type of crude oil traded are standardized so that "light sweet crude" is the same no matter who produces it. As I write this, I see that the standard terms of coffee futures involve 37,500 pounds of coffee per contract with expiration months in March, May, July, September, and December. Corn futures contracts cover 5,000 bushels each, expressed as a price per-bushel with a minimum "tick size" of ¼ of 1 cent per bushel.

Most options contracts that are near- or in-the-money are closed out before expiration because the buyer of a call option that goes in the money, for example, doesn't want to come up with the cash to buy the stock at the strike price any more than the seller wants to go buy the stock and deliver it.

With futures, all buyers and sellers need to reverse/offset their contracts before expiration to avoid making or accepting delivery of grain, live cattle, or light sweet crude, etc. With futures both sides are obligated to perform the contract if they're holding at expiration. Of course, speculators and hedgers go through brokers, who remind their customers with open long or short positions to close them out before expiration, just as my broker-dealer does for everyone trading options. Even if a retail investor forgot to liquidate a contract to buy 400,000 pounds of live hogs, he would not see a semi-truck pull up to his front door the next day. Rather, he would receive a receipt good for 400,000 pounds of live hogs. Even the hedgers typically liquidate their futures contracts rather than taking delivery of corn, soybeans, etc.

These days the underlying instrument for futures contracts is not just the raw materials/commodities used to produce other products. Stock indexes, interest rates, currencies, and other financially based instruments are used to create **financial futures**. For example, rather than trading S&P 500 index options, a speculator could trade the S&P 500 futures contracts, e.g., the E-Mini S&P and the E-Mini NASDAQ-100. Or, he could speculate on interest rate movements or foreign currency values. There are even contracts for emissions credits, weather, and bandwith available.

As with all derivatives, futures are a "zero-sum game," meaning if one side makes $30,000 it's because the other side lost $30,000. The contracts are also sometimes called "wasting assets," along with options. That is somewhat different from common stock, where one investor can earn dividends over time and sell the stock to someone else, who might end up doing the same before passing it on to another investor. Also, futures give traders leverage, putting them at risk without having to put down much of their own money initially.

Remember that options, on the other hand, are paid in full. If you buy 3 ORCL Oct 40 calls @2, you must pay the full $600 upfront (3 times the $200 represented by the "@2").

Not so with futures. A futures contract is not something that you buy or sell, really. Rather, both sides agree to the daily margin settlement that will occur as the price of the commodity moves day by day. The futures exchange requires both parties to put up an initial amount of cash, called either margin or a good faith deposit—usually between 5 and 15% of the contract value. Then, since the futures price will change daily, the difference in the strike price and the daily futures price is settled daily also.

On the other hand, if you buy those ORCL Oct 40 calls for $2 a share, you don't lose anything right now if they start trading for, say, $1 a share. I mean, it stinks, but until the contract expires, it's just a "paper loss" when you're trading options. However, with futures the exchange will pull money out of one party's margin account and put it into the other's so that each party has the appropriate daily loss or profit. If the margin account goes below a certain value, a margin call is made and the account owner has to deposit more margin to keep the game going. This process of recalculating values daily is known as marking to market, just as it's called in a margin account for stocks and bonds.

When you buy an option, you can only lose what you pay. For example, no matter how far ORCL drops, you can only lose the $2-per-share premium. With a long futures position, however, you would continue to lose as the price of the commodity continues to drop.

As with options, the buyer would only pay the contract price—and the seller receive it—upon delivery. But, as with options, most futures contracts do not lead to delivery. Futures traders offset (reverse) their trades before settlement to avoid having to provide or accept delivery of the actual commodity itself. Maybe 1% of all contracts lead to delivery of the underlying commodity.

Forwards

A **forward** is like a futures contract in that it is a derivative that specifies a price for something for delivery at a specified future date. However, a forward is not traded on an exchange. Also, forward contracts are not standardized the way options and futures contracts are standardized by the exchanges on which they trade. On the options and futures exchanges, we find clearinghouses, which act as a buffer between every buyer and seller. I mean—how do you know for sure the other side can deliver 100,000 shares of ORCL or a million barrels of light sweet crude? You don't, but luckily the options and futures exchanges have all the buyers and sellers going through clearinghouses, which guarantee the performance of every contract, period.

So, forwards are side deals between two parties. How do you know the other side is good for the contract if there's no exchange enforcing margin requirements, settlement dates, and guaranteeing that all contracts are good?

That's the counterparty risk that forwards present to both sides of the contract. On a regulated exchange, options and futures traders do not have to worry about the financial strength of the other side of the contract. The advantage of trading in forwards is the flexibility they allow both sides of the contract—the expiration date, the size of the contract, the terms of the contract, etc., are up to the two parties as opposed to the standardized contracts available on the commodity futures and options exchanges. Some companies have a specific need for a type of derivative that may not be offered on the options or futures exchanges. If that is the case, they may want to structure a private derivative contract with another party called a "forward."

INVESTMENT VEHICE	FEATURES	RISKS	TAX IMPLICATIONS	LOW/MED/HIGH RISK
Common stock	Claim on earnings/dividends Voting rights Pre-emptive rights Unlimited gain	Market Business Legislative	Dividends taxable Capital gains taxable	High
Preferred stock	Fixed-Income No voting rights No pre-emptive rights	Interest-rate risk Credit risk Reinvestment risk	Dividends taxable Capital gains taxable	Low-Med
ADRs	Common stock in foreign companies Purchased in US $s Traded on American	All risks of common stock PLUS, currency exchange risk	Dividends taxable Capital gains taxable Foreign Gov't	High

INVESTMENT VEHICE	FEATURES	RISKS	TAX IMPLICATIONS	LOW/MED/HIGH RISK
	markets		could tax Investor receives credit for US taxes	
REITs	Stock in operating real estate portfolio High dividend yields	All risks of common stock	Dividends are ordinary (not qualified) Capital gains taxable	High
Corporate Bonds	A loan to a corporation Receive interest-only, principal with last payment	Interest rate Credit Reinvestment Call Inflation	Interest taxable as ordinary income all three levels Capital gains taxable	Med
Municipal Bonds	A loan to a state, city, school district, park district, etc. Tax-exempt interest	Interest rate Credit Reinvestment Call Inflation Legislative	Interest exempt at federal and (maybe) state level Capital gains taxable	Low-Med
Treasuries	A loan to the US Government Guaranteed interest, principal	No credit risk All *other* risks to bondholders	Interest taxable at federal level Capital gains taxable all levels	Low

INVESTMENT VEHICE	FEATURES	RISKS	TAX IMPLICATIONS	LOW/MED/HIGH RISK
Zero Coupons	Bought at discount, mature at par No reinvestment risk	Interest Rate Credit Inflation Liquidity	Tax on annual accretion	Depends on issuer
Money Market Securities	Short-term debt securities High liquidity	Purchasing Power Risk/Inflation Risk	Taxable all levels (unless T-Bills or Muni)	Low
Mortgage-Backed Securities	Interests in a pool of mortgages Monthly income and principal	Prepayment Reinvestment Credit (not GNMA) Inflation	Taxable all levels	Low-Med
CMOs	Debt securities based on pools of mortgage-backed securities or mortgages	Complexity Illiquidity Interest Rate Reinvestment	Taxable at all levels	Med
Options	Derivatives based on stock, indexes, currencies, etc.	Capital risk	Gains/losses generally short-term	High
Non-qualified Variable Annuities	Insurance-and-Securities Product No limits on income or contributions	Risks to stock and bond investors, depending on subaccount	Tax-deferred earnings Earnings taxed as ordinary income	Med-High depending on subaccount allocations

INVESTMENT VEHICE	FEATURES	RISKS	TAX IMPLICATIONS	LOW/MED/HIGH RISK
		choices	No RMDs	
Fixed Annuities	Insurance Product No limits on income or contributions No RMDs	Purchasing Power Risk	Tax-deferred earnings Earnings taxed as ordinary income No RMDs	Low—obligation of insurance company
Variable Life Insurance	Cash Value and Death Benefit tied to subaccount performance Insurance-and-Securities Product	Risks to stock and bond investors depending on subaccount choices	Tax-deferred growth of cash value Death benefit not taxable to beneficiary	Med-High depending on subaccount choices
DPPs/Limited Partnerships	Tax Shelter Illiquid investments Net worth requirements	Depends on program Legislative risk (tax code) Liquidity	Tax Shelter if investor has passive income	High
Unit Investment Trusts	Portfolio of preferred stock or bonds Non-managed Redeemable	Interest rate Credit Reinvestment Call Inflation	Distributions taxed as bond interest or preferred stock dividends	Medium-High
Exchange Traded Funds	Trade-able Non-Managed	Depends on index	Tax-efficient	Depends on index

INVESTMENT VEHICE	FEATURES	RISKS	TAX IMPLICATIONS	LOW/MED/HIGH RISK
(typically)	Purchased on Margin Sold Short Low Expenses			
High-Yield/Junk Bonds	Credit quality of issuer in doubt High yields Capital Appreciation	All risks to bondholders Increased credit risk and volatility	Depends on issuer: corporate or municipal	Medium
Warrants	Right to buy issuer's stock at set price long-term Often attached to bond or preferred stock offering	Same risks as to holder of common stock Liquidity risk Time	Price-per-share added to cost basis when exercised to buy stock	High

The Primary Marketplace

Securities are issued to investors on the **primary market** to raise capital for the issuer, while securities are traded among investors on the secondary market. A security can only be issued one time, while it can then be traded an unlimited number of times over the years that follow. Typically, the media starts talking about an "IPO" only when it is about to start trading on the secondary market, where its price can become a daily news story based on the supply and demand for the shares. When you see the folks ringing the opening bell, this marks the day that the IPO shares begin to trade among investors.

This section, on the other hand, is concerned with what happens before that first opening bell is rung.

Corporate Securities Offerings

To complete an **initial public offering** on the primary market under the Securities Act of 1933 a company first registers the securities offering with the Securities and Exchange Commission. The SEC wants to see what the issuers will be telling their potential investors in the prospectus, which is part of the registration statement. They want the issuers to provide the relevant facts on the company: history, competitors, products and services, risks of investing in the company, financials, board of directors, officers, etc. And, like a fussy English instructor, they want it written in clear, readable language. Only if investors clearly understand the risks and rewards of an investment do they have a fair chance of determining a good investment opportunity from a bad one.

The issuer hires **underwriters**, also called **investment bankers**, to help them offer securities to raise money. These broker-dealers act as underwriters/investment bankers, which means they may advise the issuer how to structure the offering of securities to raise the most money possible, and/or they may help sell the IPO shares to investors. Although the underwriters could be "advising" issuers here, they are not acting as investment advisers. Investment advisers help clients invest in other people's securities—the underwriters/investment bankers are acting as broker-dealers when "advising" their underwriting clients on how many shares of common or convertible preferred stock should be issued and at what price. Even when an investment banker charges fees for advising on a securities offering, the firm is still acting within the scope of a registered broker-dealer.

The underwriters help the issuer file a registration statement with the SEC under the Securities Act of 1933. Now, the **cooling-off period**, which will usually last a minimum of 20 days, begins. The SEC is reviewing the registration statement (part of which becomes the prospectus) for clarity and to make sure that at least the boiler plate disclosures have been made. If a section looks incomplete or unclear, they'll make the issuer/underwriters rewrite it. But at no time is the SEC determining that the information is accurate or complete. They couldn't possibly do that; they don't know the issuer's history, and the financial statements the issuer provides—who knows if they're accurate? Since the SEC cannot and does not verify information, the issuer and the underwriters hold a **due diligence meeting** during the cooling-off period, a final meeting to make sure they provided the SEC and the public with accurate and full disclosure.

The issuer does not have to, but they are allowed to publish one very specific type of "advertising" during the cooling-off period—a tombstone advertisement. A tombstone lays out the basic facts: the issuer, the type of security, number of shares, amount to be raised, and then the names of the underwriters:

Even though the SEC requires issuers to register their securities offerings, they don't approve or disapprove of the securities offering or pass judgment on any aspect of the prospectus. They don't guarantee accuracy or adequacy of the information provided by the issuer and its underwriters. In other words, if this whole thing goes belly-up because of inaccurate or incomplete disclosure, the liability still rests with the issuers and underwriters, not the SEC. And there must be a prominent SEC legend such as the following:

Note: the "criminal offense" referred to would be various forms of fraud (securities fraud, wire fraud, mail fraud), but that doesn't mean the SEC is a criminal prosecutor—they are not. The SEC only uses civil courts and their own administrative hearings to make wayward investment advisers, insider traders, and various other ne'er-do-wells cut it out and promise not to do it again. If someone commits crimes within the securities industry, the SEC would refer the case to the Department of Justice.

If the issue of stock is authorized for listing on **NYSE, NASDAQ**, or other major exchanges, the issuer and underwriters only register with the SEC, since the securities are "federal covered securities." But, if the issue will not trade on those exchanges, the stock also must be registered with the states where it will be offered and sold. This state-level registration could be referred to as **blue sky-ing** the issue because "Blue Sky Law" is a synonym for state securities law.

So, nothing happens until the registration statement is filed with the SEC. At that point, the cooling-off period begins. During this period, investors are asked by underwriters and their registered representatives to give indications of interest, and those who do must receive a preliminary prospectus (red herring). No advertising is taking place and no sales literature is used during this cooling-off period. No binding agreements to buy or deliver securities are entered into. The due diligence meeting is held to make sure all the information in the prospectus is as accurate and complete as possible. When the issuer is finally given the effective date (release date) by the SEC, sales from the underwriters to the investors are finalized, all buyers receive a final prospectus, and the issuer receives the capital it needs, with the syndicate keeping the spread for its efforts.

➢ *Investment Banking*

An investment banking firm negotiates the terms of the underwriting deal with the company looking to go public and then acts as the **managing underwriter** of a group of underwriters collectively known as the underwriting **syndicate**. The tombstone we looked at showed some firms in large type with the rest listed below in a smaller font. The firms on top are selling the most shares, with one of them "running the books," keeping the many required records involved with this undertaking.

The managing underwriter will spell out the basic terms of the underwriting and issue a letter of intent to the issuing corporation in which the risks to and obligations of each side are spelled out. The underwriter relies on a **market-out clause,** which explains that certain types of unforeseen events will allow the underwriter to back out of the deal. If the company's drug making facilities are shut down by the FDA due to contamination, for example, the underwriter can back out of the underwriting engagement.

For municipal securities and for some corporate securities offerings, a potential managing underwriter submits a bid or responds to an RFP (request for proposals). This is known as a **competitive bid** as opposed to a **negotiated underwriting**. In a competitive bid, the syndicate who can raise the money at the lowest cost to the issuer wins. In a negotiated underwriting the managing underwriter negotiates the terms of the deal with the issuer, and then forms a group of underwriters known as the underwriting syndicate. Even though firms like Morgan Stanley and Goldman Sachs are fiercely competitive, they also routinely work with each other when underwriting securities. Sometimes Goldman Sachs is the managing underwriter; other times Goldman Sachs is just one of many underwriters in the syndicate. Depends which firm brought the deal to the table.

The syndicate often gives an issuer a **firm commitment**. This means they will bear the risk of any unsold securities and make up the difference by simply buying them for their own investment account. That's a last resort, though. The whole point of doing the underwriting is to sell all the securities as fast as possible, same way a promoter tries to sell concert tickets. But, we can see how important the market-out clause would be in a firm commitment, right? If a drug company had its facilities shut down by the FDA, they might still enjoy receiving the proceeds from some suddenly worthless stock. The market-out clause would allow the underwriters to pull out of the deal.

Underwriters act as agents for the issuer when they engage in a **best efforts, all-or-none**, or **mini-max** underwriting. Here, if the minimum amount is not raised, the underwriters are off the hook. In a best efforts underwriting, the issuer will accept what the underwriters can raise. In the other two types, money is returned to investors if the minimum amount is not raised during the offering period. Broker-dealers involved in either type of **contingency offering** (all-or-none, mini-max) must place all customer payments into an escrow account so that if the offering is canceled, investors receive their money plus their pro rata share of any interest payments. If the underwriter were to place such payments into its own account, this would be a violation of FINRA rules.

The firms in the syndicate usually handle different amounts of an offering, and their liability for any unsold shares is spelled out in an agreement among the underwriters. The agreement among underwriters is called the **agreement among underwriters**. To make sure it has at least two names, though, some refer to it as the **syndicate letter**. If each firm is only responsible for their commitment, this is known as a **western account**. On the other hand, if each firm is responsible for a certain percentage of the offering—even of the shares other firms couldn't sell—this is known as an **eastern account**. To make sure these terms have at least two names each, the western account is "divided" and the eastern account is "undivided," meaning that the liability for unsold shares is either divided up among each firm (western), or it's all for one and one for all (eastern).

Syndicate members in a firm commitment have their firm's capital at risk on the transaction—what the exam might refer to as acting in a **principal** capacity. The syndicate manager, therefore, often lines up other broker-dealers to help sell the offering. This group of sellers is referred to as the **selling group**. The selling group acts in an **agency** capacity for the syndicate, trying to sell shares but bearing no financial risk for the ones they can't place. They have customers who might want to invest—the syndicate is happy to share part of the compensation with these firms. So in a firm commitment underwriting the syndicate members have capital at risk, but selling group members never do in any type of underwriting.

> Underwriter Compensation

Readers are often shocked that securities regulators care about underwriter compensation in a securities offering and sometimes shut down an offering if the compensation is unreasonable. But, yes, securities regulators are concerned with investors. Investors can be defrauded when an issuer pulls most of the value out of the company and gives it to the underwriters either in the form of cash or generous warrants to buy shares at fractions-of-a-penny. Why would an issuer want to do that? Maybe they don't want to pay for the services with money and would rather just take it out of the value of the investors' shares by letting the warrants dilute their equity. Or, maybe the issuer owns a percentage of one of the underwriters. Moving money from this company over to that one would be a pretty neat trick for the issuer, so why not just pay top dollar for the underwriting both in terms of fees and underwriter options/warrants? Promoters are people who founded the company or have a big ownership interest in it. If the offering doesn't pass the smell test in terms of underwriter or promoter compensation, the regulators will shut it down through legal action.

How much do underwriters earn in a typical deal? Let's say the shares of common stock are sold at a **public offering price (POP)** of $20.00, and the syndicate takes 70 cents off the top as the **spread**, giving the issuer $19.30 per share. Of the 70 cents per share, let's say the following parties earn:

> Managing Underwriter: 14 cents
> Syndicate members (including Manager): 16 cents
> Any sellers (syndicate or selling group): 40 cents

Another word for purchasing shares of a new offering is to "subscribe" to the offering. If the IPO involves offering 1 million shares that are fully subscribed, then $20 million comes into the syndicate account from investors. The issuer receives $19.3 million; the syndicate splits up the other $700,000. The managing underwriter takes $140,000 for doing all the extra work, including handling all the regulatory filings and negotiating with the issuer. The members of the syndicate each earn 16 cents per-share, so that $160,000 is split up among the firms according to their participation in the offering.

Remember that the managing underwriter sells the most shares, typically, so they're making not just the manager's fee of $140,000, but also a big part of that $160,000 **underwriting fee.** Then, whichever firm is credited with a particular sale—syndicate or selling group member—gets part of the $400,000 available as the **selling concession.** The managing underwriter must sort all these details out, which is also partly why they get the manager's fee of 14 cents. If the managing underwriter makes a sale, they keep the full 70 cents per-share here. Whenever any syndicate member's shares get sold, they earn 16 cents, but if they want the concession of 40 cents, they must make the sale. If a selling group member makes a sale, they get the concession, with the syndicate members splitting up the underwriting fee of 16 cents in our example. So, the most the managing underwriter can make selling a share of the IPO is $.70. The most any other syndicate member could make is 70 cents minus the manager's fee of 14 cents. The most that a selling group member firm could make on any sale is the concession—or whatever part of it they are entitled to in their agreement with the managing underwriter.

Also, while the selling group (or syndicate) members generally keep the concession when they sell a security, these firms can also pass it down one more level and use another broker-dealer to make the sale. If so, they share part of the concession with them and call this piece the **reallowance,** which is usually half the concession. So, it's not a fourth piece of the spread; it's just the part of the third and fattest piece—the selling concession—that is shared on occasion with firms not in the syndicate or selling group. But, FINRA has strict rules that no one can buy the securities offered below the public offering price unless they're a member firm. All "non-members" must receive the same price that any member of the public would receive. Firms might be tempted to give their biggest customers special deals, but, again, only member firms can receive such special pricing.

Note that the numbers chosen here are merely an illustration. Different offerings have different compensation structures. Speculative stocks generally are underwritten with larger spreads than an A-rated corporate bond. If the underwriting syndicate is making a firm commitment to the issuer, they expect a larger spread than in a best efforts deal in which they bear no financial risk for unsold securities. Also, in a large offering of securities, the spread per-share is typically smaller, as the underwriters can spread costs among a larger dollar amount and make up the smaller spread in volume sales to investors. For a good "real world" example, we can pull up the prospectus for Facebook's IPO. When we do, we see that the shares were sold to investors at a POP of $38, with the spread to the underwriters at about 42 cents per share.

FINRA insists that the terms of the offering among the various underwriters be spelled out clearly. As they state in their rules:

> "Selling syndicate agreements or selling group agreements shall set forth the price at which the securities are to be sold to the public or the formula by which such price can be ascertained, and shall state clearly to whom and under what circumstances concessions, if any, may be allowed."

FINRA has a system of arbitration handling disputes among member firms—this is one place where disputes can easily arise and are, therefore, to be minimized as much as possible.

Here is a tombstone for a small offering of a technology stock from many years ago:

If the three underwriters sold all 2.875 million shares for $4 each, the issuer, RandomAccess, probably received about $10 million, with the three broker-dealers keeping the rest.

> Corporate Financing Department

FINRA's **CFD (Corporate Financing Department)** reviews the fairness of compensation that member firms earn when underwriting securities. As usual, not all offerings are subject to this review—only equity and convertible securities offerings are automatically subject to review. Non-convertible bond and preferred stock offerings are subject only if they are rated below investment-grade. The syndicate manager/lead underwriter files the following information with FINRA's Corporate

This announcement is neither an offer to sell nor a solicitation of an offer to buy any of these Securities. The offer is made only by the Prospectus.

August 18, 1993

2,875,000 Shares
Common Stock

2,875,000 Shares to be offered to the public. The Company engages in the business of selling microcomputer products and providing associated technical services, training and repair to a defined market segment.

✱ RandomAccess ™

NASDAQ/NMS Symbol (RNDM)

Price $4.00 per Share

CHATFIELD DEAN & CO.
MEMBER: NASD SIPC

Foster Jeffries & Co., Inc. • Walford and Company, Inc.

218

Financing Department in connection with an offering of securities:

> The spread
> Expenses reimbursed by the underwriter
> Non-accountable expenses
> Amount of any stock, warrants, or options received as part of compensation
> Right of first refusal to participate in future underwritings with the issuer
> All other items of value

The Corporate Financing Department will also look at any items of value the underwriters received during the 180-day period before filing the registration statement. If so, were the items given in connection with the offering? The CFD will presume they were connected if received within that 180-day window. That doesn't mean if something was received 181 days before filing it was automatically okay. The information filed above with the CFD must be filed within one business day after filing a registration statement for the offering with the SEC.

What would the Corporate Financing Department consider to be unreasonable compensation for member firms to receive from issuers in connection with securities underwritings?

> Options/warrants to be exercised below the public offering price
> Options/warrants lasting > 5 years
> Options/warrants that, when exercised, give underwriters > 10% of offering
> Non-accountable expenses > 3% of underwriting spread
> Right-of-first-refusal lasting > 3 years
> Freely transferable stock (if > 1% of securities being offered)
> Green shoe (over-allotment) clause allowing underwriters to buy > 15% of total offering

Not all expenses should be reimbursed. The underwriters typically cover the fees associated with "blue sky-ing" the issue, for example, which means to register the offering with any state securities departments requiring registration. These expenses should be reimbursed by the issuer. But, as part of the spread, the syndicate should cover the costs involved with soliciting investors—it would be *un*reasonable for those expenses to be "reimbursed."

> ## Specific Types of Securities Offerings

In a **registered secondary** offering the key word is *secondary*. As with all secondary or "non-issuer" transactions, the proceeds are not going to the issuer; rather, they are going to, for example, a former CEO or board member who is now offering his or her restricted shares to the public. The restricted shares were not registered; now they are being registered and offered to investors on the secondary market. Remember that if the issuing corporation does an additional offer of stock, it is *not* a "**secondary offering**." Rather, it is a "subsequent primary distribution." When the issuer gets the proceeds, the word is "primary," not "secondary."

Often when a company is offering securities, so are certain large shareholders such as the venture capital firms that financed the company along the way. If so, we call this a **combined offering**, since it's both primary and secondary, with proceeds going to both the issuer and to persons who are not the issuer.

A specific type of firm commitment is called a **standby underwriting**. While a broker-dealer cannot buy IPO shares for its own account just because it wants to, they can act as a standby purchaser for the issuer, buying any shares the public doesn't want. Usually, when we see the phrase "standby" on the exam, we associate it with an additional offering of stock, which inherently involves a **rights offering**. Shareholders are owners of a certain percent of a company's profits; therefore, if new shares are sold to other people, the % owned by existing shareholders would be decreased or "diluted" if they didn't get first right of refusal on a certain number of shares. That's why issuers performing an additional offering of stock typically do a rights offering that provides existing shareholders the right to buy their % of the new shares—or not. To ensure that all of these rights are used/subscribed to, a standby underwriter may be engaged to agree to buy any rights that shareholders don't use and exercise them to buy the rest of the shares being offered.

Some offerings of securities are registered now but will be sold gradually at the current "market price." That means that if you buy in the first round, you might end up paying more, or less, than the investors who buy shares at the then-current "market price." What if there is no "market" for the shares being offered in an **at the market** offering? Then, the SEC has a real problem with broker-dealers or their associated persons telling investors they're buying the security "at the market." If the stock doesn't trade on an exchange, the broker-dealer may not tell the customer the security is being offered to (or purchased from) the customer at the so-called "market price." That would be a "manipulative, deceptive, or other fraudulent device or contrivance," according to the SEC. If the firm is the only firm willing to make a bid/offer on the stock, that, by definition, means there is no actual market for the security.

An issuer might want to register a certain number of securities now but sell them gradually or on demand over the next few years. If so, the issuer can use a **shelf registration.** For example, if they want to borrow money by issuing bonds, they might want to get them registered now but wait and hope that interest rates will drop over the next few years, at which point they can issue the bonds and borrow the money at more attractive rates in the future, with the offering already on-deck and ready to go. Or, if the company has a dividend reinvestment program (DRIP) in place, or must continuously issue shares when executives and key employees exercise stock options, they are likely to use a shelf registration.

Some issuers register the securities, which are then effective for the next two years. A handful of large issuers can register now and then sell their securities over the next three years. This second type of issuer is known as a well-known seasoned issuer (WKSI), and they are granted more flexibility than mere seasoned issuers, let alone unseasoned issuers or non-reporting issuers. As those terms imply, the more that is known about the issuer, the less information that is required of them, and vice versa. When a well-known seasoned issuer files the automatic shelf registration statement for a shelf offering, it is considered effective immediately. The form used for these offerings is either an S-3 or an F-3.

> Overallotments

If there is heavy demand for a security, the underwriters may want to sell more shares than initially registered with the SEC. If so, a **green shoe clause** negotiated between the issuer and the underwriters can be invoked, allowing the syndicate to sell up to 15% more shares than were registered initially.

This green shoe clause must be disclosed in the registration statement filed with the SEC and the prospectus. Without such a provision the demand for the new securities could become excessive, making the market price excessively volatile.

A high-risk way of "over-allotting" is for the syndicate manager to sell shares short, with the obligation to repurchase them later in the secondary market. If the stock price rises above the IPO price in the secondary market, however, the syndicate will sustain losses when covering the short positions—buying them back for more than they sold the borrowed shares. The syndicate will share any of those losses due to selling shares short as stipulated in the agreement among underwriters, the contract that binds the various broker-dealers in the joint effort to underwrite the issuer's securities. The managing underwriter also needs to notify FINRA of this activity for any "OTC equity security."

When a new issue of stock comes out, there is much concern on the part of the issuer and the underwriters that investors do not suddenly start dumping the stock as if it's radioactive waste. As with houses, if everybody decides they need to sell right now, the price can plummet. So, investors are strongly encouraged against flipping (making a quick sale of) their IPO shares on the secondary market. The managing underwriter can also lean on the member firms and their associated persons by taking back the selling concession earned on shares that customers flip/sell quickly to other investors, but FINRA rules state that the syndicate managing member firm cannot assess a penalty bid at all unless the "penalty bid" applies to the entire syndicate—not just this one firm or registered representative. Special records must be kept on any penalty bids or other disincentives assessed on the associated persons of a member firm.

> When-Issued

The term **when-issued** is an abbreviation for the longer form of securities that are traded "when, as, and if issued." As the name implies, when-issued refers to a transaction made conditionally, because a security has not yet been issued—only authorized. U.S. Treasury securities—sold at auctions—new issues of stocks and bonds, and stocks that are offered continuously or over time are all examples of when-issued securities.

> Stabilization

Normally, anyone caught trying to artificially move the price of a security on the secondary market is subject to regulatory problems, civil liability to other traders, and sometimes even criminal penalties. If a few big traders of some small-company stock get together and come up with a plan to enter large buy orders at certain times throughout the day to boost the price, they are engaging in market manipulation.

On the other hand, right after a new offering of securities, the lead underwriter is allowed to prop up the price of the stock on the secondary market to some extent through **stabilization**. If the public offering price or POP is $10, but the stock starts trading on NASDAQ or NYSE for only $9.50, the managing/lead underwriter can place bids to buy the stock to provide a floor price for the investors nice enough to buy the IPO. Now, the bid can't be higher than the POP of $10, and it also can't be higher than the highest *independent* bid for the stock. That means the bid had better be bona fide and cannot come from a subsidiary of the managing underwriter's firm, for example. If another market maker is quoting $9.50, the managing underwriter can bid $9.50, but not $9.51. And, should the price rise to the public offering price again, no bids above the POP could be placed.

These quotes are known to change by the second or fractions of seconds, but each time the managing/lead underwriter places a bid to buy the stock on the secondary market, they must keep it no higher than the highest current bid for the stock.

Stabilizing bids are always one-sided, meaning there is no ask/offer price. Remember, the syndicate is trying to support the stock with *buying* pressure. Since this is an unusual situation, stabilizing bids must be identified as stabilizing bids on the NASDAQ trading system. Before the managing underwriter enters any stabilizing bids, the firm must first submit a request to NASDAQ MarketWatch to enter one-sided stabilizing bids. It is typically the managing underwriter who enters stabilizing bids, but whether it's that firm or another syndicate member, remember that only one firm can be placing stabilizing bids.

What if there *is* no independent market maker for the stock? Then, no stabilizing bids can be placed, period. The syndicate also must disclose any plans for stabilization in a legend (box of text) in the offering document that refers to disclosures in the "plan of distribution" section of the prospectus regarding stabilization activities.

Records must be kept by broker-dealers engaging in stabilization activities. The SEC requires the following in formation be kept for 3 years:

> The name and class of any security stabilized or any security in which syndicate covering transactions have been effected or a penalty bid has been imposed
>
> The price, date, and time at which each stabilizing purchase or syndicate covering transaction was effected by the manager or by any participant in the syndicate or group, and whether any penalties were assessed
>
> The names and the addresses of the members of the syndicate
>
> Their respective commitments, or, in the case of a standby or contingent underwriting, the percentage participation of each member of the syndicate

The managing underwriter must also furnish information to the other syndicate members, including:

> the name and class of any security being stabilized
>
> date and time at which the first stabilizing purchase was effected by the manager or by any participant in the syndicate
>
> date and time when stabilizing was terminated

Usually, it's the managing/lead underwriter entering the stabilizing bids, but if any other member of the syndicate does so, they need to notify the syndicate manager within 3 business days of "the price, date, and time at which such stabilizing purchase or syndicate covering transaction was effected, and shall in addition notify the manager of the date and time when such stabilizing purchase or syndicate covering transaction was terminated."

An offer of securities involves publishing and delivering a prospectus to interested investors. The Securities Act of 1933 states that a prospectus must "contain the information contained in the registration statement."

> Information required in a registration statement

The Securities Act of 1933 and the rules thereunder guide the registration process for issuers, as does **Regulation S-K**. Regulation S-K provides guidance on forward-looking statements made by an issuer and lays out the information required in various types of securities registration statements. Regulation S-K makes it clear that to file full disclosure of risks and business plans an issuer necessarily must make projections. While such projections can provide clarity, the issuer also must have a reasonable basis for making projections about, say, a proposed merger, or projections of earnings for a key business unit.

Aiding investor understanding is key, and the SEC explains their concerns like this, "When management chooses to include its projections in a Commission filing, the disclosures accompanying the projections should facilitate investor understanding of the basis for and limitations of projections. In this regard investors should be cautioned against attributing undue certainty to management's assessment, and the Commission believes that investors would be aided by a statement indicating management's intention regarding the furnishing of updated projections."

To give investors an idea of how big a gap could exist between management's previous projections and reality, the SEC stipulates that, "Management also should consider whether disclosure of the accuracy or inaccuracy of previous projections would provide investors with important insights into the limitations of projections. In this regard, consideration should be given to presenting the projections in a format that will facilitate subsequent analysis of the reasons for differences between actual and forecast results."

Most American companies use a Form S-1 to register an offer of common stock. When filling out this registration statement, the issuer is required to provide the following information about the business:

> A general description of their business: Describe the general development of the business of the registrant, its subsidiaries and any predecessor(s) during the past five years, or such shorter period as the registrant may have been engaged in business.
>
> Description of property: State briefly the location and general character of the principal plants, mines and other materially important physical properties of the registrant and its subsidiaries. In addition, identify the segment(s), as reported in the financial statements, that use the properties described.
>
> Legal proceedings: Describe briefly any material pending legal proceedings, other than ordinary routine litigation incidental to the business, to which the registrant or any of its subsidiaries is a party or of which any of their property is the subject.

Mine safety disclosure: companies involved in mining must disclose the total number of violations of mandatory health or safety standards that could significantly and substantially contribute to the cause and effect of a coal or other mine safety or health hazard for which the operator received a citation from the Mine Safety and Health Administration.

Securities of the registrant: identify the principal United States market or markets in which each class of the registrant's common equity is being traded. Where there is no established public trading market for a class of common equity, furnish a statement to that effect. Also indicate the approximate number of shareholders and any dividends paid over the previous two years.

Description of registrant's securities: provide legal description of the securities in terms of rights of holders of common stock, preferred stock, debt securities, etc.

Financial information: provide financial information (balance sheet, income statement, cash flow, etc.) for the previous five years or life of operations.

Management's discussion and analysis of financial condition and results of operations: discuss registrant's financial condition, changes in financial condition and results of operations.

Changes in and disagreements with accountants on accounting and financial disclosure: provide disclosure on any auditing accountants who were removed, resigned, etc.

Quantitative and qualitative disclosures about market risk: discuss market risk and risk factors for the registrant's securities.

Management and certain security holders: list the names and ages of all directors of the registrant and all persons nominated or chosen to become directors; indicate all positions and offices with the registrant held by each such person. List the names and ages of all executive officers of the registrant and all persons chosen to become executive officers; indicate all positions and offices with the registrant held by each such person; state his term of office as officer and the period during which he has served as such and describe briefly any arrangement or understanding between him and any other person(s) (naming such person) pursuant to which he was or is to be selected as an officer. Identify certain significant employees who are not officers and disclose the same information required of corporate officers.

Executive compensation: provide details of executive officers' compensation, cash, stock, options, etc.

Security ownership of certain beneficial owners and management: options and shares held by management and large shareholders.

Corporate governance: discuss whether directors are independent.

The issuer must also provide the following information on the offer of securities:

Name of registrant

Title and amount of securities

Offering price of the securities

Market for the securities

Risk factors

State legend: Any warnings required of state regulators.

Commission legend: A legend that indicates that neither the Securities and Exchange Commission nor any state securities commission has approved or disapproved of the securities or passed upon the accuracy or adequacy of the disclosures in the prospectus and that any contrary representation is a criminal offense.

Underwriting: information on underwriters of the securities.

Date of prospectus

Prospectus subject to completion legend: if a preliminary prospectus.

Use of proceeds: what will the issuer do with the proceeds of the offering? As the SEC states, "State the principal purposes for which the net proceeds to the registrant from the securities to be offered are intended to be used and the approximate amount intended to be used for each such purpose. Where registrant has no current specific plan for the proceeds, or a significant portion thereof, the registrant shall so state and discuss the principal reasons for the offering."

Selling security holders: if any of the securities are being offered by security holders, provide information on each one.

Issuers must provide a table of contents on either the inside front or outside back cover of the prospectus to help investors navigate the document. As the SEC states, "It must show the page number of the various sections or subdivisions of the prospectus. Include a specific listing of the risk factors section required by Item 503 of this Regulation S-K."

> Prospectus delivery

Dealers have prospectus delivery requirements, so the SEC requires that, "On the outside back cover page of the prospectus advise dealers of their prospectus delivery obligation, including the expiration date specified by . . . the Securities Act of 1933." The final prospectus must be delivered to all buyers of an IPO no later than completion of the transaction. It also must be delivered to buyers on the secondary market—the investors buying from the IPO investors—for a certain amount of time, depending on which market it trades on. Since there isn't much required of or known about Pink Quote or OTCBB stocks, the prospectus for an IPO must be delivered for 90 days on the secondary market, even after the offering period closes. For additional offerings of these stocks, the prospectus must be provided on the secondary market for 40 days. For NYSE and NASDAQ securities IPOs require the prospectus be delivered for 25 days, but for additional offers there is no requirement to deliver the prospectus on the after- or secondary market.

Broker-dealers must respond promptly to any written request for a preliminary or final prospectus. Any associated persons expected to solicit sales must be provided with copies of the preliminary prospectus and also the final prospectus—if the information is materially different from the preliminary prospectus. If the broker-dealer is the managing underwriter, they must provide sufficient copies of these documents to all syndicate and selling group members requesting them. Because of prospectus delivery requirements after the offering period, the managing underwriter also must provide copies of these disclosure documents to firms who will make a market in or trade heavily in the security.

The prospectus for an IPO is often retired soon after the offering is completed. But, the prospectus for a mutual fund or variable annuity would be subject to regular updates. Therefore, if a prospectus is used more than 9 months after the effective date, the information cannot be more than 16 months old. The SEC has the authority to permit issuers to omit any item of information by their rules if they feel it's not necessary for the protection of investors to include it. By the same token the SEC has the authority to decide that a prospectus must contain whatever they stipulate through their rulemaking process and authority.

There are many different types/forms of "prospectuses," which is why the Securities Act of 1933 states, "the Commission shall have authority to classify prospectuses according to the nature and circumstances of their use or the nature of the security, issue, issuer, or otherwise, and, by rules and regulations and subject to such terms and conditions as it shall specify therein, to prescribe as to each class the form and contents which it may find appropriate and consistent with the public interest and the protection of investors." A "prospectus" can come in the form of a TV or radio broadcast, which is why the Securities Act of 1933 also states, "In any case where a prospectus consists of a radio or television broadcast, copies thereof shall be filed with the Commission under such rules and regulations as it shall prescribe."

➤ *FINRA Rules*

If the underwriters have set the POP of a stock at $10, what happens if it becomes clear the stock will probably trade much higher as soon as it opens on the secondary market? Wouldn't it be tempting to hold all the shares for their own account and reap all the profits themselves?

> Freeriding and Withholding

Might be tempting, but it's not allowed by FINRA, who calls the violation "freeriding and withholding." These public offerings must be bona fide (good and true) distributions. That means that if your firm is an underwriter or a selling group member, it must sell all the shares it is allotted to investors, no matter how tempting it might be to keep most of them for its own account. In other words, investment bankers cannot pretend to be offering stock to the public and then sort of change their minds and keep the good ones for themselves. Offering a firm commitment is fine, provided the underwriters made a good faith effort to distribute the shares to the public before buying the remainder from the issuer for their own account.

> Restricted Persons

IPO shares in a hot company could be used as rewards, or as a means to threaten people. The prohibited practice of spinning occurs when underwriting broker-dealers allocate shares of popular IPO stocks to investors who can then direct securities business to the firm as a thank-you. To prevent spinning, FINRA prohibits the practice of allocating IPO shares to officers and directors of companies if the company is an investment banking customer of the broker-dealer or becomes an investment banking customer in the next three months—or even if it's pretty clear that the IPO allocation is designed to serve as a nice present that should be reciprocated with a phone call or business lunch to discuss opportunities.

Clearly, it is not okay for an underwriting broker-dealer to try to force someone into buying 100,000 shares of an IPO by threatening to withhold shares of future offerings if he doesn't. Similarly, it would be a violation for the managing underwriter to offer to allot 1 million shares to a broker-dealer who first writes a favorable research report on the stock. These violations could get the regulators to start using fancy phrases like "quid pro quo," which means you-scratch-my-back-I'll-scratch-yours in the original Latin. *Quid pro quo allocations* of IPO shares are not allowed. Why should the public investor be exposed to some bogus "research report" that is almost certainly overly enthusiastic due to the conflict of interest? Turns out they shouldn't be and that's why quid pro quo allocations are not allowed. You've likely noticed that virtually anything that threatens the integrity of the securities markets is not allowed by the SEC, FINRA or both.

To that end, broker-dealers acting to distribute the shares to the public might prefer to hang onto most of them for their own account if the stock has a lot of demand. No, the underwriting syndicate must make a bona fide public offering as opposed to pretending nobody wants the shares and just keeping them for themselves.

To make sure that public offerings of stock have integrity FINRA has imposed rules that will likely prevent you, dear reader, from buying IPO shares, period. The FINRA rules apply only to initial public offerings of common stock—not to debt securities, preferred stock, mutual funds, or *additional* offers of common stock. So, we're only talking about the companies coming out-of-the-starting-gates with an IPO here. Even if it's a bond that converts to common stock—not subject to this rule.

Who is defined as a **restricted person** and, therefore, restricted from buying IPOs?

broker-dealer member firms
employees of broker-dealer member firms
anyone/any entity owning 10% or more of a broker-dealer member firm
finders and fiduciaries acting on behalf of the managing underwriter (e.g., attorneys, accountants, financial consultants)
portfolio managers (mutual funds, banks, pension funds, insurance company , etc.) buying for their own account
any immediate family member of anyone above

So, if you own 10% or more of a FINRA member broker-dealer, or if you are a broker-dealer, or if you merely work for a broker-dealer, or have someone in your immediate family who fits any of those descriptions, you are basically not buying into an initial public offer of common stock. What does "immediate family member" include? First, it includes anyone who receives material financial support from a restricted person. Then, it includes: parents and in-laws, spouses, siblings, and children of a restricted person. So, if your sister works for Morgan-Stanley, you are a restricted person as an immediate family member. On the other hand, the following family members are considered too distant to worry about: aunts and uncles, grandparents, cousins. What if you have one of those old college buddies that just can't seem to catch a break? Whether he lives with you is irrelevant; remember that, among other reasons, you might want to keep your financial support to under 25% of his income. Yes, "material support" means providing more than 25% of an individual's personal income for the prior year.

The exam might bring up the fact that while a receptionist for a member firm is a restricted person, if that individual is in a joint account, and that individual's ownership is no more than 10%, then the account can buy an equity IPO under the "de minimis rule." You can see why broker-dealers who engage in underwriting activities need initial and annual statements obtained in the past 12 months or sooner from their customers verifying that they either are or are not a "restricted person". These are known as pre-conditions for sale of an equity IPO.

Nothing is ever simple in this business. Even though I just said that broker-dealers are not allowed to buy shares of an equity IPO, there are exceptions. If a broker-dealer—usually one of the underwriters—signs an agreement to act as a standby purchaser, then they can help an offering that is selling weakly by promising to buy any shares the public doesn't want. This arrangement must be in writing; it must be disclosed in the final prospectus; and the managing underwriter must state in writing that it was unable to find any other purchasers for the stock.

So, can a broker-dealer buy an equity IPO? No, except when they can—e.g., by acting as a standby purchaser with a bona fide agreement in writing that is disclosed in the prospectus. Note that securities purchased through a standby agreement may not be re-sold to investors for at least three months. See? These regulators—they think of everything!

The FINRA rules surrounding equity IPOs are designed to make sure that broker-dealers, their employees, and their family members don't unfairly profit from the process at the expense of public investors. If the offer of securities is considered to be an issuer-directed sale, however, things are different.

First, if the issuer is selling directly to investors, without any underwriters getting involved, then the parties on our restricted list are good to go. For example, the exam might mess with you by asking if the issuer can sell an equity IPO directly to one or two member broker-dealers buying for their own investment purposes. Absolutely. The rules kick in when member broker-dealers act as underwriters, stepping in between the issuer and public investors to make the spread. Provided no underwriter "solicits or sells any new issue securities in the offering, and has no involvement or influence . . . in the issuer's allocation decisions with respect to any of the new issue securities in the offering" then the *issuer* can sell directly to restricted persons, even a FINRA member broker-dealer firm. Also, an issuer-directed sale would include a program in which at least 10,000 persons are allowed to participate, and each can buy up to the same number of shares. If anyone does not buy shares, then the selection system must be random—not benefiting any restricted persons. But, in this case, restricted persons can buy the offering, provided it doesn't become disproportionate and tilted toward the restricted persons vs. everyone else in terms of the percentage of investors subscribing to the offering of shares.

A special problem arises from these rules in terms of dilution of equity. Remember that shareholders have the preemptive right to maintain their proportionate ownership of a company. That means when a company offers more shares to investors, existing investors must receive subscription rights so they can subscribe to their percentage of the new shares being offered. If a restricted person already happens to have an equity stake in the company (they invested back when the issuer was still a private company), then it wouldn't be fair to prevent them from at least maintaining their existing percentage of ownership. So, under anti-dilution provisions shares of an equity IPO can be sold to a restricted person if he/it has held an equity stake in the issuer or a company the issuer recently acquired for at least 12 months, and "the sale of the new issue to the account shall not increase the account's percentage equity ownership in the issuer above the ownership level as of three months prior to the filing of the registration statement in connection with the offering," and the sale of the new issue involves no special terms, and the securities cannot be re-sold for at least three months.

That might sound excessive, but if, say, Morgan-Stanley's private equity group owns a company that is bought by a larger entity that is then going public, Morgan-Stanley should be able to maintain their percentage of ownership along with any other investor. And they can, provided everything is done properly and all required records are maintained.

Also, it's not the underwriters' fault if the public just isn't that into this IPO. Therefore, if the managing underwriter or other syndicate members end up buying the unsold shares of an undersubscribed offering and hold them in their investment account, that is not only okay, but is also common practice. The idea is that they can't pretend they couldn't sell all the good IPOs to end up keeping them for themselves—that, as we saw, is a violation.

FINRA rules state: the book-running managing underwriter of a new issue shall be required to file the following information in the time and manner specified by FINRA with respect to new issues:

> the initial list of distribution participants and their underwriting commitment and retention amounts on or before the offering date; and
> the final list of distribution participants and their underwriting commitment and retention amounts no later than three business days after the offering date.

A "distribution participant" is "an underwriter, prospective underwriter, broker, dealer, or other person who has agreed to participate or is participating in a distribution."

An IPO is not to be treated as a quick buy-and-flip opportunity. If some investors are immediately selling their shares on the secondary market, that can push the market price of the stock downward. This is what FINRA must say about the process:

> The term "flipping" refers to the practice of selling new issues into the secondary market at a profit within 30 days following the offering date. Because these sales create downward pressure on the secondary market trading price, underwriters and selling group members may seek to discourage such sales. Under most syndicate selling agreements, a managing underwriter is permitted to impose a "penalty bid" on syndicate members to reclaim the selling concession for allocations that were flipped. Separately, and independent of any syndicate penalty bid, some firms have sought to recoup selling concessions from particular brokers when their <u>customers</u>—typically retail customers—flip a new issue. [FINRA rules prohibit] any member from recouping any portion of a commission or credit paid or awarded to an associated person for selling shares of a new issue that are subsequently flipped by a customer, unless the managing underwriter has assessed a penalty bid on the entire syndicate. FINRA believes that it is only appropriate for a firm to recoup a particular broker's compensation for selling a new issue in connection with a customer's decision to flip a security when the firm itself is required to forfeit its compensation to the managing underwriter(s).

> Research Analysts and Research Reports

As we saw earlier, many of the large broker-dealers have research analysts writing and publishing research reports that explain why an investor might consider investing in a particular stock. A research report is a form of marketing the broker-dealer uses to get its name before the eyes of investors and give them a clear idea of why they might want to invest some money through the broker-dealer.

In olden days many research analysts were nothing but cheerleaders trying to support the price of an issuer's stock as a favor for doing investment banking deals with the broker-dealer. That kind of thing happened a lot in the dot-com era, but ever since then FINRA has clamped down on research analyst activities in the following ways:

research analysts may not participate in road shows

research analysts may not have compensation tied to investment banking activity generated by subject companies

a committee that reports to the firm's board of directors must review and approve at least annually research analysts' compensation

the committee must document in writing the basis used to set each analyst's compensation

the investment banking department may not set the compensation for research analysts or serve on the committee mentioned above

research analysts and member firms may not promise favorable research coverage in exchange for the issuer doing investment banking business

Research analysts can only contact the companies whose stock they're researching to do basic fact-checking. The analysts may not share any information with the issuer on the price target for the stock that will be printed in the report, or any proposed rating (buy/hold/outperform, etc.) or even the research summary. Again, the analyst cannot offer to provide a favorable rating on the stock in exchange for the issuer's investment banking business, or threaten to give the stock a negative rating if they don't use the firm's services. The analyst must disclose in research reports or public appearances if he or anyone in his immediate family has any financial interest in the company being researched and if their firm owned 1% or more of any class of the subject company's equity securities at the close of the previous month.

The personal trading of research analysts is restricted by FINRA rules. Now, the employing broker-dealers can easily say absolutely-no-trading-in-any-company-you-research. But, at a minimum they must follow the FINRA rules that prohibit research analysts and their immediate family from investing in a company's securities prior to its IPO if it operates in the same industry sector covered by the research analyst. Also, for 30 days before publishing a research report and for 5 days after publishing it the analyst and his immediate family are prohibited from trading in the stock covered by the report. This time-frame runs from the publication of a research report, or even from the time the analyst updates his rating or price target on the stock. The regulators are simply trying to prevent analysts and their immediate families from trying to use the temporary buzz provided by a research report to help them make quick trading profits whether the reports contain any actual "research" or not.

To prevent investment banking and research reports from getting thrown together into the mix, broker-dealers must provide lots of disclosure on their research reports. For example, they need to explain their rating systems and give percentages as to how many of their recommendations end up in each category. They also need to disclose the fact, if applicable, that they received within the previous 12 months fees for investment banking services or acted as manager or co-manager for an offering of the issuer's stock. Also, the firm needs to disclose on the research report if they intend to seek investment banking business within the next 3 months of publishing the research report.

Also, if a member firm acted as manager or co-manager of a securities offering for an issuer, they generally may not issue any research reports on that stock for 40 days following an IPO or 10 days following an additional issue.

Member broker dealers are required to make a formal attestation/statement to FINRA that they have adopted and implemented procedures to comply with rules on research analysts. Specifically, the compensation of the firm's research analyst needs to be discussed.

Exempt Securities
The Securities Act of 1933 is a piece of federal legislation, so it's not surprising that the federal government is not required to abide by it. That's right, government securities are exempt from this act. T-Bills, T-Notes, T-Bonds, STRIPS, and TIPS are not required to be registered. Neither are municipal securities, issued by states, counties, cities, and school districts, etc.

Why is that? First, the U.S. Treasury Department was issuing Treasury Bonds 150 years before the SEC was even created, and the SEC and Treasury are both part of the U.S. Government, after all.

Also, companies go out of business all the time, and when their sales dry up, the bonds go into default, and the shares of common stock are no longer worth the paper they're printed on. That's not the case when the U.S. Treasury sells a T-note or T-bond. That's just a loan backed by the full faith and credit of the United States Government, as sound as the money in your wallet.

States, counties, and cities, etc.—those who issue municipal securities—also got an exemption from the registration process under the Securities Act of 1933. The federal government generally does not exert that much control over any State government, and municipal governments are not as likely to go bankrupt as corporations. So, if a school board puts out an issue of municipal securities based on fraudulent financial statements, the SEC could go after them in federal court. But, these municipal securities issuers do not file registration statements with the SEC and wait for the SEC to tell them it's okay to proceed.

Charitable/fraternal/religious/benevolent organization securities are exempt. So are bank securities, which are already regulated by bank regulators (FDIC, FRB, and Comptroller of the Currency). Securities issued by Small Business Investment Companies (SBICs) are also exempt, since they are only offered and sold to institutions and other sophisticated investors who don't require so much protection.

Short-term debt securities that mature in 270 days or less—commercial paper, bankers' acceptances, other promissory notes—are also exempt from this registration process. I mean, if a corporation had to get through the registration process just to borrow money for a few days, weeks, or months, interest rates would likely have moved before the deal could be completed. On the other hand, if they want to borrow money for several years by issuing bonds or sell ownership stakes, the regulators feel maybe they ought to slow down first and reveal a lot of material facts to investors.

Exempt Transactions

So, commercial paper, T-Notes, and municipal bonds are exempt securities. They are good to go without any paperwork being filed with the SEC. As we saw elsewhere, there are also transactions that qualify for exemptions, called exempt transactions. Unlike an exempt security that is "good to go," an exempt transaction must be claimed by the issuer with some paperwork to back up what they did or are about to do. Under **Regulation A** an issuer can sell up to $5,000,000 worth of securities in a year without having to jump through all the usual hoops. Rather than filing a standard registration statement, the issuer files an **offering circular**, a much more scaled-down document.

An issuer completing a Regulation A offering must file with the SEC a Form 1-A offering statement. Once that is filed, oral offers can be made as well as written offers that conform to the following criteria. First, the outside cover page of the material must bear the caption "Preliminary Offering Circular," the date of issuance, and the statement that, "An offering statement pursuant to Regulation A relating to these securities has been filed with the Securities and Exchange Commission. Information contained in this Preliminary Offering Circular is subject to completion or amendment. These securities may not be sold nor may offers to buy be accepted prior to the time an offering circular which is not designated as a Preliminary Offering Circular is delivered and the offering statement filed with the Commission becomes qualified. This Preliminary Offering Circular shall not constitute an offer to sell or the solicitation of an offer to buy nor shall there be any sales of these securities in any state in which such offer, solicitation or sale would be unlawful prior to registration or qualification under the laws of any such state."

The preliminary offering circular must contain substantially the information required on Form 1-A except that the following information can be omitted:

offering price
underwriting discounts or commissions
discounts or commissions to dealers
amount of proceeds, conversion rates, call prices, or other matters dependent upon the offering price

The SEC requires that, "The outside front cover page of the Preliminary Offering Circular shall include a bona fide estimate of the range of the maximum offering price and maximum number of shares or other units of securities to be offered or a bona fide estimate of the principal amount of debt securities to be offered."

And, the preliminary offering circular must be filed as part of the offering statement with the SEC.

Once the Form 1-A has been filed, the issuer can make oral offers and written offers with the preliminary offering circular. In addition, the SEC states that, "Printed advertisements may be published or radio or television broadcasts made, if they state from whom a Preliminary Offering Circular or Final Offering Circular may be obtained, and contain no more than the following information:

The name of the issuer of the security
The title of the security, the amount being offered and the per unit offering price to the public
The general type of the issuer's business
A brief statement as to the general character and location of its property.

No sales can be made of Reg A securities until the final offering circular has been qualified by the SEC, and purchasers must receive the final offering circular by confirmation of the sale.

The SEC is in charge of interstate commerce, meaning commerce among many states. Therefore, if the issuer wants to sell only to residents of one state, the SEC doesn't get involved. There is already a state securities regulator who can deal with this one. Therefore, intra-state offerings are exempt if they match this statement, "Any security which is a part of an issue offered and sold only to persons resident within a single State or Territory, where the issuer of such security is a person resident and doing business within or, if a corporation, incorporated by and doing business within, such State or Territory." These offerings would be registered with the securities regulator of that particular state or territory rather than the federal government. Notice that the state where the offering takes place is where the issuer is located and doing business. The issuer doesn't just pick a state at random in which to offer the securities.

These intra-state offerings are performed under an exemption to the Securities Act of 1933 called Rule 147. As the rule states, the offering is not required to be registered with the SEC provided "That the issuer be a resident of and doing business within the state or territory in which all offers and sales are made; and that no part of the issue be offered or sold to non-residents within the period of time specified in the rule." So, if the issuer's main business is located in the state, 80% of its gross revenue is derived there, 80% of its assets are located there, and 80% of the net proceeds will be used in that state, a Rule 147 exemption can be claimed to avoid registration with the SEC. But, as the second requirement clarified, the buyers can't sell the security to a non-resident for a time specified by the rule—which is nine months.

To be an eligible investor, the individual must be a resident of the state, or a partnership, LLC, corporation, trust or other entity that has its principal office within the state. And, if an entity is formed for the purpose of acquiring part of the offering, it would only be eligible if all of the beneficial owners of the organization are residents of the state or territory (e.g. Puerto Rico).

The SEC is out to protect the average investor from fast-talking stock operators. But, the SEC doesn't provide as much protection to sophisticated investors such as mutual funds, pension funds, or high-net-worth individuals. If anybody tries to scam these investors, they'll be in just as much trouble as if they scammed an average investor, but the SEC doesn't put up as much protection for the big, institutional investors, who can usually watch out for themselves. Therefore, if the issuer wants to avoid the registration process under the Act of 1933, they can limit the offer and sale of the securities primarily to these accredited investors. Accredited investors include institutions such as:

    banks
    broker-dealers
    insurance companies
    investment companies
    small business investment companies
    government retirement plans
    company retirement plans of a certain minimum size

An accredited investor also includes an executive officer, director, or general partner of the issuer. That seems right to me. If Amazon wants to sell shares of Amazon to Jeff Bezos and the members of the board, how much protection do these investors need from the company they themselves run?

Accredited investors also include individuals or married couples with at least $1 million net worth excluding the value of their primary residence. If not relying on net worth, an accredited investor can qualify based on income. Individuals earning at least $200,000 a year in the most recent two years and married couples earning at least $300,000—with a reasonable expectation of making at least that much this year—are also accredited investors.

The SEC creates many regulations under the various federal securities acts. Under the Securities Act of 1933, the SEC created a group of transactions exempt from the usual registration requirements. However, don't jump to conclusions. These offerings are exempt from registration requirements only; they are not completely outside the scope of the act. As **Regulation D** announces from the start, "Regulation D relates to transactions exempted from the registration requirements of section 5 of the Securities Act of 1933. Such transactions are not exempt from the antifraud, civil liability, or other provisions of the federal securities laws. Issuers are reminded of their obligation to provide such further material information, if any, as may be necessary to make the information required under Regulation D, in light of the circumstances under which it is furnished, not misleading."

Under Regulation D an issuer finds various offerings that can be completed without the usual registration requirements having to be met. Let's look at the best known exempt transactions, performed under either Rule 505 or 506.

A **Reg D/private placement** transaction is exempt based on the issuer offering to an unlimited number of accredited investors but only to a maximum of 35 **non-accredited purchasers**. Under Rule 505 the issuer can only offer and sell up to $5 million in a 12-month period. The issuer must inform all investors that they will receive "restricted securities" that cannot be sold until after a 6-month minimum holding period, which we discuss in just a few paragraphs. Also, there can be no general solicitation or advertising in connection with this private placement offering.

Even though the issuer isn't filing a registration statement with the SEC, it still must provide information to the investors. As the rule states, "Rule 505 allows companies to decide what information to give to accredited investors, so long as it does not violate the antifraud prohibitions of the federal securities laws. But companies must give non-accredited investors disclosure documents that generally are equivalent to those used in registered offerings. If a company provides information to accredited investors, it must make this information available to non-accredited investors as well. The company must also be available to answer questions by prospective purchasers."

And, even though there is no registration statement required, when the offering is completed, issuers must file a Form D that discloses the basic facts of the offering. For example, by looking up their Form D, I found out that Five Guys had sold $10 million of stock through a private placement in which they tried to raise $15 million. Beyond that, I couldn't tell you much about it, only that Five Guys takes in somewhere between $25 million and $100 million in revenue. If Five Guys does an IPO someday, then you and I will have access to all pertinent information on the issuer. You can see the Form D, by the way, at http://www.sec.gov/Archives/edgar/data/1467164/000146716409000001/xslFormDX01/primary_doc.xml

If the issuer doesn't want limits placed on the amount of money raised, they will utilize Rule 506 instead. Then, they will decide if they want to be able to solicit investors and advertise the offering to prospects or not. Under one type of Rule 506 offering the issuer will offer and sell to up to 35 non-accredited purchasers, but unlike under Rule 505 the issuer must reasonably believe the non-accredited purchasers are either sophisticated or are relying on an independent (from the issuer) purchaser representative who can explain the risks and rewards of the deal. Because the issuer will use non-accredited purchasers here, no solicitation or advertising is allowed.

If the issuer wants to be able to solicit investors, they must limit them to accredited investors only. This is the other type of exempt transaction under Rule 506.

No matter which of these exemptions is used, the issuer must file a Form D - Notice of Exempt Offering of Securities. And, investors receive "restricted shares" subject to mandatory minimum holding periods. The securities offered and sold through a private placement are not required to be registered, but FINRA requires member firms to file a copy of the **private placement memorandum (PPM)** with their Firm Gateway. The PPM must be filed no later than 15 calendar days after the first sale is made. Or, if no PPM is going to be used in connection with the offering, that fact must be reported to FINRA.

The term **restricted stock** means the investor's ability to sell the stock is restricted because of a required holding period. Stock purchased in a private placement is restricted stock, restricted in terms of the investor's ability to sell it to another party. Officers and key employees may also receive restricted shares subject to a holding period as opposed to stock options that can be exercised right away. When purchasing restricted securities investors typically receive a certificate with a legend stamped on it indicating that the securities may not be resold in the marketplace unless they are registered with the SEC or are exempt from the registration requirements.

Rule 144 provides a safe harbor exemption for those who want to sell restricted stock without violating securities law. And, remember, though a registered representative will perhaps never own restricted stock, if he executes a sale for a customer who does, he could get himself in trouble if he doesn't know and follow the rules here.

Restricted stock is subject to a holding period. If the issuer is a reporting company subject to reporting requirements at least 90 days, purchasers must hold the securities a minimum of six months before reselling them. If the issuer is not a reporting company, the minimum holding period is one year.

Once the holding period is met a non-affiliate can sell his shares if he wants to. However, as the SEC explains, "Even if you have met the conditions of Rule 144, you can't sell your restricted securities to the public until you've gotten the legend removed from the certificate. Only a transfer agent can remove a restrictive legend. But the transfer agent won't remove the legend unless you've obtained the consent of the issuer—usually in the form of an opinion letter from the issuer's counsel—that the restrictive legend can be removed. Unless this happens, the transfer agent doesn't have the authority to remove the legend and permit execution of the trade in the marketplace. To begin the legend removal process, an investor should contact the company that issued the securities, or the transfer agent for the securities, to ask about the procedures for removing a legend. Removing the legend can be a complicated process requiring you to work with an attorney who specializes in securities law."

For **affiliates** of the company Rule 144 has further requirements, whether selling restricted or **control stock**. Restricted stock is unusual because of the way it was offered to investors. For control stock, on the other hand, it's the owner himself who triggers the requirements, not the securities. Control stock is held by people who can control the issuer or could harm the market price of the stock by dumping a large amount all at once. So, whether selling restricted or control stock, affiliates must file a **Form 144** with the SEC no later than at the time of the sale. The filing is good for 90 days. Also, if the transaction is not larger than 5,000 shares and $50,000, the sale can be made without filing a Form 144. Basically, a transaction that small does not make the regulators nervous, as it won't impact the price of the stock due to the low volume of shares traded.

Typically, affiliates sell large amounts of securities, but they must comply with the volume limits under Rule 144. For exchange-traded securities affiliates are allowed to sell the issuer's stock provided they sell no more than the greater of 1% of the outstanding shares or the average weekly trading volume over the four most recent weeks. If the company has 1 billion shares outstanding, the affiliate could sell whichever is greater over the next 90 days—10 million shares or the average weekly trading volume going back four weeks. For stocks that either don't trade or trade on the OTC Bulletin Board or Pink Quote, only the 1% figure is used.

That's the amount that can be sold. As for the method of sale the rule states, "If you are an affiliate, the sales must be handled in all respects as routine trading transactions, and brokers may not receive more than a normal commission. Neither the seller nor the broker can solicit orders to buy the securities."

Also, affiliates can never sell the company's stock short. And, although control stock is not subject to a holding period, an affiliate can't take a profit on their company's stock held less than 6 months. This is called a short-swing profit, which must be turned back over to the company with the gain still being taxed by the IRS.

FINRA is concerned that agents and their firms sometimes help customers sell unregistered restricted securities, which violates federal securities law. In other words, if the customer does not conform to all the stipulations we just went over, but wants to just take his unregistered restricted shares and sell them, firms need to be sure they don't help him skirt securities law in this manner. FINRA alerts its member broker-dealers that some customers are companies trying to sell their shares illegally. If the customer deposits certificates representing a large block of thinly traded or low-priced securities, that's a red flag. If the share certificates refer to a company or customer name that has been changed or that does not match the name on the account, that's another red flag. If a customer with limited or no other assets under management at the firm receives an electronic transfer or journal transactions of large amounts of low-priced, unlisted securities, that's another red flag. Broker-dealer firms must do a reasonable inquiry to make sure that they are not helping people get around securities law. The SEC has said that "a dealer who offers to sell, or is asked to sell a substantial amount of securities must take whatever steps are necessary to be sure that this is a transaction not involving an issuer, person in a control relationship with an issuer, or an underwriter." For this purpose, it is not enough for him to accept "self-serving statements of his sellers and their counsel (attorneys) without reasonably exploring the possibility of contrary facts."

Rule 144's prohibitions on reselling restricted stock only apply to a sale to unsophisticated investors, which could completely bypass the full disclosure requirements of the Securities Act of 1933. **Rule 144a,** however, allows the restricted securities that we just discussed to be re-sold to institutional investors including banks, insurance companies, broker-dealers, investment advisers, pension plans, and investment companies without meeting the usual registration requirements under the Securities Act of 1933. So, if an investor acquires restricted securities through a private placement, he/they can re-sell them to **qualified institutional buyers** such as those mentioned without destroying the exemption the issuer is claiming from the registration requirements. As usual, the regulators want to prevent the shares from being distributed in a general public offering without registration requirements being met. When the buyers are sophisticated institutions, the regulators can ease up.

This SEC rule also states that the seller needs to be reasonably certain that the buyers are qualified institutional buyers, which generally means that the institution invests on a discretionary basis at least

$100 million, or is a registered broker-dealer, an investment company, a bank, or a federal covered investment adviser. To check that the buyers are qualified institutional buyers, the SEC says that the seller can rely on the buyer's most recent publicly available financial statements, or a certification from the CFO or other officer of the institution.

Rule 145 has to do with disclosure requirements to investors involved with a merger or a reclassification of securities. When Procter & Gamble acquired Gillette, for example, they gave the Gillette shareholders a certain number of PG shares for each share of Gillette currently held. Those PG shares must be registered on a special form (S-4), and the Gillette shareholders must receive all types of disclosure of material information. Or, if an issuer has decided to give all current warrant holders shares of convertible preferred stock instead, this is a reclassification subject to Rule 145. Remember that stock splits, stock dividends, and changes to the par value of a security are not subject to Rule 145.

To review, the Act of 1933 says that non-exempt issuers (corporations) must register their securities offerings with the SEC. Exempt securities and exempt transactions, on the other hand, all find a way around the typical registration process set forth by the Securities Act of 1933.

➢ *Crowdfunding*

Even though we just looked at concerns for non-accredited purchasers in Reg D private placements, anyone can invest in a **crowdfunding** securities offering. Because of the risks involved with this type of investing, however, investors are limited in how much they can invest during any 12-month period.

The limitation depends on net worth and annual income. If either the investor's annual income or net worth is less than $100,000, then during any 12-month period, he can invest up to the greater of either $2,000 or 5% of the lesser of his annual income or net worth.

If both his annual income and net worth are equal to or more than $100,000, then during any 12-month period, an investor can commit up to 10% of annual income or net worth, whichever is less, but not to exceed $100,000.

As when determining who is and is not an accredited investor, the value of the investor's primary residence is not included in the net worth calculation. In addition, any mortgage or other loan on a primary residence does not count as a liability up to the fair market value of the home.

Companies may not offer crowdfunding investments to investors directly. Rather, they must use a broker-dealer or funding portal registered with the SEC and also a member of the Financial Industry Regulatory Authority (FINRA).

Investors open an account with the crowdfunding intermediary to make an investment, and all written communications relating to the crowdfunding investment will be electronic.

Before an investor can make a crowdfunding investment the broker-dealer or funding portal operating the crowdfunding platform must ensure that he reviews educational materials about this type of investing. In addition, the investor must positively affirm that he understands he can lose all of the investment, and that he can bear such a financial loss.

Investors also must demonstrate that they understand the risks of crowdfunded investing. The sharing of views by the crowd is considered by some to be an integral part of crowdfunding. Broker-dealers and funding portals, through their crowdfunding platforms, are required to have communication channels transparent to the public. For example, on an online forum—relating to each investment opportunity.

In these channels, the crowd of investors can weigh in on the pros and cons of an opportunity and ask the company questions. All persons representing the company must identify themselves.

Investors have up to 48 hours prior to the end of the offer period to change their mind and cancel their investment commitment for any reason. Once the offering period is within 48 hours of ending it is too late to pull out. However, if the company makes a material change to the offering terms or other information disclosed to investors, investors are given five business days to reconfirm the investment commitment.

Investors are limited in their ability to resell their investment for the first year and may need to hold for an indefinite period. Unlike investing in companies listed on a stock exchange where investors can quickly and easily trade securities on a market, crowdfunding is similar to holding a direct participation program interest. To sell the investment an interested buyer must be located.

Issuing Municipal Securities

Municipal securities are exempt from registration requirements under the Securities Act of 1933 and the reporting requirements under the Securities Exchange Act of 1934. Both concerns, however, are for the issuers of municipal securities.

The broker-dealers who perform underwriting services for municipal securities issuers are still regulated by FINRA and the SEC. And, the rules for municipal securities firms are written by the **MSRB** or **Municipal Securities Rulemaking Board**. The MSRB writes the rules, while FINRA enforces them whenever a FINRA member firm violates them.

To issue municipal bonds, the issuer puts together a **bond resolution** in which they legally authorize the process of issuing bonds for a specific purpose. This document, or set of documents, describes the nature of the bond issue and the issuer's duties to the bondholders, as well as the issuer's rights to do X, Y, and Z. Issuing municipal bonds involves a very detailed legal process, so the issuer hires a **bond counsel** (attorney) to guide them through the legalities.

A bond counsel is a law firm specializing in public finance and the complexities of state constitutions, tax codes, etc. The bond counsel provides a **legal opinion** to the issuer in which they attest to the issuer's legal authority to issue the bonds and a statement as to whether the interest will be tax-exempt, taxable, or subject to AMT.

There are two types of opinions that the bond counsel could render: qualified and unqualified. While we always want our attorneys to be qualified, we don't want their opinions to be qualified. A **qualified opinion** means that something is in doubt so that the attorneys had to attach "qualifiers" to their opinion. What the issuer hopes for is an **unqualified opinion** from the bond counsel. That means everything looks fine to the bond counsel or that they can render their opinion without attaching any lengthy explanations to qualify it.

Municipalities are always borrowing money. They raise money by selling bonds, and those bonds are taken to the capital markets by underwriters, who keep part of the proceeds as their compensation. We call the part of the proceeds kept by the underwriters "the spread." Underwriters are the municipal securities firms who raise money for municipalities by lining up interested investors. The big underwriting firms of Wall Street typically have municipal underwriting departments. Also, there are several small firms that specialize in this particular industry, e.g., Loop Capital Markets in Chicago. How do municipalities find underwriters interested in taking their bonds to the capital markets to fund their projects?

By advertising in the daily **Bond Buyer**. When a taxing authority such as a park district wants to raise money by issuing bonds, they locate underwriters by publishing an **official notice of sale** in the Bond Buyer. In this official notice of sale the issuer announces to prospective underwriters that they would like to raise, say, $6 million. They tell the underwriters what type of bond they want to issue—GO or revenue—what they need the money for, how much principal they want to pay back each year of the serial maturity, when the bids will be accepted, where to send the bid, how much of a **good faith deposit** is required, etc. Potential lead underwriters interested in winning this business submit a bid on the **bid form** included with the official notice of sale. The bid form shows what the coupon rates must be on the bonds and how much the underwriter will pay the issuer for the bonds.

Municipalities typically award big construction projects to private contractors through a bidding process because when you are spending taxpayers' money, you owe it to the taxpayers to get the best possible deal with that money. Similarly, municipalities want the lowest debt service they can possibly get when issuing the bonds that fund such construction projects, which is why they typically award their business to the group of underwriters who can sell bonds to the public at the lowest cost. We call that cost the **net interest cost**, or NIC. That's all the municipality cares about—the lowest net interest cost, which is their cost of borrowing money from the public.

Net interest cost is the total cost of all the interest payments the issuer will make until the bonds are retired. If bonds are purchased from the issuer at a discount, that amount is added to the net interest cost, and if bonds are purchased at a premium, that amount is subtracted. In other words, if the issuer pays back more than they received, that must be added to their cost of borrowing, and when they receive more now than they pay out at maturity, that's subtracted. TIC stands for **true interest cost**. TIC factors in the time value of money. Whether the issuer is using NIC or TIC, they're looking at the cost of borrowing the money, which is all they care about.

If it's a GO, the municipality will usually take **competitive, sealed bids** from potential underwriters. If it's a revenue bond, they'll typically select a group of underwriters and hammer out the terms in a **negotiated underwriting**. What the issuer is looking for in either case is the lowest cost of borrowing available, whether measured as NIC or TIC. So, if it's a competitive underwriting, maybe the Park Board President will open the sealed bids at Park District Headquarters at noon on such-and-such a date, awarding the underwriting business to the syndicate who turned in the lowest NIC or TIC.

Why open sealed bids in public? Because, surprisingly, some politicians might otherwise try to rig the bidding process to help their cronies and make a little dirty money on the side. See, if the bids aren't sealed, maybe the mayor looks at all the bids submitted so far and calls a particular underwriting firm to tell them how low they need to bid if they want to win the business, in exchange for kickbacks in the form of cash or campaign contributions. To keep everything on the up-and-up, the process needs to be an actual sealed-bid, as it does whenever a local government is accepting bids for services.

The bidding syndicates have already made a good faith deposit, which is usually 1–2% of the par value of all the bonds. The ones who lost the bid get their deposit back, while the winning syndicate has simply made their deposit on the bonds that need to be purchased from the issuer and unloaded to investors in the near future. Most municipal underwritings are done on a **firm commitment** basis, which means the winning syndicate is going to buy all the bonds from the issuer, whether they end up selling them to investors or not. The exam may say that the underwriters act in a "principal capacity," and you'll note that the word **principal** can mean many different things on the Series 7. It means to have capital/money at risk in a transaction. The "principal" is also a supervisor of a broker-dealer. And, the "principal" amount of a debt security is what the buyer receives at maturity.

The Syndicate

For the trouble they go to finding buyers for the issuer's bonds the syndicate makes a profit known as the "spread," which is the difference between what they pay the municipality for the bonds and the price at which they sell the bonds to the public. Say the issuer gets $990 per bond from the syndicate, and the syndicate sells the bonds to the public for $1,000 each. That's a spread of $10 per bond. How does that $10 get split?

Into three pieces. One of the underwriters will act as the manager. They'll take some money right off the top, known as the **manager's fee**. Then, all syndicate members will get the next piece of the spread, known as the **additional takedown**, split according to each member's share of the bonds. Finally, whoever sells a bond gets the last and biggest piece, the **concession**. A syndicate member who sells a bond from their allotment would get the additional takedown plus the concession. Those two pieces are known together as the **total takedown**. If you want the total takedown, you must sell the bond; if somebody else sells one of your bonds, you give up or "concede" the concession, keeping only the "additional takedown," which is the piece that syndicate members get, one way or the other.

See, to make sure the bonds get sold, the syndicate might let other broker-dealers help sell them. If another broker-dealer sells a bond for the syndicate, the syndicate gives the B/D the concession. They "concede" that portion of the spread, in other words. These broker-dealers outside the syndicate make up a group of sellers, so the industry dubbed them the "selling group."

Okay. A bond point is worth $10. How much is a half-point worth?

$5. Quarter-point?

$2.50. Eighth of a point?

$1.25. And so on. So let's say the spread is $10. That means that each bond is sold for $10 more than the issuer receives—how does that $10 get split up?

Let's say the manager gets 1/8 point or $1.25. That's the Manager's Fee.

The syndicate members get 3/8 of a point or $3.75. That's the additional takedown.

Whoever sells the bond gets the 1/2 point concession, or $5.00.

So, if the managing underwriter sells a bond, they keep the whole underwriting spread of $10.00. If a syndicate member sells one of their bonds, they keep the "total takedown" or $8.75. In other words, the manager gets their $1.25, and the rest of the $10 goes to the syndicate member who sold their bond. The syndicate typically lines up broker-dealers interested in helping to sell the bonds to their customers, with no capital commitment whatsoever. These firms make up the selling group. If a selling group member sells bonds, the dealer whose bonds they sold keeps the additional takedown and gives up the selling concession to the selling group member who made the sale. In that case the member of the "selling group" keeps $5.00, the syndicate member who let them sell their bond gets $3.75, and the manager—as always—gets the manager's fee of $1.25.

Since the syndicate is at risk for these bonds, the big question is, "What happens if we don't sell all of them?" Answers to these and other questions are agreed to among the underwriters in a document called the **agreement among underwriters** or the **syndicate letter**, where the terms of the underwriting are laid out for all syndicate members to see. This agreement spells out each firm's responsibilities, the order period, and the priority of orders coming in for the bonds. As you might expect, the document governs the operations of the syndicate only, and the issuer of the bonds could not care less about it.

There are two types of syndicate accounts: western and eastern. Under a **western/divided account**, a syndicate member only must worry about selling their share of the bonds. If they sell their allotment, they are off the hook. However, in an **eastern/undivided account** all syndicate members are responsible for selling their bonds, as well as their share of any unsold bonds. If a syndicate member gets 10% of the bonds and sells its entire allotment, that's great. But if the other firms don't do so well, leaving the syndicate with 1,000 unsold bonds, the member is going to be responsible for 10% of those, too. So even though the member sold its allotment, they're going to must sell 100 more bonds, worth about $100,000. If they can't sell them, they eat them.

Sometimes the municipal securities are in hot demand, though, and now we have the opposite problem as a syndicate, which is that there are more buyers than bonds. What happens if the issue is "oversold" or "oversubscribed"? Rather than using a first-come-first-serve basis, orders are filled according to their type in the following priority:

Pre-Sale

Syndicate (or "Group Net Order")

Designated

Member

What this order priority shows is that whichever order benefits the most members of the syndicate has the highest priority. After the pre-sale orders are filled for institutional investors, the syndicate orders benefit all members of the syndicate, which is why these are filled before any designated orders benefitting a particular firm more than other members of the syndicate.

The syndicate may publish a tombstone advertisement, which lays out just the basic facts and is not considered an offer to sell the securities. A tombstone is just an announcement, including the amount of the bond issue and purpose of the proceeds, interest payment dates, maturity years and yields to maturity. The date on which interest begins to accrue is known as the **dated date** and would be included in the tombstone. The "dated date" means that buyers of the bonds may must pay accrued interest calculated from the dated date up to—not including—settlement.

Bonds are not considered to be issued until they are delivered to the buyers, so if there is lag time between the dated date on the issue and the delivery of the bonds to purchasers, purchasers will end up paying accrued interest, since their first interest payment will be larger than it should be. I would not recommend spending a lot of time trying to wrap your head around the "dated date." It's only used in a new issue. It's used to calculate accrued interest. Can't imagine how much further this exam would take the concept.

Settlement

The most detailed information about an issuer's financial condition is found in the **official statement**. This is what is delivered with final confirmation of the purchase to the investor. If the official statement isn't quite ready, the issuer can prepare a **preliminary official statement**. Either way, municipal underwriters must make sure that if an official statement is prepared it is delivered to all buyers of the bonds. As the MSRB explains, "official statements typically include information regarding the purposes of the issue, how the securities will be repaid, and the financial and economic characteristics of the issuer with respect to the offered securities. Investors may use this information to evaluate the credit quality of the securities. Although functionally equivalent to the prospectus used in connection with registered securities, an official statement for municipal securities is exempt from the prospectus requirements of the Securities Act of 1933."

There you have it. No one said the underwriters prepare the official or preliminary official statement. Rather, it is the issuer of the bonds who is responsible for that. However, assuming the official statement was prepared, the underwriters must make sure that investors receive it and receive it on time, just like with a prospectus for an offer registered under the Securities Act of 1933.

So, after the orders are taken and filled, buyers often receive **when-issued confirmations** because the bonds have not been issued yet. The confirmations prove that the buyers will receive a certain number of bonds, when they are issued. At this point, interest may be accruing from the dated date up to the settlement date, which has not occurred yet. So, the exam might have a question in which you tell it that the total dollar amount of the transaction cannot be calculated for a when-issued confirmation. Why not? If we don't know the settlement date, we can't calculate the accrued interest owed by the buyer. But, of course, the bonds are eventually ready to be delivered. On the delivery date, the purchasers make full payment for the bonds, plus any accrued interest, and the syndicate delivers the bonds, a final confirmation, and the official statement.

Refunding/Advance Refunding Issues

When do homeowners refinance their mortgage loans? When interest rates are falling. Homeowners paying 8% might get tired of servicing their debt at that rate when prevailing interest rates are falling well below 8%. Municipalities feel the same way. If a municipality is paying 8% on a bond issue when interest rates are falling to 6%, they might want to pay off the outstanding debt by issuing new, cheaper debt. If the bond issue has passed its legal call protection period, the municipality could issue new bonds at 6% and use some of the proceeds to call the bonds issued at 8%. That's known as **refunding**, which involves replacing expensive debt with cheaper debt. The new issue of bonds with lower nominal yields make up the refunding issue, which is used to eventually replace the refunded issue of bonds.

If the bond issue had not reached the first call date, the municipality could still issue cheaper debt at 6% and put the proceeds in escrow. The proceeds earn interest on Treasury securities this way, and as soon as the first call date is reached, the municipality uses the proceeds to call the outstanding bonds. Here, they've refunded the outstanding debt in advance of the first call date, which is why we call this **advance refunding** or **pre-refunding**. The bonds that are outstanding and will be called at the first or next legal call date are the "pre-refunded bonds." If the issuer creates an escrow account that is large enough to pay off all the interest and principal through the last maturity date, the outstanding bonds are considered to be **escrowed to maturity**.

Once a bond has been advance refunded or escrowed to maturity, its credit rating becomes triple-A, since the money needed to pay off the debt is already parked in an escrow account. Municipalities often invest the proceeds of an advance refunding issue of bonds in **SLGS**, which stands for "State and Local Government Series" securities. These are special securities created by the U.S. Treasury to help municipalities do an advance refunding and comply with IRS rules and restrictions on such transactions.

Also, municipal bonds issued for building projects generally pay tax-exempt interest to investors. However, a refunding issue does not offer tax-exempt interest. The U.S. Government will help states and cities borrow money to build roads, bridges and schools, but not to later do a well-timed refinance on the bonds issued to fund those infrastructure projects.

Bond Buyer

The Bond Buyer is the information source for the municipal securities primary market, meaning the new-issue market where municipalities raise money through underwriting syndicates of broker-dealers. If your firm is a municipal securities underwriter, you're receiving this newspaper and reading it every day. The exam might want you to say that the Bond Buyer provides information on the primary market, even though there is actually some secondary (trading) market information in there as well. Underwriters could see the total par value of municipal securities that are about to be offered in the near future. This is called the **visible supply**. If we're about to do a primary offering of municipal securities, we might want to know how many other bonds are trying to be absorbed by the market. We also might want to see how well the market absorbed the bonds offered last week, called the **placement ratio**. The placement ratio tells us the dollar amount sold out of the dollar amount offered the previous week. If the market tried to absorb $100 million par value of municipal securities last week but only ended up absorbing $90 million, that's a placement ratio of 90%, meaning some of the underwriters are sitting on some bonds they would rather have sold. Remember that the "placement ratio" can also be referred to as the "acceptance ratio" in a test question.

The Bond Buyer is where underwriters find official notices of sale announcing the issuer's need to raise X amount of money by a certain date in order to build a school, road, hospital, etc. Actually, what we see in the Bond Buyer is a summary official notice of sale, which gives us info on how to get the full official notice of sale, complete with a bid form that we can use to try to come up with the lowest NIC/TIC required to win the underwriting business through a competitive bid. Or, maybe we prefer to contact the issuer willing to do a negotiated underwriting in order to negotiate the terms of the underwriting engagement.

There are also various indices published in the Bond Buyer, which I'll simply list as bullet points:

- REVDEX 25: yield-based index tracking the revenue bond market. A weekly index of 25 revenue bonds with 30 years to maturity rated *A* or higher.
- 40 Bond Index: a daily price-based index that comprises 40 GO and revenue bonds. This one's based on price.
- 20 Bond Index: weekly index that comprises 20 GO bonds with 20 years to maturity rated A or higher.
- 11 Bond Index: weekly index that comprises 11 of the 20 bonds from the 20 Bond Index, rated AA or higher. These yields will be lower than yields on the 20 Bond Index because the average quality of these 11 bonds is higher.

Now What?

From this chapter the similarities and differences among common and preferred stock could provide a few exam questions. For example:

A true statement concerning preferred stock is that
   A. It is a fixed-income security, essentially the same as a corporate bond
   B. It is an equity security, with voting and preemptive rights
   C. It is both a fixed-income security and an equity security
   D. Its market price is tied to the market price of the issuer's common stock

EXPLANATION: as we saw in the chapter, preferred stock is unusual in that it is both a fixed-income security and an equity position. That right there is challenging for some folks, especially those who like things to fit into neat categories. In their minds, a security is either fixed-income or equity. And, in your industry, it is true that when folks say "fixed income," they typically mean bonds, just as they typically only mean common stock when they say they want to invest in "equities."

Oh well. Slowing down and thinking is what this test—and your job—is all about. Notice that part of Answer A is correct—preferred stock is a fixed-income security, but it is not just like a bond. A bond is a debt security whose interest has to be paid, while a preferred stock dividend has to be declared (or not) by the Board of Directors. Based on that, we can eliminate Choice A. Choice B is partly right—preferred stock is an equity security. However, it does not typically have the voting or preemptive rights enjoyed by the more junior common stock. Eliminate Choice B. Choice C looks tempting, but let's first see if we can prove Choice D to be wrong. What does the preferred stock's price have to do with the issuer's common stock? Nothing at all—not unless it happens to be convertible preferred stock, which is not the usual case. As a general rule, the two market prices are unrelated, so, yes, we can eliminate Answer Choice D, leaving us with the right answer

ANSWER: C

As always, that is just an example of what a test question could look like concerning common and preferred stock. The question would look different if presented like this:

The only accurate statement concerning preferred stock below is that:
   A. Preferred stock trades in sympathy with the issuer's common stock
   B. Preferred stock has a higher claim on the issuer's assets than either the common stock or subordinated debentures of that issuer
   C. Interest on preferred stock is typically paid semi-annually
   D. Convertible preferred stock is less interest-rate sensitive than either straight or cumulative preferred stock

EXPLANATION: your license exam is known to use some pretty fancy vocabulary such as "in sympathy" now and again. If you really don't know what it means, remember that you only have to find one true statement here. With three other answer choices, keep shopping and keep your cool. If you do know or can figure out what "in sympathy means," you know that Answer Choice A is saying exactly what Answer Choice D was saying in the previous question. And, either way we say it, it's incorrect—the issuer's preferred stock does not derive its market price from the common stock, as a general rule. Unless the question says we're looking at convertible preferred stock, there is no link between the market price of an issuer's preferred and common stock. So, we can eliminate Choice A. Answer Choice B starts out looking right but then takes a wrong turn by saying the claim is higher than that of a bondholder. That is false, so eliminate Choice B. Choice C is trying to sneak one past you. Is it paid semiannually, quarterly—wait, preferred stock doesn't receive interest at all! Preferred stock receives dividends as long as the Board declares them. Eliminate Answer C, and we're left with the only one that works,

ANSWER: D, convertible preferred stock is the exception, deriving its market value mostly from the price of the issuer's common stock. This makes interest rate moves less important to its market price.

What makes the Series 7 such a challenge is that there are so many ways it can cover any topic. And, this is just one of many topics in the chapter and on the exam outline. The trick is to learn as much detail as you can from the textbook and then take it to a higher level online with our Pass the 7 Online Practice Question Bank.

So, it's time to do the online review exercises for this chapter. After a 20-minute minimum break, come back and take the chapter review quiz. Focus on using what you know to eliminate three wrong answers to each question. After that, watch the training video lessons and move onto the next chapter in the textbook.

CHAPTER 3: Investment Recommendations & Strategies

Type of Client

Once you pass your exam and have your application as a securities agent accepted by the securities Administrator of your state, you can begin meeting with customers. Some of your customers will be human beings, and others will be businesses. Let's start with the **sole proprietor**, which is both a human being and a business.

Sole Proprietor

A handyman or a hair stylist typically pays for state and municipal licenses. Therefore, they might not want to also pay to set up a corporation or other business structure, which involves legal fees to attorneys and filing-and-renewal fees to the state. It might be tempting to just run the business as a sole proprietor. Unlike setting up a corporation or other business structure, setting up a sole proprietorship doesn't require much in terms of time and expense. The advantages of opening a business as a sole proprietorship include:

- Faster, easier, cheaper setup
- Easy tax preparation
- Income flows directly to the owner

The trouble with being in business as a sole proprietor is that the owner remains personally liable for the debts and lawsuits against the business. In other words, the owner and the business are the same

 thing. If the sole proprietorship called Harry's Hot Dogs accidentally sells 1,000 tainted wieners that send sick people to the emergency room, Harry would have a hot mess on his hands. All the lawsuits would be filed against Harry personally.

Or, if Harry hits a slow patch, the creditors who used to spot him buns, hot dogs, and condiments are going to come after him personally for the unpaid bills. Even if he has insurance, once the insurance is exhausted, the angry parties move directly to Harry, not to a corporate structure that would have added a layer of defense. So, the disadvantages of owning a business as a sole proprietor include:

- Personal liability
- Harder to obtain loans or attract investment capital due to lower financial controls

Partnerships

Many business owners are renegades who don't play well with others. So they go into business for themselves and run everything as a sole proprietorship in which they control every aspect and answer to no one. We just looked at some pros and cons of that structure. Another approach is to take on partners. In a **partnership**, the income or net loss of the business flows through directly to the owners. The business entity itself is not taxed. The percentage of profits and losses flowing through to each of the owners is stated in the partnership agreement. Does the partnership create a separate entity that shields the owners from liabilities of the business? That depends on the type of partnership.

The main difference between general and limited partnerships involves liability. In a **general partnership** two or more persons own the business jointly and are subject to creditors and lawsuits personally, just like Harry of Harry's Hot Dogs. Unless otherwise stated in the agreement, the general partners control the business jointly, equally, with one vote each. Therefore, if three college friends want to open a restaurant and maintain 33.3% ownership each, a general partnership may be the way to go. However, all three are personally liable should someone get food poisoning at the restaurant, or trip over a loose piece of carpet, etc.

Either way, a general partnership is like a sole proprietorship with more than one owner. The owners agree to be in business together. They do not shield themselves personally from debts or liabilities of the business. But the income and expenses do flow through directly to the partners rather than being taxable to the business, and there are more people to split up the work load and hold each other accountable.

Limited Partnership

To form a **limited partnership**, there must be at least one **general partner** (GP), who has personal liability for debts and lawsuits associated with the business. But a limited partnership then has **limited partners** (LPs) who maintain **limited liability** status, meaning they can only lose what they invest into the business.

By "invest into the business," I mean the money they put in as well as any debts they personally guarantee. A debt that a limited partner signs his name to is called a **recourse note**, meaning that creditors have legal recourse to come after him for the amount he guaranteed personally. A **non-recourse note**, then, would mean that the creditors have no recourse to collect this debt out of the investor's personal assets beyond any collateral that might have been pledged.

Maybe a test question will ask what a limited partner's cost basis is equal to, with the right answer something like "it equals the capital he contributes initially plus the capital he agrees to contribute in the future."

To maintain the shield of protection limited partners must stay out of day-to-day management decisions. Nevertheless, the LPs do vote on the big issues of the partnership through **partnership democracy**. Partnership democracy is used to allow the LPs to have a voice on a limited number of items, such as:

- Dissolving the partnership
- Suing the GP for negligence, breach of fiduciary duty, and other major irritations
- Inspecting certain records

The LPs can get involved with the above without jeopardizing their limited liability status, but not much else.

The General Partner has a fiduciary relationship to the LPs, which means that the GP must put the LPs' needs first. In legal terms, the GP's fiduciary duty is "two-pronged," meaning he has a duty of loyalty and a duty of good faith. His duty of loyalty means he can't compete with the partnership. His duty of good faith means he must do whatever he can to run the business successfully and in accordance with the LPs' best interests. The GP can end up getting sued by the LPs if it becomes clear that he is not meeting his duty to the limited partners, through negligence or fraud.

Since the GP has unlimited liability, the general partner is often a corporation rather than a natural person (human being). The corporate structure, as we'll see, provides a layer of protection that would be lacking otherwise.

When the limited partnership is liquidated, the senior creditors are paid first, then the unsecured creditors. The next priority is the limited partners, with the general partner last in line.

The advantages of the limited partnership structure include:

- Flow-through of income and expenses directly to the partners
- Limited partners have limited liability

The disadvantages of the limited partnership structure include:

- General partner has unlimited liability
- Distribution of profits not as flexible as within an LLC

LLC (Limited Liability Company)

A **limited liability company** (LLC) is a type of business in which the owners are called "members" and the ones who also manage the business are called "managing members." In a minute, we will see that the S-corp. is limited to 100 shareholders, while the LLC has no limit on the number of members, who can be individuals, corporations, or even other LLCs.

The owners of an LLC are protected from the debts of and lawsuits against the company, including being sued for their own negligence in operating the business.

Advantages of setting up an LLC include:

- Limited liability
- More flexible profit distributions
- No minutes required
- Avoids double taxation of income

To be structured as an LLC rather than a corporation, the LLC needs to avoid two of four corporate attributes. That means it must avoid two of the following characteristics associated with corporations:

- Perpetual life
- Centralized management
- Limited liability
- Freely transferable assets

It's almost impossible to avoid the centralized management, since there must be managing members of the LLC. It's also tough to avoid limited liability as a limited liability company. So, how do they avoid the perpetual life and freely transferable assets associated with corporations? Unlike a corporation, an LLC has a limited life. For example, when the LLC is set up, perhaps it has a triggering event after which the business is dissolved—when the last townhouse is sold, or when any of the managing members dies, maybe. Or, there could be a fixed date upon which a private investment LLC dissolves, returning cash to the members.

Regarding the "freely transferable assets," the members agree they won't sell their interests except in accordance with a strict set of rules. For example, if a member wants to sell his interest to a stranger, the other members might have the right to buy the interest first to prevent that from happening. Such an agreement is often referred to as a "right of first refusal" clause.

The disadvantages of setting up an LLC include:

- Limited life
- Harder to attract financing
- More complexity than sole proprietorship

To set up a limited liability company, the business files its articles of organization with the Secretary of State (or similar office in the state) and pays the filing fees. The owners also typically draft and sign an **operating agreement**. Similar to corporate bylaws or partnership agreements, these operating agreements spell out important points about ownership, responsibilities, and the distribution of profits.

Corporations

The limited liability company provides protection to the owners against claims on their personal assets. Corporations do the same, although they require more work in terms of having meetings of shareholders and the board of directors and keeping the minutes of those meetings.

S-Corporations

The **S-Corporation (S-corp.)** offers protection against debts and lawsuits compared to running the business as a sole proprietor. The income and expenses pass directly to the owners, so it's like a partnership or limited liability company in that sense. It avoids being taxed as a business entity, even as it provides that separate legal structure known as a corporation for the protection of the owners' personal assets. The advantages of using the S-corporation structure include:

- No corporate tax
- Liability protection
- Write-offs

The disadvantages to the S-corp. include:

- One class of stock
- 100 shareholders maximum
- Corporate meetings and minutes required

If the business is hoping to attract venture capital, the VC firms will not like the S-corporation structure with its direct flow-through of income and expenses and the limit of 100 shareholders. Also, all stock has equal voting rights and claims on profits, tying the hands of the financiers. And, even if it is a good idea, many business owners hate having to hold an annual board of directors meeting and an annual shareholders meeting, especially if shareholders and board members are required to travel far and wide to attend.

Oh well. If someone wants to create a business structure that offers protection against debts and lawsuits and avoids the double taxation of income, the S-corp. is an attractive option. To start an S-corp., the business files its articles of incorporation with the Secretary of State's office, usually by going through an attorney. More details on S-corps include:

- The corporation can have no more than 100 shareholders with a husband and wife counting as one shareholder.
- Shareholders can be individuals, estates, and certain trusts.
- Shareholders must be American residents.
- The S-corp. must be a domestic company in any state.

C-Corporations

The **C-corporation (C-Corp.)** is the traditional corporate structure. When we were talking about common stock in General Electric, Microsoft, Oracle, etc., we were talking about C-corporations. This means that Microsoft is a separate legal entity that is taxed as a corporation. The profits do not flow directly through to shareholders. The corporation gets taxed on all those billions of dollars it makes year after year. Then, when the shareholders receive dividends on the stock, they are also taxed on that income.

C-corporations also must hold annual shareholder and board of director meetings, and keep the minutes. Don't assume that C-corporations are S-corporations who wanted more than 100 shareholders. Many small companies are structured as C-corporations even if there are just a few shareholders.

Client Profile

A financial planner or a securities agent must gather key financial information about an investor before making investment recommendations:

- Income sources
- Current expenditures
- Discretionary income
- Assets
- Tax bracket

To determine how much the client can afford to invest, the investment professional looks at his income statement or statement of cash flow.

A personal cash flow statement might look like this:

Monthly Income

Salary	$7,000
Investment Income	$1,000
Other Income	$500
Total Monthly Income	$8,500

Monthly Expenditures

Taxes	$2,000
Mortgage Payment	$2,000
Living Expenses	$2,000
Insurance Premiums	$300
Loan Payments	$200
Travel/Entertainment	$300
Other Expenses	$200
Total Monthly Expenses	$7,000
Monthly Capital for Investing	$1,500

The client has **discretionary income** or excess **cash flow** of $1,500. If he has a long time horizon of, say, 10+ years, the money could go into stock mutual funds investing for growth. If he has a lower tolerance for wide fluctuations of yearly performance, he might choose growth & income, equity income, or balanced funds. And, if his time horizon is shorter, he might stay out of the stock market entirely and invest, instead, in short- or intermediate-term bond funds.

Taxes are always a factor, too. If the client is in a high marginal tax bracket, we may want to recommend municipal bonds, which generally pay interest that is tax-exempt at the federal level. A high-tax-bracket client probably doesn't want to do much short-term trading, either, since any gain taken within a year is taxed at the short-term capital gains rate (which equals his marginal tax rate). He also might want to buy stocks that pay qualified dividends rather than REITs or royalty trusts, which will force him to pay his ordinary/marginal rate on the dividends.

Or, maybe he could put the REITs and royalty trusts into a retirement plan that allows the dividends to grow tax-deferred until withdrawn, when he is in a lower tax bracket. In other words, different clients require different recommendations and strategies.

A business has both an income statement and a balance sheet. So do your clients. Assets represent what someone owns, while liabilities represent what he owes. The difference between what someone owns and what he owes is his financial **net worth**.

A client's assets include the value of his home, automobiles, personal possessions, investments, savings, and checking accounts. Liabilities include mortgages and other loan balances, credit-card balances, and, perhaps, debit balances in margin accounts.

A personal balance sheet might look like this:

Assets	
House	$400,000
Automobiles	$30,000
Personal possessions	$15,000
Stocks and Bonds	$100,000
Keogh Plan	$80,000
IRA	$20,000
Checking	$5,000
Savings Account	$5,000
Money Market	$5,000
Total Assets	$660,000

Liabilities	
Mortgage	$250,000
Auto Loans	$10,000
Credit Card Balances	$15,000
Total Liabilities	$275,000
Net Worth	$385,000

When we looked at corporate balance sheets in Chapter 1, we mentioned that analysts look only at a company's quick assets rather than including the hard-to-liquidate assets such as plant and equipment in some of their calculations. Similarly, since some assets are difficult to liquidate, we might exclude those items to calculate **liquid net worth**. Illiquid assets include real estate and private funds.

If a client has high total net worth but low liquid net worth, an investment adviser or securities agent might steer the client toward more liquid investments, like short-term debt versus a long-term zero coupon bond, or heavily traded stocks and bonds as opposed to something trading on the Non-Nasdaq OTC market.

By the way, if an investor takes $5,000 out of her savings account and pays down her mortgage or credit card debt by $5,000—how much does that increase her net worth?

Not at all. If he removes a $5,000 asset to remove a $5,000 liability, his net worth is unchanged. Net worth rises when asset values rise, and when assets provide income payments in the form of rent, interest, and dividends.

Even if the investor comes home tonight excited about a $10,000 raise, that is an item for the cash flow statement. If it ends up in a savings account, then it becomes an asset increasing financial net worth. On the other hand, if that increased income is spent on season tickets for a sports team or symphony, it was just money in and money out.

While gathering information on a client's assets, we are also uncovering his current securities holdings. Many investors have a large percentage of their portfolio tied up in one company's stock— their employer's. If a client has too much money concentrated in just one stock, an agent might advise him to sell some of that holding to diversify. Other clients will already be diversified, which is just as important to determine before recommending investments. If they already hold 20 large-cap stocks, we probably don't want to recommend that they put the rest of their discretionary income into Dow Jones Index funds, which is redundant.

Suitability

So, now that an agent or investment adviser representative has opened an account for a client, it is time to help her allocate her money to various investment vehicles. First, what are her **investment objectives?** Investment objectives include: capital preservation, income, growth & income, growth, and speculation. If the individual is in her 30s and setting up a retirement account, she probably needs growth to build up her financial net worth before reaching retirement age. If she's already in retirement, she probably needs income. If she's in her 50's and wants to retire in 10-12 years, she might be looking for both **growth & income,** which some firms consider one objective. An investment in a mutual fund by that name might be suitable, as might investments in blue chip or large-cap value stocks.

Some firms separate growth from **aggressive growth** as an investment objective. Some firms view growth as one objective that investors pursue with varying degrees of aggressiveness. Either way, aggressive growth investments include international funds, sector funds, and emerging market funds. For **speculation,** there are options and futures, and most investors should limit their exposure to these derivatives to a small % of their portfolio.

If they are saving for retirement, that generally means investors need **capital appreciation.** On the other hand, some investors already have capital and want to preserve it. This is called **capital preservation.** Investors can buy U.S. Treasury securities all on their own, without commissions. But, many chose instead to invest in U.S. Treasury mutual funds. Even though the fund is not guaranteed, the securities the fund owns are. So, it is an investment on the safer side of things, but while Treasury securities are guaranteed against default, a mutual fund is just a mutual fund.

Knowing the investor's objective is important, but that objective must be balanced with the investor's **time horizon**. In general, the longer the time horizon the more volatility the investor can withstand. If he has a three-year time horizon, he needs to stay almost completely out of the stock market and invest instead in high-quality bonds with short terms to maturity. If he's in for the long haul, on the other hand, who cares what happens this year? It's what happens over a 20- or 30-year period that matters.

With dividends reinvested, the S&P 500 has historically gained about 10% annually on average, which means the investment would double approximately every 7 years. Sure, the index can drop 30% one year and 20% the next, but we're not keeping score each year. It's where we go over the long haul that counts. A good way to see the real-world application of risk as it relates to time horizon is to pull out the prospectus for a growth fund and see if you can spot any two- or three-year periods where the bar charts are pointing the wrong way. Then compare those horrible short-term periods to the 10-year return, which is probably decent no matter which growth fund you're looking at. That's why the prospectus will remind folks that they "may lose money by investing in the fund" and that "the likelihood of loss is greater the shorter the holding period." See how important "time horizon" is?

Younger investors saving for retirement have a long time horizon, so they can withstand more ups and downs along the road. On the other hand, if the investor is 69 years old, he probably needs some income and not so much volatility. So the farther from retirement she is, the more likely your investor will be buying stock. The closer she gets to retirement, the less stock she needs and the more bonds/income investments she should be buying.

Many mutual fund companies take all the work out of retirement planning for investors by offering **target funds**. Here, the investor picks a mutual fund with a target date close to her own retirement date. If she's currently in her mid-40s, maybe she picks the Target 2040 Fund. If she's in her mid-60s, maybe it's the Target 2020 Fund. For the Target 2040, the fund is invested more in the stock market and less in the bond market than the Target 2020 fund. The fund automatically changes the allocation from mostly stock to mostly bonds as we get closer and closer to the target date. The same thing happens in an age-based portfolio used in a 529 Plan. When the child is a baby, the allocation is probably 90% growth, 10% fixed-income. As the child gets older, the portfolio gets more conservative, just as many readers have done over the years. Other names for target funds include **life-cycle funds** and **age-based portfolios**.

An investor might have the primary objective of growth or even aggressive growth. He might also have a time horizon of 10+ years. However, if he doesn't have the **risk tolerance** required of the stock market, his agent should keep him out of stocks. Remember that risk tolerance involves not only the financial resources, but also the psychological ability to sustain wide fluctuations in market value, as well as an occasional loss of principal.

The terms risk-averse, conservative, and low risk tolerance all mean the same thing—these investors cannot tolerate big market drops. They invest in fixed annuities, U.S. Treasuries, and investment-grade bonds. To invest in sector funds or emerging market funds the investor needs a high risk tolerance. Moderate risk tolerance would match up with balanced funds, equity income funds, and conservative bond funds.

Let's put the three factors together: investment objectives, time horizon, and risk tolerance. If we know that the investor in the suitability question seeks growth, we then need to know his time horizon and risk tolerance. If he's a 32-year-old in an IRA account, his time horizon is long-term. Unless he can't sleep at night knowing the account balance fluctuates, we would almost have to recommend growth funds. His risk tolerance would tell us whether to use small-cap, mid-cap, or large-cap growth funds—the higher the risk tolerance the smaller the "cap." Or, maybe we get even more aggressive with emerging market and sector funds.

If the investor is 60 years old and living on a defined benefit pension income, she might need to invest in common stock to protect her purchasing power. If so, her time horizon is long, but her risk tolerance is probably only moderate or moderate-low. So, we'd probably find a conservative stock fund—maybe a growth & income, equity income, or large-cap value fund.

If an investor seeks income primarily, we need to know her time horizon and risk tolerance. We don't buy bonds that mature beyond her anticipated holding period. If she has a 10-year time horizon, we need bonds that mature in 10 years or sooner. Buying 7-year bonds for someone with a 10-year holding period is not a problem, while going the other way is.

The investor's risk tolerance determines if we can maximize her income with high-yield bonds, or if we should be smart and buy investment-grade bond funds instead. If she needs tax-exempt income, we put some of her money into municipal bond funds. For capital preservation nothing beats U.S. Treasury or GNMA securities. Money market mutual funds are safe—though not guaranteed by the US Government or anyone else—but they pay low yields. Money market mutual funds are for people who want to not only preserve capital but also make frequent withdrawals from the account.

See, even though money is safer in a 30-year Treasury bond than in a money market mutual fund, the big difference is that the market price of a T-Bond fluctuates (rates up, price down), while the money market mutual fund stays at $1 per-share.

So if **liquidity** is a major concern, the money market mutual fund is better than T-Bonds, T-Notes, and even T-Bills, all of which have to be sold at whatever price. With the money market mutual fund investors can write checks, and the fund company will redeem the right number of shares to cover it.

Total liquidity. Then again, that total liquidity comes at a price. While there are no ongoing fees to hold Treasury Notes (and no commissions to buy them directly from the U.S. Treasury), money market mutual funds usually have annual expenses of about 75 basis points.

The questionnaire that the client fills out when opening an account with your firm will try to gauge what is more important—going for large returns or maintaining a stable principal? Earning a high level of income or making sure he gets his money back from the investment? Does he need to withdraw a large portion of his portfolio at a moment's notice? If so, put that portion in money market securities and short-term bonds.

Client Recommendations

To work with some of the preceding information let's look at 10 different case studies and see what we would recommend for each investor. As in the real world of investing, none of this is scientific.

But, if we follow basic industry guidelines, we can match the questions on your exam closely enough to get you prepared.

Our first investor is a divorced 71-year-old man who recently sold a small landscaping business for $300,000 after capital gains taxes. Although he loved to work 12-hour days for decades, those days are behind him now. This customer does not trust the stock market and also remembers that his father lost a bunch of money in bonds back in the late '70s. This $300,000 is the money your customer plans to live on as a supplement to social security. His house has a mortgage balance of $25,000 and his living expenses are reasonable, although he will need a new automobile in the next few years and both a roof replacement and a new water heater for his 30-year-old house.

- INVESTMENT OBJECTIVES: capital preservation, income
- TIME HORIZON/LIQUIDITY: long-term, high liquidity needs
- RISK TOLERANCE: low

This investor is clearly not interested in risking a loss of his investment principal. If you make aggressive recommendations to him, it's not just a bad idea, but also a potential arbitration or civil court proceeding.

If capital preservation is the main objective, your recommendation has to address that first and foremost. Anything that conflicts with that goal is to be rejected. U.S. Treasury securities provide capital preservation, so we'll either buy them directly or through a mutual fund. Easy enough.

His next objective is income. Do U.S. Treasury securities provide income? Yes. Are they liquid? Yes, but if he anticipates frequent withdrawals from the account, we'd have to avoid long-term T-Bonds and stick to the more liquid 2-year U.S. Treasury Notes or even U.S. Treasury Bills, which have maturities of just a few weeks. Depending on the four answer choices in the suitability question, we might even end up choosing a money market mutual fund here. Why not? That's a safe place to park his money, it does provide income, and it is completely liquid.

What we can eliminate for this investor: equity funds, high-yield bond funds, municipal bond funds, and long-term bond funds. The municipal bond funds aren't risky, but if we see nothing about the investor's needs for tax-exempt income, we can't recommend them.

What we might recommend for this investor: T-Bills, short-term T-Notes, investment-grade bonds/bond funds with shorter maturities, money market mutual funds.

Our next investor is a 53-year-old school teacher who got a little too enthusiastic running half-marathons in her 40s and now lacks the energy to teach on her feet all day. She does not want to start taking withdrawals from her 403(b) account before age 59 but is ready to switch to part-time teaching now or perhaps even an administrative support position for the next 5–7 years, both of which would pay half or less of her current salary.

- INVESTMENT OBJECTIVES: income, capital preservation
- TIME HORIZON/LIQUIDITY: 5–7 years, moderate liquidity
- RISK TOLERANCE: moderate

This investor needs income, so I'm already thinking of bonds or bond mutual funds. Preferred stock might work, too, but my bias is with the bonds and bond funds. Remember that bond interest has to be paid while preferred stock dividends are paid if the board of directors declares them out of profits/net income. The investor's secondary objective is capital preservation, so I don't like junk bonds. I also don't see "capital appreciation" or growth as an objective, so why bring up stocks here? All we really have to do for this investor is recommend investment-grade bonds or bond funds that match her 5–7-year time horizon. So, if I see an intermediate-term investment-grade bond fund as an answer choice, I like that one. Right?

What we can eliminate for this investor: growth stock and growth stock funds, high-yield bonds, money market mutual funds (yields are too low given her moderate liquidity needs).

What we might recommend for this investor: intermediate-term investment-grade bonds and bond funds. A balanced fund would also work. Most balanced funds invest as if the investors are all conservative and in need of income, but they also invest a big % in the stock market. I don't see where this investor is telling us she needs to be in equities at all. Remember—it's her money. If she's happy in the bond market, and you're earning commissions or advisory fees, why stick your neck out? Make your case, but meeting the client's needs sometimes means doing what she wants to do regardless of what you would like her to do. Few parents can get their kids to do what they would like them to do—why would we expect adults we barely know to be totally compliant with our wishes?

Our third investor is the mother of our second investor, and is also a school teacher. Only this investor is a retired teacher. Her teacher's pension allows her to pay bills, but she also finds herself having to do without more often than she would like. Age 73, she remembers the rampant inflation of the 1970s and is afraid that her pension checks might not keep up with the price of groceries, gas, electric, clothing, etc.

- INVESTMENT OBJECTIVES: purchasing power protection
- TIME HORIZON/LIQUIDITY: long-term, moderate liquidity needs
- RISK TOLERANCE: moderate

Growth, capital appreciation, and purchasing power protection all mean the same thing, and they all point to the stock market. Don't all retirees need income investments? Not if they're already receiving a fixed income. A teacher's pension is a fixed income. And, like most fixed annuities, it may or may not keep up with the rising cost of living. So, we need to be in the stock market. And many of the stocks we like here are going to end up paying dividends. But, that is not necessarily what we're after. I mean, it's a good sign that a company can pay a dividend—means they earn regular profits. But, what we need here is growth or capital appreciation. And, we need to get it without getting too aggressive.

In other words, this is an easy recommendation. We want a diversified, professionally managed portfolio of large-cap stocks. Maybe the right answer choice will be something like "50% domestic large-cap stock fund, 50% international large-cap stock fund." That seems aggressive, but with her pension providing the fixed-income piece, this sort of allocation will address her purchasing power concerns without getting too crazy.

What we can eliminate for this investor: small cap funds, aggressive growth investments in general, bonds and bond funds, money market mutual funds.

What we might recommend for this investor: large cap growth stock or funds, blue chip stock or funds.

Our fourth investor is a 64-year-old man who retired last year with a modest pension benefit and a small Traditional IRA account that he does not want to touch until he's required to—at age 70½. This investor recently sold a five-bedroom house in an affluent neighborhood and bought a relatively inexpensive condominium near the shopping, restaurants, and theater district of the college town in which he was born and raised. He has been drawing down the proceeds of the sale (even after the purchase of the condo) and now has approximately $400,000 left to invest with you.

This investor is in excellent physical shape and plans to spend the next several years hiking the Appalachian Trail, kayaking the Boundary Waters, snorkeling in Costa Rica, etc. Since he has no plans to take a part-time job, the investor needs income to fund the travel he plans to do over the next several years. He does not need to make withdrawals of principal from this account, but he does plan to spend every dollar of income that he earns from whatever investments you and he choose. And, he knows that his living expenses will likely rise over time and he, therefore, needs his principal to keep up with the rising cost of living.

- INVESTMENT OBJECTIVES: high income, capital appreciation
- TIME HORIZON/LIQUIDITY: long-term, low liquidity needs
- RISK TOLERANCE: moderate-high

If this investor wants high income, we have to start in the bond market. Since his risk tolerance and time horizon are appropriate, we might recommend a high-yield bond fund. Chances are we don't want to pick individual "junk" or "high-yield" bonds, since each individual issue is somewhat susceptible to default; however, a well-managed and well-diversified mutual fund with a proven track record should be able to maximize the portfolio's income and minimize the rate of default. If the bonds mature at par, or at least rise in market value as the issuer's financial health improves, there will be capital appreciation.

Or, the exam question might give an allocation like this: 50% high-yield bonds, 50% stocks. That would work for me. Or, even 25% high-yield bonds, 25% investment-grade bonds, 50% stocks. If the best answer choice appeared to be "REITs," I could also live with that—they are known for high income and, as stocks, they do offer capital appreciation. However, that makes me nervous since REITs pay dividends, meaning the company has to make a profit to pay them. Bond interest, on the other hand, is a legal obligation that has to be paid just like your mortgage and credit card bills have to be paid.

Our fifth investor has a 13-year-old daughter who is an excellent student dreaming of one day attending Dartmouth, Yale, or Duke. This investor has a 529 Plan opened for her daughter's education, but so far only $10,000 has gone into the account, with the investments currently worth only $7,255.43 after some bad market years and the regular expenses of the plan. She knows she needs to build up the balance of the account but would be more comfortable reinvesting regular income checks from her investments as opposed to waiting for some promise of "capital appreciation" entirely. She has some confidence in the stock and bond markets. She also knows they are both unpredictable and should, therefore, never be used as a reserve or spending account.

- INVESTMENT OBJECTIVES: capital appreciation/growth, income
- TIME HORIZON/LIQUIDITY: 5–10 years, low liquidity needs
- RISK TOLERANCE: moderate

Since capital appreciation is the primary objective, we have to look at stocks or equity mutual funds for this investor. But, since she also has a secondary objective of income, we don't buy pure growth funds; we buy "growth & income" funds. Or, maybe the answer is something like "70% stocks, 30% bonds." A large-cap value fund is appropriate, also. In fact, there are many potential answer choices that could work for this investor—just make sure you put the capital appreciation first, and the income second.

What we can eliminate for this investor: bonds and bond funds, money market mutual funds.

What we might recommend for this investor: growth & income funds, stock index funds, blue chip equity funds. Equity income and balanced funds are pretty close as recommendations, but those funds would put income first, while a growth & income fund, believe it or not, puts growth first. An answer choice of "60% stock, 40% bonds" would also work. Again, there are many possible answers to an investor like this one. As always, weed out the answer choices that don't work first.

Our sixth investor is 59 years old and wants to retire at age 70. His Traditional IRA account is not well-funded and has not achieved much capital appreciation over the years. In fact, your team revealed that over the 30 years the account has been open, his contributions have equaled $50,000, with the account currently worth only $44,000. In other words, he has gotten a tax *deduction* on the contributions, but, so far, no tax *deferral.*

Oh well, customers will have a litany of complaints about their investment experience so far, but hindsight is 20/20. What matters now is the future. If the investor wants to retire in 10 years, with his account currently worth just $44,000, how can you help him? Does he have any real estate, annuities, or savings bonds to enhance his "net worth"? Unfortunately, no. Beyond a half dozen highly collectible electric guitars, the sum total of his "nest egg" is the $44,000 sitting in an IRA account. And, he has been seriously considering just taking out that money, buying a Harley, and touring the country until he runs out of gas, money, and gumption.

- INVESTMENT OBJECTIVES: capital appreciation/growth
- TIME HORIZON/LIQUIDITY: 10+ years, low liquidity needs
- RISK TOLERANCE: moderate

Before we worry about the investment vehicle first we need to convince this investor of the dire need to make his maximum IRA contribution each year until the IRS says he can't do it—which is only about 10 years away. Currently, he can contribute $6,500 a year as long as he has at least that much earned income. That number will likely rise a bit over the next 10 years, and your investment team needs to run some future value calculations to see how that amount of contributions plus a reasonable amount of growth can get him to an account large enough to help him in retirement. Frankly, though, I have my doubts—$44,000?

Anyway, once we get him on a regular monthly direct-deposit plan for his Traditional IRA account, we need to pick investment options. It seems clear that this investor will be in an equity fund, or a mix of equity funds. Also, these equity funds will be neither too aggressive nor too conservative for him. If I see an answer choice like "Mid-Cap Growth" or "Large Cap Growth," I'm tempted to choose it. An answer choice like "S&P 500 Index Fund" would also not be wrong. Basically, this guy is just a growth investor who doesn't want to get crazy chasing overvalued and overhyped stocks. Choosing a conservative stock fund makes me uneasy, too, since his account balance is going to be useless in retirement if it doesn't grow significantly through capital appreciation and regular contributions.

If the investor had a fixed annuity or a pension income to supplement this account, then we could be more aggressive with the stock picks. But, since we aren't finding any of that, we're in a tough spot. It's kind of like when you're late for an appointment: do you decide to speed or play it safe? If you speed and get by with it, you win. However, if you get caught speeding, you not only miss your goal of making the appointment, but also lose a bunch of money. Could you face this investor after talking him into some international aggressive growth fund that loses 70% of its value?

Me, neither. If the answer choices include mutual funds, we want growth funds that are neither too aggressive nor too conservative. If the choices are asset allocations, we might go with 80% stock, 20% bonds.

What we can eliminate for this investor: bonds and bond funds, money market mutual funds, aggressive growth investments (emerging markets, sector funds, etc.) small cap growth funds, conservative stock funds, balanced funds, equity income funds.

What we might recommend for this investor: large cap growth fund, blue chip equity fund, stock market index fund.

Our seventh investor is a 48-year-old woman who works in marketing for a successful mid-sized manufacturing company. Like most people her age, she has had to save for retirement mostly on her own. The company where she works offers a 401(k) plan, but they only match up to 5% of her salary, and her salary is only $53,000. Retirement seems a long way off, but she has a vague idea that she'd like to retire before she's 70. Her 401(k) plan balance is currently $127,000. She feels she cannot retire on less than $500,000, even if she makes a capital gain when selling her house and downsizing someday.

- INVESTMENT OBJECTIVES: capital appreciation/growth
- TIME HORIZON/LIQUIDITY: 20+ years, low liquidity needs
- RISK TOLERANCE: high

Again, even before we pick the investment vehicles, this investor should understand that regardless of how stingy her employer is her 401(k) account will allow her to contribute more than three times what she could contribute to a Traditional IRA account. Now, while she could definitely maximize her 401(k) contributions and also maximize her Traditional IRA with tax-deductible contributions, I don't see that she has that much money to sock away for retirement. She needs to make a reasonable contribution into her 401(k) account—as much as she can afford to.

As far as where to put those contributions, this investor will be in stocks or stock/equity mutual funds. This time, however, we want more aggressive investments. Small cap growth stocks or funds would be an ideal choice. Other correct recommendations might include sector funds, international funds, and global funds. Most stock index funds would also work—S&P Mid-Cap 400 or the Russell 2000, for example, would both be good answer choices.

What we can eliminate for this investor: bonds and bond funds, money market mutual funds, conservative stock funds, balanced funds, equity income funds.

What we might recommend for this investor: small cap growth stock/funds, stock index funds, sector funds, international funds.

Our eighth investor makes a lot of money, and has a lot of money. Then again, what's "a lot of money"? To me, $3 million of investable assets ought to do it, but for this investor there is, apparently, never enough. Since his late 20s he has been making at least six figures, and since his late 30s the thought of making a mere six figures has given him the willies. Then again, while his average income over any 10-year period has been pretty good, there always seem to be those 3- and even 5-year periods where the income drops much more than he admits to himself or his drinking buddies.

This investor is 57 years old and is not interested so much in retiring as in knowing that he could retire if he wants to. He has $1.5 million to invest with you. He has a small mortgage balance, two vacation properties, and approximately $100,000 in checking and savings that he is not interested in investing with you. His retirement accounts total about $900,000, and he plans to keep maximizing the SIMPLE-IRA he participates in as a salesman for a small software company. His father lived to age 93 and his grandfather to age 91. He does not plan to slow down or retire for at least 10 years.

- INVESTMENT OBJECTIVES: retirement income
- TIME HORIZON/LIQUIDITY: long-term, low liquidity needs
- RISK TOLERANCE: low

This investor seems like a prime candidate for a fixed annuity. If he already has close to $1 million in his retirement accounts, and plans to keep funding them a while, why not put $1.5 million into a fixed annuity that promises to pay a minimum amount each month once he throws the switch, no matter how long he lives? He's afraid that he never has enough money, and his father and grandfather lived long lives—I'd say he needs the annuity to assure he won't completely run out of money no matter how long he himself manages to live. If he were going to retire now, we'd choose an immediate annuity. Since he won't retire for at least 10 years, a deferred annuity works; he will not be hit with a surrender charge since he won't need to touch the money and there will also be no tax penalties that way.

If we saw statements about a fear of losing purchasing power/inflation, we might choose a variable annuity instead. That way, he could put some money in the stock market subaccounts and the rest in safer subaccounts, maybe. But with this investor's up-and-down income coupled with his fear of running out of money and his father's and grandfather's longevity, I think a question presenting this set of facts is crying out for a fixed annuity. Just make sure he keeps maximizing his other retirement options, and that he really doesn't need to touch the money for a while, and you can go ahead and recommend a deferred fixed or deferred indexed annuity. Knowing he'll get a minimum payment each month for the rest of his life will buy this investor a lot of sleep.

What we can eliminate for this investor: just about everything. I don't see a big need for current income or a huge need for capital appreciation/growth. He isn't complaining about high taxes, so we don't need to look at municipal bond funds or direct participation programs.

What we might recommend for this investor: fixed annuity or equity indexed annuity from an insurance company with a high claims-paying ability (AM Best Rating).

Investor Number Nine is a 75-year-old widow with a financial net worth of $5 million. Her income sources include rental income from a few real estate LLC interests she inherited from her husband, plus the IRA account now worth $1.2 million after she inherited and combined her husband's IRA with her own. She takes the required minimum distribution from the IRA each year, but that falls far short of funding her rather expensive lifestyle. Because she likes to shop, eat out, attend the theater, and decorate her townhouse, this investor needs income. However, since her annual income is close to $1 million, she ends up losing over 1/3 of that to the federal government and close to 5% to her state government. This investor is slightly concerned about a loss of purchasing power, though receiving income from her investments is clearly the main objective.

- INVESTMENT OBJECTIVES: tax-exempt income, purchasing power protection
- TIME HORIZON/LIQUIDITY: intermediate-to-long-term, low liquidity needs
- RISK TOLERANCE: low

Since she needs income that is tax-exempt, we will recommend municipal bonds. We can either buy them a la carte or as a packaged set. If she's truly in a high-tax state, there may be an open- or closed-end fund designed for residents of that state. For example, if she lives in Maryland, there will be municipal bond funds for residents of that state. The income dividends they generate would, therefore, be exempt from both federal and state income taxes for this investor. Now, to deal with her concern over inflation/loss of purchasing power, we can put a small percentage of her account into a conservative equity fund, possibly a low-cost S&P 500 Index fund.

What we can eliminate for this investor: aggressive investments, a large concentration in growth stocks/growth funds, taxable bonds (corporate or U.S. Treasury).

What we might recommend for this investor: municipal bonds primarily issued inside her state of residence or municipal bond funds designed for investors residing in her state.

Our tenth and final investor, a widow, has an annual income of $95,000, her mortgage is paid off, and she does not like to shop or eat out. She is 68 years old and lives comfortably on bond interest and dividend checks from a handful of stocks her husband picked decades ago. She works part-time, earning approximately $10,000 a year. She would like to continue to fund a tax-deferred account whose balance can pass directly to her only granddaughter upon her death.

- INVESTMENT OBJECTIVES: tax-deferral, estate planning

- TIME HORIZON/LIQUIDITY: long-term, low liquidity needs
- RISK TOLERANCE: moderate to high

It might seem strange to put her risk tolerance at "moderate to high," but why not?

She is already living comfortably on her investment income. She just wants to keep putting some money away that will grow tax-deferred for a rainy day, and whatever she doesn't spend in her lifetime will pass to her granddaughter. Stock funds within a Roth IRA are the answer here, most likely. The investor has earned income, enough to maximize her annual Roth IRA contribution. In a few years, she would have to stop putting money into a Traditional IRA, which is, again, why we're looking for a Roth IRA. The next-best answer would likely be an annuity. As with a Roth, she never has to take the money out, and can name the granddaughter the beneficiary of the account. Since the investor doesn't need to live on the Roth IRA, I don't mind the fact that if it's a new account, she needs to wait 5 years to make any withdrawals. As long as she doesn't need to touch the money for a bit longer, I can even live with the surrender period on a deferred annuity.

What we can eliminate for this investor: income investments, since she already has bond interest and cash dividends a-plenty. High-risk equities can be eliminated because nothing tells us she has an appetite for risk or is trying to keep up with purchasing power.

What we might recommend for this investor: equity funds within a Roth IRA, annuity.

Portfolio Management Strategies, Styles and Techniques

Strategies and Styles

To understand the difference between growth and value investments we first need to understand the following terms.

Valuation Ratios

When a fundamental analyst compares the market price of a stock to the earnings, cash flow or book value per-share, he is looking at a **valuation ratio**. Another name for a valuation ratio is a multiple. Whatever we call them, the following are comparisons between a stock's market price and some other number from one of the issuer's three financial statements.

Price-to-Earnings Ratio

When evaluating common stock, investors compare the price of the stock to the earnings per-share to see if the stock is attractively priced. This is called the price-to-earnings ratio. The higher the number, the more expensive the stock. A share of common stock is a share of the company's earnings. So, the question is, how much are people willing to pay for those earnings? If a stock trades for $25 on the secondary market when the earnings per-share = $1, the stock trades for 25 times the earnings, or a P/E ratio of 25:1.

The price-to-earnings ratio indicates how much investors value a company's profits as expressed through the market price of the stock. Are they willing to pay ten times the earnings? Twenty times the earnings? One hundred times the earnings? Stocks trading at high multiples are **growth stocks**, while those trading at low multiples are **value stocks**. Growth stocks involve more volatility than value stocks because the price is supported by enthusiasm rather than tangible measures such as book value.

Price-to-Book Ratio

We found the earnings of the company on the income statement. We can figure the **book value** on the balance sheet. If a company had to be liquidated, the equipment, factory, real estate, etc., would be sold at auction and the proceeds would be paid first to the creditors, then to the preferred stockholders. The amount that would be left for each share of common stock is the **book value per-share**. Think of this as the hard, tangible value of a share of common stock.

If the book value of a share of stock is $6, and the stock now trades for $30, it is trading at a **price-to-book ratio** of 5.

Price-to-Sales, Price-to-Cash Ratios

It isn't just that growth investors buy stocks trading at high price-to-earnings ratios. Many growth investors buy stocks in companies with no earnings at all. If the company has no earnings, it isn't worth talking about the P/E ratio. For a company with no earnings it is more practical to compare the market price of the stock to the sales the company makes (**price-to-sales**). Notice how this ties in with the income statement. Earnings represent the bottom line; sales represent the top line. Or, for companies not making a profit, many analysts pay closest attention to the price of the stock compared to the cash flow generated per-share. This is called, not surprisingly, **price-to-cash**.

So, if the company has net income and a strong balance sheet, fundamental analysts compare the stock price to the earnings and the book value. If the company is losing money as the sales and cash flow are growing, they can compare the market price to the sales or cash flow per-share.

Some analysts prefer using price-to-sales even if the company is profitable. As many famous companies have demonstrated, it is easy to manipulate earnings with creative accounting, but sales/revenue represents a number that is hard to fake. It is the top line of the income statement, remember, so it hasn't been filtered through all the subtractions for cost of goods sold, operating expenses, depreciation, amortization, or interest.

Growth Investing

Growth stocks trade at high P/E ratios. The higher the P/E ratio, the more speculative and volatile the stock. When a stock is trading at 35 or 50 times the earnings, every earnings announcement can move the stock's price dramatically.

A **growth investor** needs a long time horizon and the ability to withstand large fluctuations in the value of his investments. And he is not seeking dividend income if he is seeking capital appreciation/growth.

Value Investing

Value investors buy stocks trading at low price-to-earnings or price-to-book ratios. A value investor purchases stocks in out-of-favor corporations trading for less than they should be. For example, when GM's CEO is testifying before Congress over badly handled recalls, many traders will dump shares of GM, while value investors might decide to buy shares at currently depressed prices.

Value stocks would typically have higher dividend yields, especially if we compare large-cap value stocks to large-cap growth. Why? Large-cap companies are more likely to pay dividends to their shareholders now that their businesses are running relatively predictably. If their market price drops, suddenly the dividend yield will increase. The board of directors does not usually want to cut that dividend, so the decreasing market price will raise the dividend yield.

 The word "growth" does not imply that value investors don't also want their investments to appreciate in value. It's just that growth investors buy expensive stocks expected to rise even more in the future, while value investors buy stocks of companies currently in trouble but worth more than the market realizes. If they were into real estate rather than common stock, growth investors would buy the new townhouses going up in the hot, new part of town, while value investors would buy foreclosed properties and rehab them for a profit.

Market Capitalization (Market Cap)

Market cap is an abbreviation for **market capitalization**. A company's market capitalization is their total number of outstanding shares times today's closing price. If the company has 100 million shares outstanding, their market capitalization is $1 billion if the stock closes at $10 per-share today. The number would, then, change each day the markets are open. In our example, if the stock closes down 50 cents tomorrow, the company's market cap would be reduced by $50 million.

There are small-cap, mid-cap, and large-cap stocks investors can choose from. The smaller the cap, the higher the risk-reward ratio.

Equity Style Box

We can now put growth and value together with market capitalization by looking at the Morningstar **equity style box.** This guide for investors places equity mutual funds in one of 9 boxes to indicate how aggressive the investment is. The most aggressive box is **small cap growth** while the least aggressive is **large cap value.**

In terms of style, growth is more aggressive than value. In terms of size, the lower the market capitalization the higher the volatility.

If a portfolio manager doesn't stick to just growth or value, that fund is called a **blend fund**. A blend fund sits between growth and value in terms of volatility.

Equity mutual funds fit somewhere in the following table or box of 9 cells developed in 1992 by Morningstar. The upper-left box is the least aggressive equity fund, while the lower-right box is the most aggressive.

Large Cap Value	Large Cap Blend	Large Cap Growth
Mid Cap Value	Mid Cap Blend	Mid Cap Growth
Small Cap Value	Small Cap Blend	Small Cap Growth

The center box--Mid Cap Blend--represents the core style of investing. Also, although not a separate style zone for the equity style box, the stocks that are smaller than small-cap are known as **micro cap**. These stocks frequently trade on the less liquid and less regulated OTC equities markets. Because of the small number of shares and the relative obscurity of the companies, these stock issues are more prone to manipulation.

We could find resources online that would set the cutoffs for small, mid, and large cap. But as Morningstar explains, "Large-cap stocks are those that together account for the top 70% of the capitalization of each style zone; mid-cap stocks represent the next 20%; and small-cap stocks represent the balance. The market caps that correspond to these breakpoints are flexible and may shift from month to month as the market changes."

Many people assume investors agree on the three market capitalization categories, but not exactly. The best we can do is see what S&P uses for their large, mid, and small cap indices. The S&P 500 is a large-cap index. To be included in the index a company must have a minimum market cap of $4 billion. To be included in the S&P SmallCap 600 a company must have a market cap between $300 million to $1.4 billion. And in the middle, the S&P MidCap 400 includes companies with a market cap of $1 billion to $4.4 billion.

You probably noticed that the mid-cap range overlaps both the high end of the small-cap range ($1.4 billion) and the low end of the large-cap range ($4 billion). That's how it works with all stock classification systems, turns out. Therefore, it is difficult to write a fair test question involving precise numbers, when S&P themselves don't use such rigid cutoffs. And, as always, the test is not that concerned with rote memorization. Reasoning skills are far more important than one's ability to commit a table of data to memory on this exam.

Active vs. Passive

Growth and value are terms that refer to types of stock as well as investment styles. The terms active and passive, on the other hand, refer only to types of investment styles. If you seek particular stocks (or bonds), you are an **active** manager. If you buy "growth" or "value" index funds, you are a **passive** manager. Is the investor actively determining that one security is more attractive than another? If so, that's active portfolio management. Now, who uses active management styles—fundamental or technical analysts?

Both. We could determine that ORCL is a better investment now than MSFT by looking at the fundamentals, or we could look at technical indicators including charts, the 200-day moving average, or short interest. Either way, if we are coming down on the side of one stock versus another, we are using active stock selection or active portfolio management.

A passive management style usually involves the use of indexes rather than trying to pick one investment over another. We could buy a growth index fund or a value index fund, which is choosing a style, but we would never try to pick one growth or value stock over another. Using this passive indexing strategy, we will pay lower expenses, because these funds aren't doing a lot of trading and, therefore, don't have to charge high management fees.

Income vs. Capital Appreciation

The terms "growth" and "value" have some overlap with the terms **income** and **capital appreciation**. Growth investors tend not to care about or receive dividend income, while value investors often receive a relatively high dividend yield. But growth and value are both mostly about capital appreciation. It's just that growth investors like to buy hot companies that will continue to grow, while value investors are drawn to companies currently in trouble but about to turn things around.

Income and capital appreciation could be called styles, but they are also investment objectives. Does the investor seek income, or is he interested in buying stocks that increase in market value? Income investors invest in bonds and preferred stock. Investors seeking capital appreciation invest in common stock.

As with many categories, these are not rigid. An investment in SBUX would involve income even though it trades as a growth stock, and growth is synonymous with capital appreciation. Some companies are successful and growing, like SBUX. They have the cash flow to cover a modest dividend, but their profits and share price may continue to rise well into the future.

Or not. Which is why SBUX is not an income investment, even if it pays a dividend. An income investor would not start with large-cap dividend paying companies. An income investor would allocate most of her assets to bonds and preferred stock.

The dividend income from common stock is associated with an investor who seeks both growth and income from a common stock investment. Such an investor is known as a growth-and-income investor, as one might expect.

But, an income investor has far better options among various bonds and preferred stock. Even though REITS offer extremely high dividend yields, an income investor should not be steered in that direction, since they are a form of common stock and, therefore, too risky for a pure income investor. A REIT is appropriate for a growth and income investor with a long time horizon who can withstand wide fluctuations in market value. Income investors don't expect to see wide fluctuations in the market values of their bonds and preferred stocks. On the other hand, any investor seeking capital appreciation has to live with the volatility that goes with it.

Asset Allocation

Asset allocation is a widely-accepted tenet of investing. Virtually no one 50 years old is 100% invested in equities, or even 100% in fixed-income. The rule of thumb has been that an investor should limit his equity exposure to 100 minus his age. If he's 47, he should have no more than 53% of his portfolio allocated to equities. These days, with age expectancies getting longer, some are now saying to increase the equity exposure to 120 minus the investor's age, which would give the 47-year-old a maximum of 73% for equities. Obviously, this rule of thumb is just a little bit arbitrary and unscientific, although it is based on a solid premise—portfolios that use asset allocation drive over the bumps in the markets much better than those concentrated too heavily on one asset class.

In general, investors in their 50s will have a little less than half their portfolio allocated to stock/equities and a little more than half devoted to fixed-income and money market/cash. Within those basic asset classes the equity portion could be divided by market cap and growth/value/blend, international vs. domestic, and industry sectors. The fixed-income piece could be divided by term to maturity, credit quality, taxable versus tax-exempt, and types of issuers.

For example, after an investor completes a questionnaire through a secure area of the firm's website, maybe the computer models return the following allocation:

- Equity – 40%
  - 20% Large-Cap Value
  - 20% Small-Cap Growth
- Fixed-Income – 50%
  - 20% High-Yield
  - 20% Investment-Grade, Taxable
  - 10% High-Yield, Tax-Exempt
- Cash – 10%

If we present that allocation as a full-color pie chart, you can imagine that most investors will begin to relax and feel that someone who knows what he is doing is about to take charge of their investments. And, of course, most investors will end up doing a whole lot better using a registered investment professional to allocate and manage their portfolio, as opposed to watching some guy on TV.

Whatever the asset allocation is the investor will tweak things from time to time to **rebalance** the portfolio back to its stated percentages. To maintain the strategic mix of asset classes the agent and the investor need to sell some of the assets that have appreciated to add to the ones that have gone down and now represent a smaller % of the portfolio.

Techniques
No matter how an investor arrives at the decision to invest in X, Y, or Z, he must manage those assets using various portfolio management techniques.

Buy and Hold
Whether I'm a growth, value, passive, or active manager, I could use **buy and hold** as a portfolio management technique. The buy and hold approach results in lower transaction costs, because the investor is not trading and generating commissions/markups. Rather, he is buying, and then holding.

Plus, he avoids getting taxed at short-term capital gains rates by selling infrequently and almost always for a long-term capital gain.

Diversification
Another accepted tenet of prudent investing is called **diversification**. As we see when discussing the Uniform Prudent Investor Act, a fiduciary is expected to diversify the assets of a trust, except in those rare cases where it is more beneficial and prudent not to. A diversified portfolio of stocks would not contain all technology or pharmaceutical companies, for example. If there were a number of oil company stocks, they would be diversified between domestic and international companies, producers of oil and refiners of oil. They would not all be small cap or large cap. A bond portfolio would not be

all triple-A-rated or all junk, but would instead be diversified throughout different maturities, credit quality, and issuers that don't all come from the same industry.

Asset allocation and diversification are somewhat related. Where they differ is that asset allocation is a style that places percentages of capital into various types of stocks, bonds, and cash. Within those allocations, we use diversification to balance the risk of one investment with the characteristics of another. So, 20% large-cap growth, 20% mid-cap growth, 30% small-cap growth, and 30% long-term bond is an asset allocation. Drill down into the "20% large-cap growth" category, and the various companies owned would come from different industries to maintain diversification.

Also, diversification is not linked to asset allocation. An active stock picker using a growth style would tend to hold a diversified portfolio of stocks in companies from different industry sectors. The same is true of a value investor. That's what makes diversification a technique, while the others are considered strategies or styles. Whether I'm active or passive, growth or value, I'm almost certainly implementing the technique of diversification to reduce my risk.

We saw earlier that unsystematic risk can be reduced through diversification, while systematic risks cannot. In other words, investors reduce their legislative risk by purchasing securities issued by companies in different industry spaces. To reduce overall market risk—which is systematic— investors use options, futures, or ETFs to hedge. If the risk is that the overall market will drop, for example, investors can buy index put options, sell ETFs short, or purchase inverse ETFs designed to move opposite the overall market.

Sector Rotating

Some portfolio managers try to anticipate which sectors are about to rise and which are about to fall. The object then becomes to sell the sectors that are about to drop and buy the ones that are about to rise. Not surprisingly, this technique is called **sector rotating**. Deciding which sectors to "underweight" and which to "overweight" could be done through fundamental or technical analysis. If an industry space seems set for an expansion due to economic forces, that analyst is using fundamental analysis and probably top-down analysis, as well. Another trader may decide to sell pharmaceuticals when they are "overbought" and invest in telecommunications because they appear to be "oversold" at this point. That is technical analysis. Either way, the technique is known as sector rotating or sector rotation.

Dollar Cost Averaging

Investors often put a fixed dollar amount into securities on a regular schedule. Since stocks, bonds, and mutual funds fluctuate in price, investors using the **dollar cost averaging** technique end up buying fewer shares when they're expensive and more of their shares when they're temporarily (we hope) cheap. The test might point out that an investor's average cost is lower than the average share price…which is because of what I just said. To illustrate it clearly, though, we need a story problem. So here goes: Melody automatically invests $1,000 into a mutual fund each month. Over the past three months the Net Asset Value was $50, $40, and $25. Therefore, her average cost per-share is what amount?

We need to figure out how many shares she bought with her total dollars invested. She invested $3,000, so how many shares did she buy?

270

	SHARE PRICE	# OF SHARES
Jan: $1,000	$50	
Feb: $1,000	$40	
Mar: $1,000	$25	

In January, her $1,000 bought 20 shares. In February, her $1,000 bought 25 shares, and in March her $1,000 bought 40 shares. Therefore, her $3,000 in total acquired 85 shares. What is the average cost per-share? Whatever $3,000 divided by 85 shares equals—about $35.29.

I'm betting the question would also present the average share price as one of the false answers, because most people want to get through a question like this as fast as possible. The average cost is not $38.33. That would be the average of the three share prices, and that would only be relevant if the investor were buying, say, 100 shares of stock each month. But that is not what happens when dollar cost averaging. Here, it's not the number of shares that is fixed—it's the dollar amount. The number of shares acquired each time varies.

Investors often use the average-cost method to figure their cost basis when selling securities for capital gains/capital losses. The other methods are FIFO (First In First Out) and share identification.

Capital Market Theory

CAPM

The **Capital Asset Pricing Model** (CAPM) has something in common with the Sharpe ratio, but the two are used for different purposes. The Sharpe ratio calculates what already happened and calls it "risk-adjusted return," while CAPM calculates and predicts expected return based on some math we're about to look at.

Both concepts use the idea that an investor could put her money into a "riskless rate of return," so if she's going to put it into something risky instead, she demands a potential reward much larger than that riskless rate of return. That extra reward is known as a "risk premium."

The formula works like this. If the risk-free rate is 3%, the beta of the stock is 2, and the expected market return over the period is 10%, then the stock is expected to return 17%. To calculate that, you would take the risk-free rate and add that to the expected return minus that risk-free rate times the beta.

Even though the formula looks heavy, it does communicate a basic concept. The calculation is saying that the expected return on a stock is equal to the risk-free return an investor could get on 3-month T-Bills plus the potential return on the stock that is over and above the risk-free rate.

The numbers above are crunched like this: (3% + 2 (10% − 3%)). That's 3%, plus the sum of (20% minus 6%). 3% plus 14% equals the expected return of 17%. And, it shows that investors expect to be compensated both for the time value of money and the risk of investing in stocks.

Again, the Sharpe ratio and CAPM both incorporate the riskless rate of return. But CAPM calculates an expected return, while the Sharpe ratio adjusts actual returns for the risk the portfolio experienced. Notice how these approaches are purely mathematical, while fundamental analysis involves both a quantitative and qualitative examination of a company. A trader using CAPM and the Sharpe ratio is more interested in how a stock or a portfolio is behaving and is likely to behave in the future. Fundamental analysts are interested in determining which companies are likely to perform well in the future.

Modern Portfolio Theory

In the distant past, investors would consider the risk of any one security. **Modern Portfolio Theory**, on the other hand, looks at how an investment affects the risk/reward ratio of the entire portfolio. It also assumes that investors are risk-averse, no matter what they tell you. Since investors don't like risk, we could say that they would prefer to make, for example, 10% returns through the least risky path, or that, given a level of risk, they want the highest possible return. Using an entirely mathematical/statistical approach to investing, Modern Portfolio Theorists construct "optimal portfolios," which means that the investor is likely to get the highest possible return given the amount of volatility he is willing to bear.

If we reverse the words, we get **portfolio optimization**, which relates to a graph called an **efficient frontier**. What is considered key is the unique mix of securities in a portfolio. There are many portfolios that fall along this efficient frontier, so which one is better for the investor? It depends on the amount of volatility the investor can handle, and what potential return he thinks he will settle for. Portfolios are constructed of a percentage mix of equity, bonds, and cash, and these various mixes can, theoretically—based on historical data—determine the amount of risk, and the likely return.

Whichever risk-reward profile the investor chooses, we want the portfolio to lie along (not behind) the efficient frontier. The portfolios that lie on the lower left part of the curve are the most efficient for the low-risk–low-reward investors, while the portfolios that lie along the upper right part of the curve are the most efficient for the high-risk–high-reward investors.

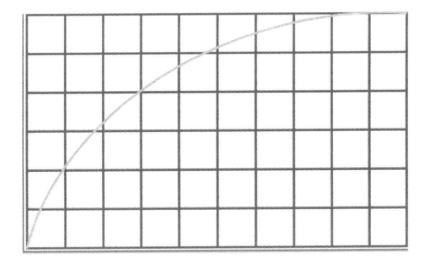

Modern Portfolio Theory is a mathematical approach to investment selection. It is interested in calculating the risk-reward nature of a portfolio by measuring expected returns, standard deviations, and correlations. Rather than thinking like a fundamental analyst that 1,000 shares of ORCL should rise next year when the company reports higher profits, Modern Portfolio Theory would, instead, calculate the likely return of a portfolio based on mathematical probabilities. Technical analysis would also be of no use to this crowd. Whether using financial statements or stock charts, to a modern portfolio theorist, either investor is actively and foolishly selecting securities.

Efficient Market Hypothesis

The **efficient market hypothesis** grew out of a Ph.D. dissertation by Eugene Fama. This school of thought assumes that at any given time in a liquid market all information about a security is already priced in, making the current market price an accurate estimate of any security's intrinsic value. Because all security prices accurately reflect their intrinsic value, attempts to outperform the overall market are based on luck rather than skill.

Efficient Market Hypothesis can be further broken down into three separate forms: weak, semi-strong, and strong. The **weak form** assumes that current stock prices fully reflect all currently available market information and contends that past price and volume data have no relationship with the future direction of security prices. It concludes that excess returns cannot be achieved using technical analysis.

The **semi-strong form** of efficient market hypothesis assumes that current stock prices adjust rapidly to the release of all new public information. It contends that security prices have factored in available market and non-market public information. It concludes that excess returns cannot be achieved using fundamental analysis, so all of that work we did in Chapter 1 on financial statements is a waste of time.

The **strong form** of efficient market hypothesis assumes that current stock prices fully reflect all public and private information. It contends that market, non-market and inside information is all factored into security prices and that no one has monopolistic access to relevant information. It assumes a perfect market and concludes that excess returns are impossible to achieve consistently.

Even if an investor possessed material non-public information, it is of no benefit to him since even that is factored into stock prices.

All three forms suggest that trying to beat the overall market is not a realistic goal. Rather, investors should seek a reasonable rate of return given the risk they are willing to take.

Behavioral Finance

Proponents of the Efficient Market Hypothesis believe that prices for securities are the result of investors implementing the information available to them in a rational manner. This seems to hold true for most market situations over the long-term. However, to explain anomalies such as speculative bubbles **behavioral finance** concludes that irrational behavior on a massive scale is the culprit.

As an excellent guide to behavioral finance by Vanguard UK explains, "The behavioral biases discussed in this guide are ingrained aspects of human decision-making processes. Many of them have served us well as ways of coping with day-to-day choices. But, they may be unhelpful for achieving success in long-term activities such as investing."

One idea of behavioral finance is that investors make decisions based on an imprecise understanding of information rather than on a perfectly rational analysis of clear and irrefutable facts. Another is that the way a problem or question is framed or presented to an investor has a profound effect on his behavior. If you think of the 24-hour news cycle these days, it is not hard to understand how some investors get mistaken notions based on the volume of the pundits on their TV screens or the number of times a story is run. Such investors could end up selling investments that are not even related to the topic they're following on-screen based on the impression they get from the pundits on financial news shows.

Or, back when companies with a dot-com in their name were hot, investors got the idea that dot-com stocks would go up forever based on the enthusiasm of such pundits, all trying to advance their speaking and publishing careers. Another name for this phenomenon is framing. The way that information is framed or presented to investors has a profound impact on their decision making.

The term recency bias or the recency effect relates to the way many investors take the data and experience of the markets recently and extrapolate the situation into the future indefinitely. If stocks have risen 20% and then 28% two years in a row, many investors assume this is the new normal and end up investing heavily just before a bear market. Bloomberg takes a weekly survey of money managers' recommended weightings for stocks/bonds/cash and found that the highest stock weighting was recommended just after the peak of the Internet stock bubble, with the lowest stock weighting coming just after the lows of the financial crisis. This suggests that recency bias is alive and well, even among institutional investors.

On the other hand, the primacy bias or primacy effect occurs when the first information or experience is given more weighting than anything that comes later. A retail investor who experiences a big profit on his first options trade could end up chasing profits far into the future no matter how many losses he later racks up. This would suggest that his first experience with options was so strongly rewarded that subsequent losses are downplayed or ignored.

Another bias that affects decision making is overconfidence. Turns out we humans tend to overrate our abilities, including our ability to make decisions. For example, when asked to rate our driving abilities, virtually no one rates himself as below average, even though--by definition--50% of drivers are below average. Overconfident investors are likely to ignore the wisdom of diversification based on their belief that they can pick market sectors or individual stocks to overweight. These investors also tend to overrate the effect that their stock picking or sector rotating has on portfolio returns.

Such investors typically trade too often, as well, based on their belief that their skills are linked to market-beating results. However, as Professor Brad Barber and Terrence Odean found by studying the habits of U.S. retail investors, investors who were in the bottom 20% for portfolio turnover had an average annual portfolio return of 18.5%, while those in the top 20% for trading activity had an average annual return of just 11.4%. (Source: Brad Barber and Terrence Odean (1999) 'The courage of misguided convictions' Financial Analysts Journal, November/December, p. 50.)

On the other hand, the bias of loss aversion can be just as self-destructive. Research suggests that investors overweight a chance of loss by as much as 2-to-1 compared to a chance of gain. For example, when surveyed, investors required a 50/50 chance of either gaining $2,500 or losing just $1,000 to make the risk of loss worth taking.

However, when a loss occurs, many investors hang onto it indefinitely, assuming the stock price will eventually return to their "breakeven" point. You might assume that retail investors tend to take a profit only after holding it long-term due to the favorable tax treatment, while, on the other hand, cutting any losses rather quickly. In fact, the same professors mentioned above found that investors sell their winners quickly while hanging onto losing positions too long. Investors are, in fact, 50% more likely to sell a winning position than to lock in a loss. That implies that they are risk-averse when holding a winner and inexplicably risk-tolerant when holding a losing position.

Which, as with most of these biases, is not what one might expect. But, it does explain why the ability to recognize these biases of investing clients could reduce the negative effects of various human quirks in financial decision making.

Tax Considerations

Most of us pay income taxes at several different rates due to the graduated, progressive income tax system in the United States. At the time of this writing, there are seven tax brackets. For most taxpayers, the first $9,275 of income is taxed at 10%. The next dollars earned up to $37,650 are taxed at 15%. The next dollars up to $91,150 are taxed at 25%, and so on.

Notice that we don't pay 25% on all our income just because we reach that bracket. Rather, we pay 25% on the dollars we make above a certain amount. If the highest rate of tax applied is 25%, then 25% is the taxpayer's **marginal tax rate**. An exam question might define an investor's marginal rate as "the rate of tax paid on the last dollar of income earned."

Beyond the different tax brackets there are also different methods of filing income taxes, and these methods affect the rate of taxes paid. For example, a single filer is pushed into the 15% tax bracket and then the 25% bracket at a certain dollar amount, while a married couple filing jointly would get to make twice those amounts before being pushed into the 15% and then the 25% bracket.

On the other hand, if they choose "married-filing-separately," the dollar amounts are different. Turns out a married couple choosing to file separately can each earn as much as single filers, until we get to those middle tax brackets and, suddenly, they get pushed into the 28% and 33% brackets sooner than if they'd stayed unattached. The reasoning for this is that married couples share expenses and should, therefore, be pushed into higher marginal brackets at lower dollar amounts. Those who disagree with the notion refer to it as the "marriage penalty."

There is another method of filing called "head of household." If the test question says that your client is now raising two children orphaned when her sister was killed in a car crash, that individual should file as "head of household" versus "single filer." For a "head-of-household" filer, the dollar amounts of income allowed before being pushed into the next tax bracket are much higher compared to a single filer. For example, using this method the individual would not reach the 15% bracket until her adjusted gross income rose above $13,250, compared to just $9,275 for the other methods ($18,550 for married filing jointly).

For a more detailed look: https://www.irs.com/articles/projected-us-tax-rates-2016.

Whatever the marginal tax bracket, what we're talking about is **ordinary income**. Ordinary income includes wages, salaries, bonuses, commissions, some dividends, and bond interest. We'll talk later about investments held within retirement accounts, but for now, let's talk about the regular, old taxable brokerage account.

There are two types of taxes on investments:

- Taxes on income
- Taxes on capital gains

Let's start with income.

Portfolio Income

Bonds pay interest, and many stocks pay dividends. This income is a major part of a portfolio's total return. Unfortunately, it is also taxable.

Dividends

Let's say you buy 1,000 shares of GE for $30 per-share. Every three months you receive a quarterly dividend of 25 cents per-share, or $250. Believe it or not, it's only taxed at a maximum rate of 15% in most cases nowadays. Before the big change to the tax code, those dividends were taxed at ordinary income rates. Many investors paying a 39% tax on dividends a few years ago are now paying no more than 15%. Imagine that. You're a wealthy individual receiving $200,000 in dividend income each year. You used to pay about $78,000 in taxes on that money; now you pay only $30,000.

But, it's also not correct to make a blanket statement such as, "Dividends are taxed at 15%." The dividends that get taxed at 15% are called **qualified dividends**. These include dividends from GE, MSFT, or most any C-corporation. But there are **ordinary dividends**, which we'll get to in a second.

First, however, why are dividends now taxed at just 15%? This relates to our look at the income statement. Remember the phrase "net income after tax"? That reminds us that corporations such as GE and MSFT pay dividends after they've paid tax on their profit. Unlike bond interest, dividends are not deducted from a company's income to reduce their tax burden. Since GE or MSFT already paid tax on the profits before paying some of them to shareholders in the form of a dividend, why should shareholders get fully taxed on that money?

Turns out they shouldn't, and they don't. We pointed out that C-corporations subject the owners to the double taxation of income, but at least, the taxation on dividends is reduced for most investors. If your marginal tax rate is 25%, 33%, or 35%, you pay only 15% on qualified dividends. But, check this out—if your tax bracket is lower than 25%, the tax you pay on qualified dividends is zero percent.

Zero. But, again, not all dividends are qualified and taxed at the kinder, gentler rates. The dividends that don't qualify for this tax treatment include ordinary dividends, which are taxed at ordinary income rates. REITs pay out 90% of their earnings pre-tax to shareholders to act as a conduit to the investors. But, since the REIT receives a tax break on the dividend, the unit holders do not. REIT investors pay ordinary dividends taxed at ordinary income rates.

For investors who reach the 39.6% marginal bracket, qualified dividends and long-term capital gains are now taxed at 20%.

Finally, I am giving you the "real-world" tax rates on dividends. The exam will likely avoid the issue entirely and say something like, "If the tax on dividends is 20%, what is Joe's after-tax return?" The exam generally wants to see if the test taker can work with a concept rather than seeing if he has memorized endless tables of data.

Bond Interest
Interest paid on corporate and government bonds is taxable at ordinary income rates. This explains why wealthier investors often try to hold their corporate bonds in tax-advantaged accounts, which we'll discuss in a few pages. Corporate bond interest is taxable at the federal, state, and local government levels, while US government bond interest is taxable at the federal level exclusively.

Corporate bond interest is taxable in states that have an income tax, and even a few cities tax the corporate bond interest that their residents earn. GNMA, FNMA, and FHLMC are taxable at the federal, state, and local levels, also, just like corporate bonds.

Taxation of municipal securities
The interest on general obligation bonds is tax-exempt at the federal level, but your state could tax the interest if you buy a bond from an out-of-state issuer. If you live in Georgia and buy a bond issued by the State of Alabama, Georgia can tax that interest. Plus, if you live in Atlanta, Georgia, and Atlanta has a tax on bond interest, your city could tax you as well.

How could you avoid being taxed by Georgia and the city of Atlanta? Buy a bond issued by Atlanta, Georgia. The state will give you a break, and so will Atlanta.

Finally, if you live in Atlanta and buy a bond issued by Valdosta, Georgia, the federal government will give you the tax break, and so will the State of Georgia, since both Valdosta and Atlanta are in that state. But, what about Atlanta—did you help them out? No, so they can tax you. How do you get Atlanta off your back? Buy one of their municipal securities. You help us finance our schools, we'll help you reduce your tax burden.

SITUATION	FEDERAL	STATE	LOCAL
Resident of Topeka, KS, buys a Toledo, OH, municipal bond	EXEMPT	TAXABLE	TAXABLE
Resident of Topeka, KS, buys a Wichita, KS, municipal bond	EXEMPT	EXEMPT	TAXABLE
Resident of Topeka, KS, buys a Topeka, KS, municipal bond	EXEMPT	EXEMPT	EXEMPT

Not all municipal securities pay tax-free interest. The ones used for public purpose/essential services do, but if the tax code says that the bond is a "private activity" bond, the interest is subject to **alternative minimum tax (AMT)**. Most municipal bond investors are subject to AMT, which would force them to add some of the interest received on a private activity bond back into their taxable income. For that reason, **private activity bonds** usually offer higher yields (before tax). An example of a private activity bond is a bond issued to finance a parking garage that will be operated by a private company, or bonds issued to build a sports stadium. If the exam says your customer wants a municipal bond but is concerned about AMT, put her into a general obligation bond, such as a school bond. Or look for the concept of "essential, public purpose."

And, some municipal bonds are taxable. For example, if a public university has already issued a certain amount of GO debt that is outstanding, additional bond issues could be taxable, requiring the issuer to offer much higher yields to investors. Or, if the bond issue is a refunding issue used to call bonds, there is no exemption for the interest paid to investors in that case, either.

So far, we have been discussing the income that securities provide to investors through interest and dividend payments.

Capital Gains

On the other hand, think of a **capital gain** as the profit you take when you sell a security for more than you bought it.

Back to our GE example. You bought 1,000 shares @$30 each. Let's say you sell 100 shares for $40 to take a vacation. If you held GE for more than 1 year, you'd realize a long-term gain of $1,000, since $10 times 100 shares = $1,000 in capital gains. Go ahead and take your vacation, and at the end of the year, you'll owe Uncle Sam 15% of that $1,000, or $150. Your state may tax the gain as well. And, if you're in the top tax bracket of 39.6%, you pay 20% to the U.S. Treasury.

If you had sold that stock within a year, the gain would be taxed at your ordinary income rate since it's a short-term capital gain. If your ordinary income rate is 25%, you owe the IRS $250. If it's 35%, you only kept $650 of that capital gain when the dust settles.

Cost Basis

A capital gain is the difference between your **proceeds** (what you sell it for) and your **cost basis** (what you paid for it). Think of your "cost basis" as all the money that has gone into an investment after being taxed. When you buy GE for $30 a share, you don't deduct that from taxable income, so $30 a share is your cost basis. You also pay a commission in most cases, so you add that to your cost basis. When you bought 1,000 shares of GE @$30, you paid a $50 commission. So, while we used round numbers above to introduce the concept, your cost basis is really $3,050 divided by 1,000 shares, or $30.05 per-share.

If an investor purchases shares of the same stock at different times and for different prices, there are different methods of determining the cost basis when he sells the stock someday. For example, if he bought 100 shares for $50, 100 shares for $60, and 100 shares for $75 over the past several years, which 100 did he just sell? The IRS assumes the method used is **first in first out (FIFO)**. That means, he just sold the shares with the $50 cost basis, leading to a much larger taxable capital gain vs. using the shares purchased for $75.

Could he use the $75 cost basis? Yes, but he and the broker-dealer would have to identify the shares with the **CUSIP number** when the sell order is placed. That method is called **share identification**.

The method many investors use is **average cost**, in which they total all the money spent on the shares and divide that by the current number of shares. This method is available only when a broker-dealer or other custodian holds the shares on the investor's behalf.

Proceeds

Broker-dealers charge commissions when customers buy and when they sell securities. So, when you buy shares of GE, you add the commission to the cost basis, and when you sell those shares of GE, you subtract the commission from your proceeds. If you sell 100 shares of GE @40 and pay a $50 commission, your proceeds would be $3,950, or $39.50 per-share. On your tax returns for the year in which you sell the stock, you would report that your proceeds were $3,950, while your cost basis on those 100 shares was $3,005. The capital gain on that sale is $945.

Holding Period

If you sell a security held for one year or less, that is a short-term gain or loss. If it's a gain, it is taxed at your marginal rate. If you hold a security for more than one year, that is considered a long-term gain or loss. If it's a gain, it is taxed at the same 15% currently used for qualified dividends for most investors (0% for low-bracket, 20% for top-bracket investors).

One advantage of a buy-and-hold investment strategy is that any gains will likely be taxed at the lower long-term capital gains rates. This helps portfolio performance.

How do you count your **holding period**? In Publication 564 the IRS explains:

To find out how long you have held your shares, begin counting on the day after the trade date on which you bought the shares. (Do not count the trade date itself.) The trade date on which you dispose of the shares is counted as part of your holding period. If you bought shares on May 6ᵗʰ of last year (trade date), and sold them on May 6ᵗʰ of this year (trade date), your holding period would not be more than 1 year. If you sold them on May 7ᵗʰ of this year, your holding period would be more than 1 year (12 months plus 1 day).

As with qualified dividends, if the investor's marginal tax rate hits 25-35%, he pays no more than 15% tax on long-term capital gains, and if his marginal rate is lower than that, he could end up paying zero percent on capital gains. Zero percent.

Capital Losses

You don't pay the tax on the day you sell the stock. Rather, you figure it into your income taxes when you file for the year. But you'll want to keep track of the gain, because the IRS will want to know, and because when you sit down with your accountant at the end of the year, you might decide to sell some other stocks at a loss to balance out that gain. You took a $945 gain on GE. If you sell another stock at a $1,000 **capital loss**, you'd end up at zero capital gains for the year.

Congratulations, you made no money this year. And, therefore, you have no capital gains taxes to pay. You could sell even more stock at a loss. If you lost, say, $10,000 for the year, you could use $3,000 of your total or net loss to offset (reduce) your adjusted gross income for the year. So, if your AGI was going to be $53,000, now it's only $50,000. That reduces your tax bill.

But you really did lose money. See the relationship? If you're paying no tax, it's because you're making no money. If you're paying taxes, it's because you're making money. Personally, I prefer the latter, but that's not the point, and many would argue that it's better to reduce your tax burden than to have the misfortune of making money in the stock market.

Some will even purposely take a net loss for the year and continue to carry the excess that's over the $3,000 limit forward. I know a few investors who have enough capital losses to last the rest of their lives, $3,000 at a time. They took about $100,000 in capital losses in 2002, and it's going to take quite some time to use that up at three grand a year.

Lucky devils.

Offsetting Gains with Losses

In any case, if an investor only made a couple of sales during the year, figuring gains and losses would be extremely easy. An exam question, of course, could be anything but. Let's use possible exam questions to show you how to deal with the tricky process of matching up gains and losses to figure an investor's net gains and net losses.

Jarod Stevens had the following results on four stock sales last year:

$15,000 in long-term gains
$5,000 in long-term losses
$5,000 in short-term gains
$13,000 in short-term losses

Therefore, the tax implications were
A. short-term capital gain of $8,000
B. long-term capital gain of $2,000
C. short-term capital gain of $2,000
D. long-term capital gain of $15,000

Step one: line up the long-term gains and the long-term losses, then line up the short-term gains with the short-term losses. Matching up the long-term gain of $15,000 with the $5,000 long-term loss leaves Jarod with $10,000 in long-term capital gains. Subtract the $13,000 short-term loss from the $5,000 short-term gain, and Jarod has $8,000 in short-term losses. Now, here's the tricky part. You can take the $10,000 long-term gain and reduce it by the $8,000 short-term loss for a net long-term gain of $2,000.

Why is that $2,000 treated as a long-term capital gain? Because the IRS defines a net long-term capital gain as any long-term capital gain that remains after subtracting any short-term losses. Or think of it this way—it's the long-term net capital gain of $10,000 that triggered the capital gains tax. Regardless, the answer is…B. I know. I don't like taxation much myself, but it could easily make the difference between a pass and a no-pass on the exam, so let's keep plodding through this.

Jarod Stevens had the following results on four stock sales this year:
$15,000 in long-term gains
$23,000 in long-term losses
$15,000 in short-term gains
$5,000 in short-term losses

Therefore, the tax implications are
A. short-term capital gain taxed at a maximum of 15%
B. no net gains or losses
C. short-term capital gain of $2,000 taxed at ordinary income rates
D. long-term capital loss of $8,000, short-term capital gain of $8,000

Line up the long-term with long-term, and the short-term with short-term. You end up with a net long-term loss of $8,000 and a net short-term gain of $10,000. The $8,000 in losses brings the total capital gain down to $2,000, which will be taxed as a short-term capital gain. Why a short-term capital gain? Because it was the short-term net gain that triggered the tax. The answer is…C.

One last time.

Jarod Stevens had the following results on four stock sales last year:

$15,000 in long-term gains
$5,000 in long-term losses
$5,000 in short-term gains
$17,000 in short-term losses

Therefore, the tax implications will be
A. short-term capital gain of $2,000
B. long-term capital gain of $2,000
C. short-term capital gain of $5,000
D. short-term capital loss of $2,000, which offsets ordinary income

Match up long-term with long-term and short-term with short-term, then net out your results. There is a net long-term gain of $10,000 and a net short-term loss of $12,000. That makes it a net loss of $2,000, which can be used to offset ordinary income.

Too bad Jarod couldn't have lost another $1,000 on our stock picks to take full advantage of our services, huh? In any case, the answer is...*D*.

Wash Sale Rules

So, the "benefit" of selling securities at a loss is that you can offset your ordinary income by up to $3,000 per year. But, to use that loss, stay out of that stock for at least 30 days. If you sell MSFT at a loss, don't buy any Microsoft stock for 30 days. And, you could not have purchased any 30 days *before* you made the sale, either.

Also, don't get clever and buy warrants, convertible bonds, convertible preferred stock or call options that convert to Microsoft common stock. Just take your capital loss and stay out of Microsoft for 30 days both before and after the sale.

What if you promise not to buy any Microsoft common stock over the next 30 days but can't stop yourself? Then, you can't use the loss now to offset ordinary income on your taxes because of wash sale rules. Never fear, though, because if you took a $7-per-share loss on Microsoft, you would add $7 per-share to your cost basis on the new purchase. If you were to repurchase MSFT @$40, your cost basis would be $47. In other words, you would eventually get the benefit of that loss you took, but not now. And, if you recall our discussion of the time value of money, now is always a better time to get those dollars rather than at some point in the future.

When you sell a bond at a loss, there is a similar rule. Either wait 30 days to buy a replacement, or, if you want to sell a GE bond at a loss and buy another GE bond, you'll need to substantially alter some features of the bond: interest rate, maturity, call feature, or some combination. Or, just buy a bond from a different issuer. The test might call this process a **bond swap**.

When an investor makes regular and frequent investments into a mutual fund, he would typically end up executing wash sales whenever selling shares for a loss. Why? Chances are he either bought or is about to buy more of the same shares with his automatic investments.

Unrealized Capital Gains

An **unrealized capital gain** is just an increase in value, a "paper gain," as some say. There is no tax to pay just because your asset has become more valuable. As with your house, you owe no capital gains tax on your securities just because they have gone up in value. Only if the investor sells the security or the house and realizes a profit would there be a capital gains tax to pay.

Capital Gain or Loss on a primary residence

Selling a house for a capital gain is usually more pleasant than doing the same with shares of stock. If a homeowner owns and lives in a primary residence any two of the previous five years leading up to the sale of the property, any capital gain taken when he sells his house is tax-free up to $250,000 for individuals and up to $500,000 for married couples. He must meet the "ownership and use tests" to claim up to those maximum amounts. But, even if he doesn't meet the two-year ownership and use tests, he may qualify for a reduced maximum amount if suffering a financial or health-related hardship.

If two people jointly own a house, each could claim up to $250,000 on his or her separate return. A married couple claiming up to $500,000 as a tax-free capital gain is required to file jointly for the year they take advantage of this maneuver. For more information look up IRS Publication 523.

What about a capital loss on a primary residence? What if you put on a $100,000 addition to your house but end up selling for less than your cost basis? That is always painful. If you wanted to take a capital loss on your primary residence, you would first need to convert it to a rental property. If you rent it out, you can take depreciation on the property as we did under our look at partnerships. And, now, if you end up selling for less than your cost basis, you do get to claim a capital loss to offset taxable capital gains for the year.

Then again, if you have no capital gains for the year, that loss doesn't help much.

Mutual Fund Taxation

The owner of the securities inside a mutual fund is the investment company itself. The fund sells pieces of this portfolio to investors in the form of common stock.

Income Dividends

So, like any common stockholder, a mutual fund holder will probably receive dividends. A stock mutual fund earns dividends from the stocks that they own. A bond fund receives regular interest payments on their fixed-income portfolio. A balanced fund earns both dividends and interest from the securities held in the portfolio. The funds pay expenses with that money and if there's a profit left over, they distribute it to the shareholders. The shareholders receive convenient **1099-DIV** statements that help keep track of this income, which will be taxable at some rate.

If it's a stock fund, the investor is taxed at ordinary or qualified dividend rates, depending on the composition of the fund.

If it's a bond fund, income checks will be taxed just like bond interest, because that's where the income is derived. If it's a government bond fund, the interest is only taxable at the federal level. If it's a corporate bond fund, the interest is taxable at all levels. And if it's a municipal bond fund, the interest is tax-exempt at the federal level, but the investor's state government often taxes the interest received on out-of-state municipal bonds. For that reason, there are many state-specific municipal bond mutual funds for residents of high-tax states such as California, Virginia, and Maryland.

Capital Gains in Mutual Funds

There are two ways that capital gains come into play for mutual funds, but before we get to that, remember that investors have no control over when the investment adviser for the fund sells a stock or bond. If the investment adviser realizes more gains than losses, the fund realizes a net gain for the year. They can either distribute this to the shareholders or not. Either way, investors are taxed on their proportional share of this capital gain. That's the trouble with investing in funds that buy low and sell high. It's called a capital gain, and the **capital gains distribution** is taxed at the investor's long-term capital gains rate.

Distributions to Shareholders

The first thing to remember is that a fund almost always makes sure that when it takes a capital gain, it's a long-term capital gain, since, as we saw, the difference to a high-tax-bracket investor could be significant. Assume it's a long-term gain on the exam. Could it be a short-term gain?

Sure, but that is the exception rather than the rule.

We've been saying that the interest on U.S. Treasury securities is exempt from state and local taxation, and it is. Notice we've said nothing about capital gains until now. Yes, capital gains (not interest payments) on U.S. Treasuries are taxable at the federal, state, and local levels.

And, on the tax-free front, even though the dividend checks received from tax-exempt municipal bond funds are usually tax-exempt at the federal level, any capital gains distributions are treated as capital gains.

Shareholder Sales

The second capital gains issue with mutual funds is within the investor's control, just as it is on a share of GE or MSFT. If she sells her mutual fund shares within a year, any gain is a short-term gain, taxed at her ordinary income rate. If she holds them for more than one year, it's a long-term gain, taxed at a maximum of 15% for most investors.

Unrealized Gains

If a mutual fund buys a stock at $10, and the stock now trades at $15, there is no tax to pay. Unrealized gains make the NAV of the fund go up, but that doesn't affect the investor unless or until A) the fund realizes a gain on the shares by selling for a profit, or B) the investor does by redeeming his shares at a higher value.

Cost Basis on Reinvestments

Many investors choose not to take the income and capital gains distributions as checks. Rather, they apply that money towards more shares of the fund, which they buy without a sales load (at the NAV). Since the distributions are taxed either way, the investor adds to her cost basis by the amount of the distribution.

Let's say she bought the ACE Equity Income Fund at $10 per-share. Last year, she received $1 in dividends and $1 in capital gains distributions per-share. If she reinvests the $2 per-share, she pays tax on that amount, and her cost basis rises by that amount, too.

Taxation of Annuities

Accumulation Period

During the accumulation phase of a deferred variable annuity, the investment grows tax-deferred. So, all the dividends and capital gains distributions from the subaccounts are reinvested into more units, just like most people reinvest distributions back into a mutual fund. If the individual dies, the death benefit is paid to the beneficiary. The death benefit is included in the annuitant's **estate** for estate tax purposes, and the beneficiary pays tax on anything above the cost basis. If the husband bought the annuity for $50,000, and it's now worth $60,000, she'll receive $60,000 and pay ordinary income rates on the $10,000 of earnings.

Sometimes people cash in their contract earlier than expected. If they're under 59½ and don't have a qualifying exemption, they will not only pay ordinary income tax on the earnings, but also a 10% penalty tax, too. So, if it's a $60,000 annuity, and a 49-year-old surrenders the contract that he bought for $50,000, he'd pay his ordinary income rate on the $10,000 of earnings and a 10% penalty of $1,000. You didn't think the IRS would, like, penalize him 10% and then take his ordinary income rate on what's left, did you? It's his ordinary income rate plus 10% of the excess over his cost basis.

Notice how only the excess over cost basis is taxed and/or penalized on a non-qualified annuity. The cost basis was taxed before it went into the account.

So, if he's not 59½ yet, the IRS is giving him all kinds of reasons not to surrender the contract. And, we already mentioned that the insurance company will keep a percentage on the back end if he surrenders during the early years of the contract. So, he can have his money if he wants to, but if he takes it out too soon, there will be penalties and taxes to deal with.

72(t) and Substantially Equal Periodic Payments

We've mentioned that the magic age for taking distributions is 59½ because, otherwise, the individual is hit with early withdrawal penalties. Remember that annuities are by nature retirement plans and are subject to the 10% penalty for early withdrawals made without a qualifying exemption. One exemption available is to utilize IRS rule "72(t)." A reference to "72t" relates to an individual taking a series of substantially equal periodic payments (SEPP). The IRS won't penalize the early withdrawal if the individual sets up a schedule whereby he or she withdraws the money by any of several IRS-approved methods.

Once he starts the SEPP program, he needs to stay on it. The IRS requires him to continue the SEPP program for five years or until he is 59½, whichever comes last. So, if the individual is 45, she'll have to keep taking periodic payments until she's 59½. If the individual is 56 when she starts, she'll have to continue for 5 years. Either that, or cut the IRS a check for the penalties she was trying to avoid.

Loans

Some insurance companies allow contract owners to take a loan against the value of the annuity during the accumulation period. Usually, the interest charge is handled by reducing the number of accumulation units owned. If the owner pays back the loan in full, the number of units goes up again. Unlike a loan against a life insurance policy, however, a loan from an annuity is treated as a distribution. In other words, it is not tax-free.

1035 Exchanges

Both annuities and insurance policies allow the contract owner to exchange their contract for another without paying taxes. That's fine, just don't forget the surrender period. If someone has a 6% surrender fee in effect, and an agent pushes them to do a 1035 exchange, the IRS won't have a problem with it, but FINRA almost certainly will.

Also, this isn't the same thing as a life insurance contract. With a life insurance policy, people often cash in part of their **cash value**. If they're only taking out what they put in—or less—the IRS treats it as part of their cost basis. In an annuity, however, if someone does a **random withdrawal** for, say, $10,000, the IRS considers that to be part of the taxable earnings first.

Most annuities are non-qualified, which means they are purchased with non-tax-deductible dollars. When you cut the check for, say, $50,000 for the annuity, you get no tax deduction from the IRS that year against adjusted gross income. In other words, that $50,000 was taxed that year, so the tax collectors won't tax that money again when you take it out someday. That $50,000 will be your cost basis. You will only pay taxes on the amount of earnings above that and only when you finally take out the money.

On the other hand, a "tax-qualified variable annuity" or "individual retirement annuity" is funded with pre-tax or tax-deductible contributions with the same maximums used for Traditional IRA accounts. Like the Traditional IRA—and unlike the non-qualified variable annuity—withdrawals from the IRA annuity account must begin at age 70½.

The IRS refers to these plans as "individual retirement annuities," and they are basically just IRAs funded with an investment into a variable annuity. Why do that? Probably for the death benefit during the accumulation phase that guarantees your beneficiaries will receive at least the amount you contributed. Or, some people like the idea of an annuity payout that lasts for as long as they live, perhaps longer.

So, most questions focus on non-qualified variable annuities funded with after-tax dollars. But, don't be shocked if you get a question about variable annuities funded with tax-deductible dollars.

Annuity Period

When the annuitant begins receiving monthly checks, part of each check is considered taxable ordinary income, and part of it is considered part of the cost basis. Once the annuitant has received all the cost basis back, each additional annuity payment will be fully taxable.

Also, if the beneficiary is receiving annuity payments through a "life with period certain" or a "joint with last survivor" settlement option, she will pay ordinary income tax on part of each monthly check, too—as always, on the "excess over cost basis."

Taxation of Life Insurance

When we pay life insurance premiums, we don't take a deduction against income, so they are made after-tax. They usually grow tax-deferred, however, which is nice. When the insured dies, the beneficiary receives the death benefit free and clear of federal income taxes. But the death benefit is added to the insured's estate to determine estate taxes. It's that simple when the beneficiary has the lump-sum settlement option, anyway. If we're talking about those periodic settlement options that generate interest, some of those payments could be taxed as interest income.

Rather than take a loan, the policyholder can also do a "partial surrender," whereby the policyholder takes out some of the cash value—not enough to make the policy lapse, of course. Depending on how much has been paid in premiums, taxes may be due on the amount withdrawn. Unlike for variable annuities, the IRS uses FIFO here, assuming the first thing coming out is the cost basis, not the earnings. Only the part taken out above the premiums paid would be taxed.

If a loan is taken out, there are no immediate tax consequences.

Taxation of Options

Three things can happen once an option contract is opened:

- Expire
- Close
- Exercise

Let's see about the tax implications of each event.

Expiration

Ordinary options expire within 9 months, so all gains and losses are short-term. If a trader buys an option this November, and it expires next April, he loses all the money he paid. It will be a short-term loss that he claims for April's tax year, which is when he "realizes" the loss. Back in November he was just putting down some money. Only in April of next year will he realize the loss.

On the other hand, if he sells an option in November that expires the following April, he realizes a **short-term capital gain** in April.

Close

Options can be closed for either a gain or a loss. The investor doesn't realize the gain or loss until both sides of the transaction have been completed. If she buys an option in November for $300 and sells it to close next April for $400, she realizes a $100 short-term capital gain in April. But, if she only sells it for $200, she would realize a $100 **short-term capital loss** in April.

Same thing for the seller of the option. When they close with a "closing purchase," they realize either a short-term capital gain or loss when they do so.

When an option is exercised, the options premium affects either the cost basis or the proceeds on the stock transaction. For example, when a call owner exercises her call, maybe she gets to buy the stock for $50 a share. If she paid $2 for the right to buy at $50, her cost basis on the stock acquired through exercise is $52. Her proceeds will only come into play if she sells the stock.

The seller of that call took in her $2 a share. Upon assignment of the contract, the seller also sells the stock for $50, meaning he's taken in a total of $52 for selling that stock. Proceeds are what you take in when you sell.

So, the premium was added to the call buyer's cost basis on the stock. The premium was added to the call seller's proceeds on the stock.

If you buy a Jun 50 put @2, you pay $2 for the right to sell stock at $50. If you exercise the put and sell the stock at $50, did you take in $50 per-share? No, you only took in $48 per-share, so $48 is your proceeds. Your cost basis is whatever you bought the stock for.

The trader who sold you that put has the obligation to buy the stock at $50. So, the cost basis on the stock will be $50 per-share, right? No, since he took in your $2 first, his cost basis is just $48.

Position	Upon Exercise	Premium	Affects
Long Call	Buys stock	Add to strike price	Raises cost base
Short Call	Sells stock	Add to strike price	Raises proceeds
Long Put	Sells stock	Subtract from strike price	Lowers proceeds
Short Put	Buys stock	Subtract from strike price	Lowers cost base

Leaps

Ordinary options expire in 9 months or sooner. Then, there are long-term options called LEAPS. Since the time value is greater on these contracts that can go out over three years, LEAPS contracts trade at much higher premiums. The strategies are the same. A trader would buy a call if he thinks the stock is going up. He would pay more for a MSFT Oct 50 call expiring in 2 or 3 years versus one expiring in 2 or 3 months.

The taxation is a little tricky. For the buyer of the contract, capital gains and losses are considered long-term. But a short seller never establishes a holding period, so any capital gains and losses for a seller of LEAPS contracts are considered short-term.

Transferred Securities

A securities issuer's transfer agent keeps track of the transfers of ownership among shareholders. Usually a transfer of ownership is the result of a sale, but there are other ways to transfer ownership of stock. Stock can be inherited, received as a gift, or received as a charitable donation.

Inherited Securities

What if your grandmother bought stock at $10 a share several decades ago and passed it to you through her will when she—you know? What is your cost basis? Whatever the stock was worth on the day your grandmother—you know. If it's worth $30 on the date of death, then that's your cost basis, $30. For an inherited stock the recipient steps up the cost basis to the fair market value on the date of death. If the recipient sells the stock for $30 when the stepped-up basis is $30, there are no capital gains taxes.

Also, if the recipient sells this stock for more than $30, the capital gain is treated as long-term no matter how long he holds it. Most estates close out within a few months. If they liquidate the securities for more than the cost basis, there is a capital gain, but it's treated as long-term, even if it all happened in a few months.

The heirs who inherit appreciated securities can either value them as of the date of death or six months after. Estates often close out within six months and would, therefore, find it easier to value the stocks and bonds as of the date they sell it to cut checks to all the beneficiaries named in the will and trigger no capital gains taxes.

If they want to value the securities as of six months after the date of death, they'll need to value all assets as of that date. That means the estate may need to pay a real estate appraiser to value the house as of the same date the securities are valued. When the house is sold, the buyer might not be willing to pay the appraised value, or even if the house is sold for the appraised value, there are generally seller's expenses. In either case, the estate could end up showing a loss on the sale of the deceased's primary residence, or on the securities for that matter.

Gifted Securities

What if Grandma decided to give you the stock while she's alive? In that case, you would take her original cost basis of $10. If the stock is worth $40 when you sell it, your gain is $30 a share. Not like when you inherited the shares. Then, your gain would have only been $10.

You would take over Grandma's holding period, and not necessarily have to hold it for 12 months plus one day to get the long-term capital gains treatment. If she has already held the stock for years, your holding period is also long-term.

Tax-deductible Charitable Donations

What if Grandma decided to donate the stock to a charity instead of giving it to her grandkids? If she does that, she deducts the fair market value of the stock on the date of the donation. If it's worth $30,000 when she donates it, she can deduct $30,000 when figuring her taxes--up to a maximum of 40% of her adjusted gross income for the year.

What should an investor do if he has a stock that has appreciated significantly and one that has gone down in value? A good tax move might be for him to donate the appreciated stock to a charity and sell the loser for a capital loss. This way he will avoid a capital gain on the appreciated stock while also getting the tax deduction. And, he can use the capital loss on the other position to offset other gains or even some of his ordinary income. From there, he can donate the cash to a charity, or, of course, find other uses for it.

If an investor is in a certain income bracket, he is subject to an "Alternative Minimum Tax," or "AMT." That means that even though people say that municipal bonds pay tax-free interest, he will report *some* municipal bond interest on his AMT form as a "tax preference item." Generally, municipal bonds that are considered "private purpose" by the tax code subject investors to reporting income on their AMT forms. That's why many tax-exempt mutual funds also buy bonds that are not subject to AMT taxes.

The following is from IRS Publication 556 – Alternative Minimum Tax.

```
The tax laws give preferential treatment to certain kinds of
income and allow special deductions and credits for certain kinds
of expenses. The alternative minimum tax attempts to ensure that
anyone who benefits from these tax advantages pays at least a
minimum amount of tax. The alternative minimum tax is a
separately figured tax that eliminates many deductions and
credits, thus increasing tax liability for an individual who
would otherwise pay less tax. The tentative minimum tax rates on
ordinary income are percentages set by law. For capital gains,
the capital gains rates for the regular tax are used. You may
have to pay the alternative minimum tax if your taxable income
for regular tax purposes plus any adjustments and preference
items that apply to you are more than the exemption amount.
```

A test question might also bring up the fact that the owner of a limited partnership interest will need to consult the instructions to his K-1 and may have to add certain tax preference items such as "accelerated depreciation" to his AMT form. The test question might say that "straight-line depreciation" would not be a tax preference item.

Progressive and Regressive

Progressive taxes include income, estate, and gift taxes. The bigger the income, estate, or gift, the higher the percentage rate the IRS charges.

Estates that are large get taxed, too. So, when Bill Gates passes away, his heirs will receive a ton of money, but the IRS will take some first in the form of estate taxes. The bigger the estate, the higher the rate of taxation. Progressive.

A **regressive** tax, on the other hand, is a flat tax. A list of regressive taxes would include sales, gas, payroll, and excise taxes. Everyone pays the same rate there. When you check out your items at Walmart, the cashier doesn't ask you your marginal tax bracket before giving you your total, right? No, it's a flat tax. Just like gas taxes are applied equally to gallons of gas whether they're pumped into a clunker or a Cadillac.

Lower-income Americans put a higher percent of their incomes into buying gasoline than high-income Americans do. If the secretary and the CEO both drive to work, they consume a similar amount of gasoline and pay a similar amount of gas taxes. If the amount of tax is, say, $800, that represents a much higher percentage of the secretary's income than it does the CEO's.

Unlike with income taxes, as the income levels drop, a flat tax represents a larger percentage of income. So, while the secretary's income might be taxed at no more than 15%, the gas and sales taxes she pays represent a much higher percent of her income than they do for the CEO in this example.

Corporate Taxes

Corporate profits are taxed at corporate tax rates. On the income statement bond interest is deducted pre-tax, while profits are taxed before dividends are paid to shareholders. Corporate profits (net income after tax) are taxed at that corporation's tax rate.

On the other hand, some companies use the IRS's Subchapter M to set themselves up as a "conduit" to investors. REITs do this. Many mutual funds do it, too. If a mutual fund has $1,000,000 in net income, for example, they often send at least 90% of it (900K) to shareholders as a dividend or "income" distribution. That way, the mutual fund company only pays tax on the remaining $100,000. The shareholders pay tax on the money the fund sends them. The company must send at least 90% of its net income to qualify for this tax treatment, and they can send more if they want.

When a corporation invests in the stocks of other companies, they receive dividends like any other investor. Unlike ordinary investors, though, the corporation receiving these dividends from shares of other companies' stock gets to exclude the first 70% from tax. That means they only get taxed on 30% of what they receive. And, if they're really an owner of the other company because they own 20% or more of it, they can exclude 80% of the income from tax. Berkshire Hathaway purchases smaller companies outright. They typically receive preferred dividends from those acquired companies, and if the smaller entity is being taxed on the net income, why should the parent company be fully taxed, too?

On the other hand, if a corporation holds the bonds of another corporation, they do not get to deduct any of the interest. That's because the company who paid the interest already deducted it from their taxable income. Municipal bond interest is tax-exempt to a corporate owner just as it is to any other owner.

Retirement Plans

In a taxable account the principal is reduced each year when the investor is taxed on interest,

dividends, and capital gains. In a tax-deferred account the principal is not taxed unless and until the individual finally takes distributions. The account balance grows faster when it is growing on a tax-deferred basis.

Tax-deferral is an advantage offered by deferred annuities and through retirement accounts. Whether one's contribution is tax-deductible, the fact that the interest, dividends, and capital gains will not be taxed each year is an advantage to the investor. That's why so many individuals participate in at least one retirement plan. Some retirement plans are started by the individual, and some are offered through an employer.

Let's start with the plans an individual can open, provided he has **earned income.** Earned income includes salary, bonuses, tips, alimony, and any income derived from actively participating in a business. It does not include passive income such as rental income from an apartment building or portfolio income such as bond interest, dividends, or capital gains.

Retirement plans are for working people who need to save up for retirement. If someone's sole source of income is rent checks or dividends, he probably doesn't need to save for retirement. And, if he does, he'll just need to do it outside a retirement account.

Individual Plans

An **IRA** is an **Individual Retirement Account,** or an Individual Retirement Arrangement.

Traditional

To contribute to a **Traditional IRA** the individual must be younger than 70 ½ and have earned income for the year. If the individual's income consists solely of dividends and bond interest, he can't make an IRA contribution for that year.

Contributions to an IRA are tax-deductible. If he contributes $5,000 to his IRA this year, that $5,000 no longer counts as taxable income. If he was going to pay tax on $52,000, now it's only $47,000 of taxable income for the year.

If he does have earned income for the year, an individual can contribute 100% of that earned income up to the current maximum. So, if she earns $1,800, then $1,800 is her maximum IRA contribution for that year. People 50 years and older can add a **catch-up contribution.** That amount is currently an extra $1,000.

At the time of writing, the maximum contribution to a Traditional IRA is $5,500, $6,500 for those 50 or older.

Penalties

Over-funding an IRA results in a 6% penalty on the amount above the maximum contribution for the year and any earnings associated with it. If the individual realizes she has over-funded her IRA for the year, she can remove the excess by the tax filing deadline the following year, or re-characterize the excess as part of the following year's contributions. If it's March 17, 2017 when she realizes she has over-funded her IRA by $1,000 for 2016, she can remove the $1,000 to avoid a penalty or fill out a form to re-characterize it as part of her 2017 contributions. If she does nothing, she pays a 6% penalty.

While we can always pull the money out of a Traditional IRA, if we take it out before age 59½, we'll pay a 10% penalty on top of the ordinary income tax that we always pay on withdrawals from IRAs. However, the following are qualifying exemptions to the 10% penalty. Although the withdrawal is taxable, the 10% penalty is waived for withdrawals made pursuant to:

- Death
- Permanent disability
- First home purchase for residential purposes
- A series of substantially equal periodic payments under IRS Rule 72-t
- Medical expenses
- Higher education expenses

A withdrawal pursuant to death means that the IRA owner has died and someone else is receiving the account balance as a named beneficiary. The beneficiary will be taxed but will not be penalized because the account owner died before age 59 1/2.

So, an individual can't have the money until he's 59½ without paying a penalty unless he uses one of the exemptions above. That's on the front end.

On the back end, he also is required to start taking it out by the time he's 70½. If not, the IRS will impose a 50% insufficient distribution penalty. We're talking about RMDs here, or **required minimum distributions**. When someone turns 70½, he has until April 1st of the following year to take out at least the required minimum distribution. If not, the IRS will levy a 50% penalty.

That's 50% of what he should have taken out at this point, not half the account value.

The absolute latest date that an individual can take his first withdrawal from a Traditional IRA without penalty is April 1st following the year he turns 70 1/2 . However, if he does that, he must take *two* distributions that year, which can push him into a higher tax bracket and make more of his social security benefits taxable. So, it's easier to take the first distribution in the year the individual turns 70½.

Unlike the Roth IRA, no contributions can be made into the Traditional IRA after age 70½.

Roth

The **Roth IRA** is funded with non-deductible contributions. However, the money comes out tax-free in retirement if the individual is 59½ years old and has had the account at least 5 years.

In retirement, then, the withdrawals you take from a Traditional IRA are taxable income. If you withdraw $30,000, you might only keep $22,000 after-tax. A withdrawal of $30,000 from your Roth IRA, on the other hand, leaves you with $30,000 to spend.

Unlike the Traditional, for the Roth IRA there is no requirement to take a distribution by age 70½. Since the IRS isn't going to tax that money, they couldn't care less when or even if it is withdrawn. In fact, individuals can keep contributing if they have earned income. So, a 72-year-old can refrain from taking Roth IRA withdrawals and can keep making contributions into the account if she has earned income. Neither option is available, on the other hand, for her Traditional IRA.

If the individual or married couple have adjusted gross incomes above a certain amount, they cannot contribute to their Roth IRAs. Period. So, get those Roth IRA accounts started while you're young and before you strike it rich. The money you contribute in your 20s and 30s can compound for decades, even if the IRS cuts off new contributions by age 40 based on your income.

If an individual has both a Traditional and a Roth IRA, the contribution limit is the total allocated among the two accounts. As I said, that is currently either $5,500 or $6,500 depending on age.

Also, the Roth IRA allows the individual to remove her cost basis, or the amount she has contributed, after five years without penalty. So, if he has contributed $25,000 into a Roth IRA and seven years later the account is worth $40,000, he could take the $25,000 out without a penalty and keep the remainder of $15,000 in the account. He could not put that $25,000 back in, however, and would not earn the tax-deferred and tax-free returns going forward.

But, as always, it's his money.

Converting a Traditional to a Roth IRA

Some individuals start out with a Traditional IRA and then decide to convert it to a Roth IRA. This requires the individual to pay tax on the entire amount going into the new Roth IRA, since Roth IRAs are funded with after-tax dollars. Even if the individual makes too much money to contribute to his Roth IRA, he can convert a Traditional IRA to a Roth IRA.

Investment Restrictions

I'm not sure why they do it, but some people like to use their Traditional IRA to invest in collectible items such as artwork, Persian rugs, antiques, coins, gems, stamps, etc. Funds withdrawn from the IRA to buy such items are considered distributed, which means the individual would pay ordinary income rates, plus a 10% penalty if he is not yet 59½.

US-minted gold or silver bullion coins are allowed, as they have intrinsic value. Collectible coins, on the other hand, are not suitable. Municipal bonds typically make poor investments for a Traditional IRA. Municipal bonds pay tax-exempt interest, which is why their coupon payments are so low. All money coming out of the Traditional IRA is taxed, so the municipal bond's tax-advantage is destroyed and all the individual is left with is a lower coupon payment.

Rollovers and Transfers

To move an IRA from one custodian to another, the best bet is to do a **direct transfer**. Just have the custodian cut a check to the new custodian. The IRA owner can do as many of these direct transfers as he wants. If, however, he does a **rollover**, things get tricky. First, he can only do one per year, and, second, it must be completed within 60 days to avoid tax ramifications.

In a rollover, the custodian cuts a check in the individual's name. The account owner cashes it and then sends the money to the new custodian, but any shortfall is subject to taxes and a 10% penalty. If the individual withdrew $50,000 but could only come up with $10,000 sixty days later, that $40,000 difference is taxed as ordinary income, plus a penalty tax of $4,000.

Plans offered through an employer either define the benefit to be received when the employee retires or the contributions made into the account. Usually, it is only the contributions that are defined.

Defined Contribution Plans

A **defined contribution plan** only defines the contributions the employer and/or the employee can make into the plan. The employer is not defining or promising any benefit at retirement. We'll talk about **defined benefit pension plans** in a bit, but let's focus first on the more familiar defined contribution plans.

At many companies new employees receive paperwork to fill out concerning the **401(k) plan** sponsored by the employer as an employee benefit. The employees choose a few mutual funds, and tell the HR department to deduct X amount from their paychecks to go into the 401(k) account. This way, part of their salary goes straight into a retirement fund and is not taxable currently, just like the money that goes into a Traditional IRA. Pretty attractive, especially if the employer matches what the employees elect to defer from each paycheck.

The amount of the employee's contribution is known as an **elective deferral**. Employers generally match all or part of an employee's elective deferral up to a certain percentage of compensation, as stipulated in their plan literature. But, they are not required to make **matching contributions**. Why might someone choose to participate in a 401(k) even if the company was not matching contributions? Maybe he likes the higher maximum contribution limit vs. the IRA or Roth IRA.

The advantage to a business owner setting up a 401(k) plan is that a vesting schedule can be laid out over several years, meaning that the employer's contributions don't belong to the employee until he is fully vested. However, 401(k) plans come with complicated **top-heavy** rules, which means the plan cannot provide benefits to just the key, highly compensated employees. A plan in which 60% of the benefits go to key employees is a plan that shows signs of being "top-heavy," and will need to adjust things or deal with tax problems.

For-profit companies offer 401(k) plans to their employees. Non-profit organizations such as schools and hospitals offer **403(b) plans** to their employees. As with a 401(k) plan, the employee indicates how much of her paycheck should go into the 403(b) account, which simultaneously gives her a tax break now and helps her save up for retirement later. As with a 401(k) plan, the contributions go in pre-tax but come out fully taxable when the participant starts taking distributions.

While a 401(k) plan might offer participants the ability to purchase stocks and bonds a la carte, a 403(b) plan only offers annuities and mutual funds as investment vehicles. The 403(b) plans can also be referred to as **Tax-Sheltered Annuities** or **TSAs**.

Some states and cities have begun to shift the burden of funding retirement benefits to their employees. These so-called **457 plans** are for state and local government employees, e.g., police and fire workers. Contributions are tax-deductible, and the plans use the same maximum contribution limits used by 401(k) and 403(b) plans.

Profit sharing plans are also defined contribution plans, but the contributions are never required. If the company does contribute, it must be made for all eligible employees based on a predetermined formula. For example, maybe all workers receive up to 10% of their salaries when the company has a banner year. The profit-sharing plan uses much higher maximum annual contributions than the 401(k), 403(b) or Section 457 plans. Of course, that would only matter if you happened to work for a profitable and generous employer.

A **money purchase plan** is not flexible the way a profit sharing plan is. The money purchase plan requires the employer to make a mandatory contribution to each employee's account, based on his/her salary, whether the company feels like it or not. The exam might say something like "in a money purchase plan, contributions are mandatory on the part of the employer and discretionary on the part of the employee."

Keogh plans are for individuals with self-employment income or for those working for a sole proprietorship with a Keogh plan in place. They're not for S-corps, C-corps, LLCs, etc.—only sole proprietors. If the individual in the test question has side income or is self-employed, he or she can have a Keogh. They can contribute a certain percentage of their self-employment income into the Keogh.

How much? A lot. As with the SEP-IRA, the business owner can put 20% of her compensation into a Keogh, and she can put in 25% of her employees' compensation. Some readers find it shocking that there may be employees at a "sole" proprietorship. But, trust me, there can be. A "sole proprietorship" is just a business with one owner, a guy doing business as himself. The number of employees he has? Anybody's guess. Also, to avoid confusion, remember we said that Keogh plans are for sole proprietorships only; we did not say that sole proprietorships can only have a Keogh plan. A SEP-IRA or SIMPLE IRA would also be available to a sole proprietor, for example.

A small business can establish a **SEP-IRA**, which stands for "Simplified Employee Pension" IRA. This allows the business owner to make pre-tax contributions for herself and any eligible employees. Twenty-five percent of wages can be contributed to an employee's SEP, up to the current maximum. SEP contributions are not mandatory on the part of the business owner. It's just that if the business makes any contributions, they must be made to all eligible employees as stipulated in the plan agreement.

Notice how the business makes the contributions, not the employees. So, if you're self-employed, you can contribute to your own SEP-IRA, but if you're an employee at a company with a SEP-IRA, it's the company who will make the contributions on your behalf. To establish a SEP, the employer uses a model agreement put out by the IRS (download it from www.irs.gov) that they and the employees sign. It does not have to be filed with the IRS, which does not issue an opinion or approval.

Keep in mind that even though a large contribution can be made to a SEP-IRA, that amount must represent 25% of wages. In other words, we often focus on the maximum amounts that can be contributed, but to make contributions at all the small business owner must be making a profit, and when contributing for employees, the contributions are 25% of wages. That means that the only way to put a lot of money into a SEP-IRA is to earn a lot of money—since 25% of a $33,000 salary is not going to make for a large contribution.

In that case, maybe the small business owner decides to set up a **SIMPLE Plan** instead. A SIMPLE plan can be either an IRA or a 401(k). The SIMPLE plan is for businesses with no more than 100 employees and with no other retirement plan offered. In a SIMPLE plan, business owners choose to either match the employee's contributions up to 3% of compensation, or to contribute 2% of the employee's compensation if he does not make an elective deferral from his paycheck.

Unlike with a 401(k) plan, employees are immediately vested in a SEP-IRA or SIMPLE plan.

Many companies reward key employees by offering them **employee stock options.** These options do not trade among investors but are essentially free call options that allow employees to buy the company's stock at a set strike/exercise price. To keep the employee around a while, the company usually awards the options to buy the stock on a vesting schedule by which the employee gradually receives options. An **ESOP** or **employee stock ownership plan** is what it sounds like. Through these plans the company allows all workers to purchase company stock at a discount and through a payroll deduction. The stock and the dividends/cap gains generated on it grow tax-deferred, like a 401(k) plan.

Defined Benefit Plans

Defined benefit pension plans are the opposite of defined contribution plans. In a defined contribution plan the employer puts in some money and then wishes employees the best of luck with retirement. For a defined benefit plan, the employer bears all the risk and, therefore, must earn sufficient returns on their investments to pay a defined benefit to retirees and their survivors.

Maybe that defined benefit is 70% of average salary figured over the employee's last three years of service, paid out each year in retirement, plus maybe a benefit to a spouse or children if he dies within a certain time.

A defined benefit pension plan is established as a trust and does not pay tax on the income it generates. In fact, the company gets to deduct the contributions it makes into the pension fund from taxable income. Therefore, these plans do not typically invest in municipal securities, since they are already tax-advantaged accounts.

Because corporations typically try to fund these plans only as much as required, defined benefit plans require an actuary to certify that funding levels are sufficient to cover future pension fund obligations.

ERISA Issues

ERISA is a federal securities act enforced by the Department of Labor. It's a "securities law" in the sense that most retirement plans offered in the workplace offer investments in securities to the participants. ERISA is shorthand for the federal government's Employee Retirement Income Security Act. ERISA was passed in 1974 and was designed to protect employees (and their beneficiaries) who depend on pension funds for their retirement security.

A defined benefit pension plan promises to pay a predetermined amount of benefits to employees when they retire. The employer sets it up and takes on the responsibility of figuring out how to deduct X amount of company dollars now and put them into the stock and bond markets wisely enough to pay out Y amount of pension fund dollars to retirees. Generally, the pension fund hires investment advisers to manage the fund's assets. Large pension funds typically dole out portions of the plan's assets to different money management/investment advisory firms. The investment committee hires various investment advisers to manage portions of the pension fund assets, and frequently even hires advisers to help them pick the other advisers.

The 401(k), defined benefit pension, profit sharing, and Keogh plan are all plans covered by ERISA. The SIMPLE and SEP-IRA, on the other hand, are informal plans between employer and employee. Starting a 401(k) requires IRS approval, while starting a SIMPLE IRA requires the business owner to print and fill out a form for their own records.

ERISA does not require companies to have retirement plans. Rather, it establishes rules for companies who happen to have them.

Fiduciaries

A defined benefit pension plan is managed for the benefit of retirees. As the US Department of Labor explains:

Each pension plan has at least one fiduciary. The fiduciaries of a plan usually include:

- Trustee
- Investment advisers
- All individuals exercising discretion
- All members of the plan's administrative committee
- Those who select committee officials

The key to determining whether someone is a fiduciary is whether they are exercising discretion or control over the plan. Attorneys, accountants, and actuaries are generally not fiduciaries when acting in their professional roles.

The investment manager of a pension fund uses discretion/control to invest the plan assets; therefore, the investment manager is a "fiduciary" with obligations to the participants and beneficiaries of the plan. As ERISA makes clear:

- a fiduciary shall discharge his duties with respect to a plan solely in the interest of the participants and beneficiaries
- and for the exclusive purpose of: (i) providing benefits to participants and their beneficiaries; and (ii) defraying reasonable expenses of administering the plan
- with the care, skill, prudence, and diligence under the circumstances then prevailing that a prudent man acting in a like capacity and familiar with such matters would use in the conduct of an enterprise of a like character and with like aims
- by diversifying the investments of the plan so as to minimize the risk of large losses, unless under the circumstances it is clearly prudent not to do so; and
- in accordance with the documents and instruments governing the plan insofar as such documents and instruments are consistent with the provisions of this subchapter and subchapter III of this chapter.

The "documents and instruments governing the plan" might be referred to on the exam as an investment policy statement. If the policy statement says that no more than 40% of the plan assets are to be invested in equities, guess what? Don't put more than 40% into equities. Even if you ended up having a good year because of your renegade stock picks, you'd be in trouble. The only time to override the policy statement is if it clearly violates ERISA.

Also, notice how diversification is presumed to be part of a prudent investment policy, "unless under the circumstances it is clearly prudent not to do so." This is a direct link to the Uniform Prudent Investor Act, which mentions ERISA many times throughout the text. In fact, all those bullet points overlap with the Uniform Prudent Investor Act. It's just that the UPIA is talking more to the administrators of private trusts, while ERISA is concerned with the fiduciaries running pension trusts.

Either way, if you're an investment adviser managing assets on behalf of beneficiaries, you need to use skill, prudence, and absolute honesty-above-reproach. You need to keep the costs of administering the plan reasonable. Why? Well, among other reasons, as the Department of Labor explains on a helpful website, "Fiduciaries who do not follow the basic standards of conduct may be personally liable to restore any losses to the plan, or to restore any profits made through improper use of the plan's assets." The website goes on to suggest, "However, fiduciaries can limit their liability in certain situations. One way fiduciaries can demonstrate that they have carried out their responsibilities properly is by documenting the processes used to carry out their responsibilities." In other words, every time you make a decision, keep good notes and make a backup. This stock was purchased for this reason, these bonds were sold for that reason, we used this broker-dealer to execute the sale for these reasons, etc.

Safe Harbor, 404(c)

This heavy fiduciary duty implies that the plan is managing the assets on behalf of employees/participants/beneficiaries. If we're talking about a 401(k) or other defined contribution plan that lets the employee choose investments, now it's the employee's problem what happens in the stock and bond markets. As an employer, you would probably rather match your employees' contributions into a plan in which they choose all their own investment options. That way, whatever happens in the market is at their own risk.

To relieve yourself of the fiduciary duty over investment losses, your plan must make sure that participants have control, as defined by ERISA and the rules written under the Act. First, the plan needs to make a clear written statement to participants that it "intends to constitute a plan described in section 404(c) of ERISA, and that the fiduciaries of the plan may be relieved of liability for any losses which are the direct and necessary result of investment instructions given by the participant or beneficiary." Also, the plan must:

- Offer a selection of at least three investment choices with materially different risk and return characteristics
- Provide the ability to change investment allocations at least quarterly
- Provide sufficient education and information about the plan to allow participants to make informed investment decisions

To sail into these safe waters, the plan needs to provide the three bullet points above. Most plans provide at least three different investment choices, and participants can almost always change allocations among, say, the growth, income, and long-term bond funds quarterly, if not every single day. It's the third bullet point that is probably the hardest to satisfy. To make sure they have provided sufficient education to shield themselves from liability for the investment losses their employees may end up with, the company must provide detailed information on the fees and expenses charged on investments, the risk/reward nature of all the investment options, the most recent prospectus for each investment option, the name of the investment manager/adviser for the investment options, and other important information.

Unfortunately, if the company gives too much advice of a personally targeted nature, they might cross into the territory of providing investment advice—yikes! That's the fiduciary relationship they're trying to avoid. So, many companies hire third-party investment advisers or other financial service providers to educate employees sufficiently to allow them to make informed investment decisions. The act of hiring an investment adviser or a provider of investment education is itself a fiduciary action, so the parties they choose had better know what they're doing. Otherwise, the company could be liable for the losses that result from incompetent or dishonest advice.

Also, note that advisers themselves are fiduciaries when giving advice or managing assets for employees. When we're talking about relieving oneself of fiduciary duties, we're only talking about the employer, and even there we're only talking about relieving themselves of responsibility for investment losses that result from the participant's investment decisions. But, if the company provides a reputable investment adviser to participants, it is relieved of the fiduciary duty in terms of how well the investments pan out.

The employer has fiduciary duties connected to the 401(k) plan. For example, the employer must make sure that when the employees make an investment into the plan, that money is deposited promptly. Sure, it is more fun to let it all sit in the corporate money market account a few extra weeks earning interest, but that would not satisfy the fiduciary duty. Is it good for the company or for the participant? As a fiduciary, think about the participants first.

Again, the employer has other fiduciary obligations to the people participating in the plan. It's just that the employer would prefer to pass the investment risk off to the employees. And since so many employers have already passed off the investment decisions and risks to employees, the industry you're in or are entering is looking like it's on a growth path for about 20–30 years.

How do I know the employees might need your services some day? Research has shown that whatever the investment options are, employees will divide their money evenly among that number of funds. For example, if the company offers a stock fund and a balanced fund, most employees will choose to put half in each, thinking they have now "diversified." In fact, since the balanced fund usually holds about 60% stock, the employee is not nearly as "balanced" as she thinks and has a large percentage of her retirement money in the stock market. Also, if there are 10 different stock funds, most employees put 10% in each one, regardless of how redundant or risky some of them are.

Company Stock

If the company allows participants to invest in company stock, it should make sure that the following bulleted list is followed:

- The company stock is publicly traded
- The company stock is traded with enough frequency and volume so participants' instructions to buy or sell can be executed promptly
- Participants are provided information given to shareholders of company stock generally
- Voting, tendering, and similar rights are passed through to participants
- The plan designates a fiduciary to ensure information regarding the purchase, sale, and holding of company stock, and the exercise of voting, tendering, and similar rights is maintained with procedures to keep it confidential
- An independent fiduciary is appointed to address any situations where the fiduciary responsible for confidentiality determines there is a potential for undue influence on a participant's decision to vote or tender shares

A plan may not "acquire any employer security or real property, if immediately after such acquisition the aggregate fair market value of employer securities and employer real property held by the plan exceeds 10 percent of the fair market value of the assets of the plan." In other words, we don't want the pension fund for XYZ Corporation to invest more than 10% of the pension fund's assets into XYZ securities. It would be bad enough if XYZ goes down; no need to drag the pension fund with it, right? We also don't want the plan to devote an extreme percentage of assets toward buying property that is then leased to the employing corporation. Again, if the plan put 90% of its assets into buying property that the employer can't afford to make payment on, that would be a real mess.

Trading Securities

On the **primary market** underwriters raise capital for corporations by selling securities to investors. The investors would never buy those securities if they didn't have a **secondary market** where they could later turn the securities back into cash. Securities are issued on the primary market, where the issuer receives money from the investor. Securities are traded on the secondary market among investors, with no money going to the issuer.

Broker-dealers not only perform investment banking activities on the primary market, but also, they execute trades for their customers on the secondary market. The broker-dealers trade the securities through various exchanges or electronic systems.

First Market – NYSE, etc.

Within the secondary market, there are four separate components. Let's start with the **first market**, the New York Stock Exchange. There are also regional exchanges in Chicago, Philadelphia, Boston, and San Francisco that are based on the NYSE. They tend to focus on regional stocks, but they also fill orders for NYSE-listed securities, such as GE, GM, and IBM.

Big member firms have a commission house broker ready to fill orders on the exchange. He works for a brokerage house and fills their orders for a commission. The more orders he can fill, the more money he can make. Firms that don't have a commission house broker often have orders executed by an individual known as a two-dollar broker. As with all brokers, a two-dollar broker earns a commission on transactions executed rather than taking a position in securities and dealing them. Then, there are competitive floor traders who try to buy low and sell high as much as possible through the trading session.

The NYSE now uses both a manual auction and an electronic trading model. That means that even though most trading throughout the day is done electronically, the exchange also uses manual auctions at the opening, at the closing, and during times of extreme volatility. A manual auction involves human beings communicating face to face in real time, indicating their buying and selling interest in a security through open outcry.

The firms in charge of running manual auctions are known as Designated Market Makers or DMMs. As a helpful video on the NYSE website explains, DMMs are kind of like commercial airline pilots. They have to be there for the take-off and the landing, and they have to step in whenever there is turbulence. During the rest of the flight, they participate, but not in such a dominant role.

Like other market participants, DMMs trade electronically throughout the day using trading algorithms. Algorithms are computerized mathematical formulas designed to determine buying and selling opportunities and execute trades automatically. Replacing the old "specialist" model, Designated Market Makers are charged with the responsibility to maintain a fair and orderly market in particular exchange-listed securities. Their job is to provide liquidity, especially during times of market volatility.

To prevent panic, they step in ready to buy or sell securities to keep the flow of trading moving. The DMM is required to quote at the National Best Bid or Offer (NBBO) a required percentage of the time. The NBBO is what it sounds like—the best prices for the security nationwide.

Supplemental Liquidity Providers play a unique role in the trading of securities on the secondary market. Supplemental Liquidity Providers are off-floor market participants using sophisticated computerized trading strategies to create high volume on exchanges to add liquidity to the markets. As an incentive to provide liquidity, the exchange pays the Supplemental Liquidity Provider (SLP) a fee/rebate.

Consolidated Tape

As we mentioned, if I place an electronic order to buy 1,000 shares of, say, GE, my order could be filled in New York, Philadelphia, Boston, San Francisco, or Chicago. That's because they're all part of the "first market."

When an NYSE-listed security is sold, it doesn't matter whether it's sold in New York, Chicago, San Francisco, or Boston—the prices are all reported to the consolidated tape. That means that the seller has to report the price he just sold a certain number of shares within 30 seconds, whether it was sold in Philly, Boston, or the floor of the security's primary exchange.

If you've ever seen the data streaming across the bottom of the TV monitor, you've seen the prices being reported to the "tape." Yes, all that "10s GE 35.55" stuff means something. It means that someone sold (and bought) 1,000 shares of GE for $35.55 per-share. The number of round lots comes first, then the stock symbol, and then the price at which the transaction took place. Let's look at some more trades as reported to the consolidated tape:

GE36.55...10s.IBM95.04... 99s.C.75.15...13,000s.GE.36.70

The first thing we see is the stock symbol GE. If there is no number before the symbol, we know that one round lot (100 shares) of GE just traded for $36.55 per-share. In the next case "10s" means 10 round lots, or 1,000 shares. So, 1,000 shares of IBM just traded at $95.04 per-share. Next, we see that 99 round lots, or 9,900 shares of "C" (for Citigroup) just traded at $75.15 per-share. But, when the number of shares gets up to 10,000 or more, they stop talking in round lots and just list the actual number of shares. In other words a trade for 10,000 shares would not be indicated as "100s." Rather, it would be "10,000s". Therefore, we read the tape to indicate that 13,000 shares of GE just traded for $36.70 per-share.

Also note that for stocks trading at $175 a share or higher, a round lot is now just one share. For these stocks, a transaction for less than 100 shares will no longer be reported as odd-lot transactions.

As usual, things get more complicated. What if you saw the following on your exam and were asked to interpret the report?

MCD12s35 .35

That means 1200 shares of McDonald's traded at $35, followed by a trade for 100 shares at $35. Remember, if there's no number before the price, that means one round lot or 100 shares traded at that price. And then we could see something like this:

MCD35 .15

That means 100 shares of McDonald's traded at $35, followed by another round lot that traded at $35.15. In other words, there is a world of difference between "35.15" and "35 .15." In the first case, 100 shares sold at $35.15. In the second case, 100 shares sold at $35, followed by 100 shares at $35.15.

For preferred stock, a round lot is just 10 shares, and they indicate that with an "s/s." Therefore, what does the following report mean?

ABC pr 7s/s.85.05

It means that 70 shares of ABC preferred stock traded for $85.05 per-share.

The following abbreviations are also used on the consolidated tape:

- SLD: the report is out-of-sequence or late
- Halt: sometimes trading in a stock is halted, usually when big news is about to come out
- OPD: the first trade that happens after a delayed opening or a trading halt
- Pr: preferred stock (also look for the s/s)
- R/T: rights
- W/S: warrants

I have been teaching in this industry for over 16 years now. When I first started, distinguishing the NYSE/1st Market from the OTC/2nd Market was getting more complicated but not too bad. The NYSE was an **exchange** that used "open outcry" like all **auction markets** did at the time. Teaching the class in Chicago, I could usually get the students to relate to the idea of the funny-colored jackets, the bad, disheveled ties and hairstyles, and the arcane hand gestures used by swearing, snarling, spitting traders down in the pits at the options exchange, the mercantile exchange or the board of trade.

Well, this industry changes faster than most. Even though the NYSE is an auction market and is an exchange, much of the trading is done electronically. And, electronic trading is what we used to safely associate with the "OTC/2nd market," which we will discuss next.

Back in the day, we would routinely hit students with questions that neatly sorted the words "listed" and "exchange" over on one side with the NYSE/1st Market, and then the OTC/2nd Market safely on the other side, where securities were "traded" or "quoted" but never "listed" because even NASDAQ, the cream of the OTC crop, at that time was not a true "exchange." It always made for awkward moments with the smartest-guy-in-the-room when I had to explain how a NASDAQ stock could be threatened with a "de-listing," if no stocks were never "listed" on NASDAQ to begin with.

NASDAQ has been an exchange for years now, and they have routinely used the terms "listed" and "de-listed" to describe the securities trading through their electronic trading facility. The term "listed" is usually thought of in terms of what it does *not* refer to. The term "listed" now accurately refers to NYSE securities and NASDAQ securities; however, the term should not be associated with securities trading over-the-counter but not on NASDAQ, e.g., the Over-the-Counter Bulletin Board, which we'll look at in a few pages.

Issuers who want to list their securities for trading on NYSE have to meet the exchange's rigid listing criteria. If s company lists its security on the NYSE (or NASDAQ), it will be monitored closely by the exchange, and if they do not meet all obligations under exchange rules and SEC rules, their security will suddenly not be trading.

For a company doing an IPO and getting authorized to list and trade on the NYSE, the total market value for the outstanding shares is a minimum of $40 million and $100 million for other companies. We're just talking about the shares of stock themselves. A company wanting to list and stay listed on the NYSE has to meet at least one of three financial tests. One is called the "earnings test" and is based on the profitability of the issuer, as its name implies. The next is the "valuation/revenue" test that is based both on the market value of the stock and the revenue of the company issuing it. And, there is an "assets/equity" test based on market valuation, assets, and stockholder's equity.

No matter which test is being used, not that many companies can meet it for an initial listing, let alone maintain it to avoid being de-listed. Sometimes the issuing company itself will decide to de-list their security. If so, all that is required for a voluntary delisting is for the company's board of directors to approve it and for the issuer to then file a form with the SEC certifying the board's approval of the resolution.

In addition to common stock, companies also list their debt securities on the NYSE, as we see at http://www1.nyse.com/bonds/nysebonds/1095449059236.html. To meet the requirements here, the issue has to have a principal value of at least $5 million.

If the bond is convertible, it can only be listed if the underlying common stock is subject to real-time last sale reports in the US, and the par value has to be $10 million or larger. Even if the issue of debt securities meets those minimum sizes and requirements, the NYSE will only list the issue if it meets one of several criteria that require that the issuer have its stock listed on the NYSE, or that an issuer with stock listed on the exchange is either a majority owner or in common control with the other issuer, or that any NYSE-listed issuer has guaranteed the issue. There is also a criteria based on the credit rating of the issue being at least "B", which, as you probably remember or know, is a junk rating.

As the website for NYSE Bonds indicates:

> NYSE Bonds operates the largest centralized corporate bond market in the U.S., providing an opportunity for participants to trade bonds in a fair, open environment. On NYSE Bonds, firm and executable orders entered by members or sponsored participants are displayed on the order book, and executed on a strict price/time priority.

Over-the-Counter

While the first market is an "auction market," the second or Over-the-Counter market is a **negotiated market**. Since traders do not gather together on the floor of an exchange, investors need big dealers to maintain inventories of over-the-counter stocks. We call these big buyers and sellers **market makers**, because they make a market in that security possible. A market maker is a broker-dealer who carries an inventory of a security and stands ready to either buy or sell it throughout the day.

Investors are able to trade shares of MSFT, ORCL, and CSCO only because there are broker-dealers who "make a market" in those securities. A "market" is a two-sided quote, allowing buyers to buy at the ask price and sellers to sell at the bid price.

Market makers electronically publish a **bid** and **ask** (or offer) price and stand ready to take either side of the trade, for at least one round lot. For stocks a round lot is 100 shares. So if a market maker says their quote is 20.00–20.11, they stand ready to buy 100 shares at $20.00 or sell 100 shares at $20.11. The difference between where they buy and where they sell is called the **spread**.

Broker-dealers can act as **brokers**, whereby they charge commissions, or they can act as **principals** in the transaction by selling stock from their own inventory, or buying stock for their inventory.

NASDAQ

Over-the-counter stocks that meet and maintain the listing criteria trade on an electronic exchange known as **NASDAQ**, which stands for National Association of Securities Dealers Automated Quotation system.

NASDAQ has three tiers. The NASDAQ Global Market Companies is a group of over 1,450 companies that have applied for listing after meeting and continuing to meet stringent financial and liquidity requirements and agreeing to meet specific corporate governance standards. And, there is the NASDAQ Global Select Market, with even higher listing standards. The former "NASDAQ SmallCap Market" has been renamed the "NASDAQ Capital Market Companies." This group of stocks consists of over 550 companies that benefit from access to the capital markets in spite of their smaller size and less proven track records. These companies have to stay current in all their SEC filings but do not have to meet the same financial standards of the Global and Global Select Companies.

Non-NASDAQ

Stocks that do not meet NASDAQ's financial, liquidity and corporate governance standards are referred to as **Non-NASDAQ OTC securities**. These securities trade on the OTC Bulletin Board and the OTC Markets, where spreads are wider and stock prices generally more volatile. When a company no longer meets NASDAQ's listing requirements, often the stock symbol changes, and the security begins to trade in the non-NASDAQ OTC market.

Securities trading here are not referred to as listed securities. The trading facilities have no regulatory relationship with the companies whose securities trade through them. Listed securities include those trading on NASDAQ and the NYSE, not here.

Third Market

The **third market** is a term used when an NYSE-listed security is traded over-the-counter. Maybe an institutional buyer can get a better, negotiated price for an order of 10,000 IBM, a listed security, so they decide to buy it over-the-counter. When a listed security trades OTC, we refer to that situation as the "third market." The Consolidated Quotation System (CQS) displays quotations on all common stock, preferred stock, warrants, and rights that are registered on the American Stock Exchange or the New York Stock Exchange and trading in the OTC market (third market). Although executed in the over-the-counter market, these transactions must be reported to the consolidated tape.

Fourth Market

The **fourth market** involves direct trading between institutional investors, completely bypassing brokers by using **Electronic Communications Networks (ECNs)**. Institutional investors include insurance companies, mutual funds, pension funds, big trust departments, broker-dealers, etc. They're professionals with millions/billions of dollars flowing in and out of the market. Basically, ECNs work like an eBay for securities transactions by matching up buyers and sellers. Some broker-dealers use a market maker to execute client transactions during normal business hours and then use an ECN to execute orders after normal business hours (after 4 p.m.). Well-known electronic communications networks include INSTINET and NYSE ARCA. Here are some essential facts on ECNs:

- If the ECN system cannot match a buyer and seller, a client's order can have a limited ability to be executed
- Some ECNs will only accept certain types of orders, such as limit orders
- Electronic communications networks allow market participants themselves to display quotes and execute transactions

- Participants are referred to as *subscribers* and pay a fee to the ECN to trade electronically through the system
- ECNs allow subscribers to trade after-hours, quote and trade anonymously
- ECNs act in an agency capacity and do not buy or sell for their own account (not a market maker)

Dark Pools, High-Frequency Trading

The term **dark pools of liquidity** refers to large institutional orders that are concealed from the public. As an example, imagine that a large pension fund wants to sell 1 million shares of GM to another large pension fund. Executing such a large order through the NYSE could be taken as a sign to the rest of the market to dump GM, meaning that the sale itself could depress the value of the stock. Therefore, the two pension funds decide to do the trade directly between themselves or possibly through a regional exchange. To execute the trade away from the NYSE is known as doing the trade "in a dark pool."

One side claims that dark pools provide more liquidity to the market and allow large trades to be executed without destabilizing the market for that security. The other side claims that such trades deprive all market participants from knowing the true prices at which specific securities are being traded.

We looked at Supplemental Liquidity Providers and saw that they receive a rebate as a financial incentive for providing liquidity to the NYSE market. Although the rebate might be a fraction of a penny, if the SLP can execute millions of trades per day, the incentive pays off. Therefore, a Supplemental Liquidity Provider often uses powerful computers to execute a huge number of trades powered by algorithms analyzing multiple markets and automatically executing trades based on spotting certain market conditions. Such trading is known as **high-frequency trading.**

It is estimated that more than half of all exchange volume comes in the form of high-frequency trading, where the traders with the fastest computers typically come out ahead. Proponents of high-frequency trading argue that it provides the most up-to-date pricing information, thereby facilitating price disco.

Some market participants and experts, however, are concerned that algorithms merely look for trends or momentum and exploit them. They are not designed to factor in war or economic news and, therefore can mindlessly exaggerate market factors. They also do not know when to stop or alter a trade and, therefore, often lead to a distortion in the buying or selling of a security far beyond what human traders would have done on their own.

Selling Short

You've probably heard that an investor should try to buy low and sell high, right? Well, some investors take that same principle and do it in reverse: they prefer selling high, then buying back low. We call these investors "short sellers."

It works like this. You go to your friend's house and see that she has a new mountain bike that she paid too much money for. Mind if I borrow your mountain bike, you ask, to which your friend agrees.

On the way home you run into another friend, who admires the bike. She likes it so much, in fact, that she offers you two thousand dollars for it.

Sold! You take the $2,000 and put it in your pocket.

Wait a minute, that wasn't even your mountain bike! No problem. All you have to do is replace it with an identical machine. A few days later you go to the bike store to replace the borrowed bike, and—as predicted—the price has fallen to just $1,000. Perfect! You sold the bike for $2,000 and you can get out of your position by paying just $1,000, keeping the $1,000 difference as your profit. Just buy the bike for $1,000, wheel it over to your friend, and everybody's happy. Notice that you made money when the price went down. Therefore, you were "bearish" on the price of mountain bikes.

Short sellers don't sell bikes or search engines short, but they can sell the stock of companies who make bikes or search engines short. If you think Google is overpriced and headed for a drop, borrow the shares from your broker-dealer and sell them at what you think is the top. Sell Google for $700 and, you hope, buy it back later for $30, keeping $670 per-share as your profit.

However, many people tried that after Google went public at $85. When it got to $100, many were convinced the stock would only go down from there, so they sold it short at $100. Expecting to buy it back or "cover their short positions" for less than $100, these traders must have been really embarrassed to see the stock soon climb to $900 per-share.

Selling for $100 and buying for $900 is not a good business model. That's no different from buying for $900 and then selling for $100. It's just more dangerous. When you buy, you've already lost all you could ever lose. But when you sell stock short, there is no limit to how much you'll have to spend to get out of your position. I mean, reality would tell us that Google was never going to hit $10,000 a share, but, hypothetically, it could have. Higher even.

Short sellers are bearish. They profit when the stock goes down. But, they have limited upside and unlimited risk. If you sell a stock short for $5,000, $5,000 is the maximum you could make, and only if the stock went to zero. Your potential loss is unlimited, since no one can tell you for sure how high the stock could go up.

Stock is not the only thing that can be sold short. Treasury securities are frequently sold short, as are corporate bonds, ETFs (exchange-traded funds), and closed-end funds. Writers of options are "short the option" and complete the trade when they buy it back to close.

Regulation SHO

The SEC does not like it when short sellers sell shares that don't exist. Allowing them to do so would distort the downward (bearish) pressure on a stock by distorting the laws of supply & demand that determine the stock's market price. Therefore, broker-dealers must "locate" the shares their customers are selling short and document it before effecting the short sale—that means they reasonably believe the securities can be delivered by the settlement date (T + 3) as required.

In olden days, a short sale could only be executed at a price that was higher than the previous price for the security, or at the same price if the price before had been an "uptick." **Reg SHO** now requires that before executing a short sale, broker-dealers must locate the securities so that the laws of supply and demand are not distorted by "naked short selling," in which people sell stock that doesn't even exist short, artificially depressing its price. If the broker-dealer executes a short sale without reasonably believing the shares can be delivered by the lender, they have violated the rule.

In May 2010 Reg SHO was updated to impose a temporary version of the old uptick rule that applies when a "circuit breaker" is tripped for a security. Starting in May of that year if a security dropped during the day by 10% or more below its most recent closing price, short sellers would not be able to sell short at or below the current best bid price for the security. In other words, people "selling long," which means selling the shares they own, will have priority and will be able to liquidate their holdings before short sellers can jump onto the pile. As the SEC states in their unique brand of English:

```
a targeted short sale price test restriction will apply the
alternative uptick rule for the remainder of the day and the
following day if the price of an individual security declines
intra-day by 10% or more from the prior day's closing price for
that security. By not allowing short sellers to sell at or below
the current national best bid while the circuit breaker is in
effect, the short sale price test restriction in Rule 201 will
allow long sellers, who will be able to sell at the bid, to sell
first in a declining market for a particular security. As the
Commission has noted previously in connection with short sale
price test restrictions, a goal of such restrictions is to allow
long sellers to sell first in a declining market. In addition, by
making such bids accessible only by long sellers when a
security's price is undergoing significant downward price
pressure, Rule 201 will help to facilitate and maintain stability
in the markets and help ensure that they function efficiently. It
will also help restore investor confidence during times of
substantial uncertainty because, once the circuit breaker has
been triggered for a particular security, long sellers will have
preferred access to bids for the security, and the security's
continued price decline will more likely be due to long selling
and the underlying fundamentals of the issuer, rather than to
other factors.
```

As we see from that passage, there is a big difference between a customer sell order marked "long" and a sell order marked "short." That is why Reg SHO requires all sell orders to be marked properly. When a customer "sells long," he is liquidating shares that he owns. To sell short, as we see, involves borrowing shares that will be sold and then replaced later by the customer. Short sales take place only in margin accounts, not cash accounts.

Bond Trading

Corporate bonds traded over-the-counter are reported to FINRA's **TRACE** system, which stands for **Trade Reporting and Compliance Engine**. Brokerage firms are now required to report price and volume data on all corporate bond transactions to TRACE, within 15 minutes. FINRA publicly disseminates that transaction data immediately on virtually 100 percent of over-the-counter corporate bond activity (approximately 22,000 transactions and $18 billion in volume every day). Recently, FINRA fined a firm $1.4 *million* for failing to report a percentage of their bond trades to TRACE. The purpose of the TRACE system is to provide transparency to the bond market, so by failing to report the trades, the firm deprived the market of the transparency it needs to remain effective. Several smaller fines have recently been levied for failing to report trades in "TRACE-eligible securities." FINRA insists that dealers provide the market with accurate and transparent data on securities transactions, and they are quite happy to remind them with disciplinary actions and fines.

The NYSE also provides a bond trading platform:

The NYSE Bonds trading platform provides a more efficient and transparent way to trade bonds. The platform incorporates the design of the current NYSE Arca all-electronic trading system. This system provides investors with the ability to readily obtain transparent pricing and trading information, enabling them to make better investment decisions. The system has also been expanded to include the bonds of all NYSE-listed companies and their subsidiaries without the companies having to list each bond issued. NYSE Bonds operates the largest centralized bond market of any US exchange or other self-regulatory organization. It offers investors a broad selection of bonds: corporate (including convertibles), agency and government bonds.

The majority of NYSE bond volume is in corporate debt, with some 94% in straight, or non-convertible bonds, and 6% in convertible debt issues. As of Monday, December 1, 2008 all NYSE Amex (formerly American Stock Exchange) listed bonds transferred to an electronic trading platform based on NYSE Bonds called NYSE Amex Bonds. Like NYSE Bonds, this electronic trading platform is based on the design of NYSE Arca's comprehensive matching technology allowing NYSE Members to enter orders to buy or sell bonds electronically.

MSRB Rule G-14 requires that transactions in municipal bonds be reported within 15 minutes of trade execution to the MSRB's Real-time Transaction Reporting System (RTRS). The MSRB disseminates trade data about all reported municipal securities transactions almost immediately at www.investinginbonds.com. You may have noticed that for both TRACE and RTRS, bond transactions are reported within 15 minutes, but when we're talking about stock transactions, the report is due within 30 seconds. Yet another indication of the increased volatility and faster pace of the stock—as opposed to the bond—market.

Types of Orders

Market Order

If a customer wants to buy 1,000 shares quickly, he places a **market order**. A market order is filled as fast as possible, at the best available market price for the security.

Limit Order

Sometimes customers name their price by placing a **limit order**. If a stock is at 43, maybe they're interested in selling it. They'd be more interested if they could sell it for $45, so they enter a **sell limit** order above the current market price. Sell limit @45 means the investor will take 45 or better (*more* is better for a seller). If he can get 45 or 45.15, or even higher, he'll sell his stock. If the bid never rises that high, he won't sell it.

Another investor is interested in buying a stock currently trading at 30. He'd be more interested in buying it at $25, so he places a **buy limit** order below the current price. That means he'll buy the stock if he can get it for $25 or better (*less* is better for a buyer). If the ask/offer price never drops to $25 or lower, he won't buy it.

Market orders guarantee a fill but not a price. Limit orders, on the other hand, guarantee a price, but they do not guarantee the order will be filled. Many times, the stock's price fails to perform like an investor wants it to. If it's entered as a day order, the limit order either gets executed that day or it goes away. If the investor is going on vacation for three weeks and doesn't want to look at his stocks while he's gone, he can leave the order open by entering it **GTC**, which stands for good 'til canceled. If it doesn't get filled and the investor doesn't cancel it, the order remains open.

Stop Order

A buy limit order is filled only if the ask/offer price drops to the limit price or lower. A sell limit order is filled only if the bid price rises to the limit price or higher. Stop orders, on the other hand, are not based on the buying and selling interest represented by the Bid and Ask prices. Stop orders are triggered only when an actual trade occurs between two other investors at the stop price or higher for a buy stop, or at the stop price or lower for a sell stop order.

So, if the test question shows the stop price on the consolidated tape, understand that, by definition, that cannot be the customer's trade. That is the trade that put the customer's order in play. It is the "last sale" that activates the stop order. Also, any trade reported with the abbreviation "SLD" is a late report and cannot trigger a stop order.

Let's start with a **buy stop** order. A technical analyst sees that a stock is trading in a narrow range, between 38 and 40. The technical analyst sees no reason to tie up his money in a stock that is stuck in a narrow trading range, known as **consolidation**. He decides if the stock can break through resistance (40), it will continue to rise, which is why he'd like to buy it on the way up. So, he places a buy stop above the current market price.

Buy stop @41 means the market price first must reach 41 or higher, at which point the order is activated. It will be executed at the next available price, whatever that is. Stop orders have an activation or trigger price, at which point they become market orders. So, if the ticker came in like this:

40.90, 40.95, 40.99, 41.00...

his order would now be triggered or activated at 41.00. It would then be filled at the next available price, regardless. And, if the last two prices had been 40.99, 41.01, the order would have been triggered at 41.01, at which point the price has passed through the stop price of 41.

Stop orders don't guarantee a price for execution. The price named as the stop is the price that triggers or activates the order. The order—now a market order—is filled at the next available price. Again, the stop price is not the exact price, either. A "buy stop at 41" is activated at 41 or any price higher than that. It's then filled as soon as possible.

On the other hand, let's say a day trader takes a large position in a high-risk security but then decides to play it safe and limit his loss. He buys 1,000 shares at $50 a share and immediately enters a **sell stop** order at 49. This means if the stock stays above $49 he's in. As soon as it falls to 49 or lower, though, he's out. A sell stop at 49 is activated as soon as the stock's price hits 49 or lower, at which point it is sold at the next available price. The exam might tell you that a customer is bullish on a stock but fears a possible downturn in the short-term. What should she do?

Well, if she originally bought in at $20 and the stock is now at $50, she should make sure she doesn't lose too much of the $30 profit she has within her grasp. Many investors end up snatching defeat from the jaws of victory at this point, probably because they don't know how to use sell stops or "**stop loss**" orders. A sell stop at $48 or $49 would protect this paper gain, and also leave room for more upside.

If someone wants to also name the price for execution, he can enter a **stop-limit** order. Now his stop order also names the most he will pay or the least he will accept for a stock. A buy stop @50, limit 50 would start out just like a buy stop order. The stock must hit 50 or higher before it's triggered. But, by adding the limit to the order the investor is saying he won't pay more than $50 for it, period.

On the other hand, a sell stop @30, limit 30 is triggered if the stock hit 30 or lower, but the investor will not take less than $30 a share. If the order is triggered and then the bid falls lower than 30, this sell order won't get executed, and the investor will end up holding a loser that would have otherwise been sold with a sell stop (not a stop-limit) order.

Or, our technical analyst who wants to buy stock on the way up might want to place a cap on how much he pays. If so, he enters a **buy stop-limit** order. In other words, a "buy stop @41" could be filled at whatever price—probably near $41—while a "buy stop @41, limit 41" could only be filled at $41 or lower. Neither order, however, is activated unless and until the stock first trades one time at $41 or higher.

NASDAQ Level 1, 2, 3

Back to NASDAQ. There are three levels of NASDAQ quoting that the test wants you to know about. The first is called **Level** 1, which represents the best bid and the best ask. Buyers want to pay the lowest ask price and receive the highest bid price when they sell, which is what Level 1 displays. Among all market makers, Level 1 displays the highest bid and the lowest ask. That makes up a very important concept known as the "inside market" or "inside quote." Everything is based on that. When a dealer sells a security, they have to be close to that inside market, which might look like this:

Bid	Ask
19.75	20.00

Those two prices represent the highest bid and the lowest ask among all market makers currently quoting the stock. If any particular dealer sells to a customer at a price higher than 20 or buys lower than 19.75, they have to remain somewhere within 5% in order to conform to the 5% markup rule, which we'll explain in more detail.

Level 2 looks more like the following. Let's say there are three market makers quoting this stock and their quotes look like this:

	Bid	Ask
Dealer 1	19.11	20.00
Dealer 2	19.75	20.50
Dealer 3	19.23	20.25

Among the three market makers, we find the highest bid at 19.75 and the lowest ask at 20.00. That's what makes up the inside quote, shown on Level 1. So, Level 2 identifies each market maker's quote, from which Level 1 pulls the highest bid and lowest ask to provide the "inside market."

Level 3 has input fields that market makers use to enter their quotes. If you're not a market maker, you don't have Level 3. Levels 1 and 2 report quotes. Level 3 lets market makers provide quotes; it's interactive, rather than just a display.

5% Markup Guideline

As it says in the FINRA Manual, the 5% "rule" is a guideline that dealers must use to ensure that customers are charged reasonable commissions or markups/markdowns. A firm can act as either a broker or a dealer. When the firm brokers a trade, they add a commission that must be reasonable. When the firm deals stock to the customer, they must charge a markup that is reasonable.

Back to the inside market. The inside market in our example above was Bid–19.75, Ask–20.00. That's the "interdealer market," which means that among all the dealers in the security, the two best prices are $19.75 to a seller and $20.00 to a buyer. So, what happens if that one market maker does sell the stock for $20.50? That's a markup of 50 cents, and the markup generally needs to be around 5% above the "inside ask" of $20.00.

If they charged "$20.50," we could judge the fairness of that markup by simply taking the excess of 50 cents compared to/divided by $20.00. That represents a markup of 2.5%, well within the 5% guideline. If they charged $21.00, that would be exactly 5%. But, 5% is not an absolute—even if they're charging 5% or less, they could still be violating the rules. If the stock is extremely liquid— like MSFT or CSCO—maybe they shouldn't be charging anything close to 5%. Or, for some securities, a markup above 5% might be okay. The dealers can (and must) take the following into consideration when determining the fairness of a markup or commission:

- The Type of Security Involved – stocks are riskier than bonds and carry higher charges.
- Availability of the Security – inactive securities might take more time and expense to buy or sell.
- Price of the Security – low-priced securities usually end up carrying markups that are higher as a percentage of the price. A markup of 10 cents is a big percentage when the stock costs $1.00, while a markup of 50 cents is pretty low on a $100 stock.
- Amount of Money Involved – if you want to buy 50 dollars' worth of stock, you aren't going to get such a great deal.
- Disclosing the higher markup or commissions before completing the transaction usually takes care of the situation.
- Nature of the Services Provided – full-service broker-dealers can charge more in commissions and markups because they provide more services. The old "you get what you pay for" thing.

Some firms charge commissions. Some broker-dealers buy the security from the market maker and then take on a few cents for a "net" price to the customer. Either way, it's kind of six-of-one-half-dozen-of-the-other: whatever extra charge the broker-dealer is adding to the customer's price, it needs to be within about 5% of the best available price for the security.

Broker-dealers can act as an agent/broker on a transaction, in which case they add a commission. Or, they can act as a principal/dealer, in which case they add a **markup** when they sell, or a **markdown** when they buy from the customer. The 5% guideline covers the fairness of both commissions and markups. Remember that this is an either-or situation. Either the firm gets a commission *or* they get a markup—not both. In other words, they acted either as a broker (agent) or a dealer (principal). Also note that when a firm acts as a principal, they are selling a security held in their inventory to a customer—as opposed to simply matching the customer with a seller. When they act as a principal in a transaction with a retail customer, the firm has to get the customer's written consent and acknowledgment that he/she understands the significance of the terminology.

Proceeds Transaction

If a customer sells one stock and uses the proceeds to buy another on the same day, we call this a **proceeds transaction**, for obvious reasons. When applying the 5% guideline, the firm has to treat both the sale and the purchase as one transaction. In other words, they can't ding the customer 5% on the sale and on the purchase. The combined commission or markup/markdown must be in the neighborhood of 5%. The FINRA Manual says it well when it writes, "the mark-up shall be computed in the same way as if the customer had purchased for cash."

Riskless Principal Transaction

The difference between "broker" and "dealer" is important. When the firm acts as a broker, they are simply finding a buyer or seller for their customer. When the firm acts as a dealer, they are taking the other side of the trade by either buying from the customer or selling to the customer. The firm acts either as a broker or a dealer on a particular transaction, which is why the industry got all clever and named these firms broker-dealers.

So, if you need some stock, maybe the broker-dealer will simply find a seller and get you a decent price. They're acting as a broker/agent, and they would charge you a commission. A-B-C…agents are brokers and they charge commissions. If the firm already had the stock in inventory, they might deal it to you at a markup. They would indicate on your trade confirmation that they acted in a "principal" capacity. To act as a "principal" means that they're taking the other side of the trade, rather than just arranging the trade for a commission (agent/broker).

Well, sometimes a customer calls up and expresses an interest in buying, say, 1,000 shares of XYZ. The firm puts the customer on hold and then purchases the 1,000 shares for their own inventory. They get the customer back on the line, and they deal the stock to him. There was no risk on this principal transaction, since their holding period is about 3 seconds. Therefore, the industry cleverly named this situation where a principal takes no risk a **riskless principal transaction**. As long as the markup conforms to the 5% guideline, everything is hunky-dory.

The 5% markup guideline does provide guidance for markups and commissions on corporate (but not municipal) bonds. As FINRA points out in its notice to members, a broker-dealer would generally use its "contemporaneous cost" when determining the fairness of a markup to a customer. That means that they would use the prevailing market price that they themselves would or did have to pay at that time. There are, of course, exceptions to that: if interest rates, credit ratings, or news announcements change the whole reality for that debt security immediately after the dealer buys it, then the firm can factor that in. And, if there is no current market for the security, the firm would not be able—let alone required—to use their contemporaneous cost.

The guideline does not apply to anything sold with a prospectus, since that's a primary market transaction. A variable annuity or mutual fund, therefore, is sold at a public offering price, just like an IPO. The public offering price (POP) already includes all the compensation to the underwriters and selling group members. Also, municipal securities aren't covered by this 5% guideline. The firm just follows the MSRB rule, which says customer transactions must be executed at a fair and reasonable price.

Firm Quotes

When a broker-dealer contacts a market maker, they need to be really clear as to what the market maker actually means with his cryptic little phrases. For example, if the market maker simply responds with a straight answer, that's a **firm quote** that has to be honored for at least one round lot of 100 shares. If the market maker says, "Bid–20.00, Ask–20.15," that's a firm quote. He doesn't have to say "firm" to make it firm. It's what he doesn't say that makes it firm.

See, sometimes the market maker is just talking, just giving the dealer a ballpark figure. These are called **nominal quotes,** which means they are subject to being reconfirmed before the deal goes down. Also know that the market maker's firm quote is only firm for 1 round lot unless some specific number of shares is mentioned.

If the buy side says, "What's the quote on XYZ?" and the market maker says, "Bid–20, Ask–20.25," the market maker only has to sell 100 shares at $20.25. If the buy side says, "Great, we'll take 1 million shares at the offer," the market maker would only be on the hook for 100 at the stated price. Beyond that, we may need to talk. So, in a test question, if somebody asks for a quote on 500 shares, a firm quote given in response would be firm for 500 shares. But, a firm quote is only firm for 1 round lot. There may only be so many round lots available at a particular price, so larger orders may have to be negotiated.

Market Orders for IPO shares

Some IPOs go crazy on their first day of trading, rising higher and higher on the secondary market with no relationship to the IPO price. To curb the volatility FINRA does not allow broker-dealers to accept market orders to buy the stock before it starts trading on the secondary market. A limit order, however, can be accepted even before the stock starts trading on the secondary market. As FINRA states in a notice to members, limit orders protect investors and facilitate price discovery on the stock. In other words, knowing that a lot of people want to buy the stock can create pandemonium. However, knowing that people want to buy this many shares at these prices simply transmits important information to the trading markets.

Trading Ahead of Customer Limit Order

Let's say a customer wants to buy 1,000 shares of ORCL @$15. When the customer enters that limit order, maybe the firm is trading for its own account in ORCL, too. So, they have the customer order to buy 1,000 shares of ORCL @15 and when they see that the ASK is $15 and the size is (10) or 10 round lots, they go ahead and buy the stock for their own trading account.

What about the customer who wanted to buy the stock at that price? Too bad, right?

Wrong. This FINRA Rule states:

> ...will require members to handle their customer limit orders with all due care so that members do not "trade ahead" of those limit orders. Thus, members that handle customer limit orders, whether received from their own customers or from another member, are prohibited from trading at prices equal or superior to that of the limit order without executing the limit order.

Then there is further clarification of that with the following:

> A member firm that accepts and holds an unexecuted limit order from its customer (whether its own customer or a customer of another member) in a NASDAQ or exchange-listed security and that continues to trade the subject security for its own account at prices that would satisfy the customer's limit order, without executing that limit order, shall be deemed to have acted in a manner inconsistent with just and equitable principles of trade.

When we are about to place a customer order to buy a bazillion shares, we can pretty well guess that the price is about to go up. So, why not buy some shares for yourself, your firm, your wife, etc.?

Because that's a violation called front-running, or taking advantage of an order you're about to place by buying some of the stock for yourself first. As FINRA states:

It shall be considered conduct inconsistent with just and equitable principles of trade for a member or person associated with a member, for an account in which such member or person associated with a member has an interest, for an account with respect to which such member or person associated with a member exercises investment discretion, or for certain customer accounts, to cause to be executed:

(a) an order to buy or sell an option or a security future when such member or person associated with a member causing such order to be executed has material, non-public market information concerning an imminent block transaction in the underlying security, or when a customer has been provided such material, non-public market information by the member or any person associated with a member; or

(b) an order to buy or sell an underlying security when such member or person associated with a member causing such order to be executed has material, non-public market information concerning an imminent block transaction in an option or a security future overlying that security, or when a customer has been provided such material, non-public market information by the member or any person associated with a member; prior to the time information concerning the block transaction has been made publicly available.

The rule defines a block transaction as:

A transaction involving 10,000 shares or more of an underlying security, or options or security futures covering such number of shares is generally deemed to be a block transaction, although a transaction of less than 10,000 shares could be considered a block transaction in appropriate cases.

We saw that firms can't trade ahead of their customer limit orders, and it's basically the same with customer market orders.

Trading Ahead of Customer Market Orders

(a) A member must make every effort to execute a customer market order that it receives fully and promptly.

> *(b) A member that accepts and holds a market order of its own customer or a customer of another broker-dealer in a NASDAQ or exchange-listed security without immediately executing the order is prohibited from trading that security on the same side of the market for its own account, unless it immediately thereafter executes the customer market order up to the size and at the same price at which it traded for its own account or at a better price.*

This next FINRA rule is not surprising:

> **Use of Manipulative, Deceptive or Other Fraudulent Devices**
>
> *No member shall effect any transaction in, or induce the purchase or sale of, any security by means of any manipulative, deceptive or other fraudulent device or contrivance.*

It is also no surprise that the regulators feel broker-dealers should get their customers the best possible price when they buy and when they sell. As FINRA explains:

> **Best Execution and Interpositioning**
>
> *(a) In any transaction for or with a customer, a member and persons associated with a member shall use reasonable diligence to ascertain the best inter-dealer market for the subject security and buy or sell in such market so that the resultant price to the customer is as favorable as possible under prevailing market conditions. Among the factors that will be considered in determining whether a member has used "reasonable diligence" are:*
>
> *(1) The character of the market for the security, e.g., price, volatility, relative liquidity, and pressure on available communications;*
>
> *(2) the size and type of transaction;*
>
> *(3) the number of primary markets checked;*
>
> *(4) location and accessibility to the customer's broker/dealer of primary markets and quotations sources.*

This is why a customer order to buy should be filled at the lowest ask/offer price possible and a customer order to sell should be filled at the highest bid price among all market makers at the time.

The violation called "interpositioning" has to do with unnecessarily inserting a third party into a transaction. As FINRA explains:

> *(b) In any transaction for or with a customer, no member or person associated with a member shall interject a third party between the member and the best available market except in cases where the member can demonstrate that to his knowledge at the time of the transaction the total cost or proceeds of the transaction, as confirmed to the member acting for or with the customer, was better than the prevailing inter-dealer market for the security. A member's obligations to his customer are generally not fulfilled when he channels transactions through another broker/dealer or some person in a similar position, unless he can show that by so doing he reduced the costs of the transactions to the customer.*

Regulation NMS

Stocks trading on the NYSE, NYSE Amex, and NASDAQ have to meet certain criteria for size, profitability and trading activity. On the other hand, stocks trading on the Over-The-Counter Bulletin Board or the Pink Quotes do not have to meet such requirements.

Regulation NMS (National Market System) has to do with the over-the-counter trading of stocks that trade on NYSE, NYSE Amex, and NASDAQ, as opposed to Over-The-Counter Bulletin Board (OTCBB) and Pink Quote stocks. The SEC defines an **NMS security** as "any security or class of securities for which transaction reports are collected, processed, and made available pursuant to an effective transaction reporting plan, or an effective national market system plan for reporting transactions in listed options." As we can see, there is more information available through the trading day on NMS stocks compared to non-NMS stocks (OTCBB, Pink Quote).

For NMS stocks the market can see throughout the day important information including high, low, and last-sale prices, cumulative volume figures, and bid and ask quotations. As NASDAQ explains, "This is due to the fact that market makers must report the actual price and number of shares in each transaction within 90 seconds versus non-real-time reporting for non-NMS stocks." For non-NMS stocks last-sale prices and minute-to-minute volume updates are not possible, which is why the broker-dealer that I use only accepts priced buy orders for non-NMS stocks as opposed to unpriced market orders, which we will look at in more detail up ahead.

Regulation NMS is so concerned with trade reporting and updated information that, "No broker or dealer may execute any transaction in, or induce or attempt to induce the purchase or sale of, any NMS stock: on or through the facilities of a national securities exchange unless there is an effective transaction reporting plan with respect to transactions in such security executed on or through such exchange facilities; or otherwise than on a national securities exchange unless there is an effective transaction reporting plan with respect to transactions in such security executed otherwise than on a national securities exchange by such broker or dealer." To facilitate this Regulation NMS requires that "Every broker or dealer who is a member of a national securities exchange or national securities association shall promptly transmit to the exchange or association of which it is a member all information required by any effective transaction reporting plan filed by such exchange or association."

The SEC wants all market participants to have access to important information throughout the trading day. Therefore, exchanges and national securities associations are prohibited from making rules or adopting practices that "prohibit, condition or otherwise limit, directly or indirectly, the ability of any vendor to retransmit, for display in moving tickers, transaction reports or last sale data made available pursuant to any effective transaction reporting plan." However, exchanges and trading facilities can definitely charge vendors who want to retransmit this information to their customers. As long as the charges are uniform and reasonable, that is. Regulation NMS states that "Nothing in this section shall preclude any national securities exchange or national securities association, separately or jointly, pursuant to the terms of an effective transaction reporting plan, from imposing reasonable, uniform charges (irrespective of geographic location) for distribution of transaction reports or last sale data."

Under Regulation NMS exchanges are required to provide important information to vendors retransmitting it "at all times such exchange is open for trading." During trading hours exchanges must "collect, process, and make available to vendors the best bid, the best offer, and aggregate quotation sizes for each subject security listed or admitted to unlisted trading privileges which is communicated on any national securities exchange by any responsible broker or dealer."

The SEC's Regulation NMS attempts to bring uniformity to trading and reporting, as well as increase access to real-time quotations. Trading facilities and vendors who retransmit their data in NMS securities are not allowed to charge fees that are discriminatory or excessive. Because of Regulation NMS a customer of an online broker-dealer, after signing various agreements, can then access real-time quotes in both NMS stocks and listed options on a computer or handheld device. This information is also available for free at www.nasdaq.com as well as other websites. In other words, because of Regulation NMS, getting real-time quotes on all of the major stock issues has become remarkably quick and easy.

Performance Measures

There are many ways to measure the performance of an investment account.

Holding Period and Annualized Return

If it takes three years to achieve a 9% return, the investor's **holding period return** is 9%. If it takes five or seven years to achieve a 9% return, the investor's holding period return is 9%. Another name for holding period return is total profit. Based on what he invested, the investor's paper gain or loss represents a percentage of that, regardless of the holding period.

To measure the return on an annualized basis take the 9% holding period return and divide it by the number of years it took to achieve it. If the holding period is three years, divide 9% by 3 for a 3% **annualized rate of return.**

If the holding period is more than one year, divide the return by the number of years. If the period is less than one year, multiply. For example, a -3% return over Q1 is -12% annualized. Or, a 5% monthly return is 60% on an annualized basis.

Question: An investment's market value decreases from $10 to $8.50 over Q1. The investment's annualized rate of return is...?

Answer: if the market price drops from $10 to $8.50, take that $1.50 divided by the original $10. The investment just dropped 15% over one quarter. Since there are four quarters per year, multiply the 15% by four, a negative 60% annualized rate of return.

The interest rate that a bond pays is called the **nominal yield**. If a bond has a nominal yield of 5%, it pays $50 a year per $1,000 par value, usually in two semiannual installments of $25. End of story.

For investors on the secondary market, however, the story goes on in the form of **current yield**. That $50 per year the issuer pays would be more attractive if we could get it for $500 rather than for, say, $1,000. In fact, it is exactly twice as nice. Yielding $50 of income from an investment of $1,000 represents a 5% current yield, but getting that same $50 from a $500 investment is a 10% current yield.

Also, when the bond matures, it pays out $1,000. If someone bought it for $1,000 and receives $1,000 at maturity, big deal. But, if he bought it for $500 and receives $1,000 at maturity, he gained $500, on top of all the interest payments received. Now we're talking about **yield to maturity**, which is the yield an investor would receive in the form of all the interest payments plus (or minus) the difference between what they paid for the bond, and the par value the bond pays out at maturity.

Question: One of your clients purchased a GE 5s debenture of '19 @96.375. What is the current yield?

Answer: the "5s" means that the coupon rate is 5% or $50 per year. Divide that $50 of annual interest by the market price of $963.75, and you've got the current yield of about 5.2%.

For **yield to call**, remember that a call can happen sooner than the maturity date. So, for people who bought the bond at a discount from par, their yield to call is even better than current yield or yield to maturity, since they would end up making their gain sooner. But, for people who bought the bond at a premium to par, their yield to call is even worse, since they realize their loss a lot sooner.

So, the yields go in this order: nominal yield, current yield, yield to maturity, and yield to call. For a **discount bond**, they go UP in that order; for a **premium bond**, they go DOWN in that order. That is the bond see-saw covered in the discussion of debt securities, and it's also a way of measuring returns on bonds.

There is a big difference between yield and **total return** for a mutual fund, UIT, or closed-end fund investor. If an investor pays $10 for a mutual fund share and receives $1 in an income or dividend distribution, the investor's yield is 10%.

But, what if the fund share dropped $2 in the meantime? That's a drop of 20% in value! Suddenly, who cares about the 10% yield? The total return is negative. If the value drops 20% and the dividend is only 10%, the total return is −10%. So, when selling mutual fund products to investors, agents must be sure to explain how yield and total return are different. And they should never quote one without quoting the other and explaining the difference.

Let's say an investor receives a dividend of $1 and the share price appreciates $2. That represents a return of $3. Three dollars on top of $10 is a 30% total return.

Doesn't have to be a mutual fund, either. Any stock or bond would have a total return because there are only two ways that an investment can help. Number one, it pays some income and, number two, it goes up in value. That's total return. It can be positive or negative depending on how things turn out.

Question: XYZ common stock pays a quarterly dividend of 75 cents. One of your investors purchased the stock at $50 at the beginning of Q3. If the stock trades for $49 at the end of Q3, what is your investor's annualized rate of return?

Answer: how much money did the investor make over the quarter and what happened to the value of his investment? He took in 75¢, but the stock dropped $1. I'd say he's down 25¢ on a $50 investment, which is a return of negative ½%. Multiply the negative ½% by 4 to get a total annualized rate of return of - 2%.

Inflation-Adjusted, Real Return

The trouble with being a fixed-income investor is that your income is fixed. If you own a 5% bond, what happens if inflation is > than 5%?

That's a risk of being a bond investor, and we don't completely escape it in the stock market, either. When we factor in the effects of inflation, we are talking about something called either **inflation-adjusted return** or **real return**. If we receive a 4% return from a bond, is that enough to help us pay bills in retirement? Not if the price of everything is rising by more than 4%. What if we're receiving 4%, but the price of everything is rising, say, 8%?

We are falling behind. So, if inflation is rising, investors need to calculate whether the return on their investments is rising even higher and faster than the rate of inflation. The number that takes this into account is called the inflation-adjusted return or real rate of return.

To calculate it we subtract the rate of inflation from a portfolio's return. If the investment returns 8% when inflation is 3%, we have an inflation-adjusted return of 5%. If the investment returns 3% when inflation is 8%, we have an inflation-adjusted return of −5%. We may not be losing money on paper, but we are losing purchasing power.

Question: Frank Dodd's investment appreciates 2% during a period in which the Consumer Price Index (CPI) increases 3%. What is Frank's real rate of return?

Answer: Frank's return is 1 point less than the CPI. Therefore, his real rate of return is -1%.

After-Tax Return

Bond interest is often taxable, and if so, it's taxed as ordinary income. Treasury securities are taxed at ordinary income rates by the federal government. Corporate bond interest is taxable by the federal, state, and local governments. Clearly, when we cut a check for taxes, this reduces the returns on our investment. The return on an investment after-tax is referred to as the investor's **after-tax return**.

When looking at municipal securities we take the comparable taxable bond yield and multiply it by the percentage the investor keeps. If he is in the 28% federal tax bracket, he gives up 28% of the return to taxes and keeps 72%. So, if a corporate bond pays $100 a year, he keeps 72% of that, or $72 per year.

The after-tax yield on a bond paying 10% is 7.2%. Not as impressive when we factor in the taxes. The formula to calculate after-tax yield is:

$$\text{Taxable yield} * (100\% - \text{tax bracket})$$

Question: An investor purchasing a corporate bond yielding 9.5% would find that a tax-free bond yielding _____ would be equivalent? The investor is in the 25% marginal tax bracket.

Answer: take 9.5% (.095) and multiply that by the percentage the investor keeps, which is 75% or .75. What is .095 times .75? 7.125%. That is all the tax-free municipal bond would have to yield to put the same dollars in the investor's pocket.

Tax-Equivalent Yield

A municipal bond doesn't have to pay as much interest as a taxable bond, since investors don't pay federal income tax on the interest paid by most municipal bonds. Someone in a 30% marginal tax bracket would come out better with a 7% municipal bond than with a 9.5% corporate or Treasury bond.

With the municipal bond, the investor would keep $70. With the taxable bond, she would keep 70% of 9.5%, which is only $66.50. To figure a municipal bond's **tax-equivalent yield**, take the yield the bond pays and divide by (100% minus tax bracket). In other words, in our example, take the 7% and divide it by 70% (100% minus 30%) to see that the municipal bond's 7% yield is equivalent to a 10% taxable yield for this investor.

Rather than have you calculate here, the exam might ask, "What is the following formula used to calculate?"

$$\text{Tax-exempt yield} / (100\% - \text{tax bracket})$$

The formula is used to calculate "tax-equivalent yield."

Question: An investor in a 30% marginal tax bracket would find that a General Obligation bond of the State of New York paying 4% is equivalent to a taxable bond paying...?

Answer: take the 4% and turn it into .04. Divide that by 70% (100% minus tax bracket). This investor would find that a 4% tax-free yield is equivalent to a taxable yield of 5.7%.

Risk-Adjusted Return

Investors are generally **risk averse**, which means they don't like risk. Risk is measured by volatility or **standard deviation.** The more unpredictable the returns of an investment, the riskier that investment is. So, if your investment adviser/portfolio manager earns an 11% total return for the year, you can then adjust that number for the risk it took to achieve it.

The **Sharpe ratio** is the most common form of **risk-adjusted return** measures. Using the Sharpe ratio, the portfolio manager only gets credit for the return he got above the **riskless rate of return**. If the account grew 11% when 3-month U.S. Treasury Bills yielded 4%, we take the 11% minus the 4%, and we're down to 7%. We then divide that 7% by the standard deviation/risk over the period. If the standard deviation is high, the Sharpe ratio is weak; if the standard deviation is low, the Sharpe ratio is strong. The higher the Sharpe ratio, the better the risk-adjusted return of the portfolio.

Alpha is the risk-adjusted return of the portfolio compared to the benchmark. If the exam talks in terms of "positive alpha" or "negative alpha," it is referring to whether the portfolio manager is adding value (positive alpha) or not (negative alpha) with his active management. Because hedge funds try to extract big market returns in all environments, they are often marketed to investors with the phrase "alpha-driven results." How good is your portfolio manager? Alpha points to the answer of that important question.

An investor who puts his money into index funds and lets it ride is on the opposite side of the chart from investors hoping their hedge fund manager can extract gains in bull, bear, or any other type of market. The best portfolio managers turn in results that exceed the expected return on a risk-adjusted basis—positive alpha. If the expected return is 8%, and the portfolio grows 9%, this represents positive alpha of 1%.

Time- and Dollar-Weighted Return

Mutual fund prospectuses and sales literature show the total return of the fund both in bar charts and in statistical tables. While a mutual fund might have a 10% return over the past six years, the average investor in the fund might have a much different experience, depending on whether we're looking at the **time-weighted return** or the **dollar-weighted return** of the portfolio.

See, when a mutual fund has a good run, the buzz attracts a lot of new investors and new money into the fund. What happens if the fund has an amazing run for two years, attracting lots of new money, but then the fund goes flat for the next four years? What happens is this: the time-weighted return looks okay, while the dollar-weighted return does not. The time-weighted return is the average of the total return percentages. The dollar-weighted return weights the returns based on the dollars invested.

Say a growth fund with $100 million of assets has an average annual return of 20% over a three-year period. That performance attracts new assets of $1 billion. And, then, the fund goes flat for the next three years. The average return of the two three-year periods is 10%, which is the time-weighted return.

How did the average investor do? Not so well. Ten times as much money was invested into the fund after the three-year winning streak, so most of the money in the fund has made absolutely nothing while a small percentage has made a decent return. The dollar-weighted return is less than 2%.

Outside of mutual funds, an individual investor who continues to make contributions to his account would need to figure his dollar-weighted return, since some of the contributions have been invested for many years while some have been invested only a few months.

Modern Portfolio Theorists analyze data and figure out likely outcomes based on probability. One example of this is called **expected return**. If we feel an investment will most likely return 8% and has a 75% probability of doing so, we can say the investment has an expected return of 6%. In other words, 8% times the 75% probability of getting the 8% equals 6% (.75 x .08 = .06).

More likely, the exam would express three possible outcomes and say that that investment has a 75% chance of returning 8%, a 10% chance of returning 12%, and a 15% chance of returning −10%. What's the total expected return? Take 75% of 8% (6%), add it to 10% of 12% (1.2%), and add that to 15% of −10% (−1.5%). That's a total expected return of 5.7%.

What happens if we expect 5.7% and get −29.3%? That's why we don't guarantee results.

Rather than use numbers or calculations, the exam might want you to define expected return as "possible return on an investment weighted by the likelihood of the outcomes."

Sometimes expected return and standard deviation are lumped together to make vague predictions about an investment's results. For example, the expected return for the stock market (S&P 500) is, say, 10%, but the standard deviation is 15. What does that tell us about next year's stock market results? Not much, unfortunately. All it can tell us is that about two-thirds of the time, the market returns are somewhere between +25% and −5%, since we add and subtract 15 from the expected return of 10. Ninety-five percent of the time, the market is somewhere between +40% and −20% (two standard deviations). We could do "three standard deviations," but most people get scared out of stocks as soon as they see that the market can end up doing just about anything any given year. Which is, of course, what makes investing in stocks so much fun in the first place.

Question: PDQ common stock has a 40% chance of appreciating 10% and a 60% chance of appreciating 8%. Therefore, its expected return is…

Answer: just take 40% of 10 (4%) and add it to 60% of 8 (4.8%). The expected return is 8.8%.

For evaluation purposes, portfolio managers compare the performance of their portfolios to some **benchmark**, like the S&P 500 index. The most helpful comparisons compare a portfolio to a benchmark that most accurately reflects the makeup of the portfolio. In other words, if the mutual fund owns mostly technology stocks, why compare the portfolio to a pharmaceutical industry index? More accurately and more usefully, we would compare it to a technology index.

If my client invests in blue-chip companies in various industries, maybe I use a "blue chip index" such as the **Dow Jones Industrial Average**. If I manage a small-cap portfolio, I'm trying to beat the **Russell 2000**, or the S&P SmallCap 600. If I'm the manager of a mid-cap portfolio, I'm hoping to beat the S&P MidCap 400. If I'm a bond fund manager, I'm being matched up against various bond indexes.

Weighting

Indexes generally assign more weight to stocks inside the index, based either on **market cap** or the share price itself. The Dow Jones Industrial Average gives more weighting to stocks priced around

$100 than to those priced at, say, $25. So, the exam could say that the DJIA is a "price-weighted index of 30 large, mostly industrial stocks." S&P doesn't use the share price in and of itself to weight their indices; instead, they use **market capitalization**.

Of course, the concept of "weighting" is nothing new. In high school and college, you might have taken courses that made your mid-term worth 30% of the final grade, the homework 10%, class participation 10%, and the final exam 50%. In that case, the final exam was heavily "weighted" at five times the importance of either the homework or the class participation. Within the S&P 500 MSFT is weighted more heavily than many other stocks that comprise the large-cap index.

Possible Calculations

The exam might expect you to calculate a mortgage payment for a hypothetical client. Maybe you'll see something like this: Jennifer Myers is financing a $275,000 home with a 30-year fixed-rate mortgage of 6.5%. If she makes a down payment of 20%, her first monthly payment will be closest to which amount?

Okay, if Jennifer is putting down 20%, she's borrowing 80% of the purchase price. 80% of $275,000 is $220,000. The first year's interest payments will be 6.5% of $220,000 divided over 12 monthly payments. That's $14,300 in interest for the year, or about $1,191.66 per month. In interest. Is her mortgage an interest-only mortgage? If so, the answer is $1,191.66 per month. But, if it's a 30-year fixed-rate mortgage, there's no way to quickly figure how much principal is added to her payment to amortize/pay off the loan over a 30-year schedule. If the exam makes it a 30-year traditional mortgage, it must expect you to do the calculation we just did and then conclude that the payment is not all interest but is, rather, the interest plus a few hundred dollars of principal.

Therefore, you eliminate $1,191.66 and any answer that is lower than that. On the other end, if an answer is too high, like, say, $2,945.52, eliminate that one. Why? You know the interest component of the monthly payment is about $1,200—no way is $1,700 or so on top of that going toward the principal.

The monthly payment (without taxes and insurance) in this example is closest to $1,390.55.

The test might expect you to calculate how long a retiree's money will last if his IRA account earns X percent while he, meanwhile, is withdrawing Y amount. So, we need to go back to our formula for future value (FV). In our examples, we were assuming the investor would leave the money untouched so that if it compounds at 3% it's always the principal times 1.03. However, if the account is earning 3% while the account owner is withdrawing $12,000 a year, obviously, the account will be exhausted at some point. Which is, of course, the point of having a retirement account. The trick is to die before you run out of money rather than the other way around.

If the IRA is earning 3%, while the owner is withdrawing $12,000 a year from the account, how long before he runs out of retirement money? Let's say the IRA starts out at $100,000. The account grows 3% over the year, to $103,000. The client removes $12,000 at the end of the year, so the principal drops to $91,000. If that compounds at 3%, we get $93,700. The client removes $12,000, and now the account is down to $81,700. At this rate, the account will be exhausted in about 11 years.

Unfortunately, my assumptions there were extremely simple. To do a more realistic estimate of proper withdrawal rates, financial planners often use **Monte Carlo simulations** to estimate what would happen if inflation or interest rates went to this or that level. The Monte Carlo method is used in many different professions for decision making. The process uses multiple values for things like interest rates, stock market returns, inflation, etc. to come up with possible outcomes that should give the investor a more realistic plan for retirement.

Now What?

Securities agents are not tax professionals, so they can't give tax planning advice or tackle big problems related to estate planning. But, they have to talk about the tax implications of investing, accurately, and without harming the investor. Therefore, a possible question could be:

One of your customers has received a distribution from the ABCD All-American Tax-Exempt Bond Fund you recommended to her 37 months ago. If this is a distribution of net long-term capital gains, you would accurately inform the customer that
   A. The distribution is exempt from federal but not state taxation
   B. The distribution is exempt from state but not federal taxation
   C. The distribution is exempt from both federal and state taxation
   D. The distribution is subject to both federal and state taxation
EXPLANATION: with the name "tax-exempt" right in the name of the fund, it sure is tempting to assume that all distributions from the fund are tax-exempt. Of course, nothing is ever that simple. First, even if this were a regular distribution from the interest payments received by the fund, it would be subject to state taxation. Right there, we can eliminate Choice B and Choice C. Again, if this were an income/dividend distribution coming from the bond interest received by the fund, then the answer would be A. However, this is a capital gains distribution, and, therefore, it is subject to taxation at both the federal and state levels. Eliminate Choice A, leaving us with
ANSWER: D

If the agent in the situation above gets in a hurry one day, he might accidentally tell this client to spend the distribution on a new Cadillac, thinking it is all tax-exempt. Later, when the customer finds out it was subject to her long-term capital gains rate of maybe 15 or even 20%, well, that's the kind of problem that agents and their regulators would rather avoid.

Registered representatives sell a lot of mutual funds. A test question might ask something like this:

A mutual fund investor receives a dividend distribution of $500 and a long-term capital gains distribution of $250. What is true if the investor reinvests both distributions into more shares of the fund?
   A. She defers taxation until the new shares of the fund are ultimately sold
   B. The full amount of the reinvestment is added to her cost basis
   C. The amount of any taxes due is added to her cost basis
   D. The dividend is added to the cost basis, while the capital gains distribution is subtracted

EXPLANATION: even though Choice A is tempting, remember that mutual funds offer no tax deferral. Tax-deferral is provided by various tax-advantaged account. Eliminate Choice A. Choice B kind of seems logical at first maybe—let's put in on the side. Choice C looks even more logical—again, put it on the side. Choice D makes no sense at all, so we can eliminate that one. Okay, so we know it's either B or C. Do we add the full amount of the reinvestment or just the amount of the taxes paid on the reinvestment? What is "cost basis"? Cost basis can be thought of as all the money that has gone into an investment and been taxed. What you pay for a stock or bond is your cost basis. What you pay for a mutual fund is your cost basis. And then, since your dividends and capital gains are taxable whether you reinvest or spend the check, you add the full amount of the distribution to your ever-rising cost basis any time you reinvest. Eliminate Choice C, leaving us with

ANSWER: B

It's time to do the online review exercises. After a break, take the chapter review quiz. Then, watch the related training video lessons before moving onto the fourth chapter.

CHAPTER 4: Serving Customers

Now that we have looked at all the securities available to investors and the many factors that affect their value, let's talk about what a registered representative does for a living in relation to these investment options.

Customer Accounts

The job of a registered representative is to open accounts for customers, help them determine suitable investments, and execute purchases and sales of stocks, bonds, mutual funds, and annuities, etc.

Let's start with the first step, opening accounts.

Opening Accounts

You have heard their names on TV or seen them in magazine ads: Charles Schwab, TD Ameritrade, E-trade, Goldman Sachs, Fidelity, etc. Maybe you've seen branch offices for such firms at the mall, or on one of the floors at your office building. What is happening inside these offices? Customers are investing in the stocks, bonds, mutual funds, and options that we have looked at in earlier chapters. Maybe the customer was pulled in by an advertisement on TV or the car radio. Maybe she was recommended by a friend. Whatever pulled her toward the front door, your job is to get her to sign up for a new account.

➤ *New Account Form*

You, the registered representative, will fill out the new account form, often over the telephone. You should obtain the following information from the new customer:

> Full name and address
> Home and work phone numbers
> Social security or Tax ID number
> Employer, occupation, employer's address
> Net worth
> Investment objectives (speculation, growth, income, growth & income, preservation)
> Estimated annual income
> Bank/brokerage firm reference
> Whether employed by a bank or broker-dealer
> Third-party trading authorization (if any)
> Citizenship (doesn't must be an American)
> Whether the customer is of legal age (not a minor child)
> How account was obtained (referring broker-dealer, investment adviser)
> Whether customer is an officer, director, or 10% shareholder of a publicly traded company

As a registered representative for a broker-dealer, you are supervised by **principals**, people who have passed not only their Series 7 but also their Series 24, 9/10, what have you. The principal has sign-off power over all kinds of important matters, and one thing a principal must always sign off on is a new account. So, the registered representative is listed on the new account form, but it's the principal/branch manager who must sign it to accept the new account. Surprisingly, there is no rule that says the customer must sign it. And, of course, that statement is always true except when it isn't. What we mean is that the customer can open a **cash account** without signing the new account form, but if she's opening a **margin account** or wants to trade options, she must sign it.

And, even though the customer is not required to sign the new account form for a pay-as-you-go cash account, she does need to verify that the information recorded is accurate, and she must sign that acknowledgment. The firm is required to send the customer a copy of the new account form within 30 days of opening the account and within 30 days of any major change in the information. Every 36 months the firm must verify the customer's information, too. Why? Making suitable recommendations to customers is your main job. If you're looking at customer information that is no longer accurate, your recommendations will most likely be unsuitable. For example, one of your customers used to trade a lot of speculative stocks because he owned a seat on the Chicago Board of Trade and had an annual income of just under $2 million. Turns out, the guy went bust last year, had his 70-foot yacht repossessed, did a short sale on a high-rise condominium, and is now living in his parents' basement in Western Springs. So, if you're still recommending high-risk securities to this guy, you're probably making unsuitable recommendations.

Unsuitable recommendations frequently lead to fines and suspensions from FINRA, and customers have been known to recover the money they lost by filing an arbitration claim. So, as the NYSE has been saying for centuries, the first rule for the registered representative is to "know thy customer." Since customers' situations change frequently, you and your firm need to keep up with the changes.

The Series 7 will likely ask some questions based on the bullet list above. For example, can the customer list only a PO Box? No. Even though your firm can send correspondence to the customer's PO Box—account statements, proxy statements, trade confirmations—your firm still needs to get a residential/street address from the customer. What if the customer refuses to provide a social security or other tax ID number? The account can still be opened, but the firm must notify him that the IRS is going to demand that a certain percentage of any interest, dividends, or capital gains must be withheld by the broker-dealer—known as a **backup withholding**. If the customer sells 100 shares of ABC for a profit, he won't be able to pull all of it out in cash at this time. Rather, a percentage will go to the IRS.

Surprisingly, even in today's climate, customers can open **numbered accounts**. This does not mean that the customer remains anonymous. Rather, it means that the customer does not want a lot of people at the firm talking about his or her financial business. The customer would need to sign a written statement acknowledging that she owns the account identified only with a number, and your firm must keep that on file. Whether an account is identified by a name or a number, remember that account information is considered confidential. This is the customer's personal business, and you know how touchy some people get over financial matters. So, the information you obtain on a customer can only be released with the customer's written permission, or if there is a legal requirement to turn it over—the SEC, FINRA, a divorce or probate court, or your state regulator, for example, has subpoenaed the information. But, if somebody calls up claiming to be the customer's fiancée and just wants to know how much dividend income she should expect this month, do not release any information to him.

Unfortunately, sometimes customers end up losing money by following the recommendations of their registered representatives. Sometimes, the customer assumes the rep was not at fault. Other times, this being America, the customer demands her money back. FINRA has a system in place to handle such disputes, called **arbitration**. Members of the securities industry are automatically required to use arbitration to handle disputes between firms or between registered representatives and their employing broker-dealers. But a customer only must use arbitration if she has signed a **pre-dispute arbitration agreement**. If your firm somehow failed to get her signature on that agreement, the customer would be free to sue you and your firm in civil court, where her attorneys could keep filing appeal after appeal until you cry uncle. To avoid the lengthy and expensive process of civil court, broker-dealers use arbitration. The pre-dispute clause must make it clear that the customer generally gets only one attempt at arbitration—no appeals—and that the arbitrators are not required to explain their decisions, and that many of them come from the industry.

So, if she loses, say, $100,000 following her registered representative's recommendations, the arbitrators could decide a whole range of outcomes. Maybe she gets $100,000, maybe she shares half the blame and gets $50,000. Maybe she gets nothing at all, and the arbitrators won't even explain why they decided against her. You can probably see why this arbitration thing needs to be clearly explained before the firm tries to hold the customer to the process by signing on the dotted line.

Finally, if the test asks about the customer's educational background, remember that it is not relevant. Educated people frequently do the dumbest things with their money, and high school dropouts have been known to make money in the market even as all the MBAs, CFAs, and CFPs consistently lose their shirts. So, we won't ask for the customer's educational level or record it on the new account form.

> *Instructions for Securities, Cash, and Mail*

> Securities

When a customer buys securities, somebody must hold them. There are three basic ways this can happen:

Transfer and ship
Transfer and hold in safekeeping
Hold in street name

Maybe Grandma wants to put the cute, colorful Disney stock certificates right over the baby crib in the spare bedroom. If so, she'll request that you register the certificates in her name and ship them—**transfer and ship**. I, myself, don't want the responsibility of protecting the certificates from damage or misplacement. I mean, I could get them re-issued by the transfer agent if I lost them, but that's a pain in the neck, and there will be fees involved. So, rather than having the securities shipped, I could have the broker-dealer transfer the securities into my name and then hold them in the firm's vault (**transfer and hold**). The firm would likely charge a fee to do that. So, what I do is what most customers do these days—have the broker-dealer hold the securities in **street name**. The exam might say that the firm in this case is the "nominal owner" and the customer is the "beneficial owner" of the securities. And, as we're about to see, shareholders can now use the **direct registration** method.

Whatever the customer chooses, the fact is that most customers these days have never seen a stock or bond certificate because their broker-dealer holds them in street name (name of the firm) and may have them on deposit at centralized "depositories" such as the **Depository Trust Company (DTC)**. From there, the securities are transferred through electronic book/journal entries only, which explains why many registered representatives have also never seen a stock or bond certificate. It also explains why good record keeping is such a concern for your firm's principals and for FINRA. From the Depository Trust Company's website at www.dtc.org we see how things currently work in terms of how a customer can register/hold securities:

> With the implementation of direct registration, investors have three securities ownership options:
>
> *Physical Certificates*: Certificates are registered and issued in the investor's name. The investor will receive all mailings directly from the issuer or its transfer agent, including dividend or interest payments, annual reports, and proxies.
>
> *Street Name Registration*: Securities are registered in the street name of the investor's broker-dealer. While no physical certificate will be issued to the investor, the broker-dealer will issue, at least quarterly, account statements of the investor's holdings. The broker-dealer will pay dividends or interest to the investor, as well as provide the investor with mailing material from the issuer or transfer agent.
>
> *Direct Registration*: This option allows the investor to be registered directly on the books of the transfer agent without the need of a physical certificate to evidence the security ownership. While the investor will not receive a physical certificate, he or she will receive a statement of ownership and periodic (at least yearly) account statements. Dividend or interest payments, proxy materials, annual reports, etc., will be mailed from the issuer or its transfer agent.

Direct registration, then, is a relatively new development. The website referenced here mentions that since the NYSE allowed their listed companies to issue spin-off stock and stock-split shares as book-entry statements instead of certificates, some 300 companies have decided to allow shareholders to use direct registration with the transfer agent, rather than via their broker-dealer under the street name method.

> Cash

Stocks have been known to pay dividends. Bonds pay interest to the account. So, if the securities are held in street name by the broker-dealer, the customer needs to indicate whether the firm should credit her account or send a check. Also, customers will sell securities from time to time, so the customer needs to indicate what should be done with the cash in the account. It can be "swept" into a money-market account (usually a government/Treasury money market account for ultimate safety).

Alternatively, the cash can be sent to the customer, or it can simply be credited to her cash balance until she decides how to reinvest the proceeds into more securities.

> Mail

The firm will be sending the customer monthly or (at least) quarterly **account statements** confirming the positions in the account and the value of the securities and the cash. Also, any time the customer buys or sells, a **trade confirmation** will be mailed to the customer's address of record. These days, statements and confirmations are often sent by email, but a customer must sign off on this method, which is much faster and cheaper for the firm to use. Confirmations and statements must be sent to the customer, unless the customer has instructed the firm in writing to send them elsewhere, e.g., his financial planner/investment adviser. Or, if the customer gives written instructions to hold back on delivering such mail while she is traveling, the firm can hold it for a reasonable length of time as instructed by the customer.

➢ Accounts for Industry Personnel and Immediate Family

The new account card asks if the customer or a family member works for a broker-dealer. If so, the employer will be notified in writing. If the member firm belongs to the NYSE, permission to open the account is required. For MSRB and FINRA firms, notification is required before the firm opening the account can proceed. For NYSE and MSRB firms, duplicate trade confirmations will automatically be sent to the employer, but for FINRA firms, duplicates are sent only upon request from the employer.

Account Transfers

Customers frequently transfer their accounts to other firms. This is generally done through something called an **ACAT**, which stands for **Automated Customer Account Transfer**. The ACAT provides instructions to the broker-dealer for transfer and delivery. The firm receiving the request has one business day to validate the instructions or take exception to them. The following are the reasons that the firm might "take exception" to the transfer instructions:

Customer's signature is invalid or missing
Account title does not match the carrying firm's account number
Social security number does not match
Account number is wrong

Once the account and positions have been validated, the firm has three additional business days to complete the transfer. FINRA states that:

> *The receiving member and the carrying member must immediately establish fail-to-receive and fail-to-deliver contracts at then-current market values upon their respective books of account against the long/short positions that have not been delivered/received and the receiving/carrying member must debit/credit the related money amount. The customer's security account assets shall thereupon be deemed transferred.*

In English, they're saying that at this point, both sides need to establish what has not been received or delivered in terms of money and securities, based on current market prices, and at that point the account is deemed to have been transferred, even if the carrying broker-dealer must send cash and/or securities at a later date.

SIPC

I mentioned that my broker-dealer was holding my cash and securities. What if it turned out that they were on the brink of bankruptcy and started pledging my securities and draining my cash position to keep their creditors off their backs? If the firm went belly-up, the creditors who now have my cash and/or securities aren't likely to let go of them.

Luckily, my accounts are covered by SIPC. Perhaps you've seen the little "SIPC" sign in the office of a broker-dealer? It stands for the Securities Investor Protection Corporation, a non-profit, industry-funded insurance company. It provides coverage of each customer account up to a total of $500,000, of which only $250,000 may be cash. So, if the investor has securities worth $200,000 and a cash position of $300,000, SIPC will cover all the securities but only $250,000 of the cash.

Commodities are not considered securities and are not covered. Mutual funds are held by the transfer agent, so if the broker-dealer fails, they weren't holding customer mutual fund shares, anyway.

If a broker-dealer goes belly up, a trustee is appointed and on that day they value each account and cover each separate customer up to the full amount. A separate customer means a separate account title. If an individual has a TOD account, an IRA account, and then a joint account with his wife, those are three separate accounts all covered up to the maximum. A cash account and a margin account would not be two separate accounts, however. When a cash account is turned into a margin account, the account number does not change. Margin is just the approval to trade on credit.

One of the most important points about SIPC is that it is *not* the same thing as the FDIC. In fact, at SIPC's website (www.sipc.org) there is a link under "Who We Are" called "Why We Are NOT the FDIC." Securities investments are not protected by FDIC. You have probably seen that warning on the first page of most mutual fund prospectuses, too. FDIC insures bank deposits. When a bank also sells securities, they must use disclaimers such as "No bank guarantee," "not FDIC insured," or "may lose value" so that customers understand just how far they have wandered from the safety and security of a bank deposit, CD, etc., even if they are in the same building.

If a broker-dealer is affiliated with a bank—as many are—customers are usually given the option of having their un-invested cash "swept" into either a non-FDIC-insured money market mutual fund or an FDIC-insured deposit account. Either way, the customer's cash is considered "safe," but a registered representative still must know the difference between SIPC on one hand and the FDIC on the other.

Death of a Customer

What should you do if one of your customers dies?

> Cancel all open orders
> Mark the account "deceased"

Freeze the account
Await proper legal papers

What should you do if you get a phone call from a young woman claiming to be the executor of your elderly customer's—apparently her grandmother's—estate? Well, definitely, don't start transferring or liquidating assets based on a phone call. Until you and the back office people see the information below, just sit tight. The proper legal papers authorizing you to transfer or sell securities are:

Certified copy of death certificate
Letters testamentary (court appointment)
Inheritance tax waivers

A certified copy of the death certificate proves the customer is dead. If the broker-dealer just took people's word for it, imagine how many elderly investors could have their accounts drained by sleazy family members! Inheritance tax waivers show that the estate is not subject to estate tax, and the court appointment verifies that the executor does, in fact, have the legal authority to execute legal and financial transactions on behalf of the deceased.

If it's a discretionary account (discussed up ahead), the discretion is terminated upon the death of the customer. If it's a custodial account for a minor, the assets are not immediately transferred to the child's parents. Rather, they become part of the child's estate.

Protecting Seniors and Other Vulnerable Adults from Financial Exploitation

FINRA has proposed rules designed to protect certain investors from caregivers or family members who might try to exploit their assets held by a broker-dealer. If adopted, the rule will apply both to senior investors and any adult with a physical or mental impairment that renders him unable to protect his own interests. New rules will require member firms to make reasonable efforts to obtain the name and contact information for a trusted contact person upon opening a customer's account. Then, if the firm ever suspects that financial exploitation could be occurring, they will notify the customer's trusted contact. Although firms will not be required to spot potential exploitation and prevent it, they will be granted safe harbor for putting a temporary hold on an account if they suspect financial exploitation is going on.

Rather than discuss the details of a rule that had not been finalized at the time of this writing, let's talk about what FINRA is already doing to protect such investors. As their website explains, "On April 20, 2015, FINRA launched a toll-free senior hotline – 1-844-57-HELPS – to provide older investors with a supportive place to get assistance from knowledgeable FINRA staff related to concerns they have with their brokerage accounts and investments. To date, FINRA has received over 1500 calls on issues including how to find information on their brokers, calls from children of deceased parents trying to locate assets or having difficulty moving assets from a brokerage firm, concerns from seniors ranging from routine poor service complaints to routine sales practice issues at firms, and fraud raised by a senior and/or child on behalf of senior investors."

Individual Account

When the account is owned by an individual, a registered representative may only discuss the account with and take orders from the individual owner. For an **individual account** the only way a registered representative could take orders from another party is if the individual account owner grants **power of attorney** or **trading authorization** to him, and the firm keeps the signed authorization on file.

Pay-On-Death

A **transfer on death** or **pay-on-death account** provides a way to transfer assets without the hassle and cost of probate. If an investor sets up an account this way, the executor or administrator of the estate will not have to take any action to ensure that the securities transfer to the designated beneficiaries when the account owner passes away. With TOD registration the investor maintains complete control of the assets during his lifetime. The named beneficiaries have no access to or control over the assets while the account owner is alive. A "POD" or "payable on death" account is the same idea applied to a bank or credit union account. As we saw, a pay-on-death bank account can also be referred to as a "Totten trust."

A related idea is the **durable power of attorney** that an individual can grant to someone else. A durable power of attorney would stay in force even after the individual was declared mentally incompetent. The person granted this durable power of attorney can make healthcare, financial, and legal decisions for someone who is incapacitated.

So, if your customer were incapacitated due to dementia, an agent could accept orders from the person granted durable power of attorney, after verifying that the person has been granted that power by the customer.

The durable power of attorney goes into effect if the individual becomes incapacitated. The power ends when the individual dies.

Joint Accounts

When two or more individuals jointly own the assets in the account, we call it a joint account. All the owners sign a joint account agreement. We can accept orders from any of the parties, and we can send mail to any of the parties. But, when we cut a check or distribute securities, they must be made out to all names on the account. In other words, if the account is entitled Barbara Williams and JoAnne Stevens, **Joint Tenants in Common,** do not cut the check to Barbara and tell her to settle with JoAnne next time they have lunch. Cut the check to "Barbara Williams and JoAnne Stevens, as Joint Tenants in Common."

A **Joint Tenants with Rights of Survivorship** (JTWROS or JTROS) account gives the survivor rights to all the assets. When one account owner dies, the surviving owner owns all the assets.

However, if the account is a Joint Tenants in Common (JTIC) account, when one party dies, at least part of the assets go to that person's estate. For JTIC accounts, the account owners indicate what % each party owns in the account agreement. For JTWROS, that wouldn't matter, as all assets go to the survivor.

Married couples often use either joint tenants in common or joint tenants with rights of survivorship accounts. However, such accounts also do not require the account owners to be married and may have more than two owners. On the other hand, a **tenancy in the entirety** account can only be established by a married couple. What separates these accounts from the other two is that while they are alive neither spouse can sell or give away his interest in the property without the consent of the other spouse, and creditors of either spouse cannot attach and sell one debtor spouse's interest in the property--only creditors of the married couple can do that.

If a test question says that one of your customers has an individual account at your firm and is now deceased, know that in a "common law" state, his wife only has a claim on half the assets if she is listed as an account owner. On the other hand, if we're in a "community property" state, the wife owns half of whatever the customer earned while they were married, whether he thought to name her on the account or not. In a transfer-on-death account, the deceased customer would have named a beneficiary, but that is subject to challenge, especially in "community property" states. Assets the now deceased husband had before the marriage would generally not be subject to a claim by the wife.

Discretionary Accounts

When a registered representative can trade the customer's account without talking to the customer first, we call this situation a **discretionary account**. In other words, what is purchased and sold for the customer is up to the agent's and firm's discretion. That means if the registered representative decides to buy 1,000 shares of MSFT, he can do so without first contacting the customer. The customer must sign a discretionary authorization form to grant this authority to the agent and firm, and the account must be reviewed more frequently, but that's about it. From then on, the registered representative can buy or sell securities for the customer without first talking to him.

On the other hand, unless the account is a discretionary account, the only thing that can be determined for the customer is the time or price at which to execute a specific transaction. So, if a customer calls you up and says, "Buy me some computer chip manufacturers today," do you need discretionary authority before you buy 100 shares of Intel?

Yes. If you choose the particular security (or the number of shares), that requires discretionary authority. If a customer calls up and says, "Buy 1,000 shares of Intel today," do you need discretionary authorization? No, your customer told you what to buy and how much of it to purchase. The only thing left for you to decide is the best time and price at which to do it, and time/price discretion does not require discretionary authorization over the account. The order involves "time/price discretion," in other words, but it doesn't require the account to be established as a discretionary account. These market orders that don't have to be placed immediately are called "market not held orders." They are only good for that day and may not be executed tomorrow or the next day without talking to the customer again.

When entering a discretionary order, the registered representative marks the order ticket "discretionary" at the broker-dealer, and a particular principal would be assigned to make sure the securities purchased are appropriate and that the agent isn't churning the account. Remember that having the power to choose investments is often convenient—not only for you but also for the customer—but the securities professional still must purchase what is suitable for the customer given her objectives, time horizon, risk tolerance, and capital resources. If a registered representative purchases unsuitable investments for a discretionary account, it's not just a bad idea—it's a violation of SEC, SRO, and state securities regulations.

Investment Advisory Accounts

Investment advisers typically have the discretion to enter trades for their clients' accounts, and those accounts are often held in custody by a broker-dealer independent of the advisory firm. The broker-dealer would need to verify that the investment adviser has discretionary authorization to enter transactions in those accounts. It would be the broker-dealer sending customers their account statements, at least monthly, by the way, rather than the adviser. And, the broker-dealer can pay the adviser the customer's advisory fee, provided the adviser sends a billing statement to both the broker-dealer and the customer.

Health Savings Accounts

As nice as it is to take money out of a Roth IRA tax-free, remember that there was no tax deduction back when that money went in. With the Health Savings Account (HSA), on the other hand, contributions are deductible and withdrawals used to pay medical expenses are tax-free.

The account receives favorable tax treatment and is tied to an insurance policy called a high deductible health plan (HDHP). To be eligible for one of these accounts the individual can be covered under no other plan and must be below the eligibility age for Medicare. HSAs are owned by the individual, even though these plans are frequently offered through an employer. If an employee changes jobs, his HSA is portable—it's his account. There is no pressure to spend any amount of money from one's health savings account each year. Even if there is money in the account, the individual is not required to use the account to pay for medical expenses. Many people choose instead to pay expenses out-of-pocket and let the account balance continue to grow tax-deferred until they really need it in their golden years.

Saving For Education

529 Savings Plan

The **529 savings plan** allows investors to save/invest for education. Usually it is a family member putting money away for a child's education, but the beneficiary does not have to be a child, or even a blood relative of the donor. In fact, an individual can set up a 529 plan for him or herself. The person who opens the account is the owner. The beneficiary is the person who will use the money for education. For 529 savings plans, the owner controls the assets.

Contributions are made after-tax (non-deductible), but the withdrawals used for qualified education expenses are tax-free at the federal level. Notice how I said "federal level." The plans are state-specific, so some states may tax the withdrawals. That means that if Grandma lives in New Jersey and buys a Wisconsin plan, New Jersey could end up taxing the money that the grandkids use for college. Then again, New Jersey might allow Grandma to deduct her contributions for purposes of state income taxes. So, you don't want to buy into a 529 savings plan without first checking how it will be taxed by the state.

And, even with the federal taxation, the withdrawals for education must be qualified withdrawals that cover tuition, room & board, books, etc. The expenses must be directly related to education; otherwise, the account owner will be subject to a 10% penalty plus ordinary income tax on any earnings withdrawn. If the beneficiary decides he doesn't need the money, the account can name a second beneficiary without tax problems, if the second beneficiary is related to the first.

And there is one area that can lead to confusion. Remember that when setting up a 529 plan it makes no difference whether the account owner is related to the beneficiary. It's just that if an individual starts a 529 plan for a beneficiary and then discovers that the child has no intention of going to college, then if he wants to avoid tax implications, he can only change the beneficiary to a blood relative of the beneficiary. If he wants to change beneficiaries to someone not related, he would have to deal with the 10% penalty and ordinary income tax ramifications.

When the donor is putting money into a 529 savings plan on behalf of her granddaughter, she is making a gift. Gifts over a certain amount are taxable to the one making the gift. With a 529 savings plan, this grandmother can contribute up to the gift tax exclusion without incurring gift taxes, and can even do a lump-sum contribution for the first five years without incurring gift tax hassles. In other words, if the annual gift tax exclusion is $14,000, she can put in $70,000 for the next five years. If she and Grandpa are married-filing-separately, they could put in twice that amount, or $140,000, without any gift tax issues. Note that if someone uses the five-year-up-front method, they can't make any more gifts to the beneficiary for the next five years without dealing with gift taxes.

The owner of the plan maintains control over the assets, deciding when withdrawals will be made. The money can be withdrawn to cover higher education expenses, such as tuition, books, and room and board. Bear in mind that it doesn't have to be "college," necessarily—just any school higher than high school, basically. So, if the exam asks if you can use the assets to go to heating & air-conditioning school, tell it that as long as the school is an accredited post-secondary institution eligible to participate in a student aid program, the answer is yes.

Prepaid Tuition

If you're sure that Junior won't mind going to college in-state, you might want to lock him in as a future Boilermaker, Hoosier, or Sycamore through a plan whereby you pay for his tuition credits now for any public school in the fine state of Indiana. I didn't say you were locking him into being *accepted* at IU or Purdue, but he would get to go to a state school with a certain number of credits already paid for. Parents worried about the ever-rising cost of tuition, then, can pay today's prices and redeem the credits more than a decade into the future.

These tuition credits cover tuition and fees only. If the child gets a scholarship or doesn't need the money because of something tragic like death or disability, a refund is typically provided plus a modest rate of interest. The exam could refer to prepaid tuition plans as "defined benefit plans." You pay for the tuition credits now, and then you hope the state can afford to provide the benefit of education when your child needs it.

Coverdell Education Savings Account

A **Coverdell Education Savings Account** (CESA) also allows for after-tax contributions (non-deductible), but the current maximum is only a few thousand dollars per year per child. While the 529

Plan is for higher education only, the Coverdell plan can be used for elementary, secondary, and higher education expenses. The distributions are tax-free at the federal level if used according to the plan guidelines. As with the 529 plan, the Coverdell ESA account can be used for education expenses, including tuition, books, and room and board. In a Coverdell contributions must stop on the beneficiary's 18th birthday, and the assets must be used for education or distributed to him by age 30. Also, there are income limits on the donors of a CESA, similar to the limits placed on people trying to fund their Roth IRAs.

So, should you use a 529 plan or a CESA? Generally, it would come down to the amount of money you want to contribute. If you're going to contribute only a few thousand dollars, you might as well use the CESA. If you want to put large amounts of money away, you'll pretty much have to use the 529 plan. Either way, you'll get tax deferral and tax-free withdrawals at the federal level, assuming you do everything according to plan.

UGMA/UTMA Accounts

If a donor wants to donate money for the benefit of a minor, all she has to do is set up the account as either an **UGMA** or **UTMA** account. UGMA stands for "Uniform Gifts to Minors Act" and UTMA stands for "Uniform Transfers to Minors Act." All states except Vermont and South Carolina have now adopted UTMA laws, which supersede UGMA laws. Either way, the child is going to eventually be in control of the assets, either at age 18 in a few states or age 21 in most states. There are even a few states that allow the transfer to happen as late as age 25, but that is the maximum and also not typical. The state used is typically where the minor resides, although it could be where the custodian resides.

Setting up the account requires no supporting documentation. The donor needs the minor's social security number and also provides the tax ID number of the custodian. The donor often manages the account as the custodian, although the two could be different parties, as well. If the donor is trying to minimize the size of his estate to avoid estate taxes, he will typically appoint another party as the custodian. Otherwise, the assets would be counted under his estate.

Either way, the account is opened as either UGMA or UTMA, making sure there's just one adult custodian and one minor child per account. You can't have two adults as custodians, and you can't have more than one minor child per account. You also can't have a corporation or a partnership acting as the custodian. Only an adult human being can serve in that role. And, that adult is a fiduciary, meaning if he "invests" the money at the racetrack or tries to engage in naked options, he could be forced to refund any losses caused by his lack of prudence.

If the exam asks what happens if you want to establish an UTMA for your niece, whose parents "oppose the gift," tell it that if you have the minor's social security number, you can open the account. The minor's parents have no access to the account that you will set up and/or manage as custodian. In fact, one cold probably keep them in the dark entirely about the existence of the account.

A proper title for an UTMA account would look like this: Mark Michelson, as Custodian for Michael Michelson under the Illinois Uniform Transfers to Minors Act. The adult custodian is the "nominal owner" while the beneficiary is the "beneficial owner" of this account. The gifts are considered "irrevocable and indefeasible," which means they cannot be taken back or treated as loans to be repaid. When the beneficiary reaches the state's age of majority (adulthood), there is nothing the donor or custodian can do to stop him from selling off all the securities and buying a Corvette. In a formal trust account—which we'll discuss up ahead—that sort of thing can be avoided. But an UTMA/UGMA account is a "trust" whose terms are drawn up in state law, as opposed to a formal trust account in which the trust documents stipulate the terms.

Of course, there is no reason to assume all young adults would be foolish with the account assets. Parents might set up an UTMA account so that the child at age 21 has money to make a down payment on a house or start a business. But, what the parents intended as a down payment on a house could, again, be spent on anything the new adult wants, period.

Since the child won't be needing the money for, say, eight years, surely the adult custodian can sort of "borrow" from the account from time to time as needed, if she repays it eventually, with interest, right?

Wrong. These accounts receive special tax consideration, so if the custodian is pretending the account is an UTMA account, but uses it to get interest-free loans, the IRS might start talking about tax fraud, back taxes, and penalties-plus-interest.

If the question asks if room and board would be a legitimate expense to be covered by an UTMA account, the answer is no. Room and board is something parents are expected to provide to their children, and not through some tax-advantaged account. Approximately the first $1,000 of income is exempt from taxation no matter how old the beneficiary is. The next $1,000 or so of income is taxed at the child's income tax rate. Seriously. Then, if there is more than about $2,000 and the child is under age 18, it will be taxed at the higher of the child's or the parents' tax rate. Or, if the child is over 18, that income is taxed at his tax rate.

So, I don't expect that level of detail in a test question, but I would expect a question asking about whether this account is tax-deferred or not. No. Some of the income is taxed favorably, period. Another tax consideration is that the donor can reduce the size of his estate by transferring assets to an UTMA/UGMA; however, if he wants to be sure the assets are excluded from his estate, he should appoint someone else as custodian.

Setting up UTMA/UGMA accounts requires no legal work, making it much cheaper than establishing a formal trust account. These days, investors typically use 529 Plans to save for college rather than custodial accounts, because assets in an UTMA/UGMA count against the child's chances of receiving financial aid more so than assets in a 529 Savings Plan.

Calculating Educational Funding Needs

When a financial planner estimates the educational funding needs for a client, she uses the following five inputs:

- Current tuition cost per year
- Education inflation rate
- Number of years of college attendance

- Number of years before college begins
- Expected investment return

Because tuition has historically risen even faster than the general rate of inflation, the calculation uses a specific rate for education costs, above the rate of the CPI.

Ownership and Estate Planning Techniques

Estates

When someone dies, the IRS and state tax collectors may end up taxing the value of assets (house, farmland, bank account, stock, life insurance, etc.) owned at the time of death.

Wait, how can the IRS can tax a dead person?

They can't. A dead person is not a person. The dead person's possessions become part of a **legal person** known as an **estate**. The estate is what can be taxed.

An estate is a legal entity in the same way that a trust, a corporation, or a partnership is a legal entity. None of those entities is a human being, but all are "legal persons" in the eyes of the law.

Think of it this way: Otis Redding is not a legal person. However, the Estate of Otis Redding *is* a legal person. The estate is a legally recognized entity. Like a corporation, it has an FEIN (federal employee identification number) and pays taxes on all those royalties received from songs like "Dock of the Bay," "R-E-S-P-E-C-T," and "Hard to Handle."

Like a corporation, the assets of the estate are separate from the assets of the beneficiaries of the deceased person's will. So, if some bass player files a claim that Otis Redding owes him $8,000,000, what happens if all the estate assets are only worth $1,000,000?

The bassist should have tried to collect sooner. Maybe he'll get every dollar of that eight million claim through the courts, but the children do not have to make up the difference. The estate is a separate legal entity, just like a corporation.

When Grandma dies, her checking and savings accounts, CDs, real estate, life insurance, etc., all go into a new legal entity called an estate. If you were named the executor of the estate, it's your job to get several death certificates and do all the paperwork required to transfer her checking and savings to a new bank account entitled, say, Jason Miller, Executor for the Estate of Maude L. Miller, Deceased. If Grandma owned stocks and bonds, they need to be re-titled in the name of the estate, as well. This will require affidavits, signature guarantees, stock powers, letters of office; the whole nine yards. When you effect these transfers of ownership, make sure you have plenty of original death certificates and that the court appointment/letters of office are no more than 60 days old.

You've probably heard the phrase that the only certainties in life are death and taxes. When we talk about estates, we're talking about both. When someone dies, the assets go into his/her estate and taxation is a concern. We'll look at the strategy of establishing trusts to minimize estate taxes in a few minutes, but, first, let's make sure we understand how an estate is treated for the purposes of taxation.

Think of an estate account as a short-term account where safe, short-term debt securities are generally the only appropriate investments. T-Bills and other money market instruments are usually the right recommendation for an estate account. Assuming no tax or legal problems, the assets of the estate will soon be distributed to the heirs/beneficiaries. What happens if the stocks, bonds, CDs, etc., earn income in the meantime? That income is taxable to the estate. But, the legal fees charged by the estate attorney may well cancel that income out. If, however, the estate earns $5,000 in dividend income when the legal bills are just $2,000, there is $3,000 of taxable income there. The estate will file a tax return (a 1041) for that income.

Will the value of the estate itself be taxed? First, we start with the gross estate—the value of the assets before taking deductions. The following are included in the value of the gross estate:

- house, farmland, savings account, checking account, investment accounts, clothing, oil paintings, Harley, etc.
- value of insurance and annuity contracts
- assets placed in revocable trusts
- does not include assets placed in irrevocable trusts (except certain property transferred within three years of death!)

So, we add those values and then start subtracting things to reduce the value of this estate. If we reduce the value enough, we might avoid paying any estate taxes. The following reduce the gross estate:

- Funeral and administrative expenses
- Debts owed at the time of death
- Any charitable gifts made after death
- The marital deduction

The "marital deduction" means that husbands and wives pass their property to one another at death without paying estate taxes, which seems fair enough. It's when the assets then go from the "second to die" to the heirs that things get dicey. So, after we've added up the value of all the assets (gross estate) and subtracted the first three bullet points above, maybe what's left is $1 million. Will we have to pay estate taxes?

No. Currently, there is a lifetime credit of $5 million for estates, indexed for inflation. Since the taxable estate is below that number, we avoid paying estate taxes on the estate itself, as an entity or "person."

How are the heirs taxed once they inherit their share? Remember that when Grandma died, we took the fair market value of her securities as our cost basis, which we enjoyed. When we sell the stocks and bonds for more than that fair market value, the excess is a long-term capital gain, even if we realize it two or three months from now.

Generally, the state only goes after estate taxes when the estate is large enough to be taxed at the federal level.

What if several months ago Grandma had gone in for her regular checkup and found out from her doctor that she had maybe two months to live? To avoid estate taxes, couldn't she just start handing out envelopes of cash to all the kids and grandkids?

Sure. In fact, the IRS is fine with that. See, the gifts that Grandma gives to individuals while she is alive are also taxable if they are over a certain amount. That number is forever changing but is currently $14,000. Whatever the amount is, there is an "annual gift-tax exclusion," which means that if Grandma gives anyone other than her husband a gift worth more than that amount, she must start chipping away at her lifetime gift tax credit. The amount of the credit that was used up over her lifetime will reduce the amount of the credit you and the other beneficiaries can use when trying to reduce the size of the estate to avoid paying estate taxes.

The IRS defines a **gift** as "transferring property to someone else and expecting nothing in return." The IRS also points out that the following can be considered gifts:

- selling something at less than its value
- making an interest-free or reduced-interest loan

Wait, so when Grandma sold Uncle Bill the back forty for $70,000 below market value, this could have been considered a "gift" to Uncle Bill?

Absolutely. So, when Grandma goes around giving people things worth more than the current annual exclusion, she files a return and tells the IRS that she's using part of her lifetime credit. What if the gift is worth no more than the current exclusion of $14,000?

Then nobody needs to know anything. In the following cases, no gift taxes would be due and no returns would have to be filed:

- Gifts made to a spouse
- Gifts that do not exceed current exclusion amount
- Paying tuition costs for someone else—payable directly to educational institution
- Paying medical costs for someone else—payable directly to the care provider
- Political and charitable donations

Gift Splitting

The IRS is clear on the topic of **gift splitting**, so let's use their Publication 950 from www.irs.gov to make the point:

> Harold and his wife, Helen, agree to split the gifts that they made during the previous tax year. Harold gives his nephew, George, $24,000, and Helen gives her niece, Gina, $18,000. Although each

> gift is more than the annual exclusion ($14,000), by gift splitting
> they can make these gifts without making a taxable gift.

That means is that half of $24,000 ($12,000) and half of $18,000 ($9,000) would be less than the annual exclusion of $14,000, so they can treat each gift as half from Harold and half from Helen. No gift taxes would be due and none of the lifetime credits would have to be used up, but the IRS requires that they file a gift tax return.

Trusts

There are many horrible ways to die, none of which needs to be mentioned for our purposes here. From a financial planning standpoint, however, the worst way to die would be to die without a will or trust. Folks who do this are said to have died **intestate**. If that happens, not only do the deceased's assets go through the probate process, but, first, an administrator of the estate has to be named by the probate court.

At least with a will the deceased's wishes are stated, and—if there are no challenges—the distribution of assets will be made according to the stated will of the now deceased individual. When someone dies with a will, an executor is named. Although that saves some time with the probate process, it puts the estate through that process.

What's the problem with probate? The probate process makes the estate assets and their distribution a public record. It delays the distribution of the assets. And, it can easily consume 4% of the estate's value, as the beneficiaries watch money that would have gone to them get eaten up in legal and accounting fees.

So, before we look at all the different types of trusts, remember that what they all have in common is avoiding the probate process. Like an estate or a corporation, a trust is a separate legal entity with its own FEIN. The trust holds assets, just as a corporation or an estate holds assets. The person who administers and oversees the investments of the trust is the "trustee." The one who grants the assets to the trust is called the "grantor." And the ones who benefit from the trust are called the "beneficiaries."

When an adult sets up an UTMA/UGMA account, the minor owns and controls the assets at the age of adulthood/majority, which is usually no later than age 21. If he sets up a trust, on the other hand, he can specify all types of things in the trust agreement about when the beneficiary is to receive distributions and how much he is to receive. The exam might point out other advantages of establishing trusts:

- Faster and less costly way to transfer property upon death, when compared to a will
- Avoids probate court process (time, expense), especially if property is owned in several different states
- Eliminates challenges to estate—just specifically disinherit anyone who poses a challenge to your wishes upon your death
- Keeps transfer of property private
- Reduces amount of estate taxable to heirs

Revocable, Irrevocable

Reducing the amount of the taxable estate can come down to the difference between revocable and irrevocable trusts. In general, assets placed in an irrevocable trust do not count as part of the estate, while assets placed in a revocable trust do count. What's the difference? If the trust is revocable, the person who set it up (grantor) can revoke the assets and change the terms of the trust documents. Therefore, not only are those assets taxable to the grantor while he/she is alive, but when he/she dies, those assets do count towards the value of the estate, even if the assets were never "taken back." If a grantor sets up an irrevocable trust, the assets cannot be revoked.

Remember that the assets placed in an irrevocable trust are no longer taxable to the grantor while he is alive, and when he dies, the assets do not count towards the value of the estate that the heirs are hoping to keep below the amount that triggers estate taxes.

The irrevocable trust will either distribute income to the beneficiaries, or it won't. Either way, the interest, dividends, and capital gains generated are taxable. If the income is distributed to the beneficiaries, they include it on their own income tax forms. If the income is not distributed, it is taxable to the trust.

In a revocable trust, or even in an irrevocable trust where the grantor or grantor's spouse benefits from the income, the grantor is subject to taxation while he is alive. In fact, because the IRS basically ignores the trust structure for revocable trusts, they are often called **grantor trusts,** because there is really no separation between the grantor and the trust at this point. Unlike with the simple and complex trusts we are about to discuss, a grantor trust is not treated as a separate entity.

Simple vs. Complex

For purposes of paying federal income taxes all trusts are either simple or complex. A **simple trust** is required to distribute all income to the beneficiaries annually. No charitable donations can be made from a simple trust, and distributions from the principal or **corpus** of the trust are not regularly made to the beneficiaries.

A **complex trust** can make charitable donations and make regular distributions to the beneficiaries from the corpus or principal of the account. A complex trust also routinely retains some of the income generated by the account rather than distributing it the way a simple trust is required to do. If the trust does any of the three things mentioned, it is treated as a complex trust (charitable donations, retain income for corpus, distribute from corpus). In either case, income that is distributed to the beneficiaries is taxable to them, while income retained by the trust is taxable to the trust itself.

Although we don't associate the simple trust with distributions from corpus, the trustee can use his discretion to make a distribution of, say, a capital gain on a large stock sale to the beneficiaries. In any year that the trustee does so the trust is treated as a complex trust under the tax code.

Inter Vivos, Testamentary

A trust can be established while the grantor is alive or through his will when he dies. A trust established while the grantor is alive is called an **inter vivos** trust, while a trust established upon the death of the grantor through the terms of a will is known as a **testamentary trust.** An inter vivos trust can be either revocable or irrevocable. A testamentary trust is an irrevocable trust. In fact, all revocable trusts become irrevocable upon the death of the grantor, who is no longer able to revoke.

Inter vivos trusts are sometimes called "living trusts" while testamentary trusts are sometimes called "will trusts."

Split Trusts

If a married couple wanted to leave money to their children and their favorite charity, rather than forming separate trusts, they could form a **split trust**. A split trust or "split-interest trust" is a type of trust account that names both charitable and non-charitable beneficiaries. The most common types of split trusts are **charitable remainder trusts** and **charitable lead trusts.** A charitable remainder trust is an irrevocable trust that can be set up in two ways. With both accounts the priority is to leave adequate funds to the non-charitable beneficiaries, while also leaving a donation to the named charitable organization. In a charitable remainder annuity trust the beneficiaries receive fixed payments for a stated period, after which the remaining assets are distributed to the charity.

In a charitable remainder unitrust the non-charitable beneficiaries receive a stated percentage of the account's fair market value for a set time period after which the remaining assets are distributed to the charitable beneficiary or beneficiaries. Typically, the grantor is also the income beneficiary of the charitable remainder trust. That means he gets to take a charitable deduction on the amount contributed to the trust immediately and then live off the prescribed income stream for the rest of his life, knowing the remainder goes to a charitable beneficiary.

A charitable lead trust is set up when the priority is to leave assets to the named charitable beneficiary/beneficiaries, while the non-charitable beneficiaries will wait for their distributions. A charitable lead trust can also be set up as either an annuity or a unitrust. Either way, the designated charitable beneficiaries receive regular distributions of assets from the trust at scheduled intervals for a stated time. Once the organizations have received the pre-set number of donations, the trust distributes the remaining assets to the non-charitable beneficiaries.

Pooled income funds are trusts that enable donors to pool their donations into an investment fund. Unlike the other split trusts, a pooled income fund is owned by the charitable organization that benefits from it. The donors themselves are the beneficiaries of the trust, receiving distributions from the income generated by the fund while alive. When the donors pass away, their share of the fund is then distributed to the charity. This type of trust allows donors to enjoy investment income throughout their lives while ultimately benefiting a charitable organization.

Totten Trusts

If you were to ask a banker how you can pass assets to your loved ones and avoid probate, chances are you would hear the term **Totten trust.** A Totten trust is really a payable-on-death (POD) bank account. If someone wants the assets in the account to pass upon his death to a named beneficiary, a Totten trust can be set up. All that is required is some paperwork establishing the account as a payable-on-death account, which the bank keeps on file. The POD beneficiary has no rights to the assets while the grantor is alive, and when the account owner passes away, the beneficiary typically needs to go to the bank with a death certificate and a photo ID. The bank could place a brief hold on the funds, but the transfer of assets does not go into the probate process.

A Totten trust is a bank account whose balance will pass to a named beneficiary. It is a revocable trust.

Bypass Trusts

For a wealthy couple avoiding estate taxes can be a challenge both when the first spouse dies and when the second spouse passes. A bypass trust transfers the maximum amount subject to the unified credit into a trust whose income can be used by the surviving spouse over his or her lifetime. The surviving spouse cannot demand a distribution from corpus, but the trustee could use his discretion to make such a distribution.

When the surviving spouse dies, the assets in the bypass trust do not count towards his or her estate. In other words, when set up correctly, the assets that pass to a bypass trust avoid estate taxes for both spouses.

AB Trusts

Although not as common today, spouses used to frequently create AB or "split" trusts to avoid estate taxes. In this rather complex scheme, when one spouse dies, two trusts are created. One trust is irrevocable, the other revocable. As with any irrevocable trust, the surviving spouse may not change the terms of Trust A. The surviving spouse typically only receives the income generated by the irrevocable trust. Trust B—the revocable living trust—would be under his or her control.

Unfortunately, the surviving spouse would have to hire a tax attorney to determine how best to divide the spouses' assets into the A and B trusts and would have to keep records for the irrevocable trust and file tax returns annually.

QPRT, Q-TIP

One way for a wealthy person to reduce estate tax liability while staying in his home for a while is to create a Qualified Personal Residence Trust (QPRT). This maneuver would allow him to transfer the property to the trust at today's value as opposed to the almost certainly higher value in the future. The grantor retains tenancy for 10 years, after which the property passes to the beneficiaries of the trust. The home could not be seized by creditors, as it would now be owned by a trust. Creditors could only claim the value of the remaining term of tenancy—the rental income, for example—but could not seize the property itself.

People who are in a second (or third, etc.) marriage often want to provide for their spouse's income needs after death but also provide for their children of a previous marriage. This is often done by establishing a Qualified Terminable Interest Property trust or Q-TIP. The Q-TIP provides that the surviving spouse will receive a prescribed lifetime income stream from the trust when the other spouse dies. The trust principal then passes to the children after the spouse dies or remarries. Q-TIPs are common with second marriages because they preserve assets for the benefit of the children from an earlier marriage, rather than the spouse's children or family. Q-TIPs can also protect a spouse when the grantor believes he or she may waste the assets during the spouse's lifetime.

To qualify for the marital deduction, income from the Q-TIP must be used only for the benefit of the surviving spouse during his or her lifetime. Estate taxes on the principal are then deferred until the surviving spouse dies. In other words, passing the income to the surviving spouse does not trigger estate tax liability. That happens when the assets transfer to the next generation.

Crummey Trusts

We talked about the annual gift tax exclusion amount earlier. And, we saw that the value of a life insurance policy is included in the gross estate, unless some fancy estate planning is performed, that is. A **Crummey Trust** is an irrevocable life insurance trust designed to pay the premiums on a life insurance policy owned by a trust and also get around the annual gift tax exclusion amount. In a Crummey Trust the beneficiaries have the stated right to withdraw the gifts made to the trust for a certain time. Because they never do that, the gifts are used to pay the premiums on the life insurance policy, which is owned by the trust to keep its value separate from the estate of the deceased.

Uniform Prudent Investor Act

Trustees are sometimes family members and sometimes financial institutions. Either way, a trustee is a **fiduciary** who can be sued for negligence or self-dealing by the beneficiaries of the trust. The **Uniform Prudent Investor Act** is a piece of model legislation that provides guidance to trustees interested in avoiding such lawsuits and regulatory actions. While in earlier times a "prudent investor" was expected to avoid risk, as the Uniform Prudent Investor Act (UPIA) clarifies, the trustee's job is to consider the risk-reward nature of a portfolio so that a risky security here might be balanced out by an uncorrelated and safer security over there. For example, junk bonds might fit into an overall portfolio if balanced out by U.S. Treasury Notes. Therefore, there is no list of prohibited investments. Rather, the trustee needs to read the trust documents and manage the risk/reward nature of the portfolio in a way that best meets the needs of the beneficiary or beneficiaries of the trust.

Diversification is considered a major part of any prudent investment strategy, and a trustee would only choose not to diversify if he had a good reason. For example, maybe he needs to wait until a short-term capital gain can be turned into a long-term capital gain before selling and rebalancing.

Some executors and trustees are just family members who have no training or experience in financial matters. While they would be held liable for fraud or self-dealing at the expense of the beneficiaries, their level of skill and care would not be assumed to be as high as that of bank's trust department. So, the UPIA clarifies that amateur fiduciaries are not held to the same standard as professional fiduciaries in terms of exercising skill and care in financial matters. Again, though, a test question could have an amateur fiduciary spending the interest payments received on Treasury Bonds when that money should, instead, be going into the estate account and eventually distributed to the other beneficiaries. That is a matter of self-dealing and "breach of fiduciary duty" regardless of her knowledge of the securities industry. If the executor decides to just move into the house of the deceased rather than get it sold for the benefit of the estate, this would also be a breach of fiduciary duty, no matter how often it probably happens in the day-to-day world.

In olden days, no responsibilities could be passed off, but the UPIA points out that a trustee could manage the investments of a pension trust while an insurance company handles payouts and actuarial calculations, for example.

Disclaiming an Inheritance

You could see a test question presenting a situation in which the wife of a recently deceased husband does not want or need the assets she is set to receive from the husband's will or trust agreement. If she wants the assets to bypass her and go to the next generation, she needs to formally disclaim the inheritance without ever touching or benefiting from the assets. This means she must do it in writing and within 9 months of the death of the deceased individual. If she does it correctly according to federal and state law, the assets are treated as if she never touched them. However, the decision to disclaim the inheritance is irrevocable. She cannot come back later asking for help from the trust. Also, she does not get to designate who receives the assets. That is up to the probate court or the trust agreement.

Generation Skipping Tax Issues

As we have seen, when assets pass from parents to the next generation, estate taxes could be due. Therefore, if someone tries to bypass that generation and leave assets to a family member who is two generations younger, the transfer is subject to both a generation-skipping tax and the estate tax. The person who is two generations younger is known as a "skip person," and an unrelated person is a skip person if he or she is more than 37.5 years younger than the one transferring assets. But, skip persons end up being off the hook if the parent dies before the transfer is made. That's right, if the generation to whom assets would have otherwise been transferred is already deceased, there was no end-run around the tax code, eliminating the generation-skipping tax.

Individuals and married couples can pass a certain amount to a skip person that is exempted from the generation-skipping tax, both numbers indexed for inflation. To leave assets for a skip person and avoid tax liability, many wealthy people establish generation-skipping trusts, whose sole purpose is to receive the maximum amount exempt from the generation-skipping tax and then provide benefits from there to the named beneficiaries.

Qualified Domestic Relations Order

As the IRS explains on their website (www.irs.gov),

> *A qualified domestic relations order (QDRO) is a judgment, decree, or court order (including an approved property settlement agreement) issued under a state's domestic relations law that:*
>
> 1. *Recognizes someone other than a participant as having a right to receive benefits from a qualified retirement plan (such as most pension and profit-sharing plans) or a tax-sheltered annuity,*
>
> 2. *Relates to payment of child support, alimony, or marital property rights to a spouse, former spouse, child, or other dependent of the participant, and*

> 3. Specifies certain information, including the amount or part of
>   the participant's benefits to be paid to the participant's spouse,
>   former spouse, child, or other dependent.

The topic of **qualified domestic relations orders** typically comes up during a divorce proceeding. When an attorney works out a divorce settlement agreement that divides various assets among the two soon-to-be-divorced spouses, he or she needs to include a qualified domestic relations order (QDRO) related to pension/retirement accounts. As the IRS defined above, the QDRO recognizes someone other than the plan participant—whom he or she is divorcing—as having a right to receive benefits from a qualified retirement plan. The QDRO states the percentage and/or number of payments the ex-spouse is to receive, which in most cases is 50% of the value of assets that was gained while the two were married—up to the divorce.

The smart move for tax purposes is for the ex-spouse to roll the money received into his or her own Traditional IRA. If this is pursuant to the QDRO, the spouse whose retirement account is being depleted avoids any taxes, and the ex-spouse whose retirement account is being augmented can defer the taxes until he or she takes withdrawals.

On the other hand, a painful move would be for a spouse to give a former spouse money from his retirement account without a QDRO in place. If that happens, the distribution is taxable to the spouse whose retirement account is being depleted and subject to a 10% penalty if he's not over 59 ½ years of age.

According to a helpful website (www.divorcesupport.about.com/od/pensionfundsandbenefits/f/qdro.htm):

A QDRO as part of a divorce decree should state the following:

- Name and mailing address of the "plan participant" (you) and the "alternate payee" (your ex)
- Each retirement qualified plan account to be split up under your divorce.
- Name of each plan to which the order applies.
- Dollar amount or percentage of benefits to be paid from each account to the alternate payee.
- Number of payments or the benefits period covered by the QDRO.

Margin Accounts

Investing "on **margin**" is a high-risk strategy that involves buying securities on credit, hoping to make more on the securities positions than the broker-dealer charges in interest on the margin loans. Broker-dealers love **margin accounts** because they open a whole new line of business. Suddenly they're credit card companies, and they don't even have to issue the little plastic cards. Plus, credit card companies have no collateral from their customers. In a margin account, customers pledge the assets they are buying on credit to the lender, the broker-dealer. If things turn south, the broker-dealer can sell the stock or bond to recover the money they lent. So, the interest rate they charge is lower than what we pay on a credit card, since they have collateral backing the loan.

People talk about the "equity" in their houses. Maybe they bought the house for $200,000 and borrowed $180,000 to do that. If so, their account starts out like this:

$200,000 Market Value

• $180,000 Money Owed
_____

$20,000 Equity

Equity equals the difference between what someone owns (assets) and owes (liabilities). Let's say that this home's value increased 15% for three years running. At this point the value of the asset has risen while the amount owed has dropped. The account now looks like this:

$304,175 Market Value

• $170,000 Money Owed
_____

$134,175 Equity

What can these homeowners do with that equity? They can borrow against it.

In a margin account, we don't buy houses on credit. Rather we buy stocks and bonds on credit. If their market value rises, we win. What if their market value drops? Then, we have a problem. This is, of course, where margin accounts get their bad name.

A "margin account" is a different type of account than a "cash account." In a **cash account**, customers must pay in full when they purchase securities, and they cannot sell short in a cash account. If the account is approved for margin trading, the customer can buy securities on credit and sell them short.

REG T

The Securities Exchange Act of 1934 gave the Federal Reserve Board the authority to regulate margin accounts. The "Fed" regulates credit, and one form of credit is the margin account, in which the broker-dealer fronts the customer half the purchase price of a security.

To purchase stock on margin, the broker-dealer follows **Regulation T (Reg T)**, which states that a listed stock can be pledged as collateral by the customer in exchange for a loan from the broker-dealer up to a maximum percentage of its value. Reg T tells broker-dealers how much credit they can extend to their customers—that percentage has been 50% for quite some time. The industry sometimes refers to the amount that a customer puts down as the "Fed call."

When a customer buys $200,000 of stock, he puts down ½ or $100,000. The other ½ or $100,000 is provided by the broker-dealer, who looks forward to charging interest on that $100,000 for as long as the customer would like to owe them. The amount that the customer puts down is referred to as "the margin." The "margin" refers to the amount of money the investor is required to deposit; the rest of the market value is extended on credit.

Regulation T requires 50% of the purchase price to be deposited by the customer within two business days after the settlement date of the transaction. Any market price change between the purchase of the security and the required payment would not affect the amount of the deposit the customer is required to make. If the stock purchased on margin rises from, say, $50 to $60, or drops from, say, $50 to $40, the margin call is based on $50 per-share; it is figured at the time of purchase.

Long Positions

Say a customer bought 1,000 shares @40 and made the required Reg T deposit of half or $20,000. At that point the customer's account looks like this:

$$\text{LMV} \quad - \quad \text{Dr} \quad = \quad \text{Equity} \quad \text{Reg T Deposit}$$

$$\$40,000 - \$20,000 = \$20,000 \qquad \$20,000$$

LMV stands for "long market value." It could be referred to as "market value" or "current market value." The "Dr" stands for "debit register," which can also be called the "debit balance." This is the amount the customer borrowed and owes his broker-dealer, like the mortgage balance that the homeowner owes the lender. So, the long market value of the stock he bought is $40,000. He made the required Reg T deposit of half—20K—the broker-dealer fronted him the other half. Do you suppose the broker-dealer wants that money back?

You bet, so it's a debit (Dr) to the client's account until he pays it off.

He "owns" an asset worth 40K and he owes 20K to the lender. That's why his equity is $20,000. Just like if you owed $80,000 on your mortgage when your house was worth $100,000—the difference of $20,000 is your equity.

Equity, Excess Equity

The investor has $20,000 of equity. What happens if the stock rises, to, say, $50 a share? The account looks like this:

$$\text{LMV} \quad - \quad \text{Dr} \quad = \quad \text{Equity}$$

$$\$50,000 - \$20,000 = \$30,000$$

The amount owed to the broker-dealer (Dr) didn't change. The long market value of the stock went up, increasing the equity dollar-for-dollar. Now, let's compare the equity of $30,000 to Reg T, which is 50% of the market value or "LMV." Reg T wants to see 50% equity in the account. Does this customer have at least half his "LMV" as equity? Half of 50K is $25,000. The customer has $30,000 of equity. That's **excess equity** of $5,000. Like this:

$$\text{LMV} \quad - \quad \text{Dr} \quad = \quad \text{Equity} \quad - \quad \text{Reg T} \quad = \text{Excess Equity}$$

$$\$50,000 - \$20,000 = \$30,000 - \$25,000 = \quad \$5,000$$

Since this customer has excess equity of $5,000, $5,000 is credited to a special line item called "**SMA**." SMA, which stands for **Special Memorandum Account,** is a line of credit that the customer can tap. I mean he can withdraw $5,000 of his cash, like it's in a savings account, right? Not at all. The $5,000 is just a number. But, if the customer wants to borrow that *amount* of money, he can. And whenever he borrows from SMA, that amount is added to the debit balance/debit register. See why customers love margin accounts, especially when the markets are moving in the proper direction? The customer can just tell the broker-dealer to cut him a check for $5,000, which will be added to his tab, like this:

$$LMV \quad - \quad Dr \quad = \quad Equity$$

$$\$50,000 - \$25,000 = \$25,000$$

Borrowing the cash didn't affect the long market value of the securities. We added the amount borrowed to the debit balance, which reduced equity and wiped out the SMA. SMA can be used as a cash advance that will be repaid with interest. Or, SMA can be used as an initial margin requirement for the purchase of more stock. So, instead of borrowing the cash, the customer could have used the $5,000 SMA credit to purchase $10,000 of stock. If so, the account would have looked like this:

LMV	Dr	Equity	SMA
$60,000	$30,000	$30,000	$0

If the customer buys more stock, that adds to the market value of securities held long in the account. Why did his Dr go up by $10,000? Because the customer in our example used his line of credit (SMA) as his margin deposit, and the broker-dealer fronted him the other half, or $5,000, which is also added to the Debit. So, he borrowed $5,000 from his line of credit (SMA), plus $5,000 that the broker-dealer fronted him for the additional stock purchase. In other words, when the stock moves your way, you can end up using borrowed money to borrow more money. When dividends, interest, or capital gains distributions from mutual funds come into the account, that income is applied to the debit balance. Therefore, SMA is affected by such income being applied to the debit.

Reg T demands that a customer put up 50% of the long market value initially. After that, what happens if the customer's equity dips below 50%?

Not much. Even though the account is called "restricted," there really aren't many restrictions. The customer is required to put up ½ to buy more stock. If the customer sells stock, he can withdraw/borrow ½ the proceeds.

Surprisingly, when the market value of a securities position drops, that does not affect SMA. It reduces the market value of the stock and, therefore, the equity, but SMA is just a line of credit. It does not get taken away. The customer can always use SMA so long as using it does not take him below the minimum maintenance requirement, which we're about to look at.

Minimum Maintenance

Reg T tells us what to put down on an initial transaction, and any excess above Reg T gives the customer "SMA." But, SMA and excess equity are terms used when the market is cooperating with the margin customer. What happens when the market goes the wrong way? Suddenly, the customer's equity is deficient, and he either must throw more cash on the fire or start liquidating securities.

Reg T requirements apply initially and then help us figure if the customer has SMA. The customer's larger concern is the SRO 25% minimum maintenance requirement. The regulators say that a customer's equity cannot go lower than 25% of the long market value. If it does, the customer gets a maintenance call to bring the equity up to the minimum 25%. If the customer can't deliver the cash, the firm sells securities equal to four times the amount of the maintenance call. The following numbers should help to clarify the concept of the minimum maintenance requirement:

LMV	Dr	Equity	Minimum	Call	Liquidate
40,000	20,000	20,000	10,000	0	0

At this point, the customer has twice as much equity as the minimum (25% of long market value).

If the stock goes from 40K down to 30K, we're okay:

LMV	Dr	Equity	Minimum	Call	Liquidate
30,000	20,000	10,000	7,500	0	0

But, if the long market value falls to 24K, we're in trouble:

LMV	Dr	Equity	Minimum	Call	Liquidate
24,000	20,000	4,000	6,000	2,000	8,000

The SROs demand $6,000 in equity, which is ¼ of $24,000, and the customer has only $4,000. So, the customer gets a maintenance call informing him that he needs to deliver $2,000. If the customer does that, the account looks like this:

LMV	Dr	Equity	Minimum	Call	Liquidate
24,000	18,000	6,000	6,000	0	0

He paid down the debit by $2,000 and now he has $6,000 in equity, the bare minimum of 25% of market value. If he didn't have the cash, the firm would have liquidated $8,000 worth of securities. If so, the account would have looked like this:

LMV	Dr	Equity	Minimum Maintenance
16,000	12,000	4,000	4,000

Whereas, it used to look like this:

LMV	Dr	Equity	Minimum Maintenance

24,000	20,000	4,000	6,000

Selling the $8,000 worth of securities reduced the LMV and the Dr by an equal amount, leaving the customer with exactly 25% equity. By the way, since the firm might have to sell a customer's stock in a hurry, they hold the customer's securities in "street name." That means the securities are registered in the name of the firm for the beneficial ownership (FBO) of the customer, who hasn't exactly paid for them yet.

Also, the 25% requirement is the minimum maintenance. Many broker-dealers require a higher minimum maintenance than just 25% to protect themselves. The one I use requires 33.3% as a minimum equity, in fact. The regulators are fine with that, so long as the firm does not let equity drop below 25%.

Account at Maintenance

In the example above the investor received a maintenance call when the market value dropped to $24,000. Luckily, he doesn't have to wait for such a drastic outcome before realizing the phone is about to ring. Back when he established the long position the market value was $40,000 and the debit balance $20,000.

At that point we can calculate the **account at maintenance** by dividing the debit by .75.

When we divide $20,000 by .75, we see that the lowest account value allowed before a maintenance call is $26,667. To double check that, we can take the equity that would be in the account--$6,667--and see if that is 25% of $26,667.

Bingo. Below that value the customer will be contacted by his agent to pay down the debit balance to bring the equity back to the minimum requirement.

Short Positions

When a customer sells short, he is selling borrowed securities in anticipation that he can replace them at a lower price. So, if he wants to sell short $10,000 worth of securities, he must deposit half that value, or $5,000 to meet the Reg T requirement. If he did so, his account would look like this:

Cr	$15,000
SMV	– $10,000
Equity	$5,000

The "Cr" stands for the "**credit**" and the "**SMV**" stands for "**short market value**," or, perhaps, we could just call it the "market value." In any case, when the customer sells short $10,000 worth of securities, that $10,000 is credited to the customer's account. Remember, he sold some stock—someone paid him $10,000.

So, our investor gets the proceeds from the sale, and deposits another 50% of that to meet the Reg T requirement. The $10,000 he took in for selling the stock, plus a $5,000 cash deposit, equals a total credit of $15,000.

If the "SMV" goes down, as the investor hopes, he'll have more equity. For example, if the SMV dropped to just $5,000, the customer's equity would increase by $5,000, like this:

Cr	$15,000
SMV	− $5,000
Equity	$10,000

The credit didn't change. He started with a credit of $15,000, and that's all the credit he's going to have. It's the market value (SMV) that changed, dropping in the desired direction for our short seller.

And if the market value of the securities sold short were to increase, his equity would shrink, like this:

Cr	$15,000
SMV	− $11,000
Equity	$4,000

How high can the SMV go before a customer gets one of those nasty maintenance calls? For short accounts, customers need 30% of their SMV as equity. If the customer's SMV is $11,000, he needs at least $3,300 in equity. You can find the highest SMV at maintenance by taking the "Cr" and dividing it by 1.3. Since the customer has a credit of $15,000, just divide that by 1.3, and you see that the highest SMV without a maintenance call is $11,538. If the securities' value doesn't exceed that number, his account will remain properly margined.

Combined Equity

To find combined equity, find the equity for the long positions and add it to the equity for the short positions. You can also remember that the formula for combined equity is:

$$LMV + Cr - Dr - SMV$$

Which is just another way of saying, "Add the two things that go on top and subtract the two things that go on the bottom." So, if a customer had an LMV of $20,000, a Cr of $20,000, a Dr of $10,000, and SMV of $10,000, his combined equity is $20,000:

$$LMV + Cr - Dr - SMV$$

$$20,000 + 20,000 - 10,000 - 10,000$$

In other words, he has $10,000 equity on the long positions, and $10,000 equity on the short positions. He must have 25% equity for the long, and 30% for the short. This customer is okay on both fronts. Each day the markets are open, the margin department recalculates requirements by marking to the market. If market values have gone the wrong way, the customer might receive a margin call. If market values have gone the right way, the customer might see SMA increase.

Marginable Securities, Accounts

Not everything can be purchased "on margin," but that doesn't mean it can't be purchased within a margin account. A "margin account" is an account that has been approved for margin. The following securities are "marginable," meaning they can be purchased using margin:

- NYSE, NASDAQ, AMEX stocks
- OTC securities on the FRB's approved list

The following can be purchased inside a margin account, but must be paid in full:

- Non-NASDAQ OTC securities
- Options
- IPOs or any new issue for 30 days
- Mutual fund shares

Watch out re: the above bullet list. If the exam question asks if options can be purchased "on margin," the answer is no. If the question asks if options can be purchased "in a margin account," the answer is yes. Also, a retirement account cannot be set up as a margin account, since it would be rather crazy to let retirees lose money that quickly, losing perhaps more than they initially deposit into the account. UGMA/UTMA accounts also may not be established as margin accounts.

Brokerage Office Procedures

Broker-dealers process orders, and each order passes through the following departments:

Order Room
Purchasing and Sales
Margin
Cashiering

When you, the registered representative, talk your customer into buying 10,000 shares of ABC, you will present the order for execution to the **order room**. We also call this the "wire room" because the order is then wired to the appropriate trading facility. Once the order has been executed, the order room forwards a confirmation or "execution report" back to you and also to the next department—purchasing & sales. After the order has been executed the "P&S" department inputs the transaction to the customer's account. The "P&S" department also mails (or emails) the trade confirmation to the customer, and that trade confirmation must be delivered no later than the settlement date. **Purchasing and sales** is also responsible for billing.

Now, you might think that something called the **margin department** would only handle transactions in margin accounts, but all transactions are sent through the margin department, whether for cash or margin accounts. The margin or "credit" department calculates the amount owed by the customer and the date the money is due. This department also calculates any money due to a customer. The **cashiering department (cashier)** processes all securities and payments delivered to the firm. This department also issues checks to customers. When the margin department issues a request, the cashiering department also forwards certificates (stocks, bonds) to the transfer agent. Basically, the cashiering department handles all receipts and distributions of cash and securities.

Another department that the test might bring up is the **reorganization department,** sometimes referred to as "reorg." When a merger takes place, shareholders of, for example, Gillette, must replace their shares with a certain number of shares of Procter & Gamble. The reorganization department makes this switch. It also handles bond calls and tender offers. A **tender offer** is a formal offer by a company or third party to purchase up to a certain amount of an issuer's stock at a fixed price for a limited time. The SEC requires anyone who owns more than 5% of a class of an issuer's securities to file a Form 13D, and anyone who will own more than 5% through a tender offer must file a Form TO. If the tender offer is a takeover bid, the subject company must also file a formal response to the offer with the SEC. If enough securities owners "tender" or present their shares to the purchaser, the tender offer will be completed. If not, the offer is withdrawn.

We wrote that the registered representative presents an order to the order/wire room. He does so by filling out and submitting an **order ticket/trade ticket**. An order ticket would contain at least the following information:

Account number
Registered representative number
Buy or Sell
If a sell: long or short
Stock or bond symbol
Number of shares, bonds
Exchange where security should be executed
Special instructions (if any)
Whether solicited, unsolicited, or discretionary

That last bullet item is a potential powder keg. See, some unscrupulous registered representatives have been known to place customer orders that no customer ever ordered. They do this by marking the ticket "unsolicited" and pretending that the customer called in the order. I guess they're hoping the customer doesn't watch his account closely, but all it takes is one customer to notice a trade he never placed and suddenly the registered rep is being disciplined for executing unauthorized transactions. It is not uncommon for such a registered representative to be barred from any further association with any FINRA firm, as he probably should be. It's the Wall Street equivalent of spending your friend's money without his permission.

Finally, the exam might ask a question about what information a registered representative needs to maintain. If so, tell it that a registered representative must maintain a record of each individual customer's current holdings and also a cross-indexed list of securities owned across the board with the names of customers and number of shares associated with it. So, he needs a list of which securities Joe Smith owns: MSFT, IBM, and ORCL. He also needs a cross-indexed list that shows, for example, MSFT and then which customers own how many shares of that stock.

A brokerage firm is a busy place to work. With registered representatives taking customer orders by telephone and/or reviewing the orders placed online, what are the odds that some of these transactions will end up going wrong? Pretty high. That's why every trade must be confirmed with the customer.

➢ *Trade Confirmations*

A **trade confirmation** confirms a transaction for the customer's review:

Account #	Transaction #	Capacity	Account Executive	
26597-5	006530698	Agent	GH	
Activity	Quantity	CUSIP	Price	Principal Amt.
Bought	10,000	3890227	$25.49	254,900.00
Trade Date	Settlement Date	Interest	Commission	Net Amount
04/22/2003	04/25/2003	N/A	$10.99	254,910.99
Symbol	Trade Description			
LGTO	Legato Systems, Inc.			

Notice how this document confirms the trade and tells the customer everything he needs to know about the transaction: the stock, the number of shares, the price of the stock, the commission, and the total price paid or received on the transaction, etc. I think of it as an invoice—a bill of sale; this is what we did for you, this is what it cost you, please keep this as a record of the transaction. Trade confirmations must be delivered no later than settlement, which is the completion of the transaction (T + 3 for stock, corporate bonds, and municipal bonds). Confirmations are often delivered by email these days, a much faster and cheaper method. Also, when we said that the firm can hold customer mail, this is one of the pieces of mail that might need to be held. Customers should also save their trade confirmations, to make it easier to report capital gains and losses each year, or to straighten out a sloppy broker-dealer who suddenly claims that you don't own 10,000 shares of IBM anymore. Oh yeah? Well here's my confirmation of the purchase—unless you have confirmation of a sale, guess what—I own 10,000 shares of IBM.

An SEC rule under the Securities Exchange Act of 1934 requires that a customer trade confirmation contain the following information:

> The date and time of the transaction (or the fact that the time of the transaction will be furnished upon written request to such customer) and the identity, price, and number of shares or units (or principal amount) of such security purchased or sold by such customer

> For a transaction in an NMS stock, a statement of whether payment for order flow is received by the broker or dealer and a statement that the source and nature of the compensation will be provided upon request

> In the case of any transaction in a debt security subject to redemption before maturity, a statement to the effect that such debt security may be redeemed in whole or in part before

maturity, that such a redemption could affect the yield represented and the fact that additional information is available upon request

That the broker or dealer is not a member of the Securities Investor Protection Corporation (SIPC), or that the broker or dealer clearing or carrying the customer account is not a member of SIPC, if such is the case

Whether the broker or dealer is acting as agent for such customer, as agent for some other person, as agent for both such customer and some other person, or as principal for its own account; and if the broker or dealer is acting as principal, whether it is a market maker in the security

If the broker or dealer is acting as agent for such customer, for some other person, or for both such customer and some other person:

The name of the person from whom the security was purchased, or to whom it was sold, for such customer or the fact that the information will be furnished upon written request of such customer

The amount of any remuneration received or to be received by the broker from such customer in connection with the transaction unless remuneration paid by such customer is determined pursuant to written agreement with such customer, otherwise than on a transaction basis

If acting in a principal capacity and not a market maker, the firm must disclose:

the difference between the price to the customer and the dealer's contemporaneous purchase (for customer purchases) or sale price (for customer sales) when executing riskless principal transactions

for stocks trading on an exchange or subject to last sale price reporting, the difference between the price to the customer and the last reported price

FINRA now requires additional information to be provided for fixed-income transactions in certain cases. For non-municipal fixed-income securities--which includes corporate and agency debt for purposes of the rule--in which the member firm acts in a principal capacity with a non-institutional customer the member must disclose the member's mark-up or mark-down from the prevailing market price for the security on the customer confirmation.

Well, not in all cases, as usual. FINRA states that "This information is required if the member also executes one or more offsetting principal transaction(s) on the same trading day on the same side as the customer trade, the aggregate size of which meets or exceeds the size of the customer trade." So, if the firm executes a lot of principal transactions in fixed-income securities throughout the day, this concern must be monitored closely. A firm that performs few such transactions, or never acts in a principal capacity with customers, would not have this concern.

> Execution Errors

The registered rep must check execution reports with order tickets. If the customer wanted to buy 1,000 shares of Cisco and ended up buying 1,000 shares of Sysco, well that's not what the customer ordered and is not, therefore, the customer's trade. The firm would eat that one. Likewise, if the customer had entered a buy-limit @30 but the firm accidentally bought the stock for more than $30 a share, the customer would not be required to accept the transaction. Or, if she had ordered 100 shares but the firm bought 10,000 shares, those extra zeroes would not be her problem. Firms must maintain an error account to keep track of, and deal with, these errors that can and do occur.

A single customer might have several different accounts at the firm. Or, maybe the firm has 10 customers named Joe Smith. Whatever the case, sometimes a security is purchased for the wrong account. If so, the registered representative needs to talk to a principal. The principal can grant permission to **"cancel and re-bill"** the transaction, which means to simply put the transaction in the proper account and keep good notes.

> ### > Reporting Errors

So, an error in the execution of the trade is one thing. On the other hand, if the registered representative merely gives the customer a mistaken report when the firm, in fact, did exactly as instructed, that's just a mistaken report. If the customer's order was filled as instructed, it's the customer's trade. Even if the firm sent a trade confirmation that was erroneous, that confirmation can be fixed and re-sent. The customer doesn't get to walk away from the trade based on some minor technicality.

➤ *Account Statements*

At the least, a broker-dealer must send account statements to their customers quarterly. It would only be that infrequently if there had been no activity in the account—an **inactive account**. Since there is usually activity in the account, most account statements are sent monthly. If any of the following had occurred in the account during the month, a monthly statement would be sent:

> Purchases or sales of securities
> Dividend and/or interest received
> Addition or withdrawal of cash or securities
> Margin interest charged to a margin account

The account statement shows:

> All positions in the account
> All activity since the last statement (purchases, sales, interest and dividends, etc.)
> All credit and debit balances

Account statements must contain a message to customers asking them to verify the statement and promptly report any discrepancy or error that they notice. This way, unauthorized transactions or plain old mistakes can be spotted and fixed sooner. As in, I don't remember talking to anyone about buying 1,000 shares of XYZ—what's going on here? And, it also ties in with SIPC protection. Remember that a customer's account is protected based on their account balance as of the day the trustee is appointed. The customer will need to show his/her account balance, and it would be a bad time to discover a major error *after* the broker-dealer had already gone belly up. *No, but I could have sworn I owned two hundred and fifty thousand dollars' worth of ORCL* isn't going to cut it. FINRA tells broker-dealers that they must:

> *advise all new customers that they may obtain information about SIPC, including the SIPC brochure, by contacting SIPC. Such members also must provide SIPC's Web site address and telephone number. Members must provide this disclosure to new customers, in writing,*

➤ *Proxies*

Back in olden days small shareholders weren't likely to cast votes at the annual meeting, unless they happened to live near corporate headquarters. The Securities Exchange Act of 1934 covered a whole lot of ground, and part of the ground covered had to do with public corporations/issuers letting shareholders vote by proxy. This way, I don't have to travel to Redwood Shores, California, just to cast my votes at the Oracle annual shareholder meeting. Instead, I can fill out the form I get from my broker-dealer and let them vote per my instructions. Usually these proxies go ahead and tell me how management thinks I should vote.

Of course, I can vote however I want with my number of shares. Or if I sign the proxy and fail to indicate how I want to cast my votes, then the board of directors/management of the company gets to use those votes as they see fit. If the matter is of no major importance, the broker-dealer can cast the votes on behalf of their customer, if the customer has failed to return the proxy at least 10 days prior to the annual meeting. A major issue, such as whether HP and Compaq should merge, would be a different matter. We're talking more like the decision to retain KPMG as the firm's auditor.

The Securities Exchange Act of 1934 also requires public companies to report quarterly and annually. So, the broker-dealer will end up forwarding those reports as well as proxy materials to their customers, but they won't charge the customers. This stuff is all a cost that the issuer must bear. Another name for a proxy is an "absentee ballot," by the way.

➤ *Annual Reports*

As we said, most broker-dealers hold customer securities in "street name," which is the name of the broker-dealer, for benefit of the customer. My stocks, for example, are registered to TD Ameritrade, FBO Robert Walker. Shareholders must receive annual reports from the issuers whose securities they hold, and the issuing corporations will send the reports to the broker-dealer, who must be sure the customer receives them. I have a thick stack of annual reports next to my desk from issuers such as Starbucks, Oracle, and a couple of REITs. TD Ameritrade mailed me those reports, just as they mail me proxy materials, either by mail or email. Again, we mentioned that customers can request a mail hold when traveling. Such mail would include trade confirmations, account statements, proxies, and annual reports.

➤ *Holding a Customer's Mail*

With all this mail coming to the customer's mailing address, what happens if the customer is going to be traveling or living at another address for an extended period? For how long can the broker-dealer hold back the delivery of the mailing pieces we just looked at? The FINRA rule says that the broker-dealer can hold customer mail, provided the following requirements are met:

The member receives written instructions from the customer that include the time period during which the member is requested to hold the customer's mail.

If the time period is for > three consecutive months, the customer's instructions must include an acceptable reason for the request (e.g., safety or security concerns). Convenience is not an acceptable reason for holding mail longer than three months.

The member informs the customer in writing of any alternate methods, such as email or access through the member's website, that the customer may use to receive or monitor account activity and information and obtains the customer's confirmation of the receipt of such information.

The member verifies at reasonable intervals that the customer's instructions still apply.

During the time that a member is holding mail for a customer, the member must be able to communicate with the customer in a timely manner to provide important account information (e.g., privacy notices, the SIPC information disclosures), as necessary.

And, above all, the rule requires that "A member holding a customer's mail pursuant to this Rule must take actions reasonably designed to ensure that the customer's mail is not tampered with, held without the customer's consent, or used by an associated person of the member in any manner that would violate FINRA rules or the federal securities laws." Why would the regulators be concerned with any of that? Maybe the customer's registered representative has been executing unauthorized transactions that he would prefer she not see in an account statement or trade confirmation. Or, maybe a family member has been gaining unauthorized access to the customer's account and—like the agent—doesn't want her to see what's been going on. I still remember a case where a "friend of the family" was able to perform switches on variable annuities and conceal the heavy surrender charges by having the paperwork sent to a PO Box that he controlled. For these reasons and more, it is important to be sure the customer is requesting the firm to hold back her mail and that the customer has a legitimate reason for asking the firm to hold back the delivery of account statements, trade confirmations, etc.

Clearing and Settlement

If I want to buy 500 shares of SBUX, my broker-dealer finds a market maker who wants to sell 500 shares right now at their offer price. You know that such trades settle "T + 3" or three business days from the trade date. But, what does that part—the next three business days—involve, if the trade is already completed?

Actually, the trade is not completed. When I buy those 500 shares of SBUX, let's say at $30 a share, my online account will show the 500 shares among my positions and will debit the $15,000 plus a commission for the purchase. But, those are just numbers on a screen at this point. Until the transaction is cleared and settled, nothing is completed. The firms that clear transactions in securities are known, not surprisingly, as **clearing agencies.**

There are two types of clearing agencies: clearing corporations and depository. **Clearing corporations** include: the **National Securities Clearing Corporation, the Fixed Income Clearing Corporation,** and the **Options Clearing Corporation (OCC).** The only depository is the **Depository Trust Company** or DTC. The SEC, as usual, explains the whole thing very well at their website, like so, "Clearing Agencies are self-regulatory organizations that are required to register with the Commission. There are two types of clearing agencies -- clearing corporations and depositories. Clearing corporations compare member transactions (or report to members the results of exchange comparison operations), clear those trades and prepare instructions for automated settlement of those trades, and often act as intermediaries in making those settlements. Depositories hold securities certificates in bulk form for their participants and maintain ownership records of the securities on their own books. Physical securities are maintained in vaults, and ownership records are maintained on the books of the depository. Clearing corporations generally instruct depositories to make securities deliveries that result from settlement of securities transactions. In addition, depositories receive instructions from participants to move securities from one participant's account to another participant's account, either for free or in exchange for a payment of money."

As the above indicates, trades among firms are automatically compared and locked-in by the NSCC. If there are discrepancies, or if a member does not recognize a trade, a **DK (Don't Know)** notice must be sent to the other side. Otherwise, trades are quickly "locked in," by the NSCC, who at some point during the T + 3 cycle guarantees performance of the transaction, eliminating "counterparty risk." That means that the sell side will be paid for the transaction, period.

The final stage of the process is **settlement**. This happens at the related entity called the DTC or Depository Trust Company, which, like the NSCC, is also a subsidiary of the Depository Trust Clearing Corporation (DTCC). Settlement occurs when payment is made and securities are delivered to the accounts of both sides of the trade. The regular way of settlement is T + 3, which stands for "Trade Date plus three business days."

As you might expect, securities transactions settle "regular way," except when they settle in one of the other ways below.

➢ *Cash Settlement*

A **cash settlement** settles "**same day**," meaning the day it is traded is the day that settlement occurs. If the trade happens before 2:00 p.m., it settles by 2:30 p.m. If the trade happens after 2:00 p.m., it settles within 30 minutes.

➢ *Next Day*

For a **next-day settlement**, the cash and securities must be available by the next day following the trade. Options and U.S. Treasury securities traded on the secondary market settle regular way next-day or "T + 1."

➢ *Seller's Option*

The exam may ask you about a **seller's option**. This is where the seller likes the price they can get today but—for whatever reason—won't be able to come up with the securities for a while. In this case the seller specifies the date on which they will be able to deliver the securities and may not deliver sooner than the fourth business day following the trade (I guess it would be T + 3 if it were any earlier, right?). If the seller specifies a certain date but ends up wanting to deliver the securities earlier, they must give the buyer a one-day written notice of their intention.

➢ *Buyer's Option*

The buyer could also specify the date when payment will be made for securities and accept delivery, which is pretty much the flip-flop of the seller's option.

➤ RVP/DVP

Certain institutional accounts avoid the risk of delivering securities before payment has been made by setting up a **DVP/RVP** account that uses **Delivery Versus Payment** settlement. As the name implies, payment must be made when or before the securities purchased are delivered. That is from the buyer's perspective. From the seller's perspective, the process is **Receive Versus Payment**. The DVP system ensures that securities will be delivered only if payment is made.

➤ Good Delivery

So, the buy side must remit the funds to the clearing agency, while the sell side must deliver securities. Remember that some customers still choose to have their securities "transferred and shipped" and some use direct registration. So when they sell stock, they are in possession of the certificates and must deliver them. Or, they must direct their bank to do so. Either way, if the stock or bond certificate is registered to Joe B. Kuhl, then it must be signed exactly as: Joe B. Kuhl. Under no circumstances, can the customer sign the certificate *Joey Kuhl*, no matter how cool he may, in fact, be.

Also, a security registered to more than one individual must be signed properly by all owners, and a security registered to a trust, an estate, a corporation, etc. must be properly signed by an executor, trustee, or corporate officer.

If a customer forgets to endorse the certificate, should you put it back in the mail? No, just send her a **stock power** and have her sign that instead. If it's a bond, guess what you'd send her?

A bond power.

These are also known as powers of substitution. It is usually the power of substitution that gets signed, rather than having the customer sign the back of the stock or bond certificate. That way, if the customer messes up the signature, they haven't destroyed anything of value. They can always try again until they get it right. The transfer agent must accept (or reject) the signature as valid, so, a signature guarantee is used. This is a medallion/stamp that NYSE member firms have, as well as bank officers. The stamp means that the holder has verified this signature is valid.

The transfer agent would reject the following signatures:

    Signature of a minor child
    Signature of an individual now deceased
    Signature of just one person in a joint account

What would you do if a sale were executed, with the securities endorsed by a person who has since died? The securities must be re-issued in the name of the estate or trust, with the executor or trustee properly signing after that has been taken care of.

Clearing and settling through the DTCC and its subsidiaries makes this next concern somewhat outdated, but the exam could still ask about the units for stock certificates in terms of delivery. When certificates come in to a broker-dealer, the back office must be able to separate round lots (100s) from odd lots (<100). So, if the trade is for 540 shares, what we'd like to see is 5 certificates good for 100 shares each and 1 certificate for 40 shares. We could also take a certificate for 90 shares and immediately stack it with a certificate for 10 shares—that would make a round lot, right? So, if we received 5 certificates for 90 shares, 5 certificates for 10 shares, and one certificate for 40 shares, this would be good delivery, too. We'd take a 90 and a 10 and make a round lot five times; then we'd have the odd lot of 40 separated all by itself.

What about 6 certificates for 90 shares each? Six times ninety = 540, right?

Yes, but it's not good delivery. If you take a certificate for 90 shares and stack it with another one for 90 shares, you do not have a round lot. It must be stackable into round lots without exceeding a round lot.

If we had a certificate for 200 shares and one for 300 shares, that would be fine. 200 and 300 are immediately "breakable" into round lots of 100, right?

Bond certificates delivered between broker-dealers must be $1,000 or $5,000 par value. If there are coupons (bearer, principal-only) missing, that's a problem. The receiving broker-dealer would cop such an attitude that if the missing coupon represented $60 of interest, they would deduct $60 from the money they send to the other firm. So there. If it's a municipal bond, the legal opinion must be attached. If there was no legal opinion obtained, the certificate needs to be stamped "ex-legal." Ex- means "without," as in "ex-dividend," which means the stock is trading without the dividend.

Delivery can be rejected by the firm representing the buyer if:

> Certificates are mutilated
> Certificates don't comply with the weird round lot thing we just looked at
> All attachments are not present (affidavit of domicile, stock power, etc.)
> Signature is invalid
> Signatures are not guaranteed
> Securities are delivered prior to the settlement date

If a stock is purchased on or after the ex-dividend date, the seller is entitled to the dividend, and if the stock is purchased before the ex-date, the buyer is entitled to the dividend. Sometimes things get screwed up. The buyer purchases the stock before the ex-date, but the seller still ends up getting the dividend. In this case, the customer's broker-dealer would send a **due bill** for the dividend to the other broker-dealer and would expect them to fork over the cash that is due. The exam might also want you to point out that when securities are sent to a broker-dealer and are not in good delivery form, the broker dealer should file a **reclamation** with the other side. As the name indicates, it's time to reclaim things here and get them right.

FINRA Rules

> *Anti-Money Laundering (AML)*

Money laundering is the process of taking illegal profits and disguising them as clean money. A criminal pulling in millions of dollars of cash must be careful not to drive an $85,000 SUV while holding no job or owning no business that could explain such a sudden stroke of good fortune. Therefore, criminals use elaborate schemes to take their "dirty" money and make it "clean." Maybe they buy a car wash and write up phony receipts for non-existent customers to match that up with a few hundred thousand dollars of illegal profits that end up being "cleaned" in the wash so to speak.

The three distinct phases of money laundering are:

Placement
Layering
Integration

Placement is the first stage in the cycle in which illegally generated funds are placed into the financial system or are smuggled out of the country. The goals of the money launderer are to remove the cash from where it was acquired to avoid detection from the authorities, and to then transform it into other assets, e.g., travelers' checks, money orders, etc.

Layering is the first attempt at disguising the source of the ownership of the funds by creating complex layers of transactions. The purpose of layering is to disassociate the dirty money from the source of the crime through a complicated web of financial transactions. Typically, layers are created by moving money in and out of offshore bank accounts of shell companies, through electronic funds transfers (EFTs). Because there are over 500,000 wire transfers circling the globe every day, most of which are legitimate, there isn't enough information disclosed on any single wire transfer to know how clean or dirty the money is. This provides an excellent way for money launderers to move their dirty money. Other forms used by launderers are complex dealings with stock, commodity and futures brokers. Given the sheer volume of daily transactions, and the high degree of anonymity available, the chances of transactions being traced are insignificant. In other words, broker-dealers are great places to launder money, which is why broker-dealers need to help the federal government clamp down on terrorists and other criminals trying to layer dirty money through a flurry of trading activity.

Integration is the final stage in the process. In this stage the money is integrated into the legitimate financial system. Integration of the now-clean money into the economy is accomplished by making it appear to have been legally earned. By this stage, it is very difficult to distinguish "clean" financial assets from "dirty."

FINRA lays out the rules for preventing money laundering:

> *Anti-Money Laundering Compliance Program*
>
> *On or before April 24, 2002, each member shall develop and implement a written anti-money laundering program reasonably designed to achieve and monitor the member's compliance with the requirements of the Bank Secrecy Act, and the implementing regulations promulgated thereunder by the Department of the Treasury. Each member's anti-money laundering program must be approved, in writing, by a member of senior management.*

The Bank Secrecy Act (BSA) authorizes the U.S. Treasury Department to require financial institutions such as banks and broker-dealers to maintain records of personal financial transactions that "have a high degree of usefulness in criminal, tax and regulatory investigations and proceedings." It also authorizes the Treasury Department to require any financial institution to report any "suspicious transaction relevant to a possible violation of law or regulation." These reports, called "Suspicious Activity Reports," are filed with the Treasury Department's Financial Crimes Enforcement Network ("FinCEN").

This is done secretly (thus the law's middle name), without the consent or knowledge of bank customers, any time a financial institution determines that a transaction is suspicious. The reports are made available electronically to every U.S. Attorney's Office and to 59 law enforcement agencies, including the FBI, Secret Service, and Customs Service.

Recently, the U.S. Treasury Department used the Bank Secrecy Act (BSA) to require that for transmittals of funds of $3,000 or more, broker-dealers are required to obtain and keep certain specified information concerning the parties sending and receiving those funds. In addition, broker-dealers must include this information on the actual transmittal order. Also, any cash transactions over $10,000 require the same type of uptight record keeping. For these, broker-dealers must file a **Currency Transaction Report** (CTR) with FinCEN.

Why? Because terrorist and other criminal organizations fund their operations through money laundering. Since broker-dealers are financial institutions, they're lumped in with banks and required to do all kinds of record keeping to help the government prevent these operations.

With the passage of the "USA Patriot Act" broker-dealers and other financial institutions must help the government monitor suspicious activity that could be tied to money laundering. Broker-dealers now must report any transaction that involves at least $5,000 if the broker-dealer knows, suspects, or has reason to suspect that it doesn't pass the smell test. FINRA spells out four specific characteristics that would make a broker-dealer file a **suspicious activity report** (SAR). An SAR would be filed if the transaction falls within one of four classes:

> the transaction involves funds derived from illegal activity or is intended or conducted to hide or disguise funds or assets derived from illegal activity;
> the transaction is designed to evade the requirements of the Bank Secrecy Act
> the transaction appears to serve no business or apparent lawful purpose or is not the sort of transaction in which the particular customer would be expected to engage and for which the broker/dealer knows of no reasonable explanation after examining the available facts; or
> the transaction involves the use of the broker/dealer to facilitate criminal activity

As a FINRA notice to members announces, "To help the government fight the funding of terrorism and money laundering activities, federal law requires financial institutions to obtain, verify and record information that identifies each person who opens an account." The notice explains obligations under the **Customer Identification Program (CIP)** for financial institutions including banks and broker-dealers. The first thing member firms must do is establish a written policy for establishing and documenting the identity of each customer for whom the firm opens an account.

Under the Customer Identification Program broker-dealers must obtain an individual's name, date of birth, residential address, citizenship, and social security/taxpayer ID. If the customer is not a U.S. citizen, the firm will need:

> taxpayer identification number
> passport number and country of issuance
> alien identification card number or government-issued identification showing nationality, residence and a photograph of the customer.

Even the U.S. citizen may need to show a photo ID, just as you do when you take your Series 7 exam. Every time I have opened an online brokerage account, for example, I have had to scan my driver's license and email or fax that to the broker-dealer, who has the obligation to make sure I'm not opening up an account through which I will launder money.

The broker-dealer also must inquire if the customer is an employee of a broker-dealer or a self-regulatory organization. If so, the employer must be notified (which was already a requirement under FINRA rules).

And, the broker-dealer must inquire if the customer is a "corporate insider" of a publicly traded company. That term includes corporate officers and members of the board of directors, as well as anyone who owns 10% or more of the common stock. For example, if Jeff Bezos opens an account with your firm, he is a "corporate insider" for Amazon as well as any of the companies for which he serves on the board of directors, or owns 10% or more of the outstanding shares. Corporate insiders are constrained under the Securities Act of 1933's Rule 144. Because Mr. Bezos knows more about what's about to happen at Amazon than ordinary shareholders, the SEC wants to monitor his trading activities on AMZN very closely. First, he cannot sell any of his holdings in AMZN unless he has held the shares at least one year. A Form 144 must be filed for the proposed sale no later than at the time of sale, and he can sell only a limited amount over the next 90 days (1% of the outstanding stock or the most recent four-week average trading volume). The sale of securities also may not be advertised.

So, as you can see, it would be great to have a billionaire customer like Jeff Bezos, but your firm will have added obligations surrounding his holdings in AMZN or any company for which he either sits on the board of directors or owns 10% or more of the shares.

Some customers are human beings, others are legal entities. As the same notice to members explains, "A corporation, partnership, trust or other legal entity may need to provide other information, such as its principal place of business, local office, employer identification number, certified articles of incorporation, government-issued business license, a partnership agreement or a trust agreement."

The federal government now maintains an **Office of Foreign Asset Control** (OFAC) designed to protect against the threat of terrorism. This office maintains a list of individuals and organizations viewed as a threat to the U.S. Broker-dealers and other financial institutions now need to make sure they aren't setting up accounts for these organizations, or—if they are—they need to block/freeze the assets. As the Department of Treasury explains, "As part of its enforcement efforts, OFAC publishes a list of individuals and companies owned or controlled by, or acting for or on behalf of, targeted countries. It also lists individuals, groups, and entities, such as terrorists and narcotics traffickers designated under programs that are not country-specific. Collectively, such individuals and companies are called 'Specially Designated Nationals' or 'SDNs.' Their assets are blocked and U.S. persons are generally prohibited from dealing with them."

➤ *Security of Customer Information*

Sharing customer information with law enforcement officials is one thing. Providing it to telemarketers and identity thieves is quite another. To fight identity theft and to protect customers from having too much of their information shared with people they've never met, the SEC enacted **Regulation S-P** to put into place a requirement from the Gramm-Leach-Bliley Act. Basically:

> a financial institution must provide its customers with a notice of its privacy policies and practices, and must not disclose nonpublic personal information about a consumer to nonaffiliated third parties unless the institution provides certain information to the consumer and the consumer has not elected to opt out of the disclosure.

A "**consumer**" is basically a prospect, someone interested in establishing some type of account. A "**customer**" is someone who has now opened a financial relationship with the firm. Broker-dealers and investment advisers must deliver initial and annual notices to customers explaining their privacy policies and practices, the types of information they share and with whom, and about the opportunity and methods to opt out of their institution's sharing of their nonpublic personal information with nonaffiliated third parties. The initial notice must be provided no later than when the firm establishes a customer relationship with the individual.

For some purposes the difference between the terms consumer and customer is important. In terms of limiting the information that is shared for certain purposes we will just refer to "consumers." Consumers (and customers) can only limit certain types of information sharing between a financial institution and another party. The other party is either an affiliate or a non-affiliate, as defined in the financial institution's privacy statement. Consumers can limit the sharing of information with an affiliate for their everyday business purposes that involves the consumer's creditworthiness. The consumer can also limit the information shared to both affiliates and non-affiliates for the purpose of marketing to the consumer. Consumers do not have the right under federal law to limit the sharing of information that the financial institution engages in for the following purposes:

the financial institution's marketing purposes
joint marketing with other financial companies
affiliates' everyday business purposes involving transactions and experiences

Broker-dealers and investment advisers also need to have written supervisory procedures dealing with the disposal of consumer credit report information. Since firms typically look at a consumer's credit history before opening accounts—especially margin accounts—selling annuities, or providing financial planning services, the firms need to safely dispose of the information rather than just setting it all in a big box out back.

Broker-dealers often must respond to requests for documents under disciplinary investigations. When providing such information through a portable media device (DVD, CD-ROM, flash drive), FINRA requires that the information be encrypted. As FINRA states:

> *the data must be encoded into a form in which meaning cannot be assigned without the use of a confidential process or key. To help ensure that encrypted information is secure, persons providing encrypted information to FINRA via a portable media device are required to use an encryption method that meets industry standards for strong encryption and to provide FINRA staff with the confidential process or key regarding the encryption in a communication separate from the encrypted information itself (e.g., a separate email, fax or letter).*

Beyond responding to the regulators' requests, customer emails also need to be encrypted, and registered representatives should not go around sharing customer information with anyone who doesn't need to know it.

The **FACT Act** is short for the **Fair and Accurate Credit Transactions Act.** Under this federal legislation the three major credit reporting agencies, in cooperation with the Federal Trade Commission (FTC) set up a website at www.AnnualCreditReport.com that allows consumers to monitor their credit reports. This Act also attempts to reduce identify theft by requiring firms who collect information on individuals to safely dispose of it and by allowing individuals to place alerts on their credit history if they suspect fraudulent transactions. Broker-dealers gather information from consumers through various sales and marketing efforts. The FACT Act requires that they don't simply toss thousands of post cards or computer hard drives containing personal and financial information about consumers out in a dumpster behind the branch office. For example.

The FACT Act requires the various agencies charged with its implementation to "identify patterns, practices, and specific forms of activity that indicate the possible existence of **identity theft**." The guidelines must be updated as often as necessary and cannot be inconsistent with the requirement to verify a customer's identity when opening an account. Right? See how we have competing concerns there? On the one hand, we want to shield customers from unauthorized access to their identities; on the other hand, we can't be so secretive that we don't know who's who on our customer list.

The Federal Trade Commission (FTC) has implemented a red flags rule that requires broker-dealers and other financial institutions to create written "Identity Theft Protection Programs" or "ITPPs" designed to identify, detect, and respond to warning signs (red flags) that could indicate identity theft. The four elements of a firm's ITPP (Identity Theft Protection Program) require broker dealers and other financial institutions to:

> identify relevant red flags for the covered accounts that the firm offers or maintains, and incorporate those red flags into its ITPP;
> detect red flags that have been incorporated into the ITPP of the financial institution or creditor;
> respond appropriately to any red flags that are detected to prevent and mitigate identity theft; and

update the ITPP and its red flags periodically to reflect changes in identity theft risks to customers and the firm.

Broker-dealers must design their Identity Theft Protection Program and have it approved by the Board of Directors of the firm or a designated member of senior management. The principals who approve the program must be involved in its oversight, development, implementation and administration. The firm must train staff to implement the ITPP. If the broker-dealer utilizes any third-party providers to help them with their responsibilities under the red flag rules, the firm must oversee those arrangements carefully.

➢ *Confirmations*

We've seen that corporate stock, corporate bonds and municipal bonds settle "T + 3," and that the broker-dealer must deliver a trade confirmation by settlement, or what the passage below calls "completion of each transaction." FINRA frequently incorporates SEC rules, as they do here:

> *A member at or before the completion of each transaction with a customer shall give or send to such customer written notification disclosing (a) whether such member is acting as a broker for such customer, as a dealer for his own account, as a broker for some other person, or as a broker for both such customer and some other person; and (b) in any case in which such member is acting as a broker for such customer or for both such customer and some other person, either the name of the person from whom the security was purchased or to whom it was sold for such customer and the date and time when such transaction took place or the fact that such information will be furnished upon the request of such customer, and the source and amount of any commission or other remuneration received or to be received by such member in connection with the transaction.*

➢ *Control Relationship*

This next one doesn't seem to require much explanation, so let's enjoy it in its original state:

> *A member controlled by, controlling, or under common control with, the issuer of any security, shall, before entering into any contract with or for a customer for the purchase or sale of such security, disclose to such customer the existence of such control, and if such disclosure is not made in writing, it shall be supplemented by the giving or sending of written disclosure at or before the completion of the transaction.*

➢ *Forwarding*

My online broker holds my securities in "street name," which means in the name of their clearing company. I am the beneficial owner. Therefore, when the companies whose stock I own send out proxy materials and annual reports, my broker must forward them to me, as we see below:

> *(a) A member has an inherent duty to forward promptly certain information regarding a security to the beneficial owner (or the beneficial owner's designated investment adviser) if the member carries the account in which the security is held for the beneficial owner and the security is registered in a name other than the name of the beneficial owner.*

➢ *Financial Condition*

This next rule seems to make perfect sense to me—if the member firm is holding my cash and securities, maybe I'd like to see how their financial condition is looking.

> *(a) A member shall make available to inspection by any bona fide regular customer, upon request, the information relative to such member's financial condition as disclosed in its most recent balance sheet prepared either in accordance with such member's usual practice or as required by any state or federal securities laws, or any rule or regulation thereunder.*
>
> *(b) As used in paragraph (a) of this Rule, the term "customer" means any person who, in the regular course of such member's business, has cash or securities in the possession of such member.*

➢ *Supplementary Documentation*

Margin accounts, third-party accounts and after-hours-trading accounts are special and, therefore, require special procedures by the broker-dealer. To open a margin account, not only must the broker-dealer provide the margin disclosure statement we are about to look at, but also they must get the customer to sign a **hypothecation agreement** and a **credit agreement**. The hypothecation agreement gives the broker-dealer the authority to pledge the customer's margin securities as collateral to a bank to secure the margin loan. Without this sort of agreement, a broker-dealer can never pledge a customer's securities as collateral any more than you can pledge your neighbor's house as collateral for a home equity loan to yourself. The credit agreement is exactly what it sounds like—the customer reads it and acknowledges that he understands how the whole loan program works with his signature. All short sales occur in margin accounts, and if the margin customer signs the **loan consent,** then his securities can be used as part of a lending program to short sellers, for which he will share some of the revenue his broker-dealer generates through the program.

FINRA is rightly concerned about margin accounts, as they increase the risk associated with the customer's account. Broker-dealers are, therefore, required to provide a margin disclosure statement to customers. FINRA rules state that, "No member shall open a margin account, as specified in

Regulation T of the Board of Governors of the Federal Reserve System, for or on behalf of a non-institutional customer, unless, prior to or at the time of opening the account, the member has furnished to the customer, individually, in writing or electronically, and in a separate document, the margin disclosure statement specified in this paragraph. In addition, any member that permits non-institutional customers either to open accounts on-line or to engage in transactions in securities on-line must post such margin disclosure statement on the member's Web site in a clear and conspicuous manner."

What does the disclosure statement contain? Let's take a look at the text of the FINRA rule:

Margin Disclosure Statement

Your brokerage firm is furnishing this document to you to provide some basic facts about purchasing securities on margin, and to alert you to the risks involved with trading securities in a margin account. Before trading stocks in a margin account, you should carefully review the margin agreement provided by your firm. Consult your firm regarding any questions or concerns you may have with your margin accounts.

When you purchase securities, you may pay for the securities in full or you may borrow part of the purchase price from your brokerage firm. If you choose to borrow funds from your firm, you will open a margin account with the firm. The securities purchased are the firm's collateral for the loan to you. If the securities in your account decline in value, so does the value of the collateral supporting your loan, and, as a result, the firm can take action, such as issue a margin call and/or sell securities or other assets in any of your accounts held with the member, in order to maintain the required equity in the account.

It is important that you fully understand the risks involved in trading securities on margin. These risks include the following:

*   *You can lose more funds than you deposit in the margin account. A decline in the value of securities that are purchased on margin may require you to provide additional funds to the firm that has made the loan to avoid the forced sale of those securities or other securities or assets in your account(s).*

*   *The firm can force the sale of securities or other assets in your account(s). If the equity in your account falls below the maintenance margin requirements, or the firm's higher "house" requirements, the firm can sell the securities or other assets in any of your accounts held at the firm to cover the margin deficiency. You also will be responsible for any short fall in the account after such a sale.*

- *The firm can sell your securities or other assets without contacting you.* Some investors mistakenly believe that a firm must contact them for a margin call to be valid, and that the firm cannot liquidate securities or other assets in their accounts to meet the call unless the firm has contacted them first. This is not the case. Most firms will attempt to notify their customers of margin calls, but they are not required to do so. However, even if a firm has contacted a customer and provided a specific date by which the customer can meet a margin call, the firm can still take necessary steps to protect its financial interests, including immediately selling the securities without notice to the customer.

- *You are not entitled to choose which securities or other assets in your account(s) are liquidated or sold to meet a margin call.* Because the securities are collateral for the margin loan, the firm has the right to decide which security to sell in order to protect its interests.

- *The firm can increase its "house" maintenance margin requirements at any time and is not required to provide you advance written notice.* These changes in firm policy often take effect immediately and may result in the issuance of a maintenance margin call. Your failure to satisfy the call may cause the member to liquidate or sell securities in your account(s).

- *You are not entitled to an extension of time on a margin call.* While an extension of time to meet margin requirements may be available to customers under certain conditions, a customer does not have a right to the extension.

That is the initial disclosure. Going forward, firms must annually provide either the above statement or the following abbreviated form:

Securities purchased on margin are the firm's collateral for the loan to you. If the securities in your account decline in value, so does the value of the collateral supporting your loan, and, as a result, the firm can take action, such as issue a margin call and/or sell securities or other assets in any of your accounts held with the member, in order to maintain the required equity in the account. It is important that you fully understand the risks involved in trading securities on margin. These risks include the following:

- You can lose more funds than you deposit in the margin account.

> - *The firm can force the sale of securities or other assets in your account(s).*
>
> - *The firm can sell your securities or other assets without contacting you.*
>
> - *You are not entitled to choose which securities or other assets in your account(s) are liquidated or sold to meet a margin call.*
>
> - *The firm can increase its "house" maintenance margin requirements at any time and is not required to provide you advance written notice.*
>
> - *You are not entitled to an extension of time on a margin call.*

The firm is not required to deliver the annual statement by itself but can, rather, include it in other deliveries of paper or electronic documents to the customer. Also note that the firm could decide to draft an alternative to either of the disclosures above and would be in compliance as long as the disclosures are substantially similar to the perfectly fine versions FINRA has already provided.

As we noted, any account where a third party has been granted power of attorney requires documentation of this authority being granted by the customer to someone else. This applies whether the person receiving this awesome authority is a friend, a relative, a financial planner, or the broker-dealer itself in a discretionary account.

Members of the securities industry are automatically required to use arbitration to handle disputes between firms or between registered representatives and their employers. But a customer is required to use arbitration only if she has signed a **pre-dispute arbitration agreement**. If your firm failed to get her signature on that agreement, the customer would be free to sue you and your firm in civil court, where her attorneys could keep filing appeal after appeal. The pre-dispute clause must make it clear that the customer generally gets only one attempt at arbitration—no appeals—and that the arbitrators do not must explain their decisions, and that many of them come from the industry. So, if she loses, say, $80,000 following her registered representative's recommendations, the arbitrators could decide a whole range of outcomes. Maybe she gets $80,000, or maybe she shares half the blame and gets only $40,000. Whatever she gets, the arbitrators won't must even explain why they decided against her. You can probably see why this arbitration thing needs to be clearly explained before the firm tries to hold the customer to the process by signing on the dotted line.

If the customer wants to trade options, he must receive the Options Disclosure Document and sign an options agreement serving as a contract between the broker-dealer and himself. Customers agree to make payment promptly and abide by options exchange rules for position limits, etc. by signing this agreement.

As we noted, broker-dealers sometimes open accounts for customers that have not provided tax ID numbers, but this is rare. Typically, broker-dealers request and receive a Form W-9 for U.S. citizens or a Form W-8 for non-resident aliens to get the tax ID and the name exactly right. These forms provide a taxpayer identification number—such as an FEIN—or evidence that the organization is exempt from backup withholding.

If a customer wants to engage in after-hours trading, member firms must provide disclosure of the special risks involved. The FINRA rule covering this states that, "No member shall permit a customer to engage in extended hours trading unless the member has furnished to the customer, individually, in paper or electronic form, a disclosure statement highlighting the risks specific to extended hours trading. In addition, any member that permits customers either to open accounts on-line in which such customer may engage in extended hours trading or to engage in extended hours trading in securities on-line, must post an extended hours trading risk disclosure statement on the member's Web site in a clear and conspicuous manner."

Risks that must be disclosed to customer trading after normal market orders include:

Risk of Lower Liquidity.
Risk of Higher Volatility.
Risk of Changing Prices.
Risk of Unlinked Markets.
Risk of Exaggerated Effect of News Announcements.
Risk of Wider Spreads.

Because issuers usually release news after hours, and because there is not as much trading going on, customers must understand how volatile these sessions can be and how the pricing they pay and receive is often inferior to what they would see during normal trading hours. FINRA provides a sample risk disclosure document called the Model Extended Hours Trading Risk Disclosure Statement that firms can send to customers. Or, firms can create their own disclosure document provided it discloses at a minimum all six risks above. And, either way, FINRA alerts member firms that they "may need to develop additional disclosures to address such issues as exchange-traded funds, options trading, options exercises, and the effect of stock splits or dividend payments during extended-hours trading."

Educational Communication Related to Recruitment Practices and Account Transfers

We looked at the process of transferring customer assets from one member firm to another through the ACATS system. FINRA has concerns surrounding the fact that some member firms may recruit registered representatives away from other members and then encourage the agent's existing customers to make the switch as well. FINRA "is concerned that former customers may not be aware of other important factors to consider in making a decision whether to transfer assets to the recruiting firm, including directs costs that may be incurred."

Therefore, when this situation occurs FINRA rules require delivery of an educational communication by the recruiting firm that highlights key considerations in transferring assets to the recruiting firm, and the direct and indirect impacts of such a transfer on those assets. This communication, put out by FINRA, encourages customers to make further inquiries of the registered rep, the new member and the existing brokerage firm holding his assets. The educational material must be delivered to the customer whether he was contacted by the registered representative or the recruiting firm, or even if he just transferred assets to an account assigned to the newly hired/recruited agent.

A former customer is defined here as any retail customer who had a securities account assigned to the registered person at the representative's previous firm.

As FINRA explains:

> *The educational communication would highlight the following potential implications of transferring assets to the recruiting firm: (1) Whether financial incentives received by the representative may create a conflict of interest; (2) that some assets may not be directly transferrable to the recruiting firm and as a result the customer may incur costs to liquidate and move those assets or account maintenance fees to leave them with his or her current firm; (3) potential costs related to transferring assets to the recruiting firm, including differences in the pricing structure and fees imposed by the customer's current firm and the recruiting firm; and (4) differences in products and services between the customer's current firm and the recruiting firm.*

Remember that some securities don't transfer--DPPs and certain annuities, for example. So, without this FINRA rule customers could end up being hit with surrender charges or other liquidation fees and even tax penalties simply because they trusted their registered representative without looking at any of the details.

As you may have noticed, FINRA is all about the details.

Now What?

As usual, we looked at a lot of important information in this chapter. All of it is fair game for Series 7 questions. For example:

Three of the following pieces of information would be on both a trade ticket and a trade confirmation. Which one would ONLY be recorded on the trade confirmation?
   A. Account number
   B. Commission
   C. Account executive identifier
   D. Number of shares, units

EXPLANATION: agents and member firms are not allowed to enter transactions and then decide in which accounts to place them. The account number must be indicated for each trade about to be placed. Also, a customer could have several accounts with the firm—identifying the account associated with this trade is important, so eliminate Choice A. Choice B does not necessarily look like something to be on the trade ticket, so let's put that one to the side. The registered representative (account executive) must be identified on the order ticket and on the trade confirmation. Eliminate Choice C. I don't see how an order could be placed without specifying the number of shares to be bought or sold. And, it wouldn't be much of a trade confirmation if it lacked such basic information. Eliminate Choice D, leaving us with

ANSWER: B

Broker-dealers are often related to banks, insurance companies and investment advisers, all under one parent company. Therefore, another question could ask:

A member firm has a customer interested in purchasing shares of XYZ, which happens to be a firm under common control of the member. Which of the following correctly states what the member firm should do in this case?
  A. Refuse to execute the order due to the conflict of interest
  B. Execute the order and disclose the control relationship if recommending the transaction to the customer
  C. State the nature of the control relationship orally before execution and provide written disclosure by completion of the transaction
  D. Execute the order without either commission or other remuneration
EXPLANATION: maybe a bank holding company owns this broker-dealer and also an insurance company that is publicly traded. The customer is going to buy shares of that insurance company. Because the firm is less than disinterested in this case, when a member firm executes a transaction in a security of an issuer related to the firm, disclosure needs to be provided. And, not just if the firm recommended the trade. Eliminate Choice B. It's not that the firm can't execute the order or receive compensation for doing business, so we can eliminate Choice A and Choice D, leaving us with

ANSWER: C

FINRA recently updated a rule on the holding of customer mailings—e.g., account statements, trade confirmations, proxies, and annual reports. Therefore, a question like this seems likely:

One of your elderly customers, who does not use electronic communications, calls this morning and asks you to please hold back the delivery of any account-related mailings while she is in South Africa for 61 days. Which of the following is accurate of this customer request?
  A. The customer must make the request in writing, and your firm must both send disclosure of alternative methods of monitoring the account and receive confirmation the customer received this disclosure
  B. Because she is traveling overseas for less than 3 months, you may fulfill this request with prompt principal approval
  C. Because she is traveling for more than two consecutive months, your firm will need her to supplement the request in writing
  D. With the passage of Dodd-Frank, member firms are no longer permitted to hold back the delivery of any account-related customer mailings
EXPLANATION: the former rule was very rigid—the firm could hold back customer mailings for two months if traveling domestically and three months if traveling abroad. Now, the

time frame is not the main concern. The main concern, as always, is that the firm first has this request in writing. Choice B implies this oral request can simply be approved by a principal, so eliminate Choice B. Choice C says you only need it in writing in this particular case. That is wrong, so eliminate Choice C. Choice D seems official-like with the reference to Dodd Frank, but, clearly the passage in this chapter would have read quite differently if this were the case. Eliminate Choice D, leaving us with

ANSWER: A

Exercising discretion over a customer account is a very big deal. Therefore, you might get a question like this:

At 10 AM this morning one of your customers tells you to sell 500 shares of ABC at the close of the day's trading session. ABC is a thinly traded stock, and when you go to sell the shares at the close, there is only buying interest for 300 shares. Therefore, you should

    A. Cancel the order

    B. Sell the 300 shares

    C. Sell the 300 shares to the market and purchase the other 200 for the firm's trading account

    D. Change the order to "at the open" and enter it electronically for tomorrow's trading session

EXPLANATION: questions like this are not easy. I don't see an answer that looks crazy enough to eliminate right away. Maybe you should sell whatever you can sell. Or, maybe you're not supposed to change the number of shares, so your firm should just buy the difference? This order is either executed at the close or not—you can't execute it tomorrow. Eliminate Choice D. The question doesn't say you have discretion, so you can't alter the number of shares, no matter how tempting Choices B and C might be. Eliminate them both. Cancel the order, leaving us with

ANSWER: A

Margin questions involve calculations as well as the basic facts we just covered. Remember that although Reg T is at 50%, member firms can demand a higher percentage for the initial margin. And, although 25% is the minimum maintenance for long positions, many firms require a higher percentage. Options are typically purchased and sold in margin accounts, but to buy an option the investor must pay in full. Firms do not have to consult with customers before liquidating long positions to cover a maintenance call. And, of course, a margin disclosure document must be sent to customers before opening up or approving the account for margin trading.

A question involving some basic math could look like this:

A new margin customer buys 1,000 ABC @50, making the required Reg T deposit. If ABC rises to $60 per share, what is the buying power in the account?

    A. None at this time

    B. $5,000

    C. $10,000

D. $20,000

EXPLANATION: whenever the stock rises, buying power increases. Eliminate Answer Choice A. The required Reg T deposit was $25,000. When the stock rises to $60,000, the equity rises to $35,000. On a $60,000 position Reg T is $30,000. Therefore, there is $5,000 of excess equity. Multiply that by 2, and the buying power is $10,000.

ANSWER: C

Buying power is good news for the margin customer. As we saw, margin accounts are not all about good news. So a question might ask about the downside of margin accounts—maintenance calls:

One of your customers is in a margin account with long stock positions currently worth $24,000. The debit balance is $15,000, and the minimum maintenance requirement is 25%. Therefore, you should inform your customer that he will receive a maintenance call if the stock drops to which amount?

A. $20,000
B. The customer should have already received a maintenance call
C. $19,000
D. $16,000

EXPLANATION: the equity is currently $9,000, which is well over 1/3 the current market value of $24,000. Eliminate Choice B. There are two ways to figure this problem out from here. One is to eyeball it until you come up with an answer leaving exactly 25% equity. Neither Choice C nor Choice D works on that score. Or, you can remember that to calculate the account at maintenance you divide the debit balance by 75%. $15,000 divided by .75 = $20,000. If the long market value were $20,000 and the debit $15,000, the account would have $5,000 of equity, which is exactly 25% of $20,000.

ANSWER: A

It's time to do the online review exercises for this chapter. After a break, take the chapter review quiz. Watch the lesson in the training videos and then move onto the next chapter in the textbook.

CHAPTER 5: Industry Regulations

In this chapter we will look primarily at FINRA registration requirements, standards for communications, and rules against influencing others with gifts and gratuities.

FINRA

The Securities and Exchange Commission has authority over broad aspects of the securities industry. They are granted this authority under the Securities Exchange Act of 1934. Under this landmark securities legislation the SEC requires securities exchanges such as NYSE and CBOE to register. These self-regulatory organizations in turn register and regulate their own member firms and the associated persons of those firms.

Securities have long traded both on the New York Stock Exchange and the so-called Over-The-Counter market. Back in 1938 Congress passed the **Maloney Act**, a law providing for the regulation of the over-the-counter securities markets through national associations registered with the SEC. This is one of several acts that have updated the Securities Exchange Act of 1934. The National Association of Securities Dealers (NASD) is the only association that has ever registered under the act. In 2007 the NASD and the regulatory arm of the NYSE formed FINRA, which stands for the **Financial Industry Regulatory Authority**. FINRA, along with NYSE and CBOE, is a self-regulatory organization (SRO) registered with the SEC under the Securities Exchange Act of 1934.

FINRA is organized along four major bylaws:

> rules of fair practice
> uniform practice code
> code of procedure
> code of arbitration

The rules of fair practice describe how to deal with customers without getting the regulators all bent out of shape. Commissions, markups, recommendations, advertising, sales literature, etc., are covered here. These are often referred to as "member conduct rules." The uniform practice code is the code that keeps the practice uniform. Settlement dates, delivery of securities, the establishment of the ex-date, ACAT transfers…that stuff is covered here. The exam might refer to the uniform practice code as "promoting cooperative effort," which it does. Just trying to keep the broker-dealers in Boston on the same page as the broker-dealers in Austin.

FINRA Membership

If your firm wants to join FINRA, it must:

> meet net capital requirements
> have at least two principals to supervise the firm
> have an acceptable business plan detailing its proposed activities
> attend a pre-membership interview

If your firm becomes a member of FINRA, they must agree to:

abide by the rules of the "Association"
abide by all federal and state laws
pay dues, fees, and membership assessments

What are these fees the firm must pay?

Basic membership fee
Fee for each rep and principal
Fee based on gross income of the firm
Fee for all branch offices

Membership, Registration and Qualification Requirements

FINRA's **Central Registration Depository (CRD)** is the electronic registration system for member firms, principals, and registered representatives. FINRA reminds their member firms not to file misleading information. As the FINRA Manual says:

> *Filing of Misleading Information as to Membership or Registration*
>
> *The filing with the Association of information with respect to membership or registration as a Registered Representative which is incomplete or inaccurate so as to be misleading, or which could in any way tend to mislead, or the failure to correct such filing after notice thereof, may be deemed to be conduct inconsistent with just and equitable principles of trade and when discovered may be sufficient cause for appropriate disciplinary action.*

Filing misleading information with FINRA is a major violation. Firms also must not use their association with FINRA in a way that is misleading, as we see with this rule:

Use of the FINRA Logo

Member firms may not use the FINRA logo in any manner; however, a firm may refer to itself as a "FINRA Member Firm" or "Member of FINRA." Also, if a firm refers to its FINRA membership on its website, it must provide a hyperlink to FINRA's website, which is www.finra.org.

> *Failure to Register Personnel*
>
> *The failure of any member to register an employee, who should be so registered, as a Registered Representative may be deemed to be conduct inconsistent with just and equitable principles of trade and when discovered may be sufficient cause for appropriate disciplinary action.*

As we can see above, it is a violation to use an individual in a position that requires registration unless and until the individual is registered. Who "should be so registered"?

FINRA lays that out, too:

> ### Definition of Representative
>
> Persons associated with a member, including assistant officers other than principals, who are engaged in the investment banking or securities business for the member including the functions of supervision, solicitation or conduct of business in securities or who are engaged in the training of persons associated with a member for any of these functions are designated as representatives.

There are different categories of "registered representative," too. A General Securities Representative has a Series 7 and can sell individual stocks, bonds, municipal securities, options…generally just about anything. A person with a Series 6 is called a Limited Representative–Investment Company and Variable Contracts Products. This allows the individual to sell only mutual funds and variable contracts, plus something that seldom gets mentioned: a Series 6 holder can also be part of an underwriting for a closed-end fund. Just the underwriting, though, which is done through a prospectus. Once they start trading in the secondary market between investors, they're just shares of stock, and a Series 6 holder can't sell individual shares of stock. Everything they sell must come with a prospectus and is a packaged product of some kind or another.

So, if you fit the definition of "representative," you must be registered, as FINRA indicates below:

> ### All Representatives Must Be Registered
>
> All persons engaged or to be engaged in the investment banking or securities business of a member who are to function as representatives shall be registered as such with FINRA in the category of registration appropriate to the function to be performed as specified in Rule 1032. Before their registration can become effective, they shall pass a Qualification Examination for Representatives appropriate to the category of registration as specified by the Board of Governors.

As basic as that rule seems, you might be surprised how often member firms will try to use an unlicensed employee to function as a registered representative, just "long enough for him to pass his test and get set up." Bad idea. Unless and until the individual is licensed by FINRA and the state securities regulators, he must not perform *any* of the functions of a registered representative.

As we said, firms, principals, and registered representatives submit their registration information to FINRA's Central Registration Depository (CRD). You will submit your own information to the CRD through a Form U4, which asks questions about your residential history and professional background, etc. A principal must sign the U4 application and certify that he or she has reviewed your information, which is why it's not a good idea to use a fictional work history—they check that stuff. The CRD system is used for many different purposes. FINRA uses the information to determine whether the applicant is subject to statutory disqualification or presents a risk for the firm and its customers. Member firms use the information to determine if a candidate is subject to statutory disqualification or special heightened supervision. Firms also use the information reported to check the backgrounds of candidates. Maybe most important, the information released to the public through BrokerCheck protects investors from serial offenders in the securities industry.

Candidates for registered representative and principal positions often try to conceal their criminal or regulatory problems when completing Form U4. When FINRA finds out, they usually bar the representative permanently from association with any member firm, because if the individual can't be trusted when applying, why let him meet with customers? Nip that problem in the bud.

In a recent notice to members FINRA explains that firms have the responsibility to review the information their candidates submit on Form U4 and conduct thorough background checks. Member firms are not supposed to just run a bunch of candidates through the CRD system and see which ones get past the regulators. FINRA requires that "each member firm ascertain by investigation the good character, business reputation, qualifications and experience of an applicant before the firm applies to register that applicant with FINRA and before making a representation to that effect on the application for registration." If the applicant has already been registered, member firms are required to review his most recent U5 information—the form filed when an associated person ends employment with a member firm—within 60 days of filing the candidate's U4.

When a principal or registered representative leaves a member firm or ceases to function as a principal or registered representative at the firm, a U5 must be submitted to FINRA within 30 days. The firm you're leaving completes a U5, and the firm that is hiring you completes a U4. If the exam uses the phrase "termination for cause," that means the registered rep gave the firm a good reason to fire him, including:

> Violating the firm's policies
> Violating the rules of the NYSE, FINRA, SEC, or any other industry regulator
> Violating state or federal securities laws

If the registered representative is the subject of an investigation by any securities industry regulator, the firm cannot terminate the rep until the investigation is completed. Otherwise, a shady supervisor could say, "Oh, you're being investigated by the State of New York? No problem, we'll just terminate you for cause and make the whole thing go away."

A principal of the firm already had to sign each U4 to certify that he or she had done due diligence in verifying the accuracy of the information. Recently, however, FINRA raised the bar by requiring firms to adopt written procedures on how they will verify such information, and by requiring them to complete that verification process within 30 calendar days of filing the Form U4. If the member finds information that doesn't match with what the candidate disclosed, the firm must file an amended U4 within 30 calendar days. While FINRA encourages firms to complete this process *before* filing the U4, the firm can also just pay the Late Disclosure Fee involved with filing the amended U4.

Not surprisingly, the filing of an amended U4 often triggers the whole process of FINRA deciding they might need to deny this particular application. For example, an amended U4 is often where a "no" answer to felony convictions and charges becomes two very embarrassing "yes" answers, with detailed explanations and court records detailing the unfortunate incident.

It used to be that if a customer wanted to win an arbitration claim, it was sort of understood that they needed to name the firm—not the individual representative—in the claim. This way, when the customer got paid, the registered representative had nothing to report on a U4 or U5 form. As we said, the information on the U4 and U5 is available to the public through "broker check" at www.finra.org, so it can make your sales efforts difficult if your next appointment already has her laptop out, with a PowerPoint presentation based on your recent arbitration awards to wronged customers and disciplinary proceedings for breaking the rules. Now, the firm must add the arbitration or civil litigation (lawsuit) award to the registered representative's U4/U5 form even if he or she isn't specifically named in the arbitration award. But, FINRA did raise the threshold to $15,000 (from $10,000) for the firm to report the settlement. FINRA and the SEC are also especially concerned about "willful violations" of securities law, and the new questions under the disclosure section are specifically designed to find out about those. As you might expect, if your U4 contains information about "willful violations" of securities law—maybe executing transactions that your customers don't even know about, or misleading people about the mutual funds you sold them—it can be very tough to stay in the business. FINRA uses "statutory disqualification," which means that by statute you are disqualified.

After becoming a registered representative, you will also need to put in some time earning continuing education requirements. Let's see what FINRA must say about that:

> ### Continuing Education Requirements
>
> *This Rule prescribes requirements regarding the continuing education of certain registered persons subsequent to their initial qualification and registration with FINRA. The requirements shall consist of a Regulatory Element and a Firm Element as set forth below.*

The Regulatory Element is described like so:

> *Each registered person shall complete the Regulatory Element on the occurrence of their second registration anniversary date and every three years thereafter, or as otherwise prescribed by FINRA. On each occasion, the Regulatory Element must be completed within 120 days after the person's registration anniversary date.*

What if you don't complete the Regulatory Element in that time frame?

> ### Failure to Complete

> *Unless otherwise determined by the Association, any registered persons who have not completed the Regulatory Element within the prescribed time frames will have their registrations deemed inactive until such time as the requirements of the program have been satisfied. Any person whose registration has been deemed inactive under this Rule shall cease all activities as a registered person and is prohibited from performing any duties and functioning in any capacity requiring registration.*

The Firm Element is described like this by the FINRA Manual:

> **Standards for the Firm Element**
>
> *(A) Each member must maintain a continuing and current education program for its covered registered persons to enhance their securities knowledge, skill, and professionalism. At a minimum, each member shall at least annually evaluate and prioritize its training needs and develop a written training plan.*

Active Military Duty

What happens when a registered representative volunteers or is called into active military duty? If he or she is away from the firm more than two years, does the license expire? Does he must take continuing education courses in some cave in Afghanistan? Does she lose all the commissions she could have made on her "book of business"?

Not surprisingly, FINRA and the SEC are extremely accommodating when a registered representative or principal is called away from the firm to serve Uncle Sam. Here are the basic facts:

> license is placed on "inactive status"
> continuing education requirements waived
> dues, assessments waived
> two-year expiration period does not apply—exam might refer to this as "tolling"
> can earn commissions, usually by splitting them with another rep who will service the book of business
> the "inactive" rep cannot perform any of the duties of a registered rep while on inactive status

You could see a question about a "sole proprietor" called into active military duty. If so, tell the test that the same bullet points above would apply.

Investment Banking Representative (Series 79)

A relatively new category of registered representative has been created for individuals whose activities relate only to investment banking (primary market) and not the trading of securities (secondary market). As FINRA states in their notice to members:

FINRA has developed this exam to provide a more targeted assessment of the job functions performed by the individuals that fall within the registration category. The exam will be required in lieu of the current General Securities Representative (Series 7) exam or equivalent exams by the individuals who perform the job functions described in the new registration category.

The individuals who will take this new test instead of the Series 7 are those whose activities involve:

(1) advising on or facilitating debt or equity securities offerings through a private placement or a public offering, including but not limited to origination, underwriting, marketing, structuring, syndication, and pricing of such securities and managing the allocation and stabilization activities of such offerings, or

(2) advising on or facilitating mergers and acquisitions, tender offers, financial restructurings, asset sales, divestitures or other corporate reorganizations or business combination transactions, including but not limited to rendering a fairness, solvency or similar opinion.

This registration category does not apply to those who work only in public finance (municipal securities) or direct participation programs.

Investment Advisers

When you complete your Series 7 requirements, you will become licensed to sell securities. You will not, however, be automatically registered to provide investment advice for compensation. To open a financial planning business or manage portfolios for a percentage of assets, you must pass your Series 65 or 66 exam and register your firm as an **investment adviser** or associate with an investment adviser as an **investment adviser representative**. If an agent opened up either type of sideline without informing her employer and/or getting registered, disciplinary action could be taken by FINRA and his or her state securities regulator.

As a securities agent/registered representative, some of your customers will be investment advisers entering trades on behalf of their customers. But you yourself can only work the advisory side of the financial services business if and when you are properly licensed.

Principals

Member firms need principals who review correspondence, approve every account, initial order tickets, handle written customer complaints, and make sure there's a procedural manual for the office to use. In other words, somebody at the firm is ultimately responsible for the business of the firm—that person is the principal.

FINRA says:

Here is how FINRA defines a principal:

Also, note that, in general, each member must have at least two principals taking care of the stuff that principals are supposed to take care of:

New accounts
Trades (transactions)
Communication
Written Customer Complaints

And, making sure there is a written supervisory and procedural manual.

Research Analysts

A research analyst prepares and approves the research reports put together by a member firm. You know all those "strong buy" or "market outperform" ratings and the accompanying reports that tell people whether to buy or back off a particular stock? Those are prepared by a **research analyst**. To become a research analyst one generally must get the Series 7 and then pass another license exam specifically for research analysts (Series 86 and 87). Also, note that a *supervisory analyst* must approve all research reports.

Many people in my classes ask, "If I stop selling for a while, can I just park my license at the firm until I'm ready to use it again?"

Here is how FINRA answers that:

> *A member shall not maintain a representative registration with FINRA for any person (1) who is no longer active in the member's investment banking or securities business, (2) who is no longer functioning as a representative, or (3) where the sole purpose is to avoid the examination requirement prescribed in paragraph (c).*

So, if you're out for two years or more, you must take this exam again, so (3) is saying that your firm had better not pretend you're associated just so you can skip the Series 7 requirement.

A broker-dealer also could not sponsor someone for the Series 7 exam just so the person could sit for the test and maybe tell the rest of the candidates what to expect. As the rules say:

> *A member shall not make application for the registration of any person as representative where there is no intent to employ such person in the member's investment banking or securities business.*

An "assistant representative" will also must get a license, because of the following:

> **All Assistant Representatives—Order Processing Must Be Registered**
>
> *All persons associated with a member who are to function as Assistant Representatives—Order Processing shall be registered with the Association. Before their registrations can become effective, they shall pass a Qualification Examination for Assistant Representatives—Order Processing as specified by the Board of Governors.*
>
> *(b) Definition of Assistant Representative—Order Processing*
>
> *Persons associated with a member who accept unsolicited customer orders for submission for execution by the member are designated as Assistant Representatives—Order Processing.*

Not every employee of a broker-dealer must register. The following have been granted exemptions from the painful process you're undergoing right now:

Persons Exempt from Registration

(a) The following persons associated with a member are not required to be registered with the Association:

(1) persons associated with a member whose functions are solely and exclusively clerical or ministerial;

(2) persons associated with a member who are not actively engaged in the investment banking or securities business;

(3) persons associated with a member whose functions are related solely and exclusively to the member's need for nominal corporate officers or for capital participation; and

(4) persons associated with a member whose functions are related solely and exclusively to:

(A) effecting transactions on the floor of a national securities exchange and who are registered as floor members with such exchange;

(B) transactions in municipal securities;

(C) transactions in commodities; or

(D) transactions in security futures, provided that any such person is registered with a registered futures association.

So, if you're just doing filing/temp work, you're not involved with underwriting or trading securities, you're just sitting on the board or investing in the firm, or you're a member of a futures or stock exchange filling orders for the firm, you are not required to register as a registered representative.

Supervision

FINRA makes sure that principals are supervising registered representatives. The member firm must establish and maintain written procedures to supervise the various types of business it's engaged in and must supervise the activities of registered representatives. They must also designate a principal responsible for supervising each type of business in which the firm engages, and they must designate an "OSJ" (Office of Supervisory Jurisdiction), which is an office with, yes, supervisory jurisdiction.

The firm must perform internal inspections, and I'll just let FINRA explain this one:

Each member shall conduct a review, at least annually, of the businesses in which it engages, which review shall be reasonably designed to assist in detecting and preventing violations of and achieving compliance with applicable securities laws and regulations, and with the Rules of this Association. Each member

> *shall review the activities of each office, which shall include the periodic examination of customer accounts to detect and prevent irregularities or abuses and at least an annual inspection of each office of supervisory jurisdiction. Each branch office of the member shall be inspected according to a cycle which shall be set forth in the firm's written supervisory and inspection procedures.*

Without getting bogged down in the amazing amount of verbiage used by FINRA, this is how they define office of supervisory jurisdiction (OSJ) and **branch office**:

> *Branch office: any location identified by any means to the public or customers as a location at which the member conducts an investment banking or securities business*
>
> *OSJ: "Office of Supervisory Jurisdiction" means any office of a member at which any one or more of the following functions take place:*
>
> *(A) order execution and/or market making;*
>
> *(B) structuring of public offerings or private placements;*
>
> *(C) maintaining custody of customers' funds and/or securities;*
>
> *(D) final acceptance (approval) of new accounts on behalf of the member;*
>
> *(E) review and endorsement of customer orders*
>
> *(F) final approval of advertising or sales literature for use by persons associated with the member*
>
> *(G) responsibility for supervising the activities of persons associated with the member at one or more other branch offices of the member.*

Gifts and Gratuities

FINRA does not allow member firms and their associated persons to buy influence at other firms with gifts of cash or gifts with resale value over a certain amount. Currently the amount is $100 but is expected to rise to $175 in the near future. Why would someone at your firm want to give someone at another firm a $1,000 set of titanium golf clubs? Maybe your firm would like to start getting invited to join certain municipal securities underwritings that they run as syndicate manager. Or, maybe your firm would just like the other firm to start throwing some of the smaller accounts they don't want your way? Maybe a case of expensive scotch would do the trick?

While gifts and business entertainment are not completely prohibited, we are now entering a gray area that can either be considered normal business expenses or a violation of FINRA rules on influencing or rewarding the employees of other member firms.

Here is how FINRA states the rule:

> *No member or person associated with a member shall, directly or indirectly, give or permit to be given anything of value, including gratuities, in excess of one hundred dollars per individual per year to any person, principal, proprietor, employee, agent or representative of another person where such payment or gratuity is in relation to the business of the employer of the recipient of the payment or gratuity. A gift of any kind is considered a gratuity.*

FINRA then makes it clear that what they are prohibiting here is more along the lines of a $1,000 set of golf clubs, as opposed to legitimate contracts of employment where one member employs another member's employee for legitimate purposes. As the rule then states:

> *This Rule shall not apply to contracts of employment with or to compensation for services rendered provided that there is in existence prior to the time of employment or before the services are rendered, a written agreement between the member and the person who is to be employed to perform such services. Such agreement shall include the nature of the proposed employment, the amount of the proposed compensation, and the written consent of such person's employer or principal.*

As with most sensitive issues, FINRA requires records surrounding these activities to be kept:

> *A separate record of all payments or gratuities in any amount known to the member, the employment agreement referred to in paragraph (b) and any employment compensation paid as a result thereof shall be retained by the member for the period specified by SEA Rule 17a-4.*

Note that "SEA" means "Securities Exchange Act of 1934" and "SEA Rule 17a-4" would be that SEC Rule promulgated under the Securities Exchange Act of 1934.

Political Contributions

Municipal securities are issued by states, cities, counties, school districts, etc. Therefore, many elected officials are in a position to influence which firms get to underwrite certain offerings. They could either rig the bidding process for a competitive, sealed bid, or they could manipulate the negotiated underwritings in a way that benefits those firms willing to donate to their campaign funds.

Fortunately, the securities regulators are interested in maintaining the integrity of the municipal bond underwriting process. The tax payers supporting all the school bond issues should not have to worry that some politically-connected broker-dealer is gouging them every time another bond is sold.

Therefore, if any firm makes a large political contribution, they are prohibited from doing securities business with the related issuer for a period of two years. So, if your broker-dealer is a municipal bond underwriter in New Orleans, and you make a $10,000 donation to the mayor's reelection campaign, not only must you disclose the contribution, but also you are not to do any municipal securities business with the City of New Orleans for two years. The same would apply if a political action committee controlled by your firm funneled the money to the mayor's campaign, or if one of your "municipal finance professionals" made the contribution with her own money. For purposes of this rule, a "municipal finance professional" includes principals, registered representatives, and any paid solicitors who help firms land underwriting deals.

Firms must keep records on all contributions by the firm, their municipal finance professionals, and any associated PACs (political action committees). And, they must refrain from doing business with an issuer if large donations are made, or if donations are made to politicians that the firm and its personnel are not even in a position to vote for. To that end, if the <u>municipal finance professional</u> making the contribution is eligible to vote for the mayor, governor, etc. *and* the contribution does not exceed $250, then provided the firm keeps records of this there is no reason to refrain from doing business with the related issuer. In other words, if one of the principals lives in New Orleans and is eligible to vote for the mayor, he or she could contribute up to $250 and provided the firm disclosed this to regulators in their regular reports on such contributions, the firm could continue to underwrite securities for the City of New Orleans. So, we're not allowing the firm or one of their PACs to make such a contribution; only the individuals working for the firm who are eligible to vote for that particular official. And, only up to a small amount—currently $250.

Quarterly, members who engage in municipal securities activities must file reports disclosing to FINRA the following information:

  the name and title (including any city/county/state or political subdivision) of each official of an
    issuer and political party receiving contributions or payments during such calendar quarter,
    listed by state
  the contribution or payment amount made and the contributor category of each person and entity
    making such contributions or payments during such calendar quarter
  a list of issuers with which the broker, dealer or municipal securities dealer has engaged in
    municipal securities business during such calendar quarter, listed by state, along with the
    type of municipal securities business
  records on contributions to any "bond ballot campaign" beyond the allowed $250 contribution by
    eligible municipal finance professionals

Pay-to-Play rules
The above rule is concerned with broker-dealers acting as underwriters of municipal securities, which are issued by government entities. Government entities also use the services of investment advisers, and these advisers often use broker-dealers to solicit business on their behalf. This type of service is typically called either soliciting or acting as the investment adviser's **placement agent.** A recent

FINRA rule change prohibits a covered member from engaging in distribution or solicitation activities for compensation with a government entity on behalf of an investment adviser that provides or is seeking to provide investment advisory services to that government entity within two years after a contribution to an official of the government entity is made by the covered member or a covered associate. And, this includes a person who becomes a covered associate within two years after the contribution is made.

The rule also prohibits a member or associate from soliciting or coordinating any person or political action committee (PAC) to make any contribution to an official of a government entity in respect of which the covered member is engaging in, or seeking to engage in, distribution or solicitation activities on behalf of an investment adviser, or to make any payment to a political party of a state or locality of a government entity with which the covered member is engaging in, or seeking to engage in, distribution or solicitation activities on behalf of an investment adviser.

Contributions made by a covered associate who is a natural person to government entity officials for whom the covered associate was entitled to vote at the time of the contributions, provided the contributions do not exceed $350 to any one official per election, are allowed. Unlike the earlier rule, if the covered associate was not entitled to vote for the official at the time of the contribution, the contribution must not exceed $150 per election. Primary and general elections are considered separate for purposes of the rule.

For a newly hired covered associate, FINRA will not preclude the member from engaging in placement activities if the individual made a contribution > 6 months ago and will not engage directly in solicitation activities with government entities on behalf of investment advisers.

As with the previous rule, member firms are required to keep information on political contributions and solicitation activities in their books and records so that FINRA can verify that members are not buying undue influence for their clients.

Exam Confidentiality

Some individuals become upset when they discover that practice questions can only mimic the actual exam—I didn't pay a fraternity brother to, like, steal an old exam for me. How serious is FINRA about protecting the surprise element in their exams? Let's see:

> *FINRA considers all of its Qualification Examinations to be highly confidential. The removal from an examination center, reproduction, disclosure, receipt from or passing to any person, or use for study purposes of any portion of such Qualification Examination, whether of a present or past series, or any other use which would compromise the effectiveness of the Examinations and the use in any manner and at any time of the questions or answers to the Examinations are prohibited and are deemed to be a violation of Rule 2110.*

Since that's the case, I decided to start a side business whereby I would text message my customers at the testing center for $100 per correct answer (no fee for incorrect answers). Unfortunately, FINRA says:

> *An applicant cannot receive assistance while taking the examination. Each applicant shall certify to the Board that no assistance was given to or received by him during the examination.*

FINRA Member Conduct Rules

The NYSE, NASDAQ, CBOE, and FINRA all must register with the SEC under the Securities Exchange Act of 1934. These self-regulatory organizations (SROs) in turn regulate their own member firms and the associated persons of those member firms.

Violating the FINRA member conduct rules leads to fines and sanctions that can get a firm expelled or a registered representative barred from the business. There are many ways to mistreat customers or try to operate outside the watchful eye of your principal and firm. The first thing to keep in mind is that:

> **Standards of Commercial Honor and Principles of Trade**
>
> *A member, in the conduct of his business, shall observe high standards of commercial honor and just and equitable principles of trade.*

Often other rules will state something like, "doing such and such would be considered conduct inconsistent with high standards of commercial honor and just and equitable principles of trade." For example, not paying an arbitration award would be a violation, as would cheating on your Series 7 exam.

➢ Customers' Securities or Funds

> *c) Authorization to Lend*
>
> *No member shall lend, either to himself or to others, securities carried for the account of any customer, which are eligible to be pledged or loaned unless such member shall first have obtained from the customer a written authorization permitting the lending of securities thus carried by such member.*

Margin customers sometimes sign a loan consent, which allows the broker-dealer to use the securities when lending to short sellers. The above rule requires the firm to have the customer's consent first. But, FINRA does not require separate forms here. As a recent notice to member firms states, "FINRA Rule 4330(a) requires a firm to obtain a customer's written authorization prior to lending securities that are held on margin for a customer and that are eligible to be pledged or loaned. Supplementary

Material .02 permits a firm to use a single customer account agreement/margin agreement/loan consent signed by the customer as written authorization under Rule 4330(a), provided such customer account agreement/margin agreement/loan consent includes clear and prominent disclosure that the firm may lend either to itself or others any securities held by the customer in its margin account."

The firm needs to keep their assets separate from the assets that clearly belong to the customer, and their books and records must make it clear which securities belong to which customers. A failure to do so is a violation called commingling:

> *d) Segregation and Identification of Securities*
>
> *No member shall hold securities carried for the account of any customer which have been fully paid for or which are excess margin securities unless such securities are segregated and identified by a method which clearly indicates the interest of such customer in those securities.*

FINRA rules require members to segregate and identify by customers both fully paid and "excess margin" securities. "With regard to a customer's account which contains only stocks, it is general practice for firms to segregate that portion of the stocks having a market value in excess of 140% of the debit balance therein."

So, if the "Dr" or "debit register" in a margin account is $5,000, 140% of that would be $7,000, and anything above that would be considered "excess margin" securities. So, the broker-dealer pledges $7,000 of the securities as collateral to the bank, and the rest is/are "excess margin securities."

As you already know, you and your firm do not guarantee customers against losses, nor could you afford to:

➢ *Prohibition Against Guarantees*

> *No member or person associated with a member shall guarantee a customer against loss in connection with any securities transaction or in any securities account of such customer.*

Can you share with your customers? Let's see what FINRA thinks about that:

➢ *Sharing in Accounts; Extent Permissible*

> *(1)(A) Except as provided in paragraph (f)(2) no member or person associated with a member shall share directly or indirectly in the profits or losses in any account of a customer carried by the member or any other member; provided, however, that a member or person associated with a member may share in the profits or losses in such an account if (i) such person associated with a member obtains prior*

> *written authorization from the member employing the associated person; (ii) such member or person associated with a member obtains prior written authorization from the customer; and (iii) such member or person associated with a member shares in the profits or losses in any account of such customer only in direct proportion to the financial contributions made to such account by either the member or person associated with a member.*

And then, just to keep things nice and simple, FINRA says, "Well, that whole proportionate sharing thing doesn't *always* apply," as we see right after the above otherwise clear passage:

> *(B) Exempt from the direct proportionate share limitation of paragraph (f)(1)(A)(iii) are accounts of the immediate family of such member or person associated with a member. For purposes of this Rule, the term "immediate family" shall include parents, mother-in-law or father-in-law, husband or wife, children or any relative to whose support the member or person associated with a member otherwise contributes directly or indirectly.*

➢ *Account Statements*

FINRA rules require broker-dealer member firms to send account statements to customers no less frequently than every quarter. However, it is almost always going to be at least once per month, because if there has been any "account activity," the statement must go out monthly. As we see from their definition of "account activity," it's pretty tough to imagine an account without any of that over the period of one month:

> *(c) Definitions*
>
> *For purposes of this Rule, the following terms will have the stated meanings:*
>
> *(1) "account activity" includes, but is not limited to, purchases, sales, interest credits or debits, charges or credits, dividend payments, transfer activity, securities receipts or deliveries, and/or journal entries relating to securities or funds in the possession or control of the member.*

Even if you're not trading every month, chances are you receive an interest payment or dividend. If you're in a margin account, there will be interest debited to your account, so account statements will always be sent monthly except when they're sent quarterly. What, exactly, is an "account statement"? FINRA defines it as:

> *[an account statement is a document]...containing a description of any securities positions, money balances, or account activity to each customer whose account had a security position, money balance, or account activity during the period since the last such statement was sent to the customer.*

The Series 7 will likely ask a few questions about borrowing from or lending to customers. Those words make the regulators a little nervous—I mean, how, exactly, does that registered representative define "borrowing" from a customer? Is this like an actual loan from a bank that happens to be his customer? Or, is this like a little old lady who seldom monitors her account and, therefore, probably won't even notice that the $50,000 was missing for a few weeks? We're talking, of course, about:

> ➢ *Borrowing From or Lending to Customers*

> *(a) No person associated with a member in any registered capacity may borrow money from or lend money to any customer of such person unless: (1) the member has written procedures allowing the borrowing and lending of money between such registered persons and customers of the member; and (2) the lending or borrowing arrangement meets one of the following conditions: (A) the customer is a member of such person's immediate family; (B) the customer is a financial institution regularly engaged in the business of providing credit, financing, or loans, or other entity or person that regularly arranges or extends credit in the ordinary course of business; (C) the customer and the registered person are both registered persons of the same member firm; (D) the lending arrangement is based on a personal relationship with the customer, such that the loan would not have been solicited, offered, or given had the customer and the associated person not maintained a relationship outside of the broker/customer relationship; or (E) the lending arrangement is based on a business relationship outside of the broker-customer relationship.*

How do they define "immediate family" here? Quite broadly:

> *(c) The term immediate family shall include parents, grandparents, mother-in-law or father-in-law, husband or wife, brother or sister, brother-in-law or sister-in-law, son-in-law or daughter-in-law, children, grandchildren, cousin, aunt or uncle, or niece or nephew, and shall also include any other person whom the registered person supports, directly or indirectly, to a material extent.*

As with sharing, the most important thing is to get your firm's permission before borrowing or lending with any customer. A registered representative who borrows money "under the table" from a customer will usually end up getting suspended by FINRA.

Being a member of FINRA is a big deal. Such a big deal that if a person is not a member, your firm may not extend any of the membership privileges to this mere civilian, as we see in the following FINRA rule:

> ➤ *Dealing with Non-Members*

> *(a) No member shall deal with any non-member broker or dealer except at the same prices, for the same commissions or fees, and on the same terms and conditions as are by such member accorded to the general public.*

So, if you let me buy a mutual fund below the public offering price, I would be forever grateful, but FINRA would be most upset. Only member firms can ever receive pricing better than what any member of the public would receive. To underwrite securities—including open-end funds and variable contracts—broker-dealers must be members in good standing with FINRA. When a member firm is disciplined, at what point are they considered "non-members"? FINRA states that, "a member firm will be considered as a non-member of FINRA from the effective date of any order or notice from FINRA or the SEC issuing a revocation, cancellation, expulsion or suspension of its membership. In the case of suspension, a member firm will be automatically reinstated to membership in FINRA at the termination of the suspension period." The last sentence there reminds us that suspension is imposed for a definite time period—15 days, or 60 days, for example. Therefore, as soon as the 16th or 61st business day rolls around, FINRA's registration system automatically reinstates the firm. On the other hand, if a firm is expelled, it would take much effort on their behalf to ever be allowed back into the securities industry.

In a notice to members FINRA explains, "a member firm can pay continuing commissions to its retiring registered representatives, after they cease to be associated with the firm, that are derived from accounts held for continuing customers of the retiring registered representative regardless of whether customer funds or securities are added to the accounts during the period of retirement, provided that: a bona fide contract between the member firm and the retiring registered representative providing for the payments was entered into in good faith while the person was a registered representative of the firm and such contract, among other things, prohibits the retiring registered representative from soliciting new business, opening new accounts or servicing the accounts generating the continuing commission payments and the arrangement complies with applicable federal securities laws, SEA rules and regulations."

So, the contract provides for the payment on old business and provides that the retired representative will not solicit business, open new accounts, or even try to service the accounts generating the continuing stream of commissions. He or she can only be paid on old business, done back when he or she was still in the business. A "retiring registered representative" is defined as an individual who retires from a member firm (including for total disability) and leaves the securities industry. Upon death of the retired registered representative the firm may continue to pay his stated beneficiaries or—if none was stated—make payments to the beneficiaries of the former registered representative's estate.

FINRA also has concerns about registered representatives and principals receiving compensation during a period of disqualification or sanction. FINRA states:

> A member firm may not pay or credit to any person subject to a sanction or disqualification, during the period of the sanction or disqualification or any period thereafter, any salary, commission, profit, or any other remuneration that the person might accrue, not just earn, during the period of the sanction or disqualification.

The phrase "that the person might accrue, not just earn," means what it sounds like. If a principal of the firm would have accrued profit-sharing payments over the three months he was suspended, the member firm may not pay him that remuneration. However, FINRA sometimes suspends a principal from any association with the member firm while other times they simply suspend him from performing the functions of a registered principal. The individual in that case could still work as a registered representative and receive pay during the suspension. However, if FINRA suspends the individual from association with the member firm in any capacity, we are back to the fact that the member cannot employ or pay him to do any sort of work.

As FINRA states, "a member firm may not allow a person subject to a sanction or disqualification to be associated with such firm in any capacity that is inconsistent with the sanction imposed or disqualified status, including a clerical or ministerial capacity." Also, the regulators are not heartless—a sanctioned/disqualified individual cannot be paid salary, bonuses, commissions, etc., during a suspension, but the member firm can still continue making payments pursuant to an insurance or medical plan.

FINRA won't allow members to reward people for violating securities regulations, but provided they can show the compensation was earned before the effective date of the sanction or disqualification and that the remuneration was totally unrelated to the activities leading to the disciplinary proceeding in the first place, members can make payment in that case. In other words, if the registered representative "earns" $50,000 by entering unauthorized transactions, the member firm will not be able to pay him for that sales activity. If that same individual, however, had done some bookkeeping work for the firm long before the disciplinary problem, the member could pay that compensation.

FINRA is not just talking about their own disciplinary actions here. If a registered representative is also subject to CBOE authority, for example, a disciplinary action from CBOE would trigger all of the same concerns. As FINRA states, "other disqualifications, not just suspensions, revocations, cancellations or bars, are subject to the rule (and the rule is not limited to orders issued by FINRA or the SEC)."

Broker-dealers and associated persons are prohibited from paying individuals and entities not registered or associated with a member firm referral fees or any form of compensation for helping them increase their sales efforts. So, if your friend knows people whom he can steer your way, it is not okay to share your commissions with him or pay him a flat referral fee.

> *Charges for Services*

Member firms not only must be fair and equitable in securities transactions with their customers, but also, if they charge for other services, those charges must also be reasonable and fair. FINRA states that, "Charges, if any, for services performed, including miscellaneous services such as collection of moneys due for principal, dividends, or interest; exchange or transfer of securities; appraisals, safe-keeping or custody of securities, and other services, shall be reasonable and not unrelatively discriminatory between customers."

> *FINRA Rule. Fidelity Bonds*

(a) Coverage Required

Each member required to join the Securities Investor Protection Corporation who has employees and who is not a member in good standing of the American Stock Exchange, Inc.; the Boston Stock Exchange; the Midwest Stock Exchange, Inc.; the New York Stock Exchange, Inc.; the Pacific Stock Exchange, Inc.; the Philadelphia Stock Exchange, Inc.; or the Chicago Board Options Exchange shall:

(1) Maintain a blanket fidelity bond, in a form substantially similar to the standard form of Brokers Blanket Bond promulgated by the Surety Association of America, covering officers and employees which provides against loss and has agreements covering at least the following:

(A) Fidelity

(B) On Premises

(C) In Transit

(D) Misplacement

(E) Forgery and Alteration (including check forgery)

(F) Securities Loss (including securities forgery)

(G) Fraudulent Trading

> *FINRA Rule. Outside Business Activities*

Many students seem shocked when I tell them that they'll need to notify their employing broker-dealer before doing any type of work outside the firm. As this rule stipulates:

> *No person associated with a member in any registered capacity shall be employed by, or accept compensation from, any other person as a result of any business activity, other than a passive investment, outside the scope of his relationship with his employer firm, unless he has provided prompt written notice to the member. Such notice shall be in the form required by the member.*

> ➤ *FINRA Rule. Private Securities Transactions*

FINRA wants all activities of a registered representative to be monitored, so if the registered representative is sitting in his office offering investors a chance to invest in his sister's new LLC without telling his firm, there is no way the firm could monitor his sales activities, which poses a threat to investors. That could even be the answer to a Series 7 question that asks why **selling away** is a violation—because it gives your principal/firm no opportunity to supervise your activities. So, principals and registered representatives cannot offer securities to investors that their firm knows nothing about. As this rule makes clear:

> *No person associated with a member shall participate in any manner in a private securities transaction except in accordance with the requirements of this Rule.*
>
> *(b) Written Notice*
>
> *Prior to participating in any private securities transaction, an associated person shall provide written notice to the member with which he is associated describing in detail the proposed transaction and the person's proposed role therein and stating whether he has received or may receive selling compensation in connection with the transaction.*

Once the associated person has provided written notice to the employing member firm, the firm can either approve or disapprove the activities. If they disapprove, the associated person would be subject to disciplinary action by FINRA and termination by the firm if he went ahead and sold the securities, anyway.

The member firm must follow different procedures based on whether the associated person will receive selling compensation in connection with the sales efforts. If the transactions involve compensation and the firm approves the activity, the member must record the transactions on their regular books and records as well as supervise the registered representative (or principal) as if the transactions were being done on their behalf.

On the other hand, if the transactions will not involve selling compensation, the employing firm must provide the associated person prompt written acknowledgment of receiving notification. The member firm may then, at its discretion, require the person to adhere to specified conditions in connection with his participation in the transactions. Obviously, the requirements are not nearly as stringent when the transactions do not involve selling compensation. However, if the associated person fails to provide prior written notice, this violates the rule above whether any selling compensation is received or not. For purposes of this rule, FINRA defines **selling compensation** as, "Any compensation paid directly or indirectly from whatever source in connection with or as a result of the purchase or sale of a security, including, though not limited to, commissions; finder's fees; securities or rights to acquire securities; rights of participation in profits, tax benefits, or dissolution proceeds, as a general partner or otherwise; or expense reimbursements."

➢ *FINRA Rule. Transactions for or by Associated Persons*

On the new account form, we ask if the customer is associated with a member firm. If your broker-dealer knows that the customer is associated with a member firm, or if an associate of a member firm has discretion over the account, your firm must:

> notify the employer member in writing, prior to the execution of a transaction for such account, of the executing member's intention to open or maintain such an account;
> upon written request by the employer member, transmit duplicate copies of confirmations, statements, or other information with respect to such account; and
> notify the person associated with the employer member of the executing member's intention to provide the notice and information required

You will soon be an associate of a member firm, so if you want to open an investment account with another firm, FINRA rules state:

> *A person associated with a member, prior to opening an account or placing an initial order for the purchase or sale of securities with another member, shall notify both the employer member and the executing member, in writing, of his or her association with the other member; provided, however, that if the account was established prior to the association of the person with the employer member, the associated person shall notify both members in writing promptly after becoming so associated.*

➢ *FINRA Rule. Transactions Involving FINRA Employees*

FINRA has approximately 3,400 employees, and surely some of them have investment accounts. Because FINRA is the regulator of the broker-dealer and agent dealing with such an employee's account, there are rules designed to prevent members from trying to buy favor with their regulator. When the member has actual knowledge that the account is partly or wholly owned by an employee of FINRA, they must promptly provide duplicate account statements to FINRA. Also, other than normal margin loans or loans between family members, no member can make any loans to an employee of FINRA. And, if an employee of FINRA has responsibility for any regulatory matter concerning the member, the firm would be in serious trouble if they tried to start providing expensive gifts to that employee. Anything more than, say, a key chain or pen would probably raise red flags for FINRA.

As in Major League Baseball, disputes in the sport known as investing are settled in arbitration. In other words, member firms can't sue each other in civil court if an underwriting turns sour and one member of the syndicate is convinced they are owed an additional $1 million from another member, who acted as syndicate manager in the IPO. That sort of dispute must be submitted to arbitration. That means you get one shot, no appeals. As we saw earlier, firms get their customers to sign pre-dispute arbitration agreements, but they must be very upfront about what that means in the document they're getting the customer to sign. The rule stipulates that the warning must look like this:

This agreement contains a pre-dispute arbitration clause. By signing an arbitration agreement the parties agree as follows:

(A) All parties to this agreement are giving up the right to sue each other in court, including the right to a trial by jury, except as provided by the rules of the arbitration forum in which a claim is filed.

(B) Arbitration awards are generally final and binding; a party's ability to have a court reverse or modify an arbitration award is very limited.

(C) The ability of the parties to obtain documents, witness statements and other discovery is generally more limited in arbitration than in court proceedings.

(D) The arbitrators do not must explain the reason(s) for their award.

(E) The panel of arbitrators will typically include a minority of arbitrators who were or are affiliated with the securities industry.

(F) The rules of some arbitration forums may impose time limits for bringing a claim in arbitration. In some cases, a claim that is ineligible for arbitration may be brought in court.

(G) The rules of the arbitration forum in which the claim is filed, and any amendments thereto, shall be incorporated into this agreement.

Only by getting the customer to sign this agreement would your firm know that when somebody loses money, that somebody will not be able to drag them through civil court, with appeal after appeal. Arbitration is faster and cheaper for all involved.

FINRA rules make sure that your firm provides you, the registered rep, with the same written disclosure that you are bound by FINRA Arbitration whenever you are asked to sign a U4 or U5 form.

Exaggerating Expertise

It's already, of course, a violation of FINRA rules to offer/sell securities by using manipulative/deceptive methods. But, specifically, FINRA and the state regulators are concerned about registered representatives giving themselves titles that make them sound like experts, when, in fact, maybe they're not at all. For example, FINRA warns firms that agents have been known to pay a marketing company to write a book on some financial topic and put the agent's name and bio on it, as if he wrote the thing. Kind of misleading, wouldn't you say? Or, maybe a marketing company could produce something that looks like an important financial magazine with a worldwide distribution with articles apparently written by or about *you* all over the place. Kind of misleading, too, right? And, what with the World Wide Web and all, some reps will put out webcasts that sound like radio interviews when, in fact, somebody they're paying is just feeding them questions like an infomercial. I mean, it's an excellent marketing strategy, no doubt about that. It's just, you know, misleading as far as the regulators are concerned.

So is giving yourself a credential that you sort of made up or sort of purchased from a marketing company selling certificates with credentials on them. Check your firm's compliance department before getting all creative with your marketing, especially when marketing to senior citizen investors. Putting the word "senior" into a credential you plan to use is a very dangerous thing. I'm not saying it's always bad; just saying be careful. I am saying that if you send out a form letter telling people you are "specially licensed to provide investment advice to senior citizens," you will probably be receiving a letter by registered mail from FINRA and/or your state securities regulator very soon.

Suitability Rules

FINRA is the **Self-Regulatory Organization** formed when the NASD and NYSE regulators merged several years ago. The NYSE had a "know your customer" rule, while the NASD had a "suitability" rule that governed the responsibilities of registered representatives, principals, and member firms when it comes to opening customer accounts and recommending investment options. Now, as FINRA consolidates the two rulebooks into one manual, they are also tweaking the suitability rules. So, before we look at case studies of hypothetical investors, let's understand how the regulators view your responsibilities and those of your firm.

FINRA has a "know your customer rule," and it requires firms to use "reasonable diligence" in regard to opening and maintaining customer accounts. It requires firms to know the "essential facts" on every customer, as well. Essential facts are defined as:

> *those required to (a) effectively service the customer's account, (b) act in accordance with any special handling instructions for the account, (c) understand the authority of each person acting on behalf of the customer, and (d) comply with applicable laws, regulations, and rules.*

The "know your customer" obligation starts at the beginning of the broker-dealer and customer relationship, even before any investment recommendations have been made. FINRA requires that agents have:

> *a reasonable basis to believe that a recommended transaction or investment strategy involving a security or securities is suitable for the customer, based on the information obtained through the reasonable diligence of the member or associated person to ascertain the customer's investment profile.*

This is how FINRA defines the **investment profile** mentioned in the rule above:

> *a customer's investment profile includes, but is not limited to, the customer's age, other investments, financial situation and needs, tax status, investment objectives, investment experience, investment time horizon, liquidity needs, risk tolerance, and any other information the customer may disclose to the member or associated person in connection with such recommendation.*

Notice two things that are not part of an investment profile: neither the customer's educational level nor his political affiliation.

Suitability requirements for the agent and his broker-dealer are triggered only when there is an investment **recommendation** made to the customer. As usual, defining the term "recommendation" is more complicated than one would like. FINRA is pretty straightforward in one of their regulatory notices:

> *For instance, a communication's content, context and presentation are important aspects of the inquiry. The determination of whether a "recommendation" has been made, moreover, is an objective rather than subjective inquiry. An important factor in this regard is whether—given its content, context and manner of presentation—a particular communication from a firm or associated person to a customer reasonably would be viewed as a suggestion that the customer take action or refrain from taking action regarding a security or investment strategy. In addition, the more individually tailored the communication is to a particular customer or customers about a specific security or investment strategy, the more likely the communication will be viewed as a recommendation. Furthermore, a series of actions that may not constitute recommendations when viewed individually may amount to a recommendation when considered in the aggregate. It also makes no difference whether the communication was initiated by a person or a computer software program. These guiding principles, together with numerous litigated decisions and the facts and circumstances of any particular case, inform the determination of whether the communication is a recommendation for purposes of FINRA's suitability rule.*

That also means if a customer is placing trades through your firm's online website, those are, by definition, **unsolicited orders** and not subject to any suitability obligations. I mean, how are you going to stop full-grown adults from investing their own money the way they want to? Because marking an order ticket as an "unsolicited" order transfers all the responsibility to the customer, it would be a violation for an agent to falsely mark an order that he recommended as "unsolicited" or—even worse—enter an order the customer never actually placed and mark that ticket as "unsolicited."

The suitability rule mentions securities and strategies. This means as soon as an agent recommends that a customer do—or not do—something in relation to a security or investment strategy, he has made a recommendation for purposes of the suitability rule. On the other hand, if the agent or broker-dealer put out purely educational material that explains investment strategies without actually recommending any particular security or strategy, then those materials are exempt from the suitability rule.

However, if the agent/firm is recommending that customers consider using margin or liquefied home equity to purchase securities, that is covered by the suitability rule. Even though it doesn't mention particular securities, and even though it doesn't lead to a transaction, this recommended strategy has to be suitable. And, guess what, margin accounts and liquefied home equity are not suitable for most investors.

So, the margin handbook or margin disclosure brochure simply explains how margin works—that is educational material and has to be provided to customers before they open margin accounts. On the other hand, any brochure that recommends or implies that a customer ought to actually open a margin account and buy securities on credit would be considered a recommended strategy. Therefore, it should only be sent to those for whom such a strategy might be suitable and never across the board for all customers on an agent's book of business.

By the way, an explicit recommendation to **hold** a security is just as much a recommendation as a recommendation to buy or sell a security. As FINRA states:

> *The rule recognizes that customers may rely on firms' and associated persons' investment expertise and knowledge, and it is thus appropriate to hold firms and associated persons responsible for the recommendations that they make to customers, regardless of whether those recommendations result in transactions or generate transaction-based compensation.*

However, an agent has to specifically tell a customer not to sell a security—or not to sell securities in general—before he has made an explicit recommendation to hold. The fact that the agent did not tell the customer to sell is not a recommendation to hold. FINRA adds:

> *That is true regardless of whether the associated person previously recommended the purchase of the securities, the customer purchased them without a recommendation, or the customer*

> *transferred them into the account from another firm where the*
> *same or a different associated person had handled the account.*

There are now three explicit suitability obligations spelled out in the rule:

1. Reasonable-basis suitability: the agent must use reasonable diligence to understand the potential risks and rewards associated with the recommended security or strategy and have reasonable basis to believe the recommendation is suitable for at least some investors.
2. Customer-specific suitability: the agent must have a reasonable basis to believe that a recommendation is suitable for a particular customer based on his/her profile. The profile now adds new items to the existing list (age, investment experience, time horizon, liquidity needs and risk tolerance).
3. Quantitative suitability: an agent with control over an account must make sure that a series of transactions that might make sense in isolation are not unsuitable based on an excessive number of transactions given the customer's investment profile. This would not apply to unsolicited transactions initiated by the customer.

Number 1 and Number 3 apply equally to retail and institutional investors. However, Number 2 is applied differently for the two types of customer. Above, we see how retail investors are to be handled. But, if the investor is an "institutional account," the firm can meet their "customer-specific suitability" requirement by having a reasonable basis to believe the customer is able to evaluate investment risks independently and by having the institutional customer acknowledge in writing that it is exercising independent judgment—unlike the typical retail investor, who relies on what her stockbroker tells her in most cases.

So, if an agent/firm tries to provide evidence that they had a reasonable basis to believe that a particular recommendation is suitable to at least some investors, one would think that having documentation would be important. Actually, that depends. As FINRA states in one of several member notices, the suitability rule:

> *does not include any explicit documentation requirements. The*
> *suitability rule allows firms to take a risk-based approach with*
> *respect to documenting suitability determinations. For example, the*
> *recommendation of a large-cap, value-oriented equity security*
> *generally would not require written documentation as to the*
> *recommendation. In all cases, the suitability rule applies to*
> *recommendations, but the extent to which a firm needs to evidence*
> *suitability generally depends on the complexity of the security or*
> *strategy in structure and performance and/or the risks involved.*
> *Compliance with suitability obligations does not necessarily turn on*
> *documentation of the basis for the recommendation. However, firms*
> *should understand that, to the degree that the basis for suitability is*
> *not evident from the recommendation itself, FINRA examination and*
> *enforcement concerns will rise with the lack of documentary*

evidence for the recommendation. In addition, documentation by itself does not cure an otherwise unsuitable recommendation.

So, a recommendation that an equity investor purchase shares of Walmart or a blue chip equity mutual fund would not require a lot of documentation that such an investment might be suitable for at least some investors. However, some of the mortgage-based derivatives that preceded the meltdown in September 2008? Maybe nobody should have been sold those things, regardless of the "documentation" one might try to provide backing up their "suitability."

If the agent uses reasonable diligence to obtain all the necessary information from a customer, what happens if the customer does not supply all the information requested? In that case the agent and firm have to use their best judgment to determine whether they have enough information to make suitable recommendations to that customer. Perhaps the investor refuses to supply her age—what if all other information makes it pretty clear that she should be in short-term bonds and money market mutual funds? Could the agent make those recommendations? Probably. Just keep good case notes.

Also, firms can decide that for certain categories of customers the information FINRA requires is not relevant—for example, a broker-dealer can decide to not ask for the age of customers that are not human beings but merely legal persons/entities (trusts, estates, corporations, etc.) or not ask about liquidity needs *if* the firm is only going to recommend liquid securities in the first place. As FINRA explains:

The significance of specific types of customer information generally will depend on the facts and circumstances of the particular case, including the nature and characteristics of the product or strategy at issue.

So, you want to recommend speculative growth stocks to a customer? You need as much information as you can get on him first. On the other hand, to recommend a money market mutual fund or 13-week T-bills chances are a determination that the customer needs liquidity, capital preservation, and modest income should suffice.

Some firms use product committees of really smart people to review whether a particular investment product or strategy is suitable for at least some customers. Can you, as an agent, simply rely on the committee's findings?

No. FINRA clarifies that as an agent you have a responsibility to assure that you understand the risks and rewards of a particular product or strategy before recommending it to any investor. Failure to understand either the product or the customer is a violation of the suitability rule right there.

FINRA and the SEC have determined that agents must not just make recommendations that make sense. Agents must be sure to "act in their customer's best interests." That means that the agent must never place his own interests ahead of the customer's. Examples of agents violating that rule include an agent recommending one product over another based on the higher commissions he can earn, or an agent asking customers to make loans to him so he can start a business, backed up with "promissory notes."

Now, an agent does not have to recommend the least expensive investment to a customer, as long as it is suitable, and as long as the higher expenses are not related to higher commissions to the agent. In other words, if your broker-dealer only sells three families of mutual funds, then you simply recommend the ones that are suitable from these mutual fund families. The fact that there may be other, less-expensive mutual fund families out there? Not your problem. Where an agent will be disciplined and, perhaps, barred from the business is when he pushes customers to do things that benefit the agent while potentially harming the customer. A margin account, for example, allows a customer to buy roughly twice as much stock as he otherwise could. That might lead to higher commissions to the agent, but if he puts someone in a margin account for that reason, he's in big trouble.

Similarly, don't try to put customers into four different large cap growth funds offered by four different front-end-loaded mutual fund families. If you had determined that it was suitable for the customer to pay a front-end load, you should have put all her money into one large cap growth fund to minimize the sales charges. It would be pretty clear that this move was designed to maximize the sales charges you and/or your broker-dealer earn on the transaction. And, again, that is not a good reason to use to justify a transaction to a securities regulator.

We mentioned orders that agents recommend (solicited) and those placed by the investor (unsolicited). In another chapter we will see that agents sometimes are granted discretion over the customer's account, which means they can enter orders without first discussing them with the customer. Obviously, any order placed pursuant to discretion is considered to have been recommended by the agent and subject to suitability obligations.

Code of Procedure (COP)

So, FINRA has member conduct rules that you do not want to break, especially if you end up getting caught. FINRA investigates violations of the conduct rules through **Code of Procedure**, which spells "COP." Just like on the street, if somebody breaks the rules, you can call a COP. When we mentioned words such as "suspend, expel, bar, and censure," those are all part of this Code of Procedure. Maybe a staff member of FINRA found out some rather disturbing information during a recent routine examination of a firm, or maybe one of your customers got ticked about losing 90% this year and then found out you were breaking rules along the way. Either way, you'll be notified and asked to respond to the charges in writing. All requests for information must be met within 25 days, so start writing. Remember that you must cooperate with the investigation, producing documents or testimony as required. And if it's decided that you broke a rule, you could be censured, fined, suspended, expelled, or barred.

Which is bad.

You would get to appeal, assuming you can afford the legal fees. The appeals first go to the National Adjudicatory Council (NAC), then to the SEC, and even into the federal courts. But it would be easier if you didn't get in trouble in the first place.

What is the maximum fine FINRA can impose? Trick question—for a major violation, they've never set a cap. If it's a "minor rule violation," there is a maximum fine (which changes from time to time, approx. $5,000), but no maximum will ever be set for the big violations. You would receive an offer from FINRA to use what they call "summary complaint procedure," and if you want to avoid a hearing as much as they apparently do, you need to accept it within 10 business days. Minor rule violations typically involve the failure to pay fees or file reports in a timely fashion. If you reject their offer to play nice, there will be a hearing, where any of these penalties can be assessed:

Censure
Fine
Suspension (up to 1 year) from the member firm or all member firms
Expelled (up to 10 years, for firms only)
Barred

Although "acceptance, waiver, and consent" is often used for minor rule violations (MRVs), it is also used for larger fines when the respondent does not want a hearing.

Code of Arbitration

When broker-dealers are arguing over money, they must take it to "arbitration." Under the **Code of Arbitration** members of FINRA must resolve money disputes with an arbitrator or arbitration panel, which cuts to the chase and makes their decision quickly. There are no appeals to arbitration. If they say your firm owes the other side one million dollars, your firm will must open their checkbook and cut a check for one million dollars. End of story. A customer is free to sue a firm or registered rep in civil court unless the customer signs the arbitration agreement. Once that's signed, the customer is also bound by the Code of Arbitration, which means they can't sue you in civil court. Which is why most firms get their customers to sign arbitration agreements when the new account is opened. Civil court is too costly and time-consuming. Arbitration can be very painful, but at least it's quick.

If the arbitration claim is for a small amount of money, Simplified Industry Arbitration is used. Here there is just one "chair-qualified" arbitrator and no hearing. The claims are submitted in writing, and the arbitrator reaches a decision.

Larger amounts of money are handled by three or five arbitrators, some from the industry and some from outside the industry. Evidence and testimony is examined and the arbitration panel makes a final determination. Maybe they say the lead underwriter owes your firm $1 million. Maybe they say they owe you nothing. All decisions are final and binding in arbitration, unlike civil court where the appeal process can go on and on. So, if the arbitration panel says you owe somebody $250,000, you must, like, pay them. Failure to comply with the arbitration decision could lead to a suspension, and now you're not having a good day.

The bylaw doesn't specifically mention the word "money." The precise wording looks like this:

> *any dispute, claim, or controversy arising out of or in connection*
> *with the business of any member of the Association, or arising out of*

While arbitrators generally don't explain their decision, FINRA requires arbitrators to explain their decision if both parties make a joint request. The parties to the arbitration are required to submit any joint request for an explained decision at least 20 days before the first scheduled hearing date. The chairperson of the arbitration panel writes the explained decision and receives an additional honorarium of $400 for doing so.

An alternative method for resolving disputes is called **mediation.** Let's see how FINRA describes the difference between the two processes at http://www.finra.org/ArbitrationMediation/Parties/Overview/OverviewOfDisputeResolutionProcess/:

Dispute resolution methods, including mediation and arbitration, are non-judicial processes for settling disputes between two or more parties. In mediation, an impartial person, called a mediator, assists the parties in reaching their own solution by helping to diffuse emotions and keeping the parties focused on the issues. In arbitration, an impartial judge, called an arbitrator, hears all sides of the issue, studies the evidence, and then decides how the matter should be resolved. The arbitrator's decision is final....

The mediator's role is to guide you and the other party toward your own solution by helping you to define the issues clearly and understand each other's position. Unlike an arbitrator or a judge, the mediator has no authority to decide the settlement or even compel you to settle. The mediator's "key to success" is to focus everyone involved on the real issues of settling--or the consequences of not settling. While the mediator may referee the negotiations-- defining the terms and rules of where, when, and how negotiations will occur--he or she never determines the outcome of the settlement itself.

Okay, so what if you try to mediate the issue but can't come to a resolution? FINRA tells us:

When it seems that other efforts to resolve your dispute are not working, it is then time to decide whether you will file a claim to arbitrate. Even if you choose, or are required to use, arbitration rather than a lawsuit as a means of resolving your dispute, you should consider hiring an attorney who will provide valuable instruction and advice.

Arbitrators are people from all walks of life and all parts of the country. After being trained and approved, they serve as arbitrators when selected to hear a case. Some arbitrators work in the securities industry; others may be teachers, homemakers, investors, business people, medical professionals, or lawyers. What is most important is that arbitrators are impartial to the particular case and sufficiently knowledgeable in the area of controversy. Potential arbitrators submit personal profiles to FINRA; the profiles detail their knowledge of the securities industry and investment concerns. If accepted, their names and backgrounds go into a pool from which arbitrators are selected for any given case. Arbitrators do not work for FINRA, though they receive an honorarium from FINRA in recognition of their service.

Oh, and here is a good heads-up that FINRA then provides to investors:

Caution. *When deciding whether to arbitrate, bear in mind that if your broker or brokerage firm goes out of business or declares bankruptcy, you might not be able to recover your money-even if the arbitrator or a court rules in your favor.* ***Over 80 percent of all unpaid awards involve a firm or individual that is no longer in business.***

(That is one of the reasons why it is so important to investigate the disciplinary history of your broker or brokerage firm before you invest. For tips on how to do this, please read the SEC publication entitled Check Out Your Broker located on the SEC Investor Education Web site. Through FINRA's BrokerCheck Program, investors, and others, can find out background information about brokers and brokerage firms.)

And, yes, after you pass your exam and successfully obtain registration, you, too, will be searchable in that "BrokerCheck Program" FINRA mentions. Also remember that if a registered representative violates sales practice rules, and a customer makes an arbitration claim after losing money, the firm must report it on the registered (or formerly registered) representative's U4/U5 forms. If the amount of the award is $15,000 or more, the public will be able to find out about it, even if the plaintiff (customer) names the firm and not the registered rep specifically.

The exam could also mention that broker-dealer customers are not prevented from joining a class of plaintiffs in a class-action lawsuit. Meaning, if a large broker-dealer with offices all over the nation is found to be gouging customers on mutual fund sales through hidden charges, there could be a class-action lawsuit filed that all customers could join. Also, if an agent has a sexual harassment or civil rights case to file, that is also outside the nice-and-easy scope of arbitration.

Recent Concerns

FINRA puts out notices to their member firms to remind them of their responsibilities, update them on rule changes, etc. One of the more recent topics concerning suitability has to do with the tricky situation of a firm hiring an established registered representative who brings with him a book of business in which the customers own mutual funds and/or annuities that the new firm can't service. As another rule points out, distributors must have a written sales agreement with any broker-dealer who wants to sell, and get paid on, their mutual funds and/or annuities. So, what should the firm and their newly hired registered rep do? They should probably just liquidate all the investments and put the customers into mutual funds/annuities that the firm and the rep can service and get paid on, right?

Not right. No way can the firm and the rep even consider the fact that they can receive "trail commissions" on the new funds/annuities they want to sell when making such a recommendation that a customer sell/liquidate his current holdings. Don't even factor that into your suitability determination. However, the fact that the rep and the firm can offer service on the new investments, and not the existing holdings, can be one—among many—suitability factors considered.

So, if the new funds/annuities meet all the suitability requirements, then the rep and the firm can factor their ability to offer service on the new investments into their suitability determination. But, if they talk the customer into liquidating a perfectly good annuity and incurring a stiff surrender charge just so the rep and the firm can get paid…nothing good can come of that. The firm and the rep would both probably pay five times more in disciplinary fines than they could possibly make on the annuity switch, not to mention the whole, you know, ethical thing.

Another concern the regulators have concerning suitability has to do with selling to senior citizen investors. Not to lump "senior citizens" into one big, neat category, but FINRA reminds us that senior citizens often have needs for liquidity and cannot afford big investment losses, period. They should not be hustled into deferred annuities with long surrender periods and steep surrender charges, since their liquidity needs are so high. And, they had better understand that the "subaccounts" are tied to the stock and bond markets, which have been very dangerous and scary places from time to time. Some firms and agents are so aggressive that they'll talk senior citizens into taking home equity loans or second mortgages to free up money for high-risk, speculative investments. Or, they'll talk seniors into making withdrawals from their IRAs to roll the dice maybe on oil & gas drilling partnerships, or complex derivatives no one understands.

Don't go there, FINRA is saying.

FINRA is also concerned about "variable life settlements," which are usually pitched to senior citizens. With home values and investment accounts depressed, many senior citizens are tempted to sell their variable life insurance policy to an intermediary to get their hands on a big amount of cash-money right now. FINRA reminds people that if the broker-dealer wants to get into this line of business, they must file a material change in business operations notice to FINRA. And, in case there is any doubt, a transaction involving variable life insurance is a securities transaction that requires proper licensing of individuals and registration of the securities. Firms who want to get into the variable life settlement line need to keep suitability in mind and be sure to fully inform customers that selling a variable life policy can trigger tax consequences, decreased access to insurance coverage, ineligibility for Medicaid, and the release of their private medical information. Also, there are transaction costs involved that the parties might not fully understand—FINRA wants firms and their registered representatives to be upfront and clear about such costs.

After purchasing variable life policies, the intermediary then sells the investment product to investors, and FINRA is concerned that retail investors will be attracted to the higher yields offered without understanding that the investment is almost completely illiquid—meaning, it can't be sold to anyone else. So, what if you want your money after holding the investment, say, seven years?

Too bad. You're waiting for the insured to die. The sooner he or she does so, the higher your yield.

FINRA notifies members firms:

> *Also, the yield on a related product may be adversely affected by the parties structuring the related product—by an inexpert or incomplete actuarial analysis or an incomplete assessment of the medical conditions of any insured(s) covered by any policy in which an investor has an interest, or by a failure to follow applicable law regarding life settlements that may result in legal challenges at the time a death benefit is payable. External developments, such as advances in medical research and treatment regarding certain diseases, also may reduce the yield of related products.*

The yield an investor receives on a "life settlement" is related to how long it takes the insured to die. That's what they mean by "advances in medical research and treatment," which could be good for the insured but would, by definition, reduce the yield to the investor, who must keep waiting and waiting for the macabre security to mature. Also, even if the insured conveniently dies quickly, the investor may not be able to collect due to legal challenges based on faulty structuring of the product.

Even though an "institutional investor" such as a pension fund or mutual fund is almost by definition sophisticated, FINRA reminds firms and their agents that they still have suitability requirements when servicing their institutional customers. If the products they're pitching are so new and so inherently complex that even the institutional buyers don't or couldn't reasonably understand the risks, then the firm and the agent have a responsibility to explain it in detail. And, if the buyer—institutional or not—still doesn't seem to understand the risks, don't sell it to him.

Some broker-dealers now operate in the same physical space used by banks. Bank deposits are guaranteed by the FDIC. Banks are very safe, which is why we have phrases such as, "money in the bank," or, "you can bank on it." Stocks and bonds are not safe or insured by the federal government. Therefore, FINRA rules state:

> *(c) Standards for Member Conduct*
>
> *No member shall conduct broker/dealer services on the premises of a financial institution where retail deposits are taken unless the member complies initially and continuously with the following requirements:*
>
> *(1) Setting*

Wherever practical, the member's broker/dealer services shall be conducted in a physical location distinct from the area in which the financial institution's retail deposits are taken. In all situations, members shall identify the member's broker/dealer services in a manner that is clearly distinguished from the financial institution's retail deposit-taking activities. The member's name shall be clearly displayed in the area in which the member conducts its broker/dealer services.

(2) Networking and Brokerage Affiliate Agreements

Networking and brokerage affiliate arrangements between a member and a financial institution must be governed by a written agreement that sets forth the responsibilities of the parties and the compensation arrangements. The member must ensure that the agreement stipulates that supervisory personnel of the member and representatives of the Securities and Exchange Commission and the Association will be permitted access to the financial institution's premises where the member conducts broker/dealer services to inspect the books and records and other relevant information maintained by the member with respect to its broker/dealer services.

(3) Customer Disclosure and Written Acknowledgment

At or prior to the time that a customer account is opened by a member on the premises of a financial institution where retail deposits are taken, the member shall:

(A) disclose, orally and in writing, that the securities products purchased or sold in a transaction with the member:

(i) are not insured by the Federal Deposit Insurance Corporation ("FDIC");

(ii) are not deposits or other obligations of the financial institution and are not guaranteed by the financial institution; and

(iii) are subject to investment risks, including possible loss of the principal invested; and

(B) make reasonable efforts to obtain from each customer during the account opening process a written acknowledgment of receipt of the disclosures required by paragraph (c)(3)(A).

(4) Communications with the Public

(A) All member confirmations and account statements must indicate clearly that the broker/dealer services are provided by the member.

(B) Advertisements and sales literature that announce the location of a financial institution where broker/dealer services are provided by the member or that are distributed by the member on the premises of a financial institution must disclose that securities products: are not insured by the FDIC; are not deposits or other obligations of the financial institution and are not guaranteed by the financial institution; and are subject to investment risks, including possible loss of the principal invested. The shorter, logo format described in paragraph (c)(4)(C) may be used to provide these disclosures.

(C) The following shorter, logo format disclosures may be used by members in advertisements and sales literature, including material published, or designed for use, in radio or television broadcasts, Automated Teller Machine ("ATM") screens, billboards, signs, posters, and brochures, to comply with the requirements of paragraph (c)(4)(B), provided that such disclosures are displayed in a conspicuous manner:

—Not FDIC Insured

—No Bank Guarantee

—May Lose Value

Business Continuity and Disaster Recovery Plans

To avoid panic in the financial marketplace, FINRA requires broker-dealers to prepare for disasters caused by natural disasters, terrorist attacks, power outages, etc. As the FINRA rule states: Each member must create and maintain a written business continuity plan identifying procedures relating to an emergency or significant business disruption. Such procedures must be reasonably designed to enable the member to meet its existing obligations to customers. In addition, such procedures must address the member's existing relationships with other broker-dealers and counter-parties. The business continuity plan must be made available promptly upon request to FINRA staff. FINRA then states that firms should consider such issues as:

(1) Data back-up and recovery (hard copy and electronic)

(2) All mission critical systems

(3) Financial and operational assessments

(4) Alternate communications between customers and the member

(5) Alternate communications between the member and its employees

> *(6) Alternate physical location of employees*
>
> *(7) Critical business constituent, bank, and counter-party impact*
>
> *(8) Regulatory reporting*
>
> *(9) Communications with regulators*
>
> *(10) How the member will assure customers' prompt access to their funds and securities in the event that the member determines that it is unable to continue its business.*

Firms must also provide disclosure to their brokerage customers as to how the firm would implement a business continuity and disaster recovery plan in the event of a disaster related to weather, terror attack, cyber-attack, whatever. This disclosure is provided when the customer opens the account, upon request, and also on the firm's website.

Member firms must supervise their principals and their representatives. As this rule states:

> *b) Written Procedures*
>
> *(1) Each member shall establish, maintain, and enforce written procedures to supervise the types of business in which it engages and to supervise the activities of registered representatives, registered principals, and other associated persons that are reasonably designed to achieve compliance with applicable securities laws and regulations, and with the applicable Rules of FINRA.*

Communications with the Public

Before we distinguish the various types of communications, let's understand the main points:

A principal (compliance officer) must approve the firm's communications and file them. The communications cannot be misleading in any way.

> *(1) Standards Applicable to All Communications with the Public*
>
> *(A) All member communications with the public shall be based on principles of fair dealing and good faith, must be fair and balanced, and must provide a sound basis for evaluating the facts in regard to any particular security or type of security, industry, or service. No member may omit any material fact or qualification if the omission, in the light of the context of the material presented, would cause the communications to be misleading.*

(B) No member may make any false, exaggerated, unwarranted or misleading statement or claim in any communication with the public. No member may publish, circulate or distribute any public communication that the member knows or has reason to know contains any untrue statement of a material fact or is otherwise false or misleading.

(C) Information may be placed in a legend or footnote only in the event that such placement would not inhibit an investor's understanding of the communication.

(D) Communications with the public may not predict or project performance, imply that past performance will recur or make any exaggerated or unwarranted claim, opinion or forecast. A hypothetical illustration of mathematical principles is permitted, provided that it does not predict or project the performance of an investment or investment strategy.

(E) If any testimonial in a communication with the public concerns a technical aspect of investing, the person making the testimonial must have the knowledge and experience to form a valid opinion.

Okay. Seems fair enough—don't mislead investors through any of your communications regardless of the format. The exam may also want you to know the different types of communication. Understand that all communications must be at least monitored by the firm, but that your **correspondence** with retail investors would not be approved before it went out. It would just be monitored, with filters and red-flag words built into the automatic monitoring system. If you send out, say 50 letters to existing retail investors, this is now considered retail communications, while in the past it would have been correspondence. The difference between correspondence—which does not have to be pre-approved—and retail communications—which do—has to do with the number 25. Up to 25 retail investors = correspondence. Over 25 retail investors = retail communications.

If the communications are for only institutional investors, they are considered **institutional communications.** For institutional communications each member firm simply must, "establish written procedures that are appropriate to its business, size, structure, and customers for the review by an appropriately qualified registered principal of institutional communications used by the member and its associated persons. Such procedures must be reasonably designed to ensure that institutional communications comply with applicable standards. When such procedures do not require review of all institutional communications prior to first use or distribution, they must include provision for the education and training of associated persons as to the firm's procedures governing institutional communications, documentation of such education and training, and surveillance and follow-up to ensure that such procedures are implemented and adhered to."

So, correspondence is not pre-approved but is monitored. Institutional communications may be pre-approved or not, depending on how the firm sets up its supervisory and training system. Retail communications are subject to pre-approval before being first used or filed with FINRA.

Regardless of what we call it, the communication had better not be misleading. Any statement of the benefits of an investment or strategy, for example, needs to be balanced out with the associated risks involved.

Any materials that are subject to review, approval and filing are subject to this:

> *(1) Date of First Use and Approval Information*
>
> *The member must provide with each filing under this paragraph the actual or anticipated date of first use, the name and title of the registered principal who approved the advertisement or sales literature, and the date that the approval was given.*

This is also self-explanatory:

> *(7) Spot-Check Procedures*
>
> *In addition to the foregoing requirements, each member's written and electronic communications with the public may be subject to a spot-check procedure. Upon written request from the Department, each member must submit the material requested in a spot-check procedure within the time frame specified by the Department.*

FINRA recently changed some definitions and procedures involving communications with the public. First, they added some new definitions:

> *"Retail communication" means any written (including electronic) communication that is distributed or made available to more than 25 retail investors within any 30 calendar-day period.*
>
> *"Retail investor" means any person other than an institutional investor, regardless of whether the person has an account with a member.*

Then, to protect "retail investors," FINRA requires that any "retail communication" that has not already been filed with FINRA must be approved by a principal either before its first use or before filing it with FINRA's Advertising Regulation Department. And, for new member firms retail communications must be filed with FINRA at least 10 days prior to first use. This includes the content of the firm's website, and any other communication with retail investors (radio, newspaper, magazine, etc.). A retail communication could come in the form of a group email, a form letter, a chat room, or a webinar—provided it involves more than 25 retail investors, it is probably a form of retail communications subject to prior principal approval.

A recent change says that firms who are intermediaries in selling investment company products (e.g., mutual funds, annuities) are not required to approve or file sales material that was already filed by someone else, usually the distributor of the fund. The intermediary selling the products could not alter the material significantly; otherwise, they would have changed it enough to require re-approval and re-filing, which is what they're trying to avoid in the first place. So, the many broker-dealers selling the American Funds™ are acting as intermediaries. Provided they don't alter the materials, they can just use the materials that have already been created and filed by the distributor of the funds, American Funds Distributors.

Members use television and other video formats to communicate with investors. Therefore, FINRA stipulates that, "If a member has filed a draft version or 'story board' of a television or video retail communication pursuant to a filing requirement, then the member also must file the final filmed version within 10 business days of first use or broadcast."

Specific Communications Rules

We just explored rules on communications in general. FINRA then has specific rules based on the particular investment being offered by the member.

Investment Company Products

As we just saw, new FINRA members must pre-file their retail communications at least 10 business days before first use with the Advertising Regulation Department of FINRA. That applies during their first year of association and applies to all retail communications other than freewriting prospectuses filed with the SEC—those can be filed with FINRA within 10 days but after-the-fact. Also, if a member firm has problems getting their advertising up to regulatory standards, FINRA can require that firm to pre-file all of their retail communications or just the types that are causing the problems.

After their first year of registration member firms file most of their retail communications with FINRA, but within 10 days after they have already been used. On the other hand, retail communications concerning certain investments still must be pre-filed. Not only must some of these communications be pre-filed, but also members must wait to see if any changes are demanded by FINRA and must withhold using the communications until they have been approved by the regulators. As the rule states:

> *At least 10 business days prior to first use or publication (or such*
> *shorter period as the Department may allow), a member must file*
> *the following retail communications with the Department and*
> *withhold them from publication or circulation until any changes*
> *specified by the Department have been made*

The communications subject to this heightened requirement are:

> *Retail communications concerning registered investment companies*
> *that include or incorporate performance rankings or performance*
> *comparisons of the investment company with other investment*

The rule defines "registered investment companies" as "including mutual funds, exchange-traded funds, variable insurance products, closed-end funds and unit investment trusts." So, if there is a ranking that did not come from, say, Lipper or Morningstar, but, rather, by the fund or its underwriter—FINRA wants to look very carefully at that sort of publication, before it goes out.

Specific Retail Communications

Retail communications for investment company securities that contain a ranking or performance comparison used to require members to file a copy of the ranking or comparison used when filing the retail communication with FINRA. The rule was created back when FINRA staff did not have ready access to such rankings or comparisons. Now that such information is readily available online, members simply need to maintain back-up materials supporting what was cited in their retail communications.

FINRA also used to require any retail communication involving bond mutual fund volatility to be filed 10 days prior to first use. Also, any such communication had to be preceded or accompanied by a prospectus when delivered to an investor. Now, FINRA allows these retail communications to be filed within (after) 10 days of first use and has eliminated the prospectus-delivery requirement for these communications.

Members offering and providing investment analysis tools allowing customers to make their own investment decisions used to be required to provide access to the tools to FINRA staff. Now, members simply must provide such access upon FINRA's request. Members also no longer must file report templates and the retail communications themselves with FINRA.

Communications Regarding Variable Contracts

Communications about variable contracts are subject to the FINRA standards for communications generally, as well as a few that are specific to these products. First, a statement to a customer or, say, a full-page advertisement in Forbes magazine must be clear that what is being offered or advertised is a variable annuity or variable life insurance (VLI) policy and not a traditional insurance product. Liquidity is not available on deferred variable contracts, so if a customer is sold an annuity or variable life policy thinking it makes a good short-term investment that can be liquidated for a good price, that's a problem if it turns out to be a lie. Remember that cashing in or "surrendering" a deferred variable annuity can subject the investor to a 10% penalty tax plus surrender charges/contingent deferred sales charges to the annuity company. If the customer didn't realize that, we're looking at securities fraud.

There are "guarantees" offered in variable contracts, but these guarantees are subject to the insurance company's ability to pay claims. That needs to be made clear to investors, and it needs to be made clear that "backed up by the insurance company" and "you can't lose money" are not the same thing.

Even though variable life insurance ties cash value and death benefit values to the ups and downs of the investment markets, it must be presented primarily as a life insurance product as opposed to a security. If the regulators feel that you're selling VLI as a way to invest in the stock and bond market while barely considering the more important insurance protections, you could have problems. To that end, don't compare VLI to mutual funds, stocks or bonds; compare it to other types of insurance, including term, whole life, or variable universal life (VUL) insurance.

Unlike with a mutual fund —where you never even imply what future results might be—when selling insurance, illustrations are routinely used. Chances are an agent will show illustrations of a whole life insurance policy compared to a VLI and perhaps a VUL policy. The illustrations are not guarantees, and the insurance company must be careful how they present this information. They can show a hypothetical illustration as high as a "gross rate" of 12%, provided they also show how things would work out with a "gross rate" of 0%. Whatever the maximum rate used, it must be reasonable given recent market conditions and the available investment options. Since mortality and expense charges reduce returns, illustrations must be figured using the maximum charges. Current charges may also be included.

Options-Related Materials

The Options Principal approves the new accounts and approves all the orders executed at the firm to ensure suitability. The customer must receive the OCC's **options disclosure document** either at or before the time that the "principal" approves the account. The CBOE says that the Options Principal "shall be responsible to review and to propose appropriate action to secure the member organization's compliance with securities laws and regulations and Exchange rules in respect of its options business."

CBOE Rule 9.21 follows the FINRA rules on communications more or less. It uses the same definitions for correspondence, retail communications, and institutional communications used by the FINRA rule. A registered options principal must pre-approve retail communications, while correspondence and institutional communications must be monitored according to what the firm determines is appropriate for its operations.

Also, if a firm plans to send out retail communications that are not preceded or accompanied by the Options Disclosure Document (ODD), these communications must be pre-filed with the Options Exchange at least 10 business days prior to first use.

FINRA rules require all firms to ensure that their options communications to retail investors include a statement that supporting documentation for any claims (including the benefits or performance of certain programs or the options expertise of sales persons) will be supplied upon request. As FINRA states:

> *Communications regarding standardized options that are used prior to delivery of the Options Disclosure Document must be limited to general descriptions of the options being discussed. This text, however, may contain a brief description of options, including a statement that identifies the registered clearing agency for options*

(OCC, for example) and a brief description of the general attributes and method of operation of the exchanges on which such options are traded, including a discussion of how an option is priced. Additionally, such options communications must contain contact information for obtaining a copy of the ODD and must not contain recommendations or past or projected performance figures, including annualized rates of return, or names of specific securities.

So, before the options disclosure document—known as an ODD—is delivered, the material presented to customers cannot look anything like a recommendation for a particular options strategy or position. General information on options, the Options Clearing Corporation (OCC), and the options exchanges, etc., is fine at this point.

The Options Disclosure Document can be delivered electronically—what the exam might call "by hyperlink"—if the customer has already consented to receiving communications electronically from the firm. For example, many customers receive trade confirmations, proxy statements, and account statements electronically from their broker dealer. These customers, if they started an options account, could also receive the Options Disclosure Document (Characteristics and Risks of Standardized Options) electronically.

One more point about this from the CBOE:

Any statement referring to the potential opportunities or advantages presented by options shall be balanced by a statement of the corresponding risks. The risk statement shall reflect the same degree of specificity as the statement of opportunities, and broad generalities should be avoided. Thus, a statement such as "with options, an investor has an opportunity to earn profits while limiting his risk of loss," should be balanced by a statement such as "of course, an options investor may lose the entire amount committed to options in a relatively short period of time."

The CBOE also offers the following comments about communications for options firms:

It shall not be suggested that options are suitable for all investors.

Statements suggesting the certain availability of a secondary market for options shall not be made.

That last bullet point means that sometimes you go to close out 10,000 contracts and, guess what, nobody wants to buy your 10,000 contracts. Unless you'd be interested in reducing your asking price by, say, 75%?

The **MSRB** writes rules for municipal securities brokers and dealers. This is how the Municipal Securities Rulemaking Board defines an advertisement:

```
. . . any material (other than listings of offerings) published or
used in any electronic or other public media, or any written or
electronic promotional literature distributed or made generally
available to customers or the public, including any notice,
circular, report, market letter, form letter, telemarketing
script, seminar text, press release concerning the products or
services of the broker, dealer or municipal securities dealer, or
reprint, or any excerpt of the foregoing or of a published
article.
```

As with all definitions, we must know what the term includes, and then what it does not include:

```
The term does not apply to preliminary official statements or
official statements, but does apply to abstracts or summaries of
official statements, offering circulars and other such similar
documents prepared by brokers, dealers or municipal securities
dealers.
```

The issuer—the city, school district, etc.—is in charge of the preliminary and final official statement; therefore, if the firm is merely disseminating those documents, there is no need for review or approval, since this material is not an advertisement or even a document put together by the firm. However, if the firm or another party has altered either document—making it an abstract or summary—then that document would be considered an advertisement subject to review, approval, filing, etc. Also, the first line of the definition excludes "listings of offerings," because when a broker or dealer is merely letting it be known which securities they have for sale and at what price, no advertising messages are being broadcast—just straight-up factual information communicated to other market participants.

The general rule for all advertisements concerning municipal securities is:

```
no broker, dealer or municipal securities dealer shall publish or
disseminate, or cause to be published or disseminated, any
advertisement relating to municipal securities that such broker,
dealer or municipal securities dealer knows or has reason to know
is materially false or misleading.
```

The MSRB then has specific concerns for specific types of advertisements. If a broker or dealer is advertising its services, the MSRB defines such communications as **professional advertisements,** defined as:

```
any advertisement concerning the facilities, services or skills
with respect to municipal securities of such broker, dealer or
municipal securities dealer or of another broker, dealer, or
municipal securities dealer.
```

Not surprisingly, it is a violation to "publish or disseminate, or cause to be published or disseminated, any professional advertisement that is materially false or misleading." The word "materially" reminds us that a harmless typo is one thing; leaving out important risks to entice buyers would be "materially misleading" and would subject the firm to disciplinary action by FINRA (who enforces MSRB rules on their member firms).

A **product advertisement** is defined as, "any advertisement concerning one or more specific municipal securities, one or more specific issues of municipal securities, the municipal securities of one or more specific issuers, or the specific features of municipal securities." As with professional advertisements, it is a violation to publish misleading product advertisements. And, product advertisements must conform—if applicable—to two other concerns for product advertisements: new issues, and municipal fund securities products.

For a new issue of municipal securities, the accuracy of the prices/reoffering yields of the securities is, obviously, important. Therefore, the MSRB stipulates that:

> A syndicate or syndicate member which publishes or causes to be published any advertisement regarding the offering by the syndicate of a new issue of municipal securities, or any part thereof, may show the initial reoffering prices or yields for the securities, even if the price or yield for a maturity or maturities may have changed, provided that the advertisement contains the date of sale of the securities by the issuer to the syndicate. In the event that the prices or yields shown in a new issue advertisement are other than the initial reoffering prices or yields, such an advertisement must show the prices or yields of the securities as of the time the advertisement is submitted for publication. For purposes of this rule, the date of sale shall be deemed to be, in the case of competitive sales, the date on which bids are required to be submitted to an issuer and, in the case of negotiated sales, the date on which a contract to purchase securities from an issuer is executed.

The above is concerned with accuracy at the time of sale—when the underwriting contract is awarded. The following is concerned with accuracy at the time of publication:

> Each advertisement relating to a new issue of municipal securities shall also indicate, if applicable, that the securities shown as available from the syndicate may no longer be available from the syndicate at the time of publication or may be available from the syndicate at a price or yield different from that shown in the advertisement.

Many parents and grandparents save for the educational needs of their children and grandchildren through state-sponsored educational savings plans. A State 529 Plan is considered a municipal security, specifically a **municipal fund security**. The Investment Company Act of 1940, which covers mutual funds, provides exemptions and exclusions for many investment pools. Although a municipal fund security is very similar to a mutual fund, it escapes the definitions under the Investment

Company Act. The regulator of municipal securities brokers and dealers, the MSRB, defines a municipal fund security as:

> "A municipal security that, but for section 2(b) of the Investment Company Act of 1940, would constitute an investment company. Municipal fund securities generally have features similar to mutual funds or 'fund of funds' and are not fixed income securities. Interests in local government investment pools and 529 college savings plans are examples of municipal fund securities."

Why is a municipal fund security "not [a] fixed income security"? Because, as with a mutual fund, investors are owners of the portfolio, not loaners to the portfolio. As we saw in a previous chapter, ownership is evidenced through an *equity* security. As with a bond fund registered under the Investment Company Act of 1940, the investors in the fund aren't buying bonds issued by the mutual fund. Rather, they are buying ownership interests in a managed portfolio, receiving their share of the interest payments after expenses are deducted. The same thing is going on here, when an investor puts money into a municipal fund security.

529 College Savings Plans are considered municipal fund securities. If you were a resident of Illinois, for example, you could invest in a college savings plan called Illinois BrightStart. The money you contribute qualifies for a deduction from state income taxes (not federal), and any earnings the account makes come out tax-free at both the state and federal level if used for qualified education expenses. As the MSRB states on their website:

"Under a 529 college savings plan, a person may make contributions to an account established for the purpose of meeting the qualified higher education expenses of the designated beneficiary of the account. Contributions generally are used to acquire shares or units in a state trust, with trust assets invested in a manner consistent with the trust's stated investment objectives. Shares or units typically constitute municipal fund securities. Under current federal tax law, earnings from a 529 college savings plan used for qualified higher education expenses of the designated beneficiary are excluded from gross income for federal income tax purposes."

Securities regulators are rightly concerned that some investors putting money into such plans might get the mistaken idea that they are in some sort of guaranteed savings account, or that a rate of return is somehow promised to them. To make sure investors understand that there are risks involved the MSRB requires several specific disclosures when communicating about municipal fund securities:

> Each product advertisement for municipal fund securities must include a statement to the effect that:
>
> - an investor should consider the investment objectives, risks, and charges and expenses associated with municipal fund securities before investing;
>
> - more information about municipal fund securities is available in the issuer's official statement;

```
-  the  official  statement  should  be  read  carefully  before
investing.
```

As an Ohio resident, you would likely use the Ohio 529 Plan because it allows you to deduct up to a certain amount of your contributions against income for state income tax purposes. That is why the MSRB rule states:

```
if the advertisement relates to municipal fund securities issued
by a qualified tuition program under Internal Revenue Code Section
529, a statement to the effect that an investor should consider,
before  investing,  whether  the  investor's  or  designated
beneficiary's home state offers any state tax or other benefits
that are only available for investments in such state's qualified
tuition program.
```

Some of the investor's money may be allocated to the money market, and this is a potentially confusing product. On the one hand, it isn't going to lose value; on the other hand, it could. So, the MSRB requires that:

```
if the advertisement is for a municipal fund security that the
issuer holds out as having the characteristics of a money market
fund, statements to the effect that an investment in the security
is not insured or guaranteed by the Federal Deposit Insurance
Corporation or any other government agency (unless such guarantee
is provided by or on behalf of such issuer) and, if the security
is held out as maintaining a stable net asset value, that although
the issuer seeks to preserve the value of the investment at $1.00
per share or such other applicable fixed share price, it is
possible to lose money by investing in the security.
```

Research Reports

If you're a big Wall Street broker-dealer the **research reports** your analysts put out encouraging customers to buy or sell a particular security can have a huge impact on the price of the stock. So, if your research department is about to issue a "strong buy" recommendation and a glowing report on Google tomorrow morning, why not buy a boatload of Google shares today, and then release the report tomorrow? Won't that be fun? Your customers will want to buy the stock tomorrow at higher and higher prices and, heck, you'll be right here to sell it to them, at higher and higher prices. FINRA defines a research report as:

> *any written (including electronic) communication that includes an*
> *analysis of equity securities of individual companies or industries,*
> *and that provides information reasonably sufficient upon which to*
> *base an investment decision.*

I happen to have a couple of old research reports on my desk from Bear Stearns, one recommending shares of PepsiCo, the other recommending shares of a large bank that unfortunately went belly up before I had a chance to put any money in. Anyway, as FINRA states:

Trading Ahead of Research Reports

The Board of Governors, under its statutory obligation to protect investors and enhance market quality, is issuing an interpretation to the Rules regarding a member firm's trading activities that occur in anticipation of a firm's issuance of a research report regarding a security. The Board of Governors is concerned with activities of member firms that purposefully establish or adjust the firm's inventory position in NASDAQ-listed securities, an exchange-listed security traded in the OTC market, or a derivative security based primarily on a specific NASDAQ or exchange-listed security in anticipation of the issuance of a research report in that same security. For example, a firm's research department may prepare a research report recommending the purchase of a particular NASDAQ-listed security. Prior to the publication and dissemination of the report, however, the trading department of the member firm might purposefully accumulate a position in that security to meet anticipated customer demand for that security. After the firm had established its position, the firm would issue the report, and thereafter fill customer orders from the member firm's inventory positions.

The Association believes that such activity is conduct which is inconsistent with just and equitable principles of trade, and not in the best interests of the investors. Thus, this interpretation prohibits a member from purposefully establishing, creating or changing the firm's inventory position in a NASDAQ-listed security, an exchange-listed security traded in the third market, or a derivative security related to the underlying equity security, in anticipation of the issuance of a research report regarding such security by the member firm.

In the old days research analysts often functioned as cheerleaders for a particular company's stock to drum up investment banking business for the firm. Basically, the firms were just drawing in suckers willing to prop up the stock of a company whose CEO would become so giddy he would then do mergers and acquisitions, as well as stock and bond offerings through the firm's investment banking department. To put an end to those days, FINRA now stipulates:

No research analyst may be subject to the supervision or control of any employee of the member's investment banking department, and no personnel engaged in investment banking activities may have any influence or control over the compensatory evaluation of a research analyst.

Research analysts cannot participate in efforts to solicit investment banking business. Accordingly:

> *No research analyst may, among other things, participate in any "pitches" for investment banking business to prospective investment banking customers, or have other communications with companies for the purpose of soliciting investment banking business.*

Also:

> *No member may pay any bonus, salary or other form of compensation to a research analyst that is based upon a specific investment banking services transaction.*

So, the research analysts can't put out positive reports just to help the investment banking or trading departments. Surely, they can buy a few shares of the stock for themselves, their family, and friends, right?

Wrong.

> **Restrictions on Personal Trading by Research Analysts**
>
> *(1) No research analyst account may purchase or receive any securities before the issuer's initial public offering if the issuer is principally engaged in the same types of business as companies that the research analyst follows.*
>
> *(2) No research analyst account may purchase or sell any security issued by a company that the research analyst follows, or any option on or derivative of such security, for a period beginning 30 calendar days before and ending five calendar days after the publication of a research report concerning the company or a change in a rating or price target of the company's securities; provided that:*
>
> *(A) a member may permit a research analyst account to sell securities held by the account that are issued by a company that the research analyst follows, within 30 calendar days after the research analyst began following the company for the member*

So, the research analyst who's working on a "strong buy" research report on XYZ can't receive bonuses if XYZ then does investment banking through the firm, and can't go on the "road shows" for IPOs designed to drum up interest in the new issue. Also, the firm can't establish a large inventory position in XYZ to then sell it to their customers all excited by the glowing research report. And, the analyst can't buy any XYZ ahead of releasing his research report. But, surely, as the guy's golfing buddy, with an office right next door, you can take a look at it before the firm releases it, right?

FINRA saw that problem coming a mile away and, therefore, now stipulates that:

Non-research personnel may review a research report before its publication as necessary only to verify the factual accuracy of information in the research report or identify any potential conflict of interest, provided that (A) any written communication between non-research personnel and research department personnel concerning the content of a research report must be made either through authorized legal or compliance personnel of the member or in a transmission copied to such personnel; and (B) any oral communication between non-research personnel and research department personnel concerning the content of a research report must be documented and made either through authorized legal or compliance personnel acting as intermediary or in a conversation conducted in the presence of such personnel.

But, other than that:

...no employee of the investment banking department or any other employee of the member who is not directly responsible for investment research ("non-research personnel"), other than legal or compliance personnel, may review or approve a research report of the member before its publication.

The research report can also not be sent to the subject company except according to this:

A member may submit sections of such a research report to the subject company before its publication for review as necessary only to verify the factual accuracy of information in those sections, provided that:

(A) the sections of the research report submitted to the subject company do not contain the research summary, the research rating or the price target;

(B) a complete draft of the research report is provided to legal or compliance personnel before sections of the report are submitted to the subject company; and

(C) if after submitting the sections of the research report to the subject company the research department intends to change the proposed rating or price target, it must first provide written justification to, and receive written authorization from, legal or compliance personnel for the change. The member must retain copies of any draft and the final version of such a research report for three years following its publication.

433

(3) The member may notify a subject company that the member intends to change its rating of the subject company's securities, provided that the notification occurs on the business day before the member announces the rating change, after the close of trading in the principal market of the subject company's securities.

Research reports are subject to a "quiet period," meaning firms cannot publish a research report on a newly public company until 10 days after the IPO. Some smaller firms don't have their own research analysts, so they use third parties to provide reports on various securities and then deliver them to their customers. If that is the case, the member firm needs to disclose that the research was/is provided by someone else and is third-party research. Finally, research analysts are regulated by **Regulation AC,** which requires them to certify that their research accurately reflects their own objective, non-cash-influenced views. To that end, they also need to disclose if they or any of their immediate family members received any type of compensation (cash, options, warrants, what-have-you) for making this recommendation. This regulation applies to both research reports and public appearances by research analysts.

CMOs

CMOs (collateralized mortgage obligations) are not well understood by most investors, so FINRA has specific rules stipulating that advertising and sales literature on CMOs must be filed with FINRA ten days *before* first use, subject to any revisions that FINRA demands before the firm uses the piece being submitted. The communication must refer to the securities as "collateralized mortgage obligations" and not some other name, and CMOs cannot be compared to *any* other product, since they are totally unique. The following disclosure statement must appear in an advertisement for a CMO: *The yield and average life shown above consider prepayment assumptions that may or may not be met. Changes in payments may significantly affect yield and average life. Please contact your representative for information on CMOs and how they react to different market conditions.*

FINRA has even gone so far as to offer a standardized CMO print advertisement that broker-dealers can use, but even if the firm uses that format, they still must submit the ad to FINRA prior to first use after filling in all the information to be communicated.

Broker-dealers are required to offer educational material about the features of CMOs to customers that must include:

> A discussion of the characteristics and risks of CMOs. This would include: how changing interest rates may affect prepayment rates and the average life of the security, tax considerations, credit risk, minimum investments, liquidity, and transactions costs.
> A discussion of the structure of a CMO. This would include the different types of structures, tranches, and risks associated with each type of security. It is also important to explain to a customer that two CMOs with the same underlying collateral may have different prepayment risk and different interest-rate risk.
> A discussion that explains the relationship between mortgage loans and mortgage securities.
> A glossary of terms applicable to mortgage-backed securities.

When a registered representative is cold calling investors, he needs to keep the following in mind:

> Don't call the residence of any person before 8 a.m. or after 9 p.m. in the prospect's local time zone, unless that person has given express written/signed permission, is an established customer of your firm, or is a broker-dealer
>
> Check your firm's specific do-not-call list. If the prospect is on that list, should you go ahead and dial them anyway? Only if you're planning an early retirement
>
> Check the Federal Trade Commission's national do-not-call list and do not call anyone on that list

Please note that the rules above do not apply to your existing customers, other broker-dealers, or any person who has given written permission to be called at a time outside 8 a.m. and 9 p.m. in his time zone. Some people can only be reached early-morning or late-night, and why would the regulators need to protect broker-dealers from being called by agents? Even if the customer has been placed on your firm's do-not-call list, provided he writes to you that he wants to be called you may do so. In other words, these regulations protect the general population from being hit with unwanted sales calls, but if someone has sent a written request to be called, or to be called at an unusual time of day, this is no longer troubling. Investors do have the right to make their own decisions, after all.

As you might expect, a member or person associated with a member making a call for telemarketing purposes must provide the called party with the name of the individual caller, the name of the member, an address or telephone number at which the member may be contacted, and that the purpose of the call is to solicit the purchase of securities or related service. The telephone number provided may not be a 900 number or any other number for which charges exceed local or long distance transmission charges

As FINRA makes clear, "The provisions set forth in this rule are applicable to members telemarketing or making telephone solicitations calls to wireless telephone numbers."

Also, "if a member uses another entity to perform telemarketing services on its behalf, the member remains responsible for ensuring compliance with all provisions contained in this rule."

Prior to engaging in telemarketing activities, the firm needs to:

> Create a written policy for maintaining a do-not-call list
>
> Train personnel who will be calling
>
> If anyone requests to be put on your firm-specific do-not-call list, put them on the list
>
> Identify all callers—who you are, who you work for, the fact that you are trying to interest them in securities

Obviously, these rules are a major inconvenience. For some firms, the pain is even greater. If certain sales representatives have an employment history that includes working at a "disciplined firm," the firm must start tape-recording all telephone conversations between the member's registered persons and both existing and potential customers. The firm must establish procedures for reviewing the tape recordings and must maintain the recordings for three years. At the end of each calendar quarter, such firms must report to FINRA on their supervision of the telemarketing activities. The reporting is due within 30 days of the end of each quarter.

What is a disciplined firm? Basically, any firm that has been busted by the SEC, any SRO, or the Commodity Futures Trading Commission. So, if a certain number of registered reps used to work at disciplined firms, break out the tape recorder and start taping. You can probably find a list of firms currently subject to this rule at www.finra.org.

Websites and BrokerCheck

FINRA requires member firms to include a prominent reference to FINRA's BrokerCheck and a hyperlink to it on the initial web page intended to be viewed by retail investors, as well as on any page containing a professional profile of any registered person conducting business with retail investors. Clearly, FINRA wants to encourage investors to check out their registered representatives both before and after they start investing through them. A few minutes with BrokerCheck will confirm—or not—whether the individual is licensed and with which firm, as well as any disciplinary reports or arbitration awards of $15,000 or more paid out to disgruntled customers.

The MSRB

The SEC is the ultimate securities regulator and is part of the federal government. National securities exchanges and associations such as FINRA, CBOE, etc., are self-regulatory organizations or SROs registered with the SEC under the Securities Exchange Act of 1934.

The SRO that regulates municipal securities firms is the MSRB, which stands for the Municipal Securities Rulemaking Board. This organization has much to say about how municipal securities dealers do business. They have no authority over issuers of municipal securities, which include state and city governments. Rather, they have authority over the firms and associated persons who do municipal securities business with such issuers.

But the MSRB does not enforce anything. They write the rules for municipal securities dealers and their associated persons. But, other regulators enforce these rules. For bank dealers the FDIC, FRB, and the Comptroller of the Currency enforce MSRB rules. For broker-dealers FINRA and the SEC enforce the rules.

All right, so that's who the MSRB is. Currently, they have 48 "General" rules, and they are all testable to some extent. Since they are the "General" rules, they all start with the letter "G." We'll list them in order, but we're not telling you to memorize each rule by rule number. You'll need to know what the rules mean and how they're applied.

Rule G-1. A separately identifiable department or division of a bank…is that unit of the bank which conducts all of the activities of the bank relating to the conduct of business as a municipal securities dealer.

Comment: some banks have divisions that conduct municipal securities business. The exam might refer to them as bank dealers or dealer-banks.

Rule G-2. No municipal securities dealer shall effect any transaction in, or induce or attempt to induce the purchase or sale of, any municipal security unless such municipal securities dealer and every natural person associated with such municipal securities dealer is qualified in accordance with the rules of the Board.

Comment: the firm, the principals, and the representatives have to meet the qualifications and registration requirements of the MSRB. They then clarify that with the next rule:

Rule G-3. No municipal securities dealer or person who is a municipal securities representative, municipal securities principal, municipal securities sales principal or financial and operations principal (as hereafter defined) shall be qualified for purposes of rule G-2 unless such municipal securities dealer or person meets the requirements of this rule. The term "municipal securities representative" means a natural person associated with a municipal securities dealer, other than a person whose functions are solely clerical or ministerial, whose activities include one or more of the following:

(A) underwriting, trading or sales of municipal securities;

(B) financial advisory or consultant services for issuers in connection with the issuance of municipal securities;

(C) research or investment advice with respect to municipal securities; or

(D) any other activities which involve communication, directly or indirectly, with public investors in municipal securities; provided.

Comment: the words "clerical or ministerial" are often used in regulations to distinguish between those who are actively involved in the investment business of the firm and those who are maybe just working as the receptionist or performing filing, word processing, or other general office work. As we can see, if the individual (natural person) is involved with underwriting, trading, or selling municipal securities, he is a "municipal securities representative" and must register. Also, if he is involved with financial advisory/consulting activities for issuers, providing research/advice on municipal securities, or communicating with public investors, he is a "municipal securities representative" and subject to registration requirements. This rule goes on to state that municipal securities representatives brand new to the securities business must go through a 90-day apprenticeship period. During this period, they can be paid a salary (no commissions) and can only deal with other dealers or institutional investors, not with public investors. A public investor is the "retail investor," and we protect them much more than we protect other dealers or big institutions. In fact, the basic idea is that an institutional investor will know if the apprentice screws up and will generally be quite happy to point out the mistake in a very pleasant, encouraging, professional tone of voice. The apprentice also must pass the appropriate exam within 180 days or stop all sales activities immediately. Of course, if he had already worked in the business with a Series 6 or Series 7 for at least 90 days, he would have already completed the apprenticeship period.

The term "municipal securities principal" refers to the individuals who are "directly engaged in the management, direction or supervision of" all the activities mentioned for representatives, plus:

maintenance of records with respect to the activities enumerated training of municipal securities principals or municipal securities representatives

The rule then goes into extreme detail concerning the fact that the qualification exams (52, 53, etc.) are confidential and that people who fail must wait 30 days to retest the first time, 30 days to retest the second time, and then 6 months every time after that. That's the way all of these exams work, so no surprise there.

> **Rule G-4.** No municipal securities dealer or natural person shall be qualified for purposes of rule G-2 if, by action of a national securities exchange or registered securities association, such municipal securities dealer has been and is expelled or suspended from membership or participation in such exchange or association, or such natural person has been and is barred or suspended from being associated with a member of such exchange or association for violation of any rules of such exchange or association which prohibit any act or transaction constituting conduct inconsistent with just and equitable principles of trade, or which requires any act the omission of which constitutes conduct inconsistent with such just and equitable principles of trade.

Comment: notice the phrase "conduct inconsistent with just and equitable principles of trade." That phrase is used by FINRA, the NYSE, and the MSRB. If the conduct of a firm, a principal, or a representative is not consistent with being fair to customers, and being fair among all customers, then we've got ourselves a problem. For example, there are plenty of reps out there who have told customers to cut checks for investments in their name. The rep then either puts the money in his own bank account or maybe establishes a joint account at an online broker. You know, two grand of his own money and fifty grand of the customer's money, split right down the middle. In order to conceal the fact that he's investing or simply spending the client's money, he sends bogus monthly account statements to the client making it appear that the investment is doing just fine. This would be conduct that is "inconsistent with just and equitable principles of trade."

The SEC, called "the Commission," under the Securities Exchange Act of 1934 has the power to allow or disallow any person from registration with the MSRB. But, if an agent accidentally spent all of her client's money while lying to him with bogus account statements, I would not anticipate the SEC going out of its way for her.

Rule G-5. This rule makes it clear that is a violation of MSRB rules to violate any SEC rules or rules of the other SROs that the firm belongs to. As usual, the regulators are on the same page when it comes to what constitutes "conduct inconsistent with just and equitable principles of trade."

Rule G-6. This rule states that since firms are members of FINRA, they have to meet the fidelity bond requirements of FINRA. Let's see how FINRA defines the "fidelity bond" issue: Each member required to join the Securities Investor Protection Corporation who has employees and who is not a member in good standing of the American Stock Exchange, Inc.; the Boston Stock Exchange; the

Midwest Stock Exchange, Inc.; the New York Stock Exchange, Inc.; the Pacific Stock Exchange, Inc.; the Philadelphia Stock Exchange, Inc.; or the Chicago Board Options Exchange shall:

(1) Maintain a blanket fidelity bond, in a form substantially similar to the standard form of Brokers Blanket Bond promulgated by the Surety Association of America, covering officers and employees which provides against loss and has agreements covering at least the following:

-Fidelity

-On Premises

-In Transit

-Misplacement

-Forgery and Alteration (including check forgery)

-Securities Loss (including securities forgery)

-Fraudulent Trading

Comment: so, certain firms that have employees need to meet fidelity bonding requirements just in case anyone accidentally loses securities or steals them, etc.

Rule G-7. This rule stipulates that municipal securities firms have to get all kinds of information about their principals and representatives. The firm is required to check the individual's employment history over at least the past 10 years, a record of all residences over the past five years, a record of any disciplinary history involving the SEC, state regulators, banking regulators, SROs, etc., and—of course—any felonies or misdemeanors related to forgery, fraud, burglary, perjury, bribery, etc. In other words, submit a U4, which is the standard form used whenever an agent or principal associates with a firm.

Rule G-8. Member firms must keep "account records for each customer account and account of such municipal securities dealer. Such records shall reflect all purchases and sales of municipal securities, all receipts and deliveries of municipal securities, all receipts and disbursements of cash, and all other debits and credits relating to such account." Firms also need to keep a daily itemized record of everything mentioned above in something called a "blotter" or "other records of original entry." There needs to be a record of each security carried by the member for its own account or the accounts of its customers. The firm must obtain customer account information, just as FINRA firms are required to do. In fact, if you're a broker-dealer involved in municipal securities, you're a member of FINRA. You follow both sets of rules, which are usually on the same page, more or less. The firm needs:

customer's name and address
whether customer is of legal age
tax identification or social security number

occupation

name and address of employer

information about the customer used for suitability/recommendations

signature of municipal securities representative and signature of a municipal securities principal indicating acceptance of the account

with respect to discretionary accounts, customer's written authorization to exercise discretionary power or authority with respect to the account, written approval of municipal securities principal who supervises the account, and written approval of municipal securities principal with respect to each transaction in the account, indicating the time and date of approval

whether customer is employed by another broker, dealer or municipal securities dealer

Firms like to get their customers to sign a pre-dispute arbitration agreement. Once that's signed, the customer cannot sue the firm in civil court. Instead, all claims are taken to arbitration, as they are in Major League Baseball. In arbitration, there is one decision and no appeals. The arbitrators don't have to explain their decision, and some of them come from the securities industry. Therefore, the rules state that firms must make it very clear what arbitration is and what the customer is being asked to sign.

The firm must keep records of all customer written complaints, including the action taken to resolve the complaints. Records of political contributions made to issuers must be kept; in fact, there are so many rules to be kept that we're going to move on from here.

Rule G-9. This rule explains that some records must be maintained for three years, and some for six years. Customer complaints, for example, are kept for six years, possibly because after six years it's too late for the customer to file an arbitration claim. Written and electronic communications, written agreements, customer account information, powers of attorney, transaction records, etc., are kept for three years.

Rule G-10. When the firm receives a written customer complaint, the firm must send an "investor brochure" that explains the customer's remedies, such as the arbitration mentioned above.

Rule G-11. This rule provides a large amount of detail for syndicate procedures. It seems too detailed for an exam question.

Rule G-12. This is the "uniform practice" rule, so it's also extremely detailed. It defines the terms "settlement date" and the specific types of settlement: cash, regular way, when/as/and if issued. Cash settlements occur on the day of the trade. Regular way settlement is "T + 3 business days." A "when, as, and if issued" settlement is what the buyer of a new issue receives. In other words, the bonds have been sold but not actually created and delivered yet. Dealers must confirm transactions with one another, and this rule provides an extreme level of detail on that process.

When firms deliver securities to the buyer's broker-dealer, there are rules about the denominations they have to come in and all the special ways they might have to be marked. The test could ask about a "mutilated certificate," which is not good delivery unless it is validated by the "trustee, registrar, transfer agent, paying agent or issuer of the securities or by an authorized agent or official of the issuer." If there's no legal opinion, the bond must be marked "ex-legal," or else delivery can be rejected by the other dealer. If the bonds have those old-fashioned coupons, the coupons must be attached. If you get a question about a coupon bond that is in default, tell the test that all coupons would need to be attached for purposes of good delivery: past due coupons, currently due coupons, coupons due in the future.

Rule G-13. This rule covers quotations. The phrase "bona fide" means that a quotation that is published has to be legitimate. So, don't be publishing BID prices unless you're prepared to actually buy some of those municipal securities at that price, for example. Also, make sure that your Bid and Offer prices represent your best judgment of the fair market value for those securities, rather than, say, gouging the heck out of your loyal customers. And, if a member is participating in a joint account, meaning that several firms control the same securities, the members cannot put out different quotes on these bonds to different parties. The exam might say that they cannot "indicate more than one market for the same securities."

Rule G-14. Municipal securities firms must report transactions to "RTRS," which is the MSRB's "Real-Time Transaction Reporting System." As this rule explains, reporting transactions is important for the purpose of regulatory enforcement and also provides transparency to the public, meaning it allows investors to quickly know the market price and volume for a particular security. Trades must generally be reported within 15 minutes to RTRS. Also, municipal securities firms must be sure they are not reporting transactions that did not actually occur, or reporting prices that are fictitious. See, there are always a few bad apples out there who will try to manipulate the securities markets. Maybe they purchase a block of bonds and then artificially drive up the price by having sloppy or dishonest firms publish trades that did not even occur at higher and higher prices until a buyer can be lured in to pay much more than the bonds are actually worth.

Or, two traders will form what are really two joint accounts at different firms but conceal each other's names from the account documents. Now, they spend all day buying and selling the securities back and forth, when there is really no change in ownership taking place. Municipal securities firms not only must avoid such conduct themselves, but also make sure they're not being used as pawns by criminals.

Rule G-15. When a firm executes a trade with or for a customer, they must provide a written trade confirmation no later than settlement/completion of the transaction. Confirmations must include information such as:

Name, address, telephone # of the dealer
Customer name
Purchase from or sale to the customer
Capacity in which firm acted (agent for customer, principal for own account)
Trade date and time of execution
Par value
CUSIP #
Yield and dollar price
Accrued interest
Extended principal (total amount paid for the bonds, before commissions or accrued interest)

Total dollar amount of the transaction

The trade confirmation must always disclose the most conservative or lowest yield to customers. For discount bonds, they must disclose the YTM. For premium bonds, they must disclose YTC. Only exception is if a bond has been advance refunded. In this case, we know for sure when the bond will be called, so yield-to-call is the only yield we have to disclose. No longer matters what yield to original maturity would have been at this point, since we'll never get there now that the bond has been called.

If the bond is insured against default, as many revenue bonds are, the customer must receive evidence of that insurance, either on the face of the certificate or in a document attached to the certificate.

> Rule G-16. At least once each two calendar years, each municipal securities dealer shall be examined to determine, at a minimum, whether such municipal securities dealer and its associated persons are in compliance with all applicable rules of the Board (MSRB) and all applicable provisions of the Act (Securities Exchange Act of 1934) and rules and regulations of the Commission (SEC) thereunder.

Comment: that one's very clear as is—I just added the parenthetical clarifications.

This next one is also not hard to follow:

> Rule G-17. In the conduct of its municipal securities activities, each broker, dealer, and municipal securities dealer shall deal fairly with all persons and shall not engage in any deceptive, dishonest, or unfair practice.

Comment: there isn't time or space here to imagine all the ways that a municipal securities dealer could take advantage of customers. But, let's look at one example to make the above dead language come alive. Let's say that Mrs. Jenkins, an 85-year-old customer, comes in with some bonds that nobody at the firm has ever heard of. Nobody ever trades these securities, but the firm, being so nice and all, tells Mrs. J that they will buy those bonds from her "at the market price" of $700. Is there a market price of $700? No. There is no market for the securities at all, so the firm is taking advantage of the client with the low price and deceiving her by pretending she's getting an objectively fair price for the bonds. The firm should be clear that these are illiquid securities with no active secondary market; if she still wants to sell them for $700, maybe the transaction will pass the smell test. Though not if the firm quickly resells the bonds for $900, right? Or, maybe a particular high-yield (junk) municipal bond fund pays the highest 12b-1 fees to firms and their agents. Therefore, even when conservative investors ask for recommendations, they are routinely routed to the higher-risk, high-yield mutual fund, not because it's suitable for the investors but because it's lucrative to the firm and the agents. Again with the whole "deceptive, dishonest, or unfair practice" thing.

Rule G-18. Each broker, dealer and municipal securities
dealer, when executing a transaction in municipal securities
for or on behalf of a customer as agent, shall make a
reasonable effort to obtain a price for the customer that is
fair and reasonable in relation to prevailing market
conditions.

Comment: notice how it doesn't say "the best possible price." Just says that if you're acting for a customer who wants to buy or sell a municipal security, try to make a reasonable effort to get them a good price. It might be tempting for two firms to trade favors by getting their customers to pay way too much whenever buying municipal bonds on the secondary market. Unfortunately, the regulators are saying that the firm needs to do some due diligence in obtaining a fair and reasonable price. It's not that hard for the regulators to review the prices reported throughout the day. If it's clear that a particular member firm is gouging their clients, there will be hell to pay in the form of sanctions, fines, and possibly even suspensions.

Rule G-19. This rule is sort of a re-statement of G-8. It tells the dealer which account information it must obtain before executing transactions with or for customers in municipal securities. For a non-institutional investor the firm must obtain the following:

> the customer's financial status;
>
> the customer's tax status;
>
> the customer's investment objectives; and
>
> such other information used or considered to be reasonable and necessary by such broker, dealer or
> municipal securities dealer in making recommendations to the customer.

The rule states that all recommendations to customers must be suitable and if granted discretion, the firm must be sure that what they're purchasing for their clients is suitable. And, as always, churning is considered impolite. Churning is defined as "executing transactions that are excessive in size or frequency in view of information known to such municipal securities dealer concerning the customer's financial background, tax status, and investment objectives."

This rule was recently updated to match FINRA's rule on suitability, which we explore in more detail under FINRA rules. As with the FINRA rule, investment strategies are covered as well as recommended transactions. And, there are three distinct suitability obligations: reasonable-basis, customer-specific, and quantitative.

Rule G-20. It's okay for a principal or a member firm to give gifts to their employees. But, in general, this rule forbids members from giving to anyone other than an employee or partner of the firm anything worth more than $100 per year. You can probably imagine how many exceptions I'm going to have to lay on you now. First, the rule states that an occasional ticket to a sporting, theatrical, or other entertainment event that is sponsored by the firm is okay, as long as it doesn't happen so often and so extensively that it raises questions of propriety. Second, the firm can sponsor legitimate business functions recognized as deductible expenses by the IRS. Third, gifts of reminder advertising (pens, coffee mugs, golf balls, etc.) are usually okay. A municipal firm could contract somebody for services, as long as there is a written agreement that spells out exactly what the heck this person is going to be doing for the firm and how much they'll be compensated, and the agreement is approved by the employer of the person whose services are being contracted. This rule also states that in connection with primary offerings, it is not okay to make or accept payment of non-cash compensation. Non-cash compensation would be, for example, merchandise, gifts and prizes, travel expenses, meals and lodging. But, of course, there are exceptions. Gifts that aren't preconditioned on somebody meeting a sales target can be given if they don't exceed $100. The occasional ticket to an entertainment venue is okay, as long as it's not excessive or preconditioned on meeting a sales target. And, if it's legitimate and by-the-book, an education seminar can be paid for by the "offeror" to a representative or principal, as long as the attendance is not preconditioned on the meeting of a sales target, only the associated person's expenses (not the guests') are reimbursed, the firm approves the attendance ahead of time, and the location is appropriate to the purpose of the meeting. In other words, if the offeror's headquarters are in LaCrosse, Wisconsin and the associated person works in Appleton, why again does the "seminar" always have to be held in Maui?

Again, try not to raise any question of propriety.

Finally, the member can provide non-cash compensation to its reps for doing a great job. But the rule states that the compensation has to be "based on the total production of associated persons with respect to all municipal securities within respective product types distributed by the firm. And, the credits are equally weighted for each product type."

> Rule G-21. (a) Definition of "Advertisement." For purposes of this rule, the term "advertisement" means any material (other than listings of offerings) published or designed for use in the public, including electronic, media, or any promotional literature designed for dissemination to the public, including any notice, circular, report, market letter, form letter, telemarketing script or reprint or excerpt of the foregoing. The term does not apply to preliminary official statements or official statements, but does apply to abstracts or summaries of official statements, offering circulars and other such similar documents prepared by brokers, dealers or municipal securities dealers.

Comment: advertising must be approved, but as we see above, listings of offerings are not included in this definition, and neither are preliminary or official statements. Official and preliminary official statements are prepared by the issuer of the municipal bonds—the city, county, school district, etc. The MSRB has nothing to say about issuers. Then again, if a firm creates a summary or abstract of either document, the MSRB considers that to be advertising, which must be approved by a principal.

Why? A listing of offerings would just be a statement of fact—the firm has these bonds for sale at this price. Advertising is something that presents a message that could, perhaps, be misconstrued. Rather than a straight-up statement of fact, maybe the piece exclaims, "Our firm can make you rich!" Unfortunately, that's not going to make it past compliance. How about, "Tax-relief strategies for the discerning investor." Better. See, the regulators get upset when important facts are left out of a presentation, or when an advertisement implies more safety than an investment actually provides, or higher returns than anyone is likely to see.

G-21 then goes on to define other terms mentioned on the exam outline, so let's take a look at these:

(b) *Professional Advertisements.*

(i) *Definition of "Professional Advertisement."* The term "professional advertisement" means any advertisement concerning the facilities, services or skills with respect to municipal securities of such broker, dealer or municipal securities dealer or of another broker, dealer, or municipal securities dealer.

(ii) *Standard for Professional Advertisements.* No broker, dealer or municipal securities dealer shall publish or disseminate, or cause to be published or disseminated, any professional advertisement that is materially false or misleading.

(c) *Product Advertisements.*

(i) *Definition of "Product Advertisement."* The term "product advertisement" means any advertisement concerning one or more specific municipal securities, one or more specific issues of municipal securities, the municipal securities of one or more specific issuers, or the specific features of municipal securities.

(ii) *Standard for Product Advertisements.* No broker, dealer or municipal securities dealer shall publish or disseminate, or cause to be published or disseminated, any product advertisement that such broker, dealer, or municipal securities dealer knows or has reason to know is materially false or misleading and, to the extent applicable, that is not in compliance with section (d) or (e) hereof.

So, a municipal securities broker-dealer must be careful not to publish misleading advertisements, whether they are advertising the services of the firm (professional advertisement) or advertising municipal securities (product advertisement). How could a firm mislead municipal securities investors? Perhaps they label an issue of bonds as "tax-exempt" without clarifying that they're still subject to state income taxes and AMT. That's an example of a misleading product advertisement. If they overstate the credentials or experience of the firm itself, that would be an example of misleading professional advertising. These are MSRB rules, and FINRA would enforce them on the wayward member firm by imposing sanctions and fines.

The exam outline mentions many specifics from G-21:

(d) *New Issue Product Advertisements.* In addition to the requirements of section (c), all product advertisements for new issue municipal securities (other than municipal fund securities) shall be subject to the following requirements:

(i) *Accuracy at Time of Sale.* A syndicate or syndicate member which publishes or causes to be published any advertisement regarding the offering by the syndicate of a new issue of municipal securities, or any part thereof, may show the initial reoffering prices or yields for the securities, even if the price or yield for a maturity or maturities may have changed, provided that the advertisement contains the date of sale of the securities by the issuer to the syndicate. In the event that the prices or yields shown in a new issue advertisement are other than the initial reoffering prices or yields, such an advertisement must show the prices or yields of the securities as of the time the advertisement is submitted for publication. For purposes of this rule, the date of sale shall be deemed to be, in the case of competitive sales, the date on which bids are required to be submitted to an issuer and, in the case of negotiated sales, the date on which a contract to purchase securities from an issuer is executed.

(ii) *Accuracy at Time of Publication.* Each advertisement relating to a new issue of municipal securities shall also indicate, if applicable, that the securities shown as available from the syndicate may no longer be available from the syndicate at the time of publication or may be available from the syndicate at a price or yield different from that shown in the advertisement.

In other words, it's okay to publish the reoffering yields/prices of the new issue, even if the yields/prices have since changed, as long as the announcement contains the date of sale by the issuer to the syndicate. And, if there are no more municipal securities available in this issue, an advertisement relating to this issue of securities needs to indicate that fact.

Municipal bonds are usually purchased directly only by institutions and very wealthy investors. Most investors purchase municipal securities through mutual funds. And, of course, MSRB has lots to say about these:

(e) *Municipal Fund Security Product Advertisements.* In addition to the requirements of section (c), all product advertisements for municipal fund securities shall be subject to the following requirements:

(i) *Required Disclosures.*

(A) *Substance and Format of Disclosure.* Except as described in paragraph (B) of this subsection (i), each product advertisement for municipal fund securities:

(1) *basic disclosure* – must include a statement to the effect that:

(a) an investor should consider the investment objectives, risks, and charges and expenses associated with municipal fund securities before investing;

(b) more information about municipal fund securities is available in the issuer's official statement;

(c) if the advertisement identifies a source from which an investor may obtain an official statement and the broker, dealer or municipal securities dealer that publishes the advertisement is the underwriter for one or more of the issues of municipal fund securities for which any such official statement may be supplied, such broker, dealer or municipal securities dealer is the underwriter for one or more issues (as appropriate) of such municipal fund securities; and

(d) the official statement should be read carefully before investing.

In other words, MSRB is on the same page with FINRA when it comes to mutual fund advertising—it's just that municipal securities come with an official statement that functions like a prospectus, so advertisements for "municipal fund securities" need to make mention of that. And, really, that makes perfect sense—would you expect the average mutual fund investor, regardless of net worth and income, to know or care about something as apparently dry as an "official statement"?

Rule G-22. What if somebody just happens to be a principal at an underwriting firm while also serving as mayor of the city issuing the bonds? He would be in a position to control both parties; therefore, a **control relationship** exists. In this case, the firm would have to disclose the control relationship to customers before executing transactions in that issuer's securities. If the disclosure is made verbally, a written disclosure has to be sent no later than settlement. If it's a discretionary account, this is one time when the customer would have to be notified before the trade is executed. As we'll see in a later section, a discretionary account allows the firm to execute trades without first contacting the customer. If it's a transaction in a security where a control relationship exists between the issuer and the firm, however, the customer would have to be notified in order to authorize the transaction.

Rule G-23. This rule regulates financial advisory activities. Issuers usually pay a financial firm to advise them "with respect to the structure, timing, terms and other similar matters concerning such issue or issues." These advisors charge fees for their expertise. Rule G-23 states that if the firm acts as a financial advisor to an issuer, there must be a written agreement that "sets forth the basis of compensation for the financial advisory services to be rendered." For a competitive, sealed bid (GO), the underwriter would need the written permission of their client, the issuer, in order to participate in the syndicate. For a negotiated bid (revenue bond) the financial advisory relationship has to be terminated in writing, the issuer has to consent to the advisor getting involved with the underwriting process, and the firm must disclose the underwriting compensation and the potential conflict of interest to the issuer and get a written acknowledgment from the issuer that the disclosure was received. See, if the firm changes from a disinterested adviser charging a fee to a very interested buyer of the issuer's bonds who might just like to buy the bonds a bit cheaper than they're worth, that's a different relationship where the firm isn't necessarily on the same side anymore. For a sealed, competitive bid, there is no reason to terminate the financial advisory relationship, since the issuer has to award the business to the lowest bid, end of story. For a negotiated underwriting, the firm that was just giving disinterested advice for a fee is now negotiating the price they'll pay for the issuer's bonds.

Rule G-24. Municipal securities firms sometimes perform services for an issuer and may, thereby, find out information that could be used to their advantage. For example, maybe they act as the paying agent, which means they cut the interest and principal checks to the bondholders. How much creativity would it take for this "paying agent" to send a slick, colorful marketing piece that says, "Has your bond matured? Why not buy a new one from us?" with the final principal and interest checks? Not much, of course. So, this rule states that no firm "shall use information discovered through performing [such] services for the purpose of soliciting purchases, sales, or exchanges of municipal securities or otherwise make use of such information for financial gain except with the consent of such issuer or such broker, dealer, or municipal securities dealer or the person on whose behalf the information was given."

Rule G-25. This rule is called "Improper Use of Assets." It tells firms not to offer guarantees against loss to customers. Investing in securities involves risk, and that's just the nature of the beast. Your firm cannot shield the investor from risk, acting as an insurance company. Now, the exception here is that the dealer can sell the investor a put option giving him the right to sell the bond back prior to redemption, usually for par. Or, the dealer can enter into repurchase agreements with investors. In those two cases, there would be a written agreement with all of the terms spelled out, not some empty promise that the investor "can't possibly lose when investing at this firm." A representative or principal might want to "share" in the profits and losses of a customer account, which makes the regulators rightfully nervous. If an associated person wants to share in the account of a client, he'll need to establish a joint account with the customer, and the exam might say he needs "the client's written consent, the consent of the employing firm, and must share in proportion to his investment in the account." In other words, even if you could get a joint account going with one of your customers, you can't put in $50 to his $50,000 and split everything "right down the middle."

Rule G-26 has to do with the process of transferring a customer account to another firm. We discuss the ACATS process in another chapter.

Rule G-27. Supervision. (a) Obligation to supervise. Each municipal securities dealer shall supervise the conduct of the municipal securities activities of the dealer and its associated persons to ensure compliance with Board rules and the applicable provisions of the Act and rules thereunder. Each dealer shall specifically designate one or more associated persons qualified as municipal securities principals, municipal securities sales principals, financial and operations principals in accordance with Board rules, or as general securities principals to be responsible for the supervision of the municipal securities activities of the dealer and its associated persons as required by this rule. A written record of each supervisory designation and of the designated principal's responsibilities under this rule shall be maintained and updated as required under rule G-9.

Comment: this rule also stipulates that the firm must have written supervisory procedures that "codify the dealer's supervisory system for ensuring compliance." What are the principals responsible for?

Handling of customer complaints

Supervision of municipal securities representatives

Monitoring of correspondence between representatives and customers

Approval of new accounts

Approval of all transactions on a daily basis

Required maintenance and retention of required books and records

Reviewing at least annually the written supervisory procedures of the firm

Updating the written supervisory procedures in response to rule changes by the MSRB and other regulators

Rule G-28. Transactions with Employees and Partners of Other Municipal Securities Professionals. No municipal securities dealer shall open or maintain an account in which transactions in municipal securities may be effected for a customer who such municipal securities dealer knows is employed by, or the partner of, another municipal securities dealer, or for or on behalf of the spouse or minor child of such person unless such municipal securities dealer first gives written notice with respect to the opening and maintenance of such account to the municipal securities

dealer by whom such person is employed or of whom such person is a partner.

Comment: before opening an account for someone who works for a municipal securities firm, or for the spouse or minor child of someone who works for a municipal securities firm, the municipal securities dealer must notify the employer in writing. And, after every transaction for this person, the municipal securities dealer has to send a duplicate trade confirmation to the employing dealer and has to act in accordance with any instructions that the employing broker-dealer has provided for the handling of this account. Also, this rule doesn't cover transactions in municipal fund securities, just municipal securities purchased individually.

Rule G-29. Each broker, dealer and municipal securities dealer shall keep in each office a copy of all rules of the Board (MSRB) and shall make such rules available for examination by customers promptly upon request.

Comment: yes, the MSRB Rules contain a Rule about MSRB Rules. Keep a few copies on hand and make sure you provide them to customers upon request. Why is a customer requesting a copy of the MSRB Rulebook? A, she's ticked off at something your firm did, and, B, she doesn't realize the rules are available online at www.msrb.org.

Rule G-30. (a) Principal Transactions. No broker, dealer or municipal securities dealer shall purchase municipal securities for its own account from a customer, or sell municipal securities for its own account to a customer, except at an aggregate price (including any mark-up or mark-down) that is fair and reasonable.

(b) Agency Transactions.

(i) Each broker, dealer and municipal securities dealer, when executing a transaction in municipal securities for or on behalf of a customer as agent, shall make a reasonable effort to obtain a price for the customer that is fair and reasonable in relation to prevailing market conditions.

(ii) No broker, dealer or municipal securities dealer shall purchase or sell municipal securities as agent for a customer for a commission or service charge in excess of a fair and reasonable amount.

Comment: small transactions usually carry higher mark-ups, as is the case whenever we buy in small quantities, but then the flip side is that large transactions should get a better deal. While the firm is "entitled to a profit," they aren't entitled to gouge their clients by purchasing bonds from them @98 and immediately reselling them @108, pocketing $100 per bond. Not that the regulators would give a maximum or minimum mark-up; instead, they use phrases that imply that there is some leeway here but that firms need to use their best judgment when determining what is "fair and reasonable." Basically, either the firm can do a good job of making those judgment calls, or FINRA can schedule a hearing to help them at their earliest convenience.

> Rule G-31. No municipal securities dealer shall solicit transactions in municipal securities with or for the account of an investment company as defined in the Investment Company Act of 1940, as compensation or in return for sales by such municipal securities dealer of participations, shares, or units in such investment company.

Comment: FINRA prohibits the same "shelf space programs" in its "anti-reciprocity rules" codified in FINRA Rules. What they're saying is that the firm cannot approach a municipal bond mutual fund with a pitch like this, "So, if you were willing to execute all of your trades through our firm, we would be willing to sell your fund to our investors ahead of all other funds." The point is that the mutual fund uses their investors' money to pay for everything, including trading commissions. It would be sort of nice if the fund would, then, obtain "best execution" on all of their trades, since they are using the customers' money to buy and sell portfolio securities. If they're cutting sleazy little deals with broker-dealers in which they pay high commissions in exchange for the broker-dealer pushing the fund to new investors, the mutual fund investors are being harmed. See, when the fund gathers new investors, that doesn't help the existing investors at all. It does give the fund more assets against which to charge management and 12b-1 fees, and it also gives them more assets to park in money market securities in order to generate enough interest to pay ever higher board of directors salaries. But, that's not helping the investors. Plus, the broker-dealer making this pitch should probably take the approach of recommending mutual funds to their customers based on suitability, rather than pushing whatever fund pays them the most in commissions.

Rule G-32 stipulates the information that must be disclosed to investors who purchase new issues of municipal securities. In a new offering, the dealer must deliver the official statement no later than the due date for confirmation. If the issuer is not putting an official statement together, that has to be disclosed to investors in writing. If the dealer is involved in a negotiated underwriting, they must disclose the following to investors:

The underwriting spread

The amount of any fee received by the municipal securities dealer as agent for the issuer in the distribution of the securities

The initial offering price for each maturity in the issue that is offered or to be offered in whole or in part by the underwriters

Underwriters now file Official Statements and Advance Refunding Documents to the "EMMA" electronic system that the public can access through a website. And, in those cases in which no official statement or advance refunding document will be prepared, underwriters must notify the EMMA system of that fact.

Rule G-33. This rule standardizes how accrued interest must be calculated. No need to look at that again, especially not at this level of detail.

Rule G-34. This rule is about CUSIP numbers and is probably too detailed to make a good test question.

Rule G-35. This rule makes bank dealers subject to the FINRA Code of Arbitration procedure for handling disputes.

Rule G-36. This rule was replaced with changes to Rule G-32 and the EMMA system referenced there. The status is "reserved," as you'll see at www.msrb.org.

Rule G-37. Political Contributions and Prohibitions on Municipal Securities Business. As a resident of Chicago, I find this rule especially interesting. See, a municipal underwriting firm in Chicago wouldn't take too long to figure out that the best way to get invited to the table for a bunch of lucrative, no-bid "negotiated" underwritings of municipal bonds would be to contribute, say, half of whatever they make to the mayor's political campaign. Not to mention that the governor and certain members of the state legislature might turn out to be really helpful allies in their quest to underwrite lucrative municipal bonds issued by the State of Illinois.

So, the MSRB takes the view that municipal securities dealers should not buy their way into the underwriting process:

> **(a) Purpose. The purpose and intent of this rule are to ensure that the high standards and integrity of the municipal securities industry are maintained, to prevent fraudulent and manipulative acts and practices, to promote just and equitable principles of trade, to perfect a free and open market and to protect investors and the public interest by: (i) prohibiting brokers, dealers and municipal securities dealers from engaging in municipal securities business with issuers if certain political contributions have been made to officials of such issuers; and (ii) requiring brokers, dealers and municipal securities dealers to disclose certain political contributions, as well as other information, to allow public scrutiny of political contributions and the municipal securities business of a broker, dealer or municipal securities dealer.**

If the dealer has made political contributions to an official of the issuer in the past two years, they may not underwrite any of that issuer's municipal bonds. If the contribution was made by the firm, a municipal finance professional associated with the firm, or any political action committee (PAC) controlled by the firm or any municipal finance professional with the firm, the above prohibition would apply.

Except when it wouldn't. As the MSRB explains, "this section shall not prohibit the municipal securities dealer from engaging in municipal securities business with an issuer if the only contributions made by the persons and entities noted above to officials of such issuer within the previous two years were made by municipal finance professionals to officials of such issuer for whom the municipal finance professionals were entitled to vote and which contributions, in total, were not in excess of $250 by any municipal finance professional to each official of such issuer, per election."

So, notice there are two requirements there—first, the municipal finance professional has to be eligible to vote for the official they're contributing to, and the contribution cannot exceed $250.

To make sure everything's on the up and up, member firms have to submit quarterly statements to the MSRB concerning political contributions on Form G-37. For anything other than the $250 contribution by a municipal finance professional eligible to vote for the official, the MSRB wants the name and title of each official and/or PAC receiving contributions, listed by state, amount of the contribution, and whether it was made by the firm, a municipal finance professional, a non-municipal finance executive, or a PAC controlled by any of those folks. The form also lists which issuers the firm has done underwriting business with in the preceding quarter, listed by state.

Rule G-38. Speaking of Chicago, I remember reading an interesting story in the *Sun-Times* a while back that pointed out how the mayor's brother was paid something like $180,000 a year as a "consultant" for a large Wall Street firm that happened to be the largest underwriter of Chicago municipal bonds. When the press asked the firm exactly what sort of "consulting" the mayor's brother might do for them, they got no answers. Well, that was then—this is now. In fact, if you diligently peruse these MSRB rules, you'll see how they often mention "former rule G-38." In the old days, a firm could use a so-called "consultant" as long as they followed some rather lax rules requiring a written agreement and a little bit of disclosure. Now, check out what the current Rule G-38 thinks about the use of so-called "consultants" . . .

> **Prohibited Payments. No municipal securities dealer may provide or agree to provide, directly or indirectly, payment to any person who is not an affiliated person of the municipal securities dealer for a solicitation of municipal securities business on behalf of such municipal securities dealer.**

Okay, so what is an "affiliated person of the municipal securities dealer"? Here we go:

> **The term "affiliated person of the municipal securities dealer" means any person who is a partner, director, officer, employee or registered person of the municipal securities dealer (or, in the case of a bank dealer, any person occupying a similar status or performing similar functions**

for the bank dealer) or of an affiliated company of the
municipal securities dealer.

Why would the MSRB have a rule such as this? Think how easy it would be for an underwriting firm to "hire" the immediate family of mayors, governors, and other key politicians to act as so-called "consultants" when, in fact, it's just a glorified bribe. If we give the governor's sister-in-law $125,000, she can get us the negotiated underwriting deal on about $25 million of upcoming revenue bonds. To make it look legitimate, we'll hire her as a consultant and let her work from home. As long as she sends in a few emails, maybe even a spreadsheet or two, we got ourselves a "consulting engagement" at about $40,000 an hour to a person who's never had a finance class and can't even balance her own checkbook.

And, it's not just the underwriting firms who might abuse the system. This rule protects firms from being shaken down by seedy family members of key political figures. "Hey, I hear you'd like to get in on that next big bond issue. Turns out, as the Governor's brother, I'm looking for a little, uh, you know, *consulting* work, myself, so maybe we should, you know, talk." At least now they can say that they are precluded from pursuing such a consulting arrangement due to MSRB Rule G-38.

Rule G-39. This rule stipulates that callers must identify the firm they represent and the fact that they are calling about securities investment opportunities. If someone says she isn't interested and asks to be put on the do-not-call list, put her on the do-not-call list and do-not-call her. There is a firm-specific list and a national list to be checked before dialing prospects. Prospects are not to be called before 8 a.m. or after 9 p.m. in their time zone, with limited exceptions.

Rule G-40. This rule stipulates that firms need to establish an Internet electronic mail account to allow for electronic communications with the MSRB. A Primary Electronic Mail Contact has to be established to serve as the official contact person for purposes of electronic mail communication between the municipal securities dealer and the MSRB. The firm may also establish an Optional Electronic Mail Contact. The firm needs to file a Form G-40 electronically informing the MSRB who these electronic mail contacts are.

Rule G-41. Every municipal securities dealer shall establish and implement an anti-money laundering compliance program reasonably designed to achieve and monitor ongoing compliance with the requirements of the Bank Secrecy Act ("BSA"), and the regulations thereunder.

Comment: this rule then states that if the firm complies with the anti-money laundering compliance program of FINRA, then they comply with MSRB Rule G-41.

Rule G-42. (a) Standards of Conduct.

(i) A municipal advisor to an obligated person client shall, in the conduct of all municipal advisory activities for that client, be subject to a duty of care.

(ii) A municipal advisor to a municipal entity client shall, in the conduct of all municipal advisory activities for that client, be subject to a fiduciary duty that includes a duty of loyalty and a duty of care.

(b) Disclosure of Conflicts of Interest and Other Information. A municipal advisor must, prior to or upon engaging in municipal advisory activities, provide to the municipal entity or obligated person client full and fair disclosure in writing of:

(i) all material conflicts of interest, including:

(A) any affiliate of the municipal advisor that provides any advice, service, or product to or on behalf of the client that is directly related to the municipal advisory activities to be performed by the disclosing municipal advisor;

(B) any payments made by the municipal advisor, directly or indirectly, to obtain or retain an engagement to perform municipal advisory activities for the client;

(C) any payments received by the municipal advisor from a third party to enlist the municipal advisor's recommendation to the client of its services, any municipal securities transaction or any municipal financial product;

(D) any fee-splitting arrangements involving the municipal advisor and any provider of investments or services to the client;

(E) any conflicts of interest arising from compensation for municipal advisory activities to be performed that is contingent on the size or closing of any transaction as to which the municipal advisor is providing advice; and

(F) any other actual or potential conflicts of interest, of which the municipal advisor is aware after reasonable inquiry, that could reasonably be anticipated to impair the municipal advisor's ability to provide advice to or on behalf of the client in accordance with the standards of conduct of section (a) of this rule, as applicable.

If a municipal advisor concludes that it has no known material conflicts of interest based on the exercise of reasonable diligence by the municipal advisor, the municipal advisor must provide a written statement to the client to that effect.

(ii) any legal or disciplinary event that is material to the client's evaluation of the municipal advisor or the integrity of its management or advisory personnel.

Information regarding legal or disciplinary events may be disclosed for purposes of this subsection by identification of the specific type of event and specific reference to the relevant portions of the municipal advisor's most recent Forms MA or MA-I filed with the Commission if the municipal advisor provides detailed information specifying where the client may electronically access such forms.

COMMENT: these specifications bring municipal advisors under similar fiduciary standards that investment advisers are held to under federal and state securities law. Conflicts of interest must be disclosed, and clients are owed a duty of care and loyalty. This rule specifically prohibits various business practices:

(A) receiving compensation that is excessive in relation to the municipal advisory activities actually performed;

(B) delivering an invoice for fees or expenses for municipal advisory activities that is materially inaccurate in its reflection of the activities actually performed or the personnel that actually performed those activities;

(C) making any representation or the submission of any information that the municipal advisor knows or should know is either materially false or materially misleading due to the omission of a material fact about the capacity, resources or knowledge of the municipal advisor, in response to requests for proposals or qualifications or in oral presentations to a client or prospective client, for the purpose of obtaining or retaining an engagement to perform municipal advisory activities;

(D) making, or participating in, any fee-splitting arrangement with underwriters on any municipal securities transaction as to which it has provided or is providing advice, and any undisclosed fee-splitting arrangements with providers of investments or services to a municipal entity or obligated person client of the municipal advisor; and

(E) making payments for the purpose of obtaining or retaining an engagement to perform municipal advisory activities other than: (1) payments to an affiliate of the municipal advisor for a direct or indirect communication with a municipal entity or obligated person on behalf of the municipal advisor where such communication is made for the purpose of obtaining or retaining an engagement to perform municipal advisory activities; (2) reasonable fees paid to another municipal advisor registered as such with the Commission and the Board for making such a communication as described in subparagraph (e)(i)(E)(1); and (3) payments that are permissible "normal business dealings" as described in Rule G-20.

G-43. a) Duty of Broker's Broker.

(i) Each dealer acting as a "broker's broker" with respect to the execution of a transaction in municipal securities for or on behalf of another dealer shall make a reasonable effort to obtain a price for the dealer that is fair and reasonable in relation to prevailing market conditions. The broker's broker must employ the same care and diligence in doing so as if the transaction were being done for its own account.

(ii) A broker's broker that undertakes to act for or on behalf of another dealer in connection with a transaction or potential transaction in municipal securities must not take any action that works against that dealer's interest to receive advantageous pricing.

COMMENT: As the rule implies, a broker's broker is a municipal securities firm that executes transactions in municipal securities "for or on behalf of another dealer." When doing so, the broker's broker has to employ the same care and diligence as if the transaction were being done for its own account. They also must not take any action that works against the other dealer's interest.

Rule G-44 stipulates that municipal advisors are subject to the same rules that municipal brokers and dealers are in terms of developing and regularly updating their written supervisory procedures. As the rule states:

(a) Supervisory System. Each municipal advisor shall establish, implement, and maintain a system to supervise the municipal advisory activities of the municipal advisor and its associated persons that is reasonably designed to achieve compliance with applicable securities laws and regulations, including applicable Board rules ("applicable rules"). Final responsibility for proper supervision shall rest with the municipal advisor. A municipal advisor's supervisory system shall provide, at a minimum, for the following:

(i) Written Supervisory Procedures. The establishment, implementation, maintenance and enforcement of written supervisory procedures that are reasonably designed to ensure that the conduct of the municipal advisory activities of the municipal advisor and its associated persons are in compliance with applicable rules. The written supervisory procedures shall be promptly amended to reflect changes in applicable rules and as changes occur in the municipal advisor's supervisory system, and such procedures and amendments shall be promptly communicated to all associated persons to whom they are relevant based on their activities and responsibilities

(ii) Appropriate Principal. The designation of one or more municipal advisory principals to be responsible for the supervision required by this rule.

The rule requires municipal advisors to review and update their compliance process and procedures regularly--annually, at a minimum. Each firm must have a chief compliance officer. Municipal advisors must require their chief executive officers to annually certify in writing that the firm has sufficient processes and procedures in place reasonably designed to achieve compliance with applicable rules.

Rule G-45 requires underwriters of municipal fund securities to file reports with the MSRB:

(a) Form G-45 Reporting Requirements. Each underwriter of a primary offering of municipal fund securities that are not interests in local government investment pools shall report to the Board the information relating to such offering required by Form G-45 by no later than 60 days following the end of each semi-annual reporting period ending on June 30 and December 31 and in the manner prescribed in the Form G-45 procedures below and as set forth in the Form G-45 Manual.

Rule G-46 is reserved.

Rule G-47 states:

(a) No broker, dealer, or municipal securities dealer shall sell a municipal security to a customer, or purchase a municipal security from a customer, whether unsolicited or recommended, and whether in a primary offering or secondary market transaction, without disclosing to the customer, orally or in writing, at or prior to the time of trade, all material information known about the transaction, as well as material information about the security that is reasonably accessible to the market.

The guidance to the rule points out:

Manner and Scope of Disclosure.

a. The disclosure obligation includes a duty to give a customer a complete description of the security, including a description of the features that likely would be considered significant by a reasonable investor, and facts that are material to assessing the potential risks of the investment.

b. The public availability of material information through EMMA, or other established industry sources, does not relieve brokers, dealers, and municipal securities dealers of their obligation to make the required time of trade disclosures to a customer.

c. A broker, dealer, or municipal securities dealer may not satisfy its disclosure obligation by directing a customer to an established industry source or through disclosure in general advertising materials.

d. Whether the customer is purchasing or selling the municipal securities may be a consideration in determining what information is material.

The trade disclosure in G-47 is then modified by G-48, which states that if the firm determines the customer is a Sophisticated Municipal Market Professional (SMMP), then the disclosure under G-47 is not required.

And, G-48 stipulates that the fair and reasonable price concerns under G-30 do not apply when the customer is an SMMP if:

(i) the transactions are non-recommended secondary market agency transactions;

(ii) the broker, dealer, or municipal securities dealer's services with respect to the transactions have been explicitly limited to providing anonymity, communication, order matching, and/or clearance functions; and

(iii) the broker, dealer, or municipal securities dealer does not exercise discretion as to how or when the transactions are executed.

When the transactions are with SMMPs, the requirement to ascertain the best market for a security is waived. And, when the transactions are with Sophisticated Municipal Market Professionals, the customer-specific suitability requirements under G-19 are waived, as well.

The securities markets are regulated under a handful of federal securities Acts of the United States Congress. The Securities and Exchange Commission (SEC) also makes ("promulgates") rules under these federal securities acts. Let's look at them in chronological order.

➤ *Securities Act of 1933*

The Securities Act of 1933 aims to ensure that investors have all the material information they need before buying stocks and bonds issued on the primary market and that this information is accurate and not misleading.

As the SEC explains on their website:

> Often referred to as the "truth in securities" law, the Securities Act of 1933 has two basic objectives:
>
> • require that investors receive financial and other significant information concerning securities being offered for public sale; and
>
> • prohibit deceit, misrepresentations, and other fraud in the sale of securities.

The scope of this securities law is narrower than the more far-reaching Securities Exchange Act of 1934. The Securities Act of 1933 focuses solely on the offering of securities to public investors for the very first time. The Act requires issuers to register an offering of securities with the SEC before the issuer is allowed to offer or sell their securities to the public. Because of this securities law an investor must be provided with a disclosure document that discloses everything he might need to know about the company issuing the security *before* the issuer or underwriters take his money and close the deal. Investors can read about the issuer's history, its board of directors, its products and services, its chances for success, and its chances for failure. They can look at the balance sheet and the income statement. They'll still be taking a risk if they buy—because all securities carry risk—but at least they'll be able to make an informed decision because of this full and fair disclosure.

When a corporation wants to raise capital by selling securities, they get a group of underwriters together and fill out paperwork for the federal government in the form of a **registration statement**. Part of this registration statement will become the **prospectus**, which is the disclosure brochure that investors will be provided with. An "underwriter" is just a broker-dealer that likes to take companies public, remember. Another name for an underwriter is investment banker, but they don't act like a traditional bank. No deposits or checking offered here. Their job is to raise money for their clients, other people's money.

Once the underwriters file the registration statement on behalf of the issuer, the process goes into a cooling off period, which will last 20 days or longer for most offerings. This process can drag on and on as the SEC reviews the paperwork, but no matter how long it takes, the issuer and underwriters can only do certain things during this "cooling off" period. Number one, they can't sell anything. They can't do any general advertising of the securities offering. They can <u>announce</u> that a sale is going to take place by publishing a **tombstone** ad in the financial press, because a tombstone ad is just a rectangle with some text. It announces that a sale of securities will take place at a particular offering price (or yield) and informs the reader how he/she can obtain a prospectus. But it is neither an offer to sell nor a solicitation to buy the securities. The underwriters can find out if anyone wants to give an "indication of interest," but those aren't sales. Just names on a list.

If someone gives an indication of interest, they must receive a preliminary prospectus, which contains everything that the final prospectus will contain except for the effective date and the final/public offering price or "POP." The registered rep may not send a research report along with the preliminary prospectus and may not highlight or alter it in any way. As you may know, the preliminary prospectus is also referred to as a "red herring," due to the red-text warning that information may be added or altered. The release date and the final public offering price are two pieces of information yet to be added to what's in the red herring to make it a final prospectus. But, the preliminary prospectus has virtually all the material information a potential investor would need before deciding to invest or not.

The issuer and the underwriters attend a due diligence meeting toward the end of the cooling-off period to try and make sure they provided the SEC and the public with accurate and full disclosure. Nothing gets sold until the SEC "releases" the security on the release date/effective date. Starting on that date, the prospectus must be delivered to all buyers of these new securities for a certain length of time.

And, even though the SEC makes issuers jump through all kinds of hoops, once it's all done, the SEC pretty much washes its hands of the whole affair. The SEC doesn't approve or disapprove of the security. They don't guarantee accuracy or adequacy of the information provided by the issuer and its underwriters. In other words, if this whole thing goes horribly wrong, the liability still rests squarely on the shoulders of the issuers and underwriters, not on the SEC. For that reason, there must be a disclaimer saying basically that on the prospectus. It usually looks like this:

> The Securities and Exchange Commission has not approved or disapproved of these securities. Further, it has not determined that this prospectus is accurate or complete. Any representation to the contrary is a criminal offense.

So, how does the SEC feel about the investment merits of the security? No opinion whatsoever. They just want to make sure you receive full and fair disclosure to make an informed decision to invest or to take a pass.

> Exempt Securities

The Securities Act of 1933 is a piece of federal legislation, so it's not surprising that the party who passed it gave themselves an exemption from the rule. That's right, U.S. government securities are exempt from this act. They don't have to be registered in this way. Neither do municipal securities. Charitable organization securities, such as church bonds, are exempt from the act. So are bank securities, which are already regulated by bank regulators. Securities that mature in 270 days or less—commercial paper, bankers' acceptances—are also exempt from this registration process.

An exempt security is excused from the registration requirement, but it's still a security. So, if anybody offers or sells it deceptively, that is considered securities fraud, which is always a bad idea. People can get sued and thrown in jail for fraudulent offers/sales of securities, and registered representatives have been known to lose their registration. Whether a security had to be registered or not has nothing to do with whether securities fraud transpired. Securities fraud can happen with *any* security, whether it's common stock or an exempt U.S. Treasury Bond. If the seller gets the buyer's money through lies, tricks, and deceit, we're talking about securities fraud.

> Exempt Transactions

There are exempt securities, and there are also transactions that qualify for exemptions. The transactions that qualify for exemptions are called exempt transactions. An exempt security can be offered and sold without filing any registration statement with the SEC. On the other hand, an exempt transaction must be claimed successfully by issuers and their attorneys.

➤ *Securities Exchange Act of 1934*

As I mentioned, the Securities Exchange Act of 1934 is broader in scope than the Securities Act of 1933. As the SEC explains on the same page of their website:

> With this Act, Congress created the Securities and Exchange Commission. The Act empowers the SEC with broad authority over all aspects of the securities industry. This includes the power to register, regulate, and oversee brokerage firms, transfer agents, and clearing agencies as well as the nation's securities self-regulatory organizations (SROs). The various securities exchanges, such as the New York Stock Exchange, the NASDAQ Stock Market, and the Chicago Board of Options are SROs. The Financial Industry Regulatory Authority (FINRA) is also an SRO.
>
> The Act also identifies and prohibits certain types of conduct in the markets and provides the Commission with disciplinary powers over regulated entities and persons associated with them.
>
> The Act also empowers the SEC to require periodic reporting of information by companies with publicly traded securities.

The Securities Exchange Act of 1934 gave the SEC broad powers over the securities markets. The Act gave the Federal Reserve Board the power to regulate margin. It also requires public companies to file quarterly and annual reports with the SEC. If a material event occurs before the next regular report is due, the issuer files an 8-K. There are reports filed when the officers and members of the board sell their shares. Mergers and acquisitions must be announced through various filings. You get the idea.

The Securities Exchange Act of 1934 talked about insider trading, warning investors not to pass around or use non-public information. If you knew that your sister's company was going to be purchased by Google, it would be very tempting to buy a bunch of calls on her company's stock and tell your customers to do the same. Unfortunately, the SEC could sue you for "treble damages," meaning they could try to extract three times the amount of your benefit in civil court.

The Securities Exchange Act of 1934 gives federal prosecutors the authority to prosecute <u>criminal</u> violations. So, if the insider trading activity is handled in civil court, the SEC will try to extract three times your benefit. If they turn it over to the U.S. Attorney's office for criminal prosecution, God help you. You could face criminal charges if the violation were serious enough.

> Insider Trading and Securities Fraud Enforcement Act of 1988 (ITSFEA)

Although the Act of 1934 talked about insider trading, apparently it didn't quite get the message across. So in 1988 Congress passed the **Insider Trading & Securities Fraud Enforcement Act** of 1988 and raised the penalties for insider trading, making it a criminal offense with stiff civil penalties as well. If your brother-in-law happens to be the Chief Financial Officer of a public company and over a few too many martinis lets it slip that his company is going to miss earnings estimates badly this quarter, just pretend like you didn't hear it. Tell your principal and no one else. If you start passing out that information, or if you buy a bunch of puts on the stock, you could go to federal prison. More likely, the SEC would just sue the heck out of you in federal court and try to extract a civil penalty of three times the amount of the profit made or loss avoided.

Any material information the public doesn't have, that's inside information. Don't pass it around, don't use it. People who violate the act can be held liable to what they call "contemporaneous traders." That means that if you're dumping your shares based on an inside tip, and that hurts me, we might need to have a little talk with our attorneys.

The investment banking arm of a broker-dealer has access to all kinds of material non-public information. To prevent that sensitive information from flowing to other areas of the firm, the broker-dealer is required to create a **Chinese wall** around departments that obtain such information. No, they don't build an actual wall. They just try to prevent the investment bankers working on a merger from revealing some good trading tips to the registered representatives working the telephones.

> Market Manipulation

Market manipulation is prohibited under the Securities Exchange Act of 1934 and various SEC and FINRA rules. If a few cheaters are allowed to manipulate the markets for their own advantage, the entire financial system suffers. Therefore, the exam might bring up terms such as **painting the tape,** a technique whereby individuals acting together repeatedly sell a security to one another without changing ownership of the securities. This is intended to give an impression of increased trading volume that can drive up the market price of their holdings. FINRA has a specific rule that says, "no member shall publish or circulate, or cause to be published or circulated, any…communication of any kind which purports to report any transaction as a purchase or sale of any security unless such member believes that such transaction was a bona fide purchase or sale of such security." So, if a member firm is publishing transactions designed to merely inflate the price of a security, such market manipulation would be a serious infraction that could get the member expelled from FINRA altogether. However, these days firms have such sophisticated, rapid-fire, electronic trading desks generating orders based on algorithms that they sometimes end up accidentally completing "self trades" in which the firm or in which related firms end up as both the buyer and seller on the same transaction.

And, that of course violates the rule against reporting trades that did not involve an actual change in beneficial ownership. Therefore FINRA states in a notice to members that "firms must have policies and procedures in place that are reasonably designed to review trading activity for, and prevent, a pattern or practice of self-trades resulting from orders originating from a single algorithm or trading desk, or related algorithms or trading desks."

Other forms of **market manipulation** include **capping** and **pegging**. Capping is the illegal technique of trying to depress a stock price while pegging involves trying to move a stock up to a particular price. A shady call option writer, for example, might want to help ensure that the calls expire by artificially conspiring to keep the price of the underlying stock from rising (capping). Or, the writer of a put might engage in pegging to push the put contracts out-of-the-money in his favor.

It's tough to manipulate a stock with billions of shares outstanding, but it's not so hard to do it with microcap stocks where the entire float is worth perhaps just $10 million. A few shady operators could easily end up manipulating the share price by forming secret joint accounts that allow them to drive up price and volume without any legitimate sales taking place. If all ten investors jointly own all 10 accounts, all the purchases and sales among these accounts would be completely bogus. That's a form of blatant market manipulation that could end up being prosecuted in criminal court, apart from whatever the securities regulators decide to do. The exam could refer to that form of market manipulation as "engaging in securities transactions that involve no effective change in beneficial ownership." Or, those 10 accounts could scheme to enter limit orders at prices higher and higher than the current market to get some activity on the stock noticed by other traders.

Another form of market manipulation occurs when traders spread **rumors** designed to move the stock price. Maybe they purchase put options on a stock trading on the OTC Bulletin Board and then start an ugly rumor about the company on social media to help push down the price. Or, they could buy call options on a small drug maker and then start a false rumor that the company has just developed the cure for ALS. The possibilities are endless, but if a registered representative were caught engaging in this type of activity, that would also be the end of a career.

➤ *Trust Indenture Act of 1939*

The SEC describes the **Trust Indenture Act of 1939** like so:

> This Act applies to debt securities such as bonds, debentures, and notes that are offered for public sale. Even though such securities may be registered under the Securities Act, they may not be offered for sale to the public unless a formal agreement between the issuer of bonds and the bondholder, known as the trust indenture, conforms to the standards of this Act.

As we see above, the Trust Indenture Act of 1939 is all about protecting bondholders. If a corporation wants to sell $5,000,000 or more worth of bonds that mature outside of one year, they must do it under a contract or indenture with a trustee, who will enforce the terms of the indenture to the benefit of the bondholders. In other words, if the issuer stiffs the bondholders, the trustee can get a bankruptcy court to sell off the assets of the company so that bondholders can recover some of their hard-earned money. Sometimes corporations secure the bonds with specific assets like airplanes, securities, or real estate. If so, they pledge title of the assets to the trustee, who just might end up selling them off if the issuer gets behind on its interest payments. So just remember that an indenture is a contract with a trustee, who looks out for the bondholders.

> *Investment Company Act of 1940*

The SEC summarizes this federal securities law like so:

> This Act regulates the organization of companies, including mutual funds, that engage primarily in investing, reinvesting, and trading in securities, and whose own securities are offered to the investing public. The regulation is designed to minimize conflicts of interest that arise in these complex operations. The Act requires these companies to disclose their financial condition and investment policies to investors when stock is initially sold and, subsequently, on a regular basis. The focus of this Act is on disclosure to the investing public of information about the fund and its investment objectives, as well as on investment company structure and operations. It is important to remember that the Act does not permit the SEC to directly supervise the investment decisions or activities of these companies or judge the merits of their investments.

So, mutual funds must register their securities and provide a prospectus to all investors under the Securities Act of 1933. The Investment Company Act of 1940 requires the investment company itself to register and then lays out an exhaustive array of dos and don'ts for their operations. The Investment Company Act of 1940 classified investment companies as face amount certificate companies, unit investment trusts, or management companies. As we saw in an earlier chapter, the management companies are either open-end or closed-end funds. The distinguishing factor is that the open-end funds are redeemable, while the closed-end shares trade on the secondary market among investors. The unit investment trust has no investment adviser managing the portfolio and is sometimes linked with "having no board of directors." Note that the separate account for a variable annuity is registered under this Act, too, either as an open-end fund or as a UIT.

To fit the definition of "investment company," the shares must be easily sold and the number of shareholders must exceed 100. Hedge funds go the other way to avoid fitting the definition of "investment company." That is, they don't let people sell their investment freely and they keep the number of investors under 100, because if you can escape the definition of "investment company," you can escape the hassle of registering the investments and providing lots of disclosure to the SEC and the public markets. As usual, under the Act of 1940 the average investor is protected more than the sophisticated investor. Mutual funds and variable annuities are for the average investor; therefore, they need to be registered and watched closely by the SEC. Hedge funds are for the sophisticated investor primarily, so maybe things don't need to be watched so closely with them.

➢ *Investment Advisers Act of 1940*

> This law regulates investment advisers. With certain exceptions, this Act requires that firms or sole practitioners compensated for advising others about securities investments must register with the SEC and conform to regulations designed to protect investors. Since the Act was amended in 1996 and 2010, generally only advisers who have at least $100 million of assets under management or advise a registered investment company must register with the Commission.

If you want to give people your expert advice on their specific investment situation and receive compensation for doing so, you must register under the Investment Advisers Act of 1940 or under your state securities law. Portfolio managers, financial planners, pension fund consultants, and even many sports and entertainment agents end up having to register to give investment advice to their customers. All open- and closed-end funds are managed by registered investment advisers, and pension funds typically farm out their assets to many different investment advisory firms. Because the role they play is so important and so potentially dangerous, all investment advisers must be registered unless they can qualify for some type of exemption.

Federal covered advisers are subject to the provisions of the Investment Advisers Act of 1940. A federal covered investment adviser with offices in various states only complies with the recordkeeping requirements and the net capital requirements set by the SEC.

The SEC promulgates rules under the Investment Advisers Act of 1940, and the state regulators often write their own rules in reference to the rules the SEC has already made. For example, the SEC is very specific on the dos and don'ts for investment advisers putting out advertisements. Most states tell advisers not to do anything that would violate that particular SEC rule.

The SEC doesn't care whether an investment adviser is subject to registration or not—either way, if the person fits the definition of "investment adviser," he is at least subject to the anti-fraud section of the Investment Advisers Act of 1940. If the investment adviser qualifies for an exemption, he may get to skip various filing requirements, but he would still be subject to the anti-fraud provisions of the Act. That also means that if the person is not an investment adviser, he is not subject to the Investment Advisers Act of 1940, period.

The SEC can discipline federal covered investment advisers through administrative hearings to determine if a license is to be denied, suspended or revoked. They can also represent the U.S. Government in federal court and ask a judge to issue an injunction/restraining order against an investment adviser violating various sections of the "Advisers Act." The SEC does this even more often against insider trading violators under the Securities Exchange Act of 1934. Either way, they're a busy bunch the SEC, believe you me.

Many Series 7 questions could be based on the information covered in this chapter. Maybe you will see something like this:

Which of the following statements is accurate concerning member firms making to references to FINRA or the SEC?

A. Member firms may not mention their affiliation with FINRA in any written communications of any kind
B. If a firm refers to its FINRA membership on its website, it must provide a hyperlink to FINRA's website
C. Member firms are free to use the FINRA logo in any manner that is consistent with high standards of commercial honor and just and equitable principles of trade
D. Members may refer to themselves as "approved by FINRA" or "certified by the Securities and Exchange Commission" only upon acceptance of their membership

EXPLANATION: if a broker-dealer is a member of FINRA, it seems odd that they would must keep that a secret. In fact, every broker-dealer website I visit mentions that they are members of FINRA, as well as SIPC. Eliminate Choice A. Choice B seems reasonable—let's put it to the side. Choice C tries to distract us with the fancy and familiar phrase about high standards of commercial honor. Still, members may not use the FINRA logo, period. Eliminate Choice C. Choice D tries to get us to focus on the idea of waiting for the membership to be accepted, but the bigger idea is that the SEC and FINRA don't put some stamp of approval on any firm or individual in the securities markets. If they did, that would mislead investors into thinking some firms are safer or more profitable than others based on such a stamp. Eliminate Choice D, leaving us with

ANSWER: B

Communications between a member firm and the public cause grave concerns for securities regulators. It only takes one firm putting up a website that claims to guarantee 20% monthly returns without any risk to principal, and soon we're reading about investors who have already lost millions of dollars believing the misleading communication. Therefore, you could see a question such as this:

Which of the following is an example of a retail communication subject to prior principal approval?

A. A webinar for 30 individuals who own mutual funds
B. An email to any individual investor that mentions investment strategies or objectives
C. A form letter about a new variable annuity offered by the firm sent to 30 bank and trust companies
D. A registered representative engaging in a group text with three existing customers

EXPLANATION: 30 individuals who hold mutual funds sure sounds like > 25 retail investors. Let's put that one to the side, no matter how right it looks at first glance. One email to an investor is considered correspondence, which must be monitored but not pre-approved. We can eliminate Choice B. Choice C would be a retail communication if it were sent to retail investors. Bank and trust companies are institutional investors, and institutional communications are not subject to pre-approval. Eliminate Choice C. The group text involves three retail investors, which is far short of the over-25 requirement. Eliminate Choice C, and we are left with

ANSWER: A

FINRA and the SEC are also concerned with the personal trading activities of research analysts. Therefore, you could see something like this:

A research analyst will release a strong-buy research report on ABC, a software company, in the next few weeks. Therefore, which of the following statements is accurate?

A. The analyst may receive—but not purchase—shares ahead of an IPO by an issuer also in the software industry but with no affiliation to ABC
B. The analyst may purchase shares of ABC only if the member is currently engaged in underwriting business with the company
C. Provided the head of the member's investment banking department supervises the transactions, the analyst may purchase shares of ABC freely
D. The analyst is restricted from purchasing shares of ABC for at least 30 days prior to and 5 days after publishing the research report

EXPLANATION: this question brings up several important points related to the personal trading of research analysts. First, there is to be no link between research analysts and the member's investment banking/underwriting activities, so we can eliminate Choice B and Choice C. Once we do that, Choice A looks pretty weak compared to Choice D, right? Would FINRA be okay with the pre-IPO shares because they were a gift? Or, would they prefer that the research analyst stay out of the stock he covers at least 30 days before and 5 days after publishing the research report? Eliminate Choice A, leaving us with

ANSWER: D

As we saw, there are many activities that registered representatives must not engage in. Therefore, you could see a question like this:

Which of the following statements is accurate concerning a registered representative who wants to work a few hours a week outside his employing FINRA-member firm for compensation?

A. Provided the compensation does not exceed $100 weekly, the registered representative may perform the work without notification to the member
B. The registered representative must provide prior written notice to the member firm
C. The member firm must first grant permission for this activity
D. Provided the work is performed within the financial services industry, the registered representative may perform the work without notification to the member

EXPLANATION: the dollar amount of $100 is designed to distract you with the rule on gifts to associated persons of other member firms. There is no dollar amount associated with the rule on outside employment, so eliminate Choice A. Candidates too often grow frustrated with choices as close to each other as B and C. Instead, put them both to the side and look at Choice D. Does this make sense? Or, would FINRA worry even more that the work is done in financial services? Eliminate Choice D. Now, unfortunately, both B and C look equally tempting. Series 7 questions are not only about your ability to use reasoning skills. At this point, you must know the rule. What you don't must do is assume that since this is a regulatory exam, your job is to pick the most stringent answer. The rule states that the registered representative simply must provide written notification. Even though the member can reject or restrict his activities, the rule does not require "written permission" from the member. Eliminate Choice C, leaving us with

ANSWER: B

Misusing the word "guaranteed" can do major harm to an investor. The Series 7 will, therefore, want to see if you know the important concepts surrounding guarantees in the securities industry, like this:

What is true of the word "guaranteed" as it relates to the securities industry?

- A. The word may not be used in connection with any security subject to investment risk
- B. Broker-dealers—but not their agents—may guarantee certain customers against investment losses on securities recommended by any agent of the firm
- C. Only U.S. Treasury—but never corporate—bonds may be described using this word
- D. Agents and broker-dealers may not guarantee any person against an investment loss

EXPLANATION: the word "guaranteed" can be used if used responsibly, so eliminate Choice A. Choice B seems logical—maybe these big firms can do it but not their agents? Choice D says that neither one can offer guarantees. Let's put them to the side, then, and see about Choice C. This one almost seems tempting, except that we know a corporate bond or preferred stock could be "guaranteed" by a third party promising to pay dividends, interest, or principal if the issuer is unable to. So, eliminate Choice C. Now, the question is whether a broker-dealer can guarantee customers against a loss, or maybe neither firms nor agents can offer guarantees. Broker-dealers are not insurance companies. They have far riskier business models and far different net capital requirements. Neither they nor their agents can offer to guarantee any customer against investment loss or promise a specific result. Eliminate Choice B, leaving us with

ANSWER: D

Investors need to know about the handful of registered representatives who harm investors and end up paying out big arbitration awards. Therefore, you could see a question like this:

A registered representative fails to follow through on instructions to sell a customer's mutual fund holdings after which the account drops by a total of $25,000. The customer plans to file an arbitration claim that names the member firm specifically and not the registered representative. Therefore, which of the following statements is accurate?

- A. If the amount of the award is $15,000 or more, the member must update the agent's U4/U5 information with a disclosure report concerning the incident
- B. Because the registered representative is not named, the member need not update the agent's U4/U5 information regardless of any award
- C. Because the amount of money was only $25,000, the customer may not file an arbitration claim based solely on this incident
- D. Because the amount of money was only $25,000, the member need not update the agent's U4/U5 information

EXPLANATION: at first all four answer choices look okay. $25,000 was an amount you read about. Unfortunately, you must now remember what that had to do with. Was the customer precluded from filing a claim, or was a claim of this size simply handled by simplified arbitration? That's it, right? The $25,000 figure had to do with simplified arbitration versus the bigger amounts that involve three or five arbitrators? If you're sure that's right, you can eliminate both Choices C and D. What if you're not sure? Put them to the side. Never eliminate an answer choice unless you *know* why you're eliminating it. What about the first two choices? Again, they both make sense—if the agent wasn't named, maybe the firm takes the hit? That is how things *used* to work. Trouble was, customers eventually understood that if they wanted to get paid, they should name the firm, who would then conceal from the public that the particular agent is a bad boy. Nowadays, members must disclose any arbitration award related to an agent's activities if the amount is at least $15,000, even if the claim fails to name the agent specifically. We can now eliminate Choice B. Then, we can go back and eliminate Choice C and D, leaving us with

ANSWER: A

As you can probably guess, it is once again time to do the online review exercises within our Pass The 7™ Online Practice Question Bank. After a break, come back and take the chapter review quiz. Next up, watch the lesson in the training videos and then move onto the full-length practice exams and the Go-No-Go Exams.

Glossary

8K: a special report of a material event required under the Securities Exchange Act of 1934.

10Q: a quarterly report required under the Securities Exchange Act of 1934.

10K: an annual report required under the Securities Exchange Act of 1934.

100% no-load fund: a mutual fund charging neither a sales charge nor a 12b-1 fee.

1035 contract exchange: a tax-free exchange of one annuity contract for another, one life insurance policy for another, or one life insurance policy for an annuity. The contracts do not have to be issued by the same company.

1099-DIV: a tax form sent to investors showing dividends and capital gains distributions from a mutual fund for the tax year.

12b-1 fee: annual fee deducted quarterly from a mutual fund's assets to cover distribution costs, e.g., selling, mailing, printing, advertising. An operating expense, unlike the sales charge that is deducted from the investor's check.

200-day moving average: average closing price over the previous 200 days for a stock or an index.

401(k) plan: qualified defined contribution plan offering employer-matched contributions.

403(b): qualified plan for tax-exempt, non-profit organizations.

(Section) 457 plan: qualified plan for state and municipal government employees.

529 Plans: education savings plans offering tax-deferred growth and tax-free distributions at the federal level for qualified educational expenses. Pre-paid tuition plans allow customers to purchase a certain number of tuition credits at today's prices to be used at a school within a particular state. 529 Savings Plans allow customers to contribute up to the current gift tax exclusion without paying gift taxes. Earnings grow tax-deferred and may be used for qualified education expenses (more than just tuition) later without federal taxation. States can tax the plans—so know the customer's situation!

72(t): an exemption under IRS tax code allowing people to take money from retirement plans including annuities without paying penalties, even though they aren't 59½ yet.

75-5-10 rule: diversification formula for an open- or closed-end fund advertising itself as "diversified." 75% of the portfolio must have no more than 5% of assets invested in any one security, and no more than 10% of a company's outstanding shares may be owned.

A

A-Shares: mutual fund shares sold with a front-end sales load/charge. Lower annual expenses than B- and C-shares.

Account at maintenance: the point at which a customer's equity in a margin account is just high enough to avoid a margin call.

Account Executive (AE): another name for a registered representative or agent.

Account Statement: document sent to a broker-dealer customer showing the recent value of all cash and securities, plus all recent activity in an investment account.

Accounts Payable: what the company owes its vendors, a current liability.

Accounts Receivable: what customers owe a corporation, a current asset.

Accredited Investors: large institutional investors, and individuals meeting certain income or net worth requirements allowing them to participate in, for example, a private placement under Reg D of the Securities Act of 1933, or hedge funds.

Accretion: increasing the cost basis of a discount bond for tax purposes.

Accrued Interest: the interest that the buyer of a debt security owes the seller. Bond interest is payable only twice a year, and the buyer will receive the next full interest payment. Therefore, the buyer owes the seller for every day of interest since the last payment up to the day before the transaction settles.

Accrued Taxes: taxes that are owed by a corporation, a current liability.

Accrued Wages: wages that are owed by a corporation, a current liability.

Accumulation Stage/Period: the period during which contributions are made to an annuity, during which the investor holds "accumulation units."

Accumulation Units: what the purchaser of an annuity buys during the pay-in or accumulation phase, an accounting measure representing a proportional share of the separate account during the accumulation/deposit stage.

Acid Test: another name for the quick ratio, a measure of short-term liquidity that is more stringent than the current ratio as it excludes inventory from current assets.

Ad Valorem: property tax. Literally "as to value."

Additional Takedown: the piece of the spread that goes to the various members of the syndicate when the bonds they've been allotted are sold.

Adjustable Rate Preferred Stock: preferred stock whose dividend is tied to another rate, often the rate paid on T-bills.

Adjusted Gross Income (AGI): earned income plus passive income, portfolio income, and capital gains. The amount upon which we pay income tax.

Adjustment Bond: another name for an "income bond," on which the issuer may skip interest payments without going into default.

Administrator: (1) the securities regulator of a particular state; (2) a person or entity authorized by the courts to liquidate an estate.

ADR/ADS: American Depository Receipt/Share. A foreign stock on a domestic market. Toyota and Nokia are two examples of foreign companies whose ADRs trade on American stock markets denominated in dollars. Carry all the risks of owning stocks, plus "currency exchange risk."

Advance Refunding/Pre-refunding: issuing new bonds and depositing part of the proceeds in escrow more than 90 days ahead of the first legal call date on the existing bond issue.

Advance/Decline Ratio: the number of stocks whose market prices increased versus the number of stocks whose market prices decreased during a trading session.

Affiliated Person or **Affiliates:** anyone in a position to influence decisions at a public corporation, including board members (directors), officers (CEO, CFO), and large shareholders (Warren Buffett at Coca-Cola or Wells Fargo) owning 10%+ of any class of the issuer's securities.

Age-Based Portfolio: also known as a lifecycle fund, a fund whose asset allocation shifts automatically over time to match the goal and time horizon of the investors in the fund. Many 529 Savings Plans offer age-based portfolios, similar to target-date retirement funds.

Agency Issue (Agency Bond): a debt security issued by an agency of the US Government such as GNMA or by a government sponsored enterprise, such as FNMA or FHLMC. Agency issues promote the public good through increased home ownership or increased credit to farmers.

Agency Transaction: a securities transaction in which the broker-dealer acts as an agent for the buyer or seller, completing the transaction between the customer and another party.

Agent: an individual representing a broker-dealer or issuer in effecting/completing transactions in securities for compensation. What you will be after passing your exams and obtaining your securities license.

Aggressive Growth: an investment objective associated with a willingness to bear a high amount of investment risk in exchange for potential appreciation in the value of the investment, e.g. emerging market or sector funds.

Agreement Among Underwriters: a document used by an underwriting syndicate bringing an issue of securities to the primary market. This document sets forth the terms under which each member of the syndicate will participate and details the duties and responsibilities of the syndicate manager.

AIR: Assumed Interest Rate. Used to determine the value of annuity units for annuities and the death benefit for variable life contracts.

All or None: a type of underwriting in which the syndicate will cancel the offering if a sufficient dollar amount is not raised as opposed to being responsible for the unsold shares (as in a "firm commitment"). Also a type of order on the secondary market in which the investor wants the order to be canceled if the broker cannot acquire the full number of shares on one attempt.

Alpha: the risk-adjusted return compared to the benchmark.

A.M. Best: a ratings service for insurance company claims paying ability/financial strength.

American Stock Exchange (AMEX): a private, not-for-profit corporation that handles roughly 20% of all securities trades in the U.S. One of the big secondary markets, along with NYSE, and the various NASDAQ markets.

American Style: an option that can be exercised at any time up to expiration.

Amortization: spreading the cost of an intangible item over its estimated useful life.

AMT (Alternative Minimum Tax): tax computation that adds certain "tax preference items" back into adjusted gross income. Some municipal bond interest is treated as a "tax preference item" that can raise the investor's tax liability through the AMT.

And Interest: term used for a debt security that trades subject to accrued interest, as opposed to "flat."

Annual Compliance Review: a broker-dealer's annual compliance review process that is mandatory for principals and registered representatives.

Annual Shareholder Report: a formal statement (10K) issued by a corporation to the SEC and shareholders discussing the company's results of operations, challenges/risks facing the company, any lawsuits against the company, etc. Required by the Securities Exchange Act of 1934.

Annuitant: the person who receives an annuity contract's distribution.

Annuitize: the process of changing the annuity contract from the "pay-in" or accumulation phase to the "pay-out" or distribution phase. Defined benefit pension plans generally offer their pensioners either a lump sum payment or the option to annuitize and receive monthly payments going forward.

Annuity Units: what the annuitant holds during the pay-out phase. Value tied to AIR.

Annuity: a contract between an individual and an insurance company that either guarantees income for the rest of the individual's life or allows him to invest his purchase payments into various subaccounts in return for a lump-sum or periodic payment to the insurance company.

Anticipation Notes: short-term obligations of a municipality often held by tax-exempt money market mutual funds.

Appreciation: the increase in an asset's value that is not subject to tax until realized.

Arbitrage: taking advantage of the disparity in pricing between two things. In a proposed merger, some traders bet against the acquiring company and bet on the company to be acquired in an arbitrage trade. Or, some specialized traders buy or sell convertible bonds versus the underlying security when there is a temporary price disparity.

Arbitration: settling a dispute without going to an actual court of law.

Arbitration Award: the decision rendered through FINRA Arbitration.

Articles of Incorporation: documents that a corporation files with the state disclosing the name and purpose of the business, its address, and how many shares of stock the corporation is authorized to issue.

Ask, Asked: the higher price in a quote representing what the customer would have to pay/what the dealer is asking the customer to pay. Ask/asked is also called "offer/offered."

Assessed Value: the value of property used to calculate property tax. For example, a home with a market value of $300,000 might have an assessed value of $150,000 against which the rate of tax is applied.

Asset Allocation: maintaining a percentage mix of equity, debt, and money market investments, based either on the investor's age (strategic) or market expectations (tactical).

Asset-Backed Securities: or ABS, bonds or notes backed by financial assets, e.g., credit card receivables or auto loans.

Asset Coverage: a measure from the balance sheet showing how well an issuer can meet its debt servicing obligations.

Assets: something that a corporation or individual owns, e.g., cash, investments, accounts receivable, inventory, etc.

Assignment Notice: what the seller of an option receives when the buyer exercises the contract.

Associated Person: a registered representative or principal of a FINRA member firm.

Assumed Interest Rate: see AIR.

At-The-Market: an offer of securities to be sold over time, often at different prices to different investors depending on when the investment is made.

Auction Market: the NYSE, for example, where buyers and sellers simultaneously enter competitive prices. Sometimes called a "double auction" market because buying and selling occur at the same time.

Auction Rate Securities: debt securities with a variable rate of interest or preferred stock with a variable dividend rate that is re-set at regular auctions.

Authorized Stock: the number of shares a company is allowed to issue by its corporate charter. Can be changed by a majority vote of the outstanding shares.

Automated Customer Account Transfer (ACAT): a system that provides instructions among broker-dealers for transfer and delivery of customer assets.

Automatic Reinvestment: a feature offered by mutual funds allowing investors to automatically reinvest dividend and capital gains distributions into more shares of the fund, without paying a sales charge.

Average Cost Basis: a method of figuring cost basis on securities for purposes of reporting capital gains and/or losses. The investor averages the cost for all purchases made in the stock, as opposed to identifying particular shares to the IRS when selling.

B

B-Shares: mutual fund shares charging a load only when the investor redeems/sells the shares. Associated with "contingent deferred sales charges." B-shares have higher operating expenses than A-shares by way of a higher 12b-1 fee.

Backdating: pre-dating a letter of intent (LOI) for a mutual fund in order to include a prior purchase in the total amount stated in the letter of intent. LOIs may be backdated up to 90 calendar days.

Back-end Load: a commission/sales fee charged when mutual fund or variable contracts are redeemed. The back-end load declines gradually, as described in the prospectus. Associated with "B-shares" and, occasionally, "C-shares."

Backing Away: a violation in which a market maker fails to honor a published firm quote to buy or sell a security at a stated price.

Backup Withholding: a required withholding from an investment account that results when the customer refuses/fails to provide a tax identification number.

Balance of Payments: imports versus exports and also financial transactions. A surplus = more $ coming into the country. A deficit = more $ flowing out of the country.

Balance of Trade: imports versus exports. A surplus= more exports than imports. A deficit = more imports than exports.

Balance Sheet: a financial statement of a corporation or individual showing financial condition (assets vs. liabilities) at a particular moment in time.

Balance Sheet Equation: Assets – Liabilities = Shareholders' Equity, or Assets = Liabilities + Shareholders' Equity.

Balanced Fund: a fund that maintains a mix of stocks and bonds at all times. Close to an asset allocation fund except that an asset allocation fund would typically hold a larger % in money market instruments.

Balloon Maturity: a bond issue in which some principal is paid in the early years, with most due at end of the term.

Bank Qualified Municipal Bond: municipal bonds that allow banks to deduct 80% of the interest costs incurred to buy them.

Bankers' Acceptance (BA): money-market security that facilitates importing/exporting. Issued at a discount from face-value. A secured loan.

Bar: the most severe sanction that FINRA can impose on an individual, effectively ending his/her career.

Basis: a synonym for yield. A bond trading at a "550 basis" trades at a price making its yield to maturity 5.5%.

Basis Points: a way of measuring bond yields or other percentages in the financial industry. Each basis point is 1% of 1%. Example: 2% = .0200 = 200 basis points. 20 basis points = .2% or 2/10ths of 1%.

Basis Quote: the price at which a debt security can be bought or sold, based on the yield. A bond purchased at a "5.50 basis" is trading at a price that makes the yield 5.5%.

Bear Market: a market for stock or bonds in which prices are falling and/or expected to fall.

Bear Spread: a call or put spread in which the investor benefits if the underlying instrument's value drops. For example, an investor who buys the ABC Aug 50 call and sells the ABC Aug 45 call establishes a bear spread. The spread would also happen to be a "credit spread" in this case.

Bearer Bond: an unregistered bond that pays principal to the bearer at maturity. Bonds have not been issued in this way for over two decades, but they still exist on the secondary market.

Bearish, Bear: an investor who takes a position based on the belief that the market or a particular security will fall. Short sellers and buyers of puts are "bearish." They profit when stocks go down. Seriously.

Beneficiary: the one who benefits. An insurance policy pays a benefit to the named beneficiary. IRAs and other retirement plans, including annuities, allow the owner to name a beneficiary who will receive the account value when the owner dies. A 529 plan names a beneficiary, who will use the money for educational expenses someday.

Best Efforts: a type of underwriting leaving the syndicate at no risk for unsold shares, and allowing them to keep the proceeds on the shares that were sold/subscribed to. Underwriters act as "agents," not principals, in a best efforts underwriting.

Beta Coefficient: another way of referring to "beta."

Beta: a way of measuring the volatility of a security or portfolio compared to the volatility of the overall market. A beta of more than 1 is associated with an investment or portfolio that is more volatile than the overall market. A beta of less than 1 is associated with an investment or portfolio that is less volatile than the overall market. Beta measures market risk.

Bid Form: document used to submit a competitive bid to the issuer of municipal securities.

Bid: what a dealer is willing to pay to a customer who wants to sell. Customers sell at the bid, buy at the ask.

Blend Fund: a fund that is neither a growth fund nor a value fund but a blend of both.

Blind Pool Offering: a direct participation program in which the sponsor does not identify the assets of the partnership.

Block: a large number of securities or dollar amount presented as one transaction. For purposes of different rules "block transactions" are defined differently.

Blue Chip: stock in a well-established company with proven ability to pay dividends in good economic times and bad. Lower risk/reward ratio than other common stock.

Blue Sky: state securities law, tested on the Series 63, 65, and 66 exams.

Board of Directors: the group elected by shareholders to run a mutual fund or a public company and establish corporate management policies.

Bona Fide: a Latin phrase meaning authentic, true. Or, made or presented without deception or fraud. A bona fide stock certificate, for example, as opposed to a bogus certificate made on a color laser printer.

Bond: a debt security offering interest payments—but not a share of profits—to the investor.

Bond Anticipation Note (BAN): a short-term municipal debt security backed by the proceeds of an upcoming bond issue. Often found in tax-exempt money market funds.

Bond Buyer: daily publication covering the municipal securities industry.

Bond Certificate: a paper or electronic document stating the details of a bond, e.g., the issuer's name, par value or face amount, interest rate, maturity date, and call date (if any).

Bond Counsel: tax law firm that guides a municipal issuer through the legal process of issuing bonds and determines the tax treatment of the interest based on research and knowledge of the Internal Revenue Code.

Bond Fund: a mutual fund with an objective of providing income while minimizing capital risk through a portfolio of bonds.

Bond Indenture: the contract spelling out the rights of bondholders and the obligations of the bond issuer.

Bond Point: 1% of a bond's par value. 1 bond point = $10.

Bond Ratio: a measure from the balance sheet showing how leveraged the issuer is. Found by taking long-term debt and comparing to (dividing by) total capitalization to show what % of the issuer's capitalization was derived from borrowed money vs. equity.

Bond Rating: an evaluation of a bond issue's chance of default published by companies such as Moody's, S&P, and Fitch.

Bond Resolution: a document that legally authorizes the process of issuing municipal bonds for a specific purpose.

Bond Swap: taking a loss on a bond and replacing it with a substantially different bond to avoid a wash sale.

Bonus Annuity: an anuity with special riders/enhancements attached.

Book Entry: a security maintained as a computer record rather than a physical certificate. All U.S. Treasuries and many mutual funds are issued in this manner.

Book Value per Share: the hard, tangible asset value associated with a share of common stock. Calculated from the balance sheet by taking stockholders' equity minus preferred shares, divided by the shares outstanding. Thought of as the "hypothetical liquidating value" for a share of stock.

Bottom-Up Analysis: fundamental analysis that starts at the company level rather than the overall economic view.

Brady Bonds: bonds issued by emerging-market nations and collateralized by U.S. Treasury securities to keep yields down and help such nations pay off their debt to the developed world.

Branch Office: any location identified by any means to the public or customers as a location at which the member conducts an investment banking or securities business. The small Charles Schwab or E-Trade office at the nearby mall or office complex is a "branch office." Registered with a Form BR.

Breakeven: the price at which the underlying security is above or below the strike price of the option by the amount of the premium paid or received. For example, an ABC Aug 50 call @2 has a "breakeven" of $52 for both the buyer and the seller.

Breakout: term used when a security suddenly treads above resistance, breaking out of a previous price range/pattern.

Breakpoint: a discounted sales charge or "volume discount" on mutual fund purchases offered on A-shares at various levels of investment.

Breakpoint Selling: preventing an investor from achieving a breakpoint. A violation.

Broad-Based Index: an index such as the S&P 500 or the Value Line Composite Index that represents companies from many industries.

Broker: an individual or firm that charges a commission to execute securities buy and sell orders submitted by another individual or firm.

Broker Call Loan Rate: interest rate that broker-dealers pay when borrowing on behalf of margin customers.

Brokered CDs: certificates of deposit offered by selling agents and paying competitive yields among a larger universe of banks.

Broker's Broker: a firm that holds no inventory and executes securities transactions exclusively with other broker-dealers and not with public investors.

Broker-dealer: a person or firm in the business of completing transactions in securities for the accounts of others (broker) or its own account (dealer).

Build America Bonds: taxable municipal bonds providing a tax credit to the issuer rather than a tax-exemption to the investor used for infrastructure improvements and repairs.

Bull Market: a market for stocks or bonds in which prices are rising and/or expected to rise.

Bull Spread: a call or put spread in which the investor will benefit if the underlying instrument rises in value. If the investor is "long the lower strike price," he has established a "bull spread." For example, if he buys the ABC Aug 50 call and sells the ABC Aug 55 call, he establishes a "bull spread." The spread would also happen to be a "debit spread" in this case.

Bulletin Board: OTC stocks too volatile and low-priced for NASDAQ. Stocks trading on the OTCBB do not have to meet requirements for profitability or number of shares and shareholders.

Bullish, Bull: an investor who takes a position based on the belief that the market or a particular security will rise. Buyers of stock and call options are bullish.

Business Cycle: a progression of expansions, peaks, contractions, troughs, and recoveries for the overall (macro) economy.

Business Risk: the (unsystematic) risk that the company whose stock or bond you own will not be successful as a business. Competition, poor management, obsolete products/services are all examples of business risk.

Buy Limit: an order to buy a security at a price below the current market price, executable at a specified price or lower/better.

Buy Stop: an order to buy a security at a price above the current market price triggered only if the market price hits or passes through the stop price.

Buy-to-Cover: a purchase order entered by a short seller to close out the short stock or options position.

C

C-corporation: a business entity that does not provide for flow-through to the owners but, rather, is associated with the double taxation of profits/dividends.

C-Shares: often called "level load" because of the high 12b-1 fee. Usually involve no front-end load, sometimes have a contingent deferred sales charge for 1 or 1.5 years. Appropriate for shorter-term investing only.

Call (n.): a contract that gives the holder the right to buy something at a stated exercise price.

Call (v.): to buy.

Call Premium: the price paid and received on a call option. Or, the amount above the par value paid by the issuer to call/retire a bond.

Call Protection: the period during which a security may not be called or bought by the issuer, usually lasting five years or more.

Call Provision: agreement between the issuer and the bondholders or preferred stockholders that gives the issuer the ability to repurchase the bonds or preferred stock on a specified date or dates before maturity.

Call Risk: the risk that a callable bond or preferred stock will be forcibly called when interest rates fall, reducing the investor's total return.

Call Spread: buying and selling a call on the same underlying instrument where the strike price, the expiration, or both are different.

Callable: a security that may be purchased/called by the issuer as of a certain date, e.g., callable preferred, callable bonds. Generally pays a higher rate of return than non-callable securities, as it gives the issuer flexibility in financing.

Cancel and rebill: fixing a trade error by placing the transaction in the proper customer account.

Cap: the maximum that an equity indexed annuity contract's value can rise in a given year.

Capital: money raised from investors by issuing stocks, bonds, etc.

Capital Appreciation: the rise in an asset's market price. The objective of a "growth stock investor."

Capital Appreciation Bond: another name for a zero coupon bond.

Capital Assets: items of value including securities, real estate, artwork, collectibles, etc.

Capital Gain: the amount by which the proceeds on the sale of a stock, bond, or other capital asset exceed your cost basis. If you sell a stock for $22 and have a cost basis of $10, the capital gain or profit is $12.

Capital Gains Distribution: distribution from fund to investor based on net capital gains realized by the fund portfolio. Holding period determined by the fund and assumed to be long-term.

Capital Loss: loss incurred when selling a capital asset for less than the purchase price. Capital losses offset an investor's capital gains and can offset ordinary income to a certain amount.

Capital Preservation: a conservative investment goal placing safety-of-principal above all else. Associated with U.S. Treasuries, GNMA securities, and bank CDs.

Capital Risk: the risk that an investor will lose some or all of his invested principal.

Capital Structure: the make-up of a corporation's financing through equity (stock) and debt (bonds) securities.

CAPM: short for the Capital Asset Pricing Model, often used to calculate expected return for a stock investment. Proposes that stock investors should expect the riskless rate of return plus a risk premium.

Capped Index Options: options that are automatically exercised when the underlying instrument moves by a certain amount known as the "cap interval."

Capping: a form of market manipulation that involves trying to decrease the value of a security, often so that call sellers will not be called. A violation.

Cash & Equivalents: the first current asset listed on a balance sheet representing everything that is cash or could be turned into cash immediately by the reporting company.

Cash Account: an investment account in which the investor must pay for all purchases no later than 2 business days following regular way settlement. Not a margin account.

Cash Dividend: money paid to shareholders from a corporation's current earnings or accumulated profits.

Cash Equivalent: a security that can readily be converted to cash, e.g., T-bills, CDs, and money market funds. Listed with cash as a current asset on a company's balance sheet.

Cash Flow: the cash provided or used by a business over a reporting period through operating, investing, and financing activities.

Cash Flows from Operating Activities: cash provided or used by a business through its business operations.

Cash Flows from Financing Activities: cash provided or used by a business through issuing or repurchasing securities or paying dividends and interest to investors.

Cash Flows from Investing Activities: cash provided or used by a business through investing in the business or securities of other entities.

Cash Settlement: same-day settlement of a trade requiring prior broker-dealer approval. Not the "regular way" of doing things.

Cash Value: the value of an insurance policy that may be accessed by the policyholder through a loan or a surrender.

Catastrophic Call: a provision in a municipal bond issue providing for an automatic call of the bonds due to a disaster, e.g., hurricane, flood, or loss of tax-exempt status, etc.

Catch-Up Contribution: the extra amount that a person 50 or older is allowed to contribute annually to a retirement account.

Central Registration Depository or **CRD:** the central licensing and registration system for the U.S. securities industry and its regulators, operated by FINRA. Agents, principals, and member firms are assigned CRD numbers. Broker-Check provides disclosure information from a registrant's CRD information.

CEO: chief executive officer. Individual ultimately responsible for a corporation's results.

Certificate of Deposit or **CD:** a (usually) longer-term deposit with a bank or other financial institution that typically offers compounded interest.

Certificate of Limited Partnership: a document filed by the general partner of a direct participation program with a state disclosing who the partnership is and what it does.

Certificate of Participation: or "COP," a municipal security paying a share of lease revenues to the investor as opposed to a bond backed by such revenues from a particular project.

CFO: chief financial officer. Individual in charge of a corporation's financial activities.

Channel: a type of chart pattern in which the stock's support and resistance lines run parallel either as a "channel up" or "channel down" pattern.

Chart: graphical representation of a stock's behavior in the secondary market.

Chartist: a trader using charts to spot buying and selling opportunities.

Check-writing Privileges: a privilege offered by mutual funds, especially money market funds, by which investors can automatically redeem shares by writing checks.

Chinese Wall: the separation that is supposed to exist between the investment banking department and the traders and registered representatives in order to prevent insider trading violations.

Churning: excessive trading in terms of frequency and size of transactions designed to generate commissions without regard for the customer.

Class: for example, all MSFT calls, or all IBM puts.

Clean-Up Price: a price outside the current quote for a security that is used to execute a block transaction.

Clearing Agencies: firms that clear/process transactions between clearing member firms. Includes both clearing agencies and depositories.

Clearing Corporation: a financial institution that compares member transactions (or reports to members the results of exchange comparison operations), clears those trades and prepares instructions for automated settlement of those trades, and often acts as an intermediary in making those settlements. For example, the Options Clearing Corporation or the National Securities Clearing Corporation.

Clearing Rate: the interest rate established by auction in connection with auction rate securities.

CLN: construction loan note, a type of municipal note backed by the proceeds from a construction loan for a new building project.

Closed-end Fund: an investment company that offers a fixed number of shares that are not redeemable. Shares are traded on the secondary market at a price that could be higher or lower than NAV (or even the same as NAV).

CDO: Collateralized Debt Obligation. A structured asset-backed security paying cash flows to investors in a predetermined sequence, based on how much cash flow is collected from the package of assets owned

CMO: Collateralized Mortgage Obligation: A complicated debt security based on a pool of mortgages or a pool of mortgage-backed securities. Pays interest monthly but returns principal to one tranche at a time.

Code of Arbitration: FINRA method of resolving disputes (usually money) in the securities business. All decisions are final and binding on all parties.

Code of Procedure: FINRA system for enforcing member conduct rules.

Coincident Indicator: economic indicator reflecting the current state of the economy, e.g., employment rate or personal income.

Collateral Trust Certificate: a bond secured by a pledge of securities as collateral.

Collection Ratio: the amount of taxes collected by a municipality divided by the amount of taxes assessed.

Combination Privilege: allows investors to combine purchases of many funds within the mutual fund family to reach a breakpoint/reduced sales charge.

Combination: a multiple options position that is neither a straddle nor a spread. For example, if an investor buys an ABC Aug 45 call and sells an ABC Aug 50 put, he has established a combination.

Combined Offering: an offering of securities in which both the issuer and other large shareholders will be selling to the public.

Commercial Paper: a short-term unsecured loan to a corporation. Issued at a discount from the face value. See "money market securities."

Commissions: a service charge an agent earns for arranging a security purchase or sale.

Common Stock: the most "junior security," because it ranks last in line at liquidation. An equity or ownership position that usually allows the owner to vote on major corporate issues such as stock splits, mergers, acquisitions, authorizing more shares, etc.

Competitive, Sealed Bids: process used for most general obligation bonds in which the underwriting business is awarded to the syndicate that turns in the lowest cost of borrowing to the issuer.

Compliance Department: the principals and supervisors of a broker-dealer responsible for making sure the firm adheres to SEC, exchange, and SRO rules.

Concession: the amount that the seller of a new issue of municipal bonds receives, whether a syndicate member or a selling group member.

Conduct Rules: an SRO's rules for member conduct that, if violated, may lead to sanctions and fines.

Conduit Theory (Tax Treatment): a favorable tax treatment achieved if a company (REIT, mutual fund) distributes 90%+ of net income to the shareholders.

Confirmation: document stating the trade date, settlement date, and money due/owed for a securities purchase or sale. Delivered on or before the settlement date.

Consolidated Quotation System (CQS): system used for trading in the third market.

Consolidation: a stock trading in a narrow price range, trading "sideways."

Constant Dollar Plan: a defensive investment strategy in which an investor tries to maintain a constant dollar amount in the account, meaning that securities are sold if the account value rises and purchased if it goes down.

Constructive Receipt: the date that the IRS considers an investor to have put his grubby little hands on a dividend, interest payment, retirement plan distribution, etc. For example, IRA funds are not taxable until "constructive receipt," which usually starts somewhere between age 59½ and 70½.

Consumer Price Index (CPI): a measure of inflation/deflation for basic consumer goods and services. A rising CPI represents the greatest risk to most fixed-income investors.

Consumer: for purposes of Regulation S-P, a consumer is someone considering a financial relationship with a firm.

Contingency Offering: an offer of securities that will be canceled if a certain amount is not raised, with investor funds going into an escrow account from which they are returned if the offer is, in fact, canceled. A mini-max offering is an example of a contingency offering, as is an all-or-none offering.

Contingent Deferred Sales Charge: associated with B-shares, the sales charge is deducted from the investor's check when she redeems/sells her shares. The charge is deferred until she sells and is contingent upon when she sells—the sales charges decline over time, eventually disappearing after 7 years, at which point the B-shares become A-shares.

Continuing Commissions: the practice of paying retired registered representatives and principals commissions on business written while still employed with the firm, e.g., 12b-1 fees on mutual funds and annuities.

Continuous Net Settlement: method used by clearing agencies that involves the netting of all purchases and sales in a particular security or options contract for a member firm, as opposed to forcing firms to settle with the other side of each trade. After all trading ceases for the day, a member firm is either a net buyer or net seller of ABC common stock and either owes money or securities to the clearing corporation.

Contraction: phase of the business cycle associated with general economic decline, recession or depression.

Contribution: the money you put into a retirement plan subject to the limits imposed by the plan.

Control Relationship: for municipal securities, a situation in which a person is in a position of control both for the issuer and any underwriter. For broker-dealers, a situation in which the member executes a transaction in a security of an issuer related to the broker-dealer. Both situations require full disclosure of the nature of the conflict.

Conversion Ratio: the number of shares of common stock that the holder of a convertible bond or preferred stock would receive upon conversion. A bond "convertible at $50" has a conversion ratio of 20 (20 shares of stock per $1,000 par value).

478

Conversion/Exchange Privilege: a feature offered by many mutual funds whereby the investor may sell shares of one fund in the family and use the proceeds to buy another fund in the family at the NAV (avoiding the sales load). All gains/losses are recognized on the date of sale/conversion for tax purposes.

Convertible: a preferred stock or corporate bond allowing the investor to use the par value to "buy" shares of the company's common stock at a set price.

Cooling-off Period: a minimum 20-day period that starts after the registration statement is filed with the SEC. No sales or advertising allowed during this period, which lasts until the effective or release date.

Core Inflation: The CPI minus volatile items such as food and energy prices.

Corporate Financing Department or **CFD:** department of FINRA reviewing the terms of compensation for member firms involved with a securities offering.

Corporation: the most common form of business organization, in which the business's total value is divided among shares of stock, each representing an ownership interest or share of profits.

Correspondence: under FINRA rules = a communication sent to no more than 25 retail investors in a 30-day period.

Cost Basis: the amount that has gone into an investment and has been taxed already. For stock, includes the price paid plus commissions. For a variable annuity, equals the after-tax contributions into the account. Investors pay tax only on amounts above their cost basis, and only when they sell or take "constructive receipt."

Cost of Goods Sold: or "cost of revenue," represents the expenses directly related to producing the company's product.

Coterminous: municipal issuers who overlap, e.g., a village and a school district.

Countercyclical: an industry or stock that performs better during bad economic times, e.g. discount retailers.

Counterparty Risk: the risk that the other party to a derivatives contract or repurchase agreement will not be able to meet its obligations upon exercise.

Coupon Rate: a.k.a. "nominal yield." The interest rate stated on a bond representing the percentage of the par value received by the investor each year. For example, a bond with a 5% "coupon rate" or "nominal yield" pays $50 per bond to the holder per year. Period.

Coverdell Education Savings Account: a tax-advantaged account whose earnings may be withdrawn tax-free for qualified education expenses.

Covered Call: a position in which an investor generates premium income by selling the right to buy stock the investor already owns, and at a set price.

CPI: Consumer Price Index, a measure of inflation/deflation for basic consumer goods and services. A rising CPI represents the greatest risk to most fixed-income investors.

Credit Agreement: document that must be signed by a margin customer in which all finance charges are explained in connection to the margin account.

Credit Enhancement: for example, an insured municipal bond backed by MBIA or AMBAC.

Credit Risk: a.k.a. "default" or "financial" risk. The risk that the issuer's credit rating will be downgraded, or that the issuer will default on a debt security.

Credit Spread: selling a more valuable call/put and simultaneously buying a less valuable call/put on the same underlying instrument. For example, an investor who sells an ABC Aug 50 put for $400 and buys an ABC Aug 45 put for $100 establishes a "credit put spread" for a net credit of $300.

Crossover Point: the point at which a limited partnership has exhausted the tax shelter and is now beginning to show a profit.

Cum Rights: term used when a stock trades with rights, meaning that buyers of the stock will receive rights to subscribe to the upcoming additional offer of stock.

Cumulative Preferred Stock: preferred stock where missed dividends go into arrears and must be paid before the issuer may pay dividends to other preferred stock and/or common stock.

Cumulative Voting: method of voting whereby the shareholder may take the total votes and split them up any way he chooses. Said to benefit minority over majority shareholders. Total votes are found by multiplying the number of shares owned by the number of seats up for election to the Board of Directors.

Cup Pattern: a pattern that emerges in a stock chart showing a curved trendline.

Currency Exchange Risk: the risk that the value of the U.S. dollar versus another currency will have a negative impact on businesses and investors.

Currency Transaction Report (CTR): a reported submitted to the U.S. Treasury by a broker-dealer when a customer deposits more than $10,000 cash.

Current Account: the difference between a nation's imports and exports in which a deficit = more imports than exports and a surplus = more exports than imports.

Current Asset: cash or something easily converted to cash in the short-term. Found on the balance sheet, includes cash & equivalents, accounts receivable, and inventory.

Current Liability: a debt to be paid by a corporation in the short-term, usually one year or sooner.

Current Ratio: a short-term measure of a corporation's liquidity found by dividing current assets by current liabilities; the higher the number, the more liquid the corporation.

Current Refunding: refunding a bond issue where the existing bonds are redeemed within 90 days.

Current Yield: annual interest divided by market price of the bond. For example, an 8% bond purchased at $800 has a current yield of 10%. $80/$800 = 10%.

CUSIP Number: an identification number/code for a security.

Custodial Account: an investment account in which a custodian enters trades on behalf of the beneficial owner, who is usually a minor child.

Custodian: maintains custody of a mutual fund's securities and cash. Performs payable/receivable functions for portfolio purchases and sales. In an UGMA, the custodian is the adult named on the account who is responsible for the investment decisions and tax reporting.

Customer: a person who opens an investment account with a broker-dealer.

Customer Identification Program (CIP): requirements to probably identify customers when opening accounts and documenting how the customer's identity was verified by the broker-dealer, e.g. passport or other government-issued photo ID.

Cyclical Industry: a term of fundamental analysis for an industry that is sensitive to the business cycle. Includes: steel, automobiles, mining and construction equipment.

D

Dark Pools of Liquidity: large institutional orders for securities that are concealed from the public and executed typically on the fourth market.

Dated Date: the date on which interest begins to accrue on a new issue of bonds.

Dealer: a person who buys or sells securities for his/its own account, taking the other side of the trade. A dealer buys securities from and sells securities directly to a customer, while a broker merely arranges a trade between a customer and another party.

Death Benefit: the amount payable to the beneficiary of a life insurance (or annuity) contract, minus any outstanding loans and/or unpaid premiums.

Debenture: an unsecured bond backed by the issuer's ability to pay. No collateral.

Debit Spread: buying a more expensive call/put and selling a less expensive call/put on the same underlying instrument. If an investor pays $500 to buy an XYZ Jan 50 call and receives $200 for selling an XYZ Jan 55 call, he has established the debit call spread at a net debit of $300.

Debt Limit: a self-imposed restriction on the total amount of general obligation debt that an issuer may have outstanding at any one time.

Debt per Capita: a measure that shows a bond analyst how much general obligation debt is outstanding divided by the number of residents of the municipality.

Debt Security: a security representing a loan from an investor to an issuer. Offers a particular interest rate in return for the loan, not an ownership position.

Debt Service: the schedule for repayment of interest and principal on a debt security.

Debt Statement: a statement in which a municipal issuer lists all of its outstanding debts.

Debt Ratio: a measure from the balance sheet showing how leveraged an issuer is. Found by comparing total liabilities to total assets. Similar to debt-to-equity ratio, another measure of long-term solvency.

Debt-to-Equity Ratio: a measure from the balance sheet showing how leveraged an issuer is. Found by comparing total liabilities to stockholders' equity.

Declaration Date: the date the Board declares a dividend.

Default: when the issuer of the bond is unable to pay interest or principal.

Default Risk: the risk that the issuer of the bond will not pay interest and/or principal. Measured by S&P and Moody's.

Defensive Industry: a company that can perform well even during rough economic times. For example, food and basic clothing represent two products purchased through both good and bad economic times; therefore, stocks of food and basic clothing companies would be "defensive" investments.

Deferred Annuity: an annuity that delays payments of income, installments, or a lump sum until the investor elects to receive it. Usually subject to surrender charges during the deferral period.

Deferred Compensation Plan: a non-qualified business plan that defers some of the employee's compensation until retirement. Usually for highly compensated employees.

Deficiency Letter: SEC notification of additions or corrections that an issuer must make to a registration statement before the offering can be cleared for distribution.

Defined Benefit Pension Plan: a qualified corporate pension plan that defines the benefit payable to the retiree.

Defined Contribution Plan: a qualified corporate plan that defines the contribution made on behalf of the employee, e.g., profit sharing, 401(k).

Deflation: a general drop in the level of prices across the economy, usually connected to an economic slump.

Delivery: the change in ownership of a security that takes place when the transaction settles. The seller delivers the securities purchased to the buyer.

Department of Enforcement: FINRA enforcers of the member conduct rules, a group you never want to hear from, especially by certified mail.

Depository Trust Company or **DTC:** centralized depository of securities involved with the final settlement process of a transaction in which securities and cash are moved to the appropriate parties.

Depreciation: spreading the cost of a fixed asset over its useful life by taking a series of non-cash charges on the income statement.

Depreciation Recapture: a tax collected when an asset that had been used for depreciation is sold for a capital gain.

Depression: a more severe version of a recession, e.g. America in the 1930s.

Designated Examining Authority: another name for an SRO or Self-Regulatory Organization, e.g., CBOE or FINRA.

Designated Market Maker: market participant charged with maintaining a fair and orderly market in the stocks they quote. DMMs must quote at the national best-bid-or-offer (NBBO) a specified percentage of the time, and facilitate price discovery throughout the day as well as at the open, close and in periods of significant imbalances and high volatility.

Developed Market: an international market that is more stable than an "emerging market," e.g. Japan as opposed to Brazil.

Developmental Program: an oil or gas drilling program in an area in which reserves are known to exist.

Diluted EPS: earnings per share after factoring in the dilution that would occur due to warrants and convertible securities.

Dilution of Equity: a reduction in the earnings per share of common stock, often due to convertible bonds or preferred stock being converted to common stock.

Direct Debt: the general obligation debt of a municipal issuer for which it is solely responsible.

Direct Participation Program (DPP): an investment in a limited partnership or similar pass-through entity in which the investor receives a share of income and expenses.

Direct Registration: a method of holding securities on the books of the transfer agent without the need for physical certificates to be issued to the investor.

Direct Transfer: moving the proceeds of a tax-deferred account to another custodian rather than the individual taking possession or control of the assets.

Discount: the difference between the (lower) market price for a bond and the par value.

Discount Bond: any bond traded below the par value, e.g., @97.

Discount Rate: interest rate charged by the 12 Federal Reserve Banks to member banks who borrow from the FRB.

Discretion: authority given to someone other than the account owner to make trading decisions for the account.

Discretionary: an order placed in which the agent/broker-dealer chose the asset or amount of shares to be purchased or sold.

Discretionary Income: the money left over after meeting all living expenses; what an investor has available for saving and investing based on his statement of cash flow.

Disintermediation: a situation in which money is being withdrawn from banks and savings & loans by depositors in order to reinvest the funds into higher yielding money market instruments (Treasury bills, certificates of deposit, money market funds). Disintermediation would occur when interest rates at savings banks are lower than money market instruments. The cause could be that the FRB is pursuing a "tight money policy," which is causing a rise in interest rates, creating a demand for the higher yielding money market securities.

Display Book: system of matching electronic orders automatically.

Distribution (Annuity) Stage: the period during which an individual receives payments from an annuity.

Distribution Expenses: the cost of distributing/marketing a mutual fund, including selling, printing prospectuses and sales literature, advertising, and mailing prospectuses to new/potential customers. Covered by sales charges/12b-1 fees.

Distribution: the money you take out of a retirement plan.

Distributor: a FINRA member firm that bears distribution costs of a fund, profiting from the sales charges paid by the investors; a.k.a. "sponsor," "underwriter," "wholesaler."

Diversification: purchasing securities from many different issuers, or industries, or geographic regions, to reduce "nonsystematic risk."

Diversified Mutual Fund: an open- or closed-end fund hat complies with an SEC rule so that no more than 5% of assets are invested in a particular stock or bond and so that the fund does not own more than 10% of any issuer's outstanding stock. Often called the "75-5-10 rule," where the 75 means that only 75% of the assets have to be diversified this way just to keep things nice and simple.

Dividend: money paid from profits to holders of common and preferred stock whenever the Board of Directors declares it.

Dividend Payout Ratio: the amount of dividends paid divided by the earnings per share. Stocks with high dividend payout ratios are typically found in "equity income" funds.

Dividend Yield: annual dividends divided by market price of the stock. Equivalent to current yield for a debt security.

Dividend/Income Distributions: distributions from a fund to the investors made from net investment income. Typically, may be reinvested at the NAV to avoid sales charge.

DK notice: a notice sent to the other broker-dealer when a firm does not recognize a transaction.

Do Not Reduce (DNR): a buy-limit or sell-stop order that will not be reduced for the payment of a cash dividend.

Dollar Cost Averaging: investing fixed dollar amounts regularly, regardless of share price. Usually results in a lower average cost compared to average of share prices, as investors' dollars buy majority of shares at lower prices.

Donor: a person who makes a gift of money or securities to another.

Double Barreled: a municipal bond backed by both the issuer's full faith and credit and revenues.

Dow Jones Industrial Average (DJIA): an index comprised of 30 large cap stocks weighted by share price.

Dual-Purpose Fund: a closed-end fund with two classes of stock: income shares and capital shares. The income shares receive dividends and interest, while the capital shares receive capital gains distributions.

Due Bill: document sent by a broker-dealer when a dividend payment was sent to the wrong party and belongs to the broker-dealer's customer

Due Diligence: meeting between issuer and underwriters with the purpose of verifying information contained in a registration statement/prospectus

Durable Power of Attorney: authorizing another party to make legal, health-related, and financial decisions if the individual should become incapacitated.

Duration: weighted average of a bond's cash flows showing its market-price-sensitivity to a small rise in interest rates.

DVP: a form of settlement in which payment will be made when the securities involved in the transaction are delivered and accepted.

E

Earned Income: income derived from active participation in a business, including wages, salary, tips, commissions, and bonuses. Alimony received is also considered earned income. Earned income can be used toward an IRA contribution.

Earnings Available to Common: net income after the preferred stock dividend is deducted. Used to find EPS.

Earnings per Share (EPS): the amount of earnings or "net income" available for each share of common stock. A major driver of the stock's price on the secondary market.

Eastern/Undivided Account: a syndicate account in which participants are responsible for a percentage of all bonds, even if they sell their allotment.

EBIT: from the income statement, Earnings Before Interest and Taxes. Compared to annual interest payments to arrive at "times interest earned."

EBITDA: from the income statement, Earnings Before Interest, Taxes, Depreciation and Amortization. Sometimes called "free cash flow."

Economic Indicator: economic data used to predict or confirm the health of the economy, e.g. building permits, industrial production, and consumer confidence.

EDGAR: SEC repository for public company filings including annual reports and prospectuses. Stands for Electronic Data Gathering, Analysis, and Retrieval system.

Education IRA: earlier name for the Coverdell Education Savings Account in which after-tax contributions may be made to pay qualified education expenses for the beneficiary.

Effective Date: date established by SEC as to when the underwriters may sell new securities to investors; a.k.a. "release date."

Effective Tax Rate: a taxpayer's total tax divided by his taxable income, sometimes called an "average rate of tax."

Elective Deferrals: the amount of each paycheck that a retirement plan participant directs the employer to deposit into his account, with that amount often matched in, for example, a 401(k) or SIMPLE plan up to a certain amount.

Electronic Communications Networks (ECNs): electronic trading platforms that allow institutional investors to buy and sell securities directly.

Eligibility: a section of ERISA that outlines who is/is not eligible to participate in a qualified plan. Those at least 21 years old who have worked "full time" for one year (1,000 hours or more) are eligible to participate in the plan.

Emerging Market: the financial markets of a developing country. Generally, a market with a short operating history, not as efficient or stable as developed markets. For example, Brazil, China, and India.

Employer's Contribution: the contributions to a retirement account made by the employer on behalf of an employee, whether matching or otherwise. As opposed to the participant's elective deferrals.

Employment Indicator: an economic indicator related to employment, e.g. unemployment claims or the employment rate (non-farm payroll).

Endorsement: the process of signing over title of a security to another party due to a sale, gift, donation, etc.

Engineering Report: a document used in the analysis of a municipal revenue bond addressing the design and construction of the proposed facility.

Equipment Leasing Program: a direct participation program that leases computers, mining equipment, etc.

Equipment Trust Certificate: a corporate bond secured by a pledge of equipment, e.g., airplanes, railroad cars.

Equity: ownership, e.g., common and preferred stock in a public company.

Equity Funds: mutual funds that primarily invest in equity securities.

Equity Income Fund: a mutual fund that purchases common stocks whose issuers pay consistent and, perhaps, increasing dividends. The fund has less volatility than an equity fund with "growth" as an objective.

Equity-Indexed Annuity: an insurance product offering a minimum guaranteed rate and the opportunity to participate in some of the gains of a particular index, usually the S&P 500.

Equity Options: standardized options giving the holder the right to buy or sell the underlying stock at a set price (strike/exercise price).

Equity REIT: a Real Estate Investment Trust that owns and manages real estate, as opposed to a mortgage REIT.

ERISA: the Employee Retirement Income Security Act of 1974 that governs the operation of most corporate pension and benefit plans.

Escrow Account: an account held by an escrow agent/bank on behalf of, for example, investors subscribing to a contingent offer in which proceeds will be returned if the offer of securities is canceled. Also used by homeowners to automatically pay insurance and taxes.

Escrow Receipt: evidence that securities are held by an escrow agent, sometimes used when selling call options to show the broker-dealer that the underlying shares can be delivered if the contract is assigned.

Escrowed to Maturity: a municipal bond issue in which the issuer has deposited funds sufficient to retire the bonds on the original maturity date with an escrow agent/bank.

ESOP or an Employee Stock Option Plan: a benefit plan in which the company allows all workers to purchase company stock at a discount and through a payroll deduction. The stock and the dividends/cap gains generated on it grow tax-deferred, like a 401(k) plan.

Estate: a legal entity that represents all assets held by a deceased person at the moment he died—or the assets of a debtor-in-possession, known as the "bankruptcy estate."

Estate Tax: a tax on estates over a certain amount, often called the "death tax."

ETF: or "Exchange-Traded Fund," a fund that trades on an exchange, typically an index fund tracking the S&P 500, the Dow Jones Industrial Average, etc. Unlike an open-end index fund, the ETF allows investors to sell short, trade throughout the day, and even purchase shares on margin.

ETN: an exchange-traded note, an unsecured debt security with interest payments made at maturity and tied to an underlying benchmark.

European Style: an option that may be exercised at expiration only.

Excess Equity: the amount of equity above the Reg T requirement in a margin account.

Exchange-Listed Security: a security that has met listing requirements to trade on a particular exchange such as NYSE, AMEX, or NASDAQ.

Exchange Rate: a comparison of the relative strength between two currencies.

Exchanges: any electronic or physical marketplace where investors can buy and sell securities. For example, NASDAQ, NYSE, AMEX.

Exclusion Ratio: method of determining which part of an annuity payment is taxable, and which part represents the tax-free return of the annuitant's after-tax cost basis.

Ex-Date: two days before the Record Date for corporate stock. The date upon which the buyer is not entitled to the upcoming dividend. Note that for mutual funds, this date is established by the board of directors, usually the day after the Record Date.

Exempt Security: a security not required to be registered under the Securities Act of 1933. Still subject to anti-fraud rules; not subject to registration requirements, e.g., municipal bonds and bank stock.

Exempt Transaction: a transactional exemption from registration requirements based on the manner in which the security is offered and sold, e.g., private placements under Reg D.

Exercised: an option that the buyer has used to purchase or sell securities at the strike price.

Exercise Notice: notification sent by a firm to the OCC when a customer exercises an options contract.

Existing Properties: a direct participation program that purchases operating real estate.

Expansion: phase of the business cycle associated with increased activity.

Expected Return: the calculation of what a stock should return. When calculated by CAPM, involves the risk-free rate, the beta, and the overall expected return for the market.

Expense Ratio: a fund's expenses divided by/compared to average net assets. Represents operating efficiency of a mutual fund, where the lower the number the more efficient the fund.

Expiration: when an option contract ceases to trade.

Expiration Date: the final day of trading for an options contract.

Exploratory Programs: a direct participation program that drills for oil or natural gas.

Ex-Rights: the term used when a stock begins to trade without rights attached.

Extension Risk: the risk that interest rates will rise, and the holder of a CMO or mortgage-backed security will have to wait longer than expected to receive principal.

F

Face Amount: the amount that a debt security pays out upon maturity.

Face-Amount Certificate: a debt security bought in a lump-sum or through installments that promises to pay out the stated face amount, which is higher than the investor's purchase price.

Face-Amount Certificate Company: one of the three types of investment company under the Investment Company Act of 1940. Issues face-amount certificates. Not a UIT or "management company."

Fair and Accurate Credit Transactions or **FACT Act:** federal legislation allowing consumers to monitor their credit reports and attempting to reduce identity theft.

Fair and Orderly Market: what the specialist at the NYSE is charged with maintaining.

FDIC (Federal Deposit Insurance Corporation): federal government agency that provides deposit insurance for member banks and prevents bank and "thrift" failures. Bank deposits are currently insured up to $250,000, a number that could have changed by the time you read this definition. A trip to your local bank will give you the updated number.

Feasibility Study: a study put together by a consulting firm analyzing the economic merits of a facility to be financed by revenue bonds.

Fed Funds Rate: interest rate charged on bank-to-bank loans. Subject to daily fluctuation.

Federal Covered: a security or an investment adviser whose registration is handled exclusively by the federal government (SEC) and subject only to notice filings at the state/blue sky level.

Federal Farm Credit System: organization of privately owned banks providing credit to farmers and mortgages on farm property.

Federal Open Market Committee (FOMC): council of Federal Reserve officials that sets monetary policy based on economic data. The money supply is tightened to fight inflation, loosened to provide stimulus to a faltering economy.

Federal Reserve Board: a seven-member board directing the operations of the Federal Reserve System.

Federal Reserve System: the central bank system of the United States, with a primary responsibility to manage the flow of money and credit in this country.

FEIN: or Federal Employer Identification Number, a tax identification number used by various entities including a corporation, estate, or trust.

FHLMC: a.k.a. "Freddie Mac." Like big sister Fannie Mae, a quasi-agency, public company that purchases mortgages from lenders and sells mortgage-backed securities to investors. Stock is listed on NYSE.

Fiduciary: someone responsible for the financial affairs of someone else, e.g., custodian, trustee, or registered rep in a discretionary account.

FIFO: first-in-first-out. An accounting method for valuing a company's inventory or for determining the capital gain/loss for an investor. Using FIFO, an investor indicates that, for example, the 100 shares of ABC that were sold at $55 are the first 100 shares that he purchased.

Filing Date: the date that an issuer files a registration statement with the SEC for a new issue of securities.

Fill or Kill (FOK): a specialized order to buy or sell securities at a set price that will be canceled if all the securities are not available at once at the specified price.

Final Prospectus: document delivered with final confirmation of a new issue of securities detailing the price, delivery date, and underwriting spread.

Financial Risk: another name for "credit risk," or the risk that the issuer of a bond could default.

Financial Statement: a report of a company's finances in terms of financial condition, profits, and cash flow, made public through a prospectus or 10K filing by a reporting company.

FinCEN: U.S. Treasury's "Financial Crimes Enforcement Network." Suspicious Activity Reports must be provided to FinCEN if a broker-dealer notices activity in accounts that appears suspicious or possibly related to fraud or money laundering activities.

FINRA (Financial Industry Regulatory Authority): the SRO formed when the NASD and the NYSE regulators merged.

Firm Commitment: an underwriting in which the underwriters agree to purchase all securities from an issuer, even the ones they failed to sell to investors. Involves acting in a "principal" capacity, unlike in "best efforts," "all or none," and "mini-max" offerings.

Firm Element: annual continuing education requirement for a registered representative.

Firm Quote: a quote by a dealer representing a price at which the dealer is prepared to trade.

First Market: another name for the exchange market, where the NYSE is the model.

First-In-First-Out (FIFO): an accounting method used to value a company's inventory or to determine capital gains/losses on an investor's securities transactions.

Fiscal Policy: Congress and President. Tax and Spend.

Fiscal Year: the twelve-month period used by an entity for preparing financial reports, e.g. income statements.

Fixed Annuity: an insurance product (not a security) in which the annuitant receives fixed dollar payments, usually for the rest of his or her life.

Fixed Assets: long-term assets that generate revenue but are not intended to be sold. For example, a printing press.

Fixed Exchange Rate: a system in which a country ties the value of its currency to a commodity—such as gold or silver—or to another currency, such as the peso or the dollar.

Fixed Income Clearing Corporation: a subsidiary of the Depository Trust Clearing Corporation that clears transactions in corporate, municipal, and government debt securities among member firms.

Fixed-Income Security: a security promising a stated stream of income to the investor, e.g., a bond as opposed to common stock.

Flat: term used for a debt security that trades without accrued interest, e.g. a zero coupon or a bond currently in default.

Flexible Premium: a premium that is flexible. Characteristic of "universal" insurance. Allows the policyholder to adjust the premiums and death benefit according to changing needs.

Floating Rate Currency: a system in which a country allows the value of its currency to rise and fall with supply and demand and also influenced by central bank policies, e.g. the Federal Reserve Board's monetary policy.

Floor Broker: an individual who works for a particular member of the exchange filling orders for the firm and receiving a commission per-order. Present during open-outcry auctions to open and close each session.

Flow of Funds: a statement for a revenue bond issue showing the priority of payments to be made with revenue generated from the facility.

FNMA: a.k.a. "Fannie Mae." Like little brother Freddie Mac, Fannie buys mortgages from lenders and sells mortgage-backed securities to investors. A quasi-agency, a public company listed for trading on the NYSE.

FOMC: the Federal Reserve Board's Federal Open Market Committee. Sets short-term interest rates by setting discount rate, reserve requirement and buying/selling T-bills to/from primary dealers.

Foreign Currencies: the actual currencies of various nations traded through Forex.

Forex: an exchange for trading foreign currencies, e.g. British Pound, Swiss Franc, and Yen, etc.

Footnotes: explanations provided in a corporate filing to explain the numbers presented in a balance sheet, income statement, or statement of cash flows.

Foreign Currency Options: standardized options in which the underlying instrument is a foreign currency, e.g., the yen, the euro, etc.

Foreign Exchange Risk: the risk to an American ADR holder that the American dollar will strengthen versus the currency used by the foreign corporation. For example, an American holding the Toyota ADR is at risk that the U.S. dollar will strengthen versus the yen.

Forward Pricing: the method of valuing mutual fund shares, whereby a purchase or redemption order is executed at the next calculated price. Mutual fund shares are bought and sold at the next computed price, not yesterday's stale prices.

Fourth Market, INSTINET: an ECN (electronic communications network) used by institutional investors, bypassing the services of a traditional broker. Institutional = INSTINET.

Fractional Share: a portion of a whole share of stock. Mutual fund shares typically are issued as whole and fractional shares, e.g., 101.45 shares.

Fraud: using deceit or manipulation to wrongfully take money/property from someone under false pretenses.

Free Credit Balance: the cash in a customer account that can be withdrawn.

Free-Look: period during which a contract or policyholder may cancel and receive all sales charges paid. Not a popular phrase among seasoned insurance and annuity salespersons.

Freeriding & Withholding: a violation in which underwriters fail to distribute all shares allocated in an offering of a "hot issue."

Front-end Load: a mutual fund commission or sales fee charged when shares are purchased (A-shares). The amount of the load is added to the NAV to determine the public offering price (POP).

Frozen Account: AKA "a frozen account," is an account in which purchase orders will be accepted only if the cash is in the account due to the customer's failure to comply with Reg T.

Full Faith and Credit: a phrase used to denote that there are no specific assets backing a bond issue, only the issuer's ability to repay the loan.

Fully Registered Bonds: bonds whose principal and interest payments are tracked/registered for purposes of taxation. A physical certificate with the owner's name, and interest payable automatically by the paying agent (no coupons).

Funded Debt: another term for corporate bonds backed by a sinking fund as opposed to collateral.

Funding: an ERISA guideline that stipulates, among other things, that retirement plan assets must be segregated from other corporate assets.

Fund of Funds: a mutual fund comprised of many funds within the same family.

Fund of Hedge Funds: a higher-risk mutual fund open to non-accredited investors that owns shares of hedge funds.

Fungible: interchangeable, e.g., $20 bills or shares of stock, where one is just as good as another.

G

GAN: Grant Anticipation Note, short-term debt obligation of a municipal issuer backed by funds to be received in a grant, usually from the federal government.

GDP: Gross Domestic Product, the sum total of all goods and services being produced by the domestic economy, regardless of nationality.

General Account: where an insurance company invests net premiums in order to fund guaranteed, fixed payouts.

General Obligation Bond: a municipal bond that is backed by the issuer's full faith and credit or full taxing authority.

General Partner: the manager of a DPP with unlimited liability and a fiduciary obligation to the limited partners.

General Securities Representative: an agent who passed the Series 7 and may sell virtually any security, unlike a Series 6 holder, who sells mutual funds and variable contracts only.

Generic Advertising: communications with the public that promote securities as investments but not particular securities.

Gift: the act of giving something of value or economic benefit and expecting nothing in return.

Gift Splitting: claiming a gift as coming from both husband and wife to avoid gift tax liability.

Gift Tax: a tax liability when a gift exceeds the current annual exclusion limit.

Global Fund: a mutual fund investing in companies located and doing business all across the globe, including the U.S.

GNMA: a.k.a. "Ginnie Mae," nickname for Government National Mortgage Association. A government agency (not a public company) that buys insured mortgages from lenders, selling pass-through certificates to investors. Monthly payments to investors pay interest and also pass through principal from a pool of mortgages. Recall that bonds pay interest and return principal only at maturity, while "pass-throughs" pass through principal monthly.

GNP or Gross National Product: the productivity of a nation's citizens, including those working overseas.

Good Faith Deposit: the deposit required by a municipal issuer for all syndicates submitting bids for an issue of bonds. Typically 1–2% of par value.

Goodwill: an intangible asset listed on the balance sheet representing the amount paid for an acquired entity above its hard, tangible asset value.

Grantor: the party who establishes and funds a trust account.

Green Shoe Clause: an agreement allowing the underwriters to sell additional shares if demand is high for an offering of securities.

Gross Margin: gross profit divided *into* revenue. For example, a company with $100 million in revenue and cost-of-goods-sold of $70 million has a gross margin of 30%.

Gross Profit: a company's revenues minus their "cost of goods sold." For example, a company with $100 million in revenue and cost-of-goods-sold of $70 million has a gross profit of $30 million.

Gross Revenue Pledge: less common method used by revenue bond issuers in which debt service is paid even before operations & maintenance.

Growth: investment objective that seeks "capital appreciation." Achieved through common stock, primarily.

Growth & Income: a fund that purchases stocks for growth potential and also for dividend income. Less volatile than pure growth funds due to the income that calms investors down when the ride becomes turbulent. Also, a common investment objective that seeks both growth and income.

Growth Funds: mutual funds investing in stocks expected to grow faster than the overall market and trading at high price-to-earnings multiples.

GTC or Good-Til-Canceled: a stop or limit order that will remain open until either filled or canceled by the customer.

Guaranteed Bond: bond that is issued with a promise by a party other than the issuer to maintain payments of interest and principal if the issuer cannot.

Guardian: a fiduciary who manages the financial affairs of a minor or a person declared mentally incompetent by a court of law.

H

Head and Shoulders: a chart pattern used by technical analysts to determine that a bull or bear trend is about to reverse.

Hedge: to bet the other way. If you own stock, you can hedge by purchasing puts, which profit when the stock goes down.

Hedge Fund: a private investment partnership open to accredited investors only. Illiquid investments that generally must be held one or two years before selling. Typically charge a management fee plus the first 20% of capital gains in most cases.

High-Yield: an investment whose income stream is very high relative to its low market price. A high-yield bond is either issued by a shaky company or municipal government forced to offer high nominal yields, or it begins to trade at lower and lower prices on the secondary market as the credit quality or perceived credit strength of the issuer deteriorates.

Holding Company: a company organized to invest in other corporations, e.g., Berkshire-Hathaway, which holds large stakes in other companies such as Coca-Cola, See's Candy, Dairy Queen, and Wells Fargo. Wells Fargo Corporation is, in turn, a bank holding company that owns a bank, a broker-dealer, and an investment adviser among other entities.

Holding Period: the period during which a security was held for purposes of determining whether a capital gain or loss is long- or short-term.

HOLDR: a financial product created by Merrill Lynch and traded daily on the American Stock Exchange that allows investors to buy and sell a basket of stocks in a particular sector, industry or other classification in a single transaction. Stands for Holding Company Depository Receipt.

Hold Recommendation: an explicit recommendation to refrain from selling a security currently held by an investor, subject to the agent's suitability obligations.

Howey Decision: a U.S. Supreme Court decision that defined an "investment contract" as "an investment of money in a common enterprise where the investor will profit solely through the efforts of others."

HR-10: a reference to a Keogh plan.

Hybrid REIT: a Real Estate Investment Trust that both owns operating real estate and also provides financing for real estate projects—a hybrid of an equity and a mortgage REIT.

Hybrid Security: another name for a convertible bond or convertible preferred stock, which starts as a fixed-income security but may be converted to common stock.

Hypothecate: to pledge securities purchased in a margin account as collateral to secure the loan.

Hypothecation Agreement: document that gives a broker-dealer the legal authority to pledge a margin customer's securities as collateral to secure the margin loan.

I

Identity Theft: the fraudulent use of another party's identity to make unauthorized purchases and other financial transactions.

IDR: "Industrial Development Revenue Bond," a revenue bond that builds a facility that the issuing municipality then leases to a corporation. The lease payments from the corporation back the interest and principal payments on the bonds.

Immediate Annuity: an insurance contract purchased with a single premium that starts to pay the annuitant immediately. Purchased by individuals who are afraid of outliving their retirement savings.

Immediate or Cancel Order: an order to buy or sell securities in which the customer will accept any part of the order that becomes available at a certain price, with the remainder of shares to be canceled.

Income: investment objective that seeks current income, found by investing in fixed-income securities, e.g., bonds, money market, preferred stock. An equity income fund buys stocks that pay dividends; less volatile than a growth & income fund or a pure growth fund.

Income Bond: a bond that will pay interest only if the issuer earns sufficient income and the board of directors declares the payment; a.k.a. "adjustment bond."

Income Programs: a direct participation program that invests in existing producing oil and/or natural gas wells.

Income Statement: a financial statement showing a corporation's results of operations over the quarter or year. Shows revenue, all expenses/costs, and the profit or loss the company showed over the period. Found in the annual shareholder report among other places.

Indenture: a contract that spells out the responsibilities and rights of an issuer in connection with a bond issue.

Index: a theoretical grouping of stocks, bonds, etc., that aids analysts who want to track something. The Consumer Price Index is a theoretical grouping or "basket" of things that consumers buy, used to track inflation. The Dow Jones Industrial Average is a theoretical grouping of 30 large-company stocks that analysts use to track the stock market. The S&P 500 index tracks the stock of 500 large companies and represents the overall stock market for many calculations, including beta.

Index Fund: a mutual fund or ETF providing investors a passive investment option seeking to match the performance of a particular index rather than "beating the market."

Index Option: a call or put option based on the value of a particular index, e.g., the Dow Jones Industrial Average or the S&P 500.

Indication of Interest: an investor's expression of interest in purchasing a new issue of securities after reading the preliminary prospectus; not a commitment to buy.

Individual Retirement Account (IRA): also called an "individual retirement arrangement" to make sure it has at least two names. A tax-deferred account that generally allows any individual with earned income to contribute 100% of earned income up to the current maximum contribution allowed on a pre-tax basis that reduces the current tax liability and allows investment returns to compound.

Inflation: rising prices, as measured by the Consumer Price Index (CPI). Major risk to fixed-income investors (loss of purchasing power).

Inflation-Adjusted: subtracting out the CPI or rate of inflation from an investor's return or from GDP calculations. Associated the word "real," e.g. "real rate or return" or "real GDP."

Inflation Risk: also called "constant dollar risk" or "purchasing power risk," it is the risk that inflation will erode the value of a fixed-income stream from a bond or preferred stock.

Initial Public Offering (IPO): a corporation's first sale of stock to public investors. By definition, a primary market transaction in which the issuer receives the proceeds.

Inside Information: material information about a corporation that has not yet been released to the public and would likely affect the price of the corporation's stock and/or bonds. Inside information may not be "disseminated" or acted upon.

Insider: for purpose of insider trading rules, an "insider" is anyone who has or has access to material non-public information. Officers (CEO, CFO), members of the board of directors, and investors owning > 10% of the company's outstanding shares are assumed to possess and have access to inside information. As fiduciaries to the shareholders, insiders may not use inside information to their benefit.

Insider Trading and Securities Fraud Enforcement Act (ITSFEA) of 1988: an Act of Congress that addresses insider trading and lists the penalties for violations of the Act. Insider traders may be penalized up to three times the amount of their profit or their loss avoided by using inside information.

Institutional Communication: written communication made available only to institutional investors, e.g., banks and insurance companies.

Institutional Investor: not an individual. An institution is, for example, a pension fund, insurance company, or mutual fund. The large institutions are "accredited investors" who get to do things that retail (individual) investors often do not get to do.

Insurance: protection against loss of income due to death, disability, long-term care needs, etc.

Insurance Covenant: promise by a revenue bond issuer to keep the facility properly insured.

Intangible Asset: an asset such as goodwill, patents, or trademarks.

Integration: the final stage in the money laundering process.

Interdealer: among dealers. The "interdealer market" is the highest bid and lowest asked price for a security among all dealers/market makers.

Interest Rate Options: options based on the price or yield of U.S. Treasury securities.

Interest Rate Risk: the risk that interest rates will rise, pushing the market value of a fixed-income security down. Long-term bonds and preferred stock is most susceptible.

Interest Rates: the cost of borrowing money. In order to borrow money, borrowers pay a rate called an interest rate on top of the principal they will return at the end of the term.

Interest-Rate Sensitive: a security whose price rises and falls when interest rates change, e.g. a fixed-income security such as preferred stock, or a bond.

Internal Revenue Code (IRC): tax laws for the U.S. that define, for example, maximum IRA contributions, or the "conduit tax theory" that mutual funds use when distributing 90% of net income to shareholders, etc.

Internal Revenue Service (IRS): an agency for the federal government that no one seems to like very much. Responsible for collecting federal taxes for the U.S. Treasury and for administering tax rules and regulations.

International Fund: a mutual fund investing in companies established outside the U.S.

Interpositioning: unnecessarily inserting another party between the broker-dealer and the customer. A violation.

Interstate Offering: an offering of securities in several states, requiring registration with the SEC.

In-the-money: a call option allowing an investor to buy the underlying stock for less than it is worth or a put option allowing an investor to sell the underlying stock for more than it is worth. For example, if ABC trades @50, both the ABC Oct 45 calls and the ABC Oct 55 puts are "in-the-money."

Intrastate Offering: an offering of securities completed in the issuer's home state with investors who reside in that state, and, therefore, eligible for the Rule 147 Exemption to registration with the SEC. Intrastate offerings generally register with the state Administrator.

Intrinsic Value: the amount by which an option is in-the-money. For example, if ABC trades @50, an ABC Oct 45 call has $5 of intrinsic value, regardless of what the premium might be.

Inventory: finished goods that have not yet been sold by a corporation. A current asset that is included in the current ratio but excluded in the quick ratio.

Inventory Turnover Ratio: a measure of how effectively a company manages its cost of production, found by comparing cost-of-goods-sold to the average inventory over the period.

Inverse Relationship: when one goes up, the other goes down, and vice versa. Interest Rates and Yields are inversely related to Bond Prices. Your rate of speed is inversely related to your travel time to and from the office.

Inverted Yield Curve: a rare situation in which short-term debt securities pay higher yields than longer-term debt securities.

Investment Adviser: a business or professional that is compensated for advising others as to the value of or advisability of investing in securities. The entity that manages mutual funds/separate accounts for an asset-based fee. Financial planners are also advisers.

Investment Adviser Representative or **IAR:** an individual representing an investment adviser for compensation.

Investment Banker: see "underwriter." A firm that raises capital for issuers on the primary market.

Investment Banking: the business of helping companies with mergers and acquisitions, performing IPOs and additional offerings. Investment bankers raise capital for issuers not by loaning money (like a traditional bank) but by finding investors willing to contribute to the cause.

Investment Company Act of 1940: classified Investment Companies and set rules for registration and operation.

Investment Company: a company engaged in the business of pooling investors' money and trading in securities on their behalf. Examples include unit investment trusts (UITs), face-amount certificate companies, and management companies.

Investment Grade: a bond rated at least BBB by S&P or Baa by Moody's. The bond does not have severe default risk, so it is said to be appropriate for investors, as opposed to the speculators who buy non-investment grade bonds.

Investment Objective: any goal that an investor has including current income, capital appreciation (growth), capital preservation (safety), or speculation.

Investment Profile: what an agent must learn through due diligence. Defined by FINRA as, "the customer's age, other investments, financial situation and needs, tax status, investment objectives, investment experience, investment time horizon, liquidity needs, risk tolerance, and any other information the customer may disclose to the member or associated person in connection with such recommendation."

Investment Risks: factors that may have a negative effect on a securities investment, e.g. interest rate or inflation risk.

Investment Style: an approach to investing, such as active, passive, or buy-and-hold.

IRA: Individual Retirement Account. A retirement account/arrangement for any individual with earned income. The Traditional IRA offers pre-tax contributions while the Roth IRA is funded with after-tax contributions.

Issued Shares: the number of shares that have been issued by a corporation.

Issued Stock: the shares that have been issued to investors by the corporation at this time. Often a lower number than the number of shares authorized.

Issuer: any individual or entity who issues or proposes to issue any security. For example, the issuer of Google common stock is Google.

Issuing Securities: raising capital by offering securities to investors on the primary market.

J

Joint Account: investment account owned by more than one individual. Account owners sign a joint account agreement that stipulates which % of the assets is owned by each individual. Joint accounts are either "tenants in common" or "tenants with rights of survivorship."

Joint With Last Survivor: a settlement/payout option on an annuity that requires the insurance company to make payments to the annuitants as long as they are alive.

JTIC (Joint Tenants In Common): account where the assets of the deceased party pass to the deceased's estate, not the other account owner(s).

JTWROS (Joint Tenants With Rights Of Survivorship): account where the assets of the deceased party pass to the other account owner(s).

Junk Bond: a bond backed by a shaky issuer. It was either issued by an entity with shaky credit, or is now trading at a frightfully low price on the secondary market because the issuer's credit has suddenly or recently been downgraded. Since the price is low, given the low quality of the debt, the yield is high. High-yield and junk are synonymous.

K

K-1: a tax form required of individuals who own direct participation interests (limited partnership, S-Corp).

Keogh: qualified retirement plan available to sole proprietorships.

Keynesian Economics: economic school of thought that advocates government intervention through fiscal policy as a way to stimulate demand for goods and services.

L

Lagging Indicator: an economic indicator that shows up after-the-fact to confirm a trend, e.g. duration of unemployment or inventory.

Large Cap: a stock where the total value of the outstanding shares is large, generally greater than $10 billion. For example, GE, MSFT, IBM.

Last-In-First-Out (LIFO): an accounting method used for random withdrawals from an annuity. The IRS assumes that all withdrawals represent part of the taxable "excess over cost basis" first.

Late Trading: a violation in which select investors are allowed to buy or sell mutual fund shares after the NAV has already been determined.

Layering: the phase of money laundering in which the first attempt at disguising the source of the ownership of the funds is made by creating complex layers of transactions.

Leading Indicator: an economic indicator used to predict a trend, e.g. building permits or the S&P 500 Index.

LEAPS: long-term standardized options.

Legal Opinion: the opinion of the bond counsel attesting to the municipality's legal authority to issue the bonds as well as the tax status of the bonds.

Legal Person: as opposed to a natural person—an entity including a trust, an estate, or a corporation.

Legislative Risk: the risk to an investor that laws will change and have a negative impact on an investment. For example, if municipal bonds lose their tax-exempt interest, their value would plummet.

Letter of Intent: LOI, a feature of many mutual funds whereby an investor may submit a letter or form expressing the intent to invest enough money over 13 months to achieve a breakpoint.

Level Load: an ongoing asset-based sales charge (12b-1 fee) associated with mutual fund C-shares. Appropriate for short-term investments only.

Leverage: using borrowed money to increase returns. Debt securities and margin accounts are associated with "leverage."

Leveraged Buyout: buying a company with the proceeds of a debt issue, frequently performed in private equity deals.

Liabilities: what an individual or corporation owes, e.g., credit card debt, bonds, mortgage balance, accounts payable.

LIBOR: short for the London Interbank Offered Rate, an average of the world's most creditworthy banks' interbank deposit rates for large loans with maturities between overnight and one year. LIBOR is the most frequently used benchmark for short-term interest rates.

Lifecycle Fund: an age-based portfolio whose asset allocation shifts automatically over time, e.g. a target retirement fund.

Life Only/Life Annuity: a payout option whereby the insurance/annuity company promises to make payments only for the rest of the annuitant's life.

Life with Joint and Last Survivor: a payout option whereby the insurance/annuity company promises to make payments to the annuitant for the rest of his life, then to the survivor for the rest of her life.

Life with Period Certain: a payout option whereby the insurance/annuity company promises to make payments to the annuitant for the rest of his life or a certain period of time, whichever is greater.

Life with Unit Refund: a payout option whereby the insurance/annuity company promises to make at least a certain number of payments to the annuitant or beneficiary.

Limit Orders: orders to buy or sell a security at a specified price or better.

Limited Liability: an investor's ability to limit losses to no more than the amount invested. Holders of common stock and limited partnership interests enjoy "limited liability," which means they can only lose 100% of what they invest.

Limited Partner: a person who owns a limited partnership interest. Has no managerial responsibility and is shielded from debts of—and lawsuits against—the partnership.

Limited Partnership: a form of business ownership in which income and expenses flow through directly to the partners rather than to a separate business entity.

Limited Representative: what one would be after passing the Series 6 and getting registered to represent one's broker-dealer. You will be a "general securities representative" once you pass the Series 7 exam.

Limited Tax Bonds: general obligation bonds backed by a tax whose rate may not be increased above a certain limit.

Limited Trading Authorization: an authorization for someone other than the account owner to enter purchase and sale orders but make no withdrawals of cash or securities.

Liquidation Priority: the priority of claims on a bankrupt entity's assets that places creditors (bondholders) ahead of stockholders and preferred stockholders ahead of common stockholders.

Liquidity: the degree to which an asset can be quickly converted to cash without having to sell at a discount. Also, the ability of a company to meet its short-term obligations as measured through, for example, their current or quick ratio.

Liquidity Risk: the risk of being unable to sell a security quickly for a fair price; a.k.a. "marketability risk."

Liquid Net Worth: a more stringent measure of net worth that excludes hard-to-liquidate assets such as real estate and limited partnerships.

Liquidity: ability to convert an investment to cash without taking a large hit to principal.

Limited Liability Company: a pass-through entity in which the owners are called members and which provides protection to the owners against claims on their personal assets.

Loan Consent: a document that when signed gives the broker-dealer the permission to lend a customer's securities to short sellers.

Long: to buy or own.

Long Straddle: a position created by purchasing a call and a put with the same strike price in order to bet on the volatility of the underlying instrument.

Long-Term Gain: a profit realized when selling stock held for at least 12 months plus 1 day. Subject to lower capital gains tax rates than short-term gains.

Long-Term Liability: a debt to be repaid in the long-run, e.g., the principal value of an outstanding bond issue.

Long-Term Loss: a loss realized when selling stock held for at least 12 months plus 1 day. Used to offset long-term capital gains.

Long-Term Options (LEAPS): standardized options contracts with expiration terms of several years, unlike ordinary options, which expire in nine months or sooner.

Lump Sum Payment: a settlement/payout option for annuities or insurance where the annuitant or beneficiary receives a lump sum payment. Go figure.

M

Maintenance Covenant: a promise of a revenue bond issuer to keep the facility properly maintained.

Maloney Act: An amendment to the Securities Exchange Act of 1934 creating the NASD as the self-regulatory organization (SRO) for the over-the-counter (OTC) market.

Management Company: one of the three types of Investment Companies, including both open-end and closed-end funds.

Management Fee: the % of assets charged to a mutual fund portfolio to cover the cost of the investment adviser's portfolio management services.

Manager's Fee: typically the smallest piece of the spread, paid to the managing underwriter for every share sold by the syndicate.

Margin: amount of equity contributed by a customer as a percentage of the current market value of the securities held in a margin account. Or *profit* margin, showing the percentage of revenue left on various lines of the income statement—gross margin, net profit margin.

Marginal Tax Rate: the tax rate applied to the last dollar of income earned. AKA "marginal tax bracket."

Markdown: the difference between the highest bid price for a security and the price that a particular dealer pays an investor for her security.

Market Letter: a publication of a broker-dealer sent to customers or the public and discussing investing, financial markets, economic conditions, etc.

Market Maker: a dealer in the OTC market maintaining an inventory of a particular security and a firm Bid and Ask price good for a minimum of 100 shares. Acts as a "principal" on transactions, buying and selling for its/their own account.

Market Manipulation: the illegal process of using deception or collusion to move securities prices in favor of the conspirators.

Market Momentum: the ability of the market to sustain up or downswings in price.

Market-On-Close Order: a market order for a security filled on the closing trade for the session, or as close to the closing trade as possible.

Market-On-Open Order: a market order for a security placed before the opening of the next trading session and filled at the opening market price for the security.

Market Order: an order to buy or sell a security at the best available market price.

Market-Out Clause: a stipulation in an underwriting agreement allowing the underwriter(s) to back out of a securities offering if certain catastrophic events occur.

Market Risk: a type of "systematic risk," the risk inherent to the entire market rather than a specific security. The risk that the stock market may suffer violent upheavals due to unpredictable events including natural disaster, war, disease, famine, credit crises, etc. Market risk can be reduced by hedging with options or ETFs.

Market Sentiment: a judgment of the overall mood of the market, often found through the put/call ratio and option volatility.

Marketability Risk: the risk of being unable to sell a security quickly for a fair price; a.k.a. "liquidity risk."

Marketability: a.k.a. liquidity; the ease or difficulty an investor has when trying to sell a security for cash without losing his shirt. Thinly traded securities have poor marketability.

Marking to the Market: process of calculating margin requirements based on the most current market values for the securities in a margin account.

Markup: the difference between the lowest ask/offer price for a security and the price that a particular dealer charges.

Material Information: any fact that could reasonably affect an investor's decision to buy, sell, or hold a security. For example, profits and losses at the company, product liability lawsuits, the loss of key customers, etc.

Maturity Date: the date that a bond pays out the principal, and interest payments cease. Also called "redemption."

Mediation: informal process of dispute resolution that sometimes avoids arbitration claims.

Member Firm: a broker-dealer and/or underwriting firm that belongs to FINRA or other securities association (MSRB, CBOE).

Millage Rate: the property tax rate used to calculate a property owner's tax bill.

Mini-Max: a type of best efforts underwriting where the syndicate must sell a minimum amount and may sell up to a higher, maximum amount.

Minimum Death Benefit: the minimum death benefit payable to the insured, regardless of how lousy the separate account returns are in a variable policy.

Monetarists: officials who implement monetary policy designed to fight inflation or stimulate the economy, e.g. the Federal Reserve Board.

Minimum Maintenance Requirement: the minimum amount of equity that a margin customer must maintain on either a short or a long position.

Monetary Policy: what the FRB implements through the discount rate, reserve requirement, and FOMC open market operations. Monetary policy tightens or loosens credit in order to affect short-term interest rates and, therefore, the economy.

Money Laundering: the process of turning profits from illegal enterprises into seemingly legitimate assets.

Money Market Mutual Fund: a highly liquid holding place for cash. Sometimes called "stable value" funds, as the share price is generally maintained at $1. The mutual funds invest in—surprisingly—money market securities.

Money Market: the short-term (1 year or less) debt security market. Examples include commercial paper, bankers' acceptance, T-bills.

Money Purchase: a retirement plan in which the employer must contribute a set percentage of the employee's salary, regardless of profitability.

Moody's Investors Service: one of the top three credit rating agencies for corporate and municipal bonds as well as stocks.

Moral Obligation Bond: type of revenue bond with a provision to seek emergency funding from the state legislature should the issuer run into financial problems.

Mortality Guarantee: a promise from an insurance company to pay out no matter how soon the insured dies, or to pay an annuitant no matter how long he lives.

Mortality & Expense Risk Fee: sometimes referred to as "M&E" expenses, annual charges levied by the annuity company to cover the cost of death benefits and any guaranteed income associated with an annuity.

Mortgage-backed Security: a debt security whose interest and principal is derived from a defined pool of mortgages, e.g. a FNMA security.

Mortgage Bond: a corporate bond secured by a pledge of real estate as collateral.

Mortgage REIT: a Real Estate Investment Trust engaging in the financing of projects as opposed to owning and managing properties.

Moving Average: an average found by regularly replacing the oldest data in the set with the most current information.

MSRB (Municipal Securities Rulemaking Board): the self-regulatory organization overseeing municipal securities dealers.

Multiplier Effect: the outsized effect that can occur when the FRB changes the reserve requirement.

Municipal Bond: a bond issued by a state, county, city, school district, etc., in order to build roads, schools, hospitals, etc., or simply to keep the government running long enough to hold another election.

Municipal Bond Fund: a mutual fund that invests in municipal bonds with an objective to maximize federally tax-exempt income.

Municipal Finance Professional: for purposes of rules on political contributions, the term includes principals, registered representatives, and any paid solicitors who help firms land underwriting deals.

Municipal Fund Security: a packaged product that is similar to, but not defined as, an investment company, e.g. a State 529 Plan.

Municipal Note: a short-term obligation of a city, state, school district, etc., backed by the anticipation of funds from revenues, taxes, or upcoming bond issues, e.g., TAN, RAN, BAN.

Mutual Fund: an investment company offering equity stakes in a portfolio that is usually managed actively and that always charges management fees and other expenses.

Mutual Fund Timing: a violation that occurs when a fund allows certain investors to redeem their shares frequently without being assessed any redemption fees.

N

Naked Call: a short call position that is not backed up by ownership of the shares the writer is obligated to deliver upon exercise. As opposed to a "covered call," wherein the writer already owns all shares he would be required to deliver upon exercise.

Narrow-based Index: an index focusing on a particular industry or geographic region, e.g., a transportation index.

NASD (National Association of Securities Dealers): former name of the SRO empowered with the passage of the Maloney Act of 1938. Regulates its own members and enforces SEC rules and regulations. Now called FINRA after a merger with the regulators from the NYSE.

NASDAQ: National Association of Securities Dealers Automated Quotation system. The main component of the OTC market. Stocks that meet certain criteria are quoted throughout the day on NASDAQ, e.g., MSFT, ORCL, and INTC.

National Adjudicatory Council: NAC, the first level of appeal for a party sanctioned by the DOE under FINRA's Code of Procedure.

National Securities Clearing Corporation: clearing agency for stock transactions that uses Continuous Net Settlement and guarantees the performance of all transactions between member firms.

Natural Event Risk: the risk that a weather-related or other catastrophic event will disrupt securities markets and have a material negative effect on an investor's holdings, e.g. a tsunami or a terrorist attack.

NAV or Net Asset Value: the liquidating value of an open-end mutual fund share. Found by taking Assets – Liabilities/Outstanding Shares.

Net Asset Value per Bond: a measure of asset coverage from the balance sheet showing the net tangible assets of the issuer divided by the number of bonds issued.

Negotiable: the characteristic of a security that allows an investor to sell or transfer ownership to another party. For example, savings bonds are not negotiable, while Treasury Bills are negotiable (able to be traded).

Negotiated Market: another name for the "second" or "over-the-counter" market.

Negotiated Underwriting: a municipal bond—usually a revenue bond—underwritten without a competitive, sealed bid.

Net Income: the "bottom line" of a corporation's income statement. Revenue minus all expenses. Also known as a "profit" or a "loss," depending on whether it's a positive or negative number.

Net Interest Cost: a measure of a municipal issuer's total cost of borrowing money by issuing bonds.

Net Investment Income: the source of an investment company's dividend distributions to shareholders. It is calculated by taking the fund's dividends and interest collected on portfolio securities, minus the operating expenses. Funds using the "conduit tax theory" distribute at least 90% of net investment income to avoid paying taxes on the amount distributed to shareholders.

Net Margin: or net profit margin, a company's margin of profitability found by taking net income and dividing it into revenue to show how much of each dollar of revenue made its way to the bottom line.

Net Overall Debt: a municipal issuer's direct debt plus their overlapping debt.

Net Profit: from the income statement, another name for net income or net income after tax. What is left after all expenses are deducted from revenue. The bottom line.

Net Revenue: or "net operating revenue," represents revenue after accounting for any returns or discounting. Especially relevant for the retail sector.

Net Revenue Pledge: the more common method used by the issuer of a revenue bond in which operations & maintenance are covered before debt service.

Net Worth: the difference between assets and liabilities. The term can be applied to individuals and business entities, although for business entities the terms "shareholders' equity" or "stockholders' equity" are typically used instead.

New Account Form: the form that must be filled out for each new account opened with a broker-dealer. The form specifies, at a minimum, the name of the account owner, trading authorization, method of payment, and the type of investment securities that are appropriate for this particular account.

New Construction: a type of DPP in which the partnership builds and then sells housing units.

New Issue Market: the primary market, where securities are issued to investors with the proceeds going to the issuer of the securities. Initial public offerings (IPOs), for example, take place on the "new issue market."

NHA – New Housing Authority (bonds): revenue bonds issued by a municipal government but ultimately backed by the United States Government, who guarantees rental payments for the residents of the housing project.

Nolo Contendere: a Latin phrase meaning "no contest." If an agent or applicant has pled "nolo contendere" to any felony charge or specific misdemeanors, he is subject to statutory disqualification.

No-load Fund: a mutual fund sold without a sales charge, but one which may charge an ongoing 12b-1fee or "asset-based sales charge" up to .25% of net assets.

Nominal Quote: as opposed to a firm quote, an indication of what a market participant might be willing to pay or accept for a security. Nominal quotes must be clearly identified as such.

Nominal Yield: the interest rate paid by a bond or preferred stock. The investor receives this % of the par value each year, regardless of what the bond or preferred stock is trading for on the secondary market.

Non-accredited purchaser: an investor who does not meet various SEC net worth and/or income requirements for accredited investors.

Non-Bank Qualified Municipal Bond: municipal bonds that do not allow banks to deduct 80% of the interest costs incurred to buy them.

Non-cumulative Preferred Stock: a type of preferred stock that does not have to pay missed dividends (dividends in arrears).

Nondiscrimination Covenant: a promise by a municipal revenue bond issuer that all users of a facility must pay to use it, including VIPs of the municipality.

Non-diversified Fund: a fund that doesn't care to meet the 75-5-10 rule, preferring to concentrate more heavily in certain issues.

Non-equity Options: standardized options based on things other than equity securities, e.g., indexes or foreign currency options.

Non-NASDAQ OTC Securities: over-the-counter securities that do not meet the requirements of NASDAQ. For example, OTCBB securities.

Non-systematic Risk: the risk of holding any one particular stock or bond. Diversification spreads this risk among different issuers and different industries in order to minimize the impact of a bankruptcy or unexpected collapse of any one issuer.

Normal Yield Curve: the usual situation in which yields rise as maturities lengthen for debt securities.

Not Held (order): an order to buy or sell a specific number of shares of a particular stock that leaves the time of order placement up to the broker, e.g. "Buy 300 shares of ABC this afternoon."

Note: a shorter-term debt security.

Numbered Account: an account identified with a number rather than a name. Allowed if the owner files a statement with the broker-dealer attesting to ownership.

NYSE: New York Stock Exchange, an auction market where buyers and sellers shout out competitive bid and asked/offered prices throughout the day.

O

Obsolescence Risk: the risk that an issuer's products or services will become irrelevant.

Odd Lot: an order for less than the normal unit of trading in a security, e.g. 8 shares of stock.

Odd Lot Theory: theory used by some technical analysts that assumes odd-lot investors are typically wrong.

Offer: another name for "ask," or the price an investor must pay if he wants to buy a security from a dealer/market maker.

Offer of Settlement: a respondent's offer to the disciplinary committee of FINRA to settle his or her recent rule violations.

Office of Foreign Asset Control (OFAC): federal government office that maintains a list of individuals and organizations viewed as a threat to the U.S., called Specially Designated Nationals.

Officers: high-level executives at a public corporation, e.g., the Chief Executive Officer (CEO), Chief Financial Officer (CFO), and the Chief Operating Officer (COO).

Official Notice of Sale: advertisement in the Bond Buyer in which a municipal issuer hopes to attract potential underwriters.

Official Statement: the document that discloses detailed information about a municipal bond issuer's financial condition.

OID: original issue discount. A bond purchased for less than the par value on the primary market, e.g., a zero coupon bond.

Omitting Prospectus: an advertisement for a mutual fund that typically shows performance figures without providing (omitting) the full disclosure contained in the prospectus. Therefore, it must present caveats and encourage readers to read the prospectus and consider all the risks before investing in the fund.

Open-end Fund: an investment company that sells an unlimited number of shares to an unlimited number of investors on a continuous basis. Shares are redeemed by the company rather than traded among investors.

Open Market Operations: how the FOMC achieves monetary target by buying and selling U.S. Treasury securities on the open market.

Operating Agreement: the agreement governing the structure and operation of an LLC.

Operating Expenses: expenses that a mutual fund deducts from the assets of the fund, including board of director salaries, custodial and transfer agent services, management fees, 12b-1 fees, etc.

Operating Profit: what is left after subtracting cost of goods sold and operating expenses from revenue on the company's income statement. Also referred to as EBIT, operating income and operating earnings.

Opportunity Cost: the return on the investment you could have made but didn't when you chose another one.

Option: a derivative giving the holder the right to buy or sell something for a stated price up to expiration of the contract. Puts and calls.

Option Volatility: a tool of technical analysis to measure market sentiment.

Order Room: a.k.a. "wire room." The department of a broker-dealer that places trades.

Order Ticket/Trade Ticket: a ticket filled out by a registered representative when placing an order to buy or sell securities.

Ordinary Dividend: a dividend subject to the investor's marginal tax rate, not a qualified dividend. REITs, for example, distribute ordinary dividends to the unitholders.

Ordinary Income: virtually all income that is not a capital gain or a qualified dividend. Includes wages, tips, bonuses and commissions; profit from an ownership interest in a sole proprietorship, partnership, LLC or Subchapter S corporation; interest income; alimony; gambling winnings; taxable distributions from retirement accounts, pensions and annuities; and income from rents, royalties and trusts.

Ordinary Income Rate: tax rate paid on ordinary income, as opposed to the rate paid on capital gains.

OTC/Over-the-Counter: called a "negotiated market." Securities traded among dealers rather than on physical exchanges. Includes NASDAQ and also Bulletin Board and Pink Sheet stocks, plus government, corporate, and municipal bonds.

OTC Options: exotic options traded on the over-the-counter market, where participants can choose the characteristics of the options traded.

Outstanding Shares: the number of shares a corporation has outstanding. Found by taking Issued shares minus Treasury stock.

Overallotment: allowing underwriters to sell additional shares of an offering, up to 15% more.

Overbought: a stock trading near resistance.

Oversold: a stock trading near support.

Overlapping Debt: the debt that a municipal issuer is responsible for along with a coterminous issuer.

P

PAC – Planned Amortization Class: a type of CMO (collateralized mortgage obligation) that provides more protection against extension risk vs. a TAC.

Packaged Security: a securities portfolio that pools capital from many investors and is typically managed by an investment adviser, e.g. an open-end or closed-end fund.

Paid-in Surplus: the amount above the par value that investors paid when purchasing the company's initial public offering. For example, if the stock has a par value of $1 and was sold to investors at a public offering price of $5, the paid-in surplus is $4 per share.

Painting the Tape: a form of market manipulation in which bogus trades are reported in order to affect the market price of a security. A violation.

Par, Principal: the face amount of a bond payable at maturity. Also, the face amount of a preferred stock. Preferred = $100, Bond = $1,000.

Parity: equal, e.g. when a convertible bond trades for exactly what the underlying shares are worth.

Partial Surrender: life insurance policyholder cashes in part of the cash value. Excess over premiums is taxable.

Participating Preferred Stock: preferred stock whose dividend is often raised above the stated rate.

Participation: provision of ERISA requiring that all employees in a qualified retirement plan be covered within a reasonable length of time after being hired.

Participation Rate: the percentage of the underlying index's increase credited to the account value of an equity indexed annuity.

Partnership Agreement: the agreement between the LPs and the GP for a direct participation program.

Passive Income: as opposed to "earned income," the income derived from rental properties, limited partnerships, or other enterprises in which the individual is not actively involved.

Pass-Through Certificate: a mortgage-backed security (usually GNMA) that takes a pool of mortgages and passes through interest and principal monthly to an investor.

Pattern Day Trader: anyone who trades in the same security 4 or more times in the same day over a 5-day period, and whose same-day trades account for at least 6% of his trading activity over that period.

Payable (or Payment) Date: the date that the dividend check is paid to investors.

Payroll Deduction IRA: retirement plan offered by some businesses in which employees direct the employer to deposit a certain amount of his paycheck into his IRA.

P/E or Price-to-Earnings Ratio: the market price of a stock compared to the earnings per share. Stocks trading at high P/E ratios are "growth stocks," while those trading at low P/E ratios are "value stocks."

Peak: the phase of the business cycle between expansion (good times) and contraction (bad times).

Pegging: a form of market manipulation in which parties illegally try to raise the price of a stock to a particular target, often to force the put options the parties have written on the stock to go out-of-the-money. A violation.

Penny Stock Cold Calling Rules: rules to protect consumers receiving telemarketing pitches to buy risky stocks trading below $5 a share. Rules require special disclosure and investor signatures when selling penny stocks.

Pension Plan: a contract between an individual and an employer that provides for the distribution of benefits at retirement.

Performance Figures: total return for a mutual fund over 1, 5, and 10 years, and/or "life of fund." Only past performance may be indicated, and there must be a caveat that past performance does not guarantee future results.

Period Certain: a settlement option that promises to pay either the annuitant or his beneficiaries for at least a stated period of time, no matter how soon the annuitant passes.

Periodic-Payment Deferred Annuity: method of purchasing an annuity whereby the contract holder makes periodic payments into the contract. The pay-out phase must be deferred for all periodic payment plans.

Permanent Insurance: life insurance other than "term."

PHA – Public Housing Authority (bonds): another name for NHA/New Housing Authority municipal revenue bonds.

Physical Certificates: a method of owning securities in which paper certificates are issued to and in the name of the investor.

Pink Markets: a part of the OTC market where thinly traded, volatile stocks change hands. AKA "non-NASDAQ OTC."

Placement: the first stage in the cycle of money laundering in which illegally generated funds are placed into the financial system or are smuggled out of the country.

Placement Ratio: a statistic published in the Bond Buyer showing the dollar amount of municipal securities sold on the primary market out of the dollar amount offered the previous week; a.k.a. the "acceptance ratio."

Policyholder: the owner of an insurance policy who is responsible for paying premiums.

Political Risk: the risk that a country's government will radically change policies or that the political climate will become hostile or counterproductive to business and financial markets.

POP: public offering price. For an IPO, this includes the spread to the underwriters. For a mutual fund, this includes any sales loads that go to the underwriter/distributor.

Portfolio: a batch of stocks, bonds, money market securities, or any combination thereof that an investor owns.

Position Limit: maximum number of options contracts that a trader can have on the same side of the market (bull/bear) and/or may exercise over a five day period.

Power of Substitution: a document that when signed by the security owner authorizes transfer of the certificate to another party.

Precious Metals: metals with industrial uses or intrinsic worth including gold, silver, copper, and platinum.

Precious Metals Funds: specialized mutual funds typically investing in the shares of mining/extraction companies.

Pre-dispute Arbitration Agreement: an agreement signed by the customer of a broker-dealer in which the customer agrees to use arbitration rather than civil court to settle disputes.

Pre-emptive Right: the right of common stockholders to maintain their proportional ownership if the company offers more shares of stock.

Preferred Stock: a fixed-income equity security whose stated dividends must be paid before common stock can receive any dividend payment. Also gets preference ahead of common stock in a liquidation (but behind all creditors).

Preliminary Official Statement: the official statement for a municipal bond issue subject to further additions and changes.

Preliminary Prospectus: a prospectus that lacks the POP and the effective date; a.k.a. "red herring." Used to solicit indications of interest.

Premium Bond: a bond purchased for more than the par value, usually due to a drop in interest rates.

Prepayment Risk: the risk that the mortgages underlying a mortgage-backed security will be paid off sooner than expected due to a drop in interest rates. Investors reinvest the principal at a lower rate going forward.

Preservation of Capital: an investment objective that places the emphasis on making sure the principal is not lost. Also called "safety."

Pre-Tax Plan: a retirement plan offering a tax deduction for the contribution made to the account.

Pre-Tax Margin: pre-tax profit divided into revenue.

Pre-Tax Profit: the profit shown on the income statement before taxes are subtracted.

Price-based Options: standardized interest rate options based on the price of various U.S. Treasury securities.

Price-to-Book: the market price of a stock compared to its book value per share.

Price-to-Cash: the market price of a stock compared to its cash-flow-from-operating-activities-per-share.

Price-to-Earnings: the market price of a stock compared to its earnings-per-share.

Price-to-Sales: the market price of a stock compared to its revenue-per-share.

Primary Market: where securities are issued to raise capital for the issuer.

Primary Offering: offering of securities in which the proceeds go to the issuer.

Prime Brokerage: a level of service provided to, for example, hedge funds requiring greater margin, securities lending, and other capabilities.

Prime Rate: interest rate charged to corporations with high credit ratings for unsecured loans.

Principal-Protected Fund: a mutual fund for people who want their principal protected. Involves holding the investment for several years, at which point the fund guarantees that the value of the investment will be equal to at least what the investor put in.

Private Equity Fund: an alternative investment fund open to sophisticated investors and focusing on purchasing companies both public and private.

Private Placement: an exempt transaction under Reg D (Rule 506) of the Securities Act of 1933, allowing issuers to sell securities without registration to accredited investors, who agree to hold them for a required period.

Private Placement Memorandum or PPM: the offering document for a private placement of unregistered securities.

Private Securities Transaction: offering an investment opportunity not sponsored by the firm. Requires permission from the firm and any disclosure demanded; otherwise, a violation called "selling away."

Probate: the process of "proving" the will and distributing assets of the deceased.

Proceeds Transaction: using the proceeds from a sale of securities to buy other securities on the same day.

Producer Price Index or PPI: defined by the Bureau of Labor Statistics as "the average change over time in the selling prices received by domestic producers for their output. The prices included in the PPI are from the first commercial transaction for many products and some services."

Product Advertisement: defined by the MSRB as any advertisement concerning one or more specific municipal securities, one or more specific issues of municipal securities, the municipal securities of one or more specific issuers, or the specific features of municipal securities.

Professional Advertisement: defined by the MSRB as any advertisement concerning the facilities, services or skills with respect to municipal securities of such broker, dealer or municipal securities dealer or of another broker, dealer, or municipal securities dealer.

Profit Sharing: a defined contribution plan whereby the company makes contributions at its discretion according to a prescribed formula.

Progressive Tax: a tax that increases as a percentage as the thing being taxed increases, including gift, estate, and income taxes. Not a flat tax.

Prospectus: a disclosure document that details a company's plans, history, officers, and risks of investment. It's the red herring plus the POP and the effective date.

Protective Covenants: promises from the issuer of a revenue bond to the bondholders designed to protect the bondholders against default.

Proxy Form: a form granting the power to vote according to a shareholder's instructions when the shareholder will not attend the meeting.

Proxy Statement: full disclosure document required by an issuer before soliciting votes by proxy at any annual or special shareholder meeting.

Prudent Investor Standards: guidance provided to fiduciaries investing on behalf of a third party, e.g., trustees or custodians of UTMA accounts.

PSA Model: a method of estimating the speed of prepayments on a CMO investment.

Public Offering Price (POP): the price an investor pays for a mutual fund or an initial public offering. For a mutual fund, POP = NAV + the sales charge.

Public Offering: the sale of an issue of common stock, either an IPO or an additional offer of shares.

Purchase Payment: a payment made into an annuity contract.

Purchasing Power: how much a dollar can buy relative to consumer prices.

Purchasing Power Risk: also called "constant dollar" or "inflation" risk, the risk that a fixed payment will not be sufficient to keep up with inflation (as measured through the CPI).

Put (n.): a contract giving the owner the right to sell something at a stated exercise price.

Put (v.): to sell.

Put/Call Ratio or **Puts-to-Calls:** a tool of technical analysis showing the ratio of puts purchased to calls, with a higher ratio a bearish indicator revealing that many stock investors have hedged by buying protective puts.

Put Feature: a feature of some bonds allowing the investor to sell the bond back for stated prices as of certain dates named in the indenture, protecting the investor from interest rate risk. AKA "puttable" bonds.

Put Spread: the act of buying and selling puts on the same underlying instrument where the two options are different in terms of strike price, expiration, or both.

Q

Qualified Dividend: a dividend that qualifies for a lower tax rate vs. ordinary income.

Qualified Institutional Buyers: investors meeting certain SEC criteria allowing them to participate in certain investment opportunities not open to the general public.

Qualified Opinion: opinion by the bond counsel for a municipal issuer in which some doubt or reservations are expressed.

Qualified Plan: a retirement plan that qualifies for deductible contributions on behalf of employers and/or employees and covered by ERISA. For example, 401(k), defined benefit, Keogh. Must meet IRS approval, unlike more informal "non-qualified plans."

Quick Assets: the current assets that a company could easily to convert to cash—cash & equivalents plus accounts receivable but *minus* inventory.

Quick Ratio: a more stringent measure of liquidity than the current ratio. Inventory is excluded from current assets before comparing to the company's current liabilities.

Quote, Quotation: a price that a dealer is willing to pay or accept for a security.

R

498

Random Withdrawal: a settlement option in an annuity whereby the investor takes the value of the subaccounts in two or more withdrawals, rather than one lump sum.

Rate Covenant: a promise that the issuer of a revenue bond will raise rates if necessary to cover the debt service.

Rating Service: e.g., S&P and Moody's; a company that assigns credit ratings to corporate and municipal bonds.

Raw Land: unimproved real estate providing no cash flow and no depreciation. A speculative investment in land.

Realized Gain: the amount of the "profit" an investor earns when selling a security.

Real Rate of Return: an investor's return minus the rate of inflation as measured by the CPI. AKA "inflation-adjusted return."

Recession: a significant decline in economic activity spread across the economy, lasting more than a few months, normally visible in real GDP, real income, employment, industrial production, and wholesale-retail sales declines.

Reclamation: document sent by a broker-dealer when delivery of securities is apparently in error.

Recommendation: an affirmative statement or implication that an investor should consider buying, selling, or holding a security or pursuing a particular investment strategy.

Record Date: the date determined by the Board of Directors upon which the investor must be the holder "of record" in order to receive the upcoming dividend. Settlement of a trade must occur by the record date for the buyer to receive the dividend.

Recourse Note: an obligation of a limited partnership for which a limited partner is responsible personally.

Red Herring: a.k.a. "preliminary prospectus." Contains essentially the same information that the final prospectus will contain, minus the POP and effective date.

Redeemable Security: a security that may be redeemed or presented to the issuer for payment, e.g., open-end (but not closed-end) funds.

Redemption: for mutual funds, redemption involves the sale of mutual fund shares back to the fund at the NAV (less any redemption fees, back-end loads). For bonds, the date that principal is returned to the investor, along with the final interest payment.

Redemption Fee: a charge to a mutual fund investor who sells her shares back to the fund much sooner than the fund would prefer.

Refunding: replacing an outstanding bond issue by issuing new bonds at a lower interest rate. Also known as "calling" a bond issue.

Refunding Issue: the bonds being issued to replace a more expensive and existing issue of bonds when the issuer performs a refunding.

Reg A: a laid-back and predictable form of island music. Also, an exempt transaction under the Securities Act of 1933 for small offerings of securities ($5 million issued in a 12-month period).

Reg D: an exempt transaction under the Securities Act of 1933 for private placements.

Reg FD: legislation requiring that any material non-public information disclosed by a public corporation to analysts or other investors must be made public.

Reg NMS: SEC regulation concerned with the over-the-counter trading of stocks that trade on NYSE, NYSE Amex, and NASDAQ, as opposed to Over-The-Counter Bulletin Board (OTCBB) and Pink Quote stocks. Concerns over access to quotes and prompt and accurate trade reporting for NMS stocks.

Reg SHO: SEC rule to prevent abusive short selling with its locate requirement for broker-dealers executing short sales.

Reg S-K: provides guidance on forward-looking statements made by an issuer and lays out the information required in various types of securities registration statements.

Reg T: established by the FRB as the amount of credit a broker-dealer may extend to a customer pledging a security as collateral for a margin loan. In a margin account, customers must put down ½ of the security's value, or at least $2,000.

Reg U: established by the FRB as the amount of credit a bank may extend to a broker-dealer or public customer pledging a security as collateral.

Regulatory Element: continuing education requirement completed on second anniversary of registration and every three years thereafter. Failure to complete within 120 days of anniversary leads to "inactive" status.

Registered Options and Security Futures Principal: designation for the principal responsible for options firm communications and the allocation of exercise notices.

Registered as to Principal Only: a bond with only the principal registered. Interest coupons must be presented for payment.

Registered Representative: an associated person of an investment banker or broker-dealer who effects transactions in securities for compensation.

Registered Secondary: an offering of securities by persons other than the issuer. For example, the former CEO of a corporation may offer a large block of restricted (unregistered) stock to the public through a broker-dealer.

Registrar: audits the transfer agent to make sure the number of authorized shares is never exceeded.

Registration Statement: the legal document disclosing material information concerning an offering of a security and its issuer. Submitted to SEC under Securities Act of 1933.

Regressive Tax: a flat tax, e.g., gasoline, sales, excise taxes.

Regular Way Settlement: T + 3, trade date plus three business days. T + 1 for Treasury securities.

Regulated Investment Company: an investment company using the conduit tax theory by distributing 90% or more of net investment income to shareholders.

Regulation AC: legislation requiring research analysts to certify the accuracy and truthfulness of their research reports.

Reinstatement Privilege: a feature of some mutual funds allowing investors to make withdrawals and then reinstate the money without paying another sales charge.

Reinvestment Risk: the risk that a fixed-income investor will not be able to reinvest interest payments or the par value at attractive interest rates. Happens when rates are falling.

REIT (Real Estate Investment Trust): a corporation or trust that uses the pooled capital of investors to invest in ownership of either income property or mortgage loans. 90% of net income is paid out to shareholders.

Release Date: date established by the SEC as to when the underwriters may sell new securities to the buyers; a.k.a. "effective date."

REMIC: a Real Estate Mortgage Investment Conduit, another name for a CMO.

Reorganization Department: back office operation of a broker-dealer handling changes to securities ownership due to mergers, acquisitions, bankruptcies, bond calls, and tender offers.

Repurchase Agreement: an agreement in which one party sells securities to the other and agrees to repurchase them for a higher price over the short-term.

Required Minimum Distribution (RMD): the required minimum distribution that must be taken from a retirement plan to avoid IRS penalties. Usually must occur by April 1st of the year following the individual's 70½th birthday.

Research Analyst: associated person of a member firm who prepares research reports.

Research Report: a communication put out by a member firm that analyzes the investment merits of a particular security.

Reserve Requirement: amount of money a bank must lock up in reserve, established by the FRB.

Residual Claim: the right of common stockholders to claim assets after the claims of all creditors and preferred stockholders have been satisfied.

Resistance: the point at which a stock's price starts to drop within a trading pattern.

Restricted Person: a person who is ineligible to purchase an equity IPO, including members of the brokerage industry and their immediate family members.

Restricted Stock: stock whose transfer is subject to restrictions, e.g., a holding period. Stock purchased in private placements is an example of restricted stock.

Retail Communications: any written (paper or electronic) communication made available to more than 25 retail investors in a 30-day period.

Retail Investor: any investor who is not an institutional investor.

Retained Earnings: a balance sheet item reflecting profits not distributed to shareholders over the years but, rather, reinvested into the business. Accumulated net income of the company from which dividends are declared.

Return on Equity: calculated from the balance sheet, a measure showing how much in profits each dollar of stockholders' equity generates. Found by dividing net income by stockholders' equity.

Revenue: the proceeds a company receives when selling products and services. AKA "sales" or "net revenue."

Revenue Anticipation Note (RAN): a short-term debt obligation of a municipal issuer backed by upcoming revenues.

Revenue Bond: a municipal bond whose interest and principal payments are backed by the revenues generated from the project being built by the proceeds of the bonds. Toll roads, for example, are usually built with revenue bonds backed by the tolls collected.

Reverse Repurchase Agreements: a repurchase agreement from the buyer's perspective, who resells the securities to the other side of the transaction at the agreed-upon price.

Rights of Accumulation: feature of many mutual funds whereby a rise in account value is counted the same as new money for purposes of achieving a breakpoint.

Rights Offering: additional offer of stock accompanied by the opportunity for each shareholder to maintain his/her proportionate ownership in the company.

Rights: short-term equity securities that allow the holder to buy new shares below the current market price.

Risk: the variability of returns an investment produces; e.g. standard deviation.

Risk-Averse: an investor who sacrifices potentially high returns for safety of income and principal, e.g., a T-Bond investor.

Riskless Principal Transaction: transaction in which a broker-dealer chooses to act as a principal when they could have acted as an agent for the customer.

Risk Tolerance: an investor's ability to bear investment risk in terms of financial resources, liquidity needs, investment objectives, and psychological makeup. Risk tolerance is simply an investor's ability to tolerate risk.

Rollover: moving retirement funds from a 401(k) to an IRA, or from one IRA to another. In a "60-day rollover," the check is cut to the individual, who must then send a check to the new custodian within 60 days to avoid early distribution penalties.

Roth IRA: individual retirement account funded with non-deductible (after-tax) contributions. All distributions are tax-free provided the individual is 59½ and has had the account at least five years.

Round Lot: the usual or normal unit of trading. 100 shares for common stock.

RTRS: a trade reporting system used for transactions in municipal securities on the secondary market.

Rule (and Form) 144: regulates the sale of "control stock" by requiring board members, officers, and large shareholders to report sales of their corporation's stock and to adhere to volume limits. The form is filed as often as quarterly, no later than concurrently with the sale.

Rule 144a: rule that allows restricted securities to be re-sold to institutional investors including banks, insurance companies, broker-dealers, investment advisers, pension plans, and investment companies without violating holding period requirements.

Rule 145: rule that requires corporations in a proposed merger/acquisition to solicit the vote of the shareholders of both the purchasing and the acquired corporation.

Rule 147: exemption under the Securities Act of 1933 for intra-state offerings of securities.

Rumors: the illegal practice of trying to move a stock's market price by publishing unfounded allegations about the issuer.

Russell 2,000: a small cap stock index often used as a benchmark for small cap portfolios.

RVP: receipt versus payment, a method of settlement whereby payment on the transaction is made when delivery of the securities is received and accepted.

S

Safety: an investment objective that seeks to avoid loss of principal first and foremost. Bank CDs, Treasury securities, and fixed annuities are generally suitable.

Sales: another name for revenue, the top line of an income statement.

Sales Charge, Sales Load: a deduction from an investor's check that goes to the distributors/sellers of the fund. Deducted from investor's check, either when she buys (A-shares) or sells (B-shares).

Saucer Pattern: a pattern forming in a stock chart where the trendline is curved with a more gradual slope than what is seen in the "cup" pattern.

Savings Bond: a U.S. Government debt security that is not "negotiable," meaning it can't be traded or pledged as collateral for a loan. Includes EE and HH series bonds.

Scheduled Premium: life insurance with established, scheduled premium payments, e.g., whole life, variable life. As opposed to "universal" insurance, which is "flexible premium."

S-corporation: a business entity providing flow-through to the shareholders and protection of personal assets, with a maximum number of owners.

Secondary Market: where investors trade securities among themselves and proceeds do not go to the issuer.

Secondary Offering/Distribution: a distribution of securities owned by major stockholders—not the issuer of the securities.

Sector Fund: a fund that concentrates heavily in a particular industry, e.g., the "Technology Fund." Higher risk/reward than funds invested in many industries.

Secured Bond: a corporate bond secured by collateral, e.g., mortgage bond, collateral trust certificate, equipment trust certificate.

Securities Act of 1933: regulates the new-issue or primary market, requiring non-exempt issuers to register securities and provide full disclosure.

Securities and Exchange Commission: SEC, empowered by passage of Securities Exchange Act of 1934. A government body, the ultimate securities regulator.

Securities Exchange Act of 1934: landmark securities legislation that prevents fraud in the securities markets. Created/empowered the SEC. Requires broker-dealers, exchanges and securities associations to register with SEC. Requires public companies to report quarterly and annually to SEC.

Securitization: the process of turning financial assets such as receivables or mortgages into securities that are packaged and sold to investors.

Security: an investment of money subject to fluctuation in value and negotiable/marketable to other investors. Other than an insurance policy or fixed annuity, a security is any piece of securitized "paper" that can be traded for value.

Security Index Future: futures contracts deriving their value from various indexes, often used to predict the movement of the stock movement when it opens.

Self-Regulatory Organization: SRO, e.g., FINRA and the CBOE. An organization given the power to regulate its members. Not government bodies like the SEC, which oversees the SROs.

Self-Trades: transactions that unwittingly occur within the same firm due to electronic trading algorithms.

Seller's Option: a special type of trade settlement that is not to happen sooner than the fourth business day following execution and is to occur on a future date specified by the seller, alterable only with a one-day advance written notice to the buyer.

Sell Limit: an order to sell placed above the current market price that may be executed only if the bid price rises to the limit price or higher.

Sell Stop: an order to sell placed below the current market price, activated only if the market price hits or passes below the stop price.

Selling Away: a violation that occurs when a registered representative offers investment opportunities not sponsored by the firm.

Selling Concession: typically, the largest piece of the underwriting spread going to the firm credited with making the sale.

Selling Dividends: a violation where an investor is deceived into thinking that she needs to purchase a stock in order to receive an upcoming dividend.

Selling Group: certain broker-dealers with an agreement to act as selling agents for the syndicate (underwriters) with no capital at risk.

Selling, General, and Administrative: or "SG&A expenses," general operating expenses listed on the company's income statement after Cost of Goods Sold. These are operating expenses not directly related to producing the companies products.

Semi-Annual: twice per year, or "at the half year," literally. Note that "bi-annually" means "every two years." Bond interest is paid semi-annually. Mutual funds report to their shareholders semi-annually and annually. Nothing happens "bi-annually" as a general rule of thumb.

Senior Security: a security that grants the holder a higher claim on the issuer's assets in the event of a liquidation/bankruptcy.

Separate Account: an account maintained by an insurance/annuity company that is separate from the company's general account. Used to invest customers' money for variable annuities and variable insurance contracts. Registered as an investment company under Investment Company Act of 1940.

SEP-IRA: pre-tax retirement plan available to small businesses. Favors high-income employees (compared to SIMPLE). Only employ-er contributes.

Series: e.g., a MSFT Nov 40 call. The standardized contracts available on the secondary market naming the underlying stock, the expiration, and the strike price.

Series EE Bond: a nonmarketable, interest-bearing U.S. Government savings bond issued at a discount from the par value. Interest is exempt from state and local taxation.

Series HH Bond: a nonmarketable, interest-bearing U.S. Government savings bond issued at par and purchased only by trading in Series EE bonds at maturity. Interest is exempt from state and local taxation.

Series I Bond: a savings bond issued by the U.S. Treasury that protects investors from inflation or purchasing power risk.

Settlement Options: payout options on annuities and life insurance including life-only, life with period certain, and joint and last survivorship.

Settlement: final completion of a securities transaction wherein payment has been made by the buyer and delivery has been made by the seller.

Share Identification: a method of calculating capital gains and losses by which the investor identifies which shares were sold, as opposed to using FIFO or average cost.

Sharing Arrangement: as stated in the subscription agreement, the way in which income and capital contributions are to be allocated among the GP and the LPs.

Shelf Registration: registering securities that will be sold gradually on the primary market.

Short Interest: the number of percentage of an issuer's shares that have been sold short.

Short Interest Theory: theory that a high level of short sales is a bullish indicator, as it creates potential buying pressure on a particular security.

Short Sale: method of attempting to profit from a security whose price is expected to fall. Trader borrows certificates through a broker-dealer and sells them, with the obligation to replace them at a later date, hopefully at a lower price. Bearish position.

Short-Term Capital Gain: a profit realized on a security held for 12 months or less.

Short-Term Capital Loss: a loss realized on a security held for 12 months or less, deductible against Short-Term Capital Gains.

Signature Guarantee: an official stamp/medallion that officers of a bank affix to a stock power to attest to its validity.

SIMPLE Plan: a retirement plan for businesses with no more than 100 employees that have no other retirement plan in place. Pre-tax contributions, fully taxable distributions. Both employer and employees may contribute—through elective deferrals. Set up either as an IRA or 401(k).

Simple Trust: a trust that accumulates income and distributes it to the beneficiaries annually.

Simplified Arbitration: a method of resolving disputes involving a small amount of money.

Single-Payment Deferred Annuity: annuity purchased with a single payment wherein the individual defers the payout or "annuity" phase of the contract.

Single-Payment Immediate Annuity: annuity purchased with a single payment wherein the individual goes immediately into the payout or "annuity" phase of the contract.

Sinking Fund: an account established by an issuing corporation or municipality to provide funds required to redeem a bond issue.

SIPC: Securities Investor Protection Corporation, a non-profit, non-government, industry-funded insurance corporation protecting investors against broker-dealer failure.

SLGS: "State and Local Government Series" securities, special securities created by the U.S. Treasury to help municipalities do an advance refunding and comply with IRS rules and restrictions on such transactions.

Small Cap: a stock where the total value of all outstanding shares is considered "small," typically between $50 million and $2 billion.

Sole Proprietorship: a business owned as an individual with no protection provided for the owner's personal assets.

Solicited Order: an order placed for a customer pursuant to an agent's recommendation and subject to suitability requirements.

Solvency: the ability of a corporation or municipality to meet its obligations as they come due.

Sovereign Debt: bonds issued by a national government and payable in a foreign currency.

S&P 500: a market-cap weighted index of 500 large-company stocks that is used to represent the overall market for purposes of calculating beta.

Special Assessment Bonds: revenue bonds backed by an assessment on only those properties benefiting from the project.

Specially Designated Nationals: parties whose names are on a special list with the Office of Foreign Asset Control (OFAC) of persons that U.S. entities are not to do business with.

Special Memorandum Account (SMA): a line of credit in a margin account.

Special Tax: a tax on gasoline, hotel and motel, liquor, tobacco, etc.

Special Tax Bond: a revenue bond backed by taxes on gasoline, hotel and motel, liquor, tobacco, etc.

Specialized Fund: a mutual fund specializing its investment approach beyond just "growth, value, or growth & income." Specialized funds might write covered calls, focus on particular industry groups or geographic areas, provide age-based portfolios, or track indexes for passive investments, etc.

Specified Program: a direct participation program in which the assets of the partnership are identified.

Speculation: an investment objective involving high-risk bets that an investment's market value will rise significantly. Associated with options, futures, and raw land investments.

Spin-Off: an offering of stock in a unit that is being divested from the issuer.

Sponsor: the party who puts together a direct participation program.

Spousal Account: an IRA established for a non-working spouse.

Spread: generally, the difference between a dealer's purchase price and selling price, both for new offerings (underwriting spread) and secondary market quotes. For underwritings the spread is the difference between the proceeds to the issuer and the POP.

Spread Load: sales charges for a mutual fund contractual plan that permits a maximum charge of 20% in any one year and 9% over the life of the plan.

Stabilizing/Stabilization: the surprising practice by which an underwriting syndicate bids up the price of an IPO whose price is dropping in the secondary market.

Stable Value Fund: a money market mutual fund attempting to keep the NAV at $1.

Stagflation: an unusual macroeconomic state associated with inflation *and* economic stagnation.

Standby Underwriting: a commitment by an underwriter to purchase any shares that are not subscribed to in a rights offering.

Standard & Poor's: a firm that analyses the credit quality of municipal and corporate bonds and also puts together various indices to track the performance of the stock market and various segments thereof.

Statement of Additional Information or SAI: detailed registration document for an open- or closed-end management company providing further details than what is contained in the statutory prospectus.

Statement of Cash Flows: a financial statement showing how much cash was provided/used by the company from operations, financing, and investing activities.

Statute of Limitations: a time limit that, once reached, prevents criminal or civil action from being filed.

Statutory Disqualification: prohibiting a person from associating with an SRO due to disciplinary or criminal actions within the past 10 years, or due to filing a false or misleading application or report with a regulator.

Statutory Voting: method of voting whereby the shareholder may cast no more than the number of shares owned per candidate/item.

Step-Up Bond: a bond that pays higher interest payments to investors as time goes on.

Stochastics: a tool of technical analysts measuring the momentum of stocks and stock indexes.

Stock: an ownership or equity position in a public company whose value is tied to the company's profits (if any) and dividend payouts (if any).

Stock Dividend: payment of a dividend in the form of more shares of stock; not a taxable event.

Stockholders' Equity: from the balance sheet, the difference between assets and liabilities. AKA "net worth."

Stock Market: a physical or electronic facility allowing investors to buy and sell stock, e.g. the NYSE or NASDAQ.

Stock Market Data: the information of importance to technical analysts concerning pricing patters, volume, moving averages, etc. for common stock and stock indexes.

Stock Power: document used to transfer ownership of a stock.

Stock Split: a change in the number of outstanding shares designed to change the price-per-share; not a taxable event.

Stop Loss: another name for a sell-stop order. So named because an investor's losses are stopped once the stock trades at a certain price or lower.

Stop Order: an order that is activated only if the market price hits or passes through the stop price. Does not name a price for execution.

Stop-limit Order: a stop order that once triggered must be filled at an exact price (or better).

Stopping Stock: a courtesy in which the specialist will guarantee a price for execution and allow the participant to seek a better price.

Straddle: buying a call and a put on the same underlying instrument with the same strike price and expiration…or selling a call and a put on the same underlying instrument with the same strike price and expiration. For example, an investor who buys an ABC Aug 50 call and buys an ABC Aug 50 put is establishing a "long straddle."

Straight Life Annuity: a settlement option in which the annuity company pays the annuitant only as long as he or she is alive. Also called "straight life" or "life only."

Straight Preferred: a preferred stock whose missed dividends do not go into arrears, a.k.a. "non-cumulative preferred."

Street Name: in the name of the broker-dealer holding securities on behalf of customers.

Strike Price or Exercise Price: the price at which a call or put option allows the holder to buy or sell the underlying security.

STRIPS: Separate Trading of Registered Interest and Principal of Securities. A zero coupon bond issued by the U.S. Treasury in which all interest income is received at maturity in the form of a higher (accreted) principal value. Avoids "reinvestment risk."

Subaccount: investment options available within the separate account for variable contract holders.

Subchapter M: section of the Internal Revenue Code providing the "conduit tax treatment" used by REITs and mutual funds distributing 90% or more of net income to shareholders. A mutual fund using this method is technically a Regulated Investment Company under IRC Subchapter M.

Subordinated Debenture: corporate bond with a claim that is subordinated or "junior" to a debenture and/or general creditor.

Subscription Agreement: what a potential Limited Partner/investor signs in order to invest into a DPP.

Subscription Price: the price that all buyers of a new issue will pay to buy the security being offered on the primary market.

Suitability: a determination by a registered representative that a security matches a customer's stated objectives and financial situation.

Supervision: a system implemented by a broker-dealer to ensure that its employees and associated persons comply with federal and state securities law, and the rules and regulations of the SEC, exchanges, and SROs.

Supplemental Liquidity Providers: specially designated off-floor members of the NYSE who play a unique role in the trading of securities on the secondary market. These participants use sophisticated computerized trading strategies to create high volume on exchanges in order to add liquidity to the markets. As an incentive to provide liquidity, the exchange pays the Supplemental Liquidity Provider (SLP) a fee/rebate.

504

Support: the point at which a stock's market price begins to rise within a trading pattern.

Surrender: to cash out an annuity or life insurance policy for its surrender value.

Swaps: a private agreement in which two parties agree to pay each other various cash flows, e.g. a fixed interest rate for one side versus a floating rate for the other. As opposed to an actual principal amount, swaps use a notional value to calculate interest owed by each side of the agreement.

Syndicate: a group of underwriters bringing a new issue to the primary market.

Syndicate Letter: another name for the agreement among underwriters. The document detailing the terms of operation for an underwriting syndicate.

Syndicator: the individual or entity who puts a limited partnership or other DPP together and typically manages the business.

Systematic Risk: another name for "market risk," or the risk that an investment's value could plummet due to an overall market panic or collapse. Other "systematic risks" include inflation and interest rate risk.

Systematic Withdrawal Plan: a plan to redeem mutual fund shares according to a certain time frame, monthly check amount, or number of shares, etc., until the account is exhausted.

T

T + 3: regular way settlement, trade date plus three business days.

TAC – Targeted Amortization Class: a type of CMO (collateralized mortgage obligation) that leaves the investor with greater extension risk as compared to a PAC (planned amortization class).

Target Funds: an age-based asset allocation fund that automatically rebalances to match the investors' time horizon, e.g. a "Target 2040" fund is designed for investors planning to retire in or around the year 2040.

Tax-Advantaged Account: an account that provides tax benefits for purposes of saving and investing for retirement, education, or healthcare expenses.

Tax and Revenue Anticipation Note (TRAN): a short-term debt obligation of a municipal issuer backed by future tax and revenue receipts.

Tax Anticipation Note (TAN): a short-term debt obligation of a municipal issuer backed by future tax receipts.

Tax Credit: an amount that can be subtracted from the amount of taxes owed.

Tax-Deferred: an account where all earnings remain untaxed until "constructive receipt."

Tax-Equivalent Yield: the rate of return that a taxable bond must offer to equal the tax-exempt yield on a municipal bond. To calculate, take the municipal yield and divide that by (100% – investor's tax bracket).

Tax-Exempt Bonds: municipal bonds whose interest is not subject to taxation by the federal government.

Tax Preference Item: certain items that must be added back to an investor's income for purposes of AMT, including interest on certain municipal bonds.

Tax Shelter: offsetting passive income with a share of passive losses from a direct participation program.

Tax-Sheltered Annuity (TSA): an annuity funded with pre-tax (tax-deductible) contributions. Available to employees of non-profit organizations such as schools, hospitals, and church organizations.

T-bills: direct obligation of U.S. Government. Sold at discount, mature at face amount. Maximum maturity is 1 year.

T-bonds: direct obligation of U.S. Government. Pay semi-annual interest. Quoted as % of par value plus 32nds. 10–30-year maturities.

Technical Analysis: a method of using stock market data concerning price and volume to spot buying and selling opportunities. For example, following chart patterns and short interest as opposed to following an issuer's profit margins or revenue.

Technical Analysts: stock traders who rely on market data to spot buying and selling opportunities.

Telemarketing: to market by telephone. Assuming you can get past the caller ID.

Telephone Consumer Protection Act of 1991: federal legislation restricting the activities of telemarketers, who generally may only call prospects between 8 a.m. and 9 p.m. in the prospect's time zone and must maintain a do-not-call list, also checking the national registry.

Tenants in Common: see Joint Tenants in Common, a joint account wherein the interest of the deceased owner reverts to his/her estate.

Tender Offer: an offer by the issuer of securities to repurchase the securities if the investors care to "tender" their securities for payment, or an offer to acquire the shares currently held by shareholders of another company in a merger or acquisition.

Term Life Insurance: form of temporary insurance that builds no cash value and must be renewed at a higher premium at the end of the term. Renting rather than buying insurance.

The Insured: the individual upon whose death a life insurance policy will pay out.

Third Market: exchange-listed stock traded OTC primarily by institutional investors.

Third-party Account: account managed on behalf of a third party, e.g., trust or UGMA.

Time Horizon: an investor's anticipated holding period, used to determine how much volatility can be withstood and how much liquidity is required.

Times Interest Earned: a measure of interest coverage for a bond. Found on the income statement by comparing EBIT to annual interest expense.

Time Value: the value of an option above its intrinsic value. For example, if XYZ trades @50, an XYZ Oct 50 call @1 has no intrinsic value but has $1 of time value.

Timing Risk: the risk of purchasing an investment at a peak price not likely to be sustained or seen again. Timing risk can be reduced through dollar cost averaging, rather than investing in a stock with one purchase.

Tippee: the guy who listened to the insider information.

Tipper: the guy who told him.

T-notes: direct obligation of U.S. Government. Pay semi-annual interest. Quoted as % of par value plus 32nds. 2–10-year maturities.

Tombstone: an advertisement allowed during the cooling-off period to announce an offer of securities, listing the issuer, the type of security, the underwriters, and directions for obtaining a prospectus.

Top-Down Analysis: fundamental analysis that starts with the overall economy, then moves down to industry groups and issuers to make buy or sell decisions.

Top-Heavy: a 401(k) plan, for example, where 60% or more of the benefits go to key, highly compensated employees.

Total Assets: from the balance sheet, a company's current, fixed, and intangible assets all added together.

Total Liabilities: from the balance sheet, a company's current and long-term liabilities added together.

Total Return: measuring growth in share price plus dividend and capital gains distributions.

Total Takedown: the additional takedown plus the concession.

Trade Confirmation: a document containing details of a securities transaction, e.g., price of the security, commissions, stock symbol, number of shares, registered rep code, trade date and settlement date, etc.

Trade Date: the date that a trade is executed.

Trade Reporting and Compliance Engine (TRACE): system used to report corporate bond transactions in the secondary market.

Trading Authorization: a form granting another individual the authority to trade on behalf of the account owner. Either "limited" (buy/sell orders only) or "full" (buy/sell orders plus requests for checks/securities) authorization may be granted. Sometimes referred to as "power of attorney."

Trading Post: a group of monitors around which market participants communicate on the floor of the NYSE.

Traditional IRA: individual retirement account funded typically with tax-deductible contributions.

Tranche: a class of CMO. Principal is returned to one tranche at a time in a CMO.

Transfer Agent: issues and redeems certificates. Handles name changes, validates mutilated certificates. Distributes dividends, gains, and shareholder reports to mutual fund investors.

Transfer and Hold in Safekeeping: a buy order for securities in which securities are bought and transferred to the customer's name, but held by the broker-dealer.

Transfer and Ship: a buy order for securities in which securities are purchased and transferred to the customer's name, with the certificates sent to the customer.

Transfer on Death (TOD): individual account with a named beneficiary—assets transferred directly to the named beneficiary upon death of the account holder.

Treasury Bill: see T-bill.

Treasury Bond: see T-bond.

Treasury Note: see T-note.

Treasury Receipts: zero coupon bonds created by broker-dealers backed by Treasury securities held in escrow. Not a direct obligation of U.S. Government.

Treasury Securities: securities guaranteed by U.S. Treasury, including T-bills, T-notes, T-bonds, and STRIPS.

Treasury Stock: shares that have been issued and repurchased by the corporation. Has nothing to do with the U.S. Treasury.

Trendline: the overall up or down movement of a security's price as it trades on the secondary market. Of interest to chartists/technical analysts.

Trough: phase of the business cycle representing the "bottoming out" of a contraction, just before the next expansion/recovery.

True Interest Cost: a measure of a municipal issuer's total cost of borrowing money by issuing bonds. Unlike net interest cost, true interest cost factors in the time value of money.

Trust Indenture: a written agreement between an issuer and creditors wherein the terms of a debt security issue are set forth, e.g., interest rate, means of payment, maturity date, name of the trustee, etc.

Trust Indenture Act of 1939: corporate bond issues in excess of $5 million with maturities greater than 1 year must be issued with an indenture.

Trustee: a person legally appointed to act on a beneficiary's behalf.

TSA: Tax-sheltered annuity. A retirement vehicle for 403(b) and 501c3 organizations.

Turnover: the frequency of trading within a portfolio.

Turnover Ratio: a measure of the frequency with which the investment adviser trades portfolio securities for an open- or closed-end fund.

Two-dollar Broker: an independent broker on the floor of the NYSE.

Type: option term used to separate a call from a put, the only two "types" of options.

U

U4: registration information for an associated person of a member firm. Used to apply for registration and subject to regular updating requirements.

U5: information provided to CRD when an associated person terminates employment with a member firm.

UGMA: Uniform Gifts to Minors Act. An account set up for the benefit of a minor, managed by a custodian.

UIT: Unit Investment Trust. A type of investment company where investments are selected, not traded/managed. No management fee is charged. Shares are redeemable.

Underwriter: see "investment banker." An underwriter or "investment banker" is a broker-dealer that distributes shares on the primary market.

Underwriting Spread: the profit to the syndicate. The difference between the proceeds to the issuer and the POP.

Unearned Income: income derived from investments and other sources not related to employment, e.g., savings account interest, dividends from stock, capital gains, and rental income.

Unfunded Pension Liabilities: obligations to retiring municipal workers that outweigh the funds set aside to actually pay them.

Uniform Practice Code: how FINRA promotes "cooperative effort," standardizing settlement dates, ex-dates, accrued interest calculations, etc.

Uniform Securities Act: a model act that state securities laws are based on. Designed to prevent fraud and maintain faith in capital markets through registration of securities, agents, broker-dealers, and investment advisers. Main purpose is to provide necessary protection to investors.

Unit of Beneficial Interest: what an investor in a Unit Investment Trust (UIT) owns.

Universal Life Insurance: a form of permanent insurance that offers flexibility in death benefit and both the amount of, and method of paying, premiums.

Unqualified Opinion: an opinion issued by the bond counsel expressing no doubts and requiring no qualifiers.

Unrealized Gain: the increase in the value of an asset that has not yet been sold. Unrealized gains are not taxable.

Unsecured Bond: a debenture, or bond issued without specific collateral.

Unsolicited Order: an order to buy or sell securities placed by the customer rather than recommended by the agent. Outside the agent's suitability obligations.

User Fee: a.k.a. "user charge," a source of revenue used to retire a revenue bond, e.g., park entrance fees, tolls, skybox rentals, etc.

Unsystematic Risk: an investment risk that is specific to an issuer or industry group, e.g. legislative or business risk.

UTMA: just like UGMA, only the minor typically has to wait until 21 years of age to have the assets re-registered solely in his/her name. The "T" stands for "transfer."

V

Valuation Ratio: the comparison of a stock's market price to the EPS, book value, etc.

Value: as in "value investing" or a "value fund," the practice of purchasing stock in companies whose share price is currently depressed.

Value Funds: mutual funds investing in stocks currently out of favor with investors.

Variable Annuity: an annuity whose payout varies. Investments allocated to separate account as instructed by annuitant. Similar to investing in mutual funds, except that annuities offer tax deferral. No taxation until excess over cost basis is withdrawn.

Variable Insurance: insurance whose death benefit and cash values fluctuate with the investment performance of the separate account.

Variable Life Insurance: form of insurance where death benefit and cash value fluctuate according to fluctuations of the separate account.

Variable Universal Life Insurance: flexible-premium insurance with cash value and death benefit tied to the performance of the separate account.

Vesting: a schedule for determining at what point the employer's contributions become the property of the employee.

Viatical Settlement: a.k.a. "life settlement," the sale and purchase of a life insurance policy wherein the investor buys the death benefit at a discount and profits as soon as the insured dies.

Visible Supply: total par value of municipal bonds to be issued over the next 30 days, published in the Bond Buyer.

Volatility: the up and down movements of an investment that make investors dizzy and occasionally nauseated.

Volume: total number of shares traded over a given period (daily, weekly, etc.). Of interest to technical—but not fundamental—analysts.

Voluntary Accumulation Plan: a mutual fund account into which the investor commits to depositing amounts of money on a regular basis.

Voter Approval: the process of approving the issuance of a general obligation bond by referendum.

VRDO – variable rate demand obligation: a debt security whose interest rate is regularly re-set and which can be "put" or sold back to the issuer or a designated third party for the par value plus accrued interest.

W

Warrants: long-term equity securities giving the owner the right to purchase stock at a set price. Often attached as a "sweetener" that makes the other security more attractive.

Wash Sale: selling a security at a loss but then messing up by repurchasing it within 30 days and, therefore, not being able to use it to offset capital gains for that year. Also a type of market manipulation in which a security is traded among the same or related parties without a "change in beneficial ownership" but only with the purpose of manipulating its market price.

Wedge: a chart pattern in which the support and resistance lines are converging rather than running parallel (channel).

Western/Divided Account: a syndicate account in which each participant is responsible for their share of the bonds only.

When-issued Confirmations: confirmations of a purchase on the primary market delivered before the securities have been issued.

Whole Life Insurance: form of permanent insurance with a guaranteed death benefit and minimum guaranteed cash value.

Withdrawal Plan: a feature of most mutual funds that allows investors to liquidate their accounts over a fixed time period, or using a fixed-share or fixed-dollar amount.

Working Capital: difference between a company's current assets and current liabilities measuring short-term liquidity.

Wrap Account: an account in which the customer pays one fee to cover the costs of investment advisory services, execution of transactions, etc.

Wrap Fee: the fee charged in a wrap account to cover trade execution, portfolio management and other related services.

Y

Yield: the income a security produces to the holder just for holding it.

Yield-based Options: standardized options based on the yield of various U.S. Treasury securities.

Yield Curve: a graph showing securities of similar credit quality across various maturities. In a normal yield curve, yields rise with maturities. With an inverted yield curve, short-term securities yield more than longer-term securities.

Yield Spread: the difference in yields between debt securities of different credit quality and similar maturities.

Yield to Call: the yield received on a bond if held to the date it is called.

Yield to Maturity: calculation of all interest payments plus/minus gain/loss on a bond if held to maturity.

Z

Zero Coupon Bond: a bond sold at a deep discount to its gradually increasing par value.

Z-Tranche: the last tranche to receive principal in a CMO.

44476133R00283

Made in the USA
Middletown, DE
07 June 2017